GREAT EVENTS FROM HISTORY

For Ed Wiggins —
Presented through
the good offices of
Orval Watts
With best wishes.

Frank N. Magill.

Flintridge, Calif.
8/11/75

Great Events from History

American Series

Volume 1
Unknown-1830

Edited by
FRANK N. MAGILL

Associate Editor
John L. Loos

SALEM PRESS, Incorporated
Englewood Cliffs, New Jersey

LIBRARY OF CONGRESS CATALOG CARD NUMBER: 72-86347

Published simultaneously in Canada by Salem Press (Canada) Ltd.

FIRST EDITION
First Printing

Library of Congress Cataloging in Publication Data

Magill, Frank Northen, 1907-
    Great events from history.

    Includes bibliographies.
    CONTENT: v. 1. Unknown-1830.—v. 2. 1831-1903—v. 3. 1904-1969.
    1. United States—History. I. Title.
E178.3.M25   973   73-18379

PRINTED IN THE UNITED STATES OF AMERICA

PREFACE

The three-volume American Series of GREAT EVENTS FROM HISTORY begins with the arrival of the Indians, the first Americans, from Asia and ends with the first manned lunar landing in 1969. Between these two noteworthy happenings, 336 additional events are studied in depth through the scholarly literature they have inspired. The two other three-volume sections of the overall work, the Ancient and Medieval Series and the Modern European Series, contain 336 events each. Thus the nine-volume set contains 1,010 events, each with its own coverage of relevant literature.

Unlike the other two series, which simply pick up a continuum at a given point (4000 B.C. or A.D. 1469) and proceed to follow along with an ongoing social development, the American Series, starting with the fourth article, enables one to examine the beginning and development of a brand-new society from point zero—a societal *tabula rasa,* so to speak. Furthermore, this development may be examined through contemporary sources not flawed by myth and information gaps, as well as through scholarly retrospect. Nowhere in human history has such an opportunity on so large a scale presented itself, where the record is there without guesswork—the social development as clear as an ant colony behind glass. It is a remarkable story that unfolds.

Shortly after Columbus landed, the Old World began to explore the New, then slowly fill it with its own restless masses. The open space, the freedom to expand, the fertile land, the spirit of conquest generated in the taming of the unknown led men to resent restrictions placed by the Old World, safe at home and unable to understand the challenge and fulfillment of the frontier. Soon the new men began to think seriously in terms of liberty and the right to live as they pleased, with no king and no nobility over them to thwart their aspirations. Thus began the building of a social organism so original and, despite some human failings, so successful that it is emulated in altered forms in many parts of the world today.

A glance through the chronological list of events will reveal the pattern of the remarkable story that unfolded as the incipient Republic sought to enhance its new concept in political democracy. From the beginning, in the eyes of these political innovators vigilance and broad participation in government were vital to liberty. Indeed, self-government was deemed so essential that the First General Assembly of Virginia was called only twelve years after the initial settlement of Jamestown.

The 1600's were a period of colonial settlement and growth but there was time for consideration of civilizing influences too. Massachusetts passed a compulsory school law in 1647 and Maryland insisted on religious freedom for all its people by the Act of Toleration in 1649. By 1734 freedom of the press had been established in the courts, a concept that later found its way into the new Constitution.

Having left the ways of the Old World far behind, the new men now found oppression from that source intolerable. If liberty must be purchased with the sword, so be it. Beginning with the Stamp Act Crisis in 1765, a dozen articles in this work record the key events leading up to Cornwallis' surrender and the end of British rule in the American colonies.

Out of this conflict a new nation emerged whose people were now committed more than ever to the principles of individual liberty and equal justice under the law. Dedicated leaders soon devised a Constitution by which to be governed, a living instrument that could be changed with changing conditions and that would assure rule by laws, not men.

The new nation's growth was spectacular. Soon Slater's spinning mill, Whitney's cotton gin, and McCormick's reaper would herald the modest beginnings of the greatest industrial power the world has ever known.

This was a unique social unit, a nation whose great energy was fed by waves of immigrants, each adding new vigor to the society. The receding frontier was tamed time after time as it shifted westward, each group bringing with it the church and the school. This was a people who advanced the highly civilized and unheard-of proposal of buying land from France—and later Russia—instead of warring for it. Yet at times they were tough and deadly. The fratricide of 1861-1865 was one of the bloodiest wars in history, though it was slow to develop. Fifteen events over a period of thirty years leading up to the war are examined here.

Following the war and Reconstruction, the nation knew a period of great economic growth and by the end of the nineteenth century—hardly more than a century after its founding—had become a world power. The twentieth century has seen this position of leadership expand, sometimes to the despair of those who yearn for the chance to withdraw. It is not likely, however, that the great and diverse people who tamed much of the North American continent and now have their eyes on space will soon lose their sense of spiritual leadership, their energy, their curiosity, or their desire to master the greatest frontier of all—the deep mystery of life and nature.

The articles in this work consist of four sections: (1) Quick reference material at the beginning showing type of event, time, locale, and principal personages involved if applicable; (2) Summary of Event, a "journalistic" account of the occurrence describing the basic facts of what took place and some of the causes and effects; (3) Pertinent Literature, wherein two original essay-reviews of scholarly works written about the event are presented; and (4) Additional Recommended Reading, which lists and annotates several other works that the student or researcher might profitably examine if he is interested in an in-depth study of the event. Works reviewed in Item (3) are usually books though sometimes scholarly articles are reported on instead. An effort has been made to select for review works of divergent viewpoints, especially if the event under consideration is controversial. The critical evaluations presented in Items (2) and (3) provide a review of the immediate and long-range effects of an occurrence and should enable the reader to view objectively the forces that sparked the event.

The primary objective of the editors has been to present an individual discussion and analysis of more than one thousand significant happenings whose consequences have changed the course of history in the Western world. GREAT EVENTS FROM HISTORY is not a compilation of reprinted historical material; all the material it contains was newly written expressly for this set by some one hundred and fifty history professors and scholars from more than fifty campuses throughout the United States. These contributing professors and scholars have brought their special knowledge and skill to the task of writing the capsule summaries of events and the individual evaluations of the two thousand appropriate works that are reviewed. They have made their articles accurate in reporting facts, scholarly but not dull, clear and not technical without cause, and interpretative in the presentation of the central ideas advanced in the books being reviewed. Reports of the events themselves average eight hundred to one thousand words in length while individual reviews of the literature run about six or eight hundred words each. Events are presented in chronological order in the text.

At the beginning of each volume there appears a chronological list of events for that volume. Volume three includes these six indexes: Alphabetical List of Events, Key Word Index of Events, Category Index for Type of Event, an alphabetized listing of Principal Personages, a listing by author of the Pertinent Literature Reviewed, and a listing by author of the Literature for Additional Recommended Reading. Since, unlike book titles, not all events lend themselves to a specific title universally applied, as do "Battle of . . ." or "Establishment of . . ." articles, the Key Word index should enable the user to locate many events more readily than would an alphabetical index of events whose first word was arbitrarily assigned by the editors.

The two indexes of historical literature provide a reading list of thousands of titles and thousands of authors whose works are pertinent to at least one of the events under examination. Such extensive coverage of the literature of the discipline offers a convenient source for in-depth research by the student, and for course development and class assignments by the instructor.

The three score contributors to the American Series are listed elsewhere in this volume along with their academic affiliations. My sincere appreciation goes to these professors and scholars and to the researchers and assistants whose efforts were so important to the completion of the work. I am especially indebted to Mr. Robert Edward Ostermeyer of the Graduate School, Department of History, University of Southern California, for his invaluable assistance with the project. All of us hope that the work will be useful and stimulating to those whose interest lies in the fascinating field of American history.

FRANK N. MAGILL

INTRODUCTION

History may be defined in a number of different ways. One useful definition is that it is a body of knowledge concerning the past which has been generally accepted by scholars. Of all that has been thought and done by man, only an infinitesimal part has been made a matter of record, and only a small fraction of that record has been examined and evaluated by qualified experts. From the records which they have investigated, these scholars have selected certain facts which they have decided are of sufficient importance to be considered historical facts, to be used in their accounts of the past. Thus the history of the United States is made up of those facts which historians have concluded are significant in understanding this nation's past. While there is naturally not complete agreement on every historical fact, the disagreement among historians is less about the facts than it is about their relative importance and what they mean.

The particular historical facts which should be emphasized and the way in which they should be interpreted change from time to time, for every generation looks to the past for answers to questions which seem to be of special relevance to it. Today, for example, the American people are especially concerned about matters of women's rights, race, and ecology. Historians are, therefore, studying this country's past with particular reference to the role and activities of women, blacks, and Indians and to the manner in which the people have used the nation's natural resources and treated the environment down through the years. Each historian, furthermore, studies the past in terms of his own education, experience, and philosophy of life, and his writing reflects these influences in greater or less degree.

In this work the history of the United States is viewed in terms of certain facts, or "great events," which stand out on the historical landscape as having been of extraordinary importance. The three volumes contain 336 such events. What constitutes a "great event" has, of course, been a matter of editorial judgment with which our readers are bound to have some disagreement. The events included here have not been chosen with any particular interpretation of American history in mind. The work has no special theme or thesis to present. It does not try to glorify the American past or to denigrate it. It does not view American history as having been characterized mainly by consensus or by conflict. It considers no single aspect of history as basically more important than another.

In making their selection the editors have taken a broad view of the American past. They have been careful to cover the entire span of American history, including even prehistory, from the migration to America of the Indians, the first human beings to inhabit this continent, to man's first successful landing on an extra-terrestrial body, the moon. They have included major events from all kinds of history—political, economic, social, military, diplomatic, religious, literary, and artistic. Geographically, the events which they have chosen embrace all sections, or regions, of the United States. Since ours is and has been principally a secular society which has produced little in the way of organized philosophy or abstract thought, religious and philosophical events do not figure prominently in this list of great events. By the same token, because this country represents a highly successful political experiment and has been favored by great natural wealth which its people have developed and exploited with unusual resourcefulness and energy, political and economic events loom large in the editors' selection. Although Americans have always considered themselves to be a peace-loving people, wars have been important in their history, and a significant number of events are, therefore, related to wars, and especially the Civil War and World War II. Reflecting the popular concern with the nation's recent past, one-third of all the events fall within the twentieth century.

These events were written by fifty-eight historians. The summaries are generally straightforward accounts of the events placed in their proper historical settings. The books which the authors have chosen to review not only contain full and accurate treatments of the subject, but they are often distinctive for their literary quality and/or the interpretation which they give the event. Some of the volumes are rather old, but they are still authoritative and have not been superseded by more modern studies. The editors have for the most part had a particular volume reviewed for only one event. They have deliberately included reviews of some of the great classics of American historiography, like volumes from Francis Parkman's *France and England in North America* and Charles M. Andrews' *The Colonial Period of American History*. Three historical works are considered to be so important that their publication constitutes three of the great events included in this study. Whenever an event is the subject of varying, or conflicting, interpretations, the editors have had reviewed books which present those differing interpretations.

As is true of the events themselves, there may well be some disagreement on the part of our readers with the selection of books reviewed for a particular event or listed in the additional recommended reading. The books from which the editors could choose were much greater for some events than for others, because some events of American history have attracted the interest of historians more than others. There are, for example, relatively few good books on the founding of most colonies, while there are many excellent works on all aspects of the Civil War; and much more has been written about some Presidential elections than about others. It can fairly be stated that, altogether, the summaries and book reviews contained in these three volumes constitute a comprehensive survey of American history.

The editor offers his thanks to the contributors to this work and to a small group of graduate students at Louisiana State University whose assistance was most valuable.

JOHN L. LOOS
Professor of History
Louisiana State University

LIST OF EVENTS IN VOLUME ONE
American Series

MEMBERS OF THE WRITING STAFF
American Series

―――――――

	GRADUATE SCHOOL	ACADEMIC AFFILIATION
Stephen E. Ambrose Ph.D.	University of Wisconsin	Louisiana State University, New Orleans
David L. Ammerman Ph.D.	Cornell University	Florida State University
Robert A. Becker Ph.D.	University of Wisconsin	Louisiana State University, Baton Rouge
Warren M. Billings Ph.D.	Northern Illinois University	Louisiana State University, New Orleans
James J. Bolner Ph.D.	University of Virginia	Louisiana State University, Baton Rouge
John G. Clark Ph.D.	Stanford University	University of Kansas
Michael D. Clark Ph.D.	University of North Carolina	Louisiana State University, New Orleans
Terrill J. Clements M.A.	University of Nebraska at Omaha	University of Nebraska at Omaha
Sidney L. Cohen Ph.D.	Yale University	Louisiana State University, Baton Rouge

xvii

Richard H. Collin Ph.D.	New York University	Louisiana State University, New Orleans
William J. Cooper, Jr. Ph.D.	The Johns Hopkins University	Louisiana State University, Baton Rouge
David H. Culbert Ph.D.	Northwestern University	Louisiana State University, Baton Rouge
Merle O. Davis M.A.	Louisiana State University	Louisiana State University, Baton Rouge
John H. DeBerry Ph.D.	University of Kentucky	Memphis State University
Fredrick J. Dobney Ph.D.	Rice University	St. Louis University
Maurice T. Dominguez Ph.D.	Tulane University	
John Duffy Ph.D.	University of California at Los Angeles	University of Maryland
Robert F. Erickson Ph.D.	University of Illinois	Southern Illinois University
Cecil L. Eubanks Ph.D.	University of Michigan	Louisiana State University, Baton Rouge
James E. Fickle Ph.D.	Louisiana State University	Memphis State University
James F. Findlay, Jr. Ph.D.	Northwestern University	University of Rhode Island
George Q. Flynn Ph.D.	Louisiana State University	University of Miami

John C. Gardner M.A.	Louisiana State University	Louisiana State University, Baton Rouge
Don R. Gerlach Ph.D.	University of Nebraska	University of Akron
William G. Haag Ph.D.	University of Michigan	Louisiana State University, Baton Rouge
William I. Hair Ph.D.	Louisiana State University	Florida State University
R. Don Higginbotham Ph.D.	Duke University	University of North Carolina at Chapel Hill
Donald Holley Ph.D.	Louisiana State University	University of Arkansas at Monticello
W. Turrentine Jackson Ph.D.	University of Texas	University of California at Davis
Burton Kaufman Ph.D.	Rice University	Louisiana State University, New Orleans
Jeffrey Kimball Ph.D.	Louisiana State University	Miami University, Oxford, Ohio
John L. Loos Ph.D.	Washington University, St. Louis	Louisiana State University, Baton Rouge
Anne C. Loveland Ph.D.	Cornell University	Louisiana State University, Baton Rouge
Frank N. Magill Ed.D.	University of Southern California	University of Southern California
Russell Magnaghi Ph.D.	St. Louis University	Northern Michigan University

Edward J. Maguire Ph.D.	St. Louis University	St. Louis University
Rex O. Mooney Ph.D.	Louisiana State University	Louisiana State University, Baton Rouge
Burl L. Noggle Ph.D.	Duke University	Louisiana State University, Baton Rouge
Donald K. Pickens Ph.D.	University of Texas	North Texas State University
Mark A. Plummer Ph.D.	University of Kansas	Illinois State University
Francis P. Prucha Ph.D.	Harvard University	Marquette University
Germaine M. Reed Ph.D.	Louisiana State University	Georgia Institute of Technology
Merl E. Reed Ph.D.	Louisiana State University	Georgia State University
William L. Richter Ph.D.	Louisiana State University	Cameron College
Karl A. Roider Ph.D.	Stanford University	Louisiana State University, Baton Rouge
Courtney B. Ross M.A.	Yale University	Louisiana State University, Baton Rouge
Terry L. Seip M.A.	Louisiana State University	Louisiana State University, Baton Rouge
Gustav L. Seligman Ph.D.	University of Arizona	North Texas State University

Lewis P. Simpson Ph.D.	University of Texas	Louisiana State University, Baton Rouge
Beatrice Spade M.A.	University of Colorado	Louisiana State University, Baton Rouge
Ronald N. Spector Ph.D.	Yale University	Office of the Chief of Military History
Fredrick M. Spletstoser M.A.	University of Missouri at Kansas City	Louisiana State University, Baton Rouge
Emory M. Thomas Ph.D.	Rice University	University of Georgia
Anne Trotter Ph.D.	Duke University	Memphis State University
William M. Tuttle Ph.D.	University of Wisconsin	University of Kansas
Bennett H. Wall Ph.D.	University of North Carolina	Tulane University
Major L. Wilson Ph.D.	University of Kansas	Memphis State University
Theodore A. Wilson Ph.D.	Indiana University	University of Kansas

INITIALS IDENTIFYING CONTRIBUTORS
OF SIGNED ARTICLES

A.C.L.	Anne C. Loveland	J.K.	Jeffrey Kimball
A.T.	Anne Trotter	J.L.L.	John L. Loos
B.H.W.	Bennett H. Wall	K.A.R.	Karl A. Roider
B.K.	Burton Kaufman	L.P.S.	Lewis P. Simpson
B.L.N.	Burl L. Noggle	M.A.P.	Mark A. Plummer
B.S.	Beatrice Spade	M.E.R.	Merl E. Reed
C.B.R.	Courtney B. Ross	M.D.C.	Michael D. Clark
C.L.E.	Cecil L. Eubanks	M.L.W.	Major L. Wilson
D.H.	Donald Holley	M.O.D.	Merle O. Davis
D.H.C.	David H. Culbert	M.T.D.	Maurice T. Dominguez
D.K.P.	Donald K. Pickens	R.A.B.	Robert A. Becker
D.L.A.	David L. Ammerman	R.D.H.	R. Don Higginbotham
D.R.G.	Don R. Gerlach	R.F.E.	Robert F. Erickson
E.J.M.	Edward J. Maguire	R.H.C.	Richard H. Collin
E.M.T.	Emory M. Thomas	R.M.	Russell Magnaghi
F.J.D.	Fredrick J. Dobney	R.N.S.	Ronald N. Spector
F.M.S.	Fredrick M. Spletstoser	R.O.M.	Rex O. Mooney
F.N.M.	Frank N. Magill	S.E.A.	Stephen E. Ambrose
F.P.P.	Francis P. Prucha	S.L.C.	Sidney L. Cohen
G.L.S.	Gustav L. Seligman	T.A.W.	Theodore A. Wilson
G.M.R.	Germaine M. Reed	T.J.C.	Terrill J. Clements
G.Q.F.	George Q. Flynn	T.L.S.	Terry L. Seip
J.C.G.	John C. Gardner	W.G.H.	William G. Haag
J.D.	John Duffy	W.I.H.	William I. Hair
J.E.F.	James E. Fickle	W.J.C.	William J. Cooper, Jr.
J.F.F.	James F. Findlay, Jr.	W.L.R.	William L. Richter
J.G.C.	John G. Clark	W.M.B.	Warren M. Billings
J.H.D.	John H. DeBerry	W.M.T.	William M. Tuttle
J.J.B.	James J. Bolner	W.T.J.	W. Turrentine Jackson

GREAT EVENTS FROM HISTORY

ARRIVAL OF THE INDIANS, THE FIRST AMERICANS

Type of event: Sociological: prehistoric migration
Time: Unknown
Locale: The North American continent

Summary of Event

America's native populations have been the objects of centuries of speculation and investigation. From Europe's discovery of the American "Indian" at the end of the fifteenth century to the present, the question of who the Indians are and how they came to the Western Hemisphere has intrigued scholars, poets, clergymen, and laymen. The answers to these questions range from intricate and scholarly theories to arrant nonsense.

When it became apparent that Columbus had not reached India in 1492 but had instead found a new continent, Europeans sought to explain the existence of the New World's indigenous people. Some, especially clergymen, theorized that the Indians descended from the ten lost tribes of Israel. Others maintained that the Indians' ancestors were Welshmen whom Prince Madoc had led to America. Still others insisted that the natives came from the fabled lost continents of Atlantis and Mu. Periodically, from the sixteenth to the twentieth century, each of these notions held sway and none was entirely satisfactory. But the advent of anthropology as an academic discipline at the end of the nineteenth century promised to provide more prosaic interpretations based upon careful and scientific analyses of available data. Modern techniques such as dendrochronology, the dating of organic matter by means of carbon 14 tests, and the hydration of obsidian finds have enhanced the development of sophisticated theories to answer the questions Europeans first posed half a millennium ago.

Regarding the Indians' ancestral identity, anthropologists seem to agree on only one point—that the Indians did not arise *sui generis* in North America. As proof of this contention they note that no skeletal remains of a human physical type earlier than *homo sapiens* have yet been found in the Americas. This fact also makes possible the tentative dating of man's arrival on the continent because *homo sapiens* emerged from the evolutionary process about fifty thousand years ago, but there is disagreement over whether one or several archaic genetic stocks of *homo sapiens* populated the New World. The resolution of that controversy depends on one's conception of the manner in which early man arrived in the Western Hemisphere.

At present, many scholars believe that Asians came to America during two periods: the first, between 50,000 and 40,000 B.C.; and the second, between 26,000 and 8,000 B.C. They are believed to have come by way of a great land bridge between Asia and North America which existed at the Bering Strait. This causeway was covered by water from about 40,000 to 26,000 B.C. because of a melting episode in mid-Wisconsin glacial time.

Because of the many different early cultural remains which have been

1

found, it is generally held that there were several discrete, and perhaps isolated, movements of various peoples from Asia to America, rather than one steady flow for a short period of time. It is speculated that this migration was caused by an increase in population of the tribes of central Asia which impelled them to move eastward in quest of additional sources of food. As hunters, they had to follow the game in order to support life. So, as the animals retreated into North America, primitive man followed.

Once they arrived in the New World, these early men did not have to make many significant cultural adjustments to survive, for the resources and climates of North America and Asia are believed to have been similar. Generation by generation, however, population pressure urged them ever farther southward toward the margins of the two continents, so that by 8,000 B.C. there were primitive hunters even in Tierra del Fuego. Around 5,000 B.C., the disappearance of large game animals in both North and South America produced a series of regional developments in certain areas which culminated in the emergence of several great civilizations, such as those of the Inca and Aztec. At the same time, remnants of the old hunting cultures survived in some isolated areas such as California and the tip of South America.

Pertinent Literature

Josephy, Alvin M., Jr. *The Indian Heritage of America.* New York: Alfred A. Knopf, Inc., 1968.

Studies of the Indians' origins are voluminous. Frequently such studies require an understanding of anthropology and archaeology in order to render them intelligible. For the uninitiated but curious nonspecialist, Josephy's book is a good place to begin investigation of the subject.

Josephy's long acquaintance with contemporary Indians and their affairs has led naturally to a deep appreciation of the first Americans and the writing of two other books about Indians. This feeling is apparent in *The Indian Heritage of America,* for like other people concerned with the present condition of the red man, Josephy often seems to be pleading a case. He tries to penetrate white stereotypes about the Indian, to emphasize cultural and physical diversity among Indians, and to suggest how much white America has depended upon the Indian throughout its history.

Drawing widely from historical, archaeological, anthropological, and ethnographic sources, Josephy attempts to portray the Indian as he was and as he is. He describes concepts of society which were fundamentally different from those of Europe, and he argues that these basic distinctions account for the rise of the stereotypic Indian in American folklore. His reconstruction of pre-Columbian Indian societies demonstrates the great variety of cultural syntheses which existed before 1492. In examining the impact of Indian culture upon European culture, Josephy also shows the debt contemporary white America owes to the Indian. Then he moves into a discussion of the modern Indians' ancestral origins.

Josephy presents a balanced, brief reading of available evidence and modern scholarship without advancing any new theory of his own. He does not load his discussion with technicalities, yet he manages to convey the essentials of present knowledge. He touches lightly on pre-twentieth century theses, while giving some attention to suggestions like Thor Heyerdahl's belief that some South American Indians had contacts with natives from the Pacific islands. His general conclusion is that the Americas were populated by successive waves of prehistoric Asians who crossed the Bering Strait land bridge during the latter stages of the Wisconsin glaciation. Over a twenty to thirty thousand year period, these immigrants diffused throughout the hemisphere, developing distinct cultures, languages, and social customs. In developing these conclusions, Josephy relies mostly upon the recent work of an archaeologist named Alex D. Kreiger.

In seeking to explain the variant manifestations of culture, language, and physical types which the pre-Columbian Indian displayed, Kreiger has postulated a series of staged developments through which early man has passed. According to Kreiger's theory, these stages occurred at periodic intervals and for varying lengths of time in different parts of the Americas. The occurrence of the development was uneven throughout the hemisphere, and the stages were marked by numerous local and regional variations. Within this conceptual framework, Kreiger has formulated three stages: Pre-Projectile Point, Paleo-Indian, and Protoarchaic. These stages make possible the relation of available archaeological data to a spatial sequence, and help to account for the known cultural flowerings of prehistory.

Josephy does not maintain that Kreiger's typology provides a final solution to the questions of who the Indians' ancestors were and how they came here. He believes that new finds will continue to shed light on these matters.

Jennings, Jesse D. *Prehistory of North America.* New York: McGraw-Hill Book Company, 1958.

The study of the modern American Indians' origin indicates how history and other academic disciplines working in concert can gain new knowledge. Since the prehistoric Indian has left none of the types of data which historians ordinarily employ in their reconstruction of the past, they must, as Alvin Josephy has done, turn to the work of other scholars. In this instance, anthropologists and archaeologists have produced most of the best recent work about the Indians of prehistory. Consequently, those persons who seek a wider perspective on the matter than is offered by Josephy's book should go to the vast corpus of literature which anthropology and archaeology provide. An excellent introduction to this literature is Jesse Jennings' *Prehistory of North America.*

Professor Jennings has written a basic, but sophisticated, study of North American Indian archaeology. Jennings' book is designed to acquaint the student with the mysteries of archaeology. Jennings imparts the flavor of field work and the "exciting order, consistency, and unbelievable efficiency of the many American cultures or tradi-

3

tions" which the field techniques have revealed.

Drawing upon the work of numerous scholars, Jennings concludes that man probably arrived in successive waves on the North American continent from Asia during the latter stages of the Wisconsin glaciation. As the glacier retreated, the land bridge was submerged, and the men were trapped forever. Furthermore, Jennings accepts the idea that this prehistoric man had attained a high level of evolutionary development. None of these facts explains, however, why "the Indians were more nearly homogeneous and like one another than they were like any other population segment in the rest of the world." This question cannot be answered definitively on empirical grounds, but Jennings theorizes that the homogeneous Indian population probably derived from one or more primitive Asian populations between ten thousand and forty thousand years ago, who when isolated from Asia by the retreating glacier, became the genotype for the modern Indian. Some of the known skeletal remains tend to confirm such a view, but too many links are missing to make this concept a certainty.

The tentative nature of Jennings' conclusions focuses attention on a major problem about the attempt to obtain a precise view of the Indians' origin. Such data as have been discovered are so fragmentary that any theory based upon them is suspect and subject to revision pending new discoveries. Reference to Jennings' bibliography, which is extensive, demonstrates how often new discoveries have forced revisions of old ideas and theses. — *W.M.B.*

Additional Recommended Reading

Underhill, Ruth M. *Red Man's America: A History of Indians in the United States.* Chicago: University of Chicago Press, 1960. A standard introductory study of the North American Indian emphasizing anthropological and archaeological, rather than historical, evidence.

Martin, Paul S., *et al. Indians Before Columbus: Twenty Thousand Years of North American History Revealed by Archaeology.* Chicago: University of Chicago Press, 1947. This brief summary stresses the diversity of the Indians' racial origins and maintains that prehistoric men migrated to America in successive waves across the land bridge.

Bushnell, G. H. *The First Americans: The Pre-Columbian Civilizations.* New York: McGraw-Hill Book Company, 1968. Provides useful data on the Indians' origins.

Heyerdahl, Thor. *Kon-Tiki.* Chicago: Rand-McNally & Company, 1950. Advances the thesis that some of the Indians may have established contact with people on the Pacific Islands by sailing across the Pacific in balsa rafts.

Gladwin, Harold S. *Men Out of Asia.* New York: Whittlesey House, 1947. Accepts the Asian migration thesis while positing the assumption that the high culture areas were populated by Alexander the Great's soldiers.

Kreiger, Alex D. "Early Man in the New World," in *Prehistoric Man in the New World.* Edited by Jesse D. Jennings and Edward Norbeck. Chicago: University of Chicago Press, 1964. This article contains a complex discussion of the typology described in Alvin Josephy's *The Indian Heritage of America.*

THE MAYAN CALENDAR

Type of event: Technological: chronological invention
Time: c.350 B.C.
Locale: Southern Mexico and Guatemala

Summary of Event

Throughout meso-America during the period A.D. 300 to 1500, there were several related calendrical systems in use. Those of the Maya were undoubtedly the equal or superior of any others in completeness and internal relations. Compared to the Julian calendar, the Mayan system appears complex and difficult to understand, but actually it is relatively simple. Although the origin of the Mayan calendar is unknown and lost in antiquity, the Maya developed several devices through the centuries. The one usually meant in references to the calendar is the interrelated solar year of 365 days and the sacred year of 260 days.

Basic to all Mayan calendrics is the day. All reckoning was in single days or multiples of days. The 260-day scheme, now called the *tzolkin* or "count of days," is conceived of as an interrelationship of twenty named days through a cycle of thirteen numbers (20 x 13 = 260). This scheme has no astronomical basis and seems to be an arbitrary development of unknown origin. Although independent of movements of celestial bodies, undoubtedly it was an "astrological" guide to the fates of the Maya. The life of every individual was predetermined by the portent of the day upon which he was born. Each of the twenty days in the name cycle was controlled by a deity who was either benevolent or malevolent. Not only were the fortunes, and even the names, of individuals at the mercy of the gods, but the whole country was downcast on days ruled by dangerous gods, and cheerful on the days of benign spirits.

These twenty days marched inexorably through time one after another but they were geared to a succession of thirteen numbers. Their names and numbers beginning with each sacred year were as follows: (1) *Imix,* (2) *Ik,* (3) *Akbal,* (4) *Kan,* (5) *Chicchan,* (6) *Cimi,* (7) *Manik,* (8) *Lamat,* (9) *Muluc,* (10) *Oc,* (11) *Chuen,* (12) *Eb,* (13) *Ben;* (1) *Ix,* (2) *Men,* (3) *Cib,* (4) *Caban,* (5) *Eznab,* (6) *Cauac,* (7) *Ahau,* (8) *Imix,* (9) *Ik,* and so on. It will be noted that after (13) *Ben,* the numbers revert to (1) but the names continue; after (7) *Ahau,* the names revert to the first, *Imix.* Hence, (1) *Imix* would not appear again to inaugurate a new sacred year until after twenty cycles of thirteen days or thirteen cycles of twenty days, making up 260 days.

The Maya also recognized a year (the *haab*), roughly equivalent to the solar year. It consisted of eighteen months of twenty days each and a period of five days of uncertainty and foreboding. These nineteen "months" were called the "vague year," meaning that it approximated the true solar year. It has been supposed that the Maya realized the sacred year would not serve for marking the times of planting or harvesting, or for activities related to the annual changes in the sun. It is also evident that the astron-

5

omer-priests knew that this vague year did not correspond exactly to a solar or tropical year (365 days, 5 hours, 48 minutes, and 46 seconds). To have corrected the discrepancy by adding a day every four years, as is now done, would have played havoc with the interrelationships of the *haab* and the *tzolkin.*

The nineteen month names are *Pop, Uo, Zip, Zotz, Tzec, Xul, Yaxkin, Mol, Chen, Yax, Zac, Ceh, Mac, Kankin, Muan, Pax, Kayab, Cumhu,* and *Uayeb* (the five-day period). Each of the first eighteen were twenty days long, but they were numbered from 0 to 19, for the Maya thought it more important to indicate a day that was "seating" the month before beginning that month's day count. The last month, *Uayeb,* counted (0) *Uayeb* through (4) *Uayeb.* This last day of the solar year was followed by (0) *Pop.*

The Maya moved in a world of these two important chronological systems, recognizing that their relationship wound through time in such a way that the coincident New Year's day for the sacred calendar and the vague year calendar could only be repeated when the two had gone through a cycle of years that brought (0) *Pop* and (1) *Imix* to fall again on the same day. For a 260-day and a 365-day period this would be fifty-two vague years or 18,980 elapsed days. This time interval is called the "calendar round." It is unknown what the Maya called it.

It may be seen from the foregoing that in the fifty-two-year calendar round, each day had a dual designation, one for the *tzolkin* and one for the *haab.* Thus, a given day might be (3) *Cib* and (17) *Pop.* This day would not reappear in the same combination for fifty-two years.

As indicated above, the Mayan priests were cognizant of the difference between the vague year and the solar year. Each calendar round departed from fifty-two true solar years by thirteen days. In a few centuries the conjunctions of various cycles would be greatly different from the priestly calculations. This seems to have led directly to the evolution of a simple notational positional vigesimal number system remarkable for involving a zero concept. This mathematical system enabled the Maya to make corrections in their observations and note discrepancies between astronomical events and calendrical calculations. It does not mean that the *tzolkin* or *haab* were corrected or shifted, but rather that the ceremonial days were shifted from certain times to others as necessary.

The growing sophistication of astronomy and of mathematics produced other calendrical inventions for the Maya: the *tun,* an approximate year of 360 days, and the *katun* of 20 *tuns* or 7,200 days. Both these periods formed important permutational cycles with the *tzolkin.* In addition, the Maya devised a 584-day cycle for the planet Venus, and some lesser cycles based on the moon and solar eclipses.

Several meso-American peoples borrowed their calendars from the Maya, but none utilized year counts greater in length than the calendar round of the Maya. The Maya, however, took the remarkable step of devising a count that began from a fictitious starting point in the distant past, determined to be 3113 B.C. by some modern scholars. This count is now referred to as the "long count" or "initial series" calendar. The latter designation stems from the position of six glyphs at the beginning of each inscription carved on commemorative monuments. When another four are added, the glyphs give a total for the number of days that have elapsed since the beginning of recorded time. The long count made possible calculations of the dates of events far in the future and millions of years in the past. So accurate were the astronomer-priests with the long count calculations that any given event could be noted in the chronology not to recur for 374,440 years.

The classic period of Mayan culture is defined as the interval during which the long count was used. It was gradually phased out during the closing centuries of that period and was replaced by a shortened form of notation that enabled a given day to be indicated by only three glyphs instead of the ten necessary for the long count. Nonetheless, this cycle was accurate to within one day in nearly nineteen thousand years. Still later, further curtailment brought the count down to an accuracy of only one day in 256 years, a system called the "short count" by modern students.

Pertinent Literature

Thompson, J. Eric. *Maya Hieroglyphic Writing: An Introduction.* 2nd ed. Norman: University of Oklahoma Press, 1960.

This monographic study is truly monumental, definitive, and exhaustive. The first edition, entitled *Maya Hieroglyphic Writing: An Introduction,* was published in 1950 by the Carnegie Institution of Washington. The 1960 edition is an offset process reproduction with a new preface by the author. Although much research had been done in Mayan writing in the intervening decade, Thompson comments on these new efforts only briefly in the preface. The fact that the volume was reproduced in facsimile is indicative of its fundamental value to modern students. It will remain for some decades the essential source for studies on this subject. The new edition is part of the *Civilization of the American Indian* series, published continuously since 1932, by the University of Oklahoma Press on the aboriginal cultures of North, South, and Central America.

Thompson is not only a fine scholar but also a great artist, a craftsman in love with his work. His intimate knowledge of the whole range of available source materials—carved stelae, altars, building features, codices, and artifacts—gives an almost incontrovertibly authoritative ring to his treatment, although Thompson would be the first to admit that future students are almost certain to bring great changes to our present understanding of Maya hieroglyphs.

The introductory material in Thompson's work is largely devoted to a short sketch of the history of the Mayan civilization in its tropical rainforest setting. Particular emphasis is given to the religious beliefs of the Maya, for many hieroglyphs are concerned with religion and nearly all are representations or conventionalizations of deities. A description follows of glyphic texts such as are to be found on altars, monolithic stone monuments, door lintels, walls, ceilings, pyramid stairways, façades, ball courts,

7

artifacts, and codices. This description justifiably merits special attention. So also do the paragraphs on the history of research on Mayan glyphs and the disclosure of many still untranslated sources such as some of the books of the *Chilam Balam,* which are manuscripts written in Yucatec with European characters by native Maya during the colonial period.

Mayan writing is hieroglyphic in principle, and it is as complex and perplexing as ancient Egyptian. In the chapter entitled "Principles of Maya Glyphic Writing," Thompson sets forth the characteristics of the glyphs. Hieroglyphic writing generally involves the use of homophones, that is, words of similar sound but having different meanings, such as "fly" (an insect) and "fly" (process of flight). The word *xoc* in Yucatec is a mythical fish but the word also means "to count." In Mayan the head of a fish is the main glyph which means "to count forward to" or "count back to" depending upon prefixes or suffixes attached as part of the glyph. There are several other well-established homophonic glyphs that function in a similar manner.

Not all glyphs are homophonic. Many are purely pictorial or even ideographic. "The hieroglyph for 'west' is the back of a partly opened hand over the sun symbol. The hand in that position symbolizes 'completion' or perhaps 'ending.' 'End of sun' is an ideographic sign for 'west.' " This example demonstrates that decipherment of the glyphs is fascinating work.

The most important element in the panoply of calendric devices used by the Maya was the sequence of twenty days with their associated numbers. Together they constituted a unit; separately they meant nothing. Each day was named for some deity, represented in writing by his specific glyph. The origin of these symbols and the names associated with various Maya languages constitute an engrossing detective story. Thompson discusses the several explanations for the 260-day sacred year, but he discounts an astronomical basis for its origin. Similarly, the 365-day year was inspired by agricultural activities, but each of its nineteen months had a "bearer" who tirelessly furthered the "burden of time" through eternity.

The Mayan calendar called the "calendar round" served certain purposes in itself, but the Maya were not content to stop there. Further progress was limited until a good notational system was evolved. When and where numbers were first used in meso-America is unknown, but it was probably among peoples marginal to the Maya. Thompson documents the development of a mathematical system with a base of twenty. A dot for a unit (four dots in a row meant "four") and a bar for five enabled notation up to nineteen. Twenty had a separate symbol, the moon. All these numbers could be written in more than one way. Of great significance was the use of a symbol for zero.

The mathematical base was necessary before the long count cycle could be developed. The Maya were, perhaps, more interested in the past than in the future, and a counting system that enabled them to go beyond the calendar round of fifty-two years gradually came into use. Although counting was by days, the year of 360 days, called a *tun,* entered into these lengthy calculations. In keeping with the vigesimal base of twenty, the following calculations were

meaningfully employed by the astronomer-priests:

20 tuns	= 1 katun (7,200 days)
20 katuns	= 1 baktun (144,000 days)
20 baktuns	= 1 pictun (2,880,000 days)
20 pictuns	= 1 calabtun (57,600,000 days)
20 calabtuns	= 1 kinchiltun (1,152,000,000 days)
20 kinchiltuns	= 1 alautun (23,040,000,000 days)

The long count is obviously appropriately named.

Thompson devotes the remainder of his monograph to techniques for noting distances forward and backward through time (sometimes called "secondary series" when used with initial series). Minor cycles involving Venus, the moon, and eclipses are described. The final chapter is entitled "Aids to Decipherment," and several appendices expand certain problems in the study.

De Landa, D. *Landa's* Relación de las Coasas de Yucatan: *A Translation.* Translated by Alfred M. Tozzer. Papers of the Peabody Museum of American Archaeology and Ethnology, Harvard University, Vol. XVIII. Cambridge: Harvard University Press, 1941

No studies of the Mayan calendar seem possible without an acquaintance with *Landa's Relación de las Coasas de Yucatan.* In this translation there is special emphasis on passages that give the first exact knowledge of Mayan hieroglyphic writings. No other source offers so grand a view of Mayan life and none dwells so thoroughly on the religion of these people.

Tozzer's is the eighth translation of this famous manuscript discovered in Madrid in the nineteenth century. Its value surpasses that of all other translations because of the accompanying notes. The manuscript on which the translation is based was itself a copy and probably dates from about A.D. 1616. Tozzer believes that it is an incomplete copy of the original. Nonetheless, the two hundred pages of text and Tozzer's notes give great in-

sight into the daily life of the Maya.

Four other short manuscripts are included in the volume. Each is an extract from a longer account by a Spanish *conquistador.* Fray Landa was Bishop of Yucatan from 1572 until his death in 1579. The *Relación de las Coasas de Yucatan* was written about 1566. He undoubtedly had access to other written accounts, such as Oviedo's *Historia* published in 1550, and he seems to have drawn freely from various manuscripts which are appended to this edition.

Although Tozzer's translation is scholarly and may look uninviting to the lay reader, it is intriguing and fascinating. The serious student and the desultory searcher alike will find this volume indispensable for understanding Maya life. — *W.G.H.*

Additional Recommended Reading

Coe, Michael D. *The Maya.* New York: Frederick A. Praeger Publishers, Inc., 1966. One of the *Ancient Peoples and Places* series, this up-to-date volume is a comprehensive treatment of the whole Mayan civilization. It is scholarly but readable. It has a wealth of illustrations, mostly artifacts of the classic period, but drawings of glyphs make the calendar easily understood.

The Mayan Calendar

Morley, Sylvanus G. *The Ancient Maya.* 3rd ed. Revised by George W. Brainard. Stanford: Stanford University Press, 1956. Morley was one of the great scholars of the Maya who often differed from other students. This volume is extensively illustrated and is one of the most widely read concerning ancient civilizations of meso-America. Its exposition of the Mayan calendar and mathematics is excellent.

Thompson, J. Eric. *The Rise and Fall of Maya Civilization.* Norman: University of Oklahoma Press, 1954. An interesting and lively account of Mayan history directed to the general reader without factual evidence being modified or distorted. Not only is the daily life of the prehistoric Maya compared with that of colonial Maya, but a description of the living Maya is included.

NORSEMEN DISCOVER THE NEW WORLD

Type of event: Sociological: voyages of discovery
Time: c.990-1015
Locale: Labrador and Newfoundland

Principal personages:

ERIK THE RED (fl. 982-986), founder of the Greenland settlement

BJARNI HERJOLFSON (fl. 985), first European to sight American shores

LEIF THE LUCKY (fl. 999-1000), son of Erik the Red, who organized the first Norse expedition to America

THORVALD ERIKSON (fl. 1000-1010), Leif's brother, who was killed in battle with Indians and was the first Christian to be buried in North America

THORFINN KARLSEFNI (fl. 1002-1015), Icelander who tried to found a permanent settlement in America

Summary of Event

Much of our information about the discovery of America by the Norsemen is contained in the Icelandic sagas, histories which were written to glorify and preserve the traditions of a particular family. As such they have to be used with caution. If it were not for independent verification of the voyages, such as in the account written about 1075 by Adam of Bremen, a German monk, and other mostly ecclesiastical sources, one could justifiably doubt the truth of the saga material. What now is open to question is the location of the Norsemen's landfall on the North American continent; the extent of their exploration and colonization; and the centuries during which Norsemen from the Greenland colony continued to visit America's shores.

The two sagas which deal with the Norse voyages to America are *The Greenlander's Saga,* written perhaps as early as the twelfth century and preserved as part of a fourteenth century manuscript known as *Flateyjarbok* (*The Annals of Flatey,* an island); and *Eirik the Red's Saga,* known from *Hauksbok* (*Book of Hauk Erlendsson,* c.1330) and in another version, *Skalholtsbok,* written in the second half of the fifteenth century. *Skalholtsbok* (the book from Skalholt, the seat of Iceland's bishop), though later in date, is generally regarded as the more reliable of the two versions of *Eirik's Saga.* But the saga itself appears to have been based in part on the *Greenlander's Saga* and to have added details about the motives of the Norsemen which do not have the ring of authenticity. *The Greenlander's Saga* almost certainly represents a more genuine tradition, and the six voyages it describes are the basis for the following summary.

Bjarni was the son of Herjolf, an Icelander who had migrated to Greenland about 985 along with Erik the Red. Bjarni returned to Iceland from a visit to Norway and learned that his father had sailed west to the newly discovered Greenland. He set out from Iceland with a crew and sailed west for seventy-two hours until the land disappeared. Thereafter he sailed "many more days" until land was sighted. It was a land of woods and low hills. His crew asked Bjarni if this was Greenland, and Bjarni replied that he did not think it was Greenland. So the ship departed and sailed for two more days. A second land was sighted, flat with white sandy beaches and covered with forest, and Bjarni knew that this was not Greenland either. So the ship departed again and sailed northwest for three days and reached a third land of mountains and glaciers. Bjarni still did not believe that he had reached Greenland because the land "appeared to be worthless." So the ship set out again, and after four days came to a fourth land, which Bjarni declared to be Greenland. He landed near the very spot where dwelt his father. If Bjarni had sailed to a fifth land, one may reasonably suppose that the saga would have reported a trip of five days.

Bjarni made no attempt to follow up his discoveries, but the news of what he had found provoked great interest in the Greenland colony, and after some years (certainly after A.D. 1000), an expedition was fitted out under the leadership of Leif, the son of that Erik the Red who had founded the Greenland colony and who was its chief citizen.

Reversing Bjarni's sailing directions, Leif, with a crew of thirty-five men in Bjarni's old ship, first discovered a land covered by huge glaciers and which looked like a single slab of rock. He named it Helluland, or Flat Stone Land, after the first impression he had

received of it. Thereafter Leif found a second land which was flat, covered with forests, and had wide, sandy beaches. Leif called this land Markland, after the forests which he had first observed. After two more days of sailing, Leif sighted a third land and went ashore on an island which lay to the north of it. Here Leif and his men observed a fresh meadow with dew on the grass. They tasted the dew and it was sweeter than anything they had ever tasted before.

Leif and his men decided to winter in this third land at a place on the mainland where a river flowed out of a lake. Both river and lake were full of salmon, a fact suggesting New England or points north, as salmon do not usually occur south of the Hudson river. No frost occurred that winter, and the Norsemen noted that the length of day at mid-winter was much longer than in either Greenland or Iceland. Moreover, one of Leif's men, perhaps his first mate, Tyrkir the German, accidentally discovered vines and grapes.

The following spring, Leif and his men departed for Greenland, and Leif named the land in which he had wintered "Vinland." Offshore from Greenland, Leif rescued fifteen people shipwrecked on a reef. For this deed he was thereafter known as "the lucky."

The following spring, Leif's brother Thorvald decided to explore Vinland with a crew of thirty men. After arriving there, he used houses which Leif had built as a base, and attempted to explore the coast west of this point. The men remained in Vinland all that summer and the following winter. In the spring they sailed to the east of Leif's houses. They ran aground in a storm and their ship was wrecked.

After considerable delay while the ship was repaired—on a promontory which they named Kjalarness, the (ship's) keel's point—they continued their voyage eastward. Eventually they came to a promontory between two fjords, or inlets. Because of the beauty of the place, Thorvald decided to settle permanently on the site.

Shortly thereafter, Thorvald and his men discovered three skin boats, with three men under each. The Norsemen killed eight of these *Skraelings,* a name of uncertain derivation possibly meaning "wretch" and designating the aboriginal inhabitants of North America, but one escaped. Thus ended the first confrontation of white men and Indians in North America.

The saga then reports that Thorvald and his men were overcome with drowsiness, but were awakened by a magic voice which urged them to flee. The *Skraelings* returned to the Norse camp and flailed them with arrows. The crew fled to the ship, and eventually the *Skraelings* withdrew. But Thorvald had been mortally wounded in the armpit, and by his request he was buried on the promontory by his men. They put crosses at his head and feet and called the place Krossaness. Thorvald was thus the first white man and the first Christian to die and be buried in North America. The date must have been sometime after the conversion of Greenland to Christianity in the first decade after the year 1000.

When Thorvald's crew returned home, still another brother, Thorstein, attempted to sail to Vinland to fetch back his brother's body. But the sea was stormy, and after some weeks of tossing about, the ship landed in the western (or northern) settlement of Greenland.

About a year later a ship arrived in Greenland from Norway captained by Thorfinn Karlsefni. He settled near the farm of Leif Erikson and fell in love with Gudrid, Leif's sister-in-law and the widow of Thorstein, who had died of disease.

After the marriage was celebrated, Gudrid urged Karlsefni to explore Vinland. Extensive preparations were made, with provisions for a crew of sixty men and five women. After an uneventful crossing, the mariners arrived at Leif's houses in Vinland, and passed the first season successfully. There was plenty of food, as the men captured a whale which had been stranded on the beach, and they were able to hunt game and gather grapes.

The following summer the *Skraelings* appeared. They came out of the woods one day, but a bull which the settlers had brought with them terrified the aborigines, and they attempted to hide in the Norsemen's houses. Karlsefni and his men, however, barred the way. The Skraelings then set down packs which they carried containing furs, and tried to barter. Karlsefni decided to offer them milk, and the *Skraelings* were willing to exchange all their furs for milk. Thereafter Karlsefni ordered his men to build a stockade around their homes.

During the same summer Gudrid, Karlsefni's wife, gave birth to a son, who was named Snorri. He was the first white child, so far as is known, to be born in North America.

The subsequent winter the *Skraelings* returned and again traded furs for milk. But they also tried to steal the Norsemen's weapons. Fighting broke out, many of the *Skraelings* were killed, and the survivors fled the scene. Karlsefni thereupon decided to return to Greenland the following spring.

The *Greenlander's Saga* tells of a final voyage led by two Icelanders, Helgi and Finnbogi, and by Freydis, a daughter of Erik, but the story deals mainly with Freydis' treachery, and it is probably unhistorical.

Eirik's Saga, our other literary tradition, provides additional details of the voyages which may originally have been part of the *Greenlander's Saga* but were lost before that saga was written down. Or they may have come from another source. We may assume, however, that there were continuing Norse contacts from Greenland to the North American coast until the fourteenth century, when the Greenland colony itself was extinguished. But after the failure of Karlsefni's expedition, no extensive or permanent settlement was undertaken by the Norsemen on American shores.

Pertinent Literature

The literature on the Norse exploration of North America is vast. Much of it belongs to the realm of fancy rather than fact. There are learned treatises and the lunatic fringe. Both kinds of books have been produced in quantity for more than one hundred years.

Vinland has been found, or probably could be, in anyone's backyard. At least Emil Horsfjord thought that he had found Leif Erikson's house in his backyard on Cape Cod, a belief he described in a work published in the late nineteenth century. Others have located Vinland in one of four principal places: Newfoundland, the St. Lawrence Estuary, Cape Cod, and Chesapeake Bay. Part of the problem is the meaning of the word "Vinland." With a short "i," the name could mean "meadow land," and thus Leif might have named Vinland after the first quality that he noted there, a meadow of sweet grass, as he had named Helluland and Markland after the rocks and forests which he saw there first. Most scholars are of the opinion, however, that "vin" with a long "i" means "wine." At least Adam of Bremen called the place "Wineland" in 1075, and that is a nearly contemporary source.

But grapes do not grow in Newfoundland, where remains of houses which appear to be eleventh century Norse have recently been uncovered. Thus some writers have suggested that "vin" means "wine berries," such as currants.

Another problem concerns the observations of the length of day made in Vinland by Leif Erikson and his men. Basing his assumption on a description in the sagas that the position of the sun at the time of the evening meal in Vinland could be determined, a Norwegian mathematician (who assumed that the evening meal was at four o'clock) calculated that Vinland must have been on Chesapeake Bay. And an Italian geographer insisted that *Eirik's Saga* told of Niagara Falls ("they entered a river where the sea fell down from the land") and located Vinland north of Lake Ontario.

Still other books have dealt with the finding of ninth century Norse artifacts in Canada; the Runic (Germanic alphabet) inscription found or manufactured at Kensington, Minnesota, in 1898 and dated 1362; and the stone mill (probably built around 1675) at Newport, Rhode Island, which strongly resembles medieval Swedish architecture. All of these books attempt to relate their archaeological materials to the Vinland problem, while, if anything, they should connect them with the extinction of the Norse colony on Greenland in the fourteenth century.

The pre-Columbian map, now in the possession of the Yale University Library, which was drawn in the 1440's and which shows a stylized Vinland, has done little to provide corroboration for the truth of the sagas or the location of Vinland, and it is without value as a historical source. It is probable that the name "Vinland" was applied to a rather large region, and any attempt to localize it to a single province or state is doomed to failure.

There are two recent treatises on the Vinland problem which are most worthy of consideration.

Ingstad, Helge. *Westward to Vinland: The Discovery of Pre-Columbian Norse House-Sites in North America.* New York: St. Martin's Press, 1969.

The archaeologist has long been able to make stones speak, and they usually tell him what he wants to hear. Thus Ingstad has been able to transform a site at L'Anse aux Meadows (the Bay of Meadows) on the Northwest coast of Newfoundland from a settlement which appears to be Norse, made perhaps as early as the eleventh century, into the site of Vinland itself, established in the year 1000. Or perhaps he is overstating the case. Ingstad at least admits that other places could have been the Vinland of the sagas. But other scholars have not been so cautious. Samuel Eliot Morison, for example, in a book published in 1971, states definitively that L'Anse aux Meadows and Vinland are one and the same.

Ingstad and his wife, Anne Stine, both Norwegian archaeologists, searched the coasts of Labrador, Newfoundland, and New England as far south as Narragansett Bay in search of likely landfalls for the Norsemen. The ruins of houses of Norse type were uncovered in 1960 at L'Anse aux Meadows, and from 1961 to 1968, systematic excavations were undertaken there. Five houses were unearthed at first, and later on, a smithy. Charcoal in the hearths gave a carbon 14 dating of A.D. 1080, plus or minus seventy years. The year 1010 would do well for dating the Vinland voyages, but the year 1150 would not do so well.

The Norse character of the buildings was inferred from the discovery of iron slag, rusty nails, a needle whetstone, and a stone lamp. Much, also, has been made of a spindle-hole of Greenland type.

Ingstad has also compared old maps of Vinland, which show that medieval geographers believed it to be a promontory to L'Anse aux Meadows site. It must be admitted that, in general, L'Anse aux Meadows does conform to the geographical details given in *The Greenlander's Saga* and *Eirik the Red's Saga.*

However, Ingstad is at a loss to identify the grapes of Vinland because grapes simply do not grow so far north. He therefore is willing to believe that berries are meant, even though elsewhere he does not insist that New-foundland is Vinland. In other words, despite the difficulty posed by the philological evidence, Ingstad wants to believe that he has found Vinland.

Wahlgren, Erik. "Fact and Fancy in the Vinland Sagas," in *Old Norse Literature and Mythology, A Symposium.* Edited by Edgar C. Polome, pp. 19-80. Austin: University of Texas Press, 1969.

Professor Erik Wahlgren is a phi-lologist specializing in runology and folklore. His most notable book is a study of the Kensington Rune Stone of Minnesota (*The Kensington Stone, A Mystery Solved,* Madison, Wisconsin, 1958), which he believes he has shown to be a forgery. On the basis of largely philological evidence, Wahlgren in the present essay examines the question of the prior authority of *The Greenland-er's Saga* versus *Eirik's Saga,* and shows fairly convincingly the greater trustworthiness of the former. He takes up the question of "vin" meaning meadow, wine, or berries, and votes unequivocally for wine. He argues, moreover, that while the L'Anse aux Meadows site is doubtlessly authentic, "it is probably not the Wineland of the Sagas."

Wahlgren's treatise must be re-garded as the most judicious assess-ment of the Vinland problem yet pub-lished. It is improbable that a precise location of Leif's houses in Vinland will be made without extensive archae-ological discoveries by competent ob-servers under controlled conditions. But discoveries of this sort are usually made by amateurs, if not publicity seekers or treasure hunters.

One fact is certain: the Norsemen did get here, but precisely where or when is still very much a mystery. — *S.L.C.*

Additional Recommended Reading

Magnusson, Magnus and Hermann Palsson. *The Vinland Sagas: The Norse Discovery of America.* New York: New York University Press, 1966. A translation of *The Greenland-er's Saga* and *Eirik's Saga,* with a long introduction which emphasizes the prior au-thority of the *Greenlander's Saga.*

Oleson, Tryggvi J. *Early Voyages and Northern Approaches, 1000-1632.* Vol. I: *Canadian Centenary* series. London: Oxford University Press, 1964. The Vinland problem is dealt with briefly and sanely, with Vinland itself located on Cape Cod.

Jones, Gwyn. *The Norse Atlantic Saga: Being the Norse Voyages of Discovery and Settle-ment to Iceland, Greenland, America.* London: Oxford University Press, 1964. A highly readable account by a historian of literature who expresses no firm opinion on the location of Vinland but who is mostly in favor of Newfoundland.

Morison, Samuel Eliot. *The European Discovery of America: The Northern Voyages, A.D. 500-1600.* New York: Oxford University Press, 1971. A dashing account, written by a master of prose, but uncritical, assigning without foundation dates for the various voyages and ignoring controversy of any sort.

COLUMBUS LANDS IN THE NEW WORLD

Type of event: Sociopolitical: discovery and exploration of the Western Hemisphere
Time: 1492
Locale: The Caribbean Sea

Principal personages:
CHRISTOPHER COLUMBUS (c. 1451-1506), Italian navigator in
Spanish service who discovered America in 1492
ISABELLA I, QUEEN OF CASTILE (1451-1504), who was patron-
ess of the Columbus venture

Summary of Event

At 2:00 A.M. on October 12, 1492, three Spanish ships sailing under the command of an Italian navigator named Christopher Columbus made a landfall off a small coral island in the Caribbean. Soon after daybreak Columbus landed, named the island San Salvador, and took possession of it in the name of the Spanish Crown that had subsidized his voyage. Thus was the "New World" discovered.

This land, in fact, had been discovered many times before. The first discoverers were ancestors of the American Indian tribes who followed migrating game across the land bridge between Asia and North America that existed during the ice ages. Then came the Norsemen sailing west across the Atlantic from Scandinavia and Iceland at least five hundred years before Columbus; remnants of a Viking settlement dating from A.D. 1000 have been discovered on the coast of Newfoundland. They were followed by Basque and later other European fishermen in search of whales, and later cod on the Grand Banks. A century before Columbus sailed, they may have coasted Newfoundland and Nova Scotia and come ashore occasionally to find fresh food, to make repairs, and to trade with the natives.

What sets Columbus apart is the fact that he did not sail as a common fisherman who returned home to sell his catch and then perhaps to gossip in some seaport tavern about strange lands he had seen. Columbus sailed as an agent of the Spanish Crown, and on his return he reported his discoveries to the highest levels of Spanish government, and ultimately to Europe's most learned geographers and navigators. Almost as important as his rediscovery of the Americas was the fact that Columbus made that discovery generally known in Europe and thus spurred curiosity about, and interest in, what he had found.

But what had he found? There was considerable doubt. Much of the New World would be explored by men searching for what was not there—passages to India or golden cities—and Columbus was no exception. As he sailed west in the autumn of 1492, he was not looking for a new world, but for a short water route to the riches of the East Indies, and as he waited for dawn off San Salvador on October 12, he thought he had found it. Columbus made a second voyage in 1493-1494, coasting Puerto Rico, Jamaica, and

17

Cuba, but it was not until his third voyage in 1498, when he touched the South American mainland at present-day Venezuela, that he understood he had stumbled across a new continental land mass. Even then he remained convinced to his death that the islands in the Caribbean Islands and the new continent were but a short sail from Asia and the East Indies. After a brief, disastrous term as a colonial Governor on the island of Hispaniola (from which he was sent back to Spain in chains), he made one final attempt, in 1502, to find a water route to Asia. He failed again and spent the rest of his life unsuccessfully badgering the Spanish Crown for the honors and rewards he thought were his due.

Columbus' voyages typified later explorations in many other ways. The three elements that underlay almost all efforts at discovery and colonization —God, gold and glory—underlie his expeditions as well. Spain agreed to finance his explorations in part to convert Indians to Christianity, in part from hopes of rich profits (hopefully from gold), and Columbus sailed in part at least for glory, planning through his discoveries to win entry for himself and his descendants into Spain's nobility.

Through the years, Columbus' voyages have become almost as shrouded in myth as the lands he discovered were cloaked in mystery and ignorance. Columbus did not, for example, have to argue against scholars who thought the world was flat before Queen Isabella agreed to subsidize his trip. By 1492, Europe's learned men knew the world was round. Columbus did spend several years convincing Isabella that the trip was feasible, and a council of experts did recommend to the Crown that his proposals be rejected. Ironically, the experts were in some respects right and Columbus wrong. They argued, for example, that Asia was much too far away to be reached by simply sailing west from Europe. Columbus insisted that Japan would be found no more than 2,400 nautical miles west of the Canary Islands—in other words, he expected to find Japan about where the Virgin Islands are. Thus he underestimated the distance between Europe and where he wanted to go by about three hundred percent.

However wrong his theory was, Columbus' voyages nevertheless marked the beginning of general awareness of the New World. European attitudes toward the new-found islands were not always favorable. The first response was sometimes annoyance, and the Americas were occasionally looked upon as an obstacle to be sailed around rather than a resource to be developed. But with the discovery of gold in Central and South America, attitudes changed rapidly. Thanks to Columbus, the leading nations of the Old World found a new arena for competition and conflict. As news of his discoveries spread across Europe, the history of the Western World became increasingly the history of the Old World interacting with the New—an interaction that continues to shape world history today.

Columbus Lands in the New World

Pertinent Literature

Morison, Samuel Eliot. *Admiral of the Ocean Sea: A Life of Christopher Columbus.* Boston: Little, Brown, and Company, 1951.

There are many biographies of Columbus, but Samuel Eliot Morison's *Admiral of the Ocean Sea* is certainly the best known, and in many ways most unique. Most biographers content themselves with describing the life and significance of their subjects from printed or manuscript sources, but Morison went further. He tried to recreate (as much as was possible) Columbus' experiences as a navigator so that he might better understand and describe his four voyages. Morison chartered a sailing ship of roughly the size Columbus used and retraced a good deal of the explorer's route. Morison's first-hand knowledge of what it is like to travel under sail gives his biography a richness of detail and an aura of authenticity not found in other accounts. Thus Morison makes vividly clear the difficulties and dangers of sailing west into unknown waters in the fifteenth century that are often overlooked by modern readers for whom rapid transatlantic crossings in powered ships are a common occurrence.

One of Morison's most interesting chapters is entitled simply "A Day at Sea." In it he describes the common routine of sailing ships during Columbus' time, and he recounts some of the problems mariners faced. Take for example the simple matter of telling time. There were no clocks on board the *Niña, Pinta,* and *Santa Maria* except for sand-filled hourglasses. It took the sand thirty minutes to run from one section of the glass to another, and then one of the ship's company had to be ready immediately to reverse the glass in order to keep even a roughly accurate account of the time. The sand clocks had to be checked constantly against the stars and the position of the sun to keep them even remotely accurate. Since time reckoning was important for accurate navigation, Columbus' accomplishments as a sailor are all the more impressive.

Besides the hourglass, Columbus had only the most rudimentary instruments (compass and quadrant) to work with, and navigating by the stars was a relatively new art, known and practiced by a few mathematicians, astronomers, and cartographers, but not by ordinary sea captains. Columbus did not understand, nor did he have the instruments necessary to carry out, celestial navigation on his voyage to the New World. He navigated largely by dead-reckoning; that is, by using the compass and by glancing over the side to watch debris float by in order to estimate the speed and to guess roughly how much progress his fleet made on any given day.

Morison notes that the fifteenth century was a deeply superstitious and religious age. Sailors, who risked their lives against the uncertainties of wind and tide and storm, and against the horrors of presumed sea monsters, were prone to invoke all the divine assistance they could on every voyage. The normal routine of Columbus' ships included a daily series of religious rituals, normally common prayer or singing, conducted sometimes as often as every hour.

Another particular strength of Mori-

19

son's biography is the direct manner in which he deals with certain commonplace stories about Columbus, many of which are pure myth. Furthermore, Morison does not manufacture evidence or make loose guesses merely to flesh out his story. Where the evidence on a point is nonexistent or contradictory, Morison says so clearly, whether the issue is minor ("Who did the cooking? I do not know.") or more substantive ("For fifteen years the records tell us nothing of the Colombos").

There are some drawbacks to *Admiral of the Ocean Sea*. Morison, unfortunately, fell into the trap that catches many biographers who tend to develop too close a familiarity with their subjects and too great a liking for them. As a result, they sometimes credit them with more importance than may be justified. However courageous Columbus was, however brilliant a seaman and explorer, it is doubtful that he did "more to direct the course of history than any individual since Augustus Caesar," as Morison claims. And Morison makes only a few off-hand references to pre-Columbian discoverers, and then only to debunk what he calls the "Nordic Myth"—that Columbus may have learned of the New World during a voyage to Iceland that he made in 1477.

Despite these drawbacks, *Admiral of the Ocean Sea* remains among the best biographies of Columbus. Morison wrote from his own experiences as well as from documentary sources, and his book offers the kind of insight into the experience of crossing the ocean under sail five hundred years ago that is available in no other account.

Parry, J. H. *The Age of Reconnaissance: Discovery, Exploration, and Settlement, 1450-1650. History of Civilization* series. London: Weidenfeld and Nicholson, 1963.

J. H. Parry's *The Age of Reconnaissance* is a useful volume for putting Columbus' voyages in historical perspective. Rather than concentrate on one man, as did Morison, Parry takes a broader view and surveys the causes, events, and consequences of two centuries (1450-1650) of discovery and exploration. He points out that Columbus' effort was but one incident in a continuing pattern of exploration that began long before he sailed and that pushed outward the limits of Europe's geographic knowledge in other areas than the Americas. European sailors had been working south along the West African Coast, and even west into the Atlantic to discover and settle new islands long before the *Niña, Pinta,* and *Santa Maria* set sail.

But what caused this burst of exploration? What made it possible? And why did it occur at this particular time in history? Parry deals with these and related questions in the first part of his book, "The Conditions for Discovery". The two most common motives for exploration and colonization, he explains, were the two most commonly admitted by contemporaries—religious zeal and the desire for profit. They were well summarized by a Conquistador named Bernal Diaz, who explained that he went to the New World "to serve God and His Majesty, to give light to those who were in darkness, and to grow rich as all men desire to do." Those who did not go themselves were often willing to subsidize those who did, and for the same reasons. By the middle of the fifteenth century, for example, Portuguese and Spanish merchantmen began actively seeking some way to break into the virtual monopoly on the rich East Indies trade in spices, silk, ivory, and gold, held by Italian merchantmen from Venice and Genoa. Since that trade moved through the Levant and then the Mediterranean, the Portuguese, perched on the western flank of the Iberian Peninsula, sought an all-water route to the Indies that might give them a competitive advantage of their own. As Parry notes, they never found one, for even after Africa had been rounded, the voyages involved were so long and uncertain that Italian and other Mediterranean merchants retained much of their favored position. Monarchs, too, were sometimes willing to risk their funds in order to find new lands to conquer, new resources to exploit, and new sources of wealth to tap. Out of the search for these things came Columbus' voyages.

And behind all the commercial motives or the hope of personal wealth there lay the sanction of religion. Expansion south into Africa might be profitable, but it could also be justified as a crusade of sorts against Islam. Parry notes, for example, that under Isabella, Spain was caught up in a wave of religious crusading zeal in the fifteenth century that culminated in the final expulsion of the Moors from the Iberian Peninsula in the same year that Columbus sailed. Farther south, profit and piety combined again and the search for gold and colonies also included the search for converts among Black Africans. Commerce and converts together motivated more and more explorations of the African Coast, and once the New World was

discovered the same motives combined in the same way to promote exploration and colonization there.

These motives may explain, at least in part, why men were willing to risk their lives or their money on voyages of discovery or on colonizing schemes, but they fail to explain why they were willing to do so at this particular time in history. Many historians seek to relate the Age of Discovery to the Italian Renaissance. The general expansion of knowledge and the growing curiosity about the world in general that marked the Renaissance, they argue, sparked renewed interest in geography and a new determination to fill in the blank areas on maps. They suggest, in fact, that the Age of Discovery was a direct outgrowth of the Renaissance. Parry, however, warns that the connection between the Renaissance and the Age of Discovery has been emphasized too much, that the relationship is more complex than is sometimes suggested. "Portuguese captains" he explains, "were sailing on tentative voyages of Atlantic discovery long before the Italian Renaissance had seriously affected Iberian culture," and Columbus himself "embarked on his famous enterprise with an intellectual equipment which was mainly medieval and traditional." Thus, for Parry, the Age of Discovery was only a partial reflection of the Renaissance; it was instead an age of transition that stretched across the declining years of feudalism to the Renaissance and the emergence of early modern Europe.

The remaining portions of Parry's book deal with the events of the great Age of Discovery and their consequences. Parry provides brief accounts of the major voyages, including those of Columbus, not only in the Atlantic and the South Seas but also for Africa and the Indian Ocean. The final section of the book, "The Fruits of Discovery" deals with various European nations' efforts to organize, govern, and exploit the lands their explorers had found by accident or design.

The particular value of *The Age of Reconnaissance* is that it is not only a history of discovery and European colonization; it is those things and more. It is a history of European expansion, of the impact Europeans had on the new lands they discovered, and the impact those new lands had on them. The book's wide focus and broad range allowed the author to treat Europe's thrust into the New World and Africa and Asia not as a series of disconnected events or isolated voyages, but as complex, integrated processes that involved two centuries, five continents, and many nations. — *S.L.C.*

Additional Recommended Reading

Columbus, Christopher. *The Journal of Christopher Columbus, (During His First Voyage, 1492-1493) and Documents Relating to the Voyages of John Cabot and Gaspar Corte Real.* London: The Hakluyt Society, 1960, translated by Cecil Jane. The Hakluyt Society is the foremost source for published explorers' journals, letters, and other first-person accounts of discovery and exploration. Columbus' *Journal* is the source for much of what is known about his voyages.

Crone, G. R. *The Discovery of America. Turning Points in History* series. London: Hamish Hamilton & Co., Ltd., 1969. A broad survey of New World explorations from the pre-Columbian period to the sixteenth century. Nearly one-third of the chapters deal with Columbus.

Elliott, J. H. *The Old World and the New, 1492-1650.* Cambridge: Cambridge University Press, 1970. Concentrates on the impact the discovery of America had on European thought about geography, history, religion, and the nature of man.

Oleson, Tryggvi J. *Early Voyages and Northern Approaches, 1000-1632.* Vol. I: *Canadian Centenary* series. Toronto: McClelland and Stewart, 1963. Part of the Canadian Centenary series, this volume is a good source for pre-Columbian explorations in the North Atlantic.

Penrose, Boies. *Travel and Discovery in the Renaissance, 1420-1620.* Cambridge: Harvard University Press, 1955. One of the better surveys of Renaissance exploration. Includes an informative chapter on the classical and medieval background to the Age of Discovery.

Wright, Louis B. *Gold, Glory, and the Gospel: The Adventurous Lives and Times of the Renaissance Explorers.* New York: Atheneum Publishers, 1970. A popularly written account of the New World exploration which contains an especially good discussion of the motives for exploration and colonization.

THE VOYAGES OF JOHN CABOT

Type of event: Sociopolitical: early exploration of North America
Time: 1497-1498
Locale: Bristol, England, and the coast of Newfoundland

Principal personages:
> JOHN CABOT (GIOVANNI CABATA) (1450-1498), Italian explorer in the service of England
> SEBASTIAN CABOT (1476?-1557), his son, a "genial and cheerful liar"
> HENRY VII (1457-1509), King of England

Summary of Event

The late fifteenth century was an age of intense, increasingly national rivalry. When, therefore, the news went around that Christopher Columbus by sailing west had landed on a hitherto unknown coast, all the nations fronting on the Atlantic became interested in exploring the new world and laying claim to some of the lands which Spain and Portugal planned to reserve for themselves. England, now at peace after the Wars of the Roses, with a strong government headed by that canny monarch, Henry VII, had no intention of being left out. To us, accustomed to thinking of the English as the great seafaring nation of Western Europe, it may seem strange that Henry should have turned to a foreign mariner to begin his outreach for a piece of the new world. But so he did; his choice fell on an Italian, John Cabot. Like other monarchs of the era, Henry was willing to use the services of such seamen whenever they were available.

Actually, we know very little about John Cabot. "No portrait, no personal description of him, no letter, no scrap of his handwriting, not even a signature has been found." The assiduous re-searches of several scholars have, however, turned up a few facts. It is reasonable to conclude that Cabot was born in Genoa, nursery of seamen, possibly in 1450, a year before Columbus. In 1484 he was married and living in Venice, where he had resided the fifteen years required to gain Venetian citizenship. Between 1490 and 1493, a John Cabot, possibly the navigator, resided in Valencia, Spain. We know that in 1495 he was in England trying to interest Henry VII in trans-Atlantic explorations.

It is significant that Cabot, with his wife and three sons, was then living in Bristol. Bristol, with its good harbor on the Avon river, was the second largest port in England. It faced the Western Ocean, carried on a large trade in spices, and was the headquarters of a large fishing fleet. It is little wonder that many of its inhabitants were deeply interested in western exploration.

Cabot was successful in his attempt to engage the King's interest. On March 5, 1496, Henry granted him letters patent to sail east, west, and north with five ships. As the King's lieutenant, he was to govern all lands he might find, but the King was to have one-fifth of all profits. Cabot was not to venture south, for Henry wanted no trouble with Spain or Portugal.

On or about May 20, 1497, Cabot set sail from Bristol. Instead of five ships, he had only one, the *Mathew*, a vessel of fifty tons burthen, with a crew of eighteen men. It was the equivalent of a fair-sized modern yacht. Going around the south end of Ireland, he last sighted land at Dursey Head. His plan, a favorite one with westbound mariners in that age, was to follow a parallel of latitude straight west. Dursey Head is in latitude 51° 33′.

At 5 A.M. on June 24, Cabot came in sight of land again. He had made the Atlantic crossing in thirty-one days. The exact spot where he first saw the coast of North America has been much disputed, and the dispute has been made foggy by local patriotism, various places trying to be "firsts." Samuel Eliot Morison, whose account is one of the best, concludes that what Cabot saw was Cape Dégrat on the northeast tip of Newfoundland (latitude 51° 37′ —only 4′ off the Dursey Head latitude). If that is true, he had performed a real feat of navigation, having come almost straight west from the Irish coast. Furthermore, he was only five miles from where it is believed Leif Erikson had landed in 1001. Turning south, Cabot entered Griquet Harbor, where he made his only landing. Here he formally took possession of the country in the name of Henry VII. Continuing his southward course, he skirted the whole east side of the island and rounded its southern tip into Placentia Bay. From Placentia he turned about, retraced his course to Cape Dégrat, and on July 20 left for home. After a fast passage of

fifteen days, he made landfall at Ushant on the coast of Brittany, headed north, and on August 6 was in Bristol. Cabot had not found the way to Japan or China, and he had brought back neither gold nor spices, but he had found a coast teeming with codfish—a most important fact.

Cabot wasted no time in Bristol, but hurried to London to make his report to Henry. The King gave him £10, and on the thirteenth of the following December, settled on the explorer a pension of £20 per year. That, for Henry VII, was liberality.

On February 3, 1498, Henry issued new letters patent giving Cabot authority to impress six ships for a second voyage to the new world. Cabot was now to explore more thoroughly the coast he had touched, and when he had reached the source of the spice trade, to set up a trading factory with the intent of funneling that desired commodity to English ports. Cabot succeeded in obtaining five ships with which he sailed from Bristol at the beginning of May, 1498. One ship turned back, but Cabot and the other four disappear from the pages of history. To this day, no one knows what happened to any of them.

The Cabot story does not end with the disappearance of John. Much more is known about his son Sebastian. Sebastian may, as a boy of fifteen, have accompanied his father on the first voyage. He said that he did, but his statement is not particularly good evidence. He also claimed to have made in 1508 a voyage to discover the fabled Northwest Passage, but as he was a "genial and cheerful liar," we do not know that this is true. He certainly knew how to feather his own nest. He set up as an expert adviser to would-be explorers and was paid by the kings of both England and Spain for his advice. He died in England about 1557. Eventually, John's name was practically forgotten, and historians took Sebastian to be the discoverer of North America.

The one voyage of John Cabot, for all the gaps in the story, may seem a small thing in the history of American exploration. But it had great results, for on Cabot's voyage was laid the British claim to North America. After a long interval, it became one of the foundation stones of the first British empire.

Pertinent Literature

Morison, Samuel Eliot. *The European Discovery of America: The Northern Voyages, A.D. 500-1600.* New York: Oxford University Press, 1971.

This is the best starting place for anyone who wants to know about the exploratory work of John Cabot. Samuel Eliot Morison is one of the best of living American historians, and this book is up to his high standards. As its title indicates, it is a comprehensive work, telling the story of the explorations of the North American coast from the mythical voyages of St. Brendan through the Virginia expeditions of 1585-1587. One chapter is devoted to John Cabot, and part of a second to his son Sebastian. Thus the Cabots are placed in their proper relation to the whole process of northern exploration.

It is one of Morison's great merits as an historian that he is able to combine qualities not often found in one writer. His narrative style is excellent. He makes good use of the historical imagination; but back of it lies thorough research. Thus at the end of the chapter on John Cabot, which is told as a straightforward story, he has eighteen pages of bibliography and notes. This is a critical bibliography in which Morison lists with comment the principal modern works dealing with Cabot, discusses with humor the various theo-ries as to where Cabot's explorations actually led him, and adeptly uses and reproduces early maps.

One of the most valuable features of these notes is the inclusion of the complete text of the recently discovered John Day letter. Day was an English merchant, resident at times in Bristol and Seville, who wrote a letter to Columbus in the winter of 1497-1498 in which he described at some length Cabot's first voyage. This is the only contemporary account of that event of which we know.

Morison has a particular advantage over all other historians who have dealt with the early explorations of North America. He is himself a practical sea-man who has handled sailing ships. As a result, his chapter on "English Ships and Seamen, 1490-1600" is one of the best features of the book. Furthermore, the historian himself has sailed the coast of Newfoundland and has a first-hand acquaintance with its fogs and icebergs. These facts make for lively narrative. The book is superbly illus-trated with reproductions of old maps and with modern photographs of the Newfoundland coast.

The Voyages of John Cabot

Williamson, James A. *The Cabot Voyages and Bristol Discovery Under Henry VII, with the Cartography of the Voyages by R. A. Skelton.* Cambridge: Published for the Hakluyt Society at the University Press, 1962.

This is in many ways the best single book on the Cabots for students who want to dig deeper than in Morison. Williamson was a Cabot specialist who devoted years to thorough and painstaking research of his subject. The result is a volume of over three hundred pages. Samuel Eliot Morison obviously depends on Williamson for many of his facts and makes suitable acknowledgment. On the other hand, Williamson frequently cites earlier works of Morison on exploration.

In spite of their interdependence, however, Morison and Williamson sometimes come to quite different conclusions. Williamson cites considerable evidence to prove that, after 1480, Bristol mariners were reaching out into the Atlantic in quest of something new, and he is sure, on what seems to be slim evidence, that in 1494 Nicholas Thorne and Hugh Elyot, both sailing from Bristol, anticipated Cabot and discovered a "New found Land." This opinion, of course, affects Williamson's whole estimate of Cabot's method and his achievement. Williamson is probably on safer ground when he discusses Cabot's second expedition, maintaining that it was very unlikely that all four of the ships in that expedition were lost. And, unlike Morison, Williamson is by no means certain where Cabot actually landed. He debates all the possibilities and votes at times for Cape Breton, and at other times for Maine. Otherwise, the two writers are in close agreement on the facts of the narrative.

Morison and Williamson, however, differ widely in their method of presenting those facts. Morison writes straightforward narrative. Bibliography, documentation, and scholarly argument are all placed together at the end of each chapter; the reader may take them or leave them. Williamson, on the other hand, might be said to incorporate his footnotes (and they are many) in his text. This makes his work far more difficult reading than Morison's. But these are two different kinds of books, and each writer uses the method suitable to his purpose.

One of the most interesting features of *The Cabot Voyages* is the long chapter on the career of Sebastian Cabot, in which the writer makes the point that until well into the nineteenth century John Cabot was practically forgotten, and the historians invariably treated Sebastian as the discoverer of North America.

Williamson's volume has two concluding sections which add greatly to its usefulness. More than one hundred pages are taken up by quotations from forty relevant documents, some of which are given in their entirety. Also, R. A. Skelton has contributed thirty pages on the cartography of the Cabot voyages. — *D.R.G.*

Additional Recommended Reading

Beazley, Charles R. *John and Sebastian Cabot: The Discovery of North America.* London: T. F. Unwin, 1898. This is a competent and documented study by an Oxford specialist in historical geography, and it is easier reading than Williamson. Beazley concludes, against all other modern scholars, that John Cabot returned from his second voyage.

Biddle, Richard. *A Memoir of Sebastian Cabot, with a Review of the History of Maritime Discovery.* Philadelphia: Carey and Lea, 1831. Republished at Freeport, New York: Books for Libraries Press, 1970. Originally published anonymously, this book has historical importance as the first attempt to apply serious scholarship to the Cabot story.

Hakluyt, Richard. *Divers Voyages Touching the Discovery of America and the Islands Adjacent.* Edited by John W. Jones. New York: Ben Franklin Press, 1963. A reprint of the famous Elizabethan collection of source material, first published in 1582 and a best seller in the years following.

Harrisse, Henry. *John Cabot: The Discoverer of North America and Sebastian Cabot, His Son, a Chapter in Maritime History of England Under the Tudors, 1496-1557.* London: B. F. Stevens, 1896. Written by the foremost French expert in the history of American discovery, this book is notable for its attack on the fictions and inflated reputation of Sebastian Cabot.

Winsor, Justin. *Narrative and Critical History of America.* Boston and New York: Houghton, Mifflin Co., 1884-1889. 8 vols. Vol. III, ch. I, by Charles Deane, consists of a brief narrative followed by a long discussion of authorities and is an excellent summary.

Weare, George E. *Cabot's Discovery of North America.* London: John Macqueen, 1897. A very discursive but thoroughly documented account, this work holds that Cabot landed on Cape Breton.

CARTIER AND ROBERVAL SEARCH FOR A NORTH-WEST PASSAGE

Type of event: Politico-economic: establishment of French claims in the New World
Time: 1534-1543
Locale: Gulf of St. Lawrence and the St. Lawrence river

Principal personages:
JACQUES CARTIER (1491-1557), master mariner
JEAN-FRANÇOIS DE LA ROQUE, SIEUR DE ROBERVAL (fl. 1544), soldier, courtier, colonizer
FRANÇOIS I (1494-1547), King of France 1515-1547
PHILIPPE DE CHABOT, SIEUR DE BRION (1480-1543), Admiral of France

Summary of Event

From 1492 to about 1534, the exploration of the New World was almost the exclusive domain of Italian seamen. When England and France contested the Spanish and Portuguese monopolies, they employed Cabot and Verrazano, both Italians. During the third decade of the new century, however, Italian explorers were replaced by other nationals.

As soon as John Cabot's report of the marvelous shoals of fish he had observed off the coast of Newfoundland reached the mainland of Europe, fishing boats from Brittany, Normandy, and Portugal began to brave the hazardous crossings of the North Atlantic to reap the harvest of these new and teeming waters. From these fisheries sprang the beginnings of New France.

Jacques Cartier was born probably in 1491 in Saint-Malo, one of the most notable of French fishing ports. He went to sea early and became an experienced navigator, being awarded the coveted title of master pilot. Before he appeared in the clear light of history, he evidently visited the Newfoundland fisheries and voyaged to Brazil. He was apparently well-esteemed in his native community, for it is recorded that he acted as a sponsor at no less than twenty-seven baptisms.

In 1534, when he was forty years old, Cartier was commissioned by the King of France to head an expedition across the Atlantic in search of a Northwest Passage to the Orient. Setting out on April 20 from Saint-Malo with two ships of about sixty tons burden each, Cartier made his landfall on May 10, at Cape Bonavista on the eastern coast of Newfoundland. After exploring the island, he crossed the Gulf of St. Lawrence to Cape Breton and the Prince Edward Island, landing on the Gaspé Peninsula. Here, upon the pledge of returning them, he was given two sons of a Huron chief to take to France. From Gaspé, Cartier sailed north to Anticosti Island. Returning to Newfoundland on August 15, he set sail for home and arrived at Saint-Malo on September 5. Although he had not found the Northwest Passage, Cartier had explored extensively the Gulf of St. Lawrence and its islands, and he was enthusiastic about the new country.

28

As a result of his favorable report, the French leaders began to think of planting outposts of the kingdom in these new lands. By royal command the Admiral of France commissioned Cartier Commander in Chief of a second expedition of three ships which was to sail beyond Newfoundland and discover and occupy lands for France. The little flotilla left Saint-Malo on May 19, 1535. This time the crossing was imperiled by severe storms, but Cartier reached Blanc Sablon, Newfoundland, on July 15; not until July 26, however, did all three ships assemble there. He had with him the two Indian boys he had taken from Gaspé the previous year. They had learned to speak French, and they told him of the great river which poured into the Gulf of St. Lawrence. Steering west and north of Anticosti Island, he entered the great river, the first white man to travel that highway into the North American interior.

As Cartier progressed up the St. Lawrence river, piloted by his two Huron guides, he was welcomed by natives from the shore. Passing the Island of Orleans, in mid-September he came to the Indian village of Stadaconé, the magnificent site of the future city of Quebec. Here he was greeted by Chief Donnaconna, who welcomed the return of his two sons but tried to dissuade Cartier from further ascending the river. Donnaconna feared the loss of his French ally to the chief of Hochelaga. But ambition and curiosity drove the Frenchman on; he set out on September 19 with the smallest of his vessels, a pinnace, and on October 2 came to Hochelaga (now Montreal) the metropolis of the Indians on the St. Lawrence. Here the Hurons feasted Cartier and tempted him with hints of a rich kingdom to the west called Saguenay. But from the top of Mont Royal Cartier saw that the rapids beyond blocked further travel inland, and he returned to Stadaconé, above which his men had built a fort. There they wintered rather than risk an unseasonable Atlantic passage. Autumnal brilliance gave way to months of ice and deep snow, and scurvy became rampant but was conquered with an Indian bark remedy. Musing upon the fabled riches of Saguenay, Cartier and his men resorted to treachery. In May, 1536, they kidnaped Donnaconna and four other Hurons as evidence to convince King François that further exploration would be profitable. With five other Indians, who apparently went without force, they set sail for France on May 6. The Atlantic crossing was speedy, and on July 15 Cartier was back at Saint-Malo. On this voyage he had opened the way for penetrating North America and had mapped out the principal sites of the future New France.

The King, impressed by Cartier's Huron captives, his samples of ores which promised diamonds and gold, and the reports of a land of spices and other abundant resources, determined to develop a colony in the New World —a New France. War between France and Spain interfered with his plans until 1538. Then followed three years of elaborate preparations and diplomatic difficulties. In 1540 Cartier received a royal commission to help lead the undertaking with a grant from the treasury. But in January, 1541, Jean-François de la Roque, Sieur de Roberval, was given command of the venture, and Cartier's authority could be exerted only in Roberval's absence.

They procured and equipped five vessels, and on May 23, 1541, Cartier sailed from Saint-Malo on his third voyage. Roberval was to follow later. Settlement was now the main aim, though Christian missionary efforts and the search for Saguenay were also important objectives. After a rough Atlantic crossing, the expedition entered the Gulf of St. Lawrence and then proceeded up the river and on August 23 arrived at Stadaconé (Quebec). Welcomed by the Hurons despite his earlier kidnaping exploits, Cartier proceeded to settle his colonists beyond Quebec at Cape Rouge for an easier approach to Saguenay. Two of his vessels were sent home with news and samples of spurious minerals. They reached Saint-Malo on October 3. Leaving the Vicomte de Beaupré' in command, Cartier proceeded to Hochelaga (Montreal) and explored the rapids above it. The events of the winter of 1541-1542 are unknown except for sailors' gossip later of Indian attacks, scurvy, and misery.

On April 16, 1542, Roberval with three ships and perhaps two hundred colonists sailed from La Rochelle for New France. On June 7 the expedition entered the harbor of what is now St. John's, Newfoundland. Meantime, the winter in Canada had been too much for Cartier, and he had abandoned the

settlement at Cape Rouge in June and struck out for Newfoundland. At St. John's he found Roberval's reinforcements. In spite of Roberval's order, he slipped out into the Atlantic and returned to Saint-Malo. Roberval pushed on, ascended the St. Lawrence, and rebuilt Cartier's abandoned settlement. He sent two ships home for reinforcements in September. A difficult winter followed in which Roberval was forced to resort to drastic disciplinary measures to maintain order. In June, 1543, Roberval began his search for the riches of Saguenay, but stopped when his boat was wrecked.

By mid-September, 1543, Roberval was back in France, so he probably gave up the settlement in New France by late July. His return marked the end of the first attempt of the French to settle Canada. François I died in 1547, and his son Henry II was uninterested in American exploration. The outbreak of religious wars in France prevented any further colonizing efforts for half a century. Cartier bought a manor near Saint-Malo where he lived, respected by all his neighbors, until his death in 1557. He had revolutionized cartographical knowledge by his well-recorded findings, but for the moment neither his nor Roberval's exploits were promising enough to overcome France's European preoccupations.

Pertinent Literature

Baxter, James P. *A Memoir of Jacques Cartier.* New York: Dodd, Mead and Co., 1906.

This is the best single book in English on Cartier and his explorations. Baxter was a bank president and several times mayor of Portland, Maine,

but he made himself into a competent historical scholar, specializing in early American explorations in Maine and Canada. The scholarship of this volume is both massive and thorough. It includes, besides Baxter's own narrative, a mass of primary material for the study of the Cartier and Roberval voyages. There are several hundred pages of translated documents. Of these the most fascinating is an account of Cartier's first voyage, written in the first person. Baxter concluded that this was not, as some over-enthusiastic scholars maintained, written by Cartier himself, but that Cartier's evidence is in back of it. There are also early narratives of the second and third voyages, a collection of what Baxter calls "collateral documents," a bibliography containing fifty-eight entries, and an itinerary of the three expeditions, given almost day by day. And there are maps, both early and modern. All the material for a thorough study of the subject is here within the covers of this one volume.

But to write good history one needs something more than careful research and accurate documentation. One needs historical imagination. This Baxter also has. Of the writers considered in this survey, he is the only one who formed a clear mental picture of what manner of man the explorer was: brave, calm, self-reliant, but most of all depending upon the "support of an overruling Providence." Living in nearby Maine, Baxter had the opportunity of following the Canadian tracks of Cartier and Roberval. He, therefore, describes their voyages with a graphic pen that reminds one of Francis Parkman; and there can be no higher compliment. This is good history.

Parkman, Francis. *Pioneers of France in the New World.* 4th ed. Boston: Little, Brown, and Company, 1912.

Of all that group of historians who participated in the flowering of New England—Bancroft, Palfrey, Hildreth, and others—Parkman seems to have best stood the test of time. He is still read, not out of curiosity, but by people who want to know the story and to enjoy it. The volume under consideration first appeared in 1865. It was the beginning of that noble series of works which traced the fortunes of New France from the beginning to their end with the decisive defeat of the French by the English on the Plains of Abraham.

The scholarly labor involved in this work was enormous. It was almost a virgin field, and the bibliographic aids available to the modern scholar were not in existence in the middle of the nineteenth century. Parkman ransacked the libraries of Canada, made several trips to France, and became a master of the sources. Since his time, new materials have come to light, but none of them seems to have disturbed his conclusions.

The results of Parkman's labors are meticulous scholarship set forth in magnificent prose. A sample will indicate how completely he visualized the scenes of his narrative and how vividly he pictured them for the reader. Cartier is here seeing the site of Quebec: "As he drew near the opening of the channel, the Hochelaga again spread before him the broad expanse of its waters. A mighty promontory, rugged and bare, thrust its scarped front into the surging torrent. Here, clothed in the majesty of solitude, breathing the stern poetry of the wilderness, rose the cliffs now rich with heroic memories, where the fiery Count Frontenac cast defiance at his foes, where Wolfe, Montcalm, and Montgomery fell."

In one respect, Parkman's narrative is better than that of Baxter. Baxter allowed himself to be swamped by detail. At times, to follow his narrative of Cartier's explorations, one must have before him a detailed map. Parkman accomplished his result by giving only the detail which a reader may easily carry in his mind.

In two other respects Parkman's work is superior. Unlike some historians, he was always aware of the European background of the story and constantly related American events to this background. And being singularly free from Puritan prejudice, he gave due credit to the Catholic missionary motive in French exploration and settlement. — *D.R.G.*

Additional Recommended Reading

Biggar, H. P. *The Voyages of Jacques Cartier.* Ottawa: Public Archives of Canada *Publications,* No. 11, 1924. Not a narrative, but a source book, giving the principal documents in French, with an English translation and copious notes. This and Biggar's *Collection of Documents Relating to Jacques Cartier and the Sieur de Roberval,* Public Archives of Canada *Publications,* No. 14 (Ottawa, 1930), contain all that is known of the Cartier-Roberval voyage.

Morison, Samuel Eliot. *The European Discovery of America: The Northern Voyages, A.D. 500-1600.* New York: Oxford University Press, 1971. In three superbly packed chapters, the exploits of Cartier and Roberval are summarized in considerable detail. A combination of fine scholarship, detailed bibliographical commentary, and attractive narration.

Pendergast, James F. and Bruce G. Trigger. *Cartier's Hochelaga and the Dawson Site.* Montreal and London: McGill-Queen's University Press, 1972. Analysis of archaeological data and ethno-history concerning the size and location of the Indian town visited by Cartier in 1535.

Pope, Joseph. *Jacques Cartier, His Life and Voyages.* Ottawa: A. S. Woodburn, 1890. This small volume of 168 pages is a popular essay, without documentation, but a good example of its type.

Winsor, Justin. *From Cartier to Frontenac: Geographical Discovery in the Interior of North America in Its Historical Relations, 1534-1700.* New York: Houghton, Mifflin Co., 1894. An excellent brief summary, with Winsor's usual good scholarship, especially valuable for its maps and illustrations.

Wrong, George M. *The Rise and Fall of New France.* 2 vols. New York: The Macmillan Company, 1928. This, perhaps the best general history of New France, contains an excellent chapter on Cartier, with a critical bibliography.

DE SOTO'S EXPEDITION AND THE FOUNDING OF ST. AUGUSTINE

Type of event: Sociopolitical: exploitation of Spanish conquests in the New World
Time: Sixteenth century (c.1539)
Locale: Southeastern United States

Principal personages:
JUAN PONCE DE LEÓN (1460?-1521), discoverer of Florida in 1513
ALONZO ALVAREZ DE PINEDA (fl. 1519), explorer of the Florida Gulf Coast in 1519
LUCAS VASQUEZ DE AYLLÓN (?-1526), explorer of the Atlantic Coast of Florida and the Carolinas as far as Cape Fear in 1526
PÁNFILO DE NARVÁEZ (1480?-1528), leader of the expedition which landed at Tampa in search of gold
HERNANDO DE SOTO (1500?-1542), principal Spanish explorer of the southeastern United States between Tampa Bay and the Arkansas river in 1538
GASPARD DE COLIGNY (1519-1572), French Admiral who promoted Huguenot settlements along the Atlantic Coast of Carolina and Florida in 1562-1564
JAN RIBAULT (1520?-1565), and
RENÉ GOULAINE DE LAUDONNIÈRE (fl. 1562-1586), who led the first French settlers to the area
PEDRO MENÉNDEZ DE AVILÉS (1519-1574), Spanish officer who drove the French out of Florida and who founded St. Augustine in 1565

Summary of Event

Juan Ponce de León, the discoverer of Florida, came to the New World in 1493 with Christopher Columbus' second expedition to the West Indies. Ponce settled on Hispaniola (Haiti and the Dominican Republic), but rumors of gold on neighboring Puerto Rico caused him to conquer it in 1508. Although Ponce de León was made Governor of Puerto Rico, he was soon removed from office because his appointment had been made without consulting Don Diego Columbus, the Governor of Hispaniola. The dejected Ponce then sought new fame and fortune by searching for the island of Bimini, which, according to the Indians of Hispañola, had a fountain whose waters turned men young again.

In 1513 Ponce de León sailed from Puerto Rico to seek his magic fountain, and when he came to a flower-covered coast, he named the area "La Florida." Ponce first anchored near the St. Johns river, then sailed south to the Florida Keys and some distance up the Gulf Coast. Ponce's party suffered three Indian attacks after the warriors tempted the Spaniards to land with false tales of rivers filled with gold. Beating off the

33

attackers Ponce sailed back to Puerto Rico, discovering the Bahama Channel which was used later by treasure fleets returning to Spain from Mexico, and which would ultimately necessitate the founding of St. Augustine to protect it.

Shortly after Ponce de León's voyage, Alonzo Alvarez de Pineda sailed northward looking for the strait between Florida and the mainland. Exploring the Gulf Coast extensively in 1519, Alvarez de Pineda sighted the mouth of the Mississippi river and later concluded that Florida was not an island as Ponce had believed, but a peninsula and part of the mainland. In 1520, an exploring party sent up the Atlantic Coast by Lucas Vasquez de Ayllón reached the same conclusion about the "island" of Florida. In addition the explorers brought back several Indians who proved to have fertile imaginations: they swore the land was full of gold and silver.

Encouraged by tales of riches, Ponce de León again set sail for Florida in 1521. His party included two ships, two hundred men, fifty horses, and several priests. The Indians proved to be hostile, however, and Ponce's settlement at Charlotte Bay was destroyed by war parties. In one of the attacks, the valiant seeker of the Fountain of Youth was mortally wounded. Deprived of their leader, the settlers abandoned Florida and sailed back to Puerto Rico. In 1526, Vasquez de Ayllón established San Miguel de Guadalupe on the Pee Dee river in South Carolina. Again the Indians refused to assist the Spaniards. Provisions soon gave out, sickness spread, Vasquez de Ayllón died, and the disheartened settlers abandoned the project. Thus, the first attempts to settle Spanish Florida ended in failure.

The next man who attempted to settle Florida was the new governor of Cuba and *adelantado*, or military commander, of Florida, Pánfilo de Narváez. Unlike the former expeditions which had originated in the West Indies, Narváez sailed from Spain in 1527 with six hundred colonists. When he reached Santo Domingo, one fourth of his party deserted and two of his ships were wrecked in a hurricane. The following spring, however, he sailed to Florida and landed at Tampa Bay, where he split his party into two sections. One group was to search inland for the rumored cities of gold, while the other was to sail northward and find a good harbor where both groups could rendezvous at a future date.

Narváez led the first party deeply inland searching for the golden cities. Each Indian village appeared poorer than the last, but the inhabitants all told of richer cities to the north, a ruse which coastal tribes soon learned would rid them of the greedy *conquistadores*. Narváez moved on seeking a town called Apalachen, near present-day Tallahassee. Instead of the promised wealth, all he found there were a few clay huts. By this time, Narváez realized that there was no gold in Florida, and he decided to move southward to the coast to find his ships.

Reaching the sea at Apalachee Bay, Narváez failed to find the expected ships, which had already gone back to Cuba. The marooned adventurers built several small boats and set sail for Mexico, which they erroneously believed was close at hand. With his men continually dying from starvation, disease, drowning, and occasional Indian attacks, Narváez sailed along the Gulf

Coast to Galveston Island. Here several of the ships sank and Narváez disappeared at sea. The survivors, led by Nuñez Cabeza de Vaca, were captured by Indians and passed from tribe to tribe until finally, with three companions, Cabeza de Vaca escaped his captors and completed the journey to Mexico City by land in 1536. These four men were the only survivors of the three hundred who followed Narváez inland at Tampa in 1528.

The Narváez expedition did not dampen the spirits of those who followed, especially after Cabeza de Vaca arrived in Mexico filled with the new tales of wealth he had garnered during the eight years he lived among the Indians. The next governor of Cuba and *adelantado* of Florida, Hernando de Soto, set sail from Havana for Florida in 1539. He, too, landed at Tampa Bay where he defeated the local Indians in a short battle. Leaving a base camp, de Soto and five hundred and fifty men marched inland seeking wealth and fame.

As de Soto's expedition advanced, they found that word of their defeat of the Indians at Tampa had preceded them and caused Indians to abandon their villages to hide in the woods. As Cortes had done before him, de Soto seized the chief of any inhabited town and held him to insure the peaceful conduct of each tribe. Only the village of Caliquen resisted, for which the inhabitants were enslaved in chains. The first winter found de Soto at Apalachen, the town visited by Narváez. Here the Spaniards rested until spring while smaller exploration parties visited Pensacola and Apalachee Bays.

In 1540, de Soto moved northward searching for his golden cities, a task which lasted four years during which the expedition traveled through the present-day states of Georgia, Alabama, Mississippi, Louisiana, and Arkansas. De Soto and his men were the first white men to identify the five civilized tribes (Choctaw, Chickasaw, Creek, Cherokee, and Seminole), to see the Great Smoky Mountains, and to chart and locate parts of the Mississippi and Arkansas rivers. During the arduous journey, the Spanish treated the Indians with great cruelty, resulting in many battles and casualties on both sides. Each conquered tribe promised the conquistadors that the Indians farther to the west possessed much gold and silver but, to the Spaniards' disappointment, little of the precious metals was found. Where the Arkansas river joins the Mississippi, de Soto fell victim to disease and died on May 21, 1542. To keep his body from the Indians, he was buried in the middle of the Mississippi river.

Upon de Soto's death, Luís de Moscoso assumed command of the expedition, which then wandered westward into Texas before returning to the Mississippi. Building small ships, de Moscoso's men floated down the Mississippi river to the Gulf. They followed the coast westward to Panuco (Tampico) in Mexico where, on September 10, 1543, the three hundred survivors disembarked and ended their journey.

These various expeditions established that Florida was a formidable wilderness, hard to penetrate, and teeming with plant and animal life. In addition, unlike the other areas conquered by Spain, the Florida Indians were extremely difficult to subdue and uncoöperative with exploration parties. There were few, if any, caches of gold or silver to attract future conquistadors. While the land was rich in natural vegetation, agriculture was extremely difficult in the sandy coastal soils. Finally, the region was plagued by severe storms and hurricanes during certain seasons of the year, which made shipping hazardous. These facts caused the Spaniards to ignore Florida for the next twenty years.

Spanish interest in Florida was rekindled when Jan Ribault, a Huguenot, established a French colony at Port Royal, South Carolina, in 1562. Although Ribault's settlement failed, the French government was impressed with its strategic location: it was close to the Bahama Channel used by the Spanish treasure fleets. To explore its possibilities as a base for French corsairs, Admiral Gaspard de Coligny of the French navy sent a second expedition to Florida led by René de Laudonnière, who founded Fort Caroline on the St. Johns river deep in Spanish Florida. Laudonnière, however, proved to be a poor leader. He offended the nearby Indians and could not discipline his men. Coligny quickly sent Jan Ribault and three hundred additional colonists to stabilize the new settlement.

Philip II, King of Spain, had no intention of allowing the French to take over his lands. He ordered Pedro Menéndez de Avilés, along with a dozen ships and 2,646 men, to expel the French and secure Florida for Spain. On August 28, 1565, Menéndez's fleet dropped anchor at his new settlement site, which he named San Augustín for the saint whose festival was celebrated on that day. Menéndez then sailed northward to Fort Caroline, ultimately capturing the fort and scattering its garrison. Returning to St. Augustine, Menéndez supervised the construction of the first building, a fortified Indian house, which he surrounded by a trench and a log wall—a rather modest beginning for the first permanent European settlement in the United States.

Pertinent Literature

Maynard, Theodore. *De Soto and the Conquistadores.* New York: Longmans, Green, and Co., 1930.

The Spanish conquistadors are frequently thought of as having been motivated in their conquests by the trinity of gold, glory, and God—often in that order. Theodore Maynard disagrees with this analysis. He does not deny the importance of gold in stimulating Spanish exploration of the New World, but he finds this was not the chief motive. Instead, Maynard asserts that the reason Spain became the first major colonial power (after tiny Portugal) is related to the *reconquista*—the eight-hundred-year war against the Moslems that culminated in the siege of Granada at the same time that Columbus set sail. In effect, Spain had driven the infidel from its land and now sought to turn its vast missionary enthusiasm into saving new worlds for God and the Church. Spain sought a special glory, the glory of God. To conquer the heathen, one must despoil them; hence, the significance of the search for wealth.

De Soto was one of the crusaders who went forth convinced that Spain had a divine mission in the world. This conviction helped to make him and the other explorers fearless men, terrible in battle and harsh in justice, who preserved the faith by the use of arms. The Spanish gave the Indians two simple choices: conversion and submission, or death. To the Iberians this was not cruelty but the truest form of kindness.

Although de Soto is best known for his lengthy journey in the southeastern United States, he had a long record as a good soldier under Pizarro, the conqueror of Peru. He brought the reinforcements that made that conquest possible, and continually led dangerous scouting expeditions. De Soto was always in the vanguard, a leader from the beginning. According to Maynard, de Soto opposed Pizarro's treachery and the execution of Inca leaders, preferring honorable treatment of the Indi-

ans instead. Yet de Soto was not above committing massacres on his Florida expedition or burning an Indian alive to extort information from other captives.

One of the most important factors which caused de Soto to continue his Florida expedition, in spite of the known fate of Narváez before him and in the face of hostile Indians, was his incredible ambition and stubbornness. De Soto refused to give in. His spirit alone kept the expedition moving westward long after his men had given up all hope of success. When de Soto died in 1542, his comrades were grieved but, at the same time, they rejoiced at their good fortune because they could go home at last. Only death could have defeated de Soto; he was too proud to have failed and lived.

Chatelain, Verne E. *The Defenses of Spanish Florida, 1565-1763.* Washington: Carnegie Institution of Washington, 1941.

The failures of Ponce de León and Vasquez de Ayllón, coupled with the disastrous Pánfilo de Narváez expedition and the negligible results of de Soto's search for wealth, made Florida one of the toughest challenges faced by Spaniards in the New World. Because of Florida's liabilities, its settlement had to be forced by political considerations. The Bahama Channel, discovered by Ponce de León and used regularly by the treasure fleets from Mexico and South America, attracted enemies who wished to plunder the great wealth of New Spain. Thus, protection from imperial rivals necessitated a settlement in Florida, both as an advanced naval base and to keep other powers from setting up their own bases.

The first attempt to set up a permanent naval base to protect the Bahama

Channel was made by Tristan de Luna y Arellano in 1559. Although Luna was supposed to settle Santa Elena (Port Royal) in Carolina, he landed at Pensacola. Before Luna could unload his ships, they were destroyed by a hurricane, forcing the survivors to live a harried existence until Angel de Villafañe arrived and relieved Luna of command. Villafañe loaded the colonists on his ships and set sail for the Carolina coast. Exploring as far north as Chesapeake Bay, Villafañe found no suitable site for his colony and abandoned the project to return home. Disappointed because these men had failed to establish a settlement in Florida, Philip II declared the entire area off limits to settlers in 1561.

The founding of Fort Caroline by Laudonnière changed the whole strategic position of Florida. Philip sent Pedro Menéndez de Avilés to secure the area for Spain. Establishing St. Augustine in 1565, Menéndez then ruthlessly exterminated the French colony to the north. As he marched by land on Fort Caroline, Jan Ribault led a sea expedition on St. Augustine. A storm scattered the French, and Fort Caroline's reduced garrison soon fell to the Spanish army. Menéndez then massacred several hundred shipwrecked survivors of the French fleet located in two groups at Las Matanzas (the Massacres) south of St. Augustine.

Although St. Augustine was an ideal naval base, the area had liabilities as a growing colony. It was surrounded by swamps and sloughs which prevented extensive agriculture, as did the jungle-like forests that had to be cut back regularly. The colony also suffered from the idealistic view of the Indians taken by the Spanish Crown, and the Church, which prevented private ownership of land in Florida.

Chatelain has written a superb volume covering the period from the founding of St. Augustine to the British take-over of Florida in 1763. He goes into great detail in describing the Spanish colonial system, Florida's place in it as its northernmost bastion, and the role of Menéndez in establishing St. Augustine. Chatelain is especially concerned with the military significance of the town and describes the environment, terrain, mission system, political organization, social conditions, early military defenses, and the construction of the Castillo San Marcos. A well-illustrated volume making use of both maps and photographs, Chatelain's book is worthwhile for the student or the general reader. — *W.L.R.*

Additional Recommended Reading

Bolton, Herbert E. *The Spanish Borderlands: A Chronicle of Old Florida and the Southwest.* Vol. XXIII: *The Chronicles of America.* New Haven: Yale University Press, 1921. A general study covering the whole of the Spanish exploration in the United States, including several excellent chapters on Florida.

Priestley, Herbert I. *Tristan de Luna, Conquistador of the Old South: A Study in Spanish Imperial Strategy.* Glendale, California: Arthur H. Clark Co., 1936. Focusing on the Luna expedition, Priestley analyzes Spanish imperial policy and Florida's place in securing the northern boundaries of the empire against other European powers.

Lowery, Woodbury. *The Spanish Settlements Within the Present Limits of the United States: Florida, 1562-1574.* New York: G. P. Putnam's Sons, 1905. The old classic in its field, Lowery's book is still one of the best detailed studies on the discovery and settlement of Spanish Florida.

Bennett, Charles E. *Laudonnière and Fort Caroline: History and Documents.* Gainesville: University of Florida Press, 1964. A fascinating short study on the French role along the Florida coast, which was critical in stimulating the founding of St. Augustine by Menéndez.

Trepaski, John J. *The Governorship of Spanish Florida, 1700-1763.* Durham: Duke University Press, 1964. Although Trepaski concentrates on a later period, he has good introductory material on the early exploration and settlement of Florida. Using Florida as an example, he also provides one of the most extensive treatments of the role of the colonial governor in a Spanish colony.

De Voto, Bernard. *The Course of Empire.* Boston: Houghton Mifflin Co., 1952. This volume, one of the most readable in American history, places the exploration and settlement of Florida in a continental perspective.

CORONADO'S EXPEDITION AND THE FOUNDING OF SANTA FE

Type of event: Socioeconomic: desire by the Spaniards to exploit the riches of the New World and extend their settlements
Time: Sixteenth century (c.1540)
Locale: New Mexico

Principal personages:

ÁLVAR NÚÑEZ CABEZA DE VACA (1490?-?1557), shipwrecked explorer who first heard of the fabled seven cities of gold in 1528

FRAY MARCOS DE NIZA (?-d.1558), Franciscan who led the preliminary scouting force into Arizona and New Mexico for Coronado in 1539

ESTEBANICO (also known as STEPHEN) (?-1539), Negro companion of Cabeza de Vaca, who guided the Niza expedition

FRANCISCO VÁSQUEZ DE CORONADO (1510-1554), Governor of Nueva Galicia and leader of the first major exploration of the Great Southwest from 1540 to 1542

EL TURCO (fl. 1540-1541), Indian who led Coronado to Quivira in present-day Kansas

FRAY AUGUSTÍN RODRIGUEZ (?-1581), Franciscan who lost his life in 1581 while attempting to establish the first mission in New Mexico

ANTONIO ESPEJO (fl. 1581-1583), civilian whose search for details of Rodriguez's death initiated an extensive exploration of Arizona and New Mexico in 1582 and 1583

GASPAR CASTAÑO DE SOSA (fl. 1590), acting Lieutenant Governor of Nuevo Leon, who made an illegal and unsuccessful attempt to settle New Mexico in 1590.

JUAN DE OÑATE (1549?-?1624), founder of the first permanent Spanish settlement and the first governor of New Mexico 1595-1609

PEDRO DE PERALTA (fl. 1609-1610), second Governor of New Mexico and founder of Santa Fe in 1610

Summary of Event

In April, 1530, Álvar Núñez Cabeza de Vaca arrived at the small frontier village of San Miguel de Culiacan in what is now the state of Sinaloa, Mexico. Cabeza de Vaca and his three companions were the only survivors of an expedition along the eastern Gulf Coast in 1528. Shipwrecked in Galveston Bay, the four Spaniards had passed from tribe to tribe through Texas and Northern Mexico protected by Cabeza de Vaca's ability to persuade the Indians that he was a man of "strong medicine" and supernatural powers.

40

When the Spanish authorities questioned the four explorers, they told of seven cities rich with gold located in an area to the north named Cibola. Spurred on by Cabeza de Vaca's stories, the Governor of the province of Nueva Galicia, Francisco Vásquez de Coronado, sent a scouting party into Arizona and New Mexico in 1539 to find the "Cities of Gold." The exploration was conducted by a Franciscan priest, Fray Marcos de Niza, who was guided by one of Cabeza de Vaca's companions, a Negro slave known as Estebanico.

The expedition traveled through the Gila River Valley in Arizona and then turned northwest toward the Zuni pueblos in northern New Mexico. Estebanico, who went ahead of Niza, urged the friar on with astonishing lies about the riches that reportedly lay ahead. When Niza arrived at Cibola, he found that the Indians had killed Estebanico for taking undue liberties with their women. Niza hurried back to Mexico, repeating Estebanico's unconfirmed tales of the vast quantities of gold in the Indian towns near Cibola.

Encouraged by Niza's reports, Coronado set out with a party of three hundred Spaniards and a large number of Indian allies to conquer the Cities of Gold. Bearing somewhat farther east than Niza, the hopeful conquistadors arrived in Cibola only to find nothing but a collection of mud huts and hostile Indians. Coronado overran the first pueblo, where he was wounded in the foot by an arrow. The nearby towns quickly surrendered to prevent further hostilities.

Using Cibola as his headquarters, Coronado sent out various exploration parties to find the reported gold. One of these parties, led by Captain Garcia Lopez de Gárdenas, visited the Grand Canyon region and was awed by the vast gorge which prevented further travel. None of these parties, however, found the gold it was seeking, though they did find a large city, Tiguex, near the Rio Grande, to which Coronado transferred his operations.

The Iberians were harsh in their treatment of the Indians; they turned the natives out of their houses, robbed them of their property, and seized their women. By the spring of 1541, the Indians wanted to be rid of the Spaniards and persuaded one of their band, known in Spanish as El Turco, to lead Coronado to Quivira, a city on the plains to the east. Coronado followed El Turco eastward as far as modern-day Kansas, where he strangled the guide because none of the promised gold had been found.

Upon his return to Tiguex, Coronado found that he was losing control of his large army because of his failure to find the riches promised them when they joined the expedition. He therefore returned to Mexico in 1542, with many unhappy members accusing their commander of incompetency.

Because of the disappointment of the Coronado expedition and a series of Indian revolts in northern Mexico, it was not until 1581 that another attempt was made to enter New Mexico. In that year, Fray Augustín Rodriguez of the Franciscan order left Nueva Vizcaya and journeyed into New Mexico via the Rio Grande. This was the first time the river route was used. At first the Indians were friendly, but within a year, Rodriguez was reported to have been murdered.

Seeking to substantiate Rodriguez's

death, the Franciscan order obtained the assistance of António Espejo, a man of wealth who agreed to lead and finance the search party. Arriving in the upper Rio Grande Valley in 1582 with a Franciscan friar and fourteen soldiers, Espejo confirmed Rodriguez's death. Since there was ample opportunity for further exploration, Espejo searched the entire region of northern New Mexico and Arizona, returning to Mexico by way of the Pecos river. It was during Espejo's journeys that the Spanish began to refer to "New Mexico," a name that denoted their hope to find a new region as rich as the land of the Aztecs.

Espejo's tales once again encouraged further journeys, and numerous men petitioned the viceroy to grant them licenses of exploration; but the viceroy refused to act. This reluctance on the part of the colonial administration led Gaspar Castaño de Sosa, acting governor of Nuevo Leon, to make an unlicensed exploration of New Mexico with a view to permanent settlement. Leaving Nuevo Leon in 1590 with a wagon train and 170 persons (including women and children), Castaño headed up the Pecos river for New Mexico. The journey, however, ended in failure which was compounded by the arrest of Castaño for an unlicensed and illegal entry into the northern territory.

In 1595, Juan de Oñate obtained permission to enter New Mexico. Oñate's contract provided that he and his descendants would be governor, captain general, and *adelantado* of New Mexico for two generations. He was to provide the expedition with two hundred men, provisions, livestock, horses, and medicines, all at his own expense. The King of Spain agreed to assist the new governor by lending him three field pieces, powder, ammunition, armor, and six thousand pesos.

After numerous delays, Oñate received final permission to proceed late in 1597. He was again delayed in Santa Barbara in northern Mexico, while a royal *visitador* inspected his accounts, supplies, and men to insure the contract's observance. Then in February, 1598, the eighty-three wagons began the long journey northward up the Rio Grande Valley. Arriving in mid-summer, Oñate supervised the building of San Juan and San Gabriel, the first two Spanish towns in New Mexico. The latter became the capital of the province.

After establishing the first settlements, Oñate engaged in various explorations of the Southwest, including a trip to Coronado's Quivira, and an extensive journey in Arizona where he discovered the Bill Williams river and followed the Colorado river to its mouth in the Gulf of California. Interspersed between his explorations, Oñate hanged several deserters and stormed the pueblo of Acoma with his army after the Indians had killed some of his settlers. Oñate then condemned the survivors of Acoma to twenty years' servitude, and cut off the right foot of all males over twenty-five years of age. He also amputated the right hands of two Hopi Indians captured at Acoma and sent them home as a warning to other tribes in the area.

Oñate's heavy-handed methods led to trouble, especially after he forced a group of fleeing settlers to return to his colony in 1601. Appeals were made to the Viceroy of Mexico protesting Oñate's Administration and asking that the colony be abandoned because of its poverty. The viceroy recommended that Oñate be replaced as Governor until a further investigation could be made. Indignantly, Oñate resigned his post. Later, in Spain, he was tried for various actions, convicted, and fined.

At first, the King of Spain had thought of abandoning the colony of New Mexico, but the Church worried about the fate of the Christianized Indians and demanded the King's support of God's work. The crown assented and dispatched Pedro de Peralta as Oñate's replacement. The son of a Navarre nobleman, Peralta had been graduated in canon law and did have military experience. So that the settlers could "live with some order and decency," Peralta was ordered to establish a new village "before all else." Named San Francisco de la Santa Fe, the new town was built in 1610. Surrounding a plaza lined with the public buildings, the new capital of New Mexico was governed by four *regidores* elected by the people, and two *alcaldes* elected by the *regidores*. With the installation of the Peralta regime, the existence of New Mexico was assured, providing a center for the Spanish culture so important to the Great Southwest even today.

Pertinent Literature

Bolton, Herbert E. *Coronado: Knight of Pueblos and Plains.* New York: McGraw-Hill Book Co., 1949.

Coronado's journey into the wilds of New Spain in often regarded as a wild-goose chase by historians, but Bolton disagrees. He finds Coronado's motivation, the desire for gold, no more absurd than the forces that drew the forty-niners to California seeking the same thing. While Coronado did not find the riches he sought, his search was one of the significant expeditions of the day. The conquistador opened North America to further exploration and ultimate settlement.

So revolutionary were Coronado's discoveries that European mapmakers failed to comprehend them correctly, says Bolton. Instead, they showed the Rio Grande flowing into the Pacific and placed Quivira on the Pacific coast instead of eastward in the middle of the plains. But many of these mistakes were also due to inadequate information dispensed to the world by the secretive King of Spain who jealously guarded the secrets of the New World.

The observations and compass readings made by Coronado have also been helpful to modern science. Coronado traveled on the plains by using a compass for direction. Scientists had assumed from scanty data that the magnetic declination in the 1500's was two degrees east of true north. Historians, however, using Coronado's reports on the location of Palo Duro Canyon in Texas have enabled scientists to correct this false notion. It is now agreed that the magnetic declination in 1540 as revealed by Coronado's observations was eleven degrees east of true north, about the same as it is today.

Bolton also challenges the traditional idea that the wild herds of mustangs found in the West descended from those horses left behind by Coronado. The expedition had few mares, and later Spanish explorers fail to mention horse-mounted Indians until the late seventeenth century. Bolton believes that the wild horses used by the American plains Indians were descended from animals brought by colonists into New Mexico much later than Coronado's time. Bolton believes that the delay in settling New Mexico after Coronado was caused by Spanish concern with Florida and a desire to prevent French settlement in South Carolina as much as anything else.

As to Coronado himself, Bolton finds him to be a responsible leader with important humane qualities. Coronado was a strict yet just disciplinarian, says Bolton, who became unpopular because he refused to allow his men to commit outrages on the Indian villages. He was especially kind in his concern for his Indian allies, which was unusual during this period of history. Bolton also finds Coronado to have been a brave and fearless leader in combat, one who inspired his men with his recklessness. Bolton concludes that the failure of his men to desert when they first realized Cibola was a collection of mud huts was due to their faith in Coronado's leadership. These qualities helped to exonerate him of the charge of incompetence brought against him by his enemies after the expedition returned from Mexico.

Hammond, George P. *Don Juan de Oñate and the Founding of New Mexico*. Santa Fe, New Mexico: El Palacio Press, 1927.

George P. Hammond, a Bolton student at the University of California at Berkeley, first wrote his study of Oñate as a doctoral dissertation. Hammond made an extensive search through the original documents located in the Archives of the Indies at Seville, Spain, hoping to clarify many points about early New Mexico history including the founding of Santa Fe. The closest Hammond could come to determining the date when Santa Fe was established was 1610, by Don Pedro de Peralta, who succeeded Oñate as governor.

Details about Oñate's early life are obscure. He married Doña Isabel de Tolosa, who was distantly related to Cortes and the Aztec chieftain Montezuma. Oñate had some experience fighting Indians on the frontier and owned several mines of great wealth. He was also a friend of Don Luis de Velasco II, Viceroy of Mexico. This influence helped him secure the original contract to settle New Mexico in 1595, which was modified several times before Oñate departed in 1598.

Oñate's frequent absences from the colony he set up in New Mexico and the disappointment of the settlers who fled back to Mexico resulted in his ultimate dismissal and trial on various charges. Oñate was convicted for spreading false stories about New Mexico's wealth, and for excessive cruelty in suppressing an Indian revolt and in forcing the fleeing settlers to return to New Mexico.

Hammond's work on Oñate has led to his editing a series of volumes collectively entitled the *Coronado Historical* series. Of special interest to students of sixteenth century New Mexico are three volumes coedited with Agapito Rey: *Narratives of the Coronado Expedition, 1540-1542; Don Juan Oñate: Colonizer of New Mexico, 1595-1628;* and *The Rediscovery of New Mexico, 1580-1594* (Albuquerque: University of New Mexico Press, 1940, 1953, and

1966 respectively). Each of these volumes is a collection of primary source materials, original accounts, letters, and documents relating to Spanish exploration in the Southwest. Although the general reader may not wish to examine the numerous documents, they are of value to the student. The brief introduction to each volume, moreover, provides an excellent synopsis of the events and personages instrumental in establishing the first settlements in New Mexico. — *W.L.R.*

Additional Recommended Reading

Day, A. Grove. *Coronado's Quest: The Discovery of the Southwestern States.* Berkeley: University of California Press, 1940. This first substantial biography of Coronado written in English is also available in a paperback edition.

Bishop, Morris. *The Odyssey of Cabeza de Vaca.* New York: The Appleton-Century Co., 1933. Bishop relates the story of the first Spaniard to hear of the fabulous Seven Cities of Gold which stimulated Coronado's exploits.

Bancroft, Hubert H. *History of Arizona and New Mexico, 1530-1888.* Vol. XVII: *The Works of Hubert Howe Bancroft.* New York: McGraw-Hill Book Co., 1967. 39 vols. Originally published in 1889, Bancroft's massive history of the Far West is still of immense value and interest.

Bolton, Herbert E. *The Spanish Borderlands: A Chronicle of Old Florida and the Southwest.* Vol. XXIII: *The Chronicles of America.* Edited by Allen Johnson and Allan Nevins. New Haven: Yale University Press, 1918-1951. 56 vols. Originally published in 1921, Bolton's work has chapters on Cabeza de Vaca, Coronado, and the founding of New Mexico.

Wellman, Paul I. *Glory, God, and Gold: A Narrative History.* Garden City: Doubleday and Co., 1954. Depicting in his title the objectives of the conquistadors, Wellman has produced a readable volume on Spanish exploration in the New World.

Forrest, Earle R. *Missions and Pueblos of the Old Southwest.* Glendale, Calif.: Arthur H. Clark Co., 1929; republished, Chicago: Rio Grande Press, Inc., 1962 and 1964. Concentrating on the *padres* and their missions, Forrest's book goes beyond the initial explorations and colonization period in New Mexico, but it offers the reader much interesting material on Church activities in the Southwest.

RALEIGH'S ATTEMPTS AT COLONIZATION IN THE NEW WORLD

Type of event: Political: desire to establish English colonies in the New World
Time: 1584-1591
Locale: England and Roanoke Island (part of present-day North Carolina)

Principal personages:

ELIZABETH I (1533-1603), Queen of England 1558-1603, after whom Virginia was named

SIR WALTER RALEIGH (1552?-1618), favorite of Elizabeth who sponsored several attempts at colonization in the New World

SIR HUMPHREY GILBERT (1539?-1583), Raleigh's half-brother, whose failure to colonize Newfoundland led to Raleigh's attempts to settle Roanoke Island

RICHARD HAKLUYT (1552?-1616), who advocated colonizing America

ARTHUR BARLOWE (1550?-?1620), commander of Raleigh's first exploratory expedition

SIR RICHARD GRENVILLE (1541?-1591), naval commander of Raleigh's second colonial venture

SIR RALPH LANE (1530?-1603), Governor of Raleigh's 1585 settlement at Roanoke

JOHN WHITE (fl. 1585-1593), Governor of the "Lost Colony"

Summary of Event

Sir Walter Raleigh's place in history is difficult to assess. His many accomplishments ought to have won for him rank among the greats of the golden age of Elizabeth I, but they have not, perhaps because Raleigh's versatility made him a dilettante. The tragic circumstances surrounding his execution for treason in 1616 have cloaked him in the martyr's guise. Yet Raleigh demands historians' attention because of his association with England's first halting steps toward the creation of a vast empire and with the fabled "Lost Colony."

Raleigh sprang from gentle but impoverished West Country stock whose sons would have a long and intimate connection with England's colonizing activities in the sixteenth century. In addition to Walter, his brother Carew and his half-brothers Sir John, Sir Humphrey, and Adrian Gilbert became active participants in the efforts to build an overseas empire. The precise point at which Sir Walter Raleigh began to take part in these activities is uncertain, but it is clear that when in 1578 Sir Humphrey Gilbert received a patent to settle lands "not actually possessed of any Christian prince or people," Raleigh's curiosity and interest had been aroused, for he commanded one of the ships which carried Gilbert's first group of colonists to Newfoundland. There followed a hiatus in Raleigh's colonizing endeavors during which his position at Elizabeth's court

46

steadily improved. Thus strengthened, he helped to finance his half-brother's ill-fated second colonizing venture in the spring of 1583. The failure of the expedition and Sir Humphrey's death put the onus of establishing an English settlement in America on Raleigh's shoulders.

Raleigh profited from Gilbert's experience. By the time he secured a renewal of Gilbert's patent in 1584, he had decided to pick a colonizing site farther south on the North American continent, where the climate would be more temperate. To ensure a successful planting, Sir Walter resolved to send a small survey party to explore the new site, and in April, 1584, two small ships under the command of Arthur Barlowe left England for America.

The vessels sailed south to the Canaries and then to the Caribbean Islands, where they took on water and supplies before sailing north, arriving off the North Carolina coast in early July. Several days were passed in reconnoitering the vicinity for a good harbor and a place to erect a plantation and initiate trading with the Indians. Barlowe and his men returned to England in September, bringing a glowing account of the voyage, which Richard Hakluyt would print in his *Principall Navigations, Voiages, and Discoveries of the English Nation* in 1589. Raleigh named the new land Virginia after the Virgin Queen who elevated him to knighthood.

For all the glowing accounts brought by Barlowe and his men, Raleigh still lacked the information necessary for starting a colony. Encouraged by Elizabeth's generosity, he persuaded Hakluyt to write a memorial to the Queen in the hope that she would lend financial support to a new venture. Hakluyt drafted the memorial, known as *A Discourse on Western Planting*, which raised nearly every argument for planting colonies—from the promotion of trade to the advancement of religion—which would be advanced over the next two centuries. The arguments were to no avail; Elizabeth offered no more than her encouragement.

Undaunted, Raleigh put together a second expedition. In seeking advice he turned to Hakluyt's older cousin, also named Richard. The elder Hakluyt suggested that a temporary colony of specialists in map making, botany, exploring, and similar accomplishments be sent over to prepare the way for more permanent settlers. Following this advice, Raleigh in 1585 dispatched an expedition under Sir Richard Grenville and Sir Ralph Lane, who was to govern the colony. Among the experts were a young Oxford scholar, Thomas Hariot, and an artist, John White, both of whom were to supply the English with their first accurate descriptions of the New World. The colonists made a slow crossing and arrived at Roanoke Island too late to plant crops. Damage to their supplies in unloading, coupled with Indian problems, made for a difficult winter. Furthermore, Lane proved to be an inept governor and when Sir Francis Drake arrived off Roanoke Island in the spring of 1586, Lane and his men were inclined to leave. A spring storm, which destroyed the few supplies Drake had brought, stiffened Lane's determination to depart, and he persuaded Drake to take the colonists back to England. Two weeks later, Grenville arrived with a major supply, but finding no colonists, he put the supplies ashore in the care of fifteen men and sailed off to raid Spanish shipping. Raleigh's second attempt to erect a colony had failed.

In 1587 Raleigh mounted a more elaborate effort. Raising a body of men, women, and children, he placed them under the jurisdiction of John White, whom he named as deputy governor. The presence of women and children and Raleigh's orders to erect a borough form of government in the new colony, suggest that he intended this venture to be a permanent settlement. Acting on a suggestion made by Lane, Raleigh ordered White to choose a more felicitous site than Roanoke Island on which to settle, but he was to take off the men whom Grenville had left there the year before. When White's colonists arrived at Roanoke Island, the pilot apparently refused to go farther, so White and his people unloaded and began to establish their position. For reasons which are not altogether clear, White returned to England with the ships. Unfortunately, he arrived just as war with Spain was breaking out, and it was four years before the English could resupply the Roanoke Island colony. When White finally returned to Roanoke Island in 1591, the colonists had vanished. What happened to them is probably best explained by the eighteenth century Virginia historian Robert Beverly. "It is supposed," he wrote, "that the Indians seeing them forsaken by their country and unfurnished of their expected supplies, cut them off. For to this day they were never more heard of."

After the loss of the Roanoke Island colonists, Raleigh turned his attentions elsewhere. The chief importance of his endeavors was the whetting of English interests in an overseas empire. Others would follow and succeed where Raleigh had failed.

Pertinent Literature

Quinn, David B. *Raleigh and the British Empire.* Chs. I-IV. London: Hodder & Stoughton, Ltd., 1947.

The European quest for empire in the sixteenth century was not so much an expression of the desires of individual men as of social forces. Beginning with this premise, David B. Quinn has chosen Sir Walter Raleigh as a representative figure on England's maiden voyage into imperialism, and he has concentrated upon aspects of Raleigh's life which illustrate the social movement of the time.

In order to explain England's imperialistic motivations, Quinn inquires into the history of the early Tudor period. The Tudor monarchy, he observes, aimed to establish a strong middle class based largely on commercial prosperity. Merchant capital developed rapidly between 1480 and 1550 because of the boom in the export of unfinished cloth. Then a serious slump in the export trade necessitated experimentation with new products for new markets. Thus England entered her first industrial revolution. As the developing industries raised demands for overseas markets, their profits provided the capital to finance overseas explorations. At the same time, the growing centralization of the state led to the creation of administrative machinery for collecting taxes, thus enabling the government to sponsor voyages of exploration. Other developments seemed to converge to make such voyages feasible: technology made possible the building of seaworthy ships, and intellectual progress unshackled minds from some of their superstitions about the unknown world. By the 1570's, England's overseas objectives were threefold: to continue piratical attacks on the Spanish treasure fleets and colonies; to extend commerce into Eastern Europe, Asia, and Africa; and to seek a northwest passage to Asia.

Raleigh entered the world of overseas adventure as a sort of junior partner in the ill-fated enterprise of his half-brother Sir Humphrey Gilbert. From the time when Sir Humphrey's disappearance at sea thrust him into the forefront of the exploration movement, Raleigh was, as portrayed by Quinn, very much the entrepreneur. He left the actual exploring to other men while he concentrated on raising capital and organizing men and materials.

The purely exploratory voyage to Roanoke Island in 1584 served mainly to raise the hopes of Raleigh and prospective investors concerning the commercial potential of North American resources. Raleigh, in Quinn's estimation, expected too much of the initial colonial enterprise in return for the small amount of planning, effort, and money that had gone into it. The first American colonists who journeyed to Roanoke with Sir Ralph Lane as their leader in 1585 were merely the paid servants of the investors and had no personal stake in the venture. Lane was knowledgeable in military matters but he had no experience in organizing agricultural or commercial activities. Failing to devote themselves to the growing of food, the colonists depended far too much upon the Indians for corn and fish and thereby alienated the initially friendly natives. Lane soon realized that "Mediterranean fruits" and lumber would not prove sufficiently profitable commodities to make the colony worthwhile. He considered investigation of the mainland of paramount importance. Although he soon concluded that the colony must move to a more favorable site with a suitable harbor if it were to survive, he expended his energies seeking gold in order to meet the enterprise's short-term objective of profit.

After the entire colony returned to England in 1586 without waiting for additional supplies to arrive, Raleigh understood that he must alter his ideas about colonization. His 1587 expedition, that of the Lost Colony, expressed the realization that colonists must be given an incentive to make their colony prosper. Each colonist was granted five hundred acres of land, each was encouraged to take his family so that a stable society might be developed, and a limited form of local government was established. Even during the four-year period when no communication with the Roanoke colony existed, sponsors in England were making plans to ensure its support by a continuing corporation of wealthy men.

Quinn's final assessment of Raleigh is that he was too much concerned with short-term profits to establish a permanent colony. Although Raleigh was more deeply involved in overseas exploration than any other of his English contemporaries, he was limited by his belief that colonization must pay its own way. Colonization was only one of his many activities, and he was unwilling to invest a major portion of his own fortune to bring about its success.

Quinn nevertheless acknowledges that Raleigh's efforts were important first steps toward the establishment of permanent settlements in the New World.

Wallace, Willard M. *Sir Walter Raleigh.* Princeton: Princeton University Press, 1959.

Raleigh's colonizing attempts in Virginia occupy only two chapters of Willard M. Wallace's full-length biography, which emphasizes the fact that these attempts were a small part of Raleigh's diversified life. The epitome of the Renaissance man, Raleigh was at various stages of his career a "soldier, sailor, courtier, Captain of the Queen's Guard, businessman, explorer, colonizer, Member of Parliament, devotee of science, ship designer, military engineer, musician, literary patron, historian, and poet." Raleigh's ambition to attain political power by becoming a member of the Privy Council was never realized, mainly because of his disinclination to concentrate on a single phase of human activity. Had he been willing to risk his entire fortune on his colonizing efforts, and had he been able to break away from his role as one of the Queen's favorites in order to command a Virginia expedition himself, Raleigh might not only have won enduring fame as the founder of the first permanent English settlement in America, but he might also have taken his seat on the Privy Council.

Wallace's biography, though not uncritical of its subject, is unquestionably pro-Raleigh. Consequently, the author is more inclined than some historians concerned with the colonization attempts at Roanoke Island to attribute failure to factors which Raleigh could not completely control. Much has been written, for instance, about the lack of wisdom in giving the 1585 attempt a military flavor, with the colonists serving merely as the paid servants of the investors. Wallace points out that the House of Commons in confirming Raleigh's title to Virginia in 1585 prohibited not only the sending of imprisoned debtors as colonists but also the taking of wives and indentured servants. Such prohibitions prevented the establishment of a permanent settlement by disallowing domestic activity.

Like other historians of colonization efforts, Wallace criticizes Raleigh's original concept of how such enterprises should be financed. By encouraging the commanders of the voyages to Virginia to attack Spanish bullion-carrying galleons, Raleigh diverted them from the primary task of proceeding to Virginia as quickly as possible in order to conserve supplies and to plant crops in time to reap the best possible harvest.

By 1587 Raleigh had altered much of his faulty thinking on the nature of colonization. The limited size of his ill-fated expedition of that year, Wallace conjectures, was perhaps caused by Raleigh's inability to find adequate financing. His enemies, jealous of the Queen's favor, ridiculed his enterprise, and an apathetic attitude prevailed among potential investors. Charles M. Andrews, in *Our Earliest Colonial Settlements,* accuses Raleigh of losing interest in the Roanoke Island colonists after 1587. Andrews implies that, the war with Spain notwithstanding, Raleigh and his representatives simply did not try as hard as they might have to reach America, or to find the colonists when the crossing was again possible. Wallace is more charitable, however, contending that Raleigh had lost a great deal of money in the colonizing effort, and that he felt that future endeavors must be supported either by the government or by commercial corporations. Raleigh's interest in colonization continued, nevertheless, after his withdrawal from active participation.

The remainder of Wallace's biography is primarily a detailed account of Raleigh's military and naval adventures and of the court intrigues which buffeted him about from the position of Queen's favorite to that of a convicted traitor, imprisoned in the Tower for thirteen years. Although Raleigh was opportunistic and perhaps indiscreet in some of his diplomatic dealings, he was by no means a traitor, and his trial, even when judged by seventeenth century standards, represents one of the grossest miscarriages of justice in English legal history. The Raleigh who emerges from this ordeal to take on yet another expedition to the New World, this time to Guiana in search of gold, is a figure of exceptional resiliency and optimism. Wallace's portrait of the mature Raleigh is that of a man who, despite never attaining eminence in any single endeavor, stands above many of his more powerful contemporaries because of his character. — *W.M.B.*

Additional Recommended Reading

Williamson, James A. "England and the Opening of the Atlantic," in *The Cambridge History of the British Empire*. Vol. I, ch. 2. Cambridge: The University Press, 1929-1930. This article offers an excellent brief introduction to England's interest in the New World.

Parks, George B. *Richard Hakluyt and the English Voyages*. Edited, with an introduction, by James A. Williamson. 2nd ed. New York: Frederick Ungar Publishing Co., 1961. No examination of Raleigh's activities is complete without some reference to the important work of the younger Hakluyt.

Rowse, A. L. *The Elizabethans and America*. London: Macmillan & Company, 1959. The early chapters of this book provide a valuable background for understanding the role of England in the age of exploration.

Thompson, Edward. *Sir Walter Ralegh: Last of the Elizabethans*. New Haven: Yale University Press, 1935. A standard biography of Sir Walter which is highly laudatory and apologetic.

Craven, Wesley F. *The Southern Colonies in the Seventeenth Century, 1607-1689*. Ch. 2. Baton Rouge: Louisiana State University Press, 1949. The brief account of Raleigh's activities contained in this volume emphasizes the importance of Hakluyt's writings.

Andrews, Charles M. *Our Earliest Colonial Settlements: Their Diversities of Origin and Later Characteristics*. Ch. I. Ithaca: Cornell University Press, 1964. While not uncritical of Raleigh, this appraisal of his attempts at colonization acknowledges the importance of experience to later successful efforts.

FOUNDING OF QUEBEC AND FRENCH EXPLORATION OF THE GREAT LAKES

Type of event: Politico-economic: establishment of French empire in New World
Time: 1603-1682
Locale: St. Lawrence Valley and the Great Lakes

Principal personages:
SAMUEL DE CHAMPLAIN (1567?-1635), father of New France
HENRY IV (1553-1610), King of France
CARDINAL RICHELIEU, ARMAND-JEAN DU PLESSIS (1585-1642), Chief Minister of France
JEAN NICOLET (1598-1642), trader and explorer
JEAN BAPTISTE COLBERT (1619-1683), French controller general of finances
JEAN BAPTISTE TALON (THE "GREAT INTENDANT") (1625?-1694), Intendant of New France
LOUIS JOLLIET (1645-1700), trader and explorer
DOLLIER DE CASSON (fl. seventeenth century), Sulpician missionary
JACQUES MARQUETTE (1637-1675), Jesuit missionary
RENÉ ROBERT CAVELIER, SIEUR DE LA SALLE (1643-1687), explorer and colonizer

Summary of Event

By 1600, France was in a condition to undertake the serious business of establishing settlements in Canada. Verrazano and Cartier had done the preliminary work of staking French claims in the New World, and although the early attempts at colonization had failed in the North as well as in Florida in 1562-1567, these experiments had taught the French lessons that were to prove valuable. Furthermore, by 1600 the long agony of the wars of religion in France was over, and France now had a strong king, Henry IV, who was vitally interested in colonization. The death of Philip II of Spain in 1598 also helped open the colonial field to France as well as to England as never before.

Henry IV found a superb agent in Samuel de Champlain, who well deserves the title of "father of New France." He was born about 1570 at Brouage, a port near La Rochelle. From childhood, Champlain came to know the sea, and in 1598-1599 he visited both Spain and her colonies, where he remained for more than two years learning important lessons in the art of colonization. Returning to France, he reported to the King and by his careful observations roused the monarch's enthusiasm for following the fishermen who for at least a century had been sailing to Newfoundland and the Gulf of St. Lawrence for both fish and furs. In March, 1603, Champlain first set out with royal approval for the North American coast. Ascending the St. Lawrence, at Tadoussac, at the mouth of the Saguenay where fur traders had been going to barter since the days of Cartier, he made his first contact with the natives. After going up river to Stadaconé, now deserted by its Indian inhabitants, he returned to France in September and reported to Henry IV. From this time forth, he was perpetually shifting back and forth across the Atlantic. In March, 1604, acting as geographer for the Sieur de Monts, to whom the king had granted semi-feudal rights in North America, he made his second voyage to Canada, with three ships. In 1605 under his direction a settlement was first made at St. Croix and finally at Port Royal, Acadia, on the Bay of Fundy. This was the first permanent French settlement in New France. A much delayed relief party from France barely saved Port Royal from abandonment in July, 1606. For three seasons thereafter Champlain explored North American waters.

In 1608 Champlain, with two ships, again ascended the St. Lawrence, while a third ship reinforced the Port Royal colony. This time he was prepared to make a permanent settlement on the banks of that river. On July 2, he landed at Stadaconé and erected buildings there, and the city of Quebec was born. At this point Indian politics entered the picture. In spite of their common origin, the Hurons and the Iroquois had become deadly enemies, and the Hurons were anxious to enlist Champlain as their ally against the recently formed confederacy of the Five Nations. In an evil moment for New France Champlain did so, thinking that his act was the means of securing Quebec from Iroquois attack. In June, 1609, escorted by a fleet of Huron canoes, Champlain went farther up the St. Lawrence. Arriving at the mouth of the Richelieu river, the expedition turned south into Iroquois country.

Champlain was now treading what was for the next two centuries to become the great warpath between Canada and the English provinces. On July 29, probably in the vicinity of Crown Point on the lake now bearing his name, Champlain encountered an Iroquois party. The two groups prepared for battle, and the next day Champlain fired the three musket shots which brought down three Iroquois chiefs. Thus began the eternal warfare between the Five Nations and the French —a warfare which was to affect profoundly the life of New France.

Although he had permanent residence at Quebec, Champlain continued his work of exploration. In 1609 he visited France, and in 1610 he turned again to the North American interior, but briefly. He went back to France and remained until 1611. Growing numbers of Indian traders troubled the natives, and in 1612 Champlain endeavored to secure aid from the French court in governing the new colony. In 1613 he returned to it as "Lieutenant-General for the King in New France," but again in 1614 the Viceroy found himself in the Mother Country, attending the States-General and pressing for a renewal of merchant support and of missionary effort among the Indians, whose savagery amazed and saddened him. Upon his return to Canada, Champlain made his farthest trip west in 1615, and reached Lake Huron. On the way back, he saw Lake Ontario and wintered with the Hurons. This was the last of his explorations. Fortunately, he carefully recorded his experiences, and eventually published four invaluable volumes (the last in 1632) containing full and accurate maps.

Meanwhile, since Henry IV's murder in 1610, France was plunged into turmoil. The new monarch, Louis XIII, was a child, and under the regency of Marie de Medicis religious factionalism resumed, and the French colonizing effort was placed in jeopardy. The advent of the Thirty Years' War (1618-1648) brought strong leadership to the fore in the person of Armand-Jean du Plessis, Cardinal Richelieu, who exalted the crown power and forced everyone to yield to the royal prerogative. By 1624 Richelieu had secured his position as chief minister of France, and, like Henry IV, he became deeply interested in New France. Unlike a predecessor, the Duc de Sully, who believed that colonization was folly, Richelieu backed overseas planting, which had now become a reality. The French, however, never sought the new world in such numbers as their English rivals. Not displacement of the Indian but trade with him for furs had become the French method, for Richelieu promoted commerce through a variety of trading companies which were also colonizing ventures under royal direction.

In 1629, however, English forces carried Anglo-French warfare to Quebec, where they forced Champlain to surrender. Charles I returned Canada and Acadia to France in 1632 after Champlain persuaded Richelieu that the seizure had followed Anglo-French peace agreements and that the territory was too valuable to be left in English hands. In 1633 Richelieu sent Champlain back to New France with the title of governor, an office he held only two years until his death on Christmas Day, 1635. He was buried in the city he had founded, but now no one knows where the remains of the founder of

New France lie. A noble character, devout, patient, and a thoroughgoing seaman, Champlain made New France a reality, inaugurated the continuing French policy of friendly relations with the Indians, and with surprising accuracy, mapped and described the lands he had visited.

Meanwhile, a new force had entered the life of New France. The seventeenth century in Europe witnessed a revival of the Roman Catholic Church, and revival meant missionary spirit and activity. The powerful order of Jesuits, untiring missionaries who were always looking for new worlds to conquer, began to take an interest in New France and its Indian allies. In 1613 two Jesuits, the forerunners of a devoted army of martyrs, sailed for Port Royal. Two years later the Récollets, a branch of the Franciscans, followed suit. Four Récollet friars, including Father Joseph Le Caron, set out with Champlain from France; Le Caron preceded him on the western trip of that year, and spent a winter with the Hurons. Pressing on to the lake that bears the Huron name, he and his men were the first Europeans on record to see any of the Great Lakes.

The French proved to be better at exploration and trade with the Indians than at colonization. In contrast with their English rivals to the south, they were slow at filling up the settlements on the seacoast and along the St. Lawrence. But they continued to move westward. The first to follow in the steps of Champlain appears to have been Jean Nicolet, who in 1634-1635 served as a Huron emissary to negotiate peace with the Winnebagoes on the shores of Lake Michigan. Nicolet explored as far west as the Fox and Wisconsin rivers. He was in all probability followed by fur traders and missionaries, but their names are lost to history.

The next great thrust to the west came several decades later as renewed French expansion followed the revival of the fur trade under the leadership of entrepreneurs, such as Médard Chouart, Sieur des Grosseilliers, and Pierre-Esprit Radisson. In 1665 Louis XIV and his minister Colbert, both greatly interested in New France, sent out as intendant Jean Talon, who became the strong man of the colony. Talon had a real vision of empire to match the one for which his royal master became famous, and he encouraged exploration, built forts on Lake Champlain and the Richelieu river to guard the Iroquois route to the St. Lawrence, and renewed war against the Iroquois enemies of Indian allies. In 1669 Talon sent out Louis Jolliet, a native-born Canadian, who in his search for the source of copper traveled only as far as Lake Erie. He was followed by Dollier de Casson, a courtly soldier whose physique matched the wilderness life of hardship which he embraced in his monastic order's missionary rivalry with the Jesuits. In 1671 he became superior of the Sulpicians at Montreal, and there he stayed until he died in 1701.

Under the governorship of the Comte de Frontenac (1672-1682) expansion in New France reached beyond the Great Lakes into the Missis-sippi Valley. In 1673 Louis Jolliet and Père Marquette, of the Jesuit order, set out on a notable voyage. Traversing the Great Lakes, they went down the Mississippi as far as the Arkansas. Their work was continued by Robert Cavelier, Sieur de La Salle, who in 1669, accompanied by a party of Sulpicians led by Dollier de Casson, had roamed through New York, crossed from Lake Erie to the headwaters of the Ohio, and paddled down that river toward the Mississippi. But his men deserted him, and he turned back. In 1678-1680 La Salle crossed the Great Lakes to the Illinois river, bent upon extending the borders of New France to Spanish Mexico. Not until 1682 did he lead his famous party from the Great Lakes, via the Illinois river, down the Mississippi to the Gulf of Mexico; there, on April 9, he claimed the vast interior for Louis XIV. Although the colony that La Salle proceded to establish did not last, and the great explorer himself was murdered by his own men in 1687, others such as Lemoyne d'Iberville, took up the challenge of making good the French claims to Louisiana by planting settlements. These are only the most notable of the French explorers, but the net result of their activities and those of many unsung adventurers was that by 1682 Frenchmen had roamed from the Gulf of St. Lawrence to the site of the city of New Orleans, laying claim to a far-flung empire and challenging English and Spanish rivals in America.

Pertinent Literature

Bourne, Edward G. and A. N. Bourne, eds. *The Voyages and Explorations of Samuel De Champlain, 1604-1616; Narrated by Himself.* 2 vols. New York: A. S. Barnes, 1906.

The student of the history of early French Canada is fortunate in having at his disposal an excellent narrative written by the man who is universally called "the father of New France." In 1604 Champlain published the narrative of his first voyage; this was followed by other accounts as his experience increased, and in 1632, three years before Champlain's death, a final and corrected version appeared. This material was not available in English until 1859, when the Hakluyt Society brought out an edition of the *Brief Discours*. Other versions followed, and the one under review was done with the purpose of making Champlain's works accessible in a fairly popular form.

The editing is well done. Parts of the earlier narrative are included in the translation of the 1632 version in order to produce a complete and full story. The footnotes are good. Champlain's occasional errors in dating are corrected, and all the place names are translated into modern place nomenclature so that the reader may follow Champlain's course on a modern map.

The writing is as good as the editing. One is inclined to compare this work with two other contemporary accounts of North American colonization, Bradford's *Of Plymouth Plantation* and John Smith's account of colonial Virginia. Champlain shows up well in the comparison. Bradford's charming narrative is confined to a small and less important colony, and Smith's is marred by doubts of his veracity.

Champlain gives us facts, straight and unadorned. He begins his narrative by a summary account of previous attempts at French settlement. This is done not merely to tell a complete story of French colonization efforts, but more importantly, to attempt to account for the failure of Champlain's predecessors, such as Ribaut, Laudonniere, and Roberval, and partly to arrive at a proper method of successful colonization. Thus, when Champlain himself founded a colony, a lasting one, he had what might be called a plan of colonization. As he explored, he was careful to note the nature of the country, its fitness for agriculture, its fauna and flora, its harbors—all that would help a would-be settler. As a result of spending a winter among the Hurons, Champlain provided a long chapter on Indian life done with a considerable sympathy for the natives and their customs. This contrasts sharply with the usual approach of the English settler, to whom the native was ordinarily a savage enemy to be despised, pushed out, or exterminated.

Beyond all this, the pages of this work give us a portrait of a man, "perhaps the ablest of the earlier makers of America," who was energetic, hopeful, devout, careful, tolerant of strange ways—a true humanitarian.

Wrong, George M. *The Rise and Fall of New France*. New York: The Macmillan Company, 1928.

George M. Wrong was trained for the ministry of the Anglican Church in Canada, but he never functioned as a parish priest. Devoting his life to teaching and writing, he taught first at Wycliffe College, then at the University of Toronto. Eventually he earned a reputation as the most notable of modern Canadian historians, and the volumes under review constitute his major work.

Anyone who writes about the rise and fall of New France inevitably invites comparison with Francis Parkman. It is interesting to see how Wrong eludes this comparison. Parkman was opening up new territory in historical writing. Basing his work solidly on the sources, his footnotes are long and copious, and in them he carefully discusses the sources and carries on a debate with previous writers who had covered parts of the field. Wrong has no footnotes whatsoever. This does not mean that his work is superficial. At the end of each volume there is an extensive and critical bibliography which the reader can take or leave as he pleases. Parkman was, of course, a master of historical narrative whose writing is graphic and eloquent. Wrong writes in a simple, straightforward style completely without purple passages.

The scope of Wrong's narrative is wide. He begins his account with Marco Polo, has a chapter on the Norse discoveries and Spanish explorers, then one on the English claim to North America, and another about the English on the Pacific coast. Until the middle of the eighteenth century, the English colonies were largely ignored by the English government. New France, on the contrary, was always rather rigidly controlled by Old France. A knowledge of the French history of the period is, therefore, essential to an understanding of the fate of New France. It is one of the merits of Wrong that he carefully tied Canadian and French history together. Henry IV, Cardinal Richelieu, Louis XIV, Colbert, all played their part in the drama, and all are admirably sketched into this narrative. But, argues Wrong, it was Champlain who was "the man destined to make New France a reality," and Wrong makes a good case for this thesis.

The chapter entitled "Champlain Among the Hurons" is much more than its title would indicate. It is a thorough sketch of the Indians of that name, and it is better than Parkman's description, for it is in part based on material not available to the earlier historian. Wrong, having a full comprehension of the great part played by the Roman Catholic Church in the founding of New France, discusses the Catholic revival in France in the seventeenth century, the work of the missionary orders in the founding of the colony, and the place occupied by Bishop Laval in the life of the colony. Parkman manages fairly well to escape from the Protestant bias characteristic of the New England historians of his age, but occasionally traces of it do crop up. From this fault Wrong is completely free. He has produced one of the best introductions to the history of New France that has been written. — *D. R. G.*

Additional Recommended Reading

Biggar, H. P., ed. *Works of Samuel de Champlain.* Toronto: University of Toronto Press, 1971. Contains the French text and English translation, and is probably the definitive edition.

Parkman, Francis. *La Salle and the Discovery of the Great West.* Boston: Little, Brown, and Company, 1897. This volume of Parkman's great work on New France is marked by good scholarship and sound composition.

De Champlain, Samuel. *Voyages of Samuel De Champlain.* Translated by Charles P. Otis.

New York: Ben Franklin Press, 1964. 13 vols. An excellent translation, similar in form and purpose to that by the Bournes though the Bourne notes are better.

Winsor, Justin. *From Cartier to Frontenac: Geographical Discovery in the Interior of North America in Its Historical Relations, 1534-1700.* Boston: Houghton, Mifflin Co., 1894. Like all of Winsor's works, a competent book with many good maps and illustrations, but with no notes or bibliography.

Eccles, William J. *France in America. New American Nation* series. New York: Harper & Row Publishers, 1972. This volume contains a good account of early French exploration of the St. Lawrence and Great Lakes area.

Morison, Samuel Eliot. *Samuel de Champlain: Father of New France.* Boston: Little, Brown, and Company, 1972. Based readily on Champlain's writings, this biography is written in informal style to honor one of the greatest pioneers, explorers, and colonists of all times.

SETTLEMENT OF JAMESTOWN

Type of event: Politico-economic: establishment of a British colony as a commercial enterprise
Time: May 24, 1607
Locale: Jamestown, Virginia

Principal personages:

SIR FERDINANDO GORGES (1566?-1647), leader in the English mercantile community and coauthor of the petition for chartering the Virginia Company

SIR JOHN POPHAM (1531?-1607), Lord Chief Justice of England and coauthor of the petition for chartering the Virginia Company

SIR THOMAS SMYTHE (1558?-1625), active commercial promoter in early seventeenth century England who became head of the Virginia Company in 1609

CHRISTOPHER NEWPORT (?-1617), sea captain who commanded the first voyage to Jamestown

EDWARD MARIA WINGFIELD (1560?-?1613), first president of the council in Jamestown

CAPTAIN JOHN SMITH (1580-1631), second president of the council in Jamestown

POWHATAN (1550?-1618), chieftain of the confederation of Indian tribes in the Jamestown region

SIR GEORGE SOMERS (1554-1610), veteran sea adventurer who commanded the ill-fated fleet of 1609 to Jamestown

THOMAS WEST (LORD DE LA WARR) (1577-1618), first Governor of Virginia after the reorganization of government in 1609

Summary of Event

In 1605 peace with Spain had finally been won, and in England capital was accumulating and commerce was flourishing. Captain George Weymouth had just returned from a voyage to Nantucket and Maine to explore the possibilities of a refuge for Catholics. The five Indians whom Weymouth had brought back with him and the glowing account of the expedition in James Rosier's *Relation* had attracted much attention.

Their interest having been aroused, Sir John Popham, Lord Chief Justice of England, and Sir Ferdinando Gorges, both powerful members of the mercantile community, petitioned the crown in the name of a group of adventurers for a charter incorporating two companies, one of London and one of Plymouth. The patent issued on April 10, 1606, granted them the territory known as Virginia, located between latitude 34° and 41° North. The London Company was authorized to settle between latitude 34° and 41° North, and the Plymouth Company, between latitude 45° and 38° North, but neither

59

was to settle within one hundred miles of the other. Because of Sir Walter Raleigh's explorations in the Chesapeake Bay area and Weymouth's investigations in Maine, the adventurers knew exactly what to request.

The absence, before 1618, of the official minutes of the Virginia Company, as the two companies were jointly called, has forced historians to turn to fragmentary, and usually biased, sources. It seems clear, however, that the central theme of Virginia's early history was the pursuit of England's national interest. The instructions concerning the manner in which the enterprise was to be carried out indicate that it was strictly a commercial undertaking.

On December 20, 1606, the Virginia Company of London dispatched for America three ships, the *Goodspeed,* the *Discovery,* and the *Sarah Constant,* carrying 144 men and boys. Captain Christopher Newport, a well-known sailor of fortune, was to be in charge until the expedition reached land. Entering Chesapeake Bay on April 26, 1607, the 105 survivors searched for a favorable site to settle. On May 24, they disembarked and called the place "Jamestown." Although the area was low and marshy, it was beautiful, defensible, and provided anchorage for deepwater vessels. The great James river offered the possibility of penetration into the interior for exploring and trading with natives.

Only when the settlers had landed and opened the sealed box containing their instructions, did they learn the names of their council, or local governing body, which had been appointed by the company. This council was inferior to a royal council in England appointed by the king. Unfortunately, a considerable number of the settlers were headstrong adventurers, and the lack of a concentrated authority in Virginia, combined with a plethora of would-be leaders, resulted in bickering and the formation of factions. Only the strong leadership of Captain John Smith, the second president of the council, held the settlement together after fear and suspicion led to the ousting of the council's first president, Edward Maria Wingfield.

More pressing than matters of government was the necessity of providing for the settlers' physical needs. Upon their arrival in America, they had divided themselves into three groups: the first was to concentrate on construction and fortifications; the second was to plant crops and keep watch downriver; and the third was to explore the surrounding area. Although the company hoped to find a water route through the continent to the South Sea and encouraged search for minerals, there was little time for such adventurous activity. Establishment of a settlement and development of trade were more urgent matters to be considered.

The successful accomplishment of both these aims depended upon the establishment of amicable relations with the Indians. Such good relations were not achieved easily because the settlers not only insisted upon their right to share the plentiful resources of the country with the Indians, but also tried to convert the red men to Christianity and the European way of life.

Although the strict discipline of John Smith's council presidency and the addition of more immigrants improved conditions at the settlement, the first two years must be judged as disappointing. The adventurers in London therefore embarked upon a more ambitious program to be financed on a joint-stock basis. Having negotiated a new charter, the Virginia Company, under the leadership of Sir Thomas Smythe (originally Smith), launched a vigorous campaign for financial support. Sixteen hundred persons were to emigrate to Virginia on two great expeditions in the summer of 1609. The joint-stock arrangement would allow a pooling of labor with common stock, since each person's migration to America was counted as equal to one share of stock. By this means a community of interest was developed between the adventurer in England and the colonist.

The new charter of 1609 abolished the royal council and placed control in the hands of the council of the company. A governor with absolute authority was to replace the local council in the colony.

The first great contingent of settlers, carrying with them so many hopes, set out on May 15, 1609, with Sir George Somers in command. Ironically, the ship carrying the leaders was blown away from the others in a hurricane and foundered in Bermuda, its passengers not arriving in Jamestown until nearly a year after they had set out. To make matters worse, when the other ships arrived in Virginia, Captain John Smith refused to give up his post as council president, though eventually he yielded leadership to Captain George Percy.

The arrival of almost four hundred new settlers in weakened condition placed considerable strain upon the economy of the colony and set in motion a cruel set of circumstances. When the leaders of the expedition arrived the following summer, they found only sixty settlers still living, with the settlement in ruins about them. Famine, disease, and attacks by Indians had left even the few survivors on the brink of death. Since the new arrivals were without sufficient provisions, the settlers abandoned hope of maintaining the colony and prepared to leave for England by way of Newfoundland. But as the disheartened colonists were sailing down the James river, miraculously they met Thomas West (Lord De La Warr), their new Governor, coming up. Lord De La Warr ordered the colonists to return and reëstablish the settlement. The new leadership, with additional supplies and manpower, gave the colonists courage to continue. Many difficult days lay ahead, but the Virginia Company was determined to keep the colony alive.

Pertinent Literature

Craven, Wesley F. *The Southern Colonies in the Seventeenth Century, 1607-1689.* Baton Rouge: Louisiana State University Press, 1949.

In his account of the settlement of Jamestown, Craven exhibits a rare talent for conveying genuine feeling for the event which he is describing. Craven pictures Jamestown Island as the colonists must have seen it for the first time from the James river. He describes the entire Chesapeake Bay area as John Smith probably explored it in his expedition of 1608. Yet it is not only through his descriptions of the setting and the colonists' experiences that

Craven helps the reader to understand them. He also analyzes the factors which probably prompted particular policies and activities concerning the colony within the seventeenth century setting.

Craven points out that the paucity of unbiased source materials relating to Jamestown has allowed historians to give a number of different interpretations of the reasons for the establishment of the colony. There can be no question, he states, that the pursuit of the national interest was the central theme in Virginia's early history. While he acknowledges the importance of the English mercantile community, he sees it as "an instrument for the achievement of national ends" within "a chronicle of epic proportions." Keeping this theme in mind, Craven offers new insight into the matter of the unfortunate division of authority in the original government of Jamestown. The decision to place a royal council in control was logical in the light of the stability which royal authority would give the colony. One of the most difficult tasks facing the colonists was the transplanting of forms of authority to the wilderness environment.

Despite the temptation to look upon the settlers' early exploration in search of a passage to the South Sea and of gold and mineral deposits as naïve and foolish, these projects appear logical within the context of the pursuit of the national interest. Was it not natural, asks Craven, for the settlers to explore and experiment in the hope of producing an early return to be reinvested in future endeavors?

By present-day standards the settlers' attitude toward the Indians appears as hypocritical and unfeeling, yet it was no more hypocritical than that of any other people, Craven contends. The land and resources seemed to be unlimited, and the English believed in their natural right to trade. They would simply share the rich resources with the Indians. If they did not claim the land, the Indians would be left to the Catholic missionary efforts of France and Spain. The slowness of English missionary efforts was not the result of any lack of sincerity, Craven argues. The godly intentions so loudly advertised during the campaigns for subscribers simply had to take second place to the more pressing physical needs of the colonists. The settlers were confident that the Indians would soon be converted both to Christianity and to European attitudes of economy and landholding. Powhatan was chieftain of the confederation of Indian tribes in the Jamestown region, and when he refused to coöperate, the settlers were forced to demand tribute of the Indians, but the English remained convinced that the red men would profit from exposure to European values and techniques.

Craven's description of the great campaign of 1609 to recruit subscribers to the company and emigrants to the colony is particularly vivid. Probably spurred on by appeals to their patriotic and religious sentiments, many laborers decided to go "on adventure" in hopes of gaining some land and a return from the joint stock. Others contracted with the company for wages or entered the service of particular colonists or subscribers. The great pooling of labor with common stock created a community of interest and a sense of equality between the colonists and subscribers in England. In the colony itself the pooling of resources and community effort was essential. Craven's ability to convey the hopes, the confusion, and the sufferings of the infant settlement in the wilderness enables the reader to understand the Jamestown experience more fully.

Morton, Richard L. *Colonial Virginia. The Tidewater Period, 1607-1710.* Chapel Hill: University of North Carolina Press, 1960. 2 vols.

This volume is a recent general history of Virginia's colonial period. It does not, however, present any startling new thesis about colonial Virginia, a fact much in evidence in the two chapters on the settlement of Jamestown. These chapters are, in essence, a narration of the principal events after Sir Walter Raleigh's unsuccessful colonizing activities in the 1500's until the "starving time" in the winter of 1609-1610.

Raleigh's efforts at colonizing were a consequence of English interest in the New World. Sir Walter hoped to succeed where his half-brother Sir Humphrey Gilbert had failed, but three attempts to plant a colony in the area called "Virginia" left Raleigh a broken man. Morton sees in Raleigh's failure a valuable lesson which other Englishmen quickly learned: colonization was beyond one man's means. For this reason, those persons interested in colonies turned to the chartered trading company as a device for marshaling the necessary human, material, and capital resources. By 1606, a group of men secured a charter for the company which successfully planted a colony in North America.

In analyzing the motives of the London Company's organizers, Morton does not present the detailed examination offered by Wesley Frank Craven. Instead, he catalogues the traditional reasons: trade with the natives, the desire to find a Northwest Passage to the Orient, the hope of duplicating Spain's discovery of gold and silver. Morton does, however, give a passing reference to colonization as an instrument of national policy which Craven emphasizes.

Morton's account of the landing and the colonists' first years is fairly traditional. He imputes the initial difficulties to poor choices of colonists and leaders. Wingfield, first president of the council in Jamestown, emerges as an inept leader who was hampered by his gentle background and poor health, but Morton is less condemnatory of Wingfield and the council than he is of scholars, such as Thomas Jefferson Wertenbaker and Alexander Brown.

It is John Smith who emerges as the colony's savior during the first critical year and a half. Smith's temperament and background suited him to the ordeal, and as long as the wily adventurer remained in the colony it had a chance of survival. When Smith was wounded in a gunpowder explosion, the lack of his steadying influence brought the colony close to disaster during the winter of 1609-1610.

While Smith and the other colonists struggled to make the Virginia venture succeed, Jamestown's backers in London realized that the organization of the colony's government and the lack of adequate funds were hampering the colonists' efforts. Armed with this realization, the London Company sought, and obtained from the Crown, a new charter which reorganized and refinanced the entire operation. This reorganization led to the sending of the "third supply" of men and material. The arrival of new colonists late in the summer of 1609, however, was followed by nearly total disaster the following winter. Morton argues that had these new arrivals and the other colonists been directed by a "strong and forceful leader," the winter of 1609-1610 would not have become the "starving time." Responsibility for the widespread suffering and death lay with the leaders who replaced Smith after his accident. Only the timely arrival of Thomas West (Lord De La Warr) in the spring of 1610 prevented the colony's demise.

Although Morton's treatment of the settlement of Jamestown is not as detailed as that of Craven, it does provide a clear account of the establishment of the first permanent English settlement in North America. — *W.M.B.*

Additional Recommended Reading

McCary, Ben C. *Indians in Seventeenth-Century Virginia.* Williamsburg: Virginia 350th Anniversary Celebration Corporation, 1957. Concentrating on the Powhatans, this booklet by the foremost authority on the subject describes the culture of seventeenth century Virginia Indians.

Barbour, Philip L. *The Three Worlds of Captain John Smith.* Boston: Houghton Mifflin Co., 1964. The most recent biography of John Smith, which explodes many of the myths which have grown up around him.

Smith, Bradford. *Captain John Smith, His Life and Legend.* Philadelphia: J. B. Lippincott Company, 1953. This laudatory biography presénts evidence that the adventures described by John Smith in his writings, long considered of questionable veracity, are indeed true.

Andrews, Charles M. *The Colonial Period of American History.* Vols. I-III: *The Settlements;* Vol. IV: *England's Commercial and Colonial Policy.* New Haven: Yale University Press, 1934-1938. In the first volume Andrews details events in London to provide background in understanding the founding of Virginia.

Wertenbaker, Thomas J. *Virginia Under the Stuarts, 1607-1688.* Princeton: Princeton University Press, 1914. Highly sympathetic toward the colonists and critical of the London Company, this account begins with the 1607 landing and details the early struggle for survival.

Notestein, Wallace. *The English People on the Eve of Colonization, 1603-1630.* New York: Harper & Row Publishers, 1954. A brief but penetrating analysis of the English people at the beginning of the colonizing activities.

CALLING OF THE FIRST GENERAL ASSEMBLY IN VIRGINIA

Type of event: Political: beginning of representative government in British North America
Time: July, 1619
Locale: Virginia

Principal personages:

SIR EDWIN SANDYS (1561-1629), Treasurer of the London Company, who instructed the governor of Virginia to call the first General Assembly

SIR GEORGE YEARDLEY (1587?-1627), Governor of Virginia, who presided over the first session of the General Assembly

SIR SAMUEL ARGALL (fl. 1609-1624), Deputy Governor of Virginia 1617-1619

JOHN PORY (1572-1635), Secretary of the colony and Speaker of the House of Burgesses in its first session

Summary of Event

By 1618 Virginia had been in existence for a decade, but the colony had neither prospered nor realized the expectations of the London Company which had been responsible for founding it. Twice before 1618, the London Company had been reorganized in unsuccessful efforts to make the Virginia venture turn a profit, and it was again on the verge of bankruptcy. As inducements to settlement, the company had sanctioned the introduction of private land tenure and the creation of particular plantations which had resulted in widely scattered settlements and confusion over land titles. Even so, the colony's economic base was insecure, and the colonists grew more restive, especially after 1617 when Sir Samuel Argall became governor and returned the colony to stricter discipline by rigorously enforcing the *Lawes, Divine, Morall, and Martiall.*

Against this background, the London Company in 1618 resolved anew to revitalize its Virginia venture. Led by Sir Edwin Sandys, the company embarked upon an ambitious course of action which aimed at a comprehensive reorganization of the entire colonial operation. The company embodied its plans in a series of instructions and commissions, the so-called "Great Charter," which was designed to reform land tenure, to improve local administration, and to supplant the *Lawes, Divine, Morall, and Martiall* with English common law and a more representative resident government.

Accordingly, the London Company instructed its newly appointed Governor, Sir George Yeardley, to call an assembly consisting of himself, a Council of State appointed by the company, and burgesses elected by the freemen of the colony. The assembly would meet not more than once a year, except upon "very extraordinary and important occasions." It would serve as a court of justice, and it was to have the power to enact such general laws and ordinances for the colony's welfare as

65

should seem necessary. These laws were to be subject to a gubernatorial veto and review by the London Company.

Following his arrival in Jamestown, Yeardley issued a call for the assembly, and on July 30, 1619, the first meeting of a representative legislative body in the New World convened in the church at Jamestown. It was composed of the Governor, six councilors, and twenty-two burgesses—two from each of eleven settlements ("plantations," "hundreds," and towns). The burgesses had been elected by the votes of all who were seventeen years old or older. After selecting John Pory (secretary of the colony and a member of the council) as Speaker, and taking the oaths of allegiance and supremacy, the general assembly proceeded to its business.

After deliberating on the qualifications of its members (two of whom were rejected pending clarification of their patents from the London Company), the assembly moved on to its legislative work. It adopted several revisions of the Great Charter which the company had suggested, and enacted a series of laws dealing with such matters as Indian relations, the dress and conduct of the settlers, church attendance, and measures to promote certain industries, including the manufacture of flax, hemp, silk, and wine. After resolving some criminal cases, "the intemperance of the weather and the falling sick of divers of the Burgesses" forced Yeardley to terminate the assembly after a session of only six days.

Despite the brevity of the meeting, the General Assembly of Virginia had made an important beginning. It had ushered in a new departure in colonial government, and had transformed Virginia "from a mere plantation colony, supported and governed by a trading company largely for profit, into a political community, self-supporting and partially self-governing." While the assembly would undergo modifications in its functions, and its right to exist would be challenged after the London Company lost its charter in 1625, that first meeting in July, 1619, established the precedent for the development of representative political institutions in English North America. And, except for a few interruptions, the General Assembly of Virginia has continued to this day.

Pertinent Literature

Wertenbaker, Thomas J. *Virginia Under the Stuarts, 1607-1688.* Reprint ed. New York: Russell and Russell, 1958.

Thomas Jefferson Wertenbaker was a pioneer in the study of seventeenth century Virginia history. Writing *Virginia Under the Stuarts* at a time when history had only begun to emerge as an academic discipline, his work left a profound impression on subsequent scholars. Nowhere is this fact more in evidence than in Wertenbaker's treatment of the origins of the first General Assembly.

Reaching intellectual maturity when Charles A. Beard, Carl Becker, and other historians were developing what is now known as the "progressive school of historiography," Wertenbaker shared the prevailing assumptions about the processes of history. Consequently, in his analysis of the origins of the General Assembly, Wertenbaker posited a fundamental conflict between James I, King of Great Britain, and his people over what forms of government should exist in Virginia. James, he argued, "had no desire to see the liberal institutions of the Mother Country transplanted to Virginia." Instead, the King wished to keep the colony dependent upon himself, thus augmenting the power of the Crown and making it less dependent upon Parliament.

But the London Company resisted such encroachments. Led by Sir Edwin Sandys, a liberal faction within the company attempted, through successive revisions of the company's charter, to put the government of the colony more in the people's hands. A conservative faction of the company tried to thwart these aims, but that effort was frustrated when Sandys became company treasurer in 1619 and drafted a set of instructions which gave the Virginia colonists broad jurisdiction over their affairs and allowed them to establish democratic institutions in the New World.

These instructions, or the "Virginia Magna Charta" as Wertenbaker termed them, were the cornerstones of liberty in the New World. The establishment of the first representative assembly provided a bulwark against tyranny and the royal prerogative until 1776.

Wertenbaker evinced an abiding fascination with the growth of the General Assembly, for it was through that institution that one could examine the people's struggle for political power. Viewed in these terms, Wertenbaker assumed that the General Assembly, from its inception, acquired all the characteristics of a fully grown, modern legislative assembly. From the start, he maintained, the people's representatives, the members of the House of Burgesses, began to check any encroachment on the people's rights. The entire colonial history of Virginia could be explained in terms of this ongoing struggle.

Unfortunately, few scholars have challenged Wertenbaker's assumptions; present knowledge regarding the origin and the development of the General Assembly has not yet progressed much beyond the pioneering work of Thomas Jefferson Wertenbaker.

Craven, Wesley F. *The Dissolution of the Virginia Company: The Failure of a Colonial Experiment.* Reprint ed. Gloucester, Massachusetts: Peter Smith Publisher, Inc., 1964.

One scholar who has not accepted the Wertenbaker assumptions about the origins of the General Assembly of Virginia is Wesley Frank Craven. Commencing with the premise that "the most common error in writing the history of the Virginia Company has been a failure to understand the fundamental character of that corporation," Craven constructed a thesis which de-

nies most of the arguments advanced by Wertenbaker.

Craven argues that the "true *motif* of the company's history is economic rather than political." The company's reorganization and the issuance of new instructions to Sir George Yeardley in 1618, were not prompted by the liberal political theories of Sir Edwin Sandys, but by a hard-headed desire to make the Virginia venture turn a profit. The so-called "Great Charter" represented the culmination of a two-year debate on the colony's future and the adoption of a new course of action which, it was hoped, would put Virginia on a firm economic footing. Major alterations were required in the colony's structural organization, including the creation of a general assembly.

As Craven interprets the birth of the assembly, the company envisioned that body as one of two resident councils charged with the management of local affairs. A newly created Council of State would handle daily administrative and judicial matters. The Council of State, together with the Governor and representatives from the colony's local jurisdictions, would meet annually to ratify company instructions and to enact local laws. The new government would, in short, act in a manner similar to that of the parent company.

To buttress his thesis concerning the company's purpose in altering the government of Virginia, Craven under-takes a comprehensive examination of Sir George Yeardley's instructions. He demonstrates that the portion which provided for the establishment of the assembly was only a small part of a larger plan. Most of the instructions dealt with such matters as the provision of adequate supplies, the maintenance of good morals, and most importantly, the settlement of land tenure and internal organization. Their objective was the establishment of a uniform system of management with limited local control.

Viewed in these terms, the creation of the General Assembly was not the signal event which Wertenbaker saw. In Craven's opinion, the calling of the first assembly in 1619 was "merely one of many improvements made in the colony's life" before the company's dissolution. The convening of the assembly did provide a precedent for the future, but the assembly's growth into a representative legislative body would be a slow, evolutionary process. — *W.M.B.*

Additional Recommended Reading

Morton, Richard L. *Colonial Virginia.* Vol. I: *The Tidewater Period, 1607-1710.* Ch. 4. Chapel Hill: University of North Carolina Press, 1960. This summary statement on the House of Burgesses leans toward the Wertenbaker analysis but recognizes some of Craven's revisions.

Craven, Wesley F. " '. . . And so the Form of Government Became Perfect,' " in *Virginia Magazine of History and Biography.* LXXVII (April, 1969), 131-146. Craven's most recent analysis of the origins and growth of Virginia's General Assembly.

Bruce, Philip A. *Institutional History of Virginia in the Seventeenth Century.* Vol. II, part v, chs. XIX-XXII. New York: Charles Scribner's Sons, 1910. The classic institutional study of the House of Burgesses.

Van Schreeven, William J. and George H. Reese, eds. *Proceedings of the General Assembly of Virginia, July 30-August 4, 1619, Written and Sent from Virginia to England by Mr. John Pory.* Jamestown, Virginia: The Jamestown Foundation, 1969. The newest and best edition of Pory's account of the first proceedings of the first General Assembly.

ARRIVAL OF THE FIRST NEGROES AND THE ORIGINS OF SLAVERY IN BRITISH NORTH AMERICA

Type of event: Sociological: slavery arising from the need for a labor force
Time: August, 1619
Locale: Jamestown, Virginia

Summary of Event

In 1619 a Dutch warship carrying twenty African Negroes landed at Jamestown, Virginia. These Negroes, the first to arrive in the British colonies, were put to work not as slaves but as servants. Neither the laws of the Mother Country nor the charter of the colony established the institution of slavery, though the system was developing in the British Sugar Islands at this time, and was almost one hundred years old in the Spanish and Portuguese colonies. To be sure, Negro servants were early discriminated against—their terms of service were usually longer than those of white servants, and they were the object of certain prohibitions which were not imposed on white servants—but in the early seventeenth century at least some Negro servants, like their white counterparts, gained their freedom and even acquired some property. Anthony Johnson, who was freed about a year after coming to Virginia in 1621, imported five servants thirty years later, receiving 250 acres on their head rights. Another former servant, a carpenter named Richard Johnson, obtained one hundred acres for importing two white servants in 1654. These two men were part of the small class of free Negroes that existed in Virginia throughout the colonial period.

Such cases as the two Johnsons were rare by mid-century. As early as the 1640's some Negroes were already serving for life, and their numbers increased throughout the decade. In 1640, for example, in a court decision involving three runaway servants, two of them, who were white, were sentenced to an additional four years of service, while the other, a Negro named John Punch, was ordered to serve his master "for the time of his natural Life." In the 1650's some Negro servants were being sold for life, and the bills of sale indicated that their offspring would inherit slave status. Thus slavery developed according to custom before it was legally established in Virginia.

Not until 1661 was chattel slavery recognized by statute in Virginia, and then only indirectly. The following year, the House of Burgesses passed a law declaring that children followed the status of their mothers, thereby rendering the system of slavery self-perpetuating. In 1667 the Virginia Assembly further strengthened the system by declaring that in the case of "children that are slaves by birth . . . the conferring of baptisme doth not alter the condition of a person as to his bondage or freedome; that divers masters, freed from this doubt, may more carefully endeavour the propagation of christianity." Until this time, Americans had justified enslavement of Africans on the ground that they were heathen, and had recognized conversion as a way to freedom. This act closed the last avenue to freedom, apart from manumission, available to Negro slaves. By the beginning of the eighteenth century, Virginia had established a slave code which completed the gradual process by which most Negroes were reduced to the status of chattels. Slaves could not bear arms or own property, nor could they leave the plantation without written permission from the master. Capital punishment was provided for murder and rape; lesser crimes were punished by maiming, whipping, or branding. Special courts were established for the trials of slaves, and Negroes were barred from serving as witnesses, except in cases where slaves were being tried for capital offenses.

In the other British colonies the pattern was similar to that of Virginia. Negro slavery existed early in both Maryland and the Carolinas. Georgia attempted to exclude slavery at the time of settlement, but the trustees eventually yielded to the protests of the colonists and repealed the prohibition in 1750. The Dutch brought slavery to the Middle colonies early in the seventeenth century. The advent of British rule in 1664 proved to be a stimulus to the system in New York and New Jersey; but in Pennsylvania and Delaware the religious objections of the Quakers delayed its growth somewhat and postponed legal recognition of slavery until the early eighteenth century. In seventeenth century New England the status of Negroes was ambiguous, as it was in Virginia. There were slaves in Massachusetts as early as 1638, possibly before, though slavery was not recognized by statute until 1641. New England became heavily involved in the slave trade, particularly after the monopoly of the Royal African Company was revoked in 1698. Like Virginia, all the colonies enacted slave codes in the late seventeenth or early eighteenth century, although the New England codes were less harsh than those of the Middle or Southern colonies. In all the colonies a small class of free Negroes developed alongside the institution of slavery, despite the fact that manumission was restricted.

Slavery grew slowly in the seventeenth century. In 1625 there were twenty-three Negroes in Virginia, and most of them were probably servants, not slaves. By mid-century, a decade before statutory recognition of slavery, the Negro population was only three hundred. But in 1700 there were twelve thousand Negroes and eighteen thousand whites. In the Carolinas the Negro population was about equal to the white population, whereas in New England Negroes numbered only about one thousand out of a total population of ninety thousand. The eighteenth century would see the rapid development of the system of Negro slavery, particularly in the Southern colonies where it became an integral part of the emerging plantation economy.

Arrival of the First Negroes and the Origins of Slavery

Pertinent Literature

Jordan, Winthrop D. *White Over Black: American Attitudes Toward the Negro, 1550-1812.* Chapel Hill: University of North Carolina Press, 1968.

Winthrop Jordan's monumental study of American attitudes toward the Negro sheds new light on the origins of slavery in the British colonies, long a controversial issue among American historians. The contemporary debate goes back to 1950 when Oscar and Mary Handlin published an article in the *William and Mary Quarterly* entitled "Origins of the Southern Labor System." They argued that enslavement of Negroes in the Southern colonies was a relatively late and gradual process. Originally, Negroes were servants, but whereas the condition of white servants improved throughout the seventeenth century, the status of Negroes gradually deteriorated until, in the 1660's, they had been reduced to the status of chattels. In addition, economic conditions, particularly the growth of the plantation system, conspired to degrade the condition of the Negro. In the Handlins' view, American Negro slavery did not develop in imitation of other systems, nor was it "a response to any unique qualities in the Negro himself." Rather, it was a product of the adjustment of "traditional European conceptions of servitude" to the peculiar conditions of the American environment.

In 1959, Carl Degler challenged the Handlins' thesis in an article in *Comparative Studies in Society and History* later incorporated into his survey of American history, *Out of Our Past: The Forces That Shaped Modern America*). Against the Handlins' view that enslavement of the Negro was a consequence of factors other than racism,

Degler argued "that the status of the Negro in the English colonies was worked out within a framework of discrimination." Degler demonstrated that prejudice against the Negro existed before slavery was legally established. "As a result, slavery, when it developed in the English colonies, could not help but be infused with the social attitude which had prevailed from the beginning, namely, that Negroes were inferior."

Writing in 1968, Winthrop Jordan suggested a new way of looking at an old problem. He argued that slavery and prejudice were two sides of the same coin, "twin aspects of a general debasement of the Negro." A "mutual relationship" developed between slavery and prejudice. "Rather than slavery causing 'prejudice,' or vice versa, they seem rather to have generated each other. . . . Slavery and 'prejudice' may have been equally cause and effect, continuously reacting upon each other, dynamically joining hands to hustle the Negro down the road to complete degradation."

One source of both slavery and prejudice in the colonies was the image of the Negro which the British took with them to the New World. Sixteenth and seventeenth century Britons emphasized the distinctive appearance and condition of Africans and saw them as essentially "a separate category of men." The Negro's color had long been a "symbol of baseness and evil"; the fact that he was a heathen also set him apart from the British, as did his condition of savagery, which

Britons tended to associate with beastliness and lecherousness. Transplanted to the New World, seventeenth century British colonists retained the attitude of their forefathers toward Negroes. Though British institutions provided no model for the system of chattel slavery which ultimately developed, Britons both at home and in the New World did possess a concept of slavery "formed by the clustering of several rough but not illogical equations. The slave was treated like a beast. Slavery was inseparable from the evil in men; it was God's punishment upon Ham's prurient disobedience. Enslavement was captivity, the loser's lot in a contest of power. Slaves were infidels or heathens." It is not difficult to see the implications of this concept of slavery, however vague, for the recently discovered "new men" of Africa. As Jordan observes, "On every count, Negroes qualified."

Thus the very qualities which made the Negro distinctive in the minds of sixteenth and seventeenth century British colonists also identified him as a slave, even before the system of slavery had been legally established. The practices of other nations in setting up systems of involuntary servitude reinforced the equation between Negroes and slavery. Economic necessities, especially the universal need for labor in the colonies, also played upon the settlers' ideas about Negroes and slavery. Above all, Jordan emphasizes the sense of difference which British colonists experienced between themselves and the Negro, a sense of difference in which the African's heathenism and color played the crucial role. The religious distinction was probably more significant in the early years of settlement, according to Jordan, but during the seventeenth century a shift of emphasis occurred which made the Negro's color seem the more important distinguishing characteristic.

Thus a whole range of factors—foreign models, traditional concepts of slavery and servitude, the environment of the New World, the British reaction to Negroes, and above all the "sense of difference" between the two races—led to the "unthinking decision" by which slavery was established in the British colonies. In describing the complex of rational and irrational impulses underlying that decision, Jordan has made a considerable contribution to our understanding of such a momentous event.

Greene, Lorenzo J. *The Negro in Colonial New England.* New York: Columbia University Press, 1942; reprinted, Atheneum Press, 1968.

This early work, now reprinted, studies the condition of free and slave Negroes in colonial New England. As portrayed by Greene, slavery in New England contrasts sharply with the system that existed in the rest of the colonies; the system of involuntary servitude which developed in that region was milder than that of the Middle or Southern colonies. One reason was the comparatively small number of Negroes, which in turn dictated less severe restrictions. Significantly, where the proportion of Negroes to whites was high, as in Boston and South Kingston, Rhode Island, local regulations were harsh.

Another reason for the comparative mildness of New England slavery was the religious and social philosophy of

Puritanism. New Englanders offered religious as well as legal and economic justifications for slavery, but their religion also introduced an element of ambiguity into the system. New England slavery was "a curious blending of servitude and bondage"; the slave occupied "a more or less indeterminate status, varying between that of person and that of property." As property, slaves could be bought, sold, and taxed. As persons, they had some of the legal rights enjoyed by freemen: the right to life, to own property and make contracts, to serve in the armed forces, and to testify and bring suit in the courts. A number of slaves actually sued their masters for freedom and some of them won their liberty by such means. The influence of Puritanism is also seen in the fact that masters were encouraged to provide religious and secular instruction for their slaves, and in the shaping of the family life of the slaves.

Paradoxically, although the Puritan religious and social philosophy shaped a milder system of slavery in New England than existed in the other British colonies, the condition of free Negroes in that region "was probably no more favorable than elsewhere in colonial America." Free Negroes occupied a legal status inferior to that of whites, could not vote, were excluded from the militia, and suffered economic discrimination as well. Despite these proscriptions, a number of free Negroes gained prominence in New England, including the poet Phillis Wheatley and Captain Paul Cuffee, a famous Quaker merchant, philanthropist, and colonizer of Liberia.

Greene wrote before the present debate regarding the relation between slavery and prejudice, but his contrast between the lot of slaves and that of free Negroes raises some interesting questions which, when answered, may shed further light on the complicated process which led to the general debasement of the Negro in seventeenth century America. — *A.C.L.*

Additional Recommended Reading

Herskovits, Melville J. *The Myth of the Negro Past.* Boston: Beacon Press, 1941. This pioneer work studies the African cultural heritage which the Negro brought to the New World and which survives in the United States in various forms.

Craven, Wesley F. *The Southern Colonies in the Seventeenth Century, 1607-1689.* Baton Rouge: Louisiana State University Press, 1949. In this general survey of the Southern colonies, Craven argues that prejudice on the part of white settlers led to early enslavement of the Negro.

Russell, John H. *The Free Negro in Virginia, 1619-1865.* Baltimore: The Johns Hopkins University Press, 1913. Russell was one of the first historians to argue that the early status of Negroes in Virginia approximated servitude rather than slavery. The subject of this study is the class of free Negroes which existed prior to the development of slavery in Virginia and persisted even after it was legally established in 1662.

Mannix, Daniel P. and Malcolm Cowley. *Black Cargoes: A History of the Atlantic Slave Trade, 1518-1865.* New York: Viking Press, 1962. Unique in its broad coverage, this book offers a general picture of the Atlantic slave trade from its beginnings, through its abolition in the early nineteenth century and the rise of an illegal trade, to its downfall in the 1860's when slavery was abolished in the United States.

LANDING OF THE PILGRIMS AT PLYMOUTH

Type of event: Sociological: early stages of European migration to America
Time: December 25, 1620 (1620-1626)
Locale: Plymouth, Massachusetts

Principal personages:
WILLIAM BRADFORD (1590-1657), second Governor of Plymouth and the Pilgrims' principal leader during his lifetime
WILLIAM BREWSTER (1567-1644), leader in the Scrooby congregation and elder of the Pilgrim church at Plymouth
JOHN CARVER (1576?-1621), first Governor of Plymouth
THOMAS WESTON (1575?-?1644), leader of a group of London merchant adventurers who obtained the patent and provided the financial backing for the Plymouth venture
SAMOSET (fl. early seventeenth century), Wampanoag Indian chief who first befriended the Pilgrims
SQUANTO (?-1622), Patuxent Indian who came to live at Plymouth as adviser and interpreter

Summary of Event

Meeting at the home of William Brewster, the postmaster, a small group of yeomen farmers in the village of Scrooby, England, decided in 1606 to form a congregation separate from the Church of England. Called Brownists, after Robert Browne, the founder of the Separatist movement—and considered to be radicals by their neighbors—the group was concerned more with the politics than the theology of their religion. The Church, they believed, should be essentially democratic, consisting of equal members joined together in a covenant. In 1608, the Scrooby congregation, determined to escape the scoffs of their neighbors and the harassment of the authorities, emigrated to Holland. After a brief sojourn in Amsterdam, they moved to Leyden and soon settled into the life of the city. Although they could worship freely in Holland, the "Pilgrims," as they called themselves, were disturbed by their children's loss of contact with English culture, by the difficulty of gaining entrance to the Dutch guilds, and by the threat of war with Spain.

The Pilgrims were in all likelihood familiar with stories of the explorations in the New World and with the settlement in Virginia. Although they possessed neither adequate resources, nor patrons, nor a patent, they decided to go to America. Fortunately for them, the Virginia Company was at this time attempting to cure its financial ills by offering privileges and plantations to "undertakers" who would set up private plantations. With the help of Sir Edwin Sandys, they secured a patent on June 19, 1619, and an unofficial assurance that the King would not molest them. Although the patent provided that they should settle within Anglican Virginia, they were to be allowed to live as a distinct body with their own government, subject only to the laws of the colony as a whole. They expected to obtain a grant of religious toleration. During the delay that ensued while the Pilgrims awaited royal approval of their grant, Thomas Weston, the leader of a group of London merchant adventurers, obtained a patent from the Virginia Company in the name of John Pierce, one of his associates. Approaching the Pilgrims in Leyden, he persuaded them to abandon their patent and join his group with the promise that the adventurers would supply the funds and handle the business end of the undertaking.

According to the agreement reached by the two parties, those persons going to the colony were to stand as equal partners with the London adventurers in the company. Three groups shared in the investment: seventy London adventurers who paid ten pounds sterling per share; planters who received one share each for their labor; and adventurer planters who were reckoned as having two shares each, one by purchase and a second by going to America. The adventurers in London were to exercise no civil authority over the planters.

In addition to the forty-eight officers and crew, 101 passengers departed from Plymouth, England, on September 16, 1620. The Pilgrims comprised less than half the group. There were thirty-five Pilgrims from Leyden, but of the sixty-six passengers recruited by the adventurers from London and Southampton, most were "strangers." Because the *Speedwell,* in which the Pilgrims had come from Leyden, proved unseaworthy, all had to crowd aboard the *Mayflower* at Plymouth.

On November 9, Cape Cod was sighted. Although they were outside the bounds of their patent and at first planned to continue southward to Virginia, treacherous seas convinced the immigrants that they should remain in New England. In order to avoid future difficulties with some of the "strangers" who seemed inclined toward mutiny, the Pilgrims drafted an agreement called the "Mayflower Compact," which was in the form of a Separatist Church covenant. By its terms, the forty-one signatories (nearly all the adult male passengers) formed a "civill body politick" giving them the power to enact laws for the common good and obligating all to obey such laws.

After several parties had explored the area, one group landed on December 11 at Plymouth, as it had already been named by Captain John Smith during his earlier exploration of the region. The *Mayflower* then entered the bay, and by December 25 a site had been chosen and work had begun on a common house. The Pilgrims' choice of a site for settlement was extremely fortunate. Because an epidemic had decimated the Patuxent Indians who inhabited the area around Plymouth, there was no threat of hostile neighbors, and there was cleared land ready for planting.

Although the winter of 1620-1621 was a mild one, over half the settlers, weakened by hardships experienced during the voyage, died of pneumonia, tuberculosis, or scurvy. Upon the death of Governor John Carver in the spring, William Bradford, who would be the Pilgrims' outstanding leader for thirty-five years, succeeded him in office. When members of the Wampanoag Indian tribe, most notably Samoset, appeared, they proved to be friendly and helpful. Squanto, the last of the Patuxents, became a permanent resident of Plymouth and Bradford's closest friend and agricultural adviser.

The residents of Plymouth were simple farmers and artisans almost totally lacking in formal education. None of the Pilgrim leaders had experience in government, but with the Scriptures as their guide, they sought to establish a Christian commonwealth in which civil and religious functions would be kept separate. Often disturbed by what they considered the improper and immoral activities of the "strangers" among them, the Pilgrims were concerned with maintaining the purity of their way of life. They accused the merchant adventurers of trying to undermine the religious exclusiveness of the colony. Because their original patent was useless outside Virginia, the merchant adventurers obtained from the Council of New England in June, 1621, a new patent which granted the lands to the Pilgrims and merchants jointly.

During the first year at Plymouth, the Pilgrims experienced hunger and great hardship. Their plight was complicated by the arrival of new settlers whom Thomas Weston had directed to be housed and fed until a new settlement could be established. William Bradford saw that the communal system of agriculture was not producing satisfactory results, and in 1624, he assigned to each family its own parcel of land. The final break with the London merchants came late in 1626 when the Pilgrims bought out their shares in the company.

Pertinent Literature

Smith, Bradford. *Bradford of Plymouth.* Philadelphia: J. B. Lippincott Company, 1951

Although the Pilgrims who landed at Plymouth in 1620 would have been appalled at the thought of being called democrats, their unabashed admirer Bradford Smith, credits their movement with the founding of American democracy. To the Separatist Church's emphasis upon the voluntary association of equal members bound by a covenant, and upon separation of the Church and the state, Smith attributes the principles embodied in the federal Constitution.

Smith's hero, William Bradford, epitomizes the desires and principles which motivated the Pilgrims. The story of their leader's life is the story of their flight from England and their struggle to maintain their chosen way of life at Plymouth. With convincing verisimilitude Smith conveys the atmosphere of Elizabethan England and of the life which William Bradford probably knew in the village of Scrooby. The orphaned child of a yeoman wool raiser, Bradford took an early interest in religion and joined a Separatist church in which he was influenced by William Brewster. Displaying a decided bias in favor of the Separatists, the author summarizes the events of the Reformation in England and the founding of the Puritan and Separatist movements. Unlike some other historians who contend that the Separatists were merely heckled by their neighbors, Smith relates a tale of harassment and imprisonment by the government, which forced the religious revolutionaries to flee the country.

Smith claims that the Pilgrims formed many of their democratic ideas and institutional concepts during their stay in Holland. He pictures the Dutch as thrifty, wholesome, and resourceful—generally superior to the "be-ribboned dandies" of England. Despite the advantages of the city of Leyden, the Pilgrims wished not only to escape the threat of war with Spain, but also to find a pastoral "Promised Land." Although most historians, including William Bradford, state (and the patent certainly implies) that the *Mayflower* passengers were headed for a settlement in Virginia, Smith insists that the Pilgrims had decided before setting out to avoid living under the laws of Anglican Virginia by landing in New England.

The London adventurers who financed the Plymouth enterprise are the villains of the piece. The eminent colonial historian, Charles M. Andrews, writes that it was simply consistent with good contemporary business practice for the merchants to insist that the lands and buildings in the settlement be divided among the shareholders at the end of seven years and that until then all the settlers' labor be for the common interest. But Smith pictures the adventurers as sinister charlatans bent on making bond servants of the Pilgrims. While it is true that the leader of the adventurers, Thomas Weston, later dealt unfairly with the settlers, Smith's view is colored by his sympathy for the Pilgrims' desire for independence.

One of the strongest points of this book, and the feature that makes it pleasant reading, is the author's feeling for the times. He vividly describes the discomforts aboard the incredibly crowded *Mayflower,* the construction of the houses at Plymouth, the methods of cultivation, the food served at Bradford's table, and many other facets of daily life in the colony. Though he has a tendency to become sentimental while attempting to invest Bradford with emotion, his use of dramatic technique does make the historical personages appear as real people having tempers, prejudices, and a sense of humor. Smith's Bradford barely escapes being too virtuous to be likable. The author admits that his hero was intolerant of lesser men, yet he manages to convey the Pilgrim governor's simple faith and basic practicality.

Bradford, William. *Of Plymouth Plantation, 1620-1647.* Edited by Samuel Eliot Morison. New York: Alfred A. Knopf, Inc., 1952

No portrait or description of William Bradford, the greatest of the Pilgrim leaders, has come down to us from the seventeenth century. But, in the words of Samuel Eliot Morison, Bradford himself created "as fair a permanent monument as any man could wish" in his history *Of Plymouth Plantation.*

The book was employed as a source by several colonial historians before 1730, and was deposited by one of them in a treasury of Americana in Boston's Old South Church. Apparently spirited away by the British during the Revolution, it disappeared until 1855, when it suddenly turned up in the library of the Bishop of London. Complicated negotiations finally succeeded in returning the volume to Massachusetts in 1897. It has come to be recognized not only as a priceless historical source, but also as a literary classic.

Of Plymouth Plantation is not a

spiritual autobiography. In fact, its author is extremely reticent about his personal feelings. Yet in relating the hopes, fears, and determination of his people, William Bradford reveals his own character and spirit. Bradford's religion was unquestionably the guiding force in his life. He had no doubt that God had chosen the Separatists as divine instruments for "propagating and advancing the gospel of the kingdom of Christ in those remote parts of the world." In a sense, he—as did another great religious rebel, John Milton—sought in his book to justify the ways of God to man. Satan had wrought the confusion and corruption which held sway over the Church of England during the reigns of Elizabeth and James I. But the Lord himself would assist his "free people" who joined themselves in a covenant "to walk in all His ways made known" though it might cause them hardship.

While the faith of Bradford and the Pilgrims is evident throughout the history, the work is in no way theological. The frequent allusions to God's purpose and to the Pilgrims' assurance of their role in it are those of a man whose religion was a natural part of his existence. Thus the allusions fall naturally within the relation of everyday events. Bradford's style is plain and forceful. Although we may wish that he had done so, he seldom stops to describe the appearance or condition of things, preferring to proceed with the narration of events. Yet this very sparseness of style manages to convey the sparseness of the settlement on the harsh New England coast and of the Pilgrims' plain way of life. With touching sympathy Bradford confides his concern for the apprehensions of his people and for their feelings of desolation and loneliness in the wilderness.

Bradford's business sense and practicality also come to light in his explanations of relations with the merchant adventurers in London and the other settlements in Massachusetts. He cannot hide his indignation over the unfair treatment of the Pilgrims by Thomas Weston, the leader of the adventurers. In his dealings with the adventurers, the Indians, the neighboring settlers, and the unruly members of his own settlement, he merges as a tough-minded, hard-bargaining leader. His intolerance of those outside the Separatist faith, and his harsh treatment of what he considered to be immoral behavior too easily conjure up the picture of the stern, unsmiling Pilgrim in the black cloak and tall black hat. Within the context of his religious convictions, however, these qualities are but further evidence of his belief that he was an instrument of God. — *W.M.B.*

Additional Recommended Reading

Adams, James Truslow. *The Founding of New England.* Ch. 5. Magnolia, Massachusetts: Peter Smith Publisher, Inc., 1921. And in paperback by Little, Brown, and Company. In contrast to the "democratic" tradition in historiography, Adams views the persecutions of the Pilgrims with skepticism and also presents the merchant adventurers' side of the economic question.

Andrews, Charles M. *The Colonial Period of American History.* Vol. I: *The Settlements.* Chs. 13 and 14. New Haven: Yale University Press, 1964. An excellent and detailed narrative which is particularly useful in explaining the preliminary arrangements with the London Company and the merchant adventurers.

Morison, Samuel Eliot. "The Pilgrim Fathers: Their Significance in History," in *By Land and By Sea.* New York: Alfred A. Knopf, Inc., 1953. Morison contends that the Pilgrims were of little significance in the development of American political and economic institutions, but their unflagging faith in the face of hardship contributed significantly to our spiritual tradition.

Rutman, Darrett B. *Husbandmen of Plymouth.* Boston: Beacon Press, 1967. Provides details, through extensive statistical information, of the agricultural life which was central to life at Plymouth in the early days.

Willison, George F. *Saints and Strangers.* New York: Reynal and Hitchcock, 1945. Spanning the period from William Brewster's youth to the end of the existence of Plymouth as a separate colony, this detailed account attempts to humanize the Pilgrims by emphasizing their goals and accomplishments.

Langdon, George D., Jr. *The Pilgrim Colony: A History of New Plymouth, 1620-1691.* New Haven: Yale University Press, 1966. An account which emphasizes the advantages of the early settlers over their successors in attaining political and economic power.

ALGONQUIN INDIANS SELL MANHATTAN ISLAND FOR TWENTY-FOUR DOLLARS

Type of event: Economic: desire of the Dutch to legalize their settlement at New Amsterdam and maintain good relations with the Indians
Time: May 6, 1626
Locale: Manhattan Island, New Netherland

Principal personages:
HENRY HUDSON (?-1611), English navigator who explored the Hudson river for the Dutch East India Company and thereby provided the basis for its claim to the area
CORNELIUS MAY (fl. 1624), first Governor of New Netherland, who brought settlers to the area
PETER MINUIT (1580-1638), third Governor and first Director-General of New Netherland, who purchased Manhattan Island and developed New Amsterdam
WILLEM KIEFT (1597-1647), fifth Governor of New Netherland whose efforts to levy taxes on the Indians caused a cruel Indian war
PETER STUYVESANT (1592-1672), last Dutch Governor of New Netherland, who surrendered the colony to the British

Summary of Event

In the early seventeenth century, the Netherlands, like other nations of northern Europe, sent out explorers to search for a sea route around North America to the riches of the Far East. The principal explorer for the Dutch was Henry Hudson, an Englishman, who, in 1609, explored the river which bears his name. When Hudson and other navigators failed to find the Northwest Passage, the Dutch, like other Europeans, decided to occupy the lands which they claimed in the New World and exploit their resources. While hoping to discover gold and silver as the Spanish had done in the south, the Dutch soon found that the most readily exploitable resource of the middle Atlantic coastal region which they claimed was the furs which they could obtain by trading with the na-

tives. The demand for furs and pelts was so great in Europe that one shipload could make its owners wealthy.

In the interests of further discovery and to stimulate trade, the Dutch parliament, the States-General, granted to its traders and explorers the exclusive right to make four voyages to any new lands which they might explore. Under this grant, in 1614 five ships visited the Hudson river, which the Dutch called the Mauritius. Later that same year, these traders combined as the United New Netherland Company and received a monopoly of the trade of the Hudson Valley from the States-General. Ignoring Manhattan Island, these early traders sailed up the Hudson to the site of present-day Albany, where they erected Fort Nassau on Castle Island as a base of operations and exchanged their goods for the furs of the Mohican Indians. Following the expiration of the charter of the United New Netherland Company in 1618, a succession of different companies exploited the Hudson river fur trade.

In 1621, a number of influential merchants obtained from the States-General a charter for the Dutch West India Company with the sole right to trade on the Atlantic coasts of Africa, and North and South America for twenty-four years. Although the new company was organized primarily to challenge Spanish control of Latin America, it was also interested in the Hudson river area. In 1624, the company dispatched Captain Cornelius May with a shipload of thirty families to settle in North America. Opposite Castle Island they established a trading post named Fort Orange, and formed a settlement on the Delaware river. They may also have established a trading house on Governor's Island in New York Harbor.

The first two governors, Cornelius May and William Verhulst, lived and administered the colony from the Delaware river site, but Peter Minuit, the third governor and first director-general of New Netherland, shifted his base of operations to Manhattan Island. A native of Wesel, then in the Duchy of Cleves, he was probably of French or Walloon descent. Minuit was described as a shrewd and somewhat unscrupulous man. One of his first acts upon arriving on Manhattan Island early in 1626 was to buy the land rights to the island from the Canarsee Indians for sixty guilders, or about twenty-four dollars, in trinkets. Since the Manhattan tribe, for whom it was named, had a better claim to the island

than did the Canarsee, Minuit later also bought the island from them. Through this, their first major land purchase from the Indians, the Dutch secured a semblance of a legal title to Manhattan. At the time of the purchase, it was a beautiful island, being covered with a great forest and abounding with game and wild fruits.

Minuit made New Amsterdam, at the southern tip of Manhattan, the center of Dutch activity in the area. A large fort, pentagonal in shape, surrounded on three sides by a great moat and fronting on the bay, was one of the first structures to be built. When it was finished, Minuit brought several families from Fort Orange to settle in the town, and ordered Fort Nassau on the South river, near present Gloucester, New Jersey, evacuated and the garrison transferred to New Amsterdam. Despite his vigorous administration of the colony, Minuit was recalled to Holland for examination in 1632, and was dismissed from the West India Company's service.

In the meantime, in 1629, the directorate of the company, with the approval of the States-General, issued a Charter of Freedoms and Exemptions which provided for the grant of large estates, called patroonships, to those members of the company who would settle at least fifty persons above the age of fifteen on their lands within four years. Ostensibly designed to promote farming in New Netherland, these grants were intended primarily to encourage settlers to go up the Hudson to settle and make further contacts with the Indians and thereby extend the fur trade. The furs, it was expected, would be sent down the river to New Amsterdam from where the West India

Company had the sole right to export them. With one exception, Rensselaerswyck, these patroonships were unsuccessful.

Relations with the Indians remained good, and the fur trade continued to prosper until 1641, when hostilities with the natives broke out. Called Governor Kieft's War, the fighting was caused by the Governor's attempt to collect taxes from the Algonquin tribes for Dutch "protection." The conflict was terminated by a treaty of August 29, 1645. It produced some disruption of the fur trade of the Hudson river and forced Governor Kieft to surrender some of his arbitrary power to advisory bodies in order to obtain popular support for the prosecution of the war. In 1647, Kieft was succeeded by Peter Stuyvesant, the last Dutch Governor or Director-General of New Netherland. It was he who surrendered the colony to the British in 1664.

Pertinent Literature

Trelease, Allen W. *Indian Affairs in Colonial New York: The Seventeenth Century.* Ithaca: Cornell University Press, 1960.

The purchase of Manhattan is by itself of little significance and should be viewed in the light of Dutch-Indian relations in the seventeenth century. The Dutch initially came to the New World to exploit its rich storehouse of furs. As traders, the Dutch provided the Indians with new or better articles of life. Mirrors, beads, cooking utensils, guns, ammunition, and liquor were traded for the precious pelts. These trading goods were prized by the Indians, for they improved the standard of living in the tribes.

In the early 1620's, however, Dutch policy in New Netherland changed. Although furs were still sought by the Dutch West India Company, permanent settlers were introduced. Their arrival posed a new problem for the Dutch in their relations with the Algonquin tribes: how could the Indians be induced to give up their land? It was a delicate matter. Farmers competed with the Indians for a dwindling supply of available land, while the fur traders had posed no threat to the tribal lands at all.

The Dutch solved the problem by determining that all lands had to be obtained from the tribes by purchase. Above all, land cessions were to be voluntary, not forced, nor obtained by "craft or fraud" according to the West India Company charter. There are few records extant before 1630, so it is hard to determine if the colonists followed official Dutch policy. But the first great purchase of note is the one by Peter Minuit of Manhattan Island in 1626. Four years later, the Dutch bought Fort Orange (Albany) from the Mohicans, legalizing the fort's presence although it had been built some years before.

After 1630, land purchases from the Indians were commonplace. The patroons were required to obtain title to their large land grants by purchase from the nearest tribe. Dutch insistence on the Indians' selling their lands for a mutually satisfactory price contributed much to the friendly relations between the two peoples. Only when Willem Kieft became governor in 1638 was there any major Dutch-Indian fighting, and that was caused in large part by Kieft's insistence that the tribes pay a tax for Dutch "protection." The arrival of Stuyvesant led to a strict reassertion of earlier governmental policy, and the end of most of the fighting.

Trelease's volume is a good study, not only of the Dutch era, but of Indian relations during the British era that followed. He devotes fully half of his book to Dutch policy, the early attempts at settlement, land purchases (of which Manhattan Island was the first), and the ensuing wars. Most interesting is his preliminary chapter which discusses the various Algonquin tribes and their neighbors, the powerful Iroquois, who determined much of the history of colonial New York.

Davies, D. W. *A Primer of Dutch Seventeenth Century Overseas Trade.* The Hague: Martinus Nijhoff, 1961.

One of the major faults of American history is that it is too often seen in isolation from the rest of the world. The purchase of Manhattan Island occurred because the Dutch were interested in world trade of which New Netherland provided a small, but important, part.

In this slim volume, D. W. Davies discusses the origin of Dutch sea interests, stemming from their ability to preserve fish which they traded to the interior countries of Europe. In the twentieth century, it is difficult to imagine that one of the mightiest powers of seventeenth century Europe was the Dutch Republic. Hardly anything moved by sea unless it was carried on a Dutch ship. The Dutch empire stretched around the world, and Dutch traders visited China, Africa, Australia, the Levant, the Baltic States of Europe, and North and South America. The Dutch West India Company was an important carrier for the slave trade, stimulating settlement on the Brazilian coast and also conducting the trade along the coasts of the regions now known as Delaware, New Jersey, and New York.

With regard to the company's activities in North America, Davies points out that contradictory policies were carried out in New Netherland: efforts to promote the establishment of permanent settlements and a farming economy ran counter to trading interests because settlers drove out the fur-bearing animals and ruined the fur trade. The company also showed that it was incapable of governing New Netherland when quarrels arose between the civilian population and Governors Kieft and Stuyvesant. In fact, the colony proved to be a liability to the West India Company, costing the directors over half a million guilders between 1626 and 1644 alone. — *W.L.R.*

Additional Recommended Reading

Wilson, Charles. *Profit and Power: A Study of England and the Dutch Wars.* London: Longmans, Green, and Co., 1957. A detailed study of the strategic, political, dynastic, and economic rivalries between Great Britain and the Netherlands during the seventeenth century which resulted in the Dutch loss of New Netherland.

Geyl, Pieter. *The Netherlands in the Seventeenth Century.* 2 vols. London: Ernest Benn Ltd., 1964. This work discusses the rise of the Netherlands as a European power, but contains good short sections on the Dutch colonies, including New Netherland.

Boxer, Charles R. *The Dutch Seaborne Empire, 1600-1800.* London: Hutchinson and Co., Ltd., 1965. This work includes little on New Netherland, but it is a good study of the Dutch empires and is useful for background.

Riemersma, Jelle C. *Religious Factors in Early Dutch Capitalism, 1550-1650.* The Hague: Mouton and Co., 1967. A short study in which the author analyzes the importance of Protestantism in stimulating the Dutch to set up one of the first really successful world trade empires.

Kessler, Henry H. and Eugene Rachlis. *Peter Stuyvesant and His New York.* New York: Random House, 1959. An account of the work of the controversial last Dutch governor of New Netherland.

Flick, Alexander C., ed. *History of the State of New York.* 10 vols. New York: Columbia University Press, 1933-1937. The first volume gives an excellent account of the founding of New York and includes a bibliography.

THE GREAT PURITAN MIGRATION

Type of event: Cultural: desire to establish a Puritan Commonwealth
Time: 1630-1643
Locale: Massachusetts Bay

> *Principal personages:*
> JOHN WINTHROP (1588-1649), Governor of Massachusetts and
> its leading citizen
> JOHN COTTON (1584-1652), teacher at the First Church in Boston and an eminent divine
> ANNE HUTCHINSON (1591-1643), an enthusiastic disciple of
> John Cotton
> ROGER WILLIAMS (1603?-1683), one of the founders of Rhode
> Island

Summary of Event

Credit for the successful establishment of a Puritan Commonwealth in North America belongs as much to Charles I, King of England and Puritan antagonist, as to any other single individual. On March 2, 1629, he dissolved Parliament, thereby denying the Puritans a public forum from which to continue their agitation for reforming the Church of England; a few days later he granted a royal charter to the Puritan-controlled Massachusetts Bay Company which provided the framework for establishing a colony in the New World. By thus harassing the Puritans in old England even as he allowed them to procure a beachhead in New England, Charles virtually guaranteed the success of their colonizing venture.

The charter granted to the Massachusetts Bay Company contained, contrary to established custom, no clause stipulating that the company should hold its meetings in England. This omission enabled several leading Puritan stockholders to carry the charter with them to the New World and so transfer control of both company and colony to North America. Massachusetts thus became an autonomous Commonwealth, the government of which evolved out of a transplanted joint-stock company. The stockholders who emigrated to Massachusetts became the voting citizens of the state, the board of directors, known as assistants, developed into a legislative assembly, and the company president served as governor of the colony.

The first contingent of settlers came to America in 1630. In the Great Migration which lasted until 1643, some twenty thousand people came to Massachusetts to make the greatest colonizing exodus that England has ever known.

John Winthrop, first Governor of Massachusetts Bay, realized soon after his arrival in the colony that too few members of the company had emigrated to provide a secure basis for government. In 1631, therefore, Winthrop arranged for the admission of more than a hundred settlers to the status of "freemen," as stockholders were then called in England, and this number was gradually increased as the colony grew. Although the original stockholders had hoped to contain the rights of these newly-created citizens within definite limits, such restrictions proved to be increasingly difficult to enforce. By 1644, the freemen had broadened their participation in the legislative process through the establishment of a lower house in the legislature consisting of two deputies from each town who shared, along with the governor and assistants, in the enactment of laws for the affected territory.

Despite these changes in the structure of government and the remarkable growth of the colony, Massachusetts remained safely under the control of a Puritan oligarchy. A law of 1636 helped to maintain this alliance of the Church and the state by providing that only members of an approved congregation could apply for the status of freemen. Moreover, Puritan political theory held that although the people had a right to elect their leaders, once magistrates were installed in office they held a commission from God and were responsible to Him rather than to the electorate. Therefore, as Boston's influential minister John Cotton repeatedly pointed out, the freemen had no right to deprive a man of elective office unless they found him guilty of some grave offense. The remarkable durability of Puritan magistrates attests to the effectiveness of this advice.

The difficulty of maintaining orthodoxy in a congregational system of church government presented the Puritan commonwealth with its greatest challenge during the early years of settlement. Despite John Winthrop's efforts to maintain unity within the col-

ony, zealots, such as Roger Williams, one of the founders of Rhode Island, and Anne Hutchinson, an enthusiastic disciple of John Cotton, threatened to divide the province into warring factions by convincing their respective congregations that the Church stood in need of further purification. Since each congregation was presumably independent of outside authority, it was difficult to discipline any heretic who succeeded in winning support from his or her local church.

Williams arrived in Massachusetts in 1631 and almost immediately began to challenge the purity of the New England churches, as well as the basis on which the Puritans had erected their civil government. He contended that the Massachusetts congregations retained too many contacts with the Church of England, that the civil government had no right to enforce religious uniformity, and that the King had acted illegally in granting a charter to the colony. These arguments threatened established authority and yet, because Williams enjoyed the confidence of his congregation at Salem, both the magistrates and the ministers found it difficult to deal with him.

Hutchinson presented an even greater problem. She argued that personal revelation might supplant the teachings of the ministers, and that each individual must obey the voice of God rather than the commands of either church or state. Although holding no official church position, she enjoyed the support of a majority in the Boston congregation and, like Williams, proved a thorny problem for the ministers and magistrates.

The ultimate expulsion of both Williams and Anne Hutchinson demonstrated the means by which orthodoxy would continue to protect itself in Massachusetts. The Puritans continued to insist upon the autonomy of each congregation but they managed to maintain uniformity through their control of the government. In theory the ministers of the colony exercised no authority over a particular congregation except through persuasion. They could, however, declare an individual a heretic and it then became the duty of the civil government to see that he was punished. Through this partnership of the Church and the state, formalized by the Cambridge Platform of 1649, the Puritans maintained a virtually unchallenged control of Massachusetts throughout the first half of the seventeenth century.

Pertinent Literature

Morgan, Edmund S. *The Puritan Dilemma: The Story of John Winthrop.* Boston: Little, Brown, and Company, 1958.

Professor Morgan's interesting and informative biography of Winthrop is one of the best short introductions to the early development of Massachusetts. Although Morgan's focus is on the life of the colony's first governor, he presents a well-rounded account of events in the Puritan settlement during the first two decades. He deals with the causes of the Puritan migration from England, the organization of the Church and the civil government, the internal threats precipitated by both Williams and Anne Hutchinson, and the problems faced by Massachusetts in its dealings with England and other parts of the Atlantic community.

Generally sympathetic to Winthrop, Morgan credits the Massachusetts leader with having guided the colony on a middle path between excessive zeal on one side and corruption on the other. As a young man Winthrop had come to believe that the Puritan, though he had to avoid compromising with the evils of the world, must do more than learn to discipline himself. He discerned, as Morgan explains it, that the Puritan could not withdraw from the world but must learn to live in it and work to improve it. This lesson was applied to the government of Massachusetts. Winthrop insisted that the colonists maintain the purity of their ideals, but he opposed the fanaticism of those who wanted to achieve that end through isolation and withdrawal. In so doing, Winthrop enabled Massachusetts to solve, temporarily, the problem which Morgan has labelled "the Puritan dilemma."

In discussing the government of Massachusetts, which he describes as "absolute authority resting on a consent that was renewed every year," Morgan makes a case for justifying the despotism of Puritan leadership. He admits that the "belligerent precisionism" of Thomas Dudley, the deputy governor of Massachusetts, or the "hasty temper" of John Endecott might have made such a government intolerable, but believes that under Winthrop it was efficient, just, and intelligent.

Morgan is most critical of Winthrop in his discussion of the trial of Hutchinson, a member of the Boston congregation who threatened the authority of civil and ecclesiastical leaders by her insistence that divine inspiration took precedence over the Scriptures. The author describes her as Winthrop's intellectual superior and insists that the Governor resorted to "blind dogmatism" in order to defeat her. The trial, which resulted in her banishment, is described as such a farce that "it might have been better for the reputation of her judges if they had simply banished her unheard."

Like Perry Miller in his essay "Errand into the Wilderness," Morgan regards the Civil War in England as a turning point for American Puritanism. Bewildered and outraged by the decision of the English Puritans to endorse toleration, the people of New England "found themselves suddenly alone in the wilderness." Once again Winthrop was confronted with the problem of separatism, although this time it was the danger of "a whole people lost in satisfaction with their own collective holiness." Winthrop's common sense told him that Massachusetts must not isolate itself from the world, and he used his influence to prevent self-righteousness from playing a decisive part in Massachusetts' foreign policy. He argued that the colony must display charity toward its sister settlements in North America and insisted that the Puritans must engage in business dealings with other people, regardless of religious differences.

The value of Morgan's work is less in the originality of his conclusions than in the clarity and detail of his synthesis. *The Puritan Dilemma* generally follows prevailing interpretations of the settlement of Massachusetts Bay, but it brings the story together in a succinct and comprehensive account which is otherwise unavailable. At the same time it is an outstanding biography of Winthrop which gives a personal and political picture of one of the most important figures in American colonial history.

Rutman, Darrett B. *Winthrop's Boston: A Portrait of a Puritan Town, 1630-1649.* Chapel Hill: University of North Carolina Press, 1965.

Whereas most accounts of the early Puritan settlements in North America have dealt with the principal leaders of the Massachusetts Bay colony, Professor Rutman approaches his task somewhat differently. His focus is on the city of Boston rather than the entire colony, and he repeatedly reminds his readers that it was "only the great who wrote" and that the mind of any given period is not simply a "compilation of assumptions" gleaned from the writings of leading figures. In attempting to convey a sense of what Boston was like in its early decades, Rutman has produced a volume which is remarkable for its vigorous narrative style and careful scholarship.

In describing the settlement of, and early developments in, Boston, the author presents a variety of material not readily available in other sources. He describes in detail such problems as the limited amount of land available to the inhabitants of the city, the process by which such land was distributed, the lack of adequate supplies of wood, and the duties of various town officials. Rutman is particularly interested in the early tendency of the town to assume authority over itself, and suggests that leaders, such as Winthrop, were willing to grant such local authority because of the overwhelming demands of "commonwealth duties." This interpretation places more importance on town government than most narrators have done, and demonstrates Rutman's effort to assess the influence of the "incoherent many as well as the vociferous few."

Although *Winthrop's Boston* is primarily concerned with events in the city itself, it also deals with other areas of the colony. The controversy with Anne Hutchinson, since it directly concerned the First Church in Boston, receives considerably more attention than the problems caused by Williams. Yet both are adequately covered and the narrative presents a broad general picture of the early years of Massachusetts.

In general outline Rutman's narrative does not differ significantly from other historical accounts. He presents a sympathetic picture of Puritan Massachusetts and emphasizes the importance of common-sense solutions to the problems facing the colony.

Most of the author's historical revisions stem from his determination to free himself from dependence on the writings of major figures and his attempt to deal with the total community. He is particularly concerned with denying the validity of the term "Puritan mind" when applied to the city of Boston. Rutman attempts to redress the stress on intellectual processes which has resulted from the remarkable work of Perry Miller, by demonstrating that the people who lived and worked in Boston were "ordinary people, neither wholeheartedly humanistic nor frigidly glacial, neither entirely emotional nor entirely rational."

Like many recent narratives, *Winthrop's Boston* describes a utopian scheme which began to crumble during the first decade of settlement. Outwardly, the Puritan oligarchy maintained its domination of the colony throughout the seventeenth century, but the forces of decay had long since decreed its fall. The dispersal of population, the availability of land, and the creation of a church establishment were incompatible with Winthropian ideals. Most destructive of all was Boston, with its commercial prosperity, its internal fragmentation, and the "preoccupation of the Bostonians with their own town rather than the community."

— *D.L.A.*

Additional Recommended Reading

Miller, Perry. *The New England Mind:* Vol. I: *The Seventeenth Century.* Cambridge: Harvard University Press, 1939. A brilliant study of Puritan theology by the author who has done much to explain the intellectual history of New England.

Miller, Perry. *Orthodoxy in Massachusetts, 1630-1650.* Cambridge: Harvard University Press, 1933. A brief but detailed account of Miller's theories of the establishment of congregationalism in Massachusetts Bay.

Miller, Perry. *Errand into the Wilderness.* Cambridge: Harvard University Press, 1956. Paperback edition in Harper Torchbooks. Sees the Civil War in England as a turning point for American Puritanism.

Battis, Emery. *Saints and Sectaries: Anne Hutchinson and the Antinomian Controversy in the Massachusetts Bay Colony.* Chapel Hill: University of North Carolina Press for the

Institute of Early American History and Culture, 1962. The author gives a detailed study of the Antinomian controversy with suggestions about the psychological, sociological, and physiological undercurrents of the event.

Bailyn, Bernard. *The New England Merchants in the Seventeenth Century.* Cambridge: Harvard University Press, 1955. This work is a study of the development of a mercantile community in the New England colonies and the effect which that development had on the decline of Puritan control.

Pettit, Norman. *The Heart Prepared: Grace and Conversion in Puritan Spiritual Life.* New Haven: Yale University Press, 1966. An excellent study which revises and enlarges our understanding of the process by which the Puritans prepared for and achieved conversion.

Simpson, Alan. *Puritanism in Old and New England.* Chicago: The University of Chicago Press, 1955. A lucid account of the impact of Puritanism in both England and America which provides some provocative suggestions about the relationship between them.

SETTLEMENT OF CONNECTICUT

Type of event: Sociopolitical: settlement of a new colony by migrants from another colony
Time: 1635-1662
Locale: Connecticut River Valley and coast of Long Island Sound

Principal personages:

EDWARD WINSLOW (1595-1655), Plymouth colonist who explored the Connecticut River Valley in 1632

ROBERT RICH, SECOND EARL OF WARWICK (1587-1658), President of the Council for New England, who solicited a patent for Connecticut from the council in 1632

JOHN WINTHROP, JR. (1638-1707), Founder of the settlements at Saybrook and New London, and Governor of Connecticut

THOMAS HOOKER (1586?-1647), Massachusetts Bay divine who headed the Hartford settlement and who was instrumental in framing the "Fundamental Orders"

ROGER LUDLOW (1590-1664?), Leader of Massachusetts Bay colonists who settled at Windsor in 1635, and co-founder of Stratford and Fairfield

JOHN DAVENPORT (1597-1670), Founder and co-leader of the New Haven colony

WOUTER VAN TWILLER (c.1580-c.1656), Governor-General of New Netherland who protested on behalf of the Dutch government the English settlement of Connecticut

THEOPHILUS EATON (1590-1658), English merchant and co-founder along with John Davenport of the New Haven colony

Summary of Event

As more and more immigrants arrived in the Massachusetts coastal towns, land prices rose dramatically. News of the Connecticut River Valley with its fertile bottom land and easy access to the sea attracted English settlers in large numbers. The lure of the West, so prominent in American history, was already making its appeal to the adventurous spirit of the New Englanders. Edward Winslow of New Plymouth had explored the region in 1632 choosing as a site for a trading post the present-day location of Windsor. The trading post, originally established for the purpose of tapping the valuable fur trade, symbolized the intention of English settlers to possess the entire Connecticut River Valley. The Dutch, however, also claimed the region as part of the West India Company's holdings in New Netherland. These rival claims, intensified by the increasing influx of land-hungry New Englanders, signaled a race for empire.

In 1635, a group of settlers from Massachusetts Bay colony ignored New Plymouth's claim to the region and settled around Windsor. Van Twiller, the Dutch Governor of New Netherland, protested this intrusion asserting that the question of the ownership of the disputed territory was a matter to be settled by the Dutch and British home authorities. The Dutch protest went unheeded. New Plymouth sold their claims to the Bay colony settlers and the process of settlement went on. In the fall of 1635 Hartford became the seat of fifty farmer residents of New Towne (Cambridge). English claims were now effectively supported by occupation. The Dutch authorities could only watch with growing concern the piecemeal erosion of their territorial rights.

Robert Rich, the Earl of Warwick and President of the Council for New England, had meanwhile obtained a patent for the region and had issued the deed to a group of Puritan gentlemen. On July 7, 1635, this group authorized John Winthrop, Jr. to erect a fort and dwellings at the mouth of the Connecticut river. The strategic importance of such a settlement was well recognized by the English lords. By establishing a fort at the mouth of the river, the English settlers could take advantage of both the river and coastal trade, cut off the Dutch contact with the interior, and guard Long Island Sound. When Winthrop declared that settlement must be by consent of the grantees, the Reverend Thomas Hooker and his flock at New Towne were preparing to move in. Hooker and his congregation agreed to Winthrop's terms and accepted him as the Governor of the territory. Winthrop, having no authority to permit the setting up of colonial government, agreed to a plan whereby the Massachusetts General Court served as a broker in giving the agreement legal validity. On March 3, 1636, the General Court issued a plan for government. The commission envisioned by

the court was to have governmental authority for one year. Although this governmental body was temporary, it provided for a remarkable degree of popular participation, indicative perhaps of a native American proclivity for democratic institutions.

Hooker's band of thirty-five men and their families were only partially motivated by land hunger. Dissatisfaction with the church at Massachusetts Bay and the patrician oligarchy of Bay colony divines inspired these pilgrims to seek a "christian refuge in the wilderness." Hooker's politics were quite advanced and the democratic principle, long submerged in the Bay colony, expressed itself in a popular belief that authority should reside in the hands of as many as were competent to exercise it. All Christian freeholders were allowed a voice in the government, although, once elected, leaders had an unbounded right to govern as they wished.

At the General Court called at Hartford in 1637, committees representing the three towns of Hartford, Windsor, and Wethersfield elected their magistrates and made preparations for war with the Pequot Indians. In a three-week campaign the Pequots were nearly destroyed, resulting in relative peace for forty years.

Soon after the Pequot War the second colony within the present limits of Connecticut was established. English Puritans under John Davenport, a minister, and Theophilus Eaton, a wealthy merchant, founded a "plantation" at New Haven. These emigrants had come to America to establish a new Puritan Canaan which they hoped would provide spiritual leadership and economic success. By the spring of

1638 the town limits had been set out and the infant colony was on a sound footing.

The New Haven colony adopted a republican government similar to its neighbors, and the inhabitants looked to Davenport and Eaton for leadership. Eaton, always more practical than spiritual, was the right man for the job. His sound leadership and astute financial policies enabled the colony to prosper. Eaton played a role in New Haven similar to that of John Winthrop in Massachusetts. Other settlements were soon established, and by 1644 these had attached themselves to New Haven to form the colony of New Haven.

Meanwhile, the other English settlements had adopted a number of laws, known as the "Fundamental Orders." The document, issued on January 14, 1639, included a preamble declaring a covenant among the inhabitants and enacted eleven laws which provided for a government consisting of a General Court, or legislature, meeting bi-annually, and a Governor. The franchise, following English practice, was restricted to qualified householders. Office-holding, however, was limited to "freemen" or those who could demonstrate to the General Court that they possessed substantial property. As a result, the ensuing years witnessed the growing prestige of the magistrates, and the "democratic principle," so fondly cherished in earlier times, was lost.

By the middle of the seventeenth century there were two autonomous governments in Connecticut. Expansion continued both eastward and westward along the coast and rivers. Winthrop organized the plantation of New London in 1646, and Stratford and Fairfield grew out of Roger Ludlow's plantation at Peguannack. The economy of the region was basically agricultural, with trade and industry having only secondary importance.

The governments in Connecticut, however, rested on no legal basis. Having never acquired a charter from the Commonwealth government in England, the Connecticut settlements and their governments lacked the legal status of Massachusetts Bay and Virginia. Late in 1661, Winthrop departed for England as agent for the Connecticut government, exclusive of New Haven. His mission was to seek confirmation of the old Warwick patent and then to obtain a royal patent from the newly restored Charles II. Influential backers in England helped persuade the Puritan-hating monarchy to grant the desired patent. The colony obtained a charter on May 10, 1662. This grant, based essentially upon the Fundamental Orders, was issued in utter disregard of the claims of New Netherland and New Haven. Connecticut became a corporate legal government with authority vested in the Governor and freemen.

The government of Connecticut, now resting on firm legal grounds, was determined to annex New Haven. Without a patent, New Haven could afford no agency in London. Hence, despite attempts to remain independent, New Haven formally submitted to annexation in 1664. Dutch claims were settled in the same year when an English fleet sailed up Long Island Sound and forced the surrender of the Dutch fort at New Amsterdam. By 1664 the entire Eastern Coast of North America was effectively under English dominion.

Settlement of Connecticut

Pertinent Literature

Andrews, Charles M. *The Colonial Period of American History.* Vol. II: *The Settlements.* Chs. 3-5. New Haven: Yale University Press, 1964.

Connecticut may be said to be the first of the colonies to typify the American frontier spirit—the desire to find new lands for expansion. Charles M. Andrews attributes the settlement of Connecticut not to the search for religious freedom but to the search for land. Unlike the sites of Jamestown and Plymouth, whose inhabitants had chosen hastily, the Connecticut River Valley had been highly recommended by the Indians and first explorers for its fertility. Despite many ventures into trade and industry in the early decades of settlement, life in seventeenth century Connecticut, Andrews states, was essentially agrarian.

Andrews' treatment of the settlement of Connecticut is extremely thorough. Each settlement and each leader are fitted into the complex total picture. In less certain hands the picture could easily have become confused because of the many localities and personalities which must be dealt with simultaneously. Several of Connecticut's leaders, most notably Winthrop, changed their habitations regularly, so that one has difficulty in associating a particular leader with a particular town. Without losing sight of these diverse activities, Andrews manages to focus upon the broader institutions and policies of the colony as a whole.

Theology never played a dominant role in Connecticut's early history, for its leaders adhered almost without exception to the Puritanism of Massachusetts Bay. Andrews contends, however, that Thomas Hooker, Roger Ludlow, and the other framers of the "Fundamental Orders" were dissatisfied with the authoritarianism of the Massachusetts magistrates and sought to place authority in the hands of as many as were competent to exercise it. In practice, the rights of the inhabitants were far removed from the twentieth century concept of democracy.

It is discussion of the Puritan concept of government compared with the modern idea of democracy that underlies Andrews' chapters on Connecticut. The Puritan government, Andrews emphasizes, sought to promote the welfare of the community rather than that of the individual. In the distribution of lands, the maintenance of the towns and resources, and the obligation to labor for the common benefit, one sees that the interest of the community came first. On the commonwealth level, the magistrates, once elected, retained control of affairs with little concern for the opinions of the inhabitants. The limiting of the franchise by the General Court is indicative of the government's willingness to subordinate individual rights to what it considered the need to exclude undesirable elements from influence in the community. In order to become even an "admitted inhabitant" a settler had to be a householder of "honest conversation," that is, deemed suitable by the authorities. Admission to the more prestigious status of freemanship required selection by the General Court. The court records of the period attest to the concern of the magistrates for the individual morality and behavior of the inhabitants, and to the harsh punishments meted out to those who fell short.

Yet the Connecticut leaders apparently carried with them out of the Massachusetts experience a suspicion of the all-powerful magistrate. Among the Fundamental Orders are safeguards for maintaining ultimate control in the hands of the freemen should the magistrates and governor fail to summon the General Court as prescribed.

Andrews' account of the Connecticut experience is extremely well-balanced. He acknowledges the colony's commitment to wider participation in government without confusing its progressive tendencies with democracy.

Black, Robert C., III. *The Younger John Winthrop.* New York: Columbia University Press, 1966.

In this well-written and frequently witty biography of the sometime Governor of Connecticut, Robert C. Black exhibits a tendency common to nearly all who are acquainted with his subject—to be utterly charmed by the man. Part of an age and environment which immediately evoke thoughts of sober-sided magistrates and tortuous theological controversies, Winthrop emerges unblemished by any of the Puritan stereotypes. Black succeeds admirably in investing Winthrop with human qualities and in depicting the spirit of the times in which he lived.

Chapters seven through seventeen are concerned with Winthrop's activities from the authorization by the Warwick grantees of the establishment of Saybrook in 1635 to the securing of Connecticut's charter in 1662. Yet this is by no means a simple story of life in a Connecticut settlement. Winthrop was too restless a man to remain with one project for long. Black characterizes him as one who enjoyed arranging enterprises, but who left the administration for someone else. "Bi-colonial," he remained an assistant (magistrate) in the Massachusetts government until his father's death in 1649, although he was living and holding office in Connecticut during much of the time.

Black suggests that Winthrop probably regarded politics "as less a matter of principle than of possibility." Supremely practical, he wasted no time on democratic ideas of equality when he established New London in 1646, preferring to run the government in the manner which he believed to be efficient. Although he reveled in political controversy, theological controversy did not interest him. Routinely orthodox, but more tolerant than many Puritans, he neglected to attend the Massachusetts General Court, of which he was a member during the Antinomian crisis concerning Anne Hutchinson.

Always ready to try a new business venture, Winthrop at various points in his career involved himself in the production of iron, salt, indigo, glass, and goats. Winthrop's interest in metals was more than a matter of business. The sciences, and particularly alchemy, fascinated him. Although his inability to remain interested in a single project for long precluded his engaging in serious scholarship, he owned perhaps the finest library in the colonies, enjoyed the friendship of numerous European scholars, and was the first North American to be elected to the Royal Society. In the absence of a physician, he often ministered to the medical needs of his neighbors.

Winthrop was so popular a political figure that New Haven and Connecticut vied with each other for his residence, each proffering him economic and political advantages. "Winthrop was never so naïve as to confuse public service with unintelligent self-sacrifice," writes Black. While he lived in New London, he enjoyed "one of the most generous assortments of rights and privileges ever seen in New England." Yet New Haven lured him away with her iron bogs, only to be outdone eventually by Connecticut's offer of the governorship. That Winthrop was an opportunist cannot be denied, but that he possessed a certain

irresistible charm is also certain. It is too easy to place Winthrop in the mold of the slick modern politician, long on affability but short on principle. Black has not done so, but neither has he explained why Winthrop was Connecticut's most sought-after political figure. We do know that through his diplomatic talents he obtained royal approval for Connecticut's charter. Perhaps it is too much to expect to know completely what made the man attractive to his contemporaries. In trying to find out, Black has nonetheless written a thoroughly readable and revealing study of early Connecticut politics. — *W. W. B.*

Additional Recommended Reading

Adams, James Truslow. *The Founding of New England.* Magnolia, Massachusetts: Peter Smith Publishers, Inc., 1921. Paperback edition by Little, Brown, and Company. Displaying his dislike for the Massachusetts Bay Puritans, Adams contends that the Connecticut settlers opened up the frontier to establish a more democratic way of life.

Archibald, Warren S. *Thomas Hooker.* New Haven: Yale University Press for the Tercentenary Commission of the State of Connecticut, 1933. This laudatory pamphlet traces Hooker's early years and his leadership, particularly as a preacher, in Connecticut.

Deming, Dorothy. *The Settlement of the Connecticut Towns.* New Haven: Yale University Press for the Tercentenary Commission of the State of Connecticut, 1933. Both the Connecticut and New Haven colony settlements are covered concisely in this booklet which extends the history beyond the seventeenth century.

Deming, Dorothy. *The Fundamental Orders of Connecticut.* New Haven: Yale University Press for the Tercentenary Commission of the State of Connecticut, 1934. A brief introduction by George M. Dutcher precedes the text of the Fundamental Orders with seventeenth century spelling and symbols intact.

Jones, Mary J. *Congregational Commonwealth: Connecticut, 1636-1662.* Middletown, Connecticut: Wesleyan University Press, 1968. A full-length work on Connecticut's early years which focuses on the Fundamental Orders as an expression of Puritan life and government rather than attempting to provide a much needed general study of the period.

FOUNDING OF RHODE ISLAND

Type of event: Politico-religious: establishment of Rhode Island by dissatisfied members of Massachusetts Bay colony
Time: 1636-1663
Locale: Narragansett Bay region of Rhode Island

Principal personages:

ROGER WILLIAMS (1603?-1683), founder of Providence in 1636, who remained Rhode Island's most important leader

WILLIAM CODDINGTON (1601-1678), founder of the Aquidneck Island settlements of Portsmouth and Newport

SAMUEL GORTON (1592?-1677), controversial supporter of Anne Hutchinson, who established Warwick

DR. JOHN CLARKE (1609-1676), physician and minister who helped to found Rhode Island and who as Rhode Island's agent in England secured confirmation of its charter in 1663

ANNE HUTCHINSON (1591-1643), who was banished from Massachusetts Bay colony for advocating Antinomianism, and who helped to found Portsmouth

Summary of Event

The founding of Rhode Island was more complicated than the founding of most of the other American colonies because it involved five separate settlements and unusual leaders bent on expressing their individualistic beliefs. The earliest settlers in Rhode Island represented those who were forced out of Massachusetts Bay colony for their "dangerous" opinions or who left of their own accord because they were dissatisfied with certain aspects of the Puritan oligarchy.

The first of these, with the exception of the recluse William Blakston, was Roger Williams, who was ordered to leave the Bay colony on October 9, 1635. Escaping deportation to England, he set out for the Narragansett region in January, 1636, and took refuge among the Indians for several months. Soon after purchasing land near the Seekonk river from Mas-

sasoit, he was joined by five other men. The warning from the Governor of Plymouth that they were trespassing forced them to establish a new settlement, which they called Providence, on the Great Salt river. It is not known whether Williams had an actual plantation in mind or whether he simply envisioned a trading post or Indian mission. But other outcasts were soon welcomed, and each settler was given a home lot and a farm from the land which Williams had purchased from the Indians. Providence was strictly an agricultural community. Though the colony was built without capital or outside assistance, its population and economy grew slowly. The heads of families participated in a "town meeting" type of government, and signed a compact agreeing to obey the laws passed by the will of all. The compact contained the phrase "only in civil

97

things," signifying a commitment to the separation of the Church and the state.

In April, 1638, another band of exiles led by William Coddington left Boston in search of religious freedom. They were preceded in March by Anne Hutchinson and her family. Arriving at Providence, they all arranged to purchase the island of Aquidneck from the Indians and by the following spring they had laid out the new settlement of Pocasset (Portsmouth). By seventeenth century standards the settlement had a democratic form of government with Coddington serving as judge.

Two such dominant personalities as Coddington and Anne Hutchinson could not exist in harmony for long. When their two factions split over Hutchinson's eccentric supporter, Samuel Gorton, Coddington was ousted and with his followers began the new plantation of Newport. In March, 1640, he succeeded in uniting the two settlements on Aquidneck so that they could manage their own affairs apart from Providence. The union, the most orderly civil organization in the Narragansett region, was to endure for seven years. By twentieth century standards the democracy which they proclaimed in 1641 was limited because it excluded half the adult males from participating in government. Probably because Coddington was unsuccessful in obtaining a patent for Aquidneck, the people of Portsmouth became disillusioned and broke away from Newport in 1648.

Meanwhile, the controversial Gorton, driven from both Portsmouth and Providence for defying the authority of the government, purchased Indian lands to establish Warwick. After enduring harassment and imprisonment

by Massachusetts officials, he obtained an order compelling Massachusetts to cease molesting him and lived in peace as an honored citizen of Warwick.

Of all the Rhode Island leaders, Williams emerged as the dominant figure. His efforts to maintain peace among the Indians were of inestimable service to the whole of New England. Yet the ambitions of other political leaders in the British settlements both in and around Rhode Island were to remain his chief problem. Convinced that the settlements of Rhode Island had to coöperate in order to remain intact, he worked selflessly for a federation of the four main towns. When the formation of the New England Confederation in 1643 threatened Rhode Island's integrity, Williams sailed for England to obtain a charter from the Long Parliament. The patent which he brought back in September, 1644, authorized the union of Providence, Portsmouth, and Newport as "The Incorporation of Providence Plantations." Warwick was included later.

The uncertainty of the Civil War in England delayed putting the newly authorized government into effect, but in May, 1647, an assembly of freemen met at Portsmouth to organize the government and draft laws. A federal system whereby the towns maintained their individual rights as parts of the larger community, was created. Their code of laws was one of the earliest made by a body of men in America and the first to embody in all its parts the precedents set by the laws and statutes of England. By 1650 a representative assembly composed of six delegates from each town was operating. The assembly at first also served as a judicial body until a separate court for trials was established in 1655. Town courts preserved the local peace.

Coddington continued to deal underhandedly in an attempt to separate Aquidneck from the union. In 1651 he succeeded in obtaining a lifetime appointment as Governor of Aquidneck and Conanicut Islands from the Council of State. The residents of the islands supported Williams' successful mission to England which resulted in the annulment of Coddington's patent in 1652. Distrust of central government and antagonism between the mainland and islands persisted until 1654, when Williams, with the support of Oliver Cromwell, restored the atmosphere of coöperation.

The Restoration in England imperilled the validity of Rhode Island's charter of 1644. Dr. John Clarke, its agent in London, petitioned the crown for confirmation. Confirmation of Connecticut's grant to include half of Rhode Island's territory necessitated submitting the matter to arbitration. The decision was in favor of Rhode Island and the new charter of 1663 also confirmed the colony's policy of complete liberty of conscience, the only charter to do so.

Pertinent Literature

Andrews, Charles M. *The Colonial Period of American History.* Vol. II: *The Settlements.* Ch. 1 and 2. New Haven: Yale University Press, 1964.

Most historians of early Rhode Island have chosen to concentrate on a particular settlement or leader, usually Roger Williams or Anne Hutchinson. This is understandable in the light of the mélange of territorial, political, and religious eccentricities peculiar to this colony. For this reason, Charles M. Andrews' detailed account is all the more remarkable. Andrews himself points out that Rhode Island can hardly be considered a colony in the early period. Lacking a patent and backers in England, it started with no more than Indian deeds and social compacts. It was actually five petty states "in embryo," each having its own political and religious atmosphere. Despite the complexity of the situation, Andrews succeeds in tracing in detail the development of the settlements, their unification, and the operation of the government after union was achieved. He also delineates the religious and political ideas which brought the settlements into being and made coöperation so difficult.

Because Andrews' account of Rhode Island's beginnings occupies only two chapters in a monumental four-volume work, it cannot really be said to propound a thesis. Yet Andrews' admiration for the establishment of freedom of conscience and democratic government permeates his writing. Choosing to deëmphasize the qualities which must have made Williams and Gorton difficult men with whom to deal—assurance of the rightness of their own opinions and a penchant for controversy—Andrews presents their efforts to find free expression for their beliefs and to live in peace in a sympathetic light.

The Williams whom he portrays bears no resemblance to the smug preacher who denounced the churches of Massachusetts Bay for not separating from the Church of England. According to Andrews, Williams espoused absolute liberty of conscience and respected religions with which he disagreed. Williams viewed the Church as but "one of the civil corporations that the state was bound to protect" and declared that the Church should regulate its own affairs without interference from the civil authorities. Well aware of the disorder which unbridled freedom had wrought in the early years of settlement, he came to advocate the need for responsibility with freedom.

Although Williams naturally remains the dominant figure of Andrews' narrative, Gorton emerges as a fascinating figure worthy of further study.

A pariah to the Massachusetts authorities and most of the Rhode Island leaders, he possessed a strong instinct for justice and the sanctity of English common law. Only the treacherous Coddington fails to elicit a sympathetic biography. Although his wealth and education made Newport the most prosperous of the settlements, his thirst for power nearly destroyed the colony.

It would be difficult to conceive of a better summary of Rhode Island's early years than the one in this work. Without confusing the reader, Andrews manages to weave together many diverse elements of the story and to create a feeling for the drama of the events.

Winslow, Ola E. *Master Roger Williams.* New York: The Macmillan Company, 1957.

In the prologue to her biography of Williams, Ola Elizabeth Winslow admits to making only a beginning in the process of understanding an extremely complex and controversial man. Cutting through the romantic myths which have often over-simplified Williams' ideas or have mistakenly placed them in a twentieth century context, Winslow acknowledges her subject's contributions without losing sight of his shortcomings.

That Winslow possesses an uncommon knowledge of seventeenth century life and thought is evident from the first chapter. Although only the barest details of Williams' youth and education are known, the author succeeds in reconstructing the milieu in which he matured and in which his ideas were shaped.

Separatist sympathies apparently prompted him to set out for Massachusetts Bay in 1630. But Governor Winthrop had no sooner welcomed

him than he affronted the magistrates by refusing the post of teacher in the First Church of Boston. Not only did he protest that the church was not completely separated from the Church of England, but he also denied the magistrates' authority in matters of conscience. His strange opinions were to arouse further discontent when he moved on to the pulpits of Salem and Plymouth. Because the New World actually belonged to the Indians, he declared, the King's patent for Massachusetts Bay was invalid. He could not have chosen a worse time to attack the patent, for the King was threatening to withdraw it and impose royal government. Williams' opinions were not only devoid of courtesy and common sense, but they were also dangerous to the colony. Finally, when he claimed that the magistrates had no right to administer oaths to unregenerate men, the General Court had no choice but to banish Williams from the colony. In

100

the light of seventeenth century practice, their decision was logical, and, contrary to romantic myth, he was given six weeks to depart. Many historians have read their history backwards at this point and have seen in Williams' protests the beginnings of religious freedom and the idea of separation of church and state. While Winslow acknowledges a foreshadowing of Williams' later convictions, she contends that his ideas were far from mature and that he had in no way come to respect the convictions of others.

The early Providence settlement which Williams founded with a handful of companions was by no means an immediate democracy. Williams apparently regarded himself as a proprietor and considered banning settlers of whom he did not approve. But he soon changed his mind, and Providence offered religious freedom from the start.

Because Williams was a puzzling and inconsistent person, Winslow speculates upon the reasons for his liberalization. Perhaps because the wilderness allowed him to speak freely and to be listened to, he learned to listen to others and to speak more cautiously. The reader finds the impetuous, hot-headed preacher of the Boston days evolving into the steady conciliator of Indian disputes and the selfless state-builder. As a mature leader, Williams came to understand the need for responsibility combined with freedom of conscience. During the unsettled years of factional disputes and rival claims which tormented Rhode Island, he labored selflessly for unity.

Yet Williams' appetite for controversy was never satiated. He remained the intrepid polemicist, carrying on a prolonged argument in print with John Cotton over the matter of his banishment, and advocating complete religious toleration. On his journeys to England to obtain support for the Rhode Island Charter, he became intimate with powerful Puritan politicians and entered into the religious controversy.

Master Roger Williams is first and foremost the story of a man and his ideas, not an account of the founding of Rhode Island. For a detailed narrative of the years of turmoil which preceded the confirmation of the charter in 1663, one should turn to a study such as that in the second volume of Charles M. Andrews' *The Colonial Period of American History.* Yet Winslow has gone a long way toward the goal of unraveling the complex mind of a man whom historians will probably never fully understand. — *W.M.B.*

Additional Recommended Reading

Andrews, Charles M. *Our Earliest Colonial Settlements: Their Diversities of Origin and Later Characteristics.* Ch. 4. New York: New York University Press, 1933. Like Andrews' Rhode Island study in *The Colonial Period of American History,* part of this volume details the political turmoil of the early years and the lives of the colony's principal leaders.

Brockunier, Samuel H. *The Irrepressible Democrat: Roger Williams.* New York: The Ronald Press Company, 1940. Views Roger Williams as the first great American democrat, a fighter against the tyranny of the Puritan oligarchy.

Miller, Perry. *Roger Williams: His Contribution to the American Tradition.* New York:

Atheneum Publishers, 1962. Liberally interspersed with selections from Williams' writings, Miller's study contends that Williams was concerned basically with theology, not democratic political reforms.

Morgan, Edmund S. *Roger Williams: The Church and the State.* New York: Harcourt Brace & World, Inc., 1967. Concentrating upon the thought of Roger Williams as presented in his writings, Morgan seeks "to expose the symmetry of the ideas that lay behind the polemics."

Greene, Theodore P. ed. *Roger Williams and the Massachusetts Magistrates.* Boston: D. C. Heath & Co., 1964. Part of the *Problems in American Civilization* series, this collection of readings presents disparate views from the seventeenth century to the present on the question of Williams' banishment.

Rugg, Winnifred K. *Unafraid: A Life of Anne Hutchinson.* Boston: Houghton Mifflin Co., 1930. The Rhode Island experience is treated only in the final chapters of this book, which focuses on the Antinomian controversy in the Massachusetts Bay colony.

ESTABLISHMENT OF HARVARD COLLEGE AND ENACTMENT OF THE MASSACHUSETTS SCHOOL LAW

Type of event: Cultural: beginnings of higher education and public education in America
Time: 1636-1647
Locale: Massachusetts Bay colony

> *Principal personages:*
> JOHN WINTHROP (1588-1649), Governor of Massachusetts Bay colony after 1637, and charter member of the Board of Overseers
> THOMAS DUDLEY (1576-1653), Deputy Governor of Massachusetts Bay colony, and member of the Board of Overseers 1637-1653
> RICHARD BELLINGHAM (1592?-1672), Treasurer of Massachusetts Bay colony, and member of the Board of Overseers 1637-1672
> SIR HENRY VANE (1613-1662), Governor of Massachusetts Bay colony in 1636
> NATHANIEL EATON (1609?-1674), the first professor to be appointed by the Board of Overseers but who was dismissed for cruelty and mismanagement in 1639
> JOHN HARVARD (1607-1638), the first benefactor of Harvard College
> HENRY DUNSTER (1609?-1659), the first president of Harvard College

Summary of Event

In *New England's First Fruits,* the famous tract extolling the virtues of New England to possible supporters in the old country, the Puritans proclaimed that one of their first concerns had been ". . . to advance *Learning* and perpetuate it to Posterity; dreading to leave an illiterate Ministry to the Churches, when our present Ministers shall be in the Dust." Because the Puritan church tenets emphasized interpretation and discussion of the Scriptures rather than mere ritual or emotion, it required a learned clergy. Therefore on October 28, 1636, the Massachusetts General Court passed a legislative act to found "a schoale or colledge" and voted four hundred pounds sterling for its support. The Antinomian crisis centering around Anne Hutchinson delayed action on the matter until November 15, 1637, when the Massachusetts General Court passed an order that the college be built at Newtown, soon to be renamed Cambridge. A few days later, the building of the college was committed to six magistrates and six church elders, the first Board of Overseers.

By June, 1638, Nathaniel Eaton, the professor engaged by the overseers, had moved into the house acquired for him in the midst of a cow pasture, and the Massachusetts General Court had

103

granted three lots to him for the college. Within a few months, the first classes were being taught, the building was being constructed, and a library was being assembled.

Thus the college was already operating when, on September 14, 1638, a young clergyman named John Harvard died and left his library and half of his estate, amounting to about eight hundred pounds sterling, to the new institution. Although John Harvard was certainly not responsible for the founding of the college, nor did his legacy make its establishment possible, his gift was a remarkable one for the times, and the Massachusetts General Court voted on March 13, 1639, to name the college after him.

Unfortunately, Professor Eaton's most praiseworthy accomplishment was the planting and fencing of the yard to keep the cows out and the students in. His tyrannical tenure was marred by beatings and dismal living conditions for the students who boarded at his home. Mistress Eaton's "loathsome catering," featuring such items as "goat's dung in their hasty pudding," provided an inauspicious beginning for that much-maligned institution, the college dining hall. When Eaton's cruelty finally came to the attention of the Massachusetts General Court, he was fined and dismissed, and the college closed its doors.

In 1645, Henry Dunster, a graduate of Magdalene College, Cambridge, accepted the presidency of Harvard College and soon infused life into it, providing a firm foundation for its growth. The Class of 1642 returned, a new freshman class entered, and a three-year course in the arts was established. A thorough knowledge of Greek and

Latin was required for admission. Dunster personally instructed the three classes in the arts, philosophies, and Oriental languages, and he also moderated the students' disputations. Although the Puritans believed that knowledge without Christ was vain, Harvard College was less ecclesiastical than the universities at Oxford or Cambridge, for it strove to provide a course in philosophy and the liberal arts which would be suitable either for a general education or as a basis for entering one of the professions.

Determined to establish in America the collegiate system as it was practiced in England, under which the students lived, studied, ate, and disputed together with their tutors, Dunster and the Overseers were anxious to complete the first building despite the economic depression. Donations made possible the occupation of the "Old College" in September, 1642, in time for the commencement of the first nine graduates. Within this building the students attended classes, studied, ate, and slept.

During its early years, Harvard College had serious financial problems. Lacking any sort of endowment or income-producing lands, it struggled along on tuition fees, and the ferry rents and town levies which it was granted. A fund-raising mission to England met with moderate success, and in 1644 representatives at the meeting of the United Colonies of New England agreed that all the Puritan colonies should share in supporting the college. Each family was obligated to give a peck of wheat or one shilling annually. Unquestionably, the establishment and support of a college was an ambitious undertaking for such a new, economically insecure community. Only the strong religious faith of the Puritans in the purpose of their endeavor carried it through.

Contrary to the claims of various educational historians, the Puritans took a greater interest in intellectual pursuits than other Englishmen of their day. Their concentrated system of settlement in towns rendered the accomplishment of popular education easier than in Virginia, where the population was dispersed. Even before the law required it, a number of towns established schools: Boston hired a master in 1635, and Charlestown, in 1636. The first New England school legislation, the Massachusetts Act of 1642, required the heads of families to teach their children and servants "to read and understand the principles of religion and the capital laws of the country" and to see that they were employed in useful occupations. Thus the Puritans envisioned education as serving social and economic needs: it provided training for citizenship and service in the community.

But the laissez-faire system apparently proved to be unsatisfactory, for in 1647 the Massachusetts General Court passed a law requiring every town of fifty families to appoint a schoolmaster "to teach all such children as shall resort to him to write and read." His wages were to be paid by the parents or the town, as the town should choose. Towns of one hundred families were to establish grammar schools to instruct youth "so far as they may be fitted for the Universitie." The cost of supporting the schools was a hardship on some of the smaller communities, and the uneducated complained of the ruling class trying to force its high standards upon the poor. Thus interest in public education did not work its way up from the bottom but down from the top. Only because the Puritan leaders possessed such high standards and determination was it possible for them to lay the foundations for public education in a hostile environment.

Pertinent Literature

Morison, Samuel Eliot. *The Founding of Harvard College.* Cambridge: Harvard University Press, 1935.

In his preface to this work, Samuel Eliot Morison jokes about his failure to heed the warning of an eighteenth century historian who began his "Chronological History of New-England" with the Creation and died before he reached the year 1631. Although Morison begins his history of Harvard in the Middle Ages, happily he has lived well beyond the completion of the monumental, definitive four-volume work. The first ten chapters of this first volume are concerned with the origin, history, and description of some of the great Western European universities, particularly Oxford and Cambridge, and with the colleges of Harvard's founders. They are followed by an account of the founding of Harvard College itself.

This story is related in great detail. Morison has assembled a vast amount of information, and he quotes liberally from a staggering array of sources. Not satisfied with limiting his attention to the institutional and curricular organization of the university, he delves deeply into such matters as the selection of the site, the backgrounds of the founders, the books in the library, and the architecture of the original building. The daily lives of the students, down to their diet and sleeping arrangements, as well as the rules of behavior which governed them, are the objects of careful scrutiny.

Because the beliefs and practices of the Puritan church are inextricably bound up with the reasons for the founding of Harvard College, Morison's overriding concern is the explanation of the purposes of the founders. Since the Puritans' emphasis on scriptural study and exegesis presupposed a learned clergy, the founders' immediate objective was the education of ministers. For this reason the suppression of Anne Hutchinson and the Antinomians was necessary to the establishment of the college, Morison contends, since Antinomianism was basically anti-intellectual, relying on divine revelation.

While the founders had as their long-range purpose the perpetuation of learning, it was only natural that religion should be deeply impregnated in the Harvard curriculum as it was in the Puritan way of life. The word *"Veritas"* on the Harvard coat of arms refers to divine truth, Morison explains, for the goal of each student was to be "to know God and Jesus Christ. . . ." But the curriculum was designed not only for students who planned to enter the ministry. The founders intended the course in philosophy and arts as either a general education or as preparation for the professions of divinity, law, or medicine.

The story of Harvard's quest for revenue demonstrates how great was the determination of the founders to maintain their ambitious undertaking. Morison reports in detail the sources and disposition of all known income received by the college from the original gift of four hundred pounds sterling by the General Court and John Harvard's legacy, to the six thousand pecks of wheat collected from all the families of the United Colonies of New England. He discusses at some length tuition, scholarships, and faculty salaries.

That Morison manages to present such a profusion of facts on a relatively narrow historical subject and still write an extremely witty and enjoyable book is no mean feat. Perhaps because he has been intimately associated with Harvard for so many years, he can write of its successes and failures in very familiar terms and in so doing strip it of the image of the sacred cow.

Morison, Samuel Eliot. *The Intellectual Life of Colonial New England.* New York: New York University Press, 1956.

Historians of education have tended to debunk Puritan efforts in the establishment of public education in America as attempts to enforce conformity to their religious beliefs. Samuel Eliot Morison here champions the Puritans, insisting that they did not prevent, but actually stimulated, intellectual pursuits and took a greater interest in education than other Englishmen of their time.

Morison's purpose in this volume is to describe the institutions and facilities that fostered intellectual life and what native-born or American-educated New Englanders made of these opportunities. Seeking to explain why New England alone among the

English colonies succeeded so quickly in encouraging intellectual life, Morison argues that only a rigidly controlled society possessed with great emotional drive could have accomplished this end amid the need for so much physical work. Paradoxically, the humanistic tradition fared better among the Puritans than elsewhere, nurtured by leaders who had been educated in the classics at Oxford and Cambridge.

Because the founding of Harvard in Morison's opinion is the best indication of the Puritans' high intellectual ambitions, he provides a detailed summary of the material found in his definitive work on the college's early years. He describes the first awkward attempts at administering and financing the fledgling institution, as well as the curriculum and living accommodations for the students. Yet Morison admits that New England could claim only about six hundred college students in the entire seventeenth century, since few boys could master the Latin required for entrance or could afford the cost of an advanced education.

Accurate information on colonial elementary and grammar schools is difficult to find, Morison explains, and so it is not surprising that much inaccurate history has been written about them. Early historians tended to be too lavish in their praise of colonial education. The contention of Professor Edgar W. Knight that the Massachusetts School Act of 1647 "seems rather to have been an effort to restrict the influence of Catholics and adherents to the English Church and to impose the Puritan creed upon the first generation of native-born New Englanders" typifies more recent judgments. Although

the preamble to the act begins, "It being one chief project of that old deluder, Satan, to keep men from knowledge of the scriptures, . . ." the motive behind the law was by no means solely religious. The preamble merely added religious sanction to an obligation which many members of the community were loathe to assume. Morison argues that we should take the Puritans' stated motives—to promote education as training for citizenship and service in the community—at face value rather than view them as mere propaganda. By insisting that their teachers be laymen and by placing their schools under the control of the community and the commonwealth, the Puritans actually moved forward in the process of the secularization of education.

The New England schools were not democratic, for the Puritan colonies had never considered democracy as a proper form for governing themselves. There was no provision for educating girls, and boys who could not master Latin were not allowed to continue their schooling. But in comparison with Virginia's the system was democratic. Only children who could afford it were asked to pay tuition, and even a poor boy had an opportunity to work his way through college. Yet sentiment for public education did not come up from among the poor country people; it "percolated from the top down," being forced upon the community by its ambitious leaders.

In his chapters on the elementary and grammar schools, Morison explains the methods of setting up and financing the schools and describes the curricula and books employed. This book's importance, however, lies in

107

Morison's thesis that the motives of the Puritan leaders to produce a learned clergy and a lettered people were the roots of public education and of the maintenance of the tradition of learning in America. — *W.M.B.*

Additional Recommended Reading

Adams, James Truslow. *The Founding of New England.* Boston: Atlantic Monthly Press, 1921. Disagreeing with Morison, Adams contends that the early intellectual life of New England was narrowly theological and that education was promoted only for religious ends.

Best, John H. and Robert T. Sidwell, eds. *The American Legacy of Learning: Readings in the History of Education.* Philadelphia: J. B. Lippincott Co., 1969. Included among the readings here are *New England's First Fruits,* the Harvard Regulations, and selections from the *New England Primer.*

Bailyn, Bernard. *Education in the Forming of American Society: Needs and Opportunities for Study.* Chapel Hill: University of North Carolina Press, 1960. Stresses the need for looking at elements bearing on education throughout society and allowing for changes in response to particular conditions.

Knight, Edgar W. *Education in the United States.* 2nd ed., revised. Boston: Ginn and Co., 1941. This anti-Puritan study by a professor of education argues that early New England education was neither public nor secular.

Morison, Samuel Eliot. "Harvard's Past" in *By Land and By Sea.* New York: Alfred A. Knopf, Inc., 1953. In this brief article, Morison speaks of John Harvard and the founding of Harvard College, and reasserts the importance of the institution's role in carrying the Western tradition of learning into American life.

Morison, Samuel Eliot. *Three Centuries of Harvard, 1636-1936.* Cambridge: Harvard University Press, 1963. The first few chapters of this book are a digest of the material found in the author's comprehensive *Founding of Harvard College.*

CONFEDERATION OF THE UNITED COLONIES OF NEW ENGLAND

Type of event: Political: organization for intercolonial coöperation
Time: 1643
Locale: Massachusetts Bay, Plymouth, Connecticut, and New Haven colonies

Principal personages:

JOHN WINTHROP (1588-1649), Governor of Massachusetts Bay colony and commissioner of the United Colonies of New England

THOMAS DUDLEY (1576-1653), Deputy Governor of Massachusetts Bay colony and commissioner of the United Colonies of New England

EDWARD WINSLOW (1595-1655), commissioner from Plymouth of the United Colonies of New England

WILLIAM COLLIER (c.1612-1670), commissioner from Plymouth of the United Colonies of New England

JOHN HAYNES (1594-1654), Governor of Connecticut and commissioner of the United Colonies of New England

EDWARD HOPKINS (1600-1657), Governor and Deputy Governor of Connecticut and commissioner of the United Colonies of New England

GEORGE FENWICK (1603-1657), commissioner from Connecticut of the United Colonies of New England

THEOPHILUS EATON (1590-1658), Governor of the New Haven colony and commissioner of the United Colonies of New England

THOMAS GREGSON (?-1646), commissioner from New Haven of the United Colonies of New England

THOMAS HOOKER (1586?-1647), Puritan divine and a leader in Connecticut

Summary of Event

As New England settlements expanded north, south, and west during the 1630's, territorial conflicts became inevitable. Not only did the Puritan colonies attempt to encroach upon one another's territory, but they also came into hostile contact with the Indians, the Dutch, and the French. Although the British had nearly destroyed the Indians in the brief Pequot War of 1637, the lack of coördinated effort had convinced them that some form of intercolonial coöperation was necessary for determining military policies and participation, as well as for arbitrating territorial disputes and regulating trade. Religious and political turmoil in Great Britain prevented the Mother Country from supervising colonial affairs directly, and the colonies preferred it that way. Yet in the absence of formal control from above, the Puri-

109

tan colonies saw the need for defending their expanded boundaries against foreign aggression.

The joint action in the Pequot War had apparently fostered a feeling of unity among the Puritan colonies. Furthermore, if the smaller, weaker colonies of Plymouth, Connecticut, and New Haven could enter into an agreement with the Massachusetts Bay colony as political equals, they should then be free from that powerful colony's attempts to encroach upon their territory. The Massachusetts Bay colony, in turn, would profit from a union by gaining legal approval from the other members in its efforts to annex territory in Maine.

In the late summer of 1637, a synod of New England church leaders meeting in Cambridge seriously broached the subject of union for the first time, but disagreements marred that and several other attempts to achieve union during the next few years. Fear of an Indian uprising in 1642, however, spurred Plymouth to send representatives to negotiate with the Massachusetts Bay colony about their mutual defense. About the same time, Connecticut also sent a proposal for mutual defense efforts to Massachusetts. The Massachusetts General Court, therefore, ordered the magistrates to meet with deputies of Connecticut, Plymouth, and New Haven on the matters of unification and defense.

Meeting in Boston on May 29, 1643, the representatives "readily yielded each to the other, in such things as tended to the common good," and drew up Articles of Confederation. When the last of the four General Courts ratified them on September 8, 1643, the articles became binding. The United Colonies of New England, thereby established, encompassed all the settlements along the coast and rivers from Long Island to New Hampshire. Rhode Island, which the Puritans disdainfully considered anarchical, and Maine were not included.

As stated in the preamble to the articles, the purposes of the confederation were: (1) to preserve the purity of the Puritans' religion and to worship free of interference; (2) to promote cöoperation; and (3) to provide for defense. The articles themselves specified the duties and powers of the confederation's commissioners, the structure of the confederation, and the rules of procedure. Because there was no judicial authority over all the members, each colony could interpret the articles to its own liking—a situation which was to cause problems later.

The governing body of the confederation was to consist of two commissioners chosen annually from each colony. The only qualifications demanded were that they be church members and that they bring "full power" from their general courts. Meeting in each colony successively, the commissioners were to convene each September. Anyone who had advice to offer was welcome to speak before them. Three magistrates from any colony could call a special meeting if necessary. Approval of a matter required the votes of six commissioners, although only four could declare war in a state of emergency. Thus the Massachusetts Bay colony could not veto the wishes of the other three colonies.

How much actual power did the commissioners possess? The answer to this question is essential to understanding the accomplishments and defects of the confederation. It must be remembered that the United Colonies of New England did not consider themselves a nation, but rather individual governments allied by a treaty. Each commissioner actually served as one of his colony's ambassadors. In matters of military preparation, declaration of war, and arbitration, the four colonies did surrender to the commissioners their individual power to act. Yet, while the confederation in theory possessed vague executive and judicial powers, in actuality it had only advisory powers in most areas.

The articles specified that each colony's military obligation should be in proportion to its means and population. Each must send aid if one of the other three colonies should be invaded and must participate in all "just" wars. The commissioners were empowered to decide if the confederation should wage an offensive war, and no colony could do so without their approval.

Apart from military affairs, actual power rested with the general courts of the member colonies. The commissioners could not pass legislation binding on the general courts, nor were they directly responsible to the people. They could neither levy taxes nor requisition supplies. Because the commissioners had no powers of enforcement, a colony which disagreed with a particular decision could simply nullify it by refusing to comply. To avoid conflict, the remaining colonies usually compromised.

Although lacking in power, the Board of Commissioners did perform numerous important services for the four participating colonies. It established various civil agreements of interest to all four colonies and arbitrated intercolonial disputes. Policies concerning the Indians, and regulations governing runaway slaves and the extradition of criminals were also within its domain. In the judicial realm, the Commissioners established uniform standards for probating wills, and served as an admiralty court. Their other duties included fund-raising for Harvard College, settling tariff disputes, and promoting religious orthodoxy.

Unquestionably, serious flaws were inherent in the Confederation of the United Colonies of New England. The illusion of power survived only for the first decade of its existence. Yet it was to be the longest-lived interstate confederation in American history. The leadership which the confederation provided was essential to the existence of the colonies in their early years. It concentrated the colonies' resources in military emergencies and protected the three weaker colonies from encroachment by the Massachusetts Bay colony. Most important of all, it preserved the peace in New England.

Pertinent Literature

Ward, Harry M. *The United Colonies of New England, 1643-1690,* New York: Vantage Press, 1961.

Harry M. Ward's recent study of the United Colonies of New England represents the only full-scale attempt to deal with a long-neglected subject. Beginning with an investigation of the precedents and ideas that influenced the founders, Ward moves on to a detailed explanation of the practical reasons that prompted attempts at unification. In the first half of the book he carefully chronicles the actual process of organizing the United Colonies of New England, outlines the structure of the governing body, and analyzes the duties and powers of the Board of Commissioners.

For Ward, the Confederation of the United Colonies of New England was important not merely because of its actions in settling intercolonial disputes, but also because it "was destined to implant in the minds of the colonists the idea of federal union and to serve as a precedent for the later American Union." As an independent effort of the colonies in search of a system of common government, Ward ranks it as "one of the most noble experiments of all time."

Since Holland was the center of Puritanism in the early seventeenth century, and many of the New Englanders had lived there for a time, Ward contends that the formation of the Dutch United Provinces in 1579 had no doubt influenced them in the direction of union. In the Puritan religion he also finds seeds of federal ideas. The Puritans were accustomed to reasoning in both particular and general terms, as exemplified by the dual importance of the individual congregation and the general will of the synod, and by the compromise between grace and works. The concept of a union of believers bound by a covenant under God also contributed to federal thinking. Their victory in the Pequot War in

1637 had led the New Englanders to think of themselves as God's chosen people, Ward suggests. Thus they sought to consolidate their gains. While acknowledging the Puritans' sincere desire to promote uniformity of religion, the author sees the need to survive in the wilderness as the most important reason for unification.

The extent to which the Board of Commissioners possessed actual power is a matter of prime concern to the author. In military matters and the conduct of foreign affairs the commissioners could claim sovereignty. With them lay the responsibility for negotiating with foreign powers, preparing for war and declaring it. So active was the confederation in this realm that Ward devotes several chapters to relations and conflicts with the Indians, the French, and the Dutch. Ward claims, however, that the constant activity and success of the confederation in matters of foreign affairs during its first decade created the illusion that it possessed sovereign power in other areas. In actuality, however, power resided in the four member colonies. The founders of the United Colonies of New England had failed to work out enforcement procedures and thus had provided no means for making the commissioners' decisions binding on the individual colonies. Ward, nevertheless, credits the confederation with many important achievements, most notably, the keeping of the peace. For a basic understanding of the formation, structure, and significance of the United Colonies of New England, Ward's study is essential.

Confederation of the United Colonies of New England

Osgood, Herbert L. *The American Colonies in the Seventeenth Century.* Gloucester, Massachusetts: Peter Smith Publisher, Inc., 1957.

Osgood was a progenitor of the "imperial school" of American colonial historiography, an interpretation of the period which stresses the English foundations and views colonial development from the vantage point of London. His three volumes on *The American Colonies in the Seventeenth Century* are an institutional history of England's mainland colonies. The work does not give much attention to the growth of social or intellectual institutions, nor, unlike Charles M. Andrews, does Osgood focus on the commercial relationship between Great Britain and America. His special preoccupation is with the transformation in English political institutions which was wrought by their transplantation to America. While Osgood may have slighted other facets of colonial developments, he is not unaware of an ever widening breach between the Mother Country and the colonies, which began to develop as royal control increased during the seventeenth century, with implications inherent in such a rift.

Osgood attributes the gap to several factors. By the end of the century the colonists were still subordinate to the larger policy designs of the British Empire. Their own personal and local concerns were, however, "as distinct from those of contemporary Europeans as time or space could well make them." Their culture, language, and traditions were European, but these had all been tempered by the New World experience, in which environmental factors had played a key role. The colonists, Osgood maintains, had by 1700 "become colonials in the full sense of the word but had not yet reached a developed American type."

Some of these ideas emerge in Osgood's discussion of Confederation of the United Colonies of New England. Osgood sees the organization of the Confederation as a response to border and trade disputes between the confederating colonies, their fear of Indian attacks, their proximity to the Dutch and French settlements, and a sense of mission which was "so strong among the New England Puritans." These were matters concerning which there was "no umpire or sovereign in Europe to whom [the New Englanders] would willingly have submitted their controversies, and none whose sympathy could have been enlisted in the furtherance of their cherished projects."

The confederation, in Osgood's view, illustrates how the colonists adapted themselves to their environment. Because unsettled conditions in Great Britain prevented the British from actively, or adequately, defending New England, the colonists created their own institution for that purpose. As Osgood notes, the United Colonies of New England remained viable until after the Restoration when the Mother Country took a more lively interest in colonial affairs.

Like later historians, Osgood devotes much of his discussion to the predominant position of the Massachusetts Bay colony within the United Colonies of New England. Because the Massachusetts Bay colony was the largest, the most populous, and the only New England colony with a royal charter at the time of the confederation's inception, it soon became the predominant member of the organization. And during the active life of the United Colonies of New England it was the commissioners from Massachusetts who made most of the important decisions.

Osgood concludes his examination of the United Colonies of New England with an account of the Confederation's missionary activity among the Indians. This work came to a ruinous end with the outbreak of King Philip's War in 1676.

Osgood does not reach any general conclusion about the importance of the Confederation of the United Colonies of New England. It may be inferred that he regards the attempt at colonial union as an important first step. And it did represent an effort to respond to unique New World problems. — *W.M.B.*

Additional Recommended Reading

Andrews, Charles M. *The Colonial Period of American History.* Vols. I-II: *The Settlements.* New Haven: Yale University Press, 1964. The chapters on the New England colonies contain frequent references to the affairs and problems of the Confederation of the United Colonies of New England.

Bradford, William. *Of Plymouth Plantation: The Pilgrims in America.* Edited by Harvey Wish. New York: Capricorn Books, 1962. Bradford records the Articles of Confederation and a brief account of the union in his chronicle for 1643.

Adams, James Truslow. *The Founding of New England.* Boston: Atlantic Monthly Press, 1921. Concentrates on the motives for unification and the actions of the commissioners without details of the administrative structure but with an anti-Puritan bias.

Winthrop, John. *Winthrop's Journal: History of New England, 1630-1649.* Edited by James Kendall Hosmer. New York: Barnes and Noble Inc., 1946. Winthrop's entries for the year 1643 include an account of the formation of the United Colonies of New England and the text of the Articles of Confederation. In the narrative which follows, he conveys a feeling for New England life during the years of the confederation.

PASSAGE OF THE MARYLAND ACT OF TOLERATION

Type of event: Religious: formal expression of a policy of religious toleration
Time: April 21, 1649
Locale: St. Mary's, Maryland

Principal personages:
GEORGE CALVERT (FIRST LORD BALTIMORE) (1580?-1632),
who petitioned Charles I for a charter to found a colony north
of the Potomac river
CECILIUS CALVERT (SECOND LORD BALTIMORE) (1605-1675),
son of George Calvert, and the first proprietor of Maryland
LEONARD CALVERT (1606-1647), brother of the first proprietor,
and the first Governor of Maryland

Summary of Event

In his instructions to his brother Leonard Calvert and the commissioners leading the first settlers to Maryland in 1633, the colony's first proprietor, Cecilius Calvert, second Lord Baltimore, cautioned that "they be very carefull to preserve unity and peace amongst all the passengers on Shipp-board, and that they suffer no scandall nor offence to be given to any of the Protestants. . . ." George Calvert, the First Lord Baltimore and father of Cecilius and Leonard, had died the previous year before his goal of founding a colony free from religious animosity could be realized. While the sincerity of Lord Baltimore's position is unquestionable, it was nonetheless necessary to the recruitment of Protestant settlers for the venture. It would have been impossible to find enough British Catholics willing to emigrate; so advantages had to be offered men of humbler rank, usually loyal practicing members of the Church of England, to persuade them to participate in an undertaking led by Catholic gentlemen.

Although the inability of some Catholic settlers, particularly the Jesuits, to restrain their proselytizing zeal which frequently provoked ill will, religious toleration was practiced from the first. Maryland was indeed unique. Nowhere else had anyone experimented with the concept that Protestants and Catholics could live together amicably and enjoy political and religious equality. Anyone who dared attempt to force his beliefs upon another could expect to meet the fate of one William Lewis, a Catholic who was fined heavily in 1638 for proselytizing among the Protestants. Cecilius Calvert, loyal to his father's purpose, encouraged missionary work by all Christians among the Indians, and Catholics and Protestants used the same chapel for their services of worship. That there should be no established church in Maryland Cecilius Calvert had determined; likewise, the government should not interfere in spiritual matters.

In ensuring the first of these tenets, the first proprietor became involved in a long dispute with the Jesuit missionaries in the colony. Claiming that they were exempt from the civil authority, the Jesuits wanted to obtain land di-

115

rectly from the Indians rather than through the proprietary, as the charter specified. They also demanded special privileges, such as exemption from paying quitrents, and preferred treatment for their retainers and servants. Lord Baltimore finally prevailed when the Jesuits' father provincial ordered them to renounce their claims.

The decade between 1640 and 1650 was an inauspicious time for trying to stabilize a colony founded on the principle of religious toleration. Leonard Calvert barely managed to recover the province after having been forced to flee to Virginia in 1644 when William Claiborne, a troublemaker of long standing, captured Kent Island, and Richard Ingle took St. Mary's and plundered the colony. The combination of American discord and England's Civil War was almost fatal for Lord Baltimore's proprietorship. Only through his shrewdness was he able to ward off revocation of his charter by the triumphant Puritans, and as it was, Catholics and loyalists were threatened with imprisonment and confiscation of their property.

Amid this turmoil Lord Baltimore drafted the famous document "An Act Concerning Religion," which has come to be known as the Toleration Act. The General Assembly passed the measure on April 21, 1649. Since toleration had been practiced from the colony's founding, the act represented no change in Lord Baltimore's policy. It apparently was passed in order to refute the charge by those who had tried to annul the charter that the colony was a hotbed of popery. The act had two parts, each with its own preamble, but the second part, positive in its sentiment, was apparently framed by Cecilius Calvert. This section proclaimed that no person "professing to believe in Jesus Christ shall from henceforth be any waies troubled, molested or discountenanced, for or in respect of his or her Religion, nor in the free Exercise thereof within this Province. . . ." It further provided for the punishment of anyone failing to respect these rights. The first clause of the act was added later by the General Assembly, then controlled by a Protestant-Puritan majority, to accord with an act passed by the Long Parliament in 1648 to punish heresies and blasphemies. As punishment for blasphemy, or for denying the Holy Trinity, or that Jesus Christ was the Son of God, it prescribed the penalty of death and confiscation of property. Paradoxically, the next section again emphasized toleration, prohibiting disparagement "in a reproachful manner" of any religious group and stipulating penalties for offenders. Finally, the act forbade swearing, drunkenness, recreation, and labor on the Sabbath.

"An Act Concerning Religion," therefore, did not guarantee complete religious liberty, freedom of thought, or separation of church and state. The first part, added by the General Assembly, actually represented a regression, since it formally limited toleration to Trinitarian Christians. What the act did accomplish was the official, formal expression of the toleration of Catholics and Protestants for each other's beliefs which had been practiced since 1634.

Following an investigation into the colony by Parliamentary commissioners, the Puritan-dominated Assembly which was called on October 30, 1654, repudiated Lord Baltimore's authority, repealed the Toleration Act, and replaced it with an act denying Catholics protection. When the Calverts regained control in 1657, however, Lord Baltimore promised to stand firm for "An Act Concerning Religion."

Pertinent Literature

Andrews, Matthew P. *The Founding of Maryland.* Baltimore: The Williams & Wilkins Co., 1933.

It is the contention of Matthew Page Andrews that historians who have based Maryland's claim to priority in the matter of liberty of conscience upon "An Act Concerning Religion" have failed to look carefully at the period of the colony's founding. Maryland's distinction, he claims, rests not on the act but on the actual practices of her founders and early colonists. The records of the early years offer no evidence of persecutions of groups or individuals either for their beliefs or the lack thereof. Such persecutions as did take place were directed against persons who interfered with the freedom of others or tried to enforce conformity to a particular creed.

Briefly tracing the history of attempts to keep religious freedom alive, Andrews admits that, while all seventeenth century churches probably had at least a few advocates of toleration, the Church in general was largely lacking in the qualities of charity and brotherly love. Thus George Calvert, perhaps reacting to his experience as a government official sent to enforce conformity in Ireland in the days before he became a Catholic, stands out as an enlightened man ahead of his time. In his earlier effort to establish the Avalon colony in Newfoundland as a haven for Catholics, he had welcomed Anglicans. Cecilius Calvert, says Andrews, adhered faithfully to his father's intentions and, in addition, evolved a princi-

ple of separation of church and state. In rebutting historians who argue that the Maryland charter does not provide sufficient evidence of adoption of these principles, Andrews says that even Charles I would not have openly promulgated a plan for a government free of ecclesiastical influence. Yet Cecilius Calvert cautioned the provincial commissioners as they embarked for Maryland to permit no offense among the colonists on matters of religion. The first proprietor's dispute with the Jesuits over their claims to land and special privileges is offered as further evidence of his determination to prevent clerical influence in political matters.

In Andrew's view "An Act Concerning Religion" actually introduced limits upon the previous conditions of freedom, and laid down particular beliefs from which one could not dissent without facing persecution. Andrews attributes the act to the influence of intolerant Puritan elements who immigrated to Maryland in increasing numbers after 1642 and wielded power during the Cromwellian period. Because the first part is decidedly more restrictive than the second, explains Andrews, the act represents a compromise between the tolerant ideas practiced by the early settlers and the restrictive measures advocated by the Puritans. The use of the word "Sabbath" and the prohibition against swearing also show Puritan influence, Andrews argues, since both

Catholics and Anglicans were generally less concerned about such matters.

Despite its restrictive features, "An Act of Toleration," Andrews admits, represented an advance over the religious principles of most of the Christian world, since it ensured for all Christian sects the right to practice their own religion. The freedoms granted were broader than those of Rhode Island, Andrews concludes, for political privileges were not limited by religious beliefs.

Andrews, Charles M. *The Colonial Period of American History.* Vol. II: *The Settlements.* New Haven: Yale University Press, 1964.

This work represents the culmination of a lifetime of scholarship by one of the foremost historians of the colonial period and the leading member of the "imperial school" of colonialists.

In his preface, Charles M. Andrews asserts that seventeenth century American history must be approached from "the English end." Deploring the tendency of many American historians to find something sinister in England's early relationship with the colonies, he defends as natural England's desire to protect herself against competitors and to seek her own best interests. This theme runs throughout the four-volume work, which covers the settlement and early development of each of England's Atlantic colonies and "England's Commercial and Colonial Policy." Andrews' detailed explanations of the circumstances in England which motivated particular colonial enterprises and which affected British attitudes toward the new settlements gave American colonial history a dimension which it had lacked as long as scholars insisted upon studying the colonies in isolation.

Andrews' treatment of the colonization of Maryland reflects his clear understanding of the way circumstances in England influenced events in America. Andrews gives George Calvert his due as an advocate of religious toleration, but he also sees the proprietor as a practical man. Because Catholic gentlemen willing to immigrate to the New World were scarce, Calvert was ready to offer religious toleration as an enticement to Anglicans to become part of his enterprise. Cecilius' instructions to the leaders of the expedition to ensure amity between the Protestants and Catholics show his loyalty to his father's purpose to establish a colony where men of different beliefs could live in peace.

Characterizing the Maryland experiment as an "act of religious knight-errantry," Andrews describes the turbulent religious and political climate both in England and the Chesapeake Bay region which rendered the existence of the colony so hazardous. Because of his involvement in family land disputes in England and because the Civil War was being fought, Cecilius Calvert was never able to travel to Maryland himself. Although Catholics controlled the positions of power in the colony, Protestants were consistently in the majority. In keeping with his convictions, Calvert had allowed numerous Puritans to immigrate to Maryland, perhaps in part to frustrate the aspirations of the Jesuit missionaries for power. In 1648 alone, between four hundred and six hundred Puritans came from Virginia to enjoy political and religious freedom in the settlement of Providence, which they established near Annapolis. Calvert's liberality worked against him, for the presence of so many settlers possessing strong religious and political convictions resulted in a period of anxiety and instability in Maryland, during which political power changed hands frequently.

To meet the charges of those who aimed to have his charter revoked on the grounds that the Catholics held sway in the colony, Calvert prepared "An Act Concerning Religion." The act represented no change in Calvert's policy, since he had advocated toleration for Trinitarians from the first. Yet he certainly realized that a formal declaration of toleration would aid his cause in England and attract colonists who had failed to find peace elsewhere. Perhaps, too, in light of the threat from the Protestant majority, he wished to ratify the original purposes of the colony and to protect the Catholic church. The more restrictive clause of the act,

Andrews agrees, was not Calvert's work but an addition by the Puritan-dominated Assembly.

Andrews concludes that "An Act Concerning Religion" guaranteed neither full religious liberty nor freedom of thought; it did not even separate the Church and the state. Although some men of the time envisioned these concepts as ideal, they were not, according to Andrews, part of the common consciousness. "The act went no farther than to give, as a matter of expedience and necessity, formal expression to that toleration [espoused by Lord Baltimore in 1633]."

Andrews' analysis of "An Act Concerning Religion" is particularly meaningful within the context of the chaotic situation in Maryland in the 1640's. The author's detailed description and explanation of the diverse religious and political elements which combined to create uncertainty and anxiety provide an indispensable background for understanding the act. — *W.M.B.*

Additional Recommended Reading

Craven, Wesley F. *The Southern Colonies in the Seventeenth Century, 1607-1689.* Baton Rouge: Louisiana State University Press, 1949. Chapters VI and VII provide an excellent introduction to Maryland's beginnings, especially in religious matters.

Hall, Clayton C. *The Lords Baltimore and the Maryland Palatinate.* Baltimore: John Murphy Co., 1902. The first three lectures published in this volume are devoted to the founding efforts of the first Lord Baltimore and to the administration of government under his son Cecilius Calvert, including the promotion of religious toleration.

Hanley, Thomas. *Their Rights and Liberties: The Beginnings of Religious and Political Freedom in Maryland.* Westminster, Maryland: Newman Press, 1959. In an obscure ordinance initiated by the Maryland colonists in 1639, Hanley finds evidence of the principles of religious freedom well before the Act of Toleration.

Mereness, Newton D. *Maryland as a Proprietary Province.* New York: The Macmillan Company, 1901. The concluding chapters of Part III briefly trace the policy of religious toleration in Maryland.

Hall, Clayton C., ed. *Narratives of Early Maryland, 1633-1684.* New York: Barnes and Noble Inc., 1946. This collection of original documents includes Lord Baltimore's instructions to the colonists, the text of "An Act Concerning Religion," and various first-hand accounts of the early years in Maryland.

Steiner, Bernard C. *Beginnings of Maryland.* Baltimore: The Johns Hopkins University Press, 1903. Relations between Protestants and Catholics are among subjects covered in this detailed general history.

PASSAGE OF BRITISH NAVIGATION ACTS

Type of event: Economic: attempt to increase British maritime activity
Time: 1660-1663
Locale: The British Empire

Principal personages:
CHARLES II (1630-1685), King of Great Britain 1660-1685
EARL OF CLARENDON (EDWARD HYDE) (1609-1674), Lord Chancellor appointed by Charles
THOMAS POVEY (fl. seventeenth century), influential English merchant
JOHN SHAW (fl. 1660), English financier who brought the Navigation Bill of 1660 before Parliament
SIR GEORGE DOWNING (1623-1684), Member of Parliament and Commissioner of Customs
FOURTH EARL OF SOUTHAMPTON (THOMAS WRIOTHESLEY) (1607-1667), Lord High Treasurer of England 1660-1667
GEORGE MONCK (BARON MONCK, EARL OF TORRINGTON) (1608-1670), Privy Councilor

Summary of Event

During the Elizabethan era, England, hitherto an agricultural country, began to emerge as a great nation ready to compete with the other European nations for wealth and power. The doctrine of mercantilism which the Crown adopted decreed that a nation must attain a favorable balance of trade—that is, to export more than it imported—in order to accumulate bullion for financing war efforts and maintaining national security. Because the navy was thought to be essential to the strength of the nation and because commercial maritime activity enhanced naval power, attention in the seventeenth century centered upon the promotion of English shipping. Success demanded the overthrow of the Dutch monopoly in the carrying trade.

That colonies existed for the benefit of the Mother Country and that the colonies' trade should be restricted to the Mother Country were tenets accepted by all the great commercial rivals of the seventeenth century. As England's knowledge of its colonies and of the new products to be reaped from them increased, so did its expectation of the colonies' potential contribution to its grand scheme. England lacked definite laws relating to commercial policy until 1650 when a combination of private corporate interests and the national interest motivated Parliament to enact legislation designed to attain the national goals. In an attempt to break Dutch control of commerce, Parliament in 1650 forbade foreign ships to trade with the colonies without a license. The following year, Parliament enacted a law stating, in part, that (1) only British-owned ships, of which the master and majority of the crew were British, could import goods from Asia, Africa, and America into Great Britain, Ireland, or the colonies; (2) only British ships or ships of the country of origin could import European goods into Great Britain, Ireland, or the colonies; and (3) foreign goods could be imported into England only from the place of production. Unfortunately, the act also prohibited British merchant ships from sailing from country to country to take on produce for import, and more seriously it provoked a two-year war with the Dutch. The entire period from 1651 to 1660 was marked by a great commercial struggle among the powers of western and northern Europe. Furthermore the last years before the Restoration in Great Britain were fraught with uncertainty and financial difficulties.

When Charles II came to the throne in 1660, he acted upon the urging of the merchants to promote British commerce. He established two councils, one for trade and one for plantations, consisting of lords, merchants, planters, and sea captains. Through the Crown's instructions to these councils, commercial policies were gradually defined. At the same time, Parliament gave the policies statutory authority. The first of such measures was the Navigation Act of 1660, sponsored by John Shaw, a prominent financier, and Sir George Downing, later Commissioner of Customs. Enacted by the Convention Parliament on September 13, 1660, and confirmed by the first regular Restoration Parliament on July 27, 1661, the act was in many respects similar to that of 1651. Certain defects and ambiguities in the earlier act had hindered enforcement and certain revisions were necessary. The act of 1660 provided that only British-built or British-owned ships of which the masters

and three-quarters of the crew were British could import or export goods or commodities, regardless of origin, to and from the British colonies. It further restricted shipment of certain enumerated articles produced in the colonies (sugar, tobacco, cotton, indigo, ginger, speckle wood, and dye-woods) to Great Britain or its colonies, and required ships sailing from the colonies to give bond that they would unload their cargoes in the realm. The enumeration clause was intended to increase England's customs revenues, to insure its access to raw materials, and to advance domestic industries by giving employment in the trades which employed the enumerated products.

In practice, the 1660 regulations created many problems, and shippers took advantage of loopholes and ambiguities to evade the law. Probably to facilitate enforcement, Parliament in 1662 passed the Act of Frauds. It restricted the privileges of the act of 1660 to ships built in England, except for ships bought before 1662.

Great Britain still had to clarify the dependent relationship of its colonies to the Mother Country. If the government were to recover from virtual bankruptcy incurred by the Puritans and royal debts, it could not allow the colonies to buy European products at cheaper prices, and it had to gain customs revenues from the colonial merchants. To make Great Britain the sole exporting center for colonial imports and thus constitute it a "staple," Parliament, on July 27, 1663, passed the "Act for the Encouragement of Trade." Henceforth, European goods could be imported to the colonies only from England and in English-built ships. The only exceptions to the rule were salt for the New England and Newfoundland fisheries, wine from Madeira and the Azores, and provisions, servants, and horses from Ireland and Scotland.

Because of the complexity of the Navigation Acts, administrative discretion was important in determining how they should be interpreted and enforced. In the colonies enforcement lay with the governors, who were required to send to England reports of all vessels trading within their jurisdiction together with copies of the bonds required of all ships' masters. Both colonial and English sea captains, however, found ways of continuing direct trade with Europe, and smuggling was common. In the period immediately following passage of the Navigation Acts, the colonists protested about the restriction on their markets. As English markets became glutted with colonial goods, the returns which the

colonists could expect decreased. The Puritans of the Massachusetts Bay colony objected to the acts on the basis that, since they were not represented in Parliament, they were not subject to the laws passed by Parliament. Gradually, however, most colonists adjusted to compliance, and the insurrections which occurred in the years following cannot be attributed in any large sense to the Navigation Acts.

As far as England was concerned, the legislation did achieve its purpose. Colonial trade with England and British overseas shipping increased more rapidly than before. There were sufficient causes for the American Revolution apart from the Navigation Acts, and the habits of trade which the acts established lasted beyond the eighteenth century. By the mid-nineteenth century Great Britain had become the world's greatest commercial and maritime power.

Pertinent Literature

Andrews, Charles M. *The Colonial Period of American History.* Vol. IV: *England's Commercial and Colonial Policy.* New Haven: Yale University Press, 1964.

In keeping with his consistent approach to American colonial history from the "English end," Charles M. Andrews views the Navigation Acts of 1660 and 1663 as expressions of Great Britain's goal to develop a great commercial empire. He explains British efforts within the context of seventeenth century ideas about the nature of the nation state. Free trade, international coöperation, and mutual dependence were foreign to the seventeenth century concept of the national interest. Jealous of its rivals, Great Britain sought to establish a self-sufficient empire. Colonies were expected to accept the princi-

ple that their chief purpose was to contribute to the advantage of the Mother Country.

Andrews outlines England's commercial scheme as follows: (1) the colonies were to have a monopoly of the English market; (2) England was to have a monopoly on the colonial output; (3) England was to control the carrying trade; (4) the colonies were obligated to pay English customs duties; and (5) England was to enlarge its navy and merchant marine. These principles were designed not only to enhance England's position but also to destroy the monopoly of its Dutch rival. The Dutch at this point were superior in ship-building, conducting finances, and carrying trade. In Holland trade was, in Andrews' phrase, "the national sport," while the English had heretofore regarded it as an inferior activity.

When Parliament assumed control of the colonies in 1649, it sought to further the interests of the merchant class by promoting trade and colonial enterprises. Andrews criticizes the Navigation Act of 1651 as a reactionary measure provoked by narrow London interests. It had little effect on the colonies, he claims, but harmed the English merchants by prohibiting them from stopping at various ports to pick up goods destined for the home market. At a time when England needed peace to recoup the losses of the Civil War, it foolishly provoked war with Holland. Cromwell's subordination of commercial matters to Puritan politics allowed financial problems to accumulate. With the Restoration came an urgent effort on the part of those interested in trade and the colonies to define and implement England's plans for recovery.

Andrews carefully analyzes the purposes of the Navigation Acts of 1660 and 1663, as well as the problems of their enforcement. The acts were opposed in both England and the colonies. Some English critics of the legislation argued that foreign-built ships should be admitted to English registry, and others charged that the laws worked to the advantage of only a small number of merchants and not the nation as a whole. That enumeration increased the cost of carrying colonial staples to foreign markets was a justifiable complaint.

Andrews takes a restrained view of the colonial protests, maintaining that they were confined primarily to the periods immediately following the acts' passage. Because the inhabitants of the nonroyal colonies had become accustomed to a considerable measure of commercial independence, they naturally "felt the pinch of constriction" most sharply. In Virginia, also, Governor Berkeley himself complained that the laws enriched only a few, but kept tobacco prices down, thus inflicting poverty upon the colony. Yet, says Andrews, these protests represented the first recoil from the blow the acts administered. There is no evidence that either Virginia or Maryland, both of which had enjoyed freedom of trade with the Dutch during the Civil War in England, suffered seriously from the enumeration restrictions. The Puritans of the Massachusetts Bay colony, on the other hand, considered themselves outside the jurisdiction of Parliamentary legislation since they were not represented in that body. Determined to preserve their open trading system, they simply ignored the Navigation Acts while at the same time passing laws requiring obedience to them. Only the revocation of the Massachusetts charter achieved their submission.

Andrews concludes that although the Navigation Acts may have contributed to the unrest in the American colonies, they were not directly responsible for the insurrections which occurred.

Harper, Lawrence A. *The English Navigation Laws.* New York: Octagon Books, Inc., 1964.

Lawrence A. Harper considers the English Navigation Acts an "experiment in social engineering." It is fitting, then, that he treats his subject scientifically, testing the effectiveness of the English experiment on the basis of statistical evidence. Because his investigation of the ramifications of the acts and of corollary matters is almost exhaustive, the book requires close attention. While it is not an easy book to read, it stands as a superior example of historical research, particularly in the handling of statistical material. Harper's study thus deserves its position as the definitive work on the Navigation Acts.

The seventeenth century "social engineers," as Harper calls them, believed that England must achieve a favorable balance of trade if it was to accumulate sufficient bullion to wage war. Likewise, the navy and merchant marine must be strengthened. Therefore, these advocates of mercantilism, confident that the national interest was compatible with their individual advancement, called upon Parliament to place their plans in legislative form. Harper traces the history of English shipping legislation and suggests that through a process of trial and error Parliament stumbled upon the formula for protecting England's shipping. The Navigation Act of 1651, he explains, represented simplification of earlier attempts at legislation. Parliament erred in trying to make the act comprehensive. Learning from this experience, Restoration statesmen in the acts of 1660 and 1663 avoided the "nuisance features" of the earlier measure of 1651 and made enforcement possible.

Harper emphasizes the importance of self-seeking business interests in determining the provisions of the Navigation Act of 1663, calling it "a monument to the legislative capacity for combining diverse and unrelated topics. . . ." It serves as a stumbling block, he points out, to those who claim that the old colonial system was impartially designed for the good of the British Empire.

A large portion of Harper's book is devoted to dissecting the administrative machinery employed in the enforcement of the Navigation Acts. The author contends that, given the complexity of the legislation, administrative actions actually determined how it should operate. The Privy Council, the Lords of the Treasury, and the Commissioners of Customs all helped to shape the laws in response to practical considerations. Harper concerns himself in particular with the activities of customs officials at the waterside. Their job was a frustrating one, for even otherwise-respectable people made a game of trying to outwit the enforcement agencies. The role of the Vice-Admiralty and Exchequer courts in the prosecution of smugglers when apprehended was an important one and is fully treated by Harper. Dependence on private "informers" and an insufficient number of customs personnel made enforcement of the Navigation Acts especially difficult in the colonies, and before the establishment of the Admiralty Courts there, lack of uniformity in the "rough and ready" judicial system complicated the prosecution of violaters. Colonial governors were given more responsibility than actual authority in enforcing the laws, and they were denied flexibility of action in dealing with the variety of cases which they had to handle.

Harper's primary purpose is to test whether the Navigation Acts aided the growth of England's empire and power. He specifically examines the evidence concerning their influence on the development of shipping, the training of sailors, and the employment of shipwrights. The figures which he marshals for the period before enactment of the laws, while they were in force, and after their repeal, furnish a panoramic view of English maritime history. After 1660, the total tonnage of shipping and the number of seamen increased at a more rapid rate than before, and after 1662 the shipbuilding industry grew. He denies that England would have gained a natural monopoly of colonial trade without the laws. The very resistance to these measures, he holds, is proof that they constituted a burden to the colonists and directed their trade into new channels. That enforcement was reasonably effective is indicated by the small fraction of total commerce attributable to illicit trade.
— *W.M.B.*

Additional Recommended Reading

Barnes, Viola F. *The Dominion of New England: A Study in British Colonial Policy.* New York: Frederick Ungar Publishing Co., 1960. Describes the reaction of the Puritans to English commercial policy and the problems involved in enforcing the Navigation Acts.

Beer, George L. *The Old Colonial System, 1660-1754.* Part I. Gloucester, Massachusetts: Peter Smith Publishers, Inc., 1958. A study of the establishment, development, and operation of the English colonial system, this work examines the economic and political development of the colonies as affected by imperial policy.

Clark, George N. *The Later Stuarts, 1660-1714.* Oxford: University Press, 1955. Part of *The Oxford History of England,* this volume provides an excellent background for an understanding of the economic tendencies and domestic and foreign policies of the reign of Charles II.

Dickerson, Oliver M. *The Navigation Acts and the American Revolution.* Philadelphia: University of Pennsylvania Press, 1951. Although Dickerson is primarily concerned with the eighteenth century Navigation Acts, his early chapters are valuable for a study of the seventeenth century attempts at regulation.

THE HALF-WAY COVENANT

Type of event: Religious: amendment of Puritan doctrine concerning church membership
Time: 1662
Locale: Boston, Massachusetts

Principal personages:

RICHARD MATHER (1596-1669), minister of the church in Dorchester, Massachusetts, and principal leader in devising the Half-Way Covenant

INCREASE MATHER (1639-1723), son of Richard, who opposed the Half-Way Covenant but who later changed his position

CHARLES CHAUNCY (1592-1672), president of Harvard College and leading opponent of the movement to revise membership requirements

JOHN WOODBRIDGE, JR. (fl. 1662), minister in Killingworth, Connecticut, who led his congregation beyond the Half-Way Covenant and opened membership to all

Summary of Event

One of the most compelling questions about the Puritan Commonwealth established in Massachusetts during the seventeenth century concerns the reasons for its decline. Historians have found it difficult to determine not only why the rule of the "saints" came to an end but also the time when the deterioration began. Some have contended that the system of the Church and the state established under the leadership of such men as John Winthrop and John Cotton was so well constructed that it remained almost unchanged for many years. Others believe that Puritan ideals began to falter from the beginning, and that too much stress has been placed on the pervasiveness of a group of attitudes defined as the "Puritan mind."

Among the controversial issues which have enlivened the debate over Puritan decline is the so-called "Half-Way Covenant" of 1662. The most important provision of this document, endorsed by a synod of more than eighty ministers and laymen meeting in Boston, was that children whose parents had not been admitted to full membership in a Puritan church might nevertheless be eligible for baptism.

The question of membership was one which had long plagued the churches of New England. On the one hand, Puritans believed that no one should be admitted to full communion in the Church who had not sufficiently demonstrated a personal experience by which he had become convinced that God had elected him to salvation. And yet if one believed that prospective church members must await a message from God, what part was the Church itself to play in recruiting new adherents? This problem became increasingly acute as the proportion of Puritans in New England declined in relation to the growing population of the area. It began to seem, as Jonathan Mitchel wrote, that the churches had

127

been set up "onely that *a few old Christians* may keep one another warm while they live, and then carry away the Church into the cold grave with them when they dye. . . ."

The Half-Way Covenant did not concern the admission of new members from outside the Church but attempted rather to deal with the problems raised by the children and grandchildren of the "elect." Since the Puritans believed in infant baptism they had always permitted church members to have their children brought under the care of the congregation, although each had to await the conversion experience before being admitted to full membership. It was expected that a significant number of these young people would ultimately experience conversion, but until that time, they were not permitted to participate in communion or vote on Church business. Unfortunately, this arrangement did not provide for the third generation.

During the early days of the Puritan Commonwealth, the churches did not have to concern themselves about the grandchildren of the "elect" because there were none. Nor when they did begin to appear was there any difficulty about those whose parents had been received into full communion with a church. The problem arose with those members of the third generation whose parents had not yet achieved full membership: were such infants to be baptised or not? No one could say for certain that the parents of these children would not experience a conversion at some later time, since the Puritans did not believe that God necessarily informed the "saints" of their election at any certain age. Moreover, if these infants were to be denied baptism would

it not then become necessary to expel their parents from the privileged position they had held in a church since childhood?

The answer which the Half-Way Covenant provided to this question may have confirmed a practice which was already developing in New England. It stated that, in cases where children were born to parents who had not yet attained full church membership, the congregation should baptize the new infants. Such persons could not, however, become full members of a church unless they subsequently experienced conversion. Both they and their parents enjoyed a kind of "halfway" membership which enabled the Puritans to maintain their rigid standards for full communion in a church and yet to provide for the possible conversion of new members. Infants baptised into a church were obviously more likely to achieve full membership than those who were excluded from the fold.

The Half-Way Covenant provided the Puritan Commonwealth with one of its most prolonged controversies. Although the Synod of 1662 had strongly endorsed the covenant, it was opposed by a small and determined group of ministers and temporarily refused by a significant number of congregations. Most of its opponents charged that, despite claims to the contrary, the covenant would open up a church to persons who were not among God's elect. Richard Mather, one of those most responsible for the decision of the synod, found his congregation at Dorchester skeptical about the covenant, and his sons, Increase and Eleazar, among its most vocal opponents. Another influential leader of the opposition was

Charles Chauncy, who, as president of Harvard College, was among the most respected scholars in the province. Nevertheless, despite such pockets of resistance as that evidenced by the refusal of Boston's Second Church to accept the covenant until 1693, the Puritan churches in New England gradually came to accept the idea of "half-way" membership. Not until the great religious revivals of the 1740's swept through the colonies did the covenant again come under serious attack and by then the Puritan commonwealth, as such, had ceased to exist.

Pertinent Literature

Miller, Perry. *The New England Mind.* Vol. I: *The Seventeenth Century.* New York: Macmillan Company, 1939.

Miller, Perry. *The New England Mind.* Vol. II: *From Colony to Province.* Cambridge: Harvard University Press, 1953.

Perry Miller's two volumes provide a magisterial account of intellectual life in early New England. Miller focuses on the Puritans of Massachusetts Bay colony. His richly complex study spans the entire seventeenth century.

In his first volume, Miller presents a topical survey of the major tenets of New England Puritanism. In a prose style that seldom comforts the reader, he carefully delineates the worldview of the Saints. His discussion ranges over Puritan notions about religion and learning, cosmology, anthropology, and sociology. He gives special emphasis to the Puritans' belief in covenant theology. The founders of the Bay colony, he argues, believed that they were parties to a covenant with God. Their contractual obligation to the Almighty required them to go to Massachusetts and to build a colony in the wilderness.

Miller chronicles the actual work of colonization in his second volume. He contends that the founders established their settlement with an eye to the wider world. They intended to build a model community, a "Bible Commonwealth," that would serve as an example for their European coreligionists. Miller pictures the builders of the Bay colony as men and women of high purpose and immense intellectual energy. They treated dissenters with a heavy hand and kept theological precepts foremost in mind. The church stood at the center of their lives.

According to Miller, New England Puritanism retained its pristine quality for only one generation. The passage of time and the challenges of a frontier environment changed the focus of Puritan life. Second generation Bay colonists lacked the sense of mission that inspired their immediate predecessors. Measures, such as the Half-Way Covenant, clearly reveal the decline of religious self-assurance. The Puritans continued to expand their settlements, but they labored in the name of a far less exalted purpose. Their concerns became increasingly secular. The task of building a "Bible Commonwealth" gave way to the chore of clearing the wilderness.

Perry Miller sketches the Puritan experience in bold strokes. At the same time, he shows keen appreciation for the intricacies of seventeenth century Puritan thought. His two volume work stands as a seminal contribution to both American History and the History of Ideas.

Morgan, Edmund S. *Visible Saints: The History of a Puritan Idea.* New York: New York University Press, 1963.

One of the first historians to take issue with Perry Miller's long-standing contention that the Half-Way Covenant illustrated the decline of Puritanism is Edmund Morgan. In *Visible Saints,* Professor Morgan argues that biological necessity, rather than a decline of faith, forced the Puritans to modify their membership requirements. It was inevitable that children would be born to members who had not yet achieved the status of full communicants in the Church and that some provision would have to be made for them. Morgan believes that the Half-Way Covenant is not a symptom of Puritan decline but evidence of their determination to maintain rigid standards of membership.

In pursuing this argument, the author of *Visible Saints* goes back to the founding of the colony in order to demonstrate a significant difference between the churches of Massachusetts and Puritan congregations elsewhere. Morgan contends that, until the 1630s, Puritan churches neither in Europe nor America required prospective members to recount the experience which convinced them of their election. In doing this, he again suggests revisions in the conclusions of Perry Miller, insisting that this unique requirement for membership developed in Massachusetts after the settlement rather than being imported from Europe or Plymouth.

The importance of Professor Morgan's contention about the peculiarity of membership requirements in Massachusetts churches is evident in his conclusion. If Puritan churches in Massachusetts were the first to insist that members demonstrate their "election," it is easier to understand why the colony experienced difficulties such as those which resulted in the Half-Way Covenant. Since earlier churches expected nothing more than a thorough knowledge of doctrine, it was relatively easy to prepare children for full membership in the congregation. In such churches the problem of baptized but unconverted parents did not arise. By the time children of church members had reached the age at which they might themselves become parents, they had been trained for and admitted into full communion with the Church. Not so for the congregations in Massachusetts which had come to expect something more than just an understanding of church doctrine.

By the middle of the seventeenth century, Professor Morgan believes the Massachusetts churches faced an unprecedented crisis over membership, which admitted only three possible solutions. The Puritans could have ignored the problem raised by the third generation and, by making no provision for the baptism of such persons, condemned the Church to a decline of membership which would have robbed it of its influence and perhaps its existence. They could have made it easier to obtain full membership in the Church, a solution which would have provided genuine evidence of declining zeal. Instead of choosing either of these extremes, the Puritans of Massachusetts, by adopting the Half-Way Covenant, protected their rigid criteria for full Church membership without isolating themselves from the rest of the colony.

In publishing *Visible Saints,* Professor Morgan continues an interpretative slant which he expounded in his earlier study of John Winthrop, entitled *The Puritan Dilemma.* In both studies, as the author himself explains it, the attempt has been to show that the Puritan, "while trying to live as God required, learned that he must live *in* the world, face its temptations, and share its guilt; . . ." The strength of the Massachusetts Puritans was that, like Winthrop himself, they managed to maintain much of their idealism without becoming fanatics. If Professor Morgan is correct, this golden mean is evident in the Half-Way Covenant of 1662; it permitted Massachusetts to solve the problem of Church membership and yet to avoid the dual pitfalls of compromise with the world on the one hand and withdrawal from it on the other. — *D.L.A.*

Additional Recommended Reading

Pope, Robert G. *The Half-Way Covenant: Church Membership in Puritan New England.* Princeton: Princeton University Press, 1969. The most detailed discussion of the Half-Way Covenant by an author who accepts, in general, the thesis advanced by Edmund Morgan.

Miller, Perry. *Errand into the Wilderness.* Cambridge: Harvard University Press, 1956. This collection of essays by Miller is a good introduction to Puritan theology and is especially useful for those who find his larger studies too formidable.

Murdock, Kenneth B. *Increase Mather: The Foremost American Puritan.* Cambridge: Harvard University Press, 1925. Although an older study, this is a good biography of a major Puritan divine who played an important part in the Puritan churches during their years of decline.

Morison, Samuel Eliot. *Builders of the Bay Colony.* Boston: Houghton Mifflin Co., 1930. Biographical essays on various figures in Massachusetts of the seventeenth century providing an extraordinarily readable introduction to the history of New England.

Adams, Brooks Henry. *The Emancipation of Massachusetts: The Dream and the Reality.* Cambridge: Harvard University Press, 1919. Although now outdated, this work is representative of an earlier group of historians who were hostile to Puritanism, and especially to the New England clergy.

SETTLEMENT OF THE CAROLINAS

Type of event: Sociological: takeover of the Carolinas by the British Crown in place of proprietorships aimed at personal profit
Time: 1663-1729
Locale: The eastern part of the Carolinas

Principal personages:

EARL OF SHAFTESBURY (ANTHONY ASHLEY COOPER) (1621-1683), proprietor and architect of the Carolina proprietary system

SIR JOHN COLLETON (fl.1660), wealthy Barbadian planter who took the initiative in acquiring the proprietary charter for the Carolinas

SIR WILLIAM BERKELEY (1606-1677), Governor of Virginia (1642-1676) and an original Carolina proprietor

WILLIAM DRUMMOND (fl.1664), first Governor of Albemarle County which later became North Carolina

SIR JOHN YEAMANS (1610?-1674), leader of South Carolina's Goose Creek faction

JOHN LOCKE (1632-1704), English political philosopher, who as Ashley Cooper's protégé helped to prepare the Fundamental Constitutions

JOHN CULPEPER (fl.1671-1680), leader of a rebellion against Albemarle's proprietary government in 1677

PHILIP LUDWELL (fl.1660-1704), first Governor of both Carolinas in 1691

EDWARD HYDE (c.1650-1712), first Governor of North Carolina independent of South Carolina

SIR FRANCIS NICHOLSON (1655-1728), first Royal Governor of South Carolina

Summary of Event

The introduction of large-scale sugar production to Barbados in the early 1660's forced many small planters to consider emigration. When Sir John Colleton, a wealthy Barbadian, returned to England and gained a seat on the Council for Foreign Plantations, he conceived the idea of establishing a proprietary colony and recruiting Barbadians to settle it. For fellow proprietors he turned to seven powerful Englishmen who had been associated with colonial expansion: the Earl of Shaftesbury, Sir William Berkeley, John Lord Berkeley, the Duke of Albemarle (George Monck), the Earl of Clarendon (Edward Hyde), the Earl of Craven, and Sir George Carteret. On March 24, 1663, Charles II granted to the proprietors the land between latitude 36 and 31 degrees north and extending west to the South Seas, which they called Carolina. Required only to pay a nominal annual sum to the king, the proprietors possessed vast powers—to fill offices, erect a government, establish courts, collect customs and taxes, grant land, confer titles, and determine military matters. They were obliged to guarantee the rights of Englishmen to their settlers, however, and could enact laws only with the consent of the freemen.

Having devised plans for the creation of three counties and begun negotiations with two groups of prospective settlers in Barbados and New England, the proprietors drafted a document, the "Declaration and Proposals to all that Will Plant in Carolina," which outlined a headright system of land distribution and a framework for participatory government. Sir William Berkeley received authorization to appoint a governor and council for Albemarle County (later North Carolina) and in October, 1664, he named William Drummond of Virginia Governor. A few months later, Sir John Yeamans was commissioned Governor of Clarendon County. As a further inducement to settlement, the proprietors in January, 1665, drew up the "Concessions and Agreements," which provided for a unicameral legislature including representatives of the freemen and insured religious toleration. Friction between new arrivals and the original settlers, combined with Indian hostility and news of better land to the south, led to the abandonment of Clarendon County in 1667.

Because the "Concessions and Agreements" proved unsatisfactory, the Earl of Shaftesbury in 1669 collaborated with his protégé John Locke to write "The Fundamental Constitutions of Carolina." An elaborate blueprint for government, it proposed a feudal system whereby two-thirds of the land would be held by a colonial nobility. Although a "parliament" consisting of the nobility and popular representatives would sit in the colony, the proprietors in England would constitute a Palatine Court which could veto the legislature's decisions. Certain provisions of the Fundamental Constitutions were implemented, but the proprietors never succeeded in winning the Assembly's approval of the system as a whole. Thus the actual government of Albemarle consisted of a powerful governor and council appointed by the proprietors and representatives elected by the freemen. After 1691, the popular branch of the legislature met separately and began to exercise parliamentary privileges. Until the establishment of a supreme court in 1700, the governor and council constituted the colony's highest court.

Since travel to Albemarle both by land and water was difficult, the area remained isolated and failed to develop. The proprietors, blaming the inhabitants for the region's slow growth, spent more time and money on South Carolina. The trickle of settlers to Albemarle County was due largely to uncertainty about the terms of landholding. To promote settlement of the region, the proprietors in 1668 signed the "Great Deed of Grant," placing landholding on the same basis as in Virginia, but because they themselves often violated its provisions, their efforts were unavailing. The failure of the proprietors to establish a stable, efficient government was also a great handicap to Albemarle's progress. Out of the proprietors' efforts to enforce the Navigation Acts, which were harmful to the colony's trade, there arose proprietary and antiproprietary factions. When Governor Thomas Miller of the proprietary faction attempted to assume the duties of customs collector in 1677, the opposing faction, led by John Culpeper, seized him and took control of the government. The rebellion failed, however, and the rebel governor was tried for treason in London. Shaftesbury magnanimously used his influence to bring about Culpeper's acquittal.

With the appointment of Philip Ludwell as "Governor of Carolina" in November, 1691, Albemarle's unfortunate history as a county ended. Ludwell was to reside in Charles Town, while North Carolina, governed by his deputy, was to retain a separate legislature. For the next fifteen years North Carolina enjoyed a peaceful and well-administered government. Huguenots from Virginia settled the area south of Albemarle Sound. In 1705 the Assembly incorporated Bath as the province's first town, and German Palatines and Swiss founded New Bern in 1710.

During the first decade of the eighteenth century, North Carolina was torn by religious dissension. Although toleration had prevailed from the beginning, and many dissenters had held positions of power, Anglicans were determined to establish the Church of England in the province. With the passage of the Vestry Act of 1703, Assembly members were required to take an oath of loyalty to the Church of England. In 1710 the proprietors appointed Edward Hyde Governor—the first Governor of North Carolina to be independent of the Governor of Carolina—and the legislature nullified the laws of the previous dissenter administration. The previous Governor, Thomas Cary, led an unsuccessful rebellion against Hyde.

In September, 1711, the Tuscarora Indians, seeking revenge for white encroachment on their lands, enslavement of Indians, and unfair trading practices, fell upon the already demoralized settlers from the Neuse to the Pamlico rivers. Two expeditions, aided by South Carolina and led by Colonel Jack Barnwell and Colonel James More in 1712 and 1713, finally broke the power of the Tuscarora.

Although the Indian war had placed the colony in dire financial straits, it drew the people together, and they entered a period of peace. The legislature of 1715 revised the laws in order to improve administration and avoid confusion. As the damaged towns were rebuilt, new ones were begun. Under the administration of Governor George Burrington in the mid-1720's immigration increased, and four new counties were formed. As part of the "royalizing" process throughout the colonies, the crown bought out the proprietors on July 25, 1729, and North Carolina became a royal colony.

Troubled as North Carolina's early years were, it had remained essentially a backwater, ignored by the proprietors who had taken a greater interest in its more prosperous sister to the south. After the abandonment of Clarendon County in 1667, Shaftesbury had convinced the proprietors that a larger investment was essential for success, and they decided to locate a settlement at Port Royal. Over one hundred settlers, led by Joseph West, left England in August, 1669, and in April, 1670, established Charles Town. Because the settlers were predominantly tradesmen ignorant of farming methods, a number got into debt and deserted the colony.

In response to recruitment efforts, large numbers of Barbadians immigrated to the colony, and by 1671 they contributed half its population. The new settlers soon learned agriculture, and Dr. Henry Woodward opened the way to trade with the Indians. Prosperity increased as the colonists developed a thriving trade in furs and naval stores with England, and in meat, lumber, and Indian slaves with the West Indies.

A powerful faction of Barbadians, known as the "Goose Creek men," gained control of the government and determined the colony's politics for nearly fifty years. Conflict between the proprietors and the settlers over debts, land distribution, and Indian slavery nearly brought an end to the colony late in its first decade. Attracted by the proprietors' promise of toleration, many dissenters came in, only to encounter the resentment of the conservative Anglican Barbadians, who resisted the proprietors' efforts at reform. When Governor James Colleton declared martial law in February, 1690, in an attempt to halt the abuses of the Indian trade and collect the quitrents, the Goose Creek faction ousted him and replaced him with Seth Sothel. In a revision of the government in 1691, the proprietors made Philip Ludwell Governor and declared that the freemen's representatives should meet as a separate house.

The decade of the 1690's was one of relative peace and prosperity. Rice became a staple crop, the Indian trade prospered, and Charles Town began to take on genteel trappings. By passing laws giving concessions to both sides, John Archdale, who became Governor in 1695, determined to reconcile the old factions. The Commons House of Assembly became the voice of the people and gained legislative prerogatives.

Factional rivalries were reviewed at the beginning of the eighteenth century. The selection of an Anglican governor in 1700 aroused the opposition of the dissenters to the establishment of the Church of England in the colony; in 1704, the parish vestries became seats of power. The popular division over religion was superseded by one over the issue of paper currency in 1712. As early as 1703, the colony had emitted its first bills of credit to pay for an expedition against the Spanish in Florida. Other emissions followed. The planters and tradesmen who did business solely within the colony favored the use of paper money, but the Charles Town merchants who had to pay their English creditors in specie bitterly opposed it.

The proprietors had never moved decisively to control the long-standing abuses of the Indian trade, and as a result, in 1715, the Yamasee War, the longest and costliest Indian war in the colony's history, broke out. During the conflict the people were driven from their homes to seek refuge in Charles Town. To end the abuses of the trade the Commons House of Assembly created a monopoly of the Indian trade under its own direction.

In 1718 the proprietors launched a strong attack upon some of the colony's most popular laws, disallowing measures providing for bills of credit and import duties, removing the monopoly on trade, and weakening the power of the legislature; consequently, antiproprietary sentiment crystallized in favor of royal government. All that lacked for rebellion was a final catalyst. It came in November, 1719, in the

135

form of the rumor of an imminent invasion of the colony by the Spanish. When the Assembly convened in December, it declared itself a convention and petitioned the Board of Trade to be made a royal colony. The Privy Council assumed the administration of the colony and appointed Francis Nicholson the first Royal Governor.

Although Nicholson tried to reconcile the contending factions and establish local governmental institutions, the paper money controversy and problems caused by the Navigation Acts continued to plague the colony. By 1728 the government had ceased to function. The Crown bought out the proprietors in 1729, but internal strife remained.

Pertinent Literature

Lefler, Hugh T. and Albert R. Newsome. *North Carolina: The History of a Southern State.* Chapel Hill: University of North Carolina Press, 1963.

In the preface to the first edition of this history of North Carolina, Hugh Lefler states that he and Albert Newsome were seeking to provide a comprehensive work for the general reader and the college student. Lacking a "pet theory of historical interpretation," the authors disavow any effort at revising history, preferring only "to present an accurate narrative." The resulting history is rich both in factual detail and interpretation. The chapters dealing with the proprietary period are for the most part objective in tone—critical of the proprietors, but by no means losing sight of the faults of factions within the colony.

The granting of the Carolina Proprietary Charter was Charles II's way of paying a political debt to some powerful countrymen who had supported him in the past and whose future support he wished to insure. Besides the furtherance of his personal ambitions, Charles had four motives in issuing the charter: the propagation of Christianity; the enlargement of the Empire; the promotion of English commerce; and an increase in the proprietors' fortunes. The discontent of the settlers and the ineffectiveness of the govern-

ment during the colony's earliest years must be attributed, say Lefler and Newsome, to the vacillatory policies and lack of interest of the proprietary board. Shaftesbury's interest in experimenting with various forms of government served only to create instability, they charge. Crediting the Fundamental Constitutions to John Locke, the authors find it ridiculous that Locke and Shaftesbury should have considered imposing so complicated a scheme upon a wilderness environment. Yet they acknowledge the progressive features of the proposed system: registration of births, marriages, and deaths, and of land titles; bienniel parliaments; trial by jury; and religious toleration.

The authors manage to convey successfully the feeling of isolation and confusion experienced by the early North Carolina colonists through their geographical position and also because of their inept government. Blaming the unenterprising settlers for the slow growth of the colony, the proprietors neglected it and concentrated their efforts on the southern part of their territory. Lefler and Newsome assign much of the blame concerning North Carolina's backwardness to the proprietors.

The authors specifically mention their failure to establish consistent terms of landholding or to create a strong, stable, and efficient government. All too frequently governors appointed by the proprietors were turned out by public demand.

Culpeper's rebellion must be attributed at least indirectly to the proprietors since they should have recognized the inevitability of resistance to acts so harmful to the colony's trade. Obliged to support the Crown's position that the acts must be enforced, they were actually opposing their own economic interests. When the rebel governor came to trial, the proprietors acted opportunistically and minimized the rebellion, fearing that their charter would be abrogated.

The authors do not, however, reserve criticism solely for the proprietors; they also declare that, in dealings with Indians, the settlers were often deceitful and immoral. By encroaching upon Indian lands, cheating them in trade, and taking their people as slaves, the whites invited the massacre of 1711.

The instability of the government and the open flouting of laws, so vividly depicted by the authors, make it plain why the Crown desired to take over the colony. As early as 1706, the Board of Trade declared that the proprietary colonies had not only failed to accomplish their goals but had also violated England's laws, denied colonists their full rights as Englishmen, and shirked their obligations to the Mother Country.

Lefler and Newsome's chapters on the proprietary period furnish an excellent introduction to the history of the Carolinas and provide a sound basis for an understanding of the problems of the proprietary system within the context of English expansionist policy.

Sirmans, M. Eugene. *Colonial South Carolina: A Political History, 1663-1763.* Chapel Hill: University of North Carolina Press, 1966.

Eugene Sirmans undertook a revision of the political history of colonial South Carolina because he was dissatisfied with the failure of earlier historians "to relate the internal history of the province to other events in the British empire." Those writers had depicted the colony's early history "as a struggle between colonists who wanted only to defend their liberties and proprietors who alternated between despotism and greed."

Sirmans' view of the proprietors is generally charitable. Admitting that they expected the colony to yield a handsome return from a minimum investment, Sirmans nonetheless contends that the proprietors exhibited a practical knowledge of colonial affairs. For the much maligned Fundamental Constitutions and its architect, Shaftesbury, the author has high praise. Where other historians have condemned the scheme as ridiculously impractical for a primitive environment, Sirmans points out that the proprietors had no intention of implementing its provisions immediately. Rather, they viewed it as a long-term plan to be realized only after the wilderness period had passed. The Fundamental Constitutions contained nothing of vassalage or of the many anachronistic features of feudalism, concentrating instead upon a revised form of manorialism. Shaftesbury, in keeping with contemporary English political philosophy, hoped to develop a society in which aristocracy would balance democracy. Sirmans argues that both the establishment of a landed gentry and the policy of religious toleration had far-reaching effects upon the development of South Carolina.

Sirmans' most significant contribution to a proper understanding of the proprietary period is his analysis of the role of the "Goose Creek men" in the politics of South Carolina. A group of Barbadians who had settled in the Goose Creek region, this powerful faction consistently opposed proprietary policy and was contemptuous of newer, less-experienced colonists. They had no sympathy with Shaftesbury's plan to develop the colony but were interested only in building up their own fortunes by illegal trade. The dissenters who had been attracted to the colony supported the proprietors in return for religious toleration. Opposition to the staunchly Anglican Goose Creek faction on the part of the dissenters resulted in constant antagonism and unrest during the forty-two year period of largely Goose Creek dominance. When, in 1690, the proprietors attempted unsuccessfully to halt the abuses of trade with the Indians, the Goose Creek faction forced the Governor out, replacing him with their own man. Some historians have sought to characterize this rebellious action as a popular revolt against despotic proprietors. Sirmans, on the other hand, interprets it simply as an attempt to oust an unpopular governor in order to return power to the faction which had formerly been in control. The proprietors were finally forced to compromise with the dissidents so that order might be maintained.

After 1700, the proprietors launched a campaign to establish the Church of England and forced a realignment of the old factions. In response to the complaints of dissenters, however, the Crown directed the proprietors to disallow the more discriminatory provisions of the establishment act. During this period, Sirmans explains, the parish vestry became the real seat of political power in South Carolina.

Even after the religious controversy ended in 1712, new divisions developed between the merchants, who supported the proprietors, and the planters over the issues of trade abuses and paper currency. When the proprietors came under the influence of corrupt politicians and attacked laws favorable to the planters, the popular forces were driven to seek the stabilizing influence of royal government. Sirmans sees no revolt against tyranny in this action. Political rights were not in question, he maintains; the Assembly merely rebelled against the neglect and maladministration of the proprietors.

The account of the chaotic state of politics and constantly changing administrations during the proprietary period makes for rather difficult reading at times. Undoubtedly, the author's untimely death before he was able to condense to some extent the wealth of detail which he had assembled accounts for occasional confusing sections. On the whole, however, Sirmans has presented a profoundly revealing interpretation of a most complex political situation where others in the past have found only simplistic answers. — *W.M.B.*

Settlement of the Carolinas

Additional Recommended Reading

Andrews, Charles M. *The Colonial Period of American History.* Vol. III: *The Settlements.* Chs. 5 and 6. New Haven: Yale University Press, 1964. After describing the efforts of the proprietors to establish their colony, Andrews goes on to detail the political turmoil which racked the Carolinas under proprietary government.

Powell, William S., ed. *Ye Countie of Albemarle in Carolina: A Collection of Documents, 1664-1675.* Raleigh: State Department of Archives and History, 1958. Among this collection of twenty-eight documents are letters from the proprietors and instructions to various governors.

Craven, Wesley F. *The Southern Colonies in the Seventeenth Century, 1607-1689.* Ch. 9. Baton Rouge: Louisiana State University Press, 1949. Placing the settlement of Carolina within the context of British expansionist policy, Craven sheds light upon the economics of proprietary promotional efforts.

Salley, Alexander S., Jr., ed. *Narratives of Early Carolina, 1650-1708.* New York: Barnes and Noble, Inc., 1946. Among the original accounts included in this work are descriptions of the early explorations and life in the settlements.

Powell, William S. *The Proprietors of Carolina.* Raleigh: Carolina Charter Tercentenary Commission, 1963. In addition to biographical material, this small booklet includes an introduction which gives reasons for the granting of the charter.

Rankin, Hugh F. *Upheaval in Albemarle: The Story of Culpeper's Rebellion, 1675-1689.* Raleigh: Carolina Charter Tercentenary Commission, 1962. Views the rebellion as a reaction against the new colonial policies of Charles II.

BRITISH CONQUEST OF NEW NETHERLAND

Type of event: Political: removal of the Dutch presence in North America
Time: August-September, 1664
Locale: Dutch colony in the New World

Principal personages:
PETER STUYVESANT (1592-1672), Dutch Governor of New Netherland until 1664
JAMES, DUKE OF YORK (Crowned KING JAMES II in 1685) (1633-1701), brother of Charles II and proprietor of New York after March, 1664
RICHARD NICOLLS (1624-1672), James's deputy and first Governor of New York 1664-1668

Summary of Event

The restoration of the Stuart monarchy to the British throne in 1660 ushered in an era of colonial expansion allied with a more vigorous mercantilism and attempts to make colonial administration more unified. New Netherland's existence as an alien wedge between Great Britain's North American colonies impinged upon all three objectives. Charles II's supporters viewed land grants in America as a device for recouping their lost fortunes, and the region occupied by the Dutch enticed such land-grabbers. Furthermore, the Crown's attempt to unify colonial administration was frustrated by the situation of New Netherland, for its strategic geographic location impeded communications between the Chesapeake and New England colonies and made more difficult the task of defending those colonies from the French.

Charles II and his Parliament had designed the navigation system against their commercial rivals, the Dutch, but New Netherland's existence rendered enforcement of the Acts of Trade and Navigation ineffective. Great Britain's mainland colonies used New Netherland as a means of circumventing the system, and the Dutch colony became a breeding ground for smugglers. Officials in the British colonies would not enforce the trade acts against the Dutch, and it was argued that the Crown lost ten thousand pounds annually in uncollected customs revenues.

The Crown concluded at length that the only effective remedy for these difficulties lay in wresting control of New Netherland from the Dutch. As early as 1663, the Council for Foreign Plantations, an advisory board of merchants and privy councillors, investigated the matter of Dutch power and examined the possibility of a military operation against New Netherland. Information from English residents on the eastern end of Long Island suggested that such a military undertaking would meet with little resistance from the Dutch garrison at New Amsterdam.

Based upon the council's recommendations, Charles moved swiftly. In March, 1664, he gave his brother James, Duke of York, a proprietary grant of all the land area between Delaware Bay and the Connecticut river, which included the Dutch colony. Parliament approved the grant, and in April the King nominated Colonel Richard Nicolls as Lieutenant-Governor of the proprietary, put him in charge of a small military force, and sent him on his way to America.

Nicolls and his squadron of four ships arrived off New Amsterdam in August, 1664. The Lieutenant-Governor immediately demanded the surrender of the colony, offering liberal terms as bait. Among the terms were guarantees to the inhabitants of all the rights of Englishmen, trading privileges, freedom of conscience, the continuance of Dutch customs and inheritance laws, and up to eighteen months for the settlers to decide whether to leave or not. At first, the Governor of New Netherland, Peter Stuyvesant, refused to surrender and began to make preparations for the defense of his colony. But the peg-legged Stuyvesant, having angered his people with his high-handed rule, received no support from the residents, who felt they would be no worse off under the British. Stuyvesant, therefore, on August 26, 1664, surrendered the town. A week later, the remainder of the colony fell into British hands.

In 1667, the Treaty of Breda, which ended the Second Anglo-Dutch War, confirmed the British conquest. Except for a brief loss of control during the Third Dutch War, the British retained a firm grip upon the former Dutch colony which they called New York.

Great Britain's conquest of New Netherland plugged the breach between the British colonies, thus forming a continuous English presence from Canada to the Floridas. It eliminated the Dutch as commercial rivals on the Continent and ultimately brought the British and the French into confrontation for continental supremacy.

Pertinent Literature

Keesler, Henry H. and Eugene Rachlis. *Peter Stuyvesant and His New York.* New York: Harper & Row Publishers, 1959.

It is perhaps unfortunate that scholars of Early New York history have given so little attention to the British conquest of New Netherland. There is no study devoted exclusively to the questions of why and how the British set out to wrest New Netherland from their great commercial rivals. Consequently, one must turn to more general studies of early New York or to biographies of prominent colonists.

Such a course is not without its pitfalls, as is evident in Keesler and Rachlis' chapters on the fall of New Netherland. Since their work is a biography of Stuyvesant, the account of New Netherland's capture is seen through Stuyvesant's eyes, without regard to some of the larger implications of British interest in the Dutch colony. The book says almost nothing about British reasons for the attack. Unless a student was familiar with Charles M. Andrews' *The Colonial Period of American History,* his reliance upon Keesler and Rachlis would convey a false impression of British motives.

In Chapter XIII, which Keesler and Rachlis entitle "The Plot Against New Netherland," the authors interpret British designs as the product of a feud between the New Netherlanders and the British colonists in Connecticut over which government possessed jurisdiction in the largely-English settlements on eastern Long Island and over long-standing boundary disputes. These conflicts had existed since the founding of Connecticut in 1636, and they were sources of continual irritation between the two colonies, especially when the Indians took to the warpath; in Dutch minds the notion persisted that the British encouraged the Indians to raid Dutch settlements. Prior to 1660, Stuyvesant had been able to maintain an uneasy balance through diplomacy, but the restoration of the Stuarts complicated matters when Charles II put eastern Long Island under Connecticut's jurisdiction. Thus armed, the Connecticut government aimed at securing the whole of Long Island, thereby provoking a confrontation which the British home government sought to resolve by force of arms.

These disputes obviously generated friction between the two colonies. They probably played a role in the British government's decision to seize New Netherland, but the interpretation which Keesler and Rachlis advance obscures the major consideration which motivated the British, namely, the wish to eliminate the Dutch as commercial rivals.

These chapters do, however, provide insight into Stuyvesant's final years as governor and his understanding of the threat posed by British interests. Indeed, Stuyvesant is pictured as being more perceptive about the inherent dangers of New Netherland's situation than his superiors in Amsterdam.

Bancroft, George. *History of the United States of America, from the Discovery of the Continent.* 24th ed. Boston: Little, Brown, and Company, 1872.

George Bancroft's *History of the United States* is one of the classic works in American historiography. Begun at a time when the fires of American nationalism were being kindled, it gave new meaning to the great events in America's past when the United States was in the midst of a period of tremendous growth and intellectual flowering. One of the more obvious manifestations of this ferment was the advent of Jacksonian democracy, that *mélange* of men and ideas which sought to make America the most socially and politically democratic society in the world. Bancroft's view of the past seemed to buttress those ends.

The *History of the United States* is a general examination of the American past from Columbus' discovery to the end of the American Revolution, and most of the work is given over to consideration of the Revolution's causes.

The first three volumes, however, are devoted to a discussion of colonial origins. In the case of New Netherland, Bancroft picks up the colony's beginnings with the Dutch struggle for independence in the sixteenth century, which he discusses at length. He finds much to admire in the Dutch: they had overthrown their Catholic rulers; they had established a republic in which religious diversity was tolerated; and they had transformed a tiny portion of Europe's people and land mass into the world's premier commercial power. In short, the Dutch seemed to exemplify progress. Similarly, there were praiseworthy aspects about New Netherland. The colony's government tolerated all religious sects, even Jews, and it became a haven for Europe's dispossessed.

But New Netherland was not without its flaws, for there was "no distinct legislative power to the people." In Bancroft's view, much of the colony's history prior to 1664 was that of struggle between colonial authorities and the people, who, "without a teacher, had become convinced of the right of resistance." Bancroft has few kind words for Stuyvesant, since the Governor doubted "man's capacity for self-government." Given these considerations, Great Britain's conquest of the Dutch colony represented some progress, because "English liberties were to be added to the security of property." — *W.M.B.*

Additional Recommended Reading

Andrews, Charles M. *The Colonial Period of American History.* Vol. IV: *England's Commercial and Colonial Policy.* New Haven: Yale University Press, 1964. Discusses Anglo-Dutch rivalry and relates the conquest of New Netherland to overall British efforts to create a self-contained colonial empire.

Raesly, Ellis L. *Portrait of New Netherland.* New York: Columbia University Press, 1945. Stresses the political and cultural aspects of the Dutch colony.

Wertenbaker, Thomas J. *The Founding of American Civilization: The Middle Colonies.* New York: Charles Scribner's Sons, 1938. Devotes more attention to social and cultural features of colonial life than to political matters.

Condon, Thomas J. *New York Beginnings: The Commercial Origins of New Netherland.* New York: New York University Press, 1968. A study of New Netherland emphasizing the role of the Dutch West India Company and stopping short of the British conquest of the colony.

FRENCH EXPLORATION OF THE MISSISSIPPI VALLEY

Type of event: Socioeconomic: desire of the French to exploit and Christianize the West
Time: 1673-1740's
Locale: Mississippi River Valley

Principal personages:

JEAN BAPTISTE TALON (THE "GREAT INTENDANT") (1625?-1694), who sent the first expeditions to the Great Lakes

LOUIS JOLLIET (1645-1700), explorer and trapper to whom Talon entrusted the task of finding the Mississippi river

JACQUES MARQUETTE (1637-1675), Jesuit priest who accompanied Jolliet and whose journal is the only record of the journey

LOUIS DE BUADE (COMTE DE FRONTENAC) (1620-1698), known as the "Iron Governor," who sponsored the La Salle expeditions

RENÉ ROBERT CAVELIER (SIEUR DE LA SALLE) (1643-1687), French nobleman who first followed the Mississippi river to the Gulf of Mexico and who later made an abortive attempt to found a colony there

PIERRE LEMOYNE D'IBERVILLE (SIEUR D'IBERVILLE) (1661-1706), who in 1699 established Biloxi, the first French settlement on the Gulf of Mexico

ÉTIENNE DE BOURGMOUND (fl. 1714), Governor of Detroit and later Commandant of the Missouri, who extended French control into the Osage country near present-day Independence, Missouri

CHARLES CLAUDE DU TISNÉ (fl. 1714), the first Frenchman to explore the Kansas and Republican rivers

PETER MALLET (fl. 1739-1740), and

PAUL MALLET (fl. 1739-1740), brothers who first used the Santa Fe Trail in 1739

SIEUR DE LA VÉRENDRYE (PIERRE GAULTIER DE VARENNES) (1685-1749), who explored Manitoba and the Dakotas sixty years before the Lewis and Clark expedition

Summary of Event

The exploration of the Mississippi River Valley was the logical result of France's desire to monopolize the fur trade of the St. Lawrence basin and extend its control to the rich fur-bearing rivers and lakes of the interior of North America. Expanding upon the explorations made by Samuel de Champlain in the early 1600's, Jean Nicolet opened the Ottawa river route to Lake Huron, Lake Michigan, and Green Bay in 1634. The trappers, or *"coureurs des bois"* (runners of the woods) as the French called them, were

144

forced to take this northern route to the western Great Lakes because of the constant enmity of the Iroquois Confederation. Living in upper New York, the Iroquois warriors hated the French partly because Champlain had helped Algonquin war parties to attack their villages, and partly because they wished to control the fur trade between the Europeans and the western tribes, which the French refused to allow.

The various Iroquois wars prevented the French from assuming control of the Great Lakes until 1671 when Nicholas Perrot guided Simon François Daumont, Sieur de St. Lusson, to Sault Sainte Marie where the latter formally took possession of the area for France and signed trade treaties with sixteen western tribes the following year. Perrot was the first man licensed to explore the Great Lakes by Jean Baptiste Talon, the intendant in charge of the judiciary and finances of the colonial government. Prior to Perrot's expeditions, Menard Chouart, Sieur des Groseillers, and Pierre Esprit Radisson had engaged in an illegal exploration and trade mission to Chequamegon Bay on Lake Superior from 1654 to 1660. The government, however, confiscated their sixty canoeloads of furs to discourage further unlicensed endeavors.

Talon, now wishing to extend French power, licensed two dozen traders and missionaries to go to Wisconsin. Two missions, St. Francis at Green Bay and St. Jacques on the Fox river, became the centers of French activity. Talon also engaged Louis Jolliet to explore the Mississippi river. In 1673, Jolliet, accompanied by Jacques Marquette, a Jesuit priest, left Michilimackinac and traveled across Green Bay and up the Fox river. They then made a portage from the headwaters of the Fox river to the Wisconsin river and descended the Wisconsin to its source. From there, they went down the Mississippi river in canoes as far as the mouth of the Arkansas. They identified and located numerous Indian tribes along the way. Becoming convinced that the Mississippi flowed into the Gulf of Mexico and not the Gulf of California, they turned around and ascended the Mississippi. On their return they discovered the mouth of the Illinois river and ascended it. From the Illinois they made a portage to the Chicago river through which they reëntered Lake Michigan at its southwestern end.

While Jolliet and Marquette were floating down the Mississippi, Talon was turning over the colonial government to Louis de Buade (Comte de Frontenac). Frontenac continued Talon's policy of exploration and trade, although he developed a few new concepts of his own. Frontenac's "Grand Plan" envisioned a series of forts west of the Appalachian Mountains to exclude the British from the Mississippi River Valley. He then hoped to tap the rich fur supply and ship it to France either through Quebec, or through a new city which he envisioned near the mouth of the Mississippi river.

The chief proponent of Frontenac's plan was René Robert Cavelier, Sieur de la Salle. Fluent in eight Indian languages, La Salle, like Jolliet, also believed that the Mississippi river flowed into the Gulf of Mexico. In 1669, his government authorized him to explore and prove his belief. For the next fifteen years, La Salle traveled throughout the West. First, he went down the Ohio river to the falls at Louisville. Returning to France, he obtained a five-year trade monopoly from the crown. La Salle built his own sailing ship, the *Griffon,* to supply the several forts that he constructed near the Chicago portage.

Disaster haunted La Salle and delayed his actual exploration of the Mississippi until 1682. He lost several shiploads of supplies from France in the Atlantic Ocean, and the *Griffon* sank in one of the Great Lakes. In addition, La Salle was a martinet who lacked the finesse necessary to command a body of men without trouble. His arrogance and autocratic attitude caused several mutinies, the suppression of which also delayed his departure. On April 9, 1682, however, La Salle finally found the mouth of the Mississippi, and he claimed the whole area, which he named Louisiana after Louis XIV, for France.

In 1684, following Frontenac's original proposals, La Salle departed from France with four ships, one hundred soldiers, and three hundred settlers to establish a city in Louisiana. Unfortunately, he failed to find the river's mouth from the Gulf side, and Spanish raiders, shipwreck, and desertion plagued the colonists. La Salle and the survivors finally landed at Matagorda Bay, Texas, where they were stranded through the loss of their ships. Making a futile search for the Mississippi river by land, La Salle decided that the expedition's only hope for survival was to go overland to Illinois. In 1687, the party set out on the long journey. La Salle's authoritarian leadership caused much dissension and led to his murder near the Brazos river. The rest of the party struggled onward to Illinois

where they met a relief expedition led by Henri de Tonti, a one-armed Italian who was in charge of La Salle's Illinois operations.

Meanwhile, French control of the upper Mississippi tightened with the activities of Daniel Greysolon (Sieur du Lhut, or Duluth), who explored the western end of Lake Superior and discovered the Falls of St. Anthony where the twin cities of St. Paul and Minneapolis now stand. Other Frenchmen opened up the Galena lead mines, extracted some copper from Minnesota, and founded Cahokia in 1699 and Kaskaskia in 1700. La Salle's dream city in Louisiana was made possible by Pierre Lemoyne d'Iberville, who rediscovered the mouth of the Mississippi and was instrumental in founding Fort Maurepas, or Biloxi, in 1699. His brother, Jean Baptiste Lemoyne (Sieur de Bienville), established Mobile in 1702 and New Orleans in 1718; the latter became the gateway to the interior of North America.

French activities along the Mississippi river led to the exploration and exploitation of its major tributary, the Missouri river. Although others had preceded him, Étienne de Bourgmond, sometime Governor of Detroit, made the first extensive journey up the Missouri river in 1714. After traveling eight hundred leagues upriver, Bourgmond returned to write a book on his experiences. Bourgmond was followed by Charles du Tisné who explored the Missouri river as far as the Osage villages where he traded for furs and horses. He then advanced westward on the Kansas river to the Pawnee country, but only over the protests of the Osage, who forced him to leave most of his firearms behind. The Pawnee refused to grant Tisné permission to contact the Comanche farther west. Undaunted by Tisné's failure, Bourgmond, now Commandant of the Missouri, established Fort Orleans in Carroll County, Missouri, and through adroit diplomacy managed to contact the Comanche. In 1724 he made an impressive series of treaties with several plains tribes, and even took some of their chiefs to France to see the king.

The upper Missouri river was explored separately by several explorers going westward from the shores of Lake Superior. The principal man of importance there was Pierre La Vérendrye who, with his sons, Pierre II, François, and Louis Joseph, received a government fur trade monopoly for the region in 1730. Basing their operations at Fort La Reine on the Assiniboine river in Manitoba in 1737, the La Verendrye family traveled over much of the present-day Dakotas and Wyoming, searching for a water route to the Pacific and exploiting the Indian trade. In 1743, they buried a lead plate near Pierre, South Dakota, claiming the land for France. The plate was accidentally found by a fourteen-year-old schoolgirl in 1914.

At the same time that the La Vérendryes were exploring the upper Missouri river, two brothers, Peter and Paul Mallet, were journeying to New Mexico, the farthest west any Frenchman had ventured. Passing through the Osage, Pawnee, and Comanche lands along the route made famous by Americans one hundred years later, the Mallets reached the town of Santa Fe. The suspicious Spanish immediately jailed the brothers, but in 1740 they were released to return to Louisiana. Because of Spanish hostility and the decline of the French empire, the Santa Fe Trail was seldom used for the next eighty years.

The French exploration of the Mississippi River Valley is of great significance in American history. The French takeover of the interior valley led directly to the clash with Great Britain in the French and Indian War (1754-1763), which cost France its entire American empire and ultimately resulted in the American Revolution. Although the *coureurs des bois* erroneously believed that the Platte river was the main fork of the Missouri, by 1740 they knew much about the Trans-Mississippi West that would be utilized by the American mountain men and the British Hudson Bay Company nearly a century later. In addition, the French made a lasting contribution to the culture of the north woods and Louisiana that remains today.

Pertinent Literature

Parkman, Francis. *The Discovery of the Great West: La Salle.* Edited by William R. Taylor. New York: Holt, Rinehart, and Winston Inc., 1956.

Francis Parkman is the first historian who comes to mind whenever one studies the rise and fall of New France. His works are classics in their field and have gone through numerous editions since they first appeared in the late nineteenth century. Parkman was a typical historian for his time, when most scholars were New Englanders who wrote in a literary manner, doing what they believed was a service to the nation by preserving its history. They were men of leisure who wrote history as a hobby and emphasized biography.

Most of Parkman's seven-volume history of New France was constructed around key persons, because he believed that great men molded events. The era between 1643 and 1689 revolved around La Salle because, to Parkman, he personified the extension of French power down the Mississippi river to the Gulf of Mexico. Other volumes focus on Samuel de Champlain *(Pioneers of France in the New World),* the Jesuit fathers in the Huron country *(The Jesuits in North America),* Frontenac *(Count Frontenac and New France under Louis XIV),* and Louis Joseph, Marquis de Montcalm, and his British opponent, General James Wolfe *(Montcalm and Wolfe).* The remaining two volumes in his history of New France, *The Old Regime in Canada,* and *A Half-Century of Conflict,* deal with the feudal nature of the French colonial government and Queen Anne's and King George's Wars.

Most historians write with a purpose or philosophy of history in mind, and Parkman is no exception. His main concern was with that nineteenth century demigod: progress. Parkman believed that progress was inevitable. He saw the struggle between France and Great Britain in America as a fight between the noble, progressive Anglo-Saxons and the decadent French; liberty and Protestantism versus absolutism and Catholicism.

Parkman believed that history was primarily a literary effort. Hence, his volumes make the events live again by emphasizing the romantic and heroic aspects of the past. In attaining his high literary effect, Parkman used methods considered unprofessional by more recent historians. He readily invents detail for his account, including dialogue and terrain descriptions, using his fertile imagination to fill in gaps if no actual accounts can be found. He sometimes plagiarizes other authors' works, reworking the original, but not indicating his sources. Parkman also rearranges the sequence of events to make the story more vivid and easier to follow. Throughout his work, he moralizes on events, which he sees with pro-British or American outlook.

The Discovery of the Great West: La Salle is typical of Parkman's style. He chose this explorer as his main character because La Salle was easily dramatized, not necessarily because he was historically significant. To Parkman, La Salle demonstrates gentility, veracity, disinterested patriotism, and supreme self-control. These factors together with his good breeding cause La Salle to achieve things in Parkman's eyes. Critics of Parkman, such as William R. Taylor, accuse him of distorting, suppressing contrary evidence, and quoting out of context to make a "half-crazed French explorer a tragic hero." Parkman suffered from a neurotic condition, says Taylor, which caused him to interpret La Salle, who was also neurotic, as a hero when, in fact, La Salle failed to accomplish much during his entire lifetime. Taylor implies that Parkman's history and La Salle's iron will are products of brilliant minds bordering on insanity.

Despite these shortcomings, Parkman's volumes remain among the most exciting and compelling historical works ever written. Some recent historians maintain that his work should be revised, but it would be difficult to retain Parkman's uncanny and envia-

ble ability to make history interesting.

Steck, Francis B. *The Jolliet-Marquette Expedition, 1673.* Glendale, California: Arthur H. Clark Company, 1928.

The purpose of Steck's volume is to place the Jolliet-Marquette expedition in its proper historical perspective. The author discusses three major problems: did the French truly "discover" the Mississippi river? Was Marquette or Jolliet the leader of the exploring party? Was the narrative of the journey really written by Father Marquette?

As to the first question, Steck maintains that discovery involves obtaining knowledge or sight of something not previously known or perceived. Using this criterion, he denies that Jolliet and Marquette "discovered" the Mississippi river, because its existence was first noted by the Spanish explorer Alvarez de Pineda in the early 1500's. Steck finds that the French verb *"découvir"* has been too literally translated by Englishmen. Instead of "discover," the French meant a more subtle concept; *"découvir"* also means "to explore"—hence, the Jolliet-Marquette expedition explored something already known. Far from discovery, the French government commissioned Jolliet to ascertain if the Mississippi might yield the long-sought water route to the Pacific Ocean—the fabled Northwest Passage.

The leadership of the expedition, maintains Steck, was given to Jolliet,

not Marquette. This problem arose after the 1673 journey and concerns relations between the Church and the state in New France. The Society of Jesus claimed that Marquette led the expedition, hoping that the French crown would give it a virtual monopoly of control in the new West, and exclude the Franciscans and the fur traders from their area. Being a Franciscan himself, Steck has a reason for criticizing the Jesuit plan, but he does make a convincing case for his position. The expedition, concludes Steck, was secular and was commanded by Jolliet. The author finds it ironic that Marquette's role, as amplified by the Jesuits, has been accepted without question by historians, and that Jolliet's role has been almost obliterated.

Finally, Steck asserts that the journal of the expedition, which was credited to Marquette, was not written by him at all. Using an analysis of the manuscript's handwriting, general tone, literary style, and contents, Steck charges that the document was probably written by Jolliet and amplified by others. Although Steck's account is sometimes laborious in detail, he presents an intriguing story of the Jolliet-Marquette expedition of 1673. — *W.L.R.*

Additional Recommended Reading

Eccles, William J. *Canada and Louis XIV, 1663-1701.* New York: Oxford University Press, 1964. One of the best recent studies of early Canada, covering governmental, economic, and cultural aspects of New France.

Kellogg, Louise P. *The French Regime in Wisconsin and the Northwest.* Madison: The State Historical Society of Wisconsin, 1925. Concentrating on the discovery of the Great

Lakes and Wisconsin, Kellogg discusses early exploration, mining, and the fur trade in the Old Northwest.

Terrell, John U. *La Salle: The Life and Times of an Explorer.* New York: Waybright and Talley, 1968. A popular account of La Salle's exploration of the Ohio and Mississippi River Valleys.

Crouse, Nellis M. *Lemoyne d'Iberville: Soldier of New France.* Ithaca: Cornell University Press, 1954. A biography of the man who founded the first French settlements on the Louisiana and Mississippi Gulf Coasts.

Crouse, Nellis M. *La Vérendrye: Fur Trader and Explorer.* Ithaca: Cornell University Press, 1956. An interesting account of the La Vérendrye family who did much to further French interests in Manitoba and the Dakotas.

Nasatir, Abraham P. *Before Lewis and Clark: Documents Illustrating the History of the Missouri, 1785-1804.* St. Louis: St. Louis Historical Documents Foundation, 1952. 2 vols. Primarily a collection of documents, Nasatir's introduction to the first volume is a fine narrative of the French exploration of the Missouri river between 1673 and 1804.

BACON'S REBELLION

Type of event: Military: uprising against royal authority
Time: April, 1676-January, 1677
Locale: Eastern Virginia

Principal personages:

NATHANIEL BACON (1647-1676), who commanded the rebel forces against the Indians and the royal government

SIR WILLIAM BERKELEY (1606-1677), Governor of Virginia 1642-1652 and 1660-1676

SIR HENRY CHICHELEY (fl. 1677), Lieutenant Governor of Virginia, whom Governor Berkeley placed in command of a force to pursue the Indians early in 1676 only to countermand the order

JOSEPH INGRAM (fl. 1676-1677), Commander of the rebel forces after Bacon's death

PHILIP LUDWELL (fl. 1660-1704), member of the Council of State, and close adviser to Governor Berkeley

ROBERT BEVERLEY (fl.1675-1677), clerk of the General Assembly and Berkeley's chief lieutenant in the suppression of the rebellion

SIR JOHN BERRY (fl. 1666-1667), and

FRANCIS MORYSON (fl. 1676-1677), two of the Royal Commissioners sent to investigate causes of the rebellion

HERBERT JEFFREYS (fl. 1676-1677), the third Royal Commissioner, who succeeded Berkeley as Governor

Summary of Event

In the early spring of 1676, circumstances were ripe for rebellion in Virginia. Although the complex causes of the rebellion are still being examined, it is possible to identify three principal causes for popular unrest: (1) the unstable political and social conditions resulting from a rapidly changing society; (2) the severe economic depression; and (3) Governor Sir William Berkeley's declining ability to govern effectively.

Instability was inherent in the rapid growth of population in Virginia after 1640. Competition for political power and social position increased after 1660

as the earlier settlers entrenched themselves in local political offices. Where a prosperous economy might have counteracted unstable political and social conditions, Virginia's economy stagnated after 1660. Chronic overproduction of an inferior quality of tobacco, aggravated by restrictive features of the Navigation Acts, drove the price of tobacco down. Expensive experimentation with methods of diversifying the economy and the need for defense measures against the Dutch and the Indians resulted in high taxes. In 1674 the colonists were further taxed to send agents to London to

151

lobby against the proprietary land grants to Lords Arlington and Culpepper. Circumstances conspired to exacerbate the planters' miseries, and Governor Berkeley's ineffectual leadership led to a general disaffection toward the government.

The events leading immediately to the rebellion grew out of a series of Indian raids which had begun in the summer of 1675. After forces of Virginians bent on revenge murdered numbers of friendly Susquehannocks on two separate occasions, the Indians increased the intensity of their raids throughout the fall and winter. Governor Berkeley angered the planters in the frontier settlements when he countermanded the order for a force to proceed against the marauding warriors. In keeping with Berkeley's overall Indian policy, the Assembly committed the colony to a defensive war, and the Governor ordered the erection of a chain of forts on the frontier.

In April an impatient group of upcountry planters persuaded one of their number, Nathaniel Bacon, Jr., to lead a band of volunteers against the Indians. Bacon, the ne'er-do-well son of an English gentleman, had not arrived in Virginia until 1674, but he had already been appointed to the Council of State. Governor Berkeley refused Bacon's request for a commission to raise volunteers and sent several letters warning him against becoming a mutineer. Unable to head off Bacon with his force of three hundred men, Berkeley, on May 10, 1676, declared him a rebel. On the same day, the Governor dissolved the "Long Assembly" and called for the first general elections in fifteen years, promising that the new Assembly would deal with the Indian threat and any other grievances.

Bacon's success in killing some Indians prompted the residents of Henrico County to send him to Jamestown as one of their new burgesses, but the Governor ordered his capture before he could take his seat. Bacon confessed his error and received a pardon from the Governor. Several days later he slipped off to Henrico.

The June Assembly met for twenty days and passed a series of acts dealing with the prosecution of the Indian war and with various local problems, especially concerning the misuse of political power. Although Bacon has often been credited with pushing through reform legislation, he did not return to Jamestown until June 23, when the session was nearly over. Arriving with five hundred armed men, he terrorized the Governor and the burgesses into granting him a commission to fight the Indians.

As soon as Bacon marched toward the falls of the James river, however, Berkeley again proclaimed him a rebel and tried to raise a force against him. Failing in his attempt, Berkeley fled to the eastern shore, leaving Bacon in control of the western shore. Upon arriving in Middle Plantation, Bacon issued a manifesto, the "Declaration of the People," which accused the Governor of numerous offenses against the colonists and called for his surrender. While Bacon then proceeded to seek out and fall upon the friendly Pamunkey Indians, Berkeley returned to Jamestown, and having reached agreement with Bacon's garrison, took possession of the capital. Several days later, Bacon arrived with six hundred men and besieged the town. The faintheartedness of Berkeley's men forced the Governor to concede the town. Bacon burned it on September 19. A little more than a month later, the rebellion fell apart at the news of Bacon's sudden death of the "Bloody Flux" and "Lousey Disease." Although Joseph Ingram made a bumbling attempt to lead the demoralized rebels, the last vestiges of rebellion were stamped out by February, 1677.

On January 29, the Royal Commissioners, John Berry, Francis Moryson and Herbert Jeffreys, arrived from England to investigate the uprising and restore order. Berkeley nullified the royal pardons which they brought for the rebels and ordered the execution of twenty-three men. His extreme cruelty was criticized by the commissioners, and Sir Herbert Jeffreys formally took over the government in April upon Berkeley's recall by the crown.

Pertinent Literature

Wertenbaker, Thomas J. *Torchbearer of the Revolution: The Story of Bacon's Rebellion and Its Leader.* Princeton: Princeton University Press, 1940.

For Wertenbaker, Nathaniel Bacon was "the greatest figure of the first century of American history." Begun in 1914 with the publication of *Virginia Under the Stuarts,* Wertenbaker's lifelong investigation of the rebellion resulted in the fullest statement of the "democratic" thesis about its causes. Although he employed a wide range of new sources, notably the official papers in the British Public Record Office and the British Museum, Wertenbaker's books bear the impress of the "progressive school of historiography." He views the first seventy years of Virginia history as a struggle for political, social, and economic power between democratic yeomen farmers and privileged aristocrats.

Wertenbaker's analysis of the origins of Virginia's population deals a severe blow to the long-standing notion that the colony had been peopled by Cavalier refugees from Cromwell's England. The great mass of immigrants to Virginia, according to Wertenbaker, were yeomen farmers who had escaped from oppressive conditions in England in order to gain the freedoms afforded by the New World. But by mid-century the door to advancement was closing for the humble immigrant, and the Navigation Acts were depriving him of a decent price for the tobacco he grew. Governor Berkeley had at first appeared as a friend to the colonists, supporting liberal reforms and aggressively fighting the hostile Indians. After his restoration to the governorship in 1660, however, he changed into a power-hungry despot bent on destroying representative government. In order to retain his clique of favorites in power, he refused to call new elections for fifteen years.

The man who came from England in 1674 to deliver the Virginians from oppression was, for Wertenbaker, a combination of George Washington, Thomas Jefferson, Sam Adams, Nathan Hale, and Robert E. Lee. The young Nathaniel Bacon, sentimentally idealized by Wertenbaker, was a lover of liberty and justice even as a child. Upon his arrival in Henrico County, he was immediately impressed by the suffering of the neighboring planters. Wertenbaker suggests that Berkeley, suspecting Bacon's democratic tendencies, appointed him to the council in the hope of winning him over to his side.

The Indians depicted by Wertenbaker were by no means noble savages, but cruel devils who delighted in committing atrocities. Berkeley's refusal to allow the frontier settlers to deal with the Indians was but one more example of his willingness to sacrifice the colonists' best interests for his own profit. When Bacon agreed to lead the planter volunteers against the Indians, it was tantamount to the stand of the Minutemen at Lexington. Wertenbaker describes the rebels as "poor planters ground down by excessive taxes; hardy, weatherbeaten frontiersmen; ragged freedmen, some mounted, others trudging along on foot, all united by a common misfortune and by love for their youthful leader." Whether the rebels were attacking friendly Indians or holding loyalists' wives as hostages, Wertenbaker attributes their actions to noble motives. Although Bacon did not

arrive with his men at the June, 1676, session of the General Assembly until it was nearly over, Wertenbaker credits the rebel with pushing through one liberal law after another.

The overt reason for the rebellion's failure, according to Wertenbaker, was the death of its indispensable leader. Even so, it was not without positive results. The rebellion put an end to Berkeley's corruption, fostered political reforms, and gave the English Privy Council a taste of what the colonists might do when driven to desperation. Most significantly, the uprising foreshadowed the American Revolution, showing that the forces which would one day result in Independence were active even in 1676.

Wertenbaker's extremely biased work is important both because it epitomizes the "democratic" tradition in scholarship and because it has served as a stepping-off point for later, more objective investigations into the rebellion's causes.

Washburn, Wilcomb E. *The Governor and the Rebel.* Chapel Hill: University of North Carolina Press, 1957.

The democratic thesis about the causes of Bacon's Rebellion espoused by Wertenbaker stood virtually unchallenged until this assault by Wilcomb Washburn appeared. Relying heavily upon the papers of the Marquis of Bath, Washburn reverses the molds in which Wertenbaker had cast the two principal antagonists. He absolves Governor Berkeley of major responsibility for the rebellion and places it instead upon Nathaniel Bacon and his Indian-hating followers.

Washburn finds no evidence to suggest that Berkeley was either unjust or

dishonest. Disputing Wertenbaker's claim that the Governor favored his friends with large land grants, Washburn contends that Berkeley possessed no power to do so. During his administration, land was granted almost entirely under the headright system, whereby a settler received fifty acres for each immigrant brought in. Washburn's research reveals that Bacon's followers actually possessed landholdings comparable in size to those of Berkeley's supporters. Some of the rebels had records of antagonizing the Indians by scheming to cheat them out of their rightful lands.

The colonists' principal complaints, as evidenced in the county grievances submitted to the Commissioners of Investigation after the rebellion, dealt with matters over which Berkeley had little control. Although the Governor was generally disliked in the period before the rebellion, he was not accused of graft or corruption. The severe economic depression caused by the low tobacco prices and the Navigation Acts so disturbed the planters that they centered their frustrations upon the Indian problem.

Berkeley hoped to maintain the peace with the Indians which had lasted since the 1640's. To counteract the antagonism aroused by white expansion onto Indian lands, he urged the Assembly to prohibit trade with the Indians and to authorize the building of frontier forts for defense. Washburn's thesis centers around the contention that the frontier planters hated Berkeley because he refused to wage war against basically benign Indians. Earlier historians had always overlooked the aggressiveness of the frontiersmen as a primary cause of the rebellion. Washburn argues that these planters, unlike Wertenbaker's fervent democrats, actually had no concept of the rights of others, and in fact expected to gain both privileged positions and estates when Bacon took control.

Since the "democratic" historians have always credited Bacon with pushing through the so-called reform legislation in the Assembly of June, 1676, Washburn undertakes an analysis of the laws passed there. He concludes that not only were most of the laws passed in Bacon's absence, but also that the rebel, bent only upon obtaining a commission to fight the Indians, had no interest in reforms. Moreover, the laws were not particularly revolutionary. Other sessions of the Assembly had passed similar ones to remedy injustices; in fact, the very next session repassed the June laws after the crown had disallowed them.

Washburn suggests that historians may have been influenced in their indictment of the Governor more by his harsh punishment of the rebels after the rebellion than by his actions before it. The Royal Commissioners were generally sympathetic toward the rebels and critical of Berkeley's vengeful acts. Because Berkeley died before having an opportunity to see the King, he was deprived of the chance to defend his actions. Ironically, some of his supporters eventually became known as defenders of the people against arbitrary royal governors and commissioners.

The Governor and the Rebel is an important revisionist study, exposing many of the false assumptions made by ardent admirers of Bacon. Yet Washburn's identification of the root causes of the rebellion as the aggressiveness of the frontier planters and the conflict of alien cultures is somewhat simplistic. Since his study begins only with the Indian raids of 1675, it fails to investigate the possible effect of political and social instability and economic depression upon the planters. In his attempt to expose Bacon as a demagogue, Washburn is too willing to excuse the faults of Berkeley. — *W.M.B.*

Bacon's Rebellion

Additional Recommended Reading

Beverley, Robert. *The History and Present State of Virginia.* Edited by Louis B. Wright. Chapel Hill: University of North Carolina Press, 1947. Somewhat pro-Berkeley, this perceptive study emphasizes the economic difficulties and Indian troubles which led up to the rebellion.

Craven, Wesley F. *The Southern Colonies in the Seventeenth Century, 1607-1689.* Baton Rouge: Louisiana State University Press, 1949. Emphasizing the complexity of the rebellion, Craven's well-balanced account urges further research into its causes.

Morton, Richard L. *Colonial Virginia.* Vol. I: *The Tidewater Period, 1607-1710.* Chapel Hill: University of North Carolina Press, 1960. The most recent presentation of the "Progressive" school's interpretation, this study closely parallels Wertenbaker's works.

Andrews, Charles M. ed. *Narratives of the Insurrections, 1675 to 1690.* New York: Charles Scribner's Sons, 1915. Andrews includes three contemporary accounts of the rebellion, two by eyewitnesses and finally the official narrative of the Royal Commissioners of Investigation.

Wertenbaker, Thomas J. *Virginia Under the Stuarts, 1607-1688.* Princeton: Princeton University Press, 1914. This is an earlier, more balanced presentation of the views expressed by the same author in *Torchbearer of the Revolution.*

FOUNDING OF PENNSYLVANIA

Type of event: Religious: desire of many Quakers to establish a colony
Time: 1681
Locale: Pennsylvania

> *Principal personages:*
> CHARLES II (1630-1685), King of Great Britain 1660-1685
> WILLIAM PENN (1644-1718), Proprietor of Pennsylvania
> WILLIAM MARKHAM (1635?-1704), Penn's personal agent in the
>   colony and Deputy Governor 1681-1682 and 1693-1699
> JAMES LOGAN (1674-1751), leader of the Proprietary Party
> DAVID LLOYD (1656?-1731), leader of the Popular Party
> THOMAS LLOYD (1640-1694?), president of the Council 1684-
>   1686 and 1690-1691, Deputy Governor 1691-1692
> ISRAEL PEMBERTON (1715-1779), leader of the strict Quakers
>   in the 1740's and 1750's

Summary of Event

On March 4, 1681, King Charles II of Great Britain granted to William Penn the colony of Pennsylvania. Named after his father Sir William Penn, an admiral who had aided Charles' accession, it was offered as payment of a debt of sixteen thousand pounds sterling which the King owed Sir William.

The charter given to William Penn made him Proprietor of the colony. It was similar to other proprietary charters in that it made Penn the owner and grantor of all land in the province and gave him authority to establish the form of government, appoint the governor, and initiate and promulgate laws with the advice and consent of the freemen in assembly. However, this particular charter was unique in its restriction of proprietary prerogatives. Three provisions assured the enforcement of the Navigation Acts passed by Parliament prior to the establishment of the colony: first, laws passed in the colony were to be submitted to the king for his confirmation or disallowance, and the king retained the right to hear and decide appeals from the courts of the province; second, the Church of England was assured a place in the colony; and third, the charter contained a promise that the king would not impose taxes on the colony "unless the same be with the consent of the proprietary, or chiefe governour, or assembly, or by act of Parliament." These provisions implemented Great Britain's new colonial policy of limiting provincial self-government and centralizing the British Empire as a means of securing the commercial and defensive interests of the Mother Country.

Penn's avowed purpose in establishing a colony in America was to found a "holy experiment" based on Quaker doctrines. Pennsylvania was to be a holy commonwealth, characterized by peace, brotherly love, and religious toleration, which would serve as "an example . . . to the nations. . . ." At the same time, the colony offered a haven to Quakers who were being persecuted in England for their nonconformist beliefs.

One month after receiving his charter from the King, Penn began advertising the new province to prospective settlers in England, Ireland, and Wales. *Some Account of the Province of Pennsylvania* was published in April, 1682, the first of eleven such publications designed to attract colonists. To the colony Penn dispatched his cousin William Markham, who was to serve as Deputy Governor until the Proprietor's arrival. Not until August 30, 1682, did Penn himself set sail for the colony in the ship *Welcome*, along with about one hundred colonists. Shortly before leaving England, he had obtained the Lower Counties (Delaware) from the Duke of York, an intimate friend, thereby gaining access to the Atlantic for his new colony.

Like other proprietors in the New World, Penn hoped to profit from the sale or rent of land in his colony, but his primary aim was a religious one. He was a member of the Society of Friends, or Quakers, founded by George Fox in the late 1640's. One of the many radical religious sects which emerged from the turbulence of the English Civil War, Quakerism embraced the Puritan social ethic but went beyond Puritanism in its rejection of formal creeds and worship. Quakers were mystics, believing that the Holy Spirit dwelled within each person, and that whoever yielded completely to the promptings of this divine presence, or "Inner Light," would be perfectly regenerated. Their ecclesiastical organization was based on the Puritan theory of congregationalism in that each congregation, or "meeting," was completely autonomous (though ultimately a hierarchy of meetings developed, similar in structure and purpose to that of the Presbyterians); it differed from Puritanism in its rejection of a national church. Like other sectarians, Quakers insisted on separation of church and state and viewed the meeting as a voluntary association composed only of believers. Two important social consequences of Quaker religious beliefs were equalitarianism and humanitarianism.

Before sailing to America, Penn had drawn up the "first frame of government" to serve as a constitution for the new colony. It provided for a governor appointed by the proprietor, a council of seventy-two members which was to be the source of all legislation, and an assembly of two hundred which had the power to accept or reject bills initiated by the council. Both the council and the assembly were elective bodies, with a property qualification for voting. The governor had a triple vote in the council but no veto over the actions of the council or assembly. When the two houses proved to be unwieldy, Penn issued a "second frame," or Charter of Liberties, in 1683, reducing the number of councilors to eighteen and assemblymen to thirty-six, and modifying the suffrage requirement. During the two years that Penn governed the colony, over 150 laws were passed by the legislature implementing the "holy experiment." In 1696, Governor William Markham issued a "third frame" which further modified suffrage requirements, reduced the council to twelve members and the assembly to twenty-four, and granted the latter body the right to initiate legislation. A "fourth frame," known as the

Charter of Privileges and drawn up by Penn in 1701, created a one-house legislature by vesting legislative power in the assembly, subject to the governor's veto, and limiting the council to executive and judicial powers. The council was appointed by the governor instead of being elected by the freemen.

Penn issued the Charter of Privileges in order to end almost twenty years of quarreling between council and assembly, the former asserting its superior status against the latter's demands for a greater share in the government of the colony. The assembly had considerably enlarged its power from 1692 to 1694 when the colony was under royal rule. Markham's "third frame," issued after the Crown returned Pennsylvania to Penn, also extended the prerogatives of the assembly, and the Charter of Privileges establishing a unicameral legislature represented a further triumph for that body.

With the council eliminated both as a legislative and also as an elective body, the assembly transferred its opposition to the governor. In the early eighteenth century, two parties dominated Pennsylvania politics: the Proprietary Party led by James Logan, which sought to centralize authority in the hands of the Governor and the council, and the Popular Party led by David Lloyd, which sought to expand the powers of the assembly. The main political issue was the Quaker principle of pacifism, which underwent a critical test in 1756 when warfare between Indians and Pennsylvania backwoodsmen erupted on the frontier. A declaration of war against the Delaware and Shawnee Indians by the Governor and the council resulted in the Quakers' decision to withdraw from the assembly rather than compromise their stand against war. This withdrawal ended almost seventy-five years of Quaker rule over the colony of Pennsylvania.

Pertinent Literature

Tolles, Frederick B. *Meeting House and Counting House: The Quaker Merchants of Colonial Philadelphia, 1682-1763.* Chapel Hill: University of North Carolina Press, 1948.

The thesis of this volume on Quakerism in colonial Philadelphia was suggested by George Fox's admonition to the first Pennsylvania colonists: "My friends, that are gone, and are going over to plant, and make outward plantations in America, keep your own plantations in your hearts, with the spirit and power of God, that your own vines and lilies be not hurt." Tolles interprets the history of the Holy Experiment in terms of the tension between the inward and outward plantations, a tension symbolized by the two institutions of Quaker Philadelphia, the meeting house and counting house. The first seventy-five years of the Pennsylvania colony were concerned with the cultivation of the outward plantation. The withdrawal of the Quakers from politics in 1756 was the beginning of a shift to the inward plantation. As Tolles points out, the Quaker experience in the New World exhibits with striking clarity the transformation of sect into church; what was unique about the Quakers was their ultimate return to the sectarian posture, refusing to compromise with the world and insisting on purity and perfection.

Once established in Philadelphia, Quakers achieved economic preëminence, a fact which Tolles attributes not to their early arrival in Pennsylvania but to their pursuit of the Calvinist economic ethic which they had carried over from Puritanism into their own religious and social philosophy. The Quaker economic ethic "looked upon the material world of daily toil and daily bread as God's world in which men were called to do His will," and, like the Puritan code, adjured Friends to love the world with "weaned affections." The distinctiveness of Quakerism, according to Tolles, lay in its combining "the ethical position of the Anabaptists with the Calvinist attitude toward the material world. . . ."

The fortunes derived from commerce and manufacturing fostered the rise of a Quaker aristocracy in Philadelphia, which became the embodiment of the contradiction or tension inherent in Quakerism. With economic wealth went political hegemony. In turn, wealth and political power fostered "a subtle but constantly growing tendency, more noticeable among some Friends than others, towards conformity to the world against which the primitive Friends had so vigorously and persistently protested." Thus the Quaker economic ethic produced tendencies which worked directly against the perfectionist and separatist elements of the Quaker religion. The crisis of the 1750's and the retirement of the Quakers from politics produced a resolution of the contradiction. "After seventy-five years of preoccupation with the outward plantation, they turned their attention once again to cultivating the plantation within." The Quaker withdrawal marked the beginning of a reformation of the Society to root out the spirit of compromise and concession that had penetrated all phases of Quakerism in Pennsylvania.

In seeing the failure of Penn's Holy Experiment as a consequence of the contradiction inherent in Quakerism, Tolles in effect exonerates individual Quakers from blame for the gradual attenuation of the ideals of simplicity and spirituality on which the experiment was based. Daniel Boorstin, author of *The Americans: The Colonial Experience,* sees the history of Pennsylvania Quakerism in much the same terms as Tolles, but he is less restrained and indicts the Quakers for their "abdication of political power." Boorstin admits that the Quaker withdrawal "led them to look more closely into their own hearts and to preserve more strictly the tenets of their sect," but he contends that it also demonstrated "the unfitness of their dogmas for the larger tasks of building a new society in a new world." By contrast, Tolles is unwilling to pass judgment on the experience of the Pennsylvania Quakers. Instead he offers a balance sheet, conceding that the Quakers gained in "increased spirituality and humanitarian zeal" as a result of their withdrawal to the inward plantation, but noting that the price of their action was "the loss of immediate influence upon the world, the development of a narrowly sectarian mentality, and a liability to internal strife and tension."

James, Sydney V. *A People Among Peoples: Quaker Benevolence in Eighteenth-Century America.* Cambridge: Harvard University Press, 1963.

A People Among Peoples is the story of the "new Holy Experiment" which emerged from the crisis of the 1750's. In contrast to Boorstin and Tolles, Sydney V. James maintains that Quakers did not immure themselves in "sectarian isolation," but became "active members of the civil community." After the middle of the eighteenth century Quakers turned increasingly to humanitarian concerns and enterprises as a way of making "participation in the affairs of the community compatible with membership among Friends."

James views the history of eighteenth century American Quakerism in terms of two seemingly antithetical tendencies: "the intensification of asceticism, sectarian exclusivity, and corporate solidarity, on the one hand, and a desire to use the church to improve the world around it, on the other." These two tendencies evolved simultaneously; they were combined by Quakers in the late eighteenth century to produce "a creative response to the ordeal of war and civil unrest."

Both tendencies had begun prior to the 1750's. A growing uneasiness over Quaker compromises with the world and a desire for reformation were intensified by the Great Awakening and the crisis brought on by the French and Indian War. Quakers in Pennsylvania split into two factions, compromising Friends and strict Friends, and it was the latter group, led by Israel Pemberton, that withdrew from the Assembly in 1756 in opposition to the proclamation of war against the Indians. But, according to James, though strict Quakers were concerned with purifying and unifying the Society, they did not "desire to retreat into a sectarian shell" or to remove themselves completely from public affairs. As he demonstrates, Quakerism contained an element of utopianism, as seen in the Holy Experiment, an attempt to create a reformed society by making the government the agent of Quaker influence. After their withdrawal from government, Quakers increasingly looked to their religious Society, and to various benevolent institutions and private societies, as the means by which Friends could impress their ideals upon the world.

Thus the Quaker shift to humanitarianism, which coincided with an increasing sectarianism, involved an active concern with the world. As such, it revealed a transition within the Society of Friends from "charity," defined as "the members' mutual aid and surveillance," to benevolence, a concern for the welfare of all mankind. Humanitarianism, the focus of the "second Holy Experiment," offered Quakers a way of influencing a world from which they did not wish to withdraw completely, and a way of maintaining their inner purity and solidarity against contamination by the world. At the same time, it offered them a role in American society as "a people among people," a sect among sects, contributing "to the national welfare in ways which would preserve and express their distinctive views." In James's view, the Quakers did not fail "the test of significance" in the New World. "The idealism—the pacifism, humanitarianism, and public spirit which emerged from their eighteenth-century trials—remained an example of what Americans

can achieve, and to some degree per-   best exemplifies." — *A.C.L.*
vaded the estimates of what the nation

Additional Recommended Reading

Tolles, Frederick B. and E. Gordon Alderfer, eds. *The Witness of William Penn.* New York: The Macmillan Company, 1957. A collection of excerpts from William Penn's writings on religion and politics, which will appeal to both the general and scholarly reader.

Bronner, Edwin B. *William Penn's Holy Experiment: The Founding of Pennsylvania, 1681-1701.* New York: Temple University Publications, 1962. A detailed, well-documented, chronological study of seventeenth century Pennsylvania, this volume describes the religious and political conflicts as well as the economic pressures which compromised the idealism of the Holy Experiment.

Davidson, Robert L. *War Comes to Quaker Pennsylvania, 1682-1756.* New York: Columbia University Press, 1957. Davidson records the dissolution of the Holy Experiment under the impact of "profit seeking and politics" and "the clash of rival empires," attributing the survival of the experiment for over three quarters of a century to its isolation from the imperial struggle and its lack of conflict with the Indians, the two factors which ultimately brought about its downfall.

Tolles, Frederick B. *James Logan and the Culture of Provincial America.* Boston: Little, Brown, and Company, 1957. This biography of one of the most important figures of colonial Pennsylvania reveals much of the politics and personalities of his time.

Nash, Gary B. *Quakers and Politics: Pennsylvania, 1681-1726.* Princeton: Princeton University Press, 1968. Unlike earlier historians of colonial Pennsylvania, Nash approaches his subject not from a religious angle, but from the viewpoint of the sociology of politics. This monograph is a study of "the agonizing struggle for political stability and maturity" in which Quakers engaged during the half century after settlement.

FORMATION OF THE DOMINION OF NEW ENGLAND

Type of event: Political: colonial resistance to British governmental policy
Time: June, 1686-April, 1689
Locale: New England colonies, New York, and the Jerseys

Principal personages:
> JAMES II (1633-1701), King of England from 1685 until his overthrow in 1689
> WILLIAM III (1650-1702), who acceded with Mary to the throne of England in 1689 after the "Glorious Revolution" of 1688
> EDWARD RANDOLPH (1632-1703), royal collector of customs and secretary of the Dominion of New England
> SIR EDMUND ANDROS (1637-1714), Governor of the Dominion of New England
> INCREASE MATHER (1639-1723), Puritan leader in Massachusetts

Summary of Event

Only after the Restoration of the Stuart monarchy in 1660, when Great Britain recognized the advantages of bringing the American colonies into its expanding commercial system, did the lack of an adequate colonial policy become apparent; but by then it was too late. Great Britain had permitted its colonies a large measure of local self-government and had demanded little of them. The governments in the American colonies (which had never experienced direct royal control) had become accustomed to independence and wanted no interference, even from a relatively liberal Mother Country. Massachusetts, the most independent and rebellious of the colonies, not only violated the Navigation Acts and refused to coöperate with Edward Randolph (whom the Crown had appointed collector and surveyor of customs in 1678) but also usurped powers not granted by its corporate charter and denied that the laws of Parliament applied in the Massachusetts Bay colony. The Crown had no choice but to declare its charter null and void in 1684.

By this time it had become evident that revocation of the colonial charters was necessary for the development of Great Britain's commercial plans. The Lords of Trade issued writs of *Quo Warranto* ("by what authority?") to Connecticut, Rhode Island, the Jerseys, Pennsylvania, Maryland, the Carolinas, Bermuda, and the Bahamas in preparation for nullifying their charters. Because the establishment of royal governmental machinery in each colony would have been too expensive, a plan for three unions was devised: one for New England, one for the Middle colonies, and one for the South.

Only the New England union materialized. It began in the fall of 1685 as a provisional government for Massachusetts, Maine, New Hampshire, and the Narragansett Bay region, and it was to last until a royal governor. could be commissioned and sent to America. On December 20, 1686, Sir Edmund Andros arrived to assume the

163

governorship and to organize the Dominion of New England. Rhode Island was incorporated into the union almost immediately, and Connecticut was brought in within a year. New York and the Jerseys entered in 1688. The commission and instructions drafted for Andros by the Lords of Trade provided for a governor and council appointed by the king, and a representative assembly chosen by the people, but James II had eliminated the provision for an assembly. The governor was empowered to appoint all officials, and with the council he was to legislate, levy taxes, establish courts, and sit as a supreme court. All laws were to be sent to England for approval.

Until a committee for codification could develop a uniform body of laws consistent with those of England, each colony was to operate in accordance with its old laws. In the absence of any revenue acts in effect in Massachusetts, the governor and council enacted increased customs, import and tonnage duties, excises, and land and poll taxes. The Puritans had habitually ignored or nullified laws which they disliked, and although the new taxes represented only a small increase, the selectmen of Ipswich led a revolt against them, claiming taxation without representation.

The matter of taxation was one of several areas of conflict between the Dominion government and the Puritans. In an effort to achieve conformity in the method of granting land and to make the new government self-supporting, the King had ordered that quitrents be collected on all new land granted, and that fees be charged for the compulsory confirmation of all old titles. The New Hampshire and Maine colonists welcomed the opportunity to ensure their titles, but the Puritans could not understand why the land was not theirs by right. Because Andros enforced the hated Navigation Acts, New England trade dropped off drastically. The continuing need for English manufactured goods created a drain on the colonies' hard money.

When the Dominion government attempted to make the administration of justice conform to English law, the Puritans resented the change. Jurors no longer had to be chosen from among the landowners, which meant that the leaders of the theocracy were robbed of some of their power. Even more alarming to the Puritans was the Declaration of Indulgence of April 4, 1687, granting liberty of conscience to all the King's subjects. No longer were the Puritan ministers and schools supported by the taxes of the entire population. When Andros appropriated one of Boston's Congregational churches for Anglican worship, the Puritans began to fear that the Church of England would become established in the colonies.

The Puritans regarded themselves as God's chosen people and interpreted the interference of Great Britain as a divine punishment for the younger generation's having slipped from the straight and narrow path. Thus they anticipated their eventual deliverance from their oppressors. In the spring of 1688, Increase Mather, the influential Puritan clergyman, traveled to England to petition for an assembly and other reforms. When James II was forced to publish a proclamation restoring rights to corporations, Mather and his fellow agents interpreted this concession to include colonial corporations. Mather gained the favor of the attorney-general, and the Lords of Trade agreed to promote a new charter granting more powers to the colonists.

The Glorious Revolution of 1688 and the accession of William and Mary in 1689 embodied the sign of deliverance that the Puritans had been expecting. The Lords of Trade recommended, however, that the Dominion be continued with two commissioners replacing Andros. In an effort to create the impression that the Puritans were allied with William and Mary against the Dominion and James, Mather suggested to the Massachusetts Puritans that they overthrow Andros in the name of the new sovereigns.

On April 18, 1689, when troops who had mutinied on the Maine frontier marched into Boston, insurrection broke out, and Andros was imprisoned. Within a month all the colonies had overthrown the Dominion government. On May 9, a convention of delegates from the colonies voted to restore the governments and laws of 1686.

Once back in power, the Puritan officials returned to their authoritarian policies, evoking many complaints from non-Puritans.

Both pro and anti-Dominion forces pleaded their cases before William and Mary on the question of New England's future government. Unfortunately, William was more concerned about gaining the Puritans' support for his war with the French than with colonial policy. Thus the new charter for Massachusetts was sealed on October 7, 1691. It allowed for a governor appointed by the Crown, but it also provided for an elected assembly and a council chosen by that assembly. New Hampshire became a separate royal colony, Maine and Plymouth were annexed to Massachusetts, and Connecticut and Rhode Island operated under their old charters. Massachusetts had gained a charter, but new policies insuring religious freedom and broadening the franchise had destroyed the Puritan oligarchy.

Pertinent Literature

Barnes, Viola F. *The Dominion of New England: A Study in British Colonial Policy.* New York: Frederick Ungar Publishing Company, Inc., 1960.

The fall of the Dominion of New England was a pivotal event in American history. If Great Britain had managed to maintain the Dominion, "the most complete expression of [its] colonial policy in the seventeenth century," its relationship with the colonies in the eighteenth century might well have been entirely different. Viola Florence Barnes' thesis is an important one, for its implications are far-reaching. Her book, more than a study of the reasons for the rise and fall of the Do-

minion of New England, is an analysis of the effect of seventeenth century British colonial policy upon the movement for American independence.

Unlike "democratic" historians of the past, Barnes does not view the imposition of royal government upon New England as a tyrannical act. The Puritan oligarchy which held sway in Massachusetts before the revocation of the charter was actually more restrictive of the rights of the majority of the colonists than was the Dominion government. In fact, it was in part the refusal of the theocrats to grant non-Puritan colonists the rights of Englishmen that had made nullification of the charter inevitable. The moderate faction of Puritans realized that the Dominion government represented reform and attempted to gain a share of the power within the new system. In detailed chapters devoted to legislation and taxation, justice, liberty of conscience, trade, the land system, and defense, Barnes points out that the royal government tried consistently to achieve greater uniformity, efficiency, and fairness in the administration of government than had the Puritans.

That the Dominion failed was not the result of any fault in Great Britain's basic intention, but because of its lack of understanding of Puritan psychology and of a developing American consciousness. Confident that they were God's chosen people, the Puritans believed that their authority was divinely ordained. Ironically, they wanted the protection of the laws of England but refused to acknowledge that those laws applied to them. What Great Britain regarded as privileges granted to its colonies, the Puritans claimed as rights. Although Andros has been criticized severely for strict execution of his instructions and harsh dealing with the Puritans, Barnes argues that he had no choice if he was to break the Puritans of the habit of nullifying any law they disliked.

James II's decision to eliminate a popular assembly from the Dominion government was no mere exercise in Stuart absolutism, explains Barnes. If he had allowed an assembly, the Puritan theocrats would have retained control. Moreover, France with its more tightly popular assemblies had managed to govern without popular assemblies. But Great Britain's colonial policy—or rather, the lack of it—had encouraged decentralization, and James's decision was a fatal mistake. Had he listened to advisers who were aware of the situation in the colonies, the King would have realized that the colonists accepted self-government as a right. The Dominion's revenue acts were not oppressive, and the Puritans had never balked at taxing disfranchised nonchurch members, but now, because there was no assembly, taxation without representation became a *cause célèbre*. If James had preserved the assembly, basing the right to vote on an adequate property qualification, Barnes claims that he would have retained the support of the moderate Puritans against the theocrats. As it was, all the Puritans lined up against him. Because the moderates disliked Andros' trade and land policies, they made no effort to suppress the revolt against him.

William III understood the importance of colonial policy even less than James. Concerned only with winning the colonies' support to defeat Louis XIV, William unknowingly abandoned Great Britain's last hope for controlling its colonies when he granted Massachusetts a new charter. Fortunately, the charter represented a compromise between the old Puritan oligarchy and the Dominion, which had the effect of broadening participation in government.

Had Great Britain succeeded in forcing New England into its colonial system, Barnes theorizes, the colonists might never have considered independence. Because the Dominion of New

England collapsed, the colonies were free to develop their independent institutions more fully. By the eighteenth century, colonial institutions were too deeply rooted to change.

Adams, James Truslow. *The Founding of New England.* Magnolia, Massachusetts: Peter Smith Publisher, Inc., 1921. Also in paperback by Little, Brown, and Company.

James Truslow Adams views Great Britain's seventeenth century colonial policy in the perspective of the contemporary debate over the question of sovereignty and the divine right of kings. The reign of Charles II marked the end of religion and the beginning of commerce as the most important influence in national affairs. When Charles recognized the necessity for unity and administrative control within his commercial empire, he was unaware of the error of granting colonial charters free of royal control. According to Adams, the influence of the frontier environment was paramount in the shaping of individualism and the desire for self-government among the colonists. The Puritan theory that sovereignty had its source in a contract or covenant entered into by the governed conflicted directly with the concept of the divine right of kings.

One of the foremost debunkers of the Puritans, Adams contends that the defiant attitude of Massachusetts toward the laws of England forced the Mother Country to interfere in the colony's affairs. After the first generation of Puritan leaders died, the new leaders were native Americans who felt no strong ties with England. In their narrow, provincial environment, they developed narrow, unhealthy attitudes intent upon preserving discriminatory, intolerant policies; only force could have changed the Massachusetts government. Yet, Adams points out, the growth of factions within the Puritan leadership hastened the decline of theocratic control. The merchants and urban types tended to be more progressive and favorable to the Mother Country, while the rural farmers retained their narrow attitudes.

Like Barnes, Adams justifies many of the measures which the Dominion government employed to make New England conform to the English system. Likewise, he cites several fatal blunders which invited the colonists' protests. Had the royal officials considered the importance of land to the colonists, for instance, they would have realized the error of exacting fees for confirmation of titles. Many of the colonists had left England to escape the inequities of the land system and could not understand why the King should have any claim on their property. In the light of present-day American territorial policy, says Adams, Great Britain was not acting unreasonably in denying its colonies the privilege of self-government. Its policy was nevertheless unwise, because the colonists had come to accept a representative assembly as a right.

While Barnes assesses the administration of the Dominion of New England favorably and suggests that, had William III been more concerned with colonial policy, the Dominion might have been maintained as an integral part of the English commercial system, Adams argues that the inherent weaknesses of the system would have brought its end even without the Glori-

167

ous Revolution of 1688. The very extent of the Dominion's territory, especially after the annexation of New York and the Jerseys, and the difficulty of communication all but rendered a centralized government impossible. Andros lacked able assistants to help control the distant reaches of the Dominion. The matter of taxation without the consent of the people created sufficient controversy by itself to wreck the royal government.

Adams pictures Massachusetts after the overthrow of Andros as a disaster area. Resentful of the Puritan government which drafted the men to defend the colony from the Indians but which had no funds to pay them, the people complained bitterly. Increase Mather, arguing in England for restoration of the old charter, resorted to reckless imputations and threats in the face of criticism.

The new charter which the King granted was more favorable than the old one which Mather desired to be restored. It freed Massachusetts from theological repression and opened the way for the development of liberal leadership. Whereas officeholding and the franchise had been based upon a religious test, it was now based only upon a property requirement which a majority of Massachusetts men could meet. The resulting movement toward the democratization of state and society was to provide a basis for the development of a common loyalty, a prerequisite for the movement toward independence. — *W.M.B.*

Additional Recommended Reading

Andrews, Charles M. *The Colonial Period of American History.* Vol. IV: *England's Commercial and Colonial Policy.* New Haven: Yale University Press, 1964. This detailed study of Great Britain's commercial and colonial policy provides excellent background for understanding the significance of the Dominion of New England.

Beer, George L. *The Old Colonial System, 1660-1754.* Vol. II, chs. 11 and 12. New York: The Macmillan Company, 1913. Sees the Dominion as an instrument in Great Britain's effort to enforce the Navigation Laws and thus create a self-sufficient commercial empire.

Hall, Michael G. *Edward Randolph and the American Colonies, 1676-1703.* Chapel Hill: University of North Carolina Press, 1960. Focuses upon the role which the dedicated public servant who was England's foremost expert on the colonies played in the formation and government of the Dominion.

Harper, Lawrence A. *The English Navigation Laws.* New York: Octagon Books, Inc., 1964. Part Three, "Enforcement in the Colonies," explains the changes in English policy which brought about colonial resistance, thus necessitating the imposition of royal government.

Miller, Perry. *The New England Mind.* Vol. II: *From Colony to Province.* Cambridge: Harvard University Press, 1953. Discusses the decline of Puritan power in the years following the Restoration.

Andrews, Charles M., ed. *Narratives of the Insurrections, 1675 to 1690.* New York: Barnes and Noble, Inc., 1959. Included are descriptions of the revolt against Andros, Andros' report of his administration, and Increase Mather's account of his efforts to obtain the restoration of the old Massachusetts Charter.

SALEM WITCHCRAFT TRIALS

Type of event: Legal: emotional upheaval resulting in persecution
Time: 1692-1693
Locale: Essex County, Massachusetts Bay colony

Principal personages:

SAMUEL PARRIS (1653-1720), Puritan pastor of Salem Village
NICHOLAS NOYES (fl. 1692), Puritan pastor of Salem Town
TITUBA (fl. 1692), West Indian slave in the Parris household
JOHN HATHORNE (fl. 1692), and
JONATHAN CORWIN (fl. 1692), assistants of the Massachusetts
   General Court who conducted the examinations of the ac-
   cused witches
SIMON BRADSTREET (1603-1697), provisional Governor of Mas-
   sachusetts after the fall of the Dominion of New England
SIR WILLIAM PHIPS (1651-1695), Royal Governor of Massa-
   chusetts (1692-1694)
SAMUEL SEWALL (1652-1730), Massachusetts magistrate and a
   judge at the witch trials
WILLIAM STOUGHTON (fl, 1692), Deputy Governor and presiding justice at the witch trials
INCREASE MATHER (1639-1723), pastor of the Boston Puritan
   church and President of Harvard College
COTTON MATHER (1663-1728), son of Increase, a Puritan minister interested in psychic research and author of *Wonders of
   the Invisible World*

Summary of Event

Early in 1692, a circle of young girls began to meet in the home of Samuel Parris, the Puritan pastor of Salem Village. The minister's nine-year-old daughter Betty and her eleven-year-old cousin Abigail Williams were fascinated by the Voodoo-like tales and tricks of the family's West Indian slave, Tituba, and soon they began to invite their friends to share in the entertainment. Before long, some of the girls in the circle began to behave strangely, complaining of physical maladies, reporting visions, lapsing into trances, and trembling and babbling without restraint.

Among the Puritans, inexplicable afflictions were customarily attributed to the work of the devil, so most of the inhabitants of Salem Village believed the young girls when they charged that Tituba and two other village women of doubtful respectability were practicing witchcraft upon them. Two assistants of the Massachusetts General Court, John Hathorne and Jonathan Corwin, were called upon to conduct an examination of the accused women. Placing no store in lawyers, the Puritans were governed essentially by Old Testament law. When they found a statement in the Scriptures that witches must not be allowed to live, their duty became clear. The two magistrates conducted their examination more like prosecuting attorneys than impartial investigators. They accepted the dreams and fancies of the young girls as positive evidence and concluded that a "strange tit or wart" on the body of one of the women was a "witches' tit," at which the devil and his familiars, or messengers, sucked the blood of the witch. When Tituba confessed her own connection with the devil, she implicated the other accused witches, and on March 7, all three were sent off to prison. Although many of the villagers were skeptical of the claims of the girls, the examiners, supported by Parris and Nicholas Noyes, his colleague in Salem Town, called upon other ministers of the area to consult with them.

More accusations—this time against respectable, pious women of the community—came almost immediately, and it seemed that the devil was carrying out his deception by possessing seemingly innocent persons. The panic soon enveloped not only the residents of Salem but those of neighboring towns as well. As the suspected witches confessed, they frequently accused others.

The devil's timing was faultless, for the Massachusetts Bay colony was still agitated over the loss of its charter in 1684 and the overthrow of the Dominion of New England in 1689. The weak provisional government, headed by the ailing governor, Simon Bradstreet, was merely awaiting the arrival of the new governor and did nothing to avert the crisis. When Sir William Phips, Royal Governor of Massachusetts, arrived in May, 1692, with the new Massachusetts Charter, he decided immedi-ately that proper courts must be established for the trying of witches. On the last Wednesday in May, the Governor's Council set up a General Court, which promptly appointed seven judges to constitute a special court of Oyer and Terminer to convene on June 2. The witchcraft fever had continued to spread, but the accused were confident that the distinguished judges Bartholomew Gedney, Samuel Sewall, John Richards, William Sergeant, Wait Winthrop, Nathaniel Saltonstall (later replaced by Jonathan Corwin); and Presiding Justice William Stoughton, representing some of the best minds in the colony, would deal justly with the witchcraft problem. The court, however, accepted the testimony gathered at the examination as proven fact. At the trials the judges simply heard new evidence, and a jury decided the prisoner's fate. On June 8, the General Court revived an old law making witchcraft a capital offence. Two days later, Bridget Bishop, the first condemned witch, went to the gallows.

A schism among the judges over the validity of spectral evidence necessitated a delay in the proceedings while they sought the advice of the clergy of the Boston area. Although the ministers urged caution in the handling of spectral evidence, they praised the judges and encouraged further prosecution of the witches. As the summer brought more hangings, the remaining prisoners began to fear for their lives, and several managed to escape. The judges, as good Puritans, accepted confession as evidence of possible regeneration and were merciful to those who would confess their dealings with the devil and repent, but few of the staunch Puritans were willing to belie themselves even to save their lives.

By the time the last of the twenty victims had been executed on September 22, public opinion was ceasing to support the trials. There were numerous reasons for this change: several of those who were executed in August died calmly, forgiving their accusers and judges, and protesting their innocence to the end; the court's procedures seemed to be aggravating the witchcraft problem rather than alleviating it; and as the witch hunt spread, persons were being accused whom no one could believe guilty. The panic had been confined almost exclusively to Essex County, and ministers from outside the immediate area began taking a stand against continuing the trials. Increase Mather, the great Boston divine, warned against reliance on spectral evidence and traveled to Salem to investigate the method of obtaining confessions. A petition from Andover was the first among many to call for release of the remaining prisoners and to denounce the accusing girls. On October 29, Governor Phips dismissed the Court of Oyer and Terminer. Its end marked the end of the witch hunt.

By acts of the General Court of November 23 and December 16, special sessions of the Superior Court of Judicature were ordered to complete the trials. The new circuit court was composed largely of the same judges as the recently dissolved court, but it now held spectral evidence to be inadmissible. Fifty-two accused witches came to trial early in January, 1693, and forty-nine were released immediately for lack of evidence. The Governor soon reprieved the others, and by May all the remaining prisoners had been discharged.

While some people were disappointed to see the trials end, most were relieved to return to their long-neglected work. Blaming Parris for allowing the death of innocent relatives and friends, the congregation of the Salem church voted to void his salary. In the ensuing years, many of the accusers of the condemned repented, and in 1709 and 1711, the Massachusetts General Court restored to many of those who had been accused of being witches, as well as the children of the executed victims, their good names and awarded them compensation for financial losses. The names of some, however, were never cleared.

During the Salem witchcraft trials both Increase and Cotton Mather expressed their doubts about the proceedings, especially concerning the use of spectral evidence. It was Increase Mather who insisted that the special Court of Oyer and Terminer be terminated because it might be guilty of shedding innocent blood. Cotton Mather, acting as one of the "most" cogent critics of the court's methods" while it was sitting, afterward offered a strongly partisan defense of the judges. Because of this defense, historians have incorrectly presented Cotton Mather as the instigator of the witchcraft trials. He was in fact guilty of not opposing the trials vigorously enough.

Although the Salem trials were not the last, because of the Massachusetts authorities' actions in discovering, acknowledging, and disowning their errors, the Salem experience "helped put an end to witchcraft trials in Western civilization."

Salem Witchcraft Trials

Pertinent Literature

Starkey, Marion L. *The Devil in Massachusetts: A Modern Enquiry into the Salem Witch Trials.* New York: Alfred A. Knopf, Inc., 1949.

The Devil in Massachusetts reads more like a novel than a history book. Marion L. Starkey's talent for converting the records of the Salem witchcraft trials into dramatic dialogue invests the proceedings with an element of excitement. So deftly does she delineate the principal characters that they immediately evoke the sympathy or antipathy of the reader. Yet this work is by no means a shallow, popular account. Starkey has employed previously unused source materials and reviews the evidence in the light of modern psychological findings. In her preface she reports having investigated the works of Freud and Janet and studies of hypnotism and spiritualism, in addition to interviewing staff members and patients at a mental hospital. The psychological dimension contributes significantly to an understanding of the motives of the young girls who began the whole affair.

Starkey sees the witch trials against the background of the gray New England countryside and the drab existence of the Puritan colonists. The young girls, their appetites for the different and the unusual having been aroused by Tituba's stories, no doubt craved attention and excitement. It is not their antics, but the reaction of the community to them, that the author finds remarkable. Because the natural impulses of the Puritans were repressed, she suggests, they sought catharsis in the outpouring of vengeful fervor.

The Satan of Milton's "Paradise Lost" loomed large in the Puritan cosmology, so that the Salem villagers were ready to accept the smallest misfortunes as his doing. Starkey depicts them as "bewitched by a mad hypnosis," so convinced of the presence of evil among them that they refused to believe the confessions of two of the accusing girls, forcing them to remain within the crazed circle.

Democracy was not an acceptable political system to the Puritans, but ironically, the author points out, there was "democracy among witches." As the hunt for witches expanded throughout Essex County, it took in persons of various races, religions, and classes. The pious, church-going grandmother was condemned along with the village strumpet.

Massachusetts' unsettled political climate in 1692 served to prolong the witchcraft panic. In the period following the overthrow of the autocratic government of the Dominion of New England, the provisional government was too weak to exert a calming influence on the agitated colonists. The new Royal Governor was at first too preoccupied with the threat from the French and Indians to take matters in hand. The peculiar quality of the colonial judicial system, with its reliance upon Scriptural law, its lack of conformity to English legal practice, and its disregard for lawyers, likewise allowed for gross neglect of accepted legal rights. Because the judges willingly accepted spectral evidence while the defendants based their arguments upon the events of the visible world, the trials were conducted on two separate planes, with neither side being capable of understanding the other. Strangely enough, however, the judges were not without mercy for those who confessed practicing witchcraft. Good Calvinists, they believed that, since all men are sinful, salvation comes only through repentance. Then, too, the confessed witches were valuable informers. The author speaks with unbounded admiration for those condemned persons who refused to lie to save their own lives. The finest examples of the "indomitable Puritan spirit," they would surely have been beatified had they been Catholics, she contends.

The Puritan belief that the hand of God was in all events naturally extended to the conclusion of the witch trials. At first, many who had taken

morbid delight in the prosecutions felt that God was punishing them—probably for accepting the new charter with its extension of the franchise to non-Puritans—by denying them the ability to ferret out the guilty ones among them. Cotton Mather's writings show that he had enjoyed the contact with the supernatural too much to learn something constructive from the horrible affair.

In keeping with her avowed purpose, the author presents a true Greek tragedy. In the classic pattern, good did come out of evil. The people of Massachusetts did, after all, possess the spiritual health to renounce error and to emerge from their tragedy with honor.

Kittredge, George Lyman. *Witchcraft in Old and New England*. Cambridge: Harvard University Press, 1929.

"It is easy to be wise after the fact,—especially when the fact is two-hundred years old." With this maxim George Lyman Kittredge concludes his list of theses about witchcraft. That the bulk of his study is concerned with the history of witchcraft in England prior to the Salem trials is significant to his defense of the Massachusetts Puritans. "The belief in witchcraft is the common heritage of humanity," he hypothesizes. Therefore, contrary to the assertions of earlier students of the subject, the outbreak in Salem cannot be attributed to some peculiarities of Puritan theology or to the accusers' colonial environment. On the contrary, Kittredge maintains, the affair was typical.

We of the present day, accustomed to thinking rationally, find it difficult to understand that seventeenth century

man believed in witchcraft as a fact of experience, explains Kittredge. There had always been witches. Even the law recognized their existence. As evidence that belief in witchcraft was by no means confined to Puritans, Kittredge quotes some of the leading non-Puritan scholars and scientific thinkers of the seventeenth century. Misunderstanding on this point had developed probably because so many indictments of supposed witches occurred during the term of the Puritan Matthew Hopkins as "Witch-Finder General."

Several works denying the power of the devil appeared in the seventeenth century, but only the Dutch theologian Balthasar Bekker's *The Enchanted World* offered a complete theory on which a contemporary Christian could logically reject witchcraft. Whether Bekker's argument would stand or fall, however, depended upon the soundness of his Biblical exegesis, for the seventeenth century Christian accepted the Bible as absolute, divinely-inspired truth. Since many orthodox theologians who believed in witches were more correct in their interpretation of Scripture than were Bekker and his adherents, antiwitchcraft writings had little influence upon the general public.

Historians who have attempted to single out certain prominent individuals to bear the blame for the Salem affair have failed to perceive that responsibility for prosecution of witches frequently lay with the community. Prosecution, Kittredge asserts, also required a body of evidence concerning reputed witches and their causing strange occurrences over an extended period of time. Often, accused witches themselves believed they possessed supernatural powers, or they pretended to possess them in order to impress their neighbors.

Some suspicion of witchcraft existed around Salem before 1692. The "devil-worshipping" Indians provided a constant reminder of its dangers. Kittredge finds it remarkable, therefore, that the Salem outburst came so late. Europe and England had for many years experienced spasmodic episodes concerning witchcraft. That the Salem panic was slow in coming he attributes to the extraordinary steadiness of the Puritans. Given the thesis that belief in witchcraft was almost universal at the time and the fact that outbreaks occurred regularly, what then triggered the Salem incident? Kittredge answers that such upheavals usually happen in times of political anxiety. Ever since the loss of its charter in 1684, Massachusetts had experienced division and unrest. Fear of Indian attack reinforced the feeling of insecurity.

In defense of the proponents of persecution at Salem, Kittredge argues that they held a scripturally stronger position than their antagonists, given the acceptance of the doctrines concerning supernaturalism by both sides. The admissibility of spectral evidence was an established legal principle in England. Kittredge, then, finds nothing abnormal in Salem's prosecution and condemnation of accused witches. What he does find remarkable is the rapid return to normalcy and the frank confession of error. The reversal of position by a judge and jury are without precedent in the annals of witchcraft. That the Puritans experienced only one short-lived outbreak in the century when England executed hundreds is much to the Puritans' credit, the author insists. Salem's repentance constituted a significant argument against maintaining the status of witchcraft as a recognized crime in England. — *W.M.B.*

Additional Recommended Reading

Hansen, Chadwick. *Witchcraft at Salem.* New York: George Braziller, Inc., 1969. This recent volume contains an excellent survey of the background and course of the Salem witchcraft hysteria.

Wendell, Barrett. *Cotton Mather: The Puritan Priest.* New York: Harcourt, Brace & World, Inc., 1963. This biography tells of the tragic consequences which the Salem incident had for the life of the determined minister who involved himself so deeply in the study of witchcraft.

Levin, David D. *What Happened in Salem?* New York: Harcourt, Brace & World, Inc., 1960. An excellent introduction precedes this collection, which includes selections from the trial evidence, contemporary writings relating to witchcraft, and two examples of historical fiction.

Miller, Perry. *The New England Mind.* Vol. II: *From Colony to Province.* Cambridge: Harvard University Press, 1953. In this excellent background work, Miller explains the witchcraft trials as a natural outgrowth of Puritan theology, but charges the Mathers with bringing the matter to a head.

Burr, George L. *Narratives of the Witchcraft Cases, 1648 to 1706.* New York: Barnes and Noble, Inc., 1952. Numerous selections from works of Cotton and Increase Mather are among this collection of seventeenth century writings relating to witchcraft in the colonies.

Upham, Charles W. *Salem Witchcraft.* New York: Frederick Ungar Publishing Co., 1959. Originally published in 1867, this detailed classic work is composed of three parts: a history of Salem Village, a history of witchcraft, and an account of the events of 1692-1693 in Salem.

THE GREAT AWAKENING

Type of event: Religious: desire of many people for a more pietistic faith
Time: 1730's and 1740's
Locale: American colonies

Principal personages:

GEORGE WHITEFIELD (1714-1770), Anglican missionary and philanthropist whose visit to America in 1739 sparked the Great Awakening

JONATHAN EDWARDS (1703-1758), minister from Northampton, Connecticut, and principal defender of the Great Awakening; author of *A Treatise Concerning Religious Affections* (1746), which defined the doctrine of regeneration that formed the core of the theology of the Great Awakening

CHARLES CHAUNCY (1705-1787), minister of Boston's First Church and chief critic of the Great Awakening; author of *Seasonable Thoughts on the State of Religion in New England* (1743)

WILLIAM TENNENT (1673-1745), native of Ireland, pastor of the Presbyterian church at Neshaminy, Pennsylvania, and founder of the Log College

GILBERT TENNENT (1703-1764), son of William, educated at the Log College; pastor of Presbyterian church at New Brunswick, New Jersey; and leader of the revivalist party which organized the Synod of New York in 1745

SAMUEL DAVIES (1723-1761), organizer and propagator of Presbyterianism in Virginia, and founder of the Hanover Presbytery in 1755

Summary of Event

Between 1739 and 1742 the American colonies experienced a quickening of religious faith that became known as the Great Awakening. The arrival of the young Anglican preacher George Whitefield probably sparked the religious conflagration. Whitefield, whose reputation as a great pulpit and open-air orator had preceded his visit, traveled through the colonies in 1739 and 1740. Everywhere he attracted large and emotional crowds, eliciting countless conversions as well as considerable controversy. Critics condemned his "enthusiasm," his censoriousness, and his extemporaneous and itinerant preaching, but his techniques were copied by numerous imitators both lay and clerical. They became itinerant preachers themselves, spreading the Great Awakening from New England to Georgia, among rich and poor, educated and illiterate, and in the backcountry as well as in seaboard towns and cities.

In the Middle colonies, Gilbert Tennent was the leader of the revival among the Presbyterians. His famous

176

sermon, "The Danger of an Unconverted Ministry," was widely circulated throughout the colonies. Led by Jonathan Dickinson, Presbyterians of New England background joined in the revival. In New England, the most notorious evangelist was James Davenport, whose extravagances were even denounced by Tennent and other revivalists. Jonathan Edwards, Samuel Buell, and Eleazar Wheelock, less controversial than Davenport, were also instruments of the Awakening in New England. In the Southern colonies, the Great Awakening made greatest headway on the frontier. Samuel Davies preached revivalism among the Presbyterians of Virginia and North Carolina; Shubal Stearns and Daniel Marshall drew converts to the Separate Baptist fold; and Devereux Jarratt inaugurated the Methodist phase of the Awakening.

The colonists were not unprepared for the Great Awakening. Prior to 1739, there had been indications of a religious quickening among several denominations. In the 1720's the Dutch Reformed Church in New Jersey experienced a series of revivals led by Theodore Frelinghuysen, a native of Germany who had been influenced by the pietistic movement within the Lutheran Church. In the mid-1730's, a "refreshing" occurred among the Presbyterians of New Jersey and Pennsylvania as a result of the preaching of a group of Scotch-Irish ministers led by William Tennent and trained in his Log College. The revivals continued throughout the 1730's, coinciding with the "subscription controversy" within American Presbyterianism. New England was also the scene of religious excitement before 1739.

The "harvests" of Solomon Stoddard, known as the "pope" of the Connecticut Valley, and the Northampton revival of 1734-1735, led by his grandson Jonathan Edwards, foreshadowed the later, more general awakening. Thus Whitefield's tour provided the catalyst, not the cause, of the Great Awakening, which represented the culmination of impulses that were already beginning to transform colonial Protestantism.

At first the Great Awakening was celebrated as a supernatural work, the "pouring out of the grace of God upon the land." But controversy over the origins and effects of the revival soon displaced the earlier consensus. Prorevivalists continued to defend the Great Awakening as the work of God, but opponents criticized the excesses stemming from the religious "enthusiasm" fomented by the revival. At the root of their disagreement was a conflict over the source of religious faith. Opponents of the revival tended to emphasize reason as the basic ingredient of true religion. The defenders defined religion as a matter of the heart, not the head, or of the feelings or "affections," as Jonathan Edwards called them, not the intellect. The theology of the revivalists was Calvinist, which stressed the depravity of man and the sovereignty of God. They emphasized faith rather than good conduct as the means to salvation. Regeneration was defined as an emotional, even a physical, experience wrought by God, not man, and resulting in a "New Birth" or "Change of Heart"; the change in the convert's personality in turn would be manifested in his actions.

In many cases the controversy over the Great Awakening split denominations into opposing factions. The revival produced a temporary schism among the Presbyterians—between Old Sides who opposed the Awakening and New Sides who approved it. Congregationalism was split between Old Lights and New Lights. Some pro-revivalist New Lights became Separatists, withdrawing from the established Congregational churches and forming new churches of the regenerate; most of these Separate churches ultimately became Baptist, with the result that the majority of New England Baptists shifted from an Arminian to a Calvinist theology. No denomination entirely escaped the divisive effects of the Great Awakening.

There were numerous aftereffects of the Great Awakening. Despite the anti-intellectual bias of their theology, the revivalists founded a number of educational institutions, including the College of New Jersey (later Princeton) and Dartmouth College. The Great Awakening stimulated social concern in other areas by virtue of its emphasis on "benevolence" as the outward sign of inner piety. Many revivalists encouraged philanthropic efforts to improve the condition of Negroes, Indians, orphans, and other unfortunates. Perhaps the most lasting effect of the Great Awakening was its encouragement of religious toleration and separation of church and state. Besides placing greater emphasis on the individual and his personal religious experience, the Awakening, by strengthening dissenting churches, such as the Methodists and Baptists, promoted the religious pluralism that helped to shape the distinctive character of American religion.

Pertinent Literature

Heimert, Alan E. *Religion and the American Mind: From the Great Awakening to the Revolution.* Cambridge: Harvard University Press, 1966.

The relationship between the Great Awakening and the American Revolution is the subject of this study of the eighteenth century colonial mind. Heimert argues that the split in American Protestantism caused by the Great Awakening—between the "rationalists," or "Liberals," who opposed the revival, and the "evangelicals," or "Calvinists," who defended it—mirrored a "fundamental cleavage" in the American mind generally and became objectified in the politics of the colonies. Challenging the traditional view that the religion of the Enlightenment supplied the underpinning of the Revolutionary ideology, Heimert concludes that the stimulus to rebellion came chiefly from the evangelical religion of the Awakening. "Liberalism," he explains, "was profoundly conservative, politically as well as socially . . . Conversely, 'evangelical' religion . . . provided pre-Revolutionary America with a radical, even democratic, social and political ideology. . . ." In short, "What the colonies had awakened to in 1740 was none other than independence and rebellion." Indeed, Heimert suggests that after the American Revolution evangelical religion continued to play a considerable role in American intellectual and political development; he traces its influence in Jeffersonian and Jacksonian democracy, as well as late nineteenth century Populism.

178

Thus, in Heimert's view, the dispute between evangelicals and rationalists was "not so much a dispute between theologians as a vital competition for the intellectual allegiance of the American people." The two parties' conflicting conceptions of man, history, and the good society had profound political and social, as well as religious, implications. For example, Heimert argues that the view of man implied by the Calvinist doctrine of the "new birth" was eminently more egalitarian and democratic than the elitist and rationalist view of the Liberals. Similarly, the Calvinists' optimistic view of history and their belief in the coming of the kingdom of God reinforced the impulse toward independence from Great Britain, whereas the Liberals' "cosmic pessimism" persuaded them of the necessity of maintaining ties with the Mother Country. Heimert also contrasts the "radically communitarian" and highly moralistic political and social theory of the evangelicals with the individualist and utilitarian premises of the rationalists. If the Liberals looked to John Locke for inspiration, it was the spirit of Rousseau that informed the views of the Calvinists. "The Calvinist political philosophy . . . centered finally not on the consent of the governed but on the will of the community," Heimert writes. In his view, the thrust of the evangelical impulse loosed during the Great Awakening was not only toward democracy but nationalism as well.

Heimert bases his analysis of the eighteenth century American mind on an extensive reading of the published literature of the period. His method, as he explains, is essentially that of "literary interpretation." In both its method and its thesis, *Religion and the American Mind* is a provocative and controversial work. If Heimert is correct, many of the earlier interpretations of the Great Awakening and its impact on American development stand in need of considerable revision.

Bushman, Richard L. *From Puritan to Yankee: Character and Social Order in Connecticut, 1690-1765*. Cambridge: Harvard University Press, 1967.

Like Alan Heimert, Richard Bushman considers the social and political consequences of the Great Awakening. However, his study of colonial Connecticut is only indirectly concerned with the relation between the religious revival and the American Revolution. His primary topic is the process by which Connecticut Puritans became Yankees, and the transformation of the social order which resulted from that change in character. In Bushman's view, the Great Awakening was one of the impulses which hastened the transition. The revival did in fact result in a "new birth," psychologically as well as spiritually. "The converted were new men, with new attitudes toward themselves, their religion, their neighbors, and their rulers in church and state. A psychological earthquake had reshaped the human landscape."

The basic division between New and Old Lights was that of piety versus order. According to Bushman, "The revivalists undermined the social order . . . not by repudiating law and authority but by denying them sanctifying power." The external social order, which Puritans and Old Lights believed to be divinely authorized, no longer commanded the allegiance of men who enjoyed a direct, personal relation with God as a result of regeneration. In this transfer of authority from the external order to an inward experience Bushman finds "the truly revolutionary aspect of the Awakening. . . ." Experimental religion not only diminished ecclesiastical authority and enlarged religious liberty. It also shaped the political behavior of New Lights. The loss of "faith in the divinity of earthly law and authority" accounted for the greater willingness of the New Lights to resist the Stamp Act in 1765, according to Bushman. In this willingness to resist authority lay the significance of the New Lights—and the political impact of the Great Awakening.

Bushman challenges a number of the theses advanced by Alan Heimert. Whereas Heimert treats the evangelicals as a unified group, Bushman argues that the New Lights were divided in their opposition to the traditional order. The majority were moderates whose views represented a compromise between order and piety. They disagreed with the other wing of the New Lights, radicals who advocated lay preaching and separation, though they shared their belief in the importance of the "new birth" and experimental religion. Nor does Bushman perceive so sharp a distinction between Old and New Lights as Heimert sees

between Liberals and Calvinists. For Bushman, the theological conflict between the two parties, like the debate between piety and order, was a matter of "emphasis and balance." Both Old and New Lights adhered to a Calvinist theology, though New Lights claimed their opponents were guilty of misinterpretation or outright heresy. Ironically, in some cases, as New Lights gained power, they threw off their role as defenders of dissent and religious toleration, and assumed the posture which had formerly belonged to the Old Lights, that of protecting orthodoxy.

Finally, in contrast to Heimert's contention that the cleavage between Liberals and Calvinists persisted into the Revolution, Bushman implies that political activity served to unite a society rent by religious schism. As early as 1765, the state had become "the symbol of social coherence, as once the Established churches had been." In turn, "concentration of community loyalties on the state intensified devotion to those principles on which all could agree. The contents of the social compact—liberty and property—became the rallying cry of the social order. When the opportunity to defend the common interests arose, men responded with religious fervor." — *A.C.L.*

Additional Recommended Reading

Maxson, Charles H. *The Great Awakening in the Middle Colonies.* Chicago: University of Chicago Press, 1920. An account of the Great Awakening in New York, New Jersey, and Pennsylvania with emphasis on the Dutch Reformed and Presbyterian Churches, viewed as part of an international evangelical revival in reaction against the Age of Reason.

Trinterud, Leonard J. *The Forming of an American Tradition: A Re-Examination of Colonial Presbyterianism.* Philadelphia: The Westminster Press, 1949. In this study of colonial Presbyterianism, Trinterud demonstrates the process by which "an American understanding of Presbyterianism" emerged out of the theological controversy and spiritual quickening of the Great Awakening.

Gaustad, Edwin S. *The Great Awakening in New England.* New York: Harper & Row Publishers, 1957. This brief but compact study of the Great Awakening in New England combines narrative and analysis, describing the events and personages of the revival and assessing its long-range theological and institutional effects.

Gesehr, Wesley M. *The Great Awakening in Virginia, 1740-1790.* Durham: Duke University Press, 1930. In addition to narrating the Presbyterian, Baptist, and Methodist phases of the Great Awakening in colonial Virginia, Gesehr traces the influence of the revival on the rise of political democracy and the development of educational and humanitarian impulses in the Old Dominion.

Goen, Clarence C. *Revivalism and Separatism in New England, 1740-1800: Strict Congregationalists and Separate Baptists in the Great Awakening.* New Haven: Yale University Press, 1962. A study of the separatist movement in New England during the Great Awakening, and its relation to the Congregational establishment from which it withdrew and the Baptist fellowship with which it ultimately merged.

Miller, Perry. *Errand into the Wilderness.* Chs. 6-8. Cambridge: Harvard University Press, 1956. A brilliant and provocative analysis of Edwards' contribution to the Great Awakening, the political implications of the revival, and the continuity between Edwards' and Emerson's views of the universe.

SETTLEMENT OF GEORGIA

Type of event: Socio-political: British desire to create a haven for debtors and also to establish a bulwark on the southern frontier
Time: June 20, 1732
Locale: Southeast Coast of North America

Principal personages:

JAMES EDWARD OGLETHORPE (1696-1785), British M.P. who proposed the founding of Georgia as a haven for imprisoned debtors and who served as its civil and military leader in its early days

SIR JOHN PERCEVAL (1683-1748), promoter of the Georgia venture

SIR ROBERT WALPOLE (1676-1745), Chancellor of the Exchequer of Great Britain

JAMES VERNON (fl. 1733), active Georgia trustee

BENJAMIN MARTYN (fl. 1733), secretary of the Board of Trustees for Georgia

TOMOCHICHI (1650-1739), Chief of the Yamacraw Indians who resided in the Savannah area

Summary of Event

The founding of Georgia attracted more attention in England than that of any other colony. Because the project suited the purposes of both philanthropic and imperial interests, it drew support from all segments of society. Two unrelated sets of circumstances in England and North America combined in the early 1730's to augment the Georgia enterprise.

In England economic depression and unemployment had filled the prisons with hapless debtors. When the investigations of a Parliamentary committee under the chairmanship of James Edward Oglethorpe resulted in the freeing of thousands of debtors, they had no place to go. A philanthropic society begun by Thomas Bray, founder of the Society for the Propagation of the Gospel in Foreign Parts, determined to relieve the plight of the debtors. Led by

John Perceval, later Earl of Egmont, the "Associates of the Late Dr. Bray," at the suggestion of Oglethorpe, petitioned the Crown for a tract of land south and west of Carolina between the Savannah and Altamaha rivers with the intention of establishing settlement especially for debtors.

The request came at a propitious moment, for in addition to its social purposes, the proposed colony offered a possible solution to an increasingly serious imperial problem. Having claimed Florida more than a hundred years before the settlement of Carolina, the Spaniards had gradually expanded northward, establishing presidios and missions first on the Sea Islands and then on the mainland of Georgia. The grant by Charles II of land claimed by the Spaniards to the Carolina proprietors in 1663 marked the beginning of

182

the contest for the territory between Charleston and Saint Augustine. Not only did the British have to find means of protecting their frontier against the Spanish, but they also had to contend with the hostile Yamasee Indians. Settlement of the region between the Savannah and Altamaha rivers would create a buffer for the defense of Carolina. From an economic standpoint, a new colony could contribute raw materials for English manufacturers, provide a market for their goods, and ease the Mother Country's unemployment problem.

On June 20, 1732, the Crown conferred upon the twenty-one members of the Board of Trustees for Georgia a charter empowering them to found and to manage for twenty-one years the land between the Savannah and Altamaha rivers, stretching as far westward as the South Seas. Although the government took a calculated view of their enterprise, the trustees considered it the greatest philanthropic and social experiment of their age. Numerous churches, organizations, and individuals responded to their promotional campaign with contributions.

Since the settlers were to participate in a social experiment, they were individually selected from among applicants and imprisoned debtors. Each would receive free passage to Georgia, tools, seeds, provisions until his first crop could be harvested, and fifty acres of land. The colonists were also entitled to all the rights of British subjects.

By the fall of 1732, over one hundred settlers had been chosen, and Oglethorpe himself led the expedition to America. Disembarking at Charleston, South Carolina, in January, 1733, Oglethorpe soon chose a site for the town of Savannah and reached an agreement with Tomochichi, Chief of the Yamacraw Indians who resided there. On February 12, 1733, the colonists arrived in small boats. With the aid of William Bull, a Carolinian, Oglethorpe laid out an orderly town, and the settlers began building houses. Settlement was to proceed in an orderly fashion, not in the haphazard manner of the older colonies. So that compactness might be assured, no one was allowed more than fifty acres. The communal arrangement provided that each family own a town lot with a garden and a piece of farm land nearby. Settlers held their land through "tail male," meaning that tenure was for life, and only eldest sons could inherit land. The prohibition against sale or rental of property eliminated the possibility of unselected immigrants becoming part of the community. Hoping once again to make silk production a profitable colonial enterprise, the crown required each settler to clear ten acres and plant one hundred mulberry trees within ten years.

In addition to the "charity settlers," the trustees also admitted approved "adventurers," persons who paid their own passage to the colony. Persecuted Protestants from Europe, notably Lutheran Salzburgers and Moravians, were also welcomed. After a few years, the adventurers and foreigners far outnumbered the debtor element in the population.

Authority over Georgia's affairs was officially shared by the Board of Trustees and the British government, though in practice a smaller body known as the Common Council carried on most of the work. Among the most active trustees were Oglethorpe, Perceval, James

Vernon, the Earl of Shaftesbury (Anthony Ashley-Cooper), and Benjamin Martyn, the secretary. Although the trustees were to appoint the governor, his instructions came from the King. All laws passed by the trustees had to be reviewed by the king. While the trustees held the philanthropic and social goals to be of primary importance, the government was chiefly concerned with the economic and defensive advantages which Georgia might contribute to the Empire. The trustees came to distrust Sir Robert Walpole, the Chancellor of the Exchequer, and in order to evade the authority of the government, tried, as far as possible, to govern by regulations rather than laws. In the absence of local governmental institutions, Oglethorpe acted as an authoritarian, patriarchal leader.

Inevitably, Georgia took on the military character which the Crown intended it to have, and the colonists were distracted from the business of building a stable society. Georgia's most serious problems in the early years were caused by the conflicting purposes which she was expected to fulfill.

Pertinent Literature

Coulter, E. Merton. *Georgia: A Short History.* Chapel Hill: University of North Carolina Press, 1933.

Coulter's work begins with the sixteenth century, for knowledge of the competition between Spain, France, and England for American territory is essential for understanding the situation which encouraged the founding of Georgia but which nearly destroyed it.

Coulter emphasizes the basic conflict between the idealism of the philanthropists and the pragmatism of the British government. The essential incompatibility of the two objectives made for the turbulent early history of Georgia.

In this book ample evidence is provided that Georgia bore a strong military tinge from the beginning. Oglethorpe concerned himself not only with fortifying Savannah, but also with establishing other strategic military posts. A considerable portion of his time was occupied with offensive as well as defensive expeditions against the Spanish.

Military duties were not the only concern that kept the settlers from the essential business of growing food. As in Virginia and South Carolina, the British government was determined to promote industries which would eliminate dependence on foreign markets for certain goods. So the Georgia settlers were required to plant mulberry trees with the intention of producing all the silk that England required. Again the government's efforts served only to divert the colonists from more practical and necessary activities.

Conflicting imperial interests were by no means Georgia's only problem. The trustees, who had so carefully screened the population and who had so thoughtfully planned the system of land tenure, had been sadly lacking in an understanding of human nature. By the early 1740's, dissatisfaction with the restrictions on landholding and the Indian trade, and with the prohibitions on the introduction of slaves and liquor, had resulted in a severe drop in the population and in vocal criticism and widespread violations by the colonists. Realizing the impracticality of their plans, the trustees gradually relaxed the limitations on landholdings and allowed the importation of rum and slaves, thus destroying their dream of a controlled social environment. After the first ten years, many of the original disillusioned promoters lost interest in Georgia, and contributions for her support were no longer forthcoming. In actuality, Coulter contends, Georgia was never primarily a charitable enterprise. Less than half the immigrants came at the expense of the trust, and a large proportion of those who did were foreign Protestants rather than English debtors.

In Coulter's estimation, probably the greatest blunder of the trustees was their failure to establish adequate political institutions. Hoping to evade the King's veto, they governed when possible by regulations. Oglethorpe was never formally appointed Governor, but acted as a military, rather than a civil, leader much of the time. When he did set up a government, it consisted merely of three judges to try cases and a few minor law enforcement officials. The subsequent creation of a president and assistants, actually only a court of appeals, did little to advance the level of government. The colonists had no voice at all in their affairs. Only at the very end of their tenure did the trustees recognize the folly of expecting men to sit back and accept the will of an authority imposed upon them. In the year before they surrendered their charter, the trustees finally decided to experiment in the direction of popular government.

Reasons, both well-intentioned and selfish, for the failure of Georgia during the period of trusteeship become eminently clear to the reader through Coulter's analysis of factual data.

Ettinger, Amos A. *James Edward Oglethorpe, Imperial Idealist.* Hamden, Connecticut: Archon Books, 1968.

In an age not famous for social consciousness, Oglethorpe came to prominence as a proponent of humane treatment for the downtrodden. Ettinger portrays his subject as the "guiding genius" and "dominant force" behind reform of the corrupt English prison system. An unlikely candidate for distinguished service to his government, Oglethorpe was the son of ardent Jacobites. Although the family's political intrigues on both sides of the English Channel in the cause of the deposed Stuarts appear to have had little influence upon the young Member of Parliament, Ettinger relates them in some detail with obvious amusement.

Oglethorpe's parliamentary career was distinguished primarily by his leadership of the prison investigation, but he was a fairly consistent supporter of progressive causes. So enlightened were Oglethorpe's views on free trade and equality for all parts of the British Empire that, had they been realized, the author conjectures that there might have been no desire for American independence. Nonetheless, Oglethorpe's interest in the mercantilist and imperial spheres was sincere. As an advocate of military preparedness, he opposed the pacific tendencies of Walpole and the Whigs.

Combining the qualities of the social reformer, the mercantilist, and the military man, Oglethorpe seemed to be the ideal leader for a colony which was to serve a threefold purpose: philanthropic, economic, and defensive. The inaccessibility of the records of the "Associates of the Late Dr. Bray" at the time of Ettinger's research led him to underestimate the role of that society in getting the Georgia venture underway. It is true, nevertheless, that Oglethorpe was the dominant figure in the early period of settlement and the primary reason for its temporary success. Lacking any sort of political machinery, the colonists looked to him as a moral leader, planner, judge, and general. His diplomatic skill in winning the friendship and respect of the Indians, particularly of Chief Tomochichi, was of incalculable value to the colony.

Ettinger does not lose sight, however, of Oglethorpe's shortcomings in his management of Georgia's affairs. He pictures the general as headstrong and sometimes foolishly aggressive, marching his troops back and forth against the Spanish almost in comic opera fashion. Oglethorpe's irresponsible attitude toward the Board of Trustees no doubt proved a trial to Perceval, who had assumed the task of raising and administering the funds for Georgia. Oglethorpe not only neglected to inform the trustees of affairs in the colony, but also drew drafts on their funds without notifying them. In 1736, he was called to England over three issues: the plight of the trust because of his failure to correspond, complaints by South Carolinians over restrictions placed upon their trade in Georgia, and the need for a stronger defense. With obvious admiration, the author recounts Oglethorpe's manipulation of the facts to work his way back into the favor of the trustees and the Crown to the discredit of Walpole.

Returning to Georgia with a newly-raised regiment, the general cleverly succeeded in saving the colony from the clutches of the Spanish, but only temporarily from the waning interest of the trustees. By the early 1740's, most of Oglethorpe's administrative powers had passed to far less able men.

After his return to England in 1743, Oglethorpe's participation in Georgia affairs dwindled. His life from his forty-sixth year, though enlivened by association with Samuel Johnson's literary circle and by friendships with many of the famous figures of the age, was anticlimactic.

Because Oglethorpe exhibited at times seemingly paradoxical qualities, it is much to the author's credit that he manages to portray the various facets of his subject in a relatively unbiased manner. That this is a biography of scholarly importance is further evidenced by the nearly exhaustive assemblage of source materials which Ettinger consulted. — *W.M.B.*

Additional Recommended Reading

Reese, Trevor R. *Colonial Georgia: A Study in British Imperial Policy in the Eighteenth Century.* Athens: University of Georgia Press, 1963. Georgia's internal affairs are subordinated to an examination of the colony's early history from the vantage point of British imperial policy.

McPherson, Robert G., ed. *The Journal of the Earl of Egmont: Abstract of the Trustees Proceedings for Establishing the Colony of Georgia, 1732-1738.* Athens: University of

Georgia Press, 1962. An indispensable primary source, this private record of the meeting of the Georgia trustees was kept by Perceval in addition to the official minutes.

Tailfer, Patrick. *A True and Historical Narrative of the Colony of Georgia: With Comments by the Earl of Egmont.* Edited by Clarence L. VerSteeg. Athens: University of Georgia Press, 1960. Generally known as the "Tailfer Book," this famous polemic by three disgruntled Georgia settlers, published in 1741, roundly condemns the management of the colony.

Coulter, E. Merton, ed. *The Journal of Peter Gordon, 1732-1735.* Athens: University of Georgia Press, 1963. The author of this first-hand account of the establishment of Georgia occupied a position of authority in the local government and eventually became an agent of the malcontents.

Crane, Verner W. *The Southern Frontier, 1670-1732.* Ann Arbor: University of Michigan Press, 1956. A fine background study which provides a history not only of the beginnings of the Carolinas but also of the expansion of frontier trade with the Indians and of the contest for empire.

Church, Leslie F. *Oglethorpe: A Study of Philanthropy in England and Georgia.* London: The Epworth Press, 1932. Though less satisfactory than Ettinger's work as a biography, this book does portray the situation in Georgia in greater detail.

TRIAL OF JOHN PETER ZENGER AND FREEDOM OF THE PRESS

Type of event: Legal: establishment of precedents for libel prosecutions
Time: August 4, 1734
Locale: New York

Principal personages:

JOHN PETER ZENGER (1697-1746), printer and publisher of the *New York Weekly Journal*
WILLIAM COSBY (c.1690-1736), Governor of New York
ANDREW HAMILTON (?-1741), Zenger's defense counsel
JAMES ALEXANDER (1691-1756), lawyer and leader of the anti-Cosby faction
JAMES DE LANCEY (1703-1760), Chief Justice appointed by Cosby to the Supreme Court of the Province of New York
LEWIS MORRIS (1671-1746), Chief Justice removed by Cosby from the Supreme Court of the Province of New York
RICHARD BRADLEY (fl. 1734), attorney general of the Province of New York

Summary of Event

John Peter Zenger's fame rests upon his role in what is perhaps the best known free speech case in American history. Born in Germany in 1697, Zenger emigrated to New York in 1710 and took up an apprenticeship with William Bradford, publisher of the *New York Gazette.* Bradford was then the only printer in New York and the printer for the colonial government. Upon completing his apprenticeship, Zenger traveled through the colonies and settled in Maryland during 1720-1722. He married and served for a time as the printer for the colonial administration. When his wife died, he returned to New York, where, in 1726, he established his own printing shop. Zenger later became the public printer for New York and New Jersey. He died on July 28, 1746.

Zenger's famous trial took place while he was living in New York, and grew out of a dispute between the Governor of New York and New Jersey, and the acting Governor. William Cosby was appointed Governor of the two colonies in 1731, but remained in England until 1732. During 1731-1732, Rip Van Dam, the senior member of the Governor's Council in New York, served as "acting Governor." Upon his arrival in New York, Cosby demanded that Van Dam turn over half of the stipend which he had received from the colonial legislature as "acting" Governor." When Van Dam refused, Cosby declared the colonial Supreme Court to be a court of equity and proceeded to sue Van Dam in that court. This tactic was an obvious ruse to evade the requirement of trying Van Dam before a jury of colonials hostile to the governor's authority. Two of the three justices of the Supreme Court coöperated with Cosby, but Chief Justice Lewis

Morris agreed with Van Dam's lawyers (who were later to serve as Zenger's original lawyers) that the governor had no authority to create the court of equity. Cosby was so angered by Morris' action that he removed him from office.

In the meantime, Morris and the leaders of the anti-Cosby forces began to plan the establishment of a newspaper which could counter the official *New York Gazette* in mobilizing public opinion in their favor. The paper they founded was the *New York Weekly Journal,* published by Zenger and edited by James Alexander, Morris' chief attorney and a leading figure in the opposition to Cosby. The first issue of the paper appeared in November, 1733.

Zenger's criticisms of Cosby and his actions soon brought him trouble. A few months after the journal began publication, Cosby condemned it, and in August, 1734, the Governor and his council ordered Zenger's arrest for libel. While Zenger was in prison, his second wife continued to publish the paper. After failing in their attempts to persuade a grand jury to indict him, the authorities secured from the attorney general of New York, Richard Bradley, a bill of information charging that Zenger had committed "false, malicious, and seditious, and scandalous libel" by printing two issues of his journal. One of these two issues, dated January 28, 1734, had asserted that the people of New York "think, as matters now stand, that their liberties and properties are precarious, and that slavery is likely to be entailed on them and their posterity . . . ." The second issue, dated April 8, 1734, contained a statement by a New York resident

which declared: "We see men's deeds destroyed, judges arbitrarily displaced, new courts erected without consent of the legislature by which . . . trial by jury is taken away when a governor pleases . . . ."

Zenger was given a jury trial in the colonial Supreme Court before Chief Justice James de Lancey and Justice Frederick Philipse. His first defense counsel, James Alexander and William Smith, challenged the validity of the entire proceedings on the ground that the commissions of the two judges were defective. This challenge provoked the court to disbar them, and they were replaced by Andrew Hamilton of Philadelphia as chief defense counsel. Seizing upon the bill of information's reference to the libel as "false," Hamilton first attempted to prove the truth of the assertions, but Chief Justice de Lancey ruled him out of order. The attorney then attempted to caricature the precedents relied upon by the prosecution as "Star Chamber" cases. A more successful tactic, apparently, was Hamilton's insistence that Zenger had merely exercised the "natural right" of "complaining and remonstrating," "that the restraint upon this natural right is the law only; and that those restraints can only extend to what is *false* . . . ." Accepting the defense argument, after a brief deliberation, the jury returned a verdict of "not guilty," and Zenger was released.

Zenger's case constituted a major innovation concerning the law of libel. Up to that time, the role of the jury had been limited to ascertaining whether or not the accused had in fact published the material in question. But two important new rules were derived from this case: that juries in libel cases are competent to decide on questions of "law" as well as those of "fact"; and that truth is a defense in a libel prosecution. These principles were not adopted into American law, however, until the enactment of the Sedition Act of 1798.

Pertinent Literature

Buranelli, Vincent. *The Trial of Peter Zenger*. New York: New York University Press, 1957.

This study is considered by many to be the leading commentary on the Zenger trial because of its detailed examination of the trial's underlying social and political context. Buranelli aligns himself with those writers who see the persons around Zenger, specifically Alexander and Hamilton, as playing a more substantial role in the affair than Zenger himself. Although Buranelli tends to diminish Zenger's role, he nevertheless credits the overall movement with being "one of the most significant things that ever happened on this side of the Atlantic."

Buranelli states that the foundation for the Zenger affair was laid years before the trial took place by a savage feud between two of the most influential families in colonial New York, the Morrises and the de Lanceys. The de Lanceys, an emerging merchant family, sought to take away the political authority held by the traditional landowners' group as represented by the Morrises. As mercantile interests gained power, the influence of landowners in the colonial government declined. Year after year the conflict gained momentum until the Zenger affair precipitated an open confrontation of the two factions. From the beginning of his administration as Governor, Cosby sided with the commercial group and systematically replaced advisers, judges, and assemblymen who opposed him. Among Cosby's victims was Lewis Morris, who lost his position as chief justice to James de Lancey. The Morrisite faction, including Alexander, Van Dam, and Smith, clearly saw that their influence within the colony would be destroyed unless desperate measures were adopted. Their determination led them, Buranelli claims, to Zenger's print shop.

Buranelli credits Alexander with instigating the entire Zenger affair. Alexander was apparently convinced that the landowning interest could regain lost influence in colonial affairs if it could discredit the current colonial administration in the public mind. It was for this reason that the *New York Weekly Journal* was founded. It was, as Buranelli states, the first politically independent newspaper ever published on this continent.

Although the journal was known as "Zenger's paper," it was Alexander, according to Buranelli, who was actually its editor and who wrote most of its political editorials. Alexander had previously written political articles for the *New York Gazette*. Furthermore, the content of the paper, its witty and sarcastic tone, and its barbed innuendos were too professional for a man of Zenger's meager talents.

The journal was born not to gain a free press but to gain political influence. Buranelli believes that the overall importance of the *New York Weekly Journal* and the concepts which it embodied are to be found not only in its success in achieving its original goal but, more importantly, in its subsequent influence in political and legal reforms. It was an independent newspaper which not only printed news critical of the colonial government but also justified its right to do so. In defending the newspaper, Hamilton said that the people had the right to be informed on what their government was doing, and also the right to criticize their government when they had just cause.

Buranelli finds that Zenger's trial gave rise to two principles relative to a free press: "that truth may be used as a defense in libel cases" and "that the jury has a right to decide on both the 'fact' and the 'law'." These two propositions later became accepted legal principles both in America and in England.

Alexander, James. *A Brief Narrative of the Case and Trial of John Peter Zenger, Printer of the* New York Weekly Journal. Edited by Sidney N. Katz. Cambridge: Harvard University Press, 1963.

In his introduction, Katz questions the influence of Zenger's trial on the advancement of the free press. In his view, this development would have come about "with or without Peter Zenger." Katz believes that the most important aspects of Zenger's trial lay in the social and political forces surrounding the trial, which had been gaining impetus long before the Zenger affair. He implies that the Zenger case was used as a vehicle by which Zenger's associates, specifically James Alexander and Lewis Morris, hoped to regain their political influence by impeaching the colonial administration of Governor Cosby.

Katz points out that even Zenger's associates recognized the need of the state to restrain any speech which might endanger its security or tranquility. Katz doubts whether these men were "the radical exponents of free speech" that many writers have made them out to be. Their defense of Zenger consisted in assailing the jurisdiction of the judges and questioning the validity of their commissions on the grounds that they had not been approved by the State Council. It was not a legal defense resting on points of law, but rather a forthright accusation of maladministration leveled against Cosby.

Katz states that, although Zenger's first attorneys' defense argument was unsuccessful so that they were immediately disbarred and removed from the case, this action was significant because it allowed the entry of Hamilton into the case. Katz proceeds to use Hamilton's defense of Zenger to substantiate his contention that the real influence of Zenger's trial was not on the concept of a free press but on the political issues involved. Hamilton's defense of Zenger did not rest on law but on politics. His case was not based upon the legal question whether Zenger's editorials were to be considered libelous, but rather on the political issue whether the citizens had the right to criticize their government.

Hamilton's arguments for freedom of speech assumed that there existed a basic political difference between British and American government. Since

191

the Governors in America were only representatives of the Crown, they should not be allowed the same degree of freedom from criticism that the king enjoyed. Thus the colonists had the right to criticize their government even though their British counterparts did not have that right.

Finally, Katz states that, as Hamilton cited principles of government and not of law, his defense of Zenger was not meant to appeal to the legal sense of the judges. Rather, it was intended to appeal to the common men of the jury and their emotional involvement in the political issues of the time.

Katz concludes by stating that the influence of Zenger's trial on subsequent legal reform was not as great as some have considered. For example, Katz points out that the New York Assembly between 1747 and 1770 pressured the printers to exercise their freedom of the press cautiously under the threat of trial before the assembly for failure to do so. Although Zenger's

trial did assist in restraining the use of seditious libel as a weapon to restrict the press, it by no means guaranteed freedom of the press. It was not until passage of the Fox Libel Act in 1792 that juries were granted the power to give a verdict on the question whether or not certain writings were to be considered libelous. The substance of the libel law itself was not changed until more than a century after Zenger's trial when, with the passage of Lord Campbell's Act, it was stated that the truth of a written statement could be used as a defense in cases of seditious libel.

Although Katz presents a case which diminishes the measure of the Zenger trial's influence on freedom of the press and legal reform, he concludes that the most profound effect of the case was indirect. In his defense of Zenger, Hamilton articulated current colonial feelings concerning the proper relationship between government and citizens. — *J.J.B.*

Additional Recommended Reading

Emery, Edwin. *The Press and America: An Interpretative History of Journalism.* 2nd ed. Englewood Cliffs, New Jersey: Prentice-Hall, Inc., 1962. In this detailed history of the growth of the American newspaper, the author presents some noteworthy comments on the legal aspects of the Zenger trial and questions the overall effect of the trial on the concept of the free press.

Kobre, Sidney. *The Development of the Colonial Newspaper.* Magnolia, Massachusetts: Peter Smith Publisher, Inc., 1960. This historical survey of the newspaper in colonial America provides some insight into the economic, social, and political temper of the 1730's which, combined with Zenger's trial, made possible the advancement of the free press in America.

Levy, Leonard W. *Freedom of Speech and Press in Early American History: Legacy of Suppression.* New York: Harper & Row Publishers, 1963. Levy follows Buranelli's lead in crediting James Alexander with being the architect of Zenger's defense; he also claims that the Zenger trial had little or no impact on the common law governing libel.

Mott, Frank L. *American Journalism: A History, 1690-1960.* New York: The Macmillan Company, 1962. The author, although sketchy on the historical details surrounding the trial of Zenger, is nonetheless firm in his belief that the trial did have an immense effect upon the development of the American press.

Rutherford, Livingston. *John Peter Zenger: His Press, His Trial, and a Bibliography of Zenger Imprints.* New York: Dodd, Mead & Company, 1904. Reprinted, Magnolia, Massachusetts: Peter Smith Publisher, Inc. Presents an account of the events leading to Zenger's trial and a reprint of the *First Edition of the Trial* written by Zenger and published in his *New York Weekly Journal.* The author tends to exaggerate the immediate effects of Zenger's trial on the legal and political environment of the colony.

FOUNDING OF THE AMERICAN PHILOSOPHICAL SOCIETY

Type of event: Intellectual: desire to coördinate philosophical and scientific activities in the American colonies
Time: 1744
Locale: Philadelphia

Principal personages:
BENJAMIN FRANKLIN (1706-1790), editor, inventor, politician, diplomat, and founder of the American Philosophical Society
THOMAS JEFFERSON (1743-1826), author of the Declaration of Independence and third President of the United States
JOHN ADAMS (1735-1826), second President of the United States, political philosopher and theorist, author of *A Defence of the Constitutions of the United States*
THOMAS PAINE (1737-1809), British-born revolutionary, Deist, and author of *Common Sense, The Rights of Man,* and *The Age of Reason*
BENJAMIN RUSH (1745?-1813), physician and psychologist, one of the founders of the Pennsylvania Society for Promoting the Abolition of Slavery
CADWALLADER COLDEN (1688-1776), politician, scientist, and popularizer of Newton's theories
JOEL BARLOW (1754-1812), poet and author of *The Columbiad*
JAMES MADISON (1751-1836), fourth President of the United States and one of the authors of *The Federalist*
JONATHAN MAYHEW (1720-1766), pastor of Boston's West Church and author of *A Discourse Concerning Unlimited Submission and Non-Resistance to the Higher Powers*

Summary of Event

In 1743 Benjamin Franklin proposed the establishment of an American Philosophical Society to be located in Philadelphia. "The first Drudgery of Settling New Colonies, which confines the Attention of People to mere Necessaries, is now pretty well over," he explained in the circular letter describing the organization, "and there are many in every Province in Circumstances that set them at Ease, and afford Leisure to cultivate the finer Arts, and improve the common Stock of Knowl-edge." The society was organized the following year, with its founder as secretary, but it soon lapsed into inactivity. In 1769 it merged with another organization, the American Society; the new organization was called the American Philosophical Society for Promoting Useful Knowledge. Its membership included the leading philosophers and scientists of America. As the focus of intellectual activity in the New World, it was an important agent in the shaping of the distinctive pattern of thought known as the American Enlightenment.

Like their counterparts in Britain and on the Continent, the thinkers of the American Enlightenment accepted the Newtonian conception of the universe as a rational and harmonious machine operating according to natural laws which man, by the use of his reason, could discover. They believed that at the creation, all species of life had been arranged in a "chain of beings," ranging upward from the lowest form of life to man, a little lower than the angels; and that since that time no new species had come into existence and none had become extinct. Thus the harmony and variety of nature was matched by its economy. Believing that the universe was intelligible to man, eighteenth century Americans enthusiastically took up the task of studying nature. Thomas Jefferson's *Notes on the State of Virginia,* containing his observations on almost every aspect of the Virginia environment, suggested the wide-ranging interests and empirical bent of men of the American Enlightenment.

For Jefferson and other American thinkers, to study nature was to study God, who had created it. They worshipped God as the great architect of the universe and its laws, viewing him as an essentially rational and benevolent being to whom "the most acceptable service" was, as Benjamin Franklin declared, "doing good to His other children." Under the impact of Enlightenment ideas, Puritanism gave way to Arminianism and liberal religion. Boston's leading Arminians, Charles Chauncy and Jonathan Mayhew, preached the benevolence of God, the essential goodness of man, freedom of the will, the primacy of reason in religion, and universal salvation. Deism, or natural religion, which appealed to those who shied away from organized religion, embraced similar doctrines, though it expressly repudiated the authority of Scripture and the divinity of Christ. But despite the efforts of Ethan Allen, Elihu Palmer, and Thomas Paine, Deism never made much headway in America; and outright atheism, which flourished among French *philosophes,* was rare indeed.

The "sensational" psychology of John Locke, which taught that all ideas come from experience, was the primary source of the environmentalism from which much of the thinking of the American Enlightenment emanated. Using the pseudonym J. Hector St. John, Michel Guillaume Jean de Crèvecœur wrote in his *Letters from an American Farmer* (1782): "Men are like plants; the goodness and flavor of the fruit proceeds from the particular soil and exposition in which they grow. We are nothing but what we derive from the air we breathe, the climate we inhabit, the government we obey, the system of religion we profess, and the mode of our employment." Americans of the Enlightenment used the theory of environmentalism to explain the great variety of minds and creeds in society, as well as racial differences. The theory also underlay the faith which eighteenth century men put in education as a means of individual and social improvement.

The thinkers of the American Enlightenment developed a view of human nature that was both optimistic and realistic. They emphasized man's capacity for goodness in contrast to the Puritan doctrine of innate depravity.

195

Man, they said, was endowed by his Creator with a moral sense, or faculty, which enabled him to choose right over wrong. Subscribing to a utilitarian system of ethics, they advocated the practice of virtue as the way to wealth and happiness. The belief in man's capacity for "benevolence," along with the doctrine of environmentalism, which attributed evil not to the sinfulness of man but to corrupt institutions which might be reformed, provided the impulse behind the humanitarian reform movement of the late eighteenth century.

Though they emphasized man's capacity for good, American thinkers also recognized his inherent selfishness. To check man's tendency to encroach upon his fellows, government was necessary. Its purpose was the promotion of security and happiness to society, by protecting the natural, and therefore inalienable, rights of life, liberty and property belonging to all men. But government, being the work of men, was itself inclined to infringe upon the rights and liberties of the governed by aggrandizing power at their expense. Therefore, the men of the American Enlightenment tended to agree with Thomas Paine that "Government even in its best state is but a necessary evil." As a result, they interpreted the functions of government in a negative, restrictive sense, and advocated the establishment of internal checks and balances to restrain what they believed was the natural tendency of government to assume power. They believed in government by consent of the governed. Should government fail to perform its duties, "it is the right of the people to alter or to abolish it, and to institute a new government, laying its foundation on such principles, and organizing its powers in such form, as to them shall seem most likely to effect their safety and happiness." Both the Declaration of Independence and the United States Constitution bear the lasting imprint of the political theory of the American Enlightenment and the assumptions about nature and human nature on which it was based.

Pertinent Literature

Boorstin, Daniel J. *The Lost World of Thomas Jefferson.* New York: Holt, Rinehart and Winston, Inc., 1948.

Daniel Boorstin explains in his preface that his purpose is "to discover the dominant spirit of the Jeffersonian view of the world." He bases his analysis on the printed writings of the community of eighteenth century American philosophers and scientists whom he calls "the Jeffersonian circle": David Rittenhouse, Benjamin Rush, Benjamin Smith Barton, Joseph Priestley, Charles Willson Peale, Thomas Paine, and, of course, Thomas Jefferson himself, "the human magnet" who drew the others together and "gave order and meaning to their discrete investigations."

Boorstin agrees with other historians of the Enlightenment in emphasizing the Jeffersonians' worshipful attitude toward nature. Nature was apotheosized. Viewing nature "as the complete and perfected work of divine artifice," the Jeffersonians insisted that it supplied the standard by which to judge man and society. In addition, Boorstin emphasizes the naturalistic perspective from which Jeffersonians viewed man and his relation to the universe, noting that they commonly referred to man as "creature" to signify his "integration by the common Creator into the processes of nature."

Minimizing the influence of the European Enlightenment, Boorstin finds the keynote of Jeffersonian thought in what he calls "the American task," the business of carving a nation out of the wilderness. Thus the Jeffersonians worshiped God as "Architect and Builder" of the universe, the supreme embodiment of the talents which they themselves needed to fulfill their "continental task." The preoccupation with the American task also produced the Jeffersonians' sense of tension between man and nature. Though the Jeffersonians stressed man's adaptability, his capacity for adjusting to new environments, they also recognized that "the environment was in a sense master of man." In Boorstin's view, the sense of tension between man and nature was the most important source of the Jeffersonian vision of nature as a work of art. "It explains why the mere process of nature, the intricacy and smoothness of its operation, seemed to make the search for ends outside of nature superfluous. For the shaping, subduing and organizing of the material environment, in which the Creator had been so impressively successful, seemed itself the overwhelming task of the Jeffersonians."

The preoccupation with the American task also explains the profoundly activist temper of the American Enlightenment, which in turn influenced its political philosophy. Boorstin attributes the Jeffersonians' negative, restrictive view of government to their distrust of metaphysics. "A list of 'rights' substituted for a systematic theory of government." According to Boorstin the Jeffersonians saw no need to define the positive duties of government. "Such human definition was quite superfluous, for the ends had already been defined by the Creator and revealed in nature."

In effect, Boorstin has done what the Jeffersonians were unable to do because of their "antimetaphysical bias." He has systematized and synthesized their ideas about nature, God, and man, revealing the scientific and religious assumptions underlying the political and social theory of the American Enlightenment. At the same time, he exposes what he believes are the inadequacies of Jeffersonian thought—and of certain aspects of the American liberal tradition based on it—for the twentieth century. When the American task was completed at the end of the nineteenth century, Americans lost their earlier "sense of creaturehood"; they no longer felt a sense of tension between man and nature; they no longer saw nature as "a fixed point of reference." The intellectual world of the Jeffersonians had been annihilated. Moreover, the Age of the Robber Barons revealed the logical consequences of the Jeffersonian political philosophy once it had been stripped of the "prophetic spirit" that gave eighteenth century men "their sense of community, and prevented an emphasis on 'rights' from becoming anarchy, or from making society seem a hopeless jungle." Thus, in recreating the intellectual world of Jefferson and his friends, Boorstin reminds us at the same time of the extent to which the world of eighteenth century America, with its focus on the conquest of the wilderness, is indeed a "lost world."

Koch, Adrienne. *Power, Morals, and the Founding Fathers: Essays in the Interpretation of the American Enlightenment.* Ithaca: Great Seal Books, 1961.

Power, Morals, and the Founding Fathers is a collection of essays analyzing the political and social thought of Benjamin Franklin, Thomas Jefferson, Alexander Hamilton, John Adams, and James Madison—philosophers-statesmen whom Adrienne Koch considers "touchstones for the character of the American Enlightenment." Like Boorstin, Koch treats the American Enlightenment as a distinctive pattern of thought. But, whereas Boorstin emphasizes the activist temper of the Jeffersonian circle and its distrust of philosophical speculation, Koch argues that the thought of the founding fathers represents a conjunction of "supposedly contradictory" ideas and ideals: experience and theory, pragmatism and wisdom, power and morals. "Experimental humanism" is her term for "the central vision of the founding fathers and the temper of the Enlightenment in America . . . ."

Koch is primarily concerned with the political philosophy of the American Enlightenment and the way in which it conjoined the "two conditions necessary for successful free government," power and morals. In her view, the personal conflict between Jefferson and Hamilton and between Republicans and Federalists generally stemmed from different opinions as to the proper relation between the two elements. Whereas Hamilton and Adams tended to emphasize the necessity of power over moral concerns, Jefferson and Madison tipped the scales in the other direction, frequently advocating "moral restraints on the use of power." Jefferson's defense of the right of all men to pursue happiness and of majority rule were two such "moral restraints," both deriving from a belief in "the primacy of the human being," the purposes of which were to check the power of the government.

Koch argues that Jefferson and Madison were more successful than Hamilton and Adams in maintaining a balance between power and morals, and she implies that the two Virginians viewed power in a more positive light than has usually been thought. In Jefferson's conception of America as an "empire for liberty" she finds the two elements joined "in lifelike tension," the one term "symbolizing strength for self-preservation and growth, the other indicating the object for which that national strength, that power to resist outside manipulation and aggression, is to be sought: so that freedom, under the kind of benign government that values men and respects their natural rights, can be realized in fact." Because they saw the necessity of maintaining a "dynamic balance between power and morals," Jefferson and Madison were the true realists, according to Miss Koch, not visionary idealists as they have often been called. In contrast, Hamilton was a self-admitted political failure as a result of his "all-consuming passion for power," and at the same time something of an innocent because he remained unaware "that power is a runaway tiger, difficult to dismount."

Like Boorstin, Koch finds a lesson for the present in the thought of the American Enlightenment. In effect, she urges a revitalization of the "American philosophic tradition" formulated by the founding fathers. She believes that experimental humanism, with its recognition that "morals without power are weak, just as power without morals spells long-run destruction," can serve twentieth century Americans "as a strategic guide in meeting the future," particularly the exigencies of the Cold War. — *A.C.L.*

Additional Recommended Reading

Becker, Carl L. *The Declaration of Independence: A Study in the History of Political Ideas.* New York: Harcourt, Brace & World, Inc., 1922. Analyzes the Declaration of Independence and the natural rights philosophy on which it was based.

Koch, G. Alfred. *Republican Religion: The American Revolution and the Cult of Reason.* New York: Holt, Rinehart and Winston, Inc., 1933. Reprinted in 1968 by Thomas Y. Crowell, as *Religion of the American Enlightenment.* A study of Deism and free thought in post-Revolutionary America, as revealed in the writings and activities of such men as Ethan Allen, Elihu Palmer, Thomas Paine, John Foster, and "Walking" John Stewart.

Kraus, Michael. *The Atlantic Civilization: Eighteenth Century Origins.* Ithaca: Cornell University Press, 1949. This study of the new civilization produced by the interrelationship of the New and Old World reveals the common fund of ideas shared by enlightened thinkers in both Europe and America. Kraus emphasizes the influence on America of eighteenth century concepts of political and religious freedom, economic opportunity, and humanitarianism.

Hindle, Brooke. *The Pursuit of Science in Revolutionary America, 1735-1789.* Chapel Hill: University of North Carolina Press, 1956. Describes the development of scientific interest and activity in the American colonies as a result of European influence and in response to indigenous needs.

Bailyn, Bernard. "Political Experience and Enlightenment Ideas in Eighteenth Century America," in *American Historical Review.* LXVII (January, 1962), 339-351. In this seminal article, based on his own research as well as recent revisionist interpretations of early American history, Bailyn sketches the broad outlines of a provocative new interpretation of the relation between the ideas of the Enlightenment and political developments in the American colonies.

Koch, Adrienne. *The Philosophy of Thomas Jefferson.* New York: Columbia University Press, 1943. A study of various aspects of Jefferson's philosophy in relation to European schools of thought.

THE FRENCH AND INDIAN WAR

Type of event: Military: rivalry between the British and the French which culminated in the defeat of the French in America
Time: 1754-1760
Locale: The eastern half of North America

Principal personages:

BENJAMIN FRANKLIN (1706-1790), American statesman, scientist, and philosopher, whose Plan of Union was accepted by the Albany Congress but rejected by Great Britain and the colonies

WILLIAM PITT (THE ELDER) (1708-1778), Secretary of State of Great Britain and leader of the House of Commons with full control of foreign and military affairs 1757-1761

JOHN STUART (EARL OF BUTE) (1713-1792), Prime Minister of Great Britain 1762-1763 who negotiated the Treaty of Paris

WILLIAM SHIRLEY (1694-1771), Governor of Massachusetts 1753-1756 and British Commander in Chief in America 1755-1756

JOHN CAMPBELL (EARL OF LOUDON) (1705-1782), British Commander in Chief in America 1756-1757

JEFFREY AMHERST (1717-1797), British officer who commanded army against the French fortress of Louisbourg until it surrendered in 1758, Commander in Chief in North America in 1759, and Governor General of British North America 1760-1763

JAMES WOLFE (1727-1759), British army officer who served under Amherst at the siege of Louisbourg and who commanded the expedition against Quebec which routed the French in 1759

MARQUIS LOUIS JOSEPH DE MONTCALM DE SAINT-VÉRAN (1712-1759), Commander of French troops in Canada who fought heroically to save Canada from the British but who was defeated and mortally wounded in the Battle of Quebec in 1759

Summary of Event

Before the 1750's, the rivalry between Great Britain and France in the New World had been incidental to their more significant conflicts in Europe. To thwart French territorial ambitions against the Austrian empire and the German states, Great Britain had formed and led coalitions to maintain the balance of power on the Continent. In the War of the League of Augsburg (1689-1697), and the War of the Spanish Succession (1702-1713), known in the colonies as King William's War and Queen Anne's War re-

200

spectively, neither antagonist felt any need to send large regular forces overseas. By the Treaty of Utrecht (1713), however, France acknowledged Great Britain's claim to the Hudson Bay country and gave up Nova Scotia. A later British conflict with Spain involving Georgia and the West Indies, the War of Jenkins' Ear (1739-1742), merged with the War of the Austrian Succession (1740-1748) and was called King George's War in the colonies. The British provincials, accomplishing relatively little in earlier wars against French strongholds to the north, successfully assaulted the fortress of Louisbourg on Cape Breton Island near the mouth of the St. Lawrence river; but the supposedly impregnable bastion, "the Gibraltar of the New World," reverted to France in the Treaty of Aix-la-Chapelle (1748) that restored the *status quo ante bellum.* Yet the colonists' achievement in capturing Louisbourg emphasized to both powers the increasing role that Great Britain's American subjects would have if, as was generally predicted, the shaky settlement of 1748 failed to last.

Events in America, not in Europe, brought about a resumption of hostilities in the early 1750's. The British settlers, numbering more than a million by mid-century and "multiplying like rattlesnakes," were pushing westward; already they were trickling through the mountain passes and looking toward the fertile bottom lands of the Ohio river country, a region claimed by both France and Great Britain. The French, with their small and diffused population in Canada (called "New France"), strengthened their claim by cementing their traditional Indian alliances and by erecting forts in the Ohio River Val-

ley. Initially, the British numerical advantage failed to bring positive results. Colonial disunity was demonstrated through the rejection, by both Great Britain and the colonies in general, of Benjamin Franklin's Plan of Union in 1754 even after it had been accepted by the Albany Congress. Likewise, the defeat of Washington's Virginia militia near the forks of the Ohio on July 3, 1754, and the tragic failure of the British expedition under General Braddock against Fort Duquesne on July 9, 1755, all foretold a long and difficult war for Great Britain and its American colonists. Braddock was succeeded by William Shirley, Governor of Massachusetts, as Commander in Chief of British forces in America from 1755 to 1756, who was succeeded in turn from 1756 to 1757 by John Campbell, Earl of Loudon, and until 1759, by James Abercrombie. During their tenures, expeditions against Fort Niagara, Crown Point, and Fort Ticonderoga sputtered and failed, and their French adversaries seized Oswego and Fort William Henry. Inadequate generalship and the inability of the British and Americans to galvanize their impressive advantages in human and material resources played a decisive part in the string of reversals between 1754 and 1758. Moreover, the French pursued the policy of a strategic defense, which compelled Anglo-American forces to cope with formidable obstacles in advancing men and supplies over hundreds of miles of dense, unsettled country. The French also were fortunate in that their own movements were greatly facilitated by the St. Lawrence river, providing them with a continuous waterway from Louisbourg to Niagara. In Europe, too, the French seemed to have the upper hand; their "diplomatic revolution" made an ally out of a former enemy, Austria, while England was driven into the arms of Prussia. On the high seas, a French victory over the British fleet in the Mediterranean led to the capture of Minorca.

Great Britain needed a sound logistical system and better leadership, both at home and in America, in order to win. Actually, the discredited Loudon, who was replaced by Abercrombie, had recognized the first essential requirement and had put in motion plans to build roads, create supply stations, and utilize colonial manpower—not on the battlefield but to transport supplies for armies advancing into positions from which to mount attacks against French outposts. Leadership, the second necessary ingredient, came from William Pitt, the Elder, who after 1757 was Secretary of State of Great Britain and leader of the House of Commons with full control of foreign and military affairs. Vigorous and resourceful, unmindful of tradition or military seniority, Pitt elevated younger officers over their elders and dipped lavishly into the Treasury to subsidize both the hard-pressed Frederick the Great of Prussia on the Continent and the American colonies in order to encourage greater participation of the latter in the War. Two of Pitt's hand-picked officers, Jeffrey Amherst, a former lieutenant colonel who had never before had an independent command, and thirty-one-year-old James Wolfe, took Louisbourg on July 26, 1758, the first major British victory of the War. Cut off from the mouth of the St. Lawrence river,

the French lost control of the other end of that river a short time later when Lieutenant Colonel John Bradstreet captured Fort Frontenac. Its seizure cut French supply lines to Fort Duquesne and forced the evacuation of that post, which the British occupied and renamed Fort Pitt.

The campaign of 1759—the culmination of Pitt's grand strategy for America—saw pincer movements directed at Quebec and Montreal. Quebec fell to the brilliant Wolfe, who, fatally wounded, as was the French commander, Marquis Louis Joseph de Montcalm de Saint-Véran, did not live to witness the surrender on September 18, 1759. As French efforts to recapture the city failed, a second British force was driving northward and overcame Montreal on September 8, 1760. The war for North America was over, but the international phases of the conflict continued as Great Britain inflicted crushing defeats on France's ally, Spain, at Manila and Havana. The temperamental Pitt, who lost political support once victory was assured and who was not close to the new King, George III, was out of office before the peacemaking began. John Stuart, Earl of Bute, the new Prime Minister and an intimate of the young monarch, did not share Pitt's desire to strip the Bourbon enemies of all their possessions. Even so, as a result of the Treaty of Paris, he vastly extended the British Empire by taking Canada from France and Florida from Spain, and by carving up French possessions in India. Great Britain in 1763 stood unrivaled as the foremost power in the world.

Pertinent Literature

Parkman, Francis. *Montcalm and Wolfe.* 2 vols. Boston: Little, Brown, and Company, 1884.

Montcalm and Wolfe is probably the most famous of Francis Parkman's historical works. It forms a part of his eight-volume series on *France and England in North America,* an account of the struggle between the two great European powers for supremacy in the New World, which was written over a period of more than forty years between 1851 and 1892. "The plan of the work," writes Parkman, "was formed in early youth." He "visited and examined every spot" connected with his history of the French and Indian War, which drew its title from the two famous generals who opposed each other at the Battle of Quebec. "In short, the subject has been studied as much from life and in the open air as at the library table." Born into a family of Boston patricians and educated at Harvard, Parkman possessed the financial means and the intellectual background to accomplish his long-term objective of chronicling the duel for empire between Great Britain and France; the fact that he suffered long periods of semiblindness was really a virtue, for he had to master his materials completely before beginning composition.

The devoting of his life to a gigantic undertaking, the development of a grand theme, and the use of bold, descriptive prose, make Parkman's work rank with the best historical writing of the nineteenth century, such as that of Lord Macaulay in England and of William H. Prescott, John L. Motley, and George Bancroft in the United States. Parkman, in the fashion of his period, presents detailed vignettes of the personalities who figured largely in his story. If he unabashedly favored the British cause, he admired many of the French as individuals, including Frontenac and La Salle in the early volumes and Montcalm in his treatment of the French and Indian War. The reader sees both the public and the personal sides of his characters. Parkman often, in moving prose, bids farewell to one of his heroic personalities, as with the dead Montcalm at Quebec in 1759: "Montcalm lay in his soldier's grave before the humble altar of the Ursulines, nevermore to see the home for which he yearned, the wife, mother, and children whom he loved, the olive-trees and chestnut-groves of his beloved Candiac. He slept in peace among triumphant enemies. . . ." Even the Jesuits, whose religion Parkman abhorred, aroused his admiration for their hardships and suffering, and for their bravery in the face of unbelievable torture from the Iroquois. For the Indians, however, the author had nothing but contempt, considering them treacherous, murdering fiends rather than "noble savages." Although Parkman had observed the Plains Indians firsthand on a journey resulting in his classic, *The Oregon Trail,* he never saw the red men as fighting to save their own lands or to maintain their way of life.

If Parkman's history has its serious weaknesses stemming from ideas of race, religion, and nationality current in his own day; if he and other literary craftsmen of the last century were overly imbued with the concept of history as a guide to the present and shaper of the future, his work still towers majestically over almost all the literature of American history. It endures not merely because of the rare narrative power or his prodigious research, but, more important, because he addressed himself to the fundamental question inherent in the century-long conflict for supremacy in North America: Why did the English-speaking people win? Their victory was explained, in the final analysis, by the superiority of British society in America. The absolute government, religious repression, economic restrictions, and restraints on immigration that characterized New France and retarded its growth and development, were absent from British America. The English settlers, for the reasons mentioned above, were more numerous than the French inhabitants to the north and had greater incentive. They fought to maintain the freedom they already possessed. One may question many of Parkman's details, and object that he somewhat neglected to give credit to British naval power and other European factors that helped to shape the outcome, but his overview is still reflected strongly in the writings of American historians. The most recent one-volume synthesis of the subject by a leading authority (Howard H. Peckham's *The Colonial Wars, 1689-1762*), agrees largely with Parkman.

Gipson, Lawrence H. *The British Empire Before the American Revolution.* Vol. VI: *The Years of Defeat, 1754-1757: The Great War for the Empire.* New York: Alfred A. Knopf, Inc., 1949.

Gipson, Lawrence H. *The British Empire Before the American Revolution.* Vol. III: *The Victorious Years, 1758-1760: The Great War for the Empire.* New York: Alfred A. Knopf, Inc., 1949.

Lawrence H. Gipson, who like Parkman, was an indefatigable researcher, spent the most productive years of his long life in the preparation of his own magnum opus: *The British Empire Before the American Revolution.* Gipson is concerned with a shorter time span than Parkman, roughly the quarter century before the Declaration of Independence, but Gipson's history is more broadly conceived, devoted to a detailed examination of the whole of the British Empire in the eighteenth century, including Africa, India, and the West Indies, and their administrative and economic relationships with the Mother Country. While Parkman gives his readers a glamorized picture of the final Anglo-French conflict before the American Revolution, Gipson covers the ground in the role of a dispassionate analyst, laying stress upon France's lack of seapower and her debilitating involvements on the Continent of Europe.

Gipson believes that our nationalist tradition has led us astray concerning various truths about the war. Even the name which Americans gave to the struggle, "the French and Indian War," arose from hostility to Great Britain during the American Revolution. Among the revolutionists, Thomas Paine did most to destroy the notion of Great Britain's fighting to protect the colonies after 1754; among historians, George Bancroft is the chief culprit. According to Gipson, the nationalist tradition has several components: that Great Britain's rivalry with France involved the colonists in wars of no vital interest to them; that whatever Great Britain contributed to the successful outcome, "the unlimited expanses of North America were predestined to be the heritage of the Americans . . . the war in question was but a somewhat incidental thing"; and that Great Britain's motive was only self-interest, and that its troops, unschooled in wilderness warfare, were more of a handicap than an advantage.

In striving to disavow these concepts, Gipson insists that the stakes in the war were exceedingly high. The outcome determined whether British or French civilization would prevail in North America and whether the Appalachians would be a permanent barrier to westward expansion. As for the myth of the supremacy of colonial militia over redcoats, Gipson shows that the provincial assemblies begged for royal regiments; the Americans "had much greater faith in the performances of troops trained in the regular method of warfare than in irregulars fighting in Indian fashion." Gipson also contends that this final conflict, begun by the French and directed at the Ohio River Valley, initially "had nothing to do with the old animosities of Europe." It was a peculiarly American war, as the Duke of Newcastle maintained when he said, "Let Americans fight Americans." Instead of following Newcastle's pronouncement, the Mother Country provided massive aid, its primary purpose being to preserve its empire, not to enlarge it. Thus it was not "the French and Indian War," but "the Great War for the Empire," a name the author employs throughout, as have later writers sympathetic to his viewpoint.

Critics, though sometimes finding fault with the author for his occasional criticism of Pitt's leadership and Wolfe's tactics at Quebec, among other things, have generally accepted Gipson's contention that orthodox military science and tactics predominated in a struggle that increasingly resembled "a European conflict in a New World setting." But not all specialists subscribe to his claim that Great Britain acted primarily from a spirit of altruism in hastening troops and monies to America; after all, it was British colonies that were threatened, and Britain had much to lose by their defeat or dismemberment. Certainly Pitt viewed the war as one of territorial gain for Great Britain. Whether it was a war for the British Empire or a war to acquire empire, the outcome had momentous consequences for both Great Britain and America. — *R.D.H.*

Additional Recommended Reading

Pargellis, Stanley M. *Lord Loudon in North America*. New Haven: Yale University Press, 1933. A sympathetic portrait which contributes significantly to our knowledge of supply and logistics.

Freeman, Douglas Southall. *George Washington*. Vol. V: *Victory with the Help of France*. New York: Charles Scribner's Sons, 1948. 2 vols. An excellent narrative of the first three years of the war on the Virginia frontier.

Stacey, C. P. *Quebec, 1759: The Seige and the Battle*. New York: St. Martin's Press, 1959. The bicentennial of Wolfe's victory marked the appearance of three good books on the subject, but Stacey's is the best.

Cuneo, John R. *Robert Rogers of the Rangers.* New York: Oxford University Press, 1959. A sprightly, well-documented life of a New Hampshire frontier leader whose commando-like tactics against the French have been studied in recent years by the United States Army.

Schutz, John A. *William Shirley: King's Governor of Massachusetts.* Chapel Hill: University of North Carolina Press, 1961. A perceptive biography of a popular and successful colonial administrator who met with failure upon assuming the position of Commanding General early in the French and Indian War.

Peckham, Howard H. *The Colonial Wars, 1689-1762.* Chicago: University of Chicago Press, 1964. A readable synthesis of existing scholarship.

Leach, Douglas E. *The Northern Colonial Frontier, 1607-1763.* New York: Holt, Rinehart, & Winston, Inc., 1966. An excellent book, especially strong on Indian-white relations.

PROCLAMATION OF 1763

Type of event: Political: desire to avoid further Indian wars by retarding colonial expansion
Time: October 7, 1763
Locale: London, England

Principal personages:

EARL OF HALIFAX (GEORGE MONTAGU DUNK) (1716-1771), president of the Board of Trade 1748-1761

WILLIAM PETTY (EARL OF SHELBURNE, MARQUIS OF LANSDOWNE) (1737-1805), president of Board of Trade 1763 and Secretary of State for the Southern Department 1766-1768, who opposed the British government on its American policy.

EARL OF EGREMONT (CHARLES WYNDHAM) (1710-1763), Secretary of State for the Southern Department 1761-1763

EARL OF HILLSBOROUGH, MARQUIS OF DOWNSHIRE (WILLS HILL) (1718-1793), president of the Board of Trade 1763-1765 and 1768, and Secretary of State for the Colonies 1768-1772

JEFFREY AMHERST (1717-1797), British Commander in Chief in North America from 1759, and Governor General of British North America 1760-1763

SIR WILLIAM JOHNSON (1715-1774), superintendent of Indian Affairs 1755-1774

Summary of Event

How would Britain, victorious in the French and Indian War, control the vast domain between the Appalachians and the Mississippi after 1763? The answer to this question was awaited by Indians, French Canadians, and British colonial administrators as it was by American fur traders, merchants, and land speculators. The West had increasingly occupied the attention of British and colonial officials since the Albany Congress. During the ensuing war, the Crown appointed superintendents to coördinate Indian affairs, Sir William Johnson for the Northern Department and Edmund Atkin (succeeded by John Stuart in 1762) for the Southern Department, but exigencies of the moment made the new arrangement inadequate. In the eyes of White-

hall officials, the old policy of leaving control of the frontier to the individual colonies had been chaotic and ruinous. The line of English agricultural settlement had steadily edged westward with scant regard for Indian land claims or the red man's way of life. Repeatedly, royal governors, Indian superintendents, and British military men had complained of the disregard of Indian treaties by the colonists as well as fraudulent land purchases by them, and of the mistreatment of the aborigines at the hands of white traders.

The necessity of reaching an accord with the Indians was underscored by Pontiac's Rebellion of 1763-1764. The red men, already uneasy over the defeat of their French allies, encountered repeated insults from the British Com-

207

mander in Chief, General Jeffrey Amherst, who also refused to court them with guns, ammunition, and other gifts, as was the French custom. The storm broke early in May, 1763. Striking first in the remote West and later on the Pennsylvania frontier, roving parties of Ottawas, Chippewas, Delawares, and Senecas overran one British-occupied post after another until, by the end of June, only Forts Detroit, Pitt, and Niagara still held out against the warriors. Amherst, who was soon recalled under a cloud, dispatched relief expeditions to his remaining garrisons, and several colonies raised troops to repel the invaders. The prospect of fire and sword, the diplomatic skills of William Johnson, and the breakup of the coalition of tribes, never united as to ultimate objectives, explain the restoration of peace in 1764. The Indians, treated generously, paid no penalty for Pontiac's Rebellion.

During the uprising, the government announced its new policy for the West, one that had evolved from British experience in the French and Indian War. It was the work of no single minister or subminister, although the Earl of Egremont (Charles Wyndham, Secretary of State for the Southern Department 1761-1763), William Petty, the Earl of Shelburne, President of the Board of Trade in 1763 and later Secretary of State for the Southern Department), and the Earl of Hillsborough (Wills Hill, President of the Board of Trade from 1763 to 1765 and later Secretary of State for the Colonies) were keenly interested in the matter. On October 7, 1763, King George III signed the edict known today as the Proclamation of 1763. By its terms, the recently acquired territories of Canada and East and West Florida became Crown colonies, and their inhabitants became entitled to the same rights as Englishmen at home. All colonial claims to territories west of the crest of the Appalachians were nullified, those lands, "for the present, and until our further Pleasure be known," being set aside for the Indians. Trade with the tribesmen was to be "free and open," although traders were to be licensed and were to obey such regulations as might be prescribed. Since the Proclamation of 1763 contained no provision for law enforcement in the area beyond provincial boundaries, an *ad hoc* system developed, with the trade confined to certain posts or towns under the supervision of the Indian superintendents, assisted by fort commanders whose regular troops were to enforce the trade regulations.

In the long run, this "Western policy" of Great Britain failed. Land-hungry settlers spilled over into the Indian country in defiance of the Proclamation of 1763. British troops could not guard every mountain pass, nor could they and Crown Indian agents confine white traders to specified locations. Moreover, the maintenance of Western garrisons was expensive, especially when American revenues for the army's upkeep failed to materialize and when the redcoats did not accomplish their mission. In 1768, the British government, beset by these problems and colonial rebelliousness in the East, adopted a policy of retrenchment in the West. Control of the Indian trade reverted to the individual colonies, and British troops received orders to abandon all the interior posts except Niagara, Detroit, and Michilimackinac. Almost simultaneously, the government bowed to pressure for pushing the Indian boundary westward. This shift was accomplished in the Treaty of Fort Stanwix (1768) with the Iroquois and the Treaties of Hard Labor (1768) and Lochaber (1770) with the Cherokee. No longer did the West loom uppermost in British imperial thinking.

Pertinent Literature

Alvord, Clarence W. *The Mississippi Valley in British Politics.* Glendale, Calif.: The Arthur H. Clark Co., 1917. 2 Vols.

Clarence Alvord was the first scholar to write an in-depth study of British Western policy between the final colonial war and the American Revolution. Throughout the years in question, maintains Alvord, the foremost concern of the home government was not the revolutionary agitation on the Eastern seaboard; it was rather the development of the tramontane region acquired from Great Britain's vanquished enemies. Alvord's examination of successive ministries and the relationships between leading political personalities resulted in his conclusion (reached before most scholars) that British politics revolved around factions instead of easily defined parties bearing the Whig and Tory labels. However, with the debate over the Peace of Paris in 1763, especially the question of whether to retain Canada or Guadeloupe, there emerged a "clear-cut issue": those who favored retaining Canada committed themselves to a program of westward expansion, while their opponents, who favored annexing the French West Indian Guadeloupe Island, generally opposed the opening of the North American interior. To state the matter another way, as does Alvord, the struggle involved whether or not to stand rigidly behind mercantilist principles. The mercantilists, believing that the greatest value of colonies was as mar-

kets for finished goods or as sources of raw materials needed by the Mother Country, favored the retention of the valuable sugar island of Guadeloupe over the barren wastelands of Canada. "Thus it may be said with approximate truth that all future issues concerning the Mississippi Valley were formed and the trend of partisan opinion determined during the critical period of the peace negotiations."

According to Alvord, the key to understanding the various proposals for controlling the interior before the American Revolution is to be found in the Proclamation of 1763. Of all the politicians who figure in the story of the West, Lord Shelburne, President of the Board of Trade in 1763, emerges as the most enlightened and far-seeing. Writes Alvord, "To name Lord Shelburne is to name the man who has exercised greater influence on the development of western America than any other British statesman, not excepting even William Pitt." Responsible for the more admirable features of the Proclamation of 1763, Shelburne later, as Secretary of State for the Southern Department, proposed to deal with Indian relations and colonial growing pains by creating two new colonies, one in the Illinois country and the other in the area around Detroit, which the author calls "a wise, conciliatory, and statesmanlike measure." If the book has a villain, it is Lord Hillsborough, holder of various ministerial posts before the American Revolution, a man who crossed swords with Shelburne repeatedly, who opposed new colonies in the West, and who, in the opinion of Benjamin Franklin and the author, favored a hard, uncompromising position in dealing with the colonies on all matters. The fall of Shelburne in 1768 and the ascendancy of Hillsborough ushered in the British policy of retrenchment in the interior, and ideas of systematic expansion were permanently discredited. The Quebec Act of 1774, the final ministerial effort to organize and administer the country between the Ohio and the Mississippi, denied the colonists the opportunity for attaining their legitimate aspirations in the West, as Lord Shelburne pointed out, although that part of the act was not designed with malice in mind. "If historians would interpret rightly the causes of the American Revolution," writes Alvord in bringing his work to a close, they must extend their vision beyond the East to include "the occurrences beyond the mountains, where the British ministers experimented in imperialism and sought a basis for their future colonial policy in the administration of the West."

Sosin, Jack M. *Whitehall and the Wilderness: The Middle West in British Colonial Policy, 1760-1775.* Lincoln: University of Nebraska Press, 1961.

For many years historians in piecemeal fashion have worked over the terrain covered by Alvord. They have not always agreed with the old master; nor, for that matter, have they always found unanimity among themselves. In his monumental history of the *British Empire Before the American Revolution,* Lawrence H. Gipson stresses the temporary nature of the Proclamation of 1763 that was designed to safeguard the welfare of the Indians; it did not, as Alvord contended, contain serious weaknesses which were incorporated in its final form after Shelburne had stepped down as President of the Board of Trade. On the other hand, Bernhard Knollenberg has more recently, in *Origin of the American Revolution,* resurrected the specter of British selfishness in addition to a concern for the Indian. He sees a desire on the part of certain British leaders to keep the colonists economically and politically subservient to the Mother Country by confining them to the territory east of the Appalachians. In any case, another scholar, Robin Humphreys, shows conclusively that the constructive features of the proclamation were not the brain child of one man, Shelburne, whose originality and authority Alvord exaggerated.

In 1961, Jack M. Sosin published the first comprehensive account of British Western policy since Alvord's pioneer undertaking. Sosin's conclusions are strikingly different. Discounting the significance of the Canada versus Guadeloupe debate, the author observes that many of the sixty-five pamphlets on the subject appeared after the ministry had made its choice of Canada. The Crown's ministers seldom, if ever, inaugurated programs for the interior on the basis of abstract mercantile principles. They "were primarily administrators who arrived at particular solutions for specific problems as they arose. . . ." Indeed, Sosin

210

believes that we have put undue emphasis upon the roles of prominent personages in the creation of laws and pronouncements for the back country. A host of second-line bureaucrats, such as ex-governors and subministers in the Colonial Department, exercised no small influence in decision making, as did military officers and Indian agents in America.

So it was with the Proclamation of 1763, which the ministry began to formulate before Lord Shelburne entered the picture. Sosin sees the Proclamation as an outgrowth of efforts on the part of royal officials in the colonies during the French and Indian War to win the Indians' allegiance and to maintain peace on the frontier. In fact, the British military establishment had by the early 1760's already put into practice the basic features later incorporated into the Proclamation. Sosin also disputes Alvord's contention that considerations relating to the West dominated the thinking of Whitehall policy-makers throughout the period 1763-1775. Although the ministry always sought peace and stability in the back country, the late 1760's witnessed the West's declining importance as the government shifted its primary attention to meeting the American challenge on the Eastern seaboard.

On these points Sosin's revisionist views appear to be sound and sensible. But critics have raised questions or objections to certain of the author's additional interpretations. Lord Shelburne receives rough handling from Sosin, who contends that his thinking on extending the frontiers and creating new colonies was not always consistent or enlightened. A final estimate of Shelburne as an imperial statesman will have to await extended monographic treatment of the man who has hitherto been treated sympathetically by most historians. We may also need to look more fully into the career of Lord Hillsborough, whom Sosin defends in his unwillingness to give in to the American expansionistic ambitions. American land speculators, traders, and other expansionists are seen in these pages as generally irresponsible in their lust to roll back the frontiers at the expense of the Indians and the best interests of the British Empire; but, as one reviewer remarks, we need a clearer picture of the colonists' point of view. Only when we understand the Americans' thinking can the full story emerge; only then can we say with precision the degree to which British Western policy was a factor in the origins of the American Revolution. — *W.D.H.*

Additional Recommended Reading

Abernethy, Thomas P. *Western Lands and the American Revolution.* New York: D. Appleton-Century Co., 1937. Broad in scope, Abernethy's work is now outdated in some respects.
Alden, John R. *John Stuart and the Southern Colonial Frontier: A Study of Indian Relations, War, Trade, Land Problems in the Southern Wilderness, 1754-1775.* Ann Arbor: University of Michigan Press, 1944. Alden's exhaustive study of the wilderness of the South between 1754 and 1775 is definitive.
Peckham, Howard H. *Pontiac and the Indian Uprising.* Princeton: Princeton University Press, 1947. An excellent monograph, this work invalidates part of Francis Parkman's

older treatment of the same subject.

Gipson, Lawrence H. *The British Empire Before the American Revolution*. Vol. IX: *New Responsibilities Within the Enlarged Empire, 1763-1766: The Triumphant Empire*. New York: Alfred A. Knopf, Inc., 1956. Gipson sees British Western programs as more flexible than do some writers.

Knollenberg, Bernhard. *Origins of the American Revolution, 1759-1766*. New York: The Macmillan Company, 1961. Knollenberg is much less sympathetic than Gipson to the British point of view.

Philbrick, Francis S. *The Rise of the West, 1754-1830*. New York: Harper & Row Publishers, 1965. Philbrick presents a broad survey, but at times he injects fresh interpretations.

CAROLINA REGULATOR MOVEMENTS

Type of event: Military: clashes arising from abuses in government in North Carolina and the absence of government in South Carolina
Time: 1765-1771
Locale: The back country of the Carolinas

Principal personages:

WILLIAM TRYON (1729-1788), British Governor of North Carolina 1765-1771

SAMUEL JOHNSTON (1733-1816), conservative leader in the North Carolina assembly

HERMON HUSBANDS (1724-1795), pamphleteer who stated the case for the North Carolina back country

EDMUND FANNING (1739-1818), Justice of the Peace and Recorder of Deeds of Orange County who was hated by the North Carolina Regulators

WILLIAM BULL (1710-1791), Lieutenant Governor of South Carolina who was friendly to the back country

CHARLES WOODMASON (fl. 1770's), Church of England clergyman who wrote a petition of grievances for the South Carolina frontiersmen

CHARLES GARTH (fl. 1770's), South Carolina agent in London who sought legislation to cope with the colony's interior

MOSES KIRKLAND (fl. 1770's), aggressive planter and businessman who emerged as leader of the South Carolina Regulators

Summary of Event

Conflicts between the East and the West, between old established societies and new bucolic settlements of the frontier, have been recurring phenomena of American history. The breadth and depth of these sectional antagonisms have varied sharply according to time and place. The Regulator Movements of the 1760's and 1770's in the Carolinas illustrate the complexity of the subject.

In Maryland and Virginia the frontier folk harbored no deep-seated grievances against the East. The legislatures, though dominated by tidewater aristocrats, had established counties—with courts, justices of the peace, sheriffs, and representation in the assemblies —and had enacted statutes to build roads and bridges for facilitating trade. In North Carolina, where the same political institutions made their appearance in the piedmont, there was nevertheless serious regional discord because of the malpractices of local officials, and, to a lesser extent, because of high quitrents, inadequate arteries of transportation, and underrepresentation in the legislature. Sheriffs, by failing to publish the tax rate, collected far more than the law permitted and lined their own pockets in the process; if a taxable person could not pay—and cash was ever in short supply—they

213

seized his property and sold it, rigging the auctions in favor of insiders. Here the sheriffs acted in collusion with other county officials; these "courthouse rings" moreover charged exorbitant fees for performing routine legal services. The symbol of the people's unhappiness was New York-born, Yale-educated Edmund Fanning ("by his civil robberies, He's laced his coat with gold"), Justice of the Peace and Recorder of Deeds of Orange County.

Although violence erupted as early as 1759 in the Granville District, the initial pattern of the Regulators (a name which the aroused victims of these discriminatory practices borrowed from a simultaneous but separate reform movement in South Carolina) was to lodge formal protests with the governor and the assembly. Humble in tone and legalistic in concept, these petitions were largely ignored or condemned on the seaboard. Only then, after rebuffs, did the Regulators broaden their goals to include dividing western counties and instituting secret voting so as to increase their representation in the colonial legislature. New elections, however, strengthened the hand of the Regulators and their sympathizers. James Iredell, a conservative, declared that a majority of the lower house was "of regulating principles." But the modest reforms concerning officers' fees and court costs in litigation which were enacted were inadequate without the means of enforcement at county level. Violence increased, and in September, 1770, Regulators invaded the Orange County court at Hillsborough, drove out the justices, and tried cases themselves. Fear of rebellion led the assembly to abandon its "regulating prin-

ciples" by enacting the repressive Johnston Act against unlawful gatherings and by backing Governor William Tryon in sending a militia army against the Regulators. Near the banks of the Alamance Creek, twenty miles from Hillsborough, a motley throng of a thousand farmers gathered to oppose Tryon's force of equal size. After desultory firing and ludicrous field movements on both sides, the Regulators fled, each side losing nine dead. The Regulation ended at Alamance, but subsequently justices and sheriffs in the Piedmont appear to have paid stricter attention to the law in performing their duties, for patriot leaders saw the need to placate the West to achieve unity in the face of the challenge from Great Britain in the middle 1770's.

The "back country" of South Carolina was settled somewhat later than that of the Tarheel colony, and its chief grievance was the absence of government rather than the abuses of government that plagued frontier North Carolina. In the 1760's, newcomers flooded into the back country, which was a region suffering from the aftermath of the Cherokee War of 1759-1761. Life in the "up country" (a South Carolina expression), precarious at best, threatened a total breakdown before rising lawlessness and social and economic maladjustment. The parishes of South Carolina, the units of political and ecclesiastical authority, were only theoretically extended to the back country. There were, it is true, justices of the peace, but their authority was limited to minor civil cases. The absence of courts meant a visit to Charleston if one desired to transact any form of important legal business, and the journey entailed a week on horseback or two weeks by wagon from distant stations, such as Ninety-Six. In 1767, as roving bands of outlaws terrorized the region while Charleston authorities looked the other way, leading citizens with the support of respectable elements formed an "association" for "regulating" the back country. Dedicated to law and order and to the protection of property, the Regulators, by 1768, had dealt harshly and effectively with the criminal part of the population. But many honest men felt the Regulators had gone too far by punishing immorality as well as lawlessness. An anti-Regulator group, the Moderate movement, brought the excesses of the extremist Regulators to an end so that the restoration of control by respectable property owners was completed. A direct confrontation between the Regulators and constituted authority in Charleston never took place, partly because Lieutenant Governor William Bull and others in authority recognized the need to bring tranquility to the interior. In addition, the Commons House of Assembly finally endeavored to solve back country problems, including more legislative representation and the establishment of schools. These well-intentioned undertakings ran afoul of British policy and the emerging Anglo-American conflict, but a major grievance terminated following passage of the Circuit Court Act of 1769, which created four back country courts with full jurisdiction in civil and criminal matters, and contained provisions for jury trials and the strict regulation of legal fees.

Despite obvious differences, the broad objectives of the two Regulator movements in the Carolinas were the same. Eschewing theoretical political innovations or radical social leveling, the Regulators asked principally for a redress of specific grievances, for government that was just and responsible, for the political and legal rights to which freeborn Englishmen were everywhere entitled.

Pertinent Literature

Bridenbaugh, Carl. *Myths and Realities: Societies of the Colonial South.* Baton Rouge: Louisiana State University Press, 1952.

"Too much has been made of the supposedly primitive, semibarbaric condition of the Southern back country between 1730 and 1776," writes Carl Bridenbaugh in a lengthy essay surveying the various levels of society in that region. Easy generalizations do not come readily regarding the quarter of a million Germans, Scotch-Irish, and English who settled the interior from Maryland to Georgia before the American Revolution, and who for the most part streamed down from Pennsylvania, many over the seven hundred-mile-long Great Wagon Road, which Bridenbaugh claims should be as well remembered today as the Lancaster Pike and the Santa Fe and Oregon Trails. To be sure, there was an abundance of poverty, crudity, and immorality; life was hard, ministers of the gospel few, and schoolteachers a rarity, as one can tell from reading the fascinating journal of the Reverend Charles Woodmason *(The Carolina Backcountry on the Eve of the Revolution).* As would be true in the future, the West seemed an inexorable "safety valve" for shiftless lawbreakers from the East. But men could go up the ladder, just as others could go down. Daniel Morgan, a youthful pugilist and rum-drinker involved in countless scrapes with the law, who lived with his wife-to-be for ten years before marrying her, rose to be a general in the American Revolutionary Army and a leading citizen of the Valley of Virginia. The solid core of back country society consisted of small planters who owned at most a few hundred acres. By their labors they might climb, like Daniel Morgan, to become leading men. Indeed, from the beginning there were always some inhabitants who occupied positions of prestige and influence in their rural surroundings. For, as Bridenbaugh remarks, there came along with the simple folk country gentlemen, soldiers, lawyers, land speculators, merchants, and men of culture. The only resident peer in America was Thomas, the sixth Baron Fairfax, and he built his home, Greenway Court, in the Southern interior near Winchester, Virginia, in 1752.

The author reminds us that just as settlement of the back parts of each colony took place at different times, so it was that developments within each province followed their own patterns. Here Bridenbaugh sheds light on why Maryland and Virginia escaped the Regulator troubles of the Carolinas. The interior of the Chesapeake colonies was settled early, and partly by influen-

tial aristocrats from the tidewater counties; the ideals and attitudes of the East were quickly implanted there, just as were its political institutions, and its inhabitants sometimes sent tidewater planters, such as George Washington, to represent them in the assemblies. "I have searched fruitlessly," says Bridenbaugh, "for evidence that before 1776 political sectionalism—western resentment of eastern overrepresentation and rule—was an issue, either open or covert, in Maryland or Virginia." Even the rise of Patrick Henry, as the author indicates, is no longer considered a sign of western radicalism but rather a readjustment within the ruling Virginia aristocracy.

By the time of the American Revolution, the back country had witnessed the growth of towns, the rise of commerce with the North and East, the accumulation of wealth, and the growth of slavery. If the interior had taken on certain characteristics of the other two "Souths," those the author terms "the Chesapeake Society" and the "Low Country Society" (and discusses in detail in separate chapters), the back country remained "a land of sharp contrasts and amazing antitheses." "Not until 1790 was the back country ready to crystallize into a definite society, and by that time much of its old colonial character had been modified by the exigencies of the new age, or had disappeared forever."

Brown, Richard M. *The South Carolina Regulators.* Cambridge: Harvard University Press, 1963.

This splendid monograph is the only lengthy account of either group of Regulators to appear in many years. Fortunately, Richard M. Brown chose

to examine the movement in South Carolina, for less was known about the convulsions there. Brown reveals that the Regulators were the "have's" and not the "have not's" of the back country. They were upstanding citizens concerned with protecting property rights and restoring order in a region devastated by Indian warfare and overrun by outlaws and "lower people." Are responsible men in such circumstances entitled to go outside the law, or become law unto themselves, in order to maintain their liberty? The question itself is contradictory, but so has been the reality of men's plight on several frontiers in American history. The South Carolina Regulators were among the first to face up to this predicament with a successful plan of action. Here was no East-West schism cut from traditional cloth, for the greatest opposition to the Regulators was never in Charleston, where ultimately the seriousness of back country turbulence prompted the governor and legislature to seek ways of satisfying Regulator demands. It was in the back country itself that the Regulation stirred dissatisfaction by overseeing morals, family life, and debt collections, all scarcely comparable to the criminal activity that had initially caused the Regulators to take the field. The "Moderates," themselves of the better sort, might have clashed seriously with the extreme Regulators except for a truce arranged in 1769, also the year of the Circuit Court Act that met the Regulators' deepest grievances. "The Moderate movement checked the Regulation when the latter had outlived its usefulness." Even so, as Brown demonstrates, "the larger objectives of halting the demoralization of the Back Country had been attained, a result which the Moderates did not even desire to reverse."

The author amasses a wealth of information from which he makes careful estimates as to the ages, wealth, and geographic distribution of the Regulators. They were "a coalition of small planters and leading men" who endeavored to establish "a society in which they themselves were to prosper," who took the law into their own hands "for conservative social purposes." According to the standard histories, the Regulators out of bitterness against the low country supported the British during the Revolutionary War. The conclusion is deflated in Brown's pages: "There was little genuine resentment (only a bit of 'rhetoric') directed at the Charleston ruling circle by the identifiable Regulators, of whom only five percent can definitely be classified as Tories."

Not the least of the book's virtues is the placing of the South Carolina Regulators within the framework of American vigilante movements. The Carolinians, in fact, served as "the prototype" of such undertakings, and similar organizations in the first half of the nineteenth century in Texas, Illinois, and elsewhere used the term "Regulator" and employed South Carolina precedents. If the celebrated San Francisco vigilantes of 1851 eclipsed the older name of "Regulator," the South Carolina movement, thanks to Richard M. Brown, is restored to its significant niche in the story of the search for law and order on the American frontier. — *R.D.H.*

Additional Recommended Reading

Bassett, John S. "The Regulators of North Carolina, 1765-1771," in *Annual Report for the Year 1894*. Pp. 141-212. Washington, D.C.: American Historical Association. Still useful though limited in scope.

Meriwether, Robert L. *The Expansion of South Carolina, 1729-1765*. Kingsport, Tenn.: Southern Publishers, 1940. A piece of meticulous scholarship by a leading authority on South Carolina history.

Alden, John R. *John Stuart and the Southern Colonial Frontier: A Study of Indian Relations, War, Trade, Land Problems in the Southern Wilderness, 1754-1775*. Ann Arbor: University of Michigan Press, 1944. Contains valuable information on the Cherokee War and white-Indian relations.

Woodmason, Charles. *The Carolina Backcountry on the Eve of the Revolution: The Journal and Other Writings of Charles Woodmason, Anglican Itinerant*. Edited by Richard J. Hooker. Chapel Hill: University of North Carolina Press, 1953. An itinerant Church of England clergyman who sympathized with the Regulators, Woodmason paints a vivid and sometimes amusing picture of life in the up country.

Dill, Alonzo T. *Governor Tryon and His Palace*. Chapel Hill: University of North Carolina Press, 1955. A readable and informative study of the Governor who put down the North Carolina Regulators, and of his times.

Gipson, Lawrence H. *The British Empire Before the American Revolution*. Vol. XI: *The Rumbling of the Coming Storm, 1766-1770: The Triumphant Empire*. New York: Alfred A. Knopf, Inc., 1965. Gipson devotes two chapters to what he calls "The Struggle for Political Equality" in the Carolinas.

STAMP ACT CRISIS

Type of event: Constitutional: British and American friction
Time: 1765-1766
Locale: America and Great Britain

Principal personages:

GEORGE GRENVILLE (1712-1770), head of the ministry, 1763-1765, and chiefly responsible for the program of American taxation

THOMAS WHATELY (fl. 1765), Treasury official who prepared the Stamp Act and who maintained Americans were virtually represented in Parliament

DANIEL DULANY (1722-1797), Maryland lawyer who wrote the most significant pamphlet attacking the Stamp Act and the concept of virtual representation

PATRICK HENRY (1736-1799), led the Virginia House of Burgesses in adopting resolutions against taxation that influenced other assemblies to do likewise

BENJAMIN FRANKLIN (1706-1790), colonial agent in London who told Parliament that Americans objected only to internal taxes

CHARLES WATSON WENTWORTH (MARQUIS OF ROCKINGHAM) (1730-1782), succeeded Grenville as first minister and secured the Stamp Act's repeal

Summary of Event

In 1763, the British national debt had soared to a level double its prewar figure. Besides finding revenues to meet the interest on this war debt, George Grenville, first minister, needed additional funds to administer a greatly enlarged empire. Although Parliament had never before placed direct taxes on the colonies, Grenville persuaded that body to approve the Sugar Act of 1764 and the Stamp Act of 1765. The decision to tax America was momentous in its consequences. The intensity of the colonists' opposition shocked most Englishmen, and on both sides of the Atlantic the crisis produced an atmosphere of tension and mistrust that influenced all subsequent Anglo-American relations before the War of Independence.

Grenville, a narrow-minded financial expert, amassed impressive statistics to show that the prosperous colonists were lightly taxed compared to Englishmen at home. The Sugar Act grew out of Grenville's discovery that the American customs service was costing the government more to maintain than it was collecting in revenues. The colonists were evading payment of the import duties—sixpence a gallon—on foreign molasses, which was required under the Molasses Act of 1733. Grenville revamped the customs service and ordered the Royal Navy to guard against smuggling. The Sugar

219

Act itself cut the molasses duty to threepence a gallon, a sum Grenville believed would be enforceable without ruining the New England rum industry. It was clear that colonial rum distillers needed more molasses than the British West Indian sugar islands could provide. The new statute placed additional duties upon colonial imports, increased restrictions upon colonial exports, and added further to the difficulties of smugglers by strengthening the system of Vice-Admiralty Courts. But the preamble to the Sugar Act, unlike the Molasses Act, made it clear that the law of 1764 was not designed primarily to regulate trade: it stated "that a revenue be raised" in His Majesty's dominions. Subsequently, Grenville introduced his Stamp Act, passed by Parliament and signed by the King on March 22, 1765—to be effective on November 1. Taxes fell on every kind of legal document and on playing cards, dice, and almanacs, each item to carry a stamp indicating payment of the tax. Offenders were to be tried in Vice-Admiralty Courts (without trial by jury), which formerly had jurisdiction only over affairs relating to the sea and commerce. New taxes meant payments in cash, but money, always scarce in the agriculturally oriented colonies, became tighter than ever because Grenville, in 1764, had persuaded Parliament to adopt the Currency Act that forbade the provincials to continue making their own paper money as legal tender.

The colonists found much to displease them in Grenville's program. Merchants thought the rum industry would not be able to stand the threepence duty on molasses, and they found the new customs procedures complicated and difficult, just as the currency restrictions would make silver in shorter supply than ever; nor did it seem fair to try Stamp Act offenders in courts devoid of juries and possessing authority beyond that permitted them in England. Even more important to Americans, Parliament's direct taxes seemed to deprive them of their rights as British subjects to be taxed only by their elected representatives. They were, of course, represented in their own assemblies but not in the House of Commons. They vigorously approved the pamphlet written by Maryland lawyer Daniel Dulany, who denied the contention of Englishman Thomas Whately that all residents of the empire were, in effect, represented in Parliament, which allegedly looked after the interests of all, regardless of whether one had the opportunity, as many local Englishmen did not, to vote for members of the House of Commons. American writers quoted John Locke, political philosopher of the "Glorious Revolution" of 1688, who said that the most esteemed right of people was the right of property, without which both life and liberty were endangered. The Virginia House of Burgesses, prodded by young Patrick Henry, took the lead in drafting remonstrances against Parliamentary taxation. Soon afterward the Massachusetts legislature issued a call for a congress from all the colonies to meet to consider ways of securing relief. The Stamp Act Congress, meeting October 7 to 27, 1765, at New York and attended by delegates from nine colonies, acknowledged Parliament's authority to regulate trade (to legislate) for the welfare of the whole empire while rejecting its right to tax America. By

November 1, the date the stamps were to go on sale, none were available.

The Sons of Liberty had "persuaded" almost every designated stamp distributor to resign. Colonial merchants also aided the cause by curtailing imports from Britain until the oppressive Stamp Act was repealed.

In 1766, Grenville was out of office (for reasons unrelated to America), and the ministry was under the Marquis of Rockingham, who had opposed the Stamp Act and who now listened to the outcries of British merchants suffering from the colonial economic boycott. By stressing the disruption of trade and ignoring American rioting, and by employing Benjamin Franklin's erroneous testimony that the colonists opposed only internal taxes (the Stamp Act), Rockingham secured repeal of the Stamp Act—after Parliament passed the vaguely worded Declaratory Act, a bill that affirmed Parliament's right to "make laws and statutes . . . to bind the colonies . . . in all cases whatsoever." Americans rejoiced at the outcome without knowing the Declaratory Act's precise meaning.

Pertinent Literature

Morgan, Edmund S. and Helen M. Morgan. *The Stamp Act Crisis.* Chapel Hill: University of North Carolina Press, 1953.

The turn of the twentieth century gave rise to the so-called "imperial school of American historiography," which endeavored to sweep away nationalistic stereotypes and to examine objectively the British Empire prior to the American Revolution. Products of the new graduate schools, these historians were trained and disciplined in their craft. They looked askance at George Bancroft, the most influential student of the Revolution in the previous century, a patrician scholar who had gazed on the Anglo-American rupture through patriotic glasses. The imperialists contributed impressively to our understanding of the intricate workings of "the Old Colonial System," as George L. Beer described it. Writing sympathetically of British administrators' manifold problems, the imperialists saw the Navigation Acts—designed to regulate and control imperial trade—as a sensible and equitable means of strengthening both the colonies and the Mother Country. Thus it was difficult, contrary to Bancroft's nineteenth century free trade principles, to argue that a restrictive mercantilistic policy in the eighteenth century had severely damaged the colonial economy and had driven the Americans to revolt. Broadly speaking, the imperialists explained the clashes of the 1760's and 1770's as not so much over different theories or principles as over conflicting interests. The matter of colonial rights, wrote Charles McLean Andrews, a distinguished scholar and the "dean" of the imperial school, was a "subject of more or less legal and metaphysical speculation," which had relatively little impact on the vast majority of Americans. Thirty years later Andrews' most prolific student, Lawrence H. Gipson, in his monumental *The British Empire Before the American Revolution,* also passed lightly over constitutional issues. According to Gipson, when the colonies were no longer threatened by the French in Canada after 1763, they shirked their imperial responsibilities in rejecting Parliamentary taxation. They were eager to pursue their own ends without interference from the home government. Gipson apparently sees the Revolution as an inevitable development, with growing American nationalism as the prime cause.

Revisionism is surely the life blood of historical study, and in time the fashionable opinion is cast aside or severely modified. The American Revolutionary field has witnessed the rise of the neo-whig, or neo-conservative school in the years since World War II. Deterministic histories have been replaced by articles and monographs that attempt to pinpoint the significance of individual actions and immediate controversies. The Revolution no longer appears predestined, not in the third quarter of the eighteenth century at least, especially if the Mother Country displayed more enlightened leadership. Ideas, particularly American constitutional arguments, receive careful scrutiny.

The most influential member of the neo-whig school is Edmund S. Morgan, a successor to the Early American history post at Yale University once held by Charles Andrews. None of Morgan's numerous writings has had such a vital impact as *The Stamp Act Crisis,* written with the assistance of Helen M. Morgan. The blame for the first imperial controversy is placed squarely upon George Grenville, who, although pretending otherwise, made no real effort to allow the colonies to raise revenues on their own to aid in the upkeep of the empire; in fact, the first minister discouraged Massachusetts and the

agents of various colonies in London from devising means to acquire needed revenue in America. Consequently, the Americans in Morgan's pages appear less irresponsible in facing up to their imperial obligations than they are depicted in accounts by the imperial school. Believing the actual stamp tax would have been a small expense to almost all the colonists, Morgan considers the crux of the American opposition a matter of the constitutional principle of no taxation without representation. Moreover, Morgan parts company from previous historians by demonstrating that Americans objected not only to internal taxes (the Stamp Act) but also to external taxes (the Sugar Act) as well in 1765-1766. During the following decade they consistently adhered to this constitutional principle, at the same time that they continued to recognize the need for Parliament to legislate (but not for revenue) in the interest of harmonizing the trade and commerce of the empire for the welfare of all its parts. Morgan stresses American unity in still another way by revealing that the Sons of Liberty were not, as often claimed, simply groups of lower-class men who wished to wrest control of the patriot movement from the aristocratic leaders who traditionally dominated political office. The "better and wiser" element of society was active in the Sons, working hand in glove in many cases with the artisans and mechanics who directed the street gangs. Subsequent books by the present generation of early American historians show the profound impact of *The Stamp Act Crisis* in reorienting the study of the Revolution's origins.

222

Stamp Act Crisis

Knollenberg, Bernhard. *Origins of the American Revolution, 1759-1766.* New York: The Macmillan Company, 1960.

Knollenberg's *Origins of the American Revolution* complements and amplifies Edmund Morgan's account of the first imperial crisis. Knollenberg discovers little evidence of colonial unhappiness with the British empire as it existed before the Seven Years' War. He finds no reason to doubt the colonists' sincerity in opposing taxes by Parliament on principle. The British, reasonable in asking Americans to contribute to the cost of imperial affairs, nevertheless went about exacting American cash in the wrong way: "to act unilaterally, to change a constitutional relationship established for over a century without prior effort to negotiate a settlement and without any offer of compensation or assurance against future exploitation was highhanded, reckless and unjust." But Knollenberg does modify slightly Morgan's picture of Americans consistently opposing all forms of British taxation. At any early point in the controversy, Massachusetts implicitly and Connecticut explicitly distinguished between external and internal taxes; but Americans generally did adhere to the position outlined by Morgan. There would likely have been no program of American taxation in the first place, speculates the author, had William Pitt, in 1761, and the Duke of Newcastle, in 1762, not retired from the ministry; for the two most powerful ministers were well versed in colonial affairs and opposed to controversial schemes upsetting to

imperial trade and harmony. The men responsible for the plan of taxation, as Knollenberg observes, were inexperienced in colonial matters and preoccupied with domestic distractions at the conclusion of the Seven Years' War.

Even so, there was colonial discontent prior to 1763 that did not stem from taxation. Here Knollenberg develops his most original and significant thesis: beginning in 1759, when the war was all but won and there was no further need to placate the colonists, various crown officials inaugurated certain measures that angered many colonials. The disallowance of the Twopenny Act in Virginia, the stipulation that judicial tenure in New York and New Jersey should be at the Crown's pleasure instead of during good behavior, the disallowance of an election law in South Carolina, the issuance of writs of assistance in Massachusetts to combat smuggling, the needless exploitation of white pines in New England for the Royal Navy, and the endeavors of Archbishop Thomas Secker to create an Anglican bishopric in America, when taken together, explain much of the violent reaction in the colonies at the time of the Stamp Act episode. If the Stamp Act remains the foremost issue that drove Americans to the verge of open revolt in the mid-1760's, we now know that other factors heightened the vehemence of the American opposition. — *R.D.H.*

Additional Recommended Reading

Bancroft, George. *History of the United States of America, from the Discovery of the Continent.* 6 vols. New York: Appleton-Century-Crofts, Inc., 1888. For all of Bancroft's faults, no one since his time has been so familiar with the sources and no one has attempted a history of the Revolution in such comprehensive fashion.

Beer, George L. *British Colonial Policy, 1754-1765.* New York: The Macmillan Company, 1907. One of several volumes that Beer devoted to "the Old Colonial System"; the others cover the earlier colonial period.

Andrews, Charles M. *The Colonial Background of the American Revolution: Four Essays in American Colonial History.* New Haven: Yale University Press, 1924. This thoughtful monograph consists of four essays that provide a good starting point for a study of the origins of the Revolution.

Gipson, Lawrence, H. *The Coming of the Revolution, 1763-1775.* New York: Harper & Row Publishers, 1954. Gipson's book, a part of the *New American Nation* series, is a useful condensation of themes treated in more detail in volumes IX and X of his *The British Empire Before the American Revolution.*

Malone, Joseph J. *Pine Trees and Politics: The Naval Stores and Forest Policy in Colonial New England.* Seattle: University of Washington Press, 1964. Malone now offers the full story of the white pines controversy in New England.

Bridenbaugh, Carl. *Mitre and Sceptre: Transatlantic Faiths, Ideas, Personalities, and Politics, 1689-1775.* New York: Oxford University Press, 1962. Bridenbaugh believes that American fears of an Anglican establishment throughout the colonies were a factor in the growth of American nationalism and a hitherto neglected cause of the American Revolution.

REVENUE ACT OF 1767 AND THE TOWNSHEND CRISIS

Type of event: Economic: attempt by Parliament to impose new regulations and taxation on the American colonists

Time: June 29, 1767-1770

Locale: North America and Great Britain

Principal personages:

WILLIAM PITT (THE ELDER) (1708-1778), Prime Minister of Great Britain 1766-1768

CHARLES TOWNSHEND (1725-1767), Chancellor of the Exchequer 1766-1767

GENERAL THOMAS GAGE (1721-1787), British Commander in Chief in North America

JOHN DICKINSON (1732-1808), Philadelphia lawyer whose *Letters from a Farmer in Pennsylvania* denied the constitutionality of the Townshend duties

EARL OF GUILFORD (LORD FREDERICK NORTH) (1732-1792), former Chancellor of the Exchequer who became Prime Minister of Great Britain in 1770

Summary of Event

When the Rockingham Ministry followed its repeal of the Stamp Act in 1766 by imposing fresh taxes at home, it was replaced by a coalition of diverse politicians under the ailing William Pitt, who had been elevated to the House of Lords as Lord Chatham. Pitt's prolonged absences because of bad health enabled his ministers to pursue their own individualistic ends. The Chancellor of the Exchequer, "Champagne Charlie" Townshend, dealt with the financial crisis, which became considerably worse after Parliament appeased its constituents by slashing the land tax, depriving the government of over £400,000 in yearly revenue. Seizing upon Benjamin Franklin's testimony, preceding the Stamp Act's repeal, to the effect that Americans opposed on principle only internal taxes, Townshend declared that if the colonists adhered to such a foolish distinction, then they should be saddled with external duties on tea, lead, paper, paints, and glass. The danger to Americans in the subsequent Revenue Act of 1767 containing these proposals was not in the quantity of cash to be extracted from their pockets. That sum annually, by Townshend's own admission, would be only £40,000, less than a tenth of the money lost by Parliament's cutting the land tax. The danger, as Americans saw it, was that Parliament persisted in its efforts to destroy their constitutional rights, not only by taxing them without their consent but also by a provision in the act stating that part of the amount collected was to be used of necessity to pay the salaries of judges and governors in America, thus making them independent of the financial jurisdiction of the colonial assemblies. These legislatures had developed impressive powers in

225

the eighteenth century because of their control of the purse; it was a means of keeping the Crown's appointed officials in line, of making them responsive for the most part to the will of the people they served.

The assemblies believed themselves threatened on still another front by the Quartering Act of 1765; when barracks were unavailable British troops in the colonies were to be lodged in taverns and other public houses at the expense of provincial authorities, who were also responsible for furnishing redcoats with firewood, candles, bedding, and other items. Here Parliament seemed to be taxing Americans indirectly by ordering their assemblies to levy monies for the upkeep of royal regiments. Although the American legislatures after 1765 usually provided for the army's needs, they were careful to maintain their constitutional integrity by avoiding a precise compliance with the letter of the law. But when New York (because of its location the colony most frequently called upon for support) enacted a billeting measure which the military deemed to be inadequate, Parliament suspended the colony's legislature until it bowed to the letter of the British Quartering Act. New York was not cowed, nor were the other assemblies, and when a compromise on military appropriations for New York was reached with local leaders, the ministry secured a lifting of the ban, but not before Americans realized that a dangerous precedent had been set in temporarily depriving citizens of the British Empire of their political representation.

For the colonists there were other ominous straws in the wind. Townshend brought about a reorganization of the customs service in America to guarantee collections of the new taxes as well as to achieve greater compliance with the older Navigation Acts. Previously controlled from Great Britain, customs officers in the colonies were now under a special board sitting in Boston; they would predictably be zealous in the handling of their assignment, for a third of all fines received in the Vice-Admiralty Courts went to the customs men. For that matter, additional courts were established the following year, where many merchants faced charges of violating the exceedingly complicated provisions of the Sugar Act.

If these various British measures prompted a less violent reaction in the colonies than the Stamp Act, they collectively represented an even larger threat to American rights. The point was brought home when, in response to the customs collectors' appeal for protection, the Secretary of State for the colonies, the Earl of Hillsborough (Wills Hill), ordered General Thomas Gage, British Commander in Chief in North America, to station regular troops in Boston. Even before then, however, American opinion was mobilizing in response to lawyer John Dickinson's *Letters from a Farmer in Pennsylvania,* which became popular reading throughout America. What Dickinson lacked in originality he made up for by expressing with vigor and clarity the colonists' constitutional opposition to all forms of taxation by a Parliament in which they were not represented. Other writers joined the battle, as did the assemblies with their remonstrances and petitions against the unpopular doings of the British government. The Massachusetts legislature with its so-called circular letter led the way with a bitter denunciation of Parliamentary taxation and the scheme to pay judges and governors from funds other than those appropriated by the colonial assemblies. Once more merchants formed nonimportation agreements, just as the Sons of Liberty reappeared to lend a hand with violators. Once more Englishmen saw that Parliament had created a storm without producing the intended revenue. With Townshend dead and Pitt retired from office, the ministry of Lord North, in 1770, convinced Parliament to repeal all the Townshend duties except the one on tea, a symbol of Parliament's authority to tax. North was a practical man whose way out of the crisis seemed to herald a *rapprochement* in Anglo-American relations. For the time being, the remaining tax was all but forgotten, as were other grievances, as Americans celebrated their second victory over Parliament in four years.

Pertinent Literature

Namier, Lewis B. *The Structure of Politics at the Accession of George III.* 2 vols. London: Macmillan & Company, Ltd., 1929.

Namier, Lewis B. *England in the Age of the American Revolution.* London: Macmillan & Company, Ltd., 1930.

While dedication to principle and growing unity are popular themes in our current historical literature about the American Revolution, the trend in Great Britain today is to view the eighteenth century history of the island kingdom as a time when issues counted little and ideas counted even less. Compared to a scholarly trend in vogue a half century and more ago, the change in Great Britain has been profound, for the "Whig interpretation" of the years between the revolutions of 1688 and 1776 is now *passé.* Thus it is considered erroneous to portray the Whigs as the sole defenders of Parliamentary supremacy and the Bill of Rights, as juxtaposed with the Tories in a symmetrical two-party system, while the Crown occupies a subordinate role in such political affairs as the selecting of ministers and the influencing of policy. Nor can one confidently take the next step, as did older writers, such as W. E. H. Lecky and George Otto Trevelyan, and assert that in 1760 the new monarch, George III, was out to wreck the constitutional settlement of 1688-1689; with the support of the previously discredited Tories, he allegedly tried to destroy the Whig party and to institute virtually one-man rule at the expense of his subjects on both sides of the Atlantic. He was opposed in these designs by a small but undaunted band of heroes: William Pitt, Rockingham, Edmund Burke, Charles James Fox, and their followers, men united with the American patriots in a common struggle against tyranny.

The Whig interpretation of eighteenth century British politics has received devastating blows from Sir Lewis Namier and the historical school that has grown up around him. Born a Polish Jew, Namier was an outsider looking in at the British aristocracy, an object of fascination to a man who himself lacked deep roots. Basing his research heavily upon a detailed structural analysis of constituencies, elections, and family relationships, Namier published *The Structure of Politics at the Accession of George III* in 1929, followed the next year by *England in the Age of the American Revolution.* At the time of his death in 1960 Namier and his students had launched a coöperative series that took the title of Namier's book of 1930: *England in the Age of the American Revolution, (1750-1784),* several volumes of which are now in print. To his chief lieutenant, John Brooke, Namier also left the task of completing the first three volumes of the monumental *History of Parliament;* they appeared in 1964 and cover the period 1754-1790.

Namier tells us there was no party system in the age of the Hanoverians, only factions and family groups that coalesced to obtain favors and office. It could scarcely have been otherwise when local rather than national or imperial considerations dominated men's thinking and when ideas and principles scarcely mattered. To avoid chaos and to bring about some order to the political scene, kings inevitably had to play a stabilizing role. Ministers were responsible to the monarch, and they led Parliament in his behalf. George III produced no constitutional revolution, nor did he desire one. The difference between the young George III and the first two Georges was primarily a matter of not relying on the old-line politicians, such as the Duke of Newcastle who had managed affairs for his predecessors; George III used his legitimate powers himself. Interested in the country, high-minded and hard-working, he hired and fired ministers who were personally responsible to him in the absence of a modern cabinet system. His own handling of patronage guaranteed him the dominant voice in much that Parliament did. If the King was attacked by the "Old Whigs" (really the displaced political henchmen of George II) in the years after 1760, the explanation is not that ideas and issues were at stake as they claimed, but rather that now they were the "outs" instead of the "ins."

Such an interpretation vindicates George of usurping the constitution but does not necessarily absolve him of the traditional charges of being obstinate and short-sighted. While the stature of the King rises, the luster of the American Revolution diminishes, indirectly at least. The Rockinghams and the other opponents of the post-1763 imperial policies appear to have been mainly disgruntled office-seekers after a means of bringing down the ministry. Certainly the zigs and zags of British measures between the Sugar Act and the opening shots of the American Revolution are more understandable owing to the labors of the Namierists. The absence of parties, the shifting of factions, and the involvement with internal concerns reveal why inconsistency was the rule and not the exception in handling the American problem. For yet another reason, but related to the absence of parties with programs, it would have been virtually impossible to institute a comprehensive plan for the colonies, be it repressive or enlightened; the prime function of government in the eighteenth century was to administer, not to legislate. Hence, a series of measures, often unrelated and adopted in hit-and-miss fashion, managed to inflame the colonies without bringing any benefit to the Mother Country.

The confusion and the contradictions notwithstanding, some men were fairly consistent in the way they viewed the American problem. Indeed, Herbert Butterfield has expressed a common complaint against the Namierists, reminding us that men do not live by bread alone, that principle may not have been completely absent in the age of the American Revolution. Whether the Namierists' microscopic research techniques tend to take "the mind out of history" is perhaps debatable, but some historians point to a discernible consistency in Rockingham and his followers. They opposed the taxing of America and most other harsh measures directed toward the colonies, believing such schemes disruptive and harmful to imperial unity; and for the most part during their long years on the outside, they gained absolutely no political mileage from their stand —usually contrary to the position of the King, who dispensed "the loaves and fishes."

Namier, Lewis B. and John Brooke. *Charles Townshend*. New York: St. Martin's Press, 1964.

Other men could also be consistent; by advocating the bringing of the mature and supposedly headstrong colonists to heel, as Namier himself shows in his biography of Charles Townshend, which was completed after Namier's death by John Brooke. A man of rare charm and eloquence, gay and amoral, Townshend was brilliant but erratic. Of his "champagne speech" Horace Walpole cried, "Nobody but he could have made that speech, and nobody but he would have made it if they could." His theatrics and instability aside, Townshend was one of a growing number of British administrators who desired to limit colonial self-government and to bolster royal authority throughout the British Empire. As early as 1753, he revealed aspects of the program he pushed through Parliament fourteen years later. A junior minister on the eve of the French and Indian War, he drafted instructions for the Governor of New York, Sir Danvers Osborn, that were designed for the local assembly to make permanent arrangements for salaries of the governor, judges, and other officials. The Crown-appointed executives and judges would have become financially independent of the New York legislature had Townshend's dispatch been acted upon. His "Townshend duties" of 1767 were pushed through Parliament in spite of the opposition of Pitt, the Duke of Grafton, and Lord Shelburne. They were not in fact the result of Parliament's lowering the land tax and leaving no alternative other than once again to prime the American pump. The Revenue Act of 1767, worked out a month before the government's defeat on the land tax, had nothing to do with that setback. As much as anything else, Townshend's legislation was the realization of his earlier design to bolster British control at the expense of the colonies.

Thanks to the Namierist school we know how the game of politics was played in the days of the Hanoverians. But we may wonder whether, in the third quarter of the eighteenth century, the players were capable of managing a far-flung empire, immersed as they were in factional and other parochial issues of a domestic nature. Indeed, it was not until 1774, with the passage of the Coercive Acts, that Parliament cast aside the irresolution that had marked its actions toward America since 1763. Then it pursued in earnest the imperial approach of Townshend. From that point, if not earlier, the days of the first British Empire were numbered. — *W.D.H.*

Additional Recommended Reading

Pares, Richard. *King George III and the Politicians.* Oxford: The University Press, 1953. A brilliantly written account of the Monarch's place in the political and constitutional picture, reflecting the Namierist point of view.

Brooke, John. *The Chatham Administration, 1766-1768.* New York: St. Martin's Press, 1956. This first volume in Namier's series on *England in the Age of the American Revolution* mirrors the approach and conclusions of the author's mentor.

Butterfield, Herbert. *George III and the Historians.* New York: The Macmillan Company, 1957. In this historiographical monograph, Butterfield finds serious fault with some of the conclusions of Namier and Brooke concerning parties and principles.

Ubbelohde, Carl. *The Vice-Admiralty Courts and the American Revolution.* Chapel Hill: University of North Carolina Press, 1960. According to the author of this carefully researched work, "the Vice-Admiralty Courts were a minor, but persistent, cause of the American Revolution."

Jacobson, David L. *John Dickinson and the Revolution in Pennsylvania, 1764-1776.* Berkeley and Los Angeles: University of California Press, 1965. A useful narrative of Dickinson's political ideas and activities.

Gipson, Lawrence H. *The British Empire Before the American Revolution.* Vol. XI: *The Rumbling of the Coming Storm, 1766-1770: The Triumphant Empire.* New York: Alfred A. Knopf, Inc., 1965. A detailed investigation of the second imperial crisis which deals sympathetically with Charles Townshend.

BOSTON MASSACRE

Type of event: Military: friction caused by the presence of British troops in Boston
Time: March 5, 1770
Locale: Boston, Massachusetts

Principal personages:
EARL OF HILLSBOROUGH, MARQUIS OF DOWNSHIRE (WILLS HILL) (1718-1793), Secretary of State for the colonies 1768-1772
GENERAL THOMAS GAGE (1721-1787), British Commander in Chief in North America
JOHN HANCOCK (1737-1793), wealthy Boston merchant in conflict with customs collectors
CAPTAIN THOMAS PRESTON (fl. 1770), officer of the main guard at Boston
JOHN ADAMS (1735-1826), Boston lawyer

Summary of Event

On the night of March 5, 1770, a small crowd gathered around a soldier at the guard post in front of the Customs House at Boston, accusing him of striking a boy who had made disparaging remarks about a British officer. John Adams depicted the hecklers as "a motley rabble of saucy boys, negroes and mulattoes, Irish teagues and outlandish Jack tars." The sentinel's call for aid brought a file of eight men from the 29th Regiment and Captain Thomas Preston, officer of the day. The crowd increased, especially after someone rang the bell in the old Brick Meeting House; men and boys hurled snowballs and pieces of ice at the crimson-coated regulars and taunted them to retaliate with cries of "lobster," "bloody-back," and "coward." The crowd's hostility actually stemmed from more than this particular incident; it rested on a series of occurrences between the Bostonians and the military during the seventeen months that the troops had been garrisoned in the city. If possible, the townspeople had expressed even more antipathy for the Customs Commissioners, who that very evening gazed uneasily from the windows of the Customs House on the scene before them in King Street. They were the real source of the trouble; their cries for protection had brought troops to Boston in the first place. Americans were right about the role of the commissioners, but their version of what transpired shortly after nine o'clock on the night of March 5 is highly questionable. Captain Preston probably did not order his nervous troops to fire into the angry throng. But fire they did after one of their number was clubbed on the head. Three Americans died instantly, two a short time later, and six more received wounds. The "Boston Massacre" may have been a misnomer, the result of extreme harassment of the redcoats, and triggered, according to John Adams, by an unprincipled mulatto, Crispus Attucks, "to whose mad behavior, in all

231

probability, the dreadful carnage of that night is chiefly to be ascribed." But to the people of Massachusetts it was the Boston Massacre, and Americans elsewhere wondered if their respective colonies would be the next to have a standing army in their midst, an army seemingly intent on destroying their liberties not only by its presence but also by the use of fire and sword.

At the time, however, Massachusetts had been singled out ostensibly because of the Customs Commissioners' appeal for protection. Undoubtedly another consideration made the decision to comply an easy one for London politicians: the Massachusetts Bay colony, with its spirited opposition to the Stamp Act and the Townshend Revenue Act, had long been viewed as a hotbed of sedition.

The conduct of His Majesty's revenue collectors had been such as to incite colonial opposition. They were, to use Professor Oliver M. Dickerson's epithet, "customs racketeers," a lecherous band who played fast and loose with the complicated provisions of the Sugar Act in order to win judgments in Vice-Admiralty Courts which lined their own pockets. This was substantially the opinion of New Hampshire's Governor Benning Wentworth, and the British Commander in Chief in North America, General Thomas Gage, admitted almost as much to the Secretary of State for the colonies, the Earl of Hillsborough, Marquis of Downshire (Wills Hill), who had, nevertheless, ordered the General to dispatch regulars to the Massachusetts capital.

Gage's troops met no resistance when they first landed on October 1, 1768, and despite the obvious displeasure of the populace reflected in the town fathers' reluctance to aid in securing quarters for the soldiers (soon increased by two additional regiments), there followed months of relative calm with no mob activity against either the redcoats or the customs collectors. Lord Hillsborough was nevertheless determined to deal harshly with Massachusetts, and had he been able to impose his will, Parliament would have wrought changes to equal or surpass in severity the Coercive Acts of 1774. Because of troubles in Ireland and threats from France and Spain, together with the colonial boycott of British goods in protest against the Townshend duties, the government rejected Hillsborough's schemes and eventually repealed all the Townshend taxes except the one on tea. Then, too, the employment of troops against civilians was ticklish business to George III and Englishmen in general, calling forth memories of Stuart days. With the mailed fist idea discredited, the logical step was to remove all the troops; but two regiments remained in Boston. Serious tension began to build up in the late summer and fall of 1769 when Bostonians believed that the redcoats were apparently permanent residents. The soldiers were subjected to every form of legal harassment by local magistrates, to say nothing of mounting acts of violence against the men in uniform. The redcoats in the ranks, like all European soldiers of their day, were hardly of the highest character, often recruited from the slums and the gin mills, and stories of theft, assault, and rape by the regulars were not without considerable foundation. The culmination, foreseen by the army and townspeople alike, was the Boston Massacre. Only then were the last regiments pulled out of the city, leaving behind a legacy of fear and suspicion that was revived every succeeding March 5th. "Massacre Day," as it was called, was commemorated by the tolling of bells and a patriot address that stressed the danger of standing armies.

Pertinent Literature

Shy, John. *Toward Lexington: The Role of the British Army in the Coming of the American Revolution.* Princeton: Princeton University Press, 1965.

The "Boston Massacre," dramatic and controversial, has overshadowed the broader role of the British army in North American affairs. Why did the government break precedent in 1763 and retain in the colonies a large peacetime military establishment consisting of fifteen regiments stationed at posts along the Mississippi and elsewhere ranging from Canada to the Floridas? In the absence of in-depth research on the question, historians generally accepted the "classic" interpretation advanced six decades ago by George L. Beer, who maintained that the redcoats were present to control the Indians and protect the colonists. A deeper and more recent exploration of the subject comes from Bernhard Knollenberg, who stresses that the ranger and light infantry units best trained for Indian fighting were actually disbanded at the conclusion of the French and Indian War. Although discarding the Beer thesis, Knollenberg has difficulty replacing it with a comprehensive explanation; he finds relatively little evidence that the ministry saw the army in 1763 as a means of holding the colonists in check. A general desire to increase the size of the postwar army and to place the added regiments out of the sight of British taxpayers was probably the overriding factor, according to Knollenberg.

The first book-length study of the British Army during the dozen years before Lexington and Concord did not appear until 1965. The author, John Shy, a careful student of both early American and military history, writes with clarity, vigor, and authority. Sympathetic to the British ministers of the Crown who wrestled with complex American problems, Shy is also critical of some points, and he seldom fails to present the colonists' point of view regarding events connected with the military. Shy holds that the army decision, like the Proclamation of 1763, cannot be traced to a single administrator or even to a particular ministry; instead, it evolved from Great Britain's experiences in the final Anglo-French conflict for North America. If the army's implicit mission included a defense against the Indians and a check against the resurgence of Bourbon ambitions, the chief function of the redcoats was actually to prevent war, not to wage it, and "to see that the Indians were not abused, either in trade or land." This policy contained "little of altruism or oppression, but the American Revolution would lead politicians and has continued to lead historians toward viewing the decision in these terms."

Even so, the army produced more problems than it solved. Efforts to procure American revenue through Parliamentary taxation for the soldiers' upkeep led to constitutional crises in

1765-1766 and 1767-1770. The Quartering Act of 1765, for the purpose of obtaining lodging and necessities for the military, brought additional headaches, as the colonists balked at what they considered an indirect form of British taxation. In other ways the new military policy failed to come up to expectations. Even without opposition, formidable problems of communication, transportation, and administration drastically hampered the regiments in their service as frontier policemen. So did the ambitions of fur traders, land speculators, westward-moving settlers, and colonies with expansionist objectives.

A failure on the frontier, the army fared little better when, after a ministerial reassessment of western policy in 1767, Gage transferred most of his troops to the East, leaving the colonies to handle commercial relations with the Indians. At that point two possibilities seemed to be present: to employ the troops in the older communities to uphold Parliamentary supremacy, or to withdraw them altogether. As Shy discloses, the discrediting of Hills-borough's hard-line proposals for Massachusetts suggested the latter course as the logical one. But the troops remained, largely useless because of prevalent Whig notions of militarism and legally paralyzed in the face of urban disorders, since governors were exceedingly reluctant to assume the responsibility of asking for military assistance. To the colonists, the army's role by the 1770's seemed uncertain. But its very presence in their midst aroused suspicions as never before, especially following the Boston Massacre; such suspicions were apparently confirmed in the darkest manner in 1774 when Gage again hastened forces to Boston following the "Tea Party."

One sees from Shy's account that the British Army, a European war machine, was cast into a peculiar role for which it was poorly equipped, being no more capable of policing the seaboard than the frontier. But the army's performance was only in response to Great Britain's various American programs between 1763 and 1775, most of which were well-intentioned but haphazardly planned and poorly executed.

Dickerson, Oliver M. *The Navigation Acts and the American Revolution.* Philadelphia: University of Pennsylvania Press, 1951.

The relationship between the new American Board of Customs Commissioners and the Boston Massacre is illuminated fully in Oliver M. Dickerson's work. Prior to the attempts of Grenville and Townshend to reorganize the British Empire and tap the American colonies for revenue, the laws regulating imperial navigation and the mercantilist theory that lay behind them were acceptable to the colonists, writes Dickerson. The Americans, moreover, were engaged in far less smuggling than George L. Beer and other imperialist historians believed. Except for the widely-evaded Molasses Act of 1733, the colonists willingly contributed payments under the navigation laws, which were the "cement of empire." The first revolution, not of American origins, was made by British policy makers when, with the Sugar Act of 1764, they changed the nature of the Old Colonial System by substituting money-making schemes for the regulation of commerce in the interest of all parts of the Empire. Within the altered framework, Great Britain's "most fateful decision" was the creation of an American Board of Customs Commissioners at Boston in 1767. The commissioners, paid from fines, behaved as "customs racketeers," availing themselves of every opportunity to trap lawful merchants in the maze of complicated procedures called for under the language of the Sugar Act. Their most outrageous behavior was directed against Boston's wealthy John Hancock, who nevertheless "stood his ground . . . and insisted upon his legal rights." To Dickerson there is no mystery attached to the unpopularity of the customs commissioners. Nor does he wonder why the presence of troops to defend such justly unpopular figures could culminate in violence. In a later essay, Dickerson postulates that the initial shots into the mob on March 5 may have come from inside the Custom House, but Shy seemingly dissents from this view.

If the commissioners' most serious abuses came to an end by the middle of 1770, partly because of the Boston Massacre and the departure of the redcoats, "the damage had been done." The old "commercial-colonial empire" was gone, subverted by new laws and the men who rapaciously enforced them. Writing in 1951, Dickerson exercised a guiding hand in turning studies of the origins of the Revolution back to the fundamental question of the period: why did the colonists revolt against Britain? — *R.D.H.*

Additional Recommended Reading

Beer, George L. *British Colonial Policy, 1754-1765.* New York: The Macmillan Company, 1907. Contains information about military affairs, including the once-traditional interpretation of why redcoats remained in the colonies after 1763.

Miller, John C. *Sam Adams: Pioneer in Propaganda.* Boston: Little, Brown, and Company, 1936. Stresses the role of Adams as a manipulator and agitator, whose talents indirectly at least helped lead to the bloodshed in King Street.

Alden, John R. *General Gage in America.* Baton Rouge: Louisiana State University Press, 1948. The redcoats in Boston are treated with sympathy and fairness by Alden in his two chapters relevant to the subject.

Alden, John R. *The South in the Revolution, 1763-1789.* Baton Rouge: Louisiana State University Press, 1957. The author contends that the presence of the troops in America was unnecessary in 1763, as it was also later when they were removed from the West.

Knollenberg, Bernhard. *Origins of the American Revolution, 1759-1766.* Revised ed. New York: The Macmillan Company, 1961. Until the appearance of Shy's book, Knollenberg's interpretation of the decision to maintain an army in America had not been seriously challenged.

Barrow, Thomas C. *Trade and Empire: The British Customs Service in Colonial America, 1660-1775.* Cambridge: Harvard University Press, 1967. Based upon impressive research, this work is sound and comprehensive; the author believes that smuggling was more of a problem for British officials than does Knollenberg.

BENJAMIN FRANKLIN WRITES HIS *AUTOBIOGRAPHY*

Type of event: Cultural: Franklin's desire for his son and the public to know about his rise in the world
Time: 1771-1790
Locale: Philadelphia, Pennsylvania

Principal personages:
BENJAMIN FRANKLIN (1706-1790), American statesman, scientist, and philosopher
JOSIAH FRANKLIN (1657-1745), Benjamin's father
ABIAH FOLGER (1667-1752), Benjamin's mother
JAMES FRANKLIN (1697-1735), Benjamin's brother and first employer
DEBORAH READ FRANKLIN (?-1774), Benjamin's wife
WILLIAM FRANKLIN (1731-1813), Benjamin's son to whom the first part of his *Autobiography* is addressed
WILLIAM TEMPLE FRANKLIN (1758-?), Benjamin's grandson who acquired the manuscript of the *Autobiography* upon his grandfather's death

Summary of Event

Although Benjamin Franklin begins his famous *Autobiography* by addressing it to his son William who might wish "to know the circumstances of *my* Life," he concedes that there are other motives for his literary effort. Having passed from "Poverty and Obscurity . . . to a State of Affluence and some Degree of Reputation in the World," Franklin believed that an account of his spectacular career would be "suitable" to the "Situations" of other aspiring young men and "fit to be imitated." Clearly the focus of the biography, especially the first installment, is upon the man instead of his "times." In this he was faithful to the canons of eighteenth century biography and autobiography, like James Boswell, who in his *Life of Samuel Johnson* noted that the virtues and vices of men are most easily discernible in small personal happenings rather than in important public actions. The individual doings of men explain why they rose or fell, and why they reached their varying levels of attainment.

Franklin's early reading has much to suggest concerning the thrust of his *Autobiography*. It included not only the secular literature of Franklin's day but also such classics as Plutarch's *Lives* ("time spent to great Advantage," he wrote) and religious pieces tailored to Franklin's own New England Puritan heritage. From his youth he recalled most vividly John ("Honest John") Bunyan's *Pilgrim's Progress,* an allegory of the travels of "Christian" through the perils of life and on to the glories of heaven. If Franklin's journey terminates at an earthly destination, it still lays stress upon the values which Bunyan extolled. A nonconformist in religion, Franklin retained the ethical Puritanism of his father and his for-

236

bears while shedding the formal trappings of their creed. In an opening paragraph, Franklin, ever the moralist, thanks God for his good fortune: "I desire with all Humility to acknowledge, that I owe the mention'd Happiness of my past Life to his kind Providence. . . ." Were he given the chance, however, he would, like the author bringing out a second edition, correct every *erratum* in his own story. Franklin learned from his own mistakes, and he hoped his readers would do likewise. The energetic boy Benjamin, son of a Boston candlemaker, is admonished by his father for building a wharf from stones meant for the construction of a house: he "convinc'd me that nothing was useful which was not honest." The young man Franklin, after an unhappy apprenticeship to his brother James, a printer, arrives in Philadelphia munching a roll (the best-remembered episode of the *Autobiography*) and acquires gainful employment, but his passions hurry him into wrongful "Intrigues with low women."

Surviving "this dangerous Time" of youth, Franklin matured. He "grew convinc'd that *Truth, Sincerity* and *Integrity* . . . were of the utmost Importance to the Felicity of Life"; combining with these frugality (drinking water instead of beer at mealtime) and hard work (putting in longer hours than Philadelphia's other printers), he prospered and formed valuable friendships. As publisher of the *Pennsylvania Gazette* (a "Means of Communicating Instruction") and *Poor Richard's Almanac* ("both entertaining and useful"), Franklin gave classic expression in nimble witticisms to virtues and values that were already becoming a part of the American tradition, as valid

in Quaker Philadelphia as in Puritan Boston. His scholarly and civic activities, which increasingly ate up his time, are narrated in the *Autobiography:* the Junto, "a club for mutual Improvement," and "the best School of Philosophy, Morals and Politics that then existed in the Province"; the American Philosophical Society, which struggled to survive in the early days; a subscription library, the still-flourishing Library Company of Philadelphia; an academy, now the University of Pennsylvania; and the Philadelphia Hospital, the first institution of its kind in British America. It is well to remember, as critics of the *Autobiography* forget, that success for Franklin was more than the accumulation of wealth; D. H. Lawrence missed the mark in ascribing to Franklin a desire to confine the soul to a potato patch. Personal financial independence enabled one to escape certain temptations—"it being more difficult for a Man in Want to act always honestly" —and to find higher forms of satisfaction with leisure time. At a relatively early age, Franklin himself retired from business to pursue more disinterested goals in science and public service.

Even so, Franklin's descriptions of his renowned electrical experiments and his participation in Pennsylvania politics do not constitute the most illuminating parts of the *Autobiography*. Its fame does not rest upon the presentation of vital new information, nor is it invariably accurate. Moreover, it ends in 1758 when Franklin was in England on a political mission. Ahead lay momentous years for Franklin and America—his efforts to heal the Anglo-American rift after 1763, his service in the Continental Congress, his diplomatic achievements in France, and his attendance at the Constitutional Convention of 1787. But as the personal testament of one American's progress in the world, the *Autobiography* has no close rival. "Franklin's memoirs," writes Max Farrand, "tell the story of a printer and a shopkeeper who was infinitely bigger than his job but who was not above it; of a tradesman who had risen to greatness but was not ashamed of his origin nor of his station."

Pertinent Literature

Franklin, Benjamin. *Autobiography of Benjamin Franklin.* Edited by Leonard W. Labaree *et al.* New Haven: Yale University Press, 1964.

By 1890, Franklin's autobiography had gone through at least one hundred and seventy editions, and the flow has continued in the twentieth century. By 1964 one could confidently say that the definitive edition had at last appeared, edited by Leonard W. Labaree and his associates of Yale University, who since the early 1950's had been collecting and editing a comprehensive edition of the *Franklin Papers.*

The history of the writing of the *Autobiography* and the subsequent tale of its publication are well told by Labaree. Franklin worked on his memoirs at four different times over a period of nearly nineteen years. In 1771, at the age of sixty-five, he began his narrative during a two-week visit to the home of his friend, Bishop Jonathan Shipley, near Twyford in Hampshire, England. His "little scribbling in the garden study" resulted in what scholars today know as Part I, containing a description of his life to about 1730. In this section the author is at his best, and the inner man emerges vividly before the reader. Perhaps the world-famous Franklin, who returned to his autobiographical labors in 1784, was overly conscious of his public image, for one sees somewhat less of his personal side in the later installments, which stress his external record. Part II was written in 1784 at Passy, the Paris suburb where Franklin lived as a diplomat; Part III was done in 1788 at Philadelphia, when he was eighty-three and afflicted with gout and kidney stones; and Part IV was put down between the late fall of 1789 and his death on April 17, 1790.

Franklin's manuscript of the *Autobiography* led a precarious existence. When he left for France early in the Revolutionary War, he entrusted Part I to Joseph Galloway, who thereafter departed for England as a Loyalist. Franklin himself did not know the fate of his memoirs until 1782, when a Philadelphia merchant, Abel James, wrote to the American peace commissioner that, as an executor of the estate of Mrs. Joseph Galloway (who had remained in Philadelphia), he had come into possession of the manuscript. Later, when the *Autobiography* had been completed and Franklin had died, the original work passed into the hands of his grandson, William Temple Franklin. Initial editions of the published *Autobiography,* which first appeared in 1791, were not based on Franklin's own manuscript, which disappeared from sight after William Temple Franklin for inexplicable reasons turned it over to Louis Guillaume Le Veillard, Mayor of Passy. The early editions of the *Autobiography* were taken from copies of the original made before Franklin had written Part IV. Franklin's original work was finally discovered in France by John Bigelow, American Minister in Paris 1865-1866, who published the first edition of Franklin's own manuscript in 1867 but which was inadequate in some respects. A more reliable printing did not become available until 1949 (the Parallel text edition of Benjamin Franklin's *Memoirs,* edited by Max Farrand). But the present-day reader is advised to acquire the Labaree edition in which the notes are helpful without being obtrusive. In this superb publication the reader can be confident that the text "—every word of it—was written by Franklin himself" in his "informal, easy style," characterized by his masterful "use of vivid, colloquial expression."

Granger, Bruce I. *Benjamin Franklin: An American Man of Letters.* Ithaca: Cornell University Press, 1964.

Although Bruce Granger is highly complimentary of Franklin as a man of letters, there is sharp disagreement among specialists as to the place of the Philadelphian in American literature; it is, however, a mark in his favor that an increasing number of experts in the fields of languages and literature are joining historians in the arena of Franklin studies. Between 1962 and 1964 there appeared three monographs that endeavored to evaluate the role of Franklin in the American literary tradition.

It is true, of course, that Franklin's fame rests less upon his prose than upon his endeavors as a scientist, statesman, and diplomat. But he was a prolific author and thought of himself as a writer. In preparing an outline for his *Autobiography,* he placed "My writing" at the top of the lists of subjects to be treated, and he proceeded to tell how as a youth he "grew more attentive to the *Manner* in Writing, and determin'd to endeavour at Improvement." He received assistance from reading the *Spectator,* a British periodical of essays produced by Joseph Addison and Richard Steele. From it he learned about good organization and the importance of choosing the best means of expression, often making up exercises in writing based on that publication. He was "encouraged to think [that] I might possibly in time come to be a tolerable English Writer, of which I am extreamly ambitious." Improve he did in the course of a steady outpouring of newspaper essays, pamphlets, almanacs, and personal correspondence. Witty, satirical, or straightforward, he wrote smooth, concise, well-structured prose; one usually gets the point when reading Franklin, except perhaps for some of his famous hoaxes contrived so skillfully they deceive even discerning readers.

Granger reminds us that the literary milieu of Franklin's day was predominantly neoclassical with its stress upon appeal to reason that constituted a fixed and universal part of man's nature. "I shall venture to lay it down as a Maxim," declared Franklin in 1733, *"That no Piece can properly be called good, and well written, which is void of any Tendency to benefit the Reader, either by improving his Virtue or his Knowledge. "* Yet interwoven with his reading and other European influences was the reality of life in the New World. Born into an acquisitive, highly pragmatic society, Franklin and other American writers were also profoundly influenced by what Daniel Boorstin has aptly called the "whispering of environment." Ralph Ketcham has trenchantly observed that Franklin's mental equipment "cannot be extracted and sorted out according to some analytical scheme without robbing . . . [it] of meaning. In fact, a harmony of thought and action was the seminal feature of his mind."

It is easy enough to say what Franklin was not as a writer. The *Autobiography,* like his other works, lacks a spiritual quality, but so does most of the literature produced in Hanoverian England. Franklin was not a writer in the belletristic sense as applied to lyric poetry, fiction, and drama. He seldom probed the depths of the human psyche. But if literature may be judged by utilitarian standards apart from aesthetic ones, then Franklin, in Granger's view, "was indeed an important man of letters." This is hardly a startling conclusion, although, to employ language Franklin would have approved, it is a *reasonable* one, allowing us to pass over the much-debated question of Franklin's greatness as a literary figure. Finally, it may be said as a high compliment to Franklin that people read him in his day, and they still do.

— *R.D.H.*

Additional Recommended Reading

Van Doren, Carl. *Benjamin Franklin.* New York: Viking Press, 1938. A splendid detailed biography essential to any study of Franklin.

Franklin, Benjamin. *Autobiography of Benjamin Franklin.* Edited by Max Farrand. (Parallel text ed.) Berkeley, California: University of California Press, 1949. Farrand prints the major editions of the autobiography and discusses textual problems.

Crane, Verner W. *Benjamin Franklin and a Rising People.* Boston: Little, Brown, and Company, 1954. An excellent short biography emphasizing Franklin's political and diplomatic activities.

Boorstin, Daniel J. *The Americans.* Vol. I: *The Colonial Experience.* New York: Random House, 1958. A stimulating but controversial book that plays down the significance of the Enlightenment and underscores the importance of the American environment in shaping thought and action.

Hornberger, Theodore. *Benjamin Franklin.* Minneapolis: University of Minnesota Press, 1962. A brief monograph on Franklin as a writer; Hornberger is critical of the *Autobiography* in some respects, believing that Franklin's account of his rise to prominence contains an "aura of finagling and of elasticity of conviction."

Amacher, Richard E. *Benjamin Franklin.* New York: Twayne Publishers, Inc. Amacher, like Hornberger, is concerned with the literary Franklin, but his study is longer and more sympathetic than Hornberger's.

Ketcham, Ralph L. *Benjamin Franklin.* New York: Washington Square Press, 1966. A splendid assessment of Franklin's thought, Ketcham's book is abreast of the latest scholarship, including his own as a former editor on the staff of Yale's *Franklin Papers.*

BOSTON TEA PARTY

Type of event: Economic: symbolic gesture by the colonists against Great Britain's insistence on taxing tea
Time: December 16, 1773
Locale: Boston, Massachusetts

Principal personages:

EARL OF GUILFORD (LORD FREDERICK NORTH) (1732-1792), Prime Minister of Great Britain 1770-1782, who sponsored the Tea Act of 1773

THOMAS HUTCHINSON (1711-1780), Governor of Massachusetts 1771-1774

THOMAS HUTCHINSON, JR. (fl.1773), and

ELISHA HUTCHINSON (fl.1773), sons of the Governor and two of the tea consignees

EDMUND BURKE (1729-1797), Member of Parliament, who opposed North's proposals for punishing Massachusetts

JOSEPH WARREN (1741-1775), physician prominent in patriot political organizations

SAMUEL ADAMS (1722-1803), and

JOHN HANCOCK (1737-1793), patriots who aroused Bostonians against the continued presence of the tea ships

Summary of Event

On the evening of December 16, 1773, three vessels lay at anchor in Boston Harbor. All told, they carried 342 chests containing over ninety-thousand pounds of dutiable tea worth about nine-thousand pounds sterling. Shortly after 6:00 P.M., between thirty and sixty men, calling themselves "Mohawks" and roughly disguised as Indians, boarded the ships. Hundreds of silent onlookers at the wharf saw the "Mohawks," organized into three groups, swiftly and systematically break open the tea chests and pour their contents into the sea. Since the water was only two or three feet deep, the tea began to pile up, forcing the men to rake it aside to allow room for the rest. In less than three hours they had completed their work and disappeared into the darkness; to this day the identities of most remain unknown. The "Destruction of the Tea," exclaimed John Adams next day, "is so bold, so daring . . . it must have so important Consequences and so lasting, that I cannot but consider it as an Epocha in History. . . ." Eighteen months later, the colonists were locked in military combat with Great Britain. The Boston Tea Party had ushered in a series of events that led directly to war and eventually independence.

The origins of the famous Tea Party are to be found in Parliament's repeal, in 1770, of all the external taxes embodied in the controversial Townshend Revenue Act, except the tax on tea, which was to remain principally as a symbol of the Mother Country's right

241

to extract cash from American purses. Although the colonists had won only a partial victory in their battle against the second British program of taxation (compared to a complete repeal of the earlier Stamp Act), the chances for an improvement in Anglo-American relations seemed fairly bright in the years 1771-1773. The Secretary of State for the colonies, the Earl of Hillsborough, Marquis of Downshire (Wills Hill), soothed American tempers by announcing that the British government did not intend to propose any new taxes for the colonists. These were years of renewed commercial prosperity when countless Americans drank the dutied brew; when all but a few ignored the frantic schemes of Samuel Adams and a radical minority to keep alive the old flames of resentment. There were, to be sure, occasional happenings that generated fresh ill will, such as the burning by Rhode Islanders of the royal revenue cutter *Gaspee* and the clandestine publication of Massachusetts Governor Thomas Hutchinson's correspondence expressing stern criticism of the colony's patriot leaders. But it was Parliament's Tea Act of 1773 that brought the period of quiescence to an abrupt end throughout North America.

Ironically, British politicians acted not with the purpose of disciplining the Americans but with the intention of boosting the sagging fortunes of the giant East India Company. After sundry unsuccessful attempts to help the ailing corporation with huge investments in India, the Prime Minister of Great Britain, Frederick North, Earl of Guilford ("Lord North"), secured passage of the Tea Act, which for the first time allowed the East India Company to sell tea directly to America and to do so through its own agents; previously it had sold its product to English wholesale merchants, the tea then passing into the hands of American wholesalers and retailers. By removing the profits formerly obtained by English and American middlemen, and by the added provision eliminating English duties on tea exported to the New World possessions, the company hoped to undersell Dutch-smuggled leaves in America, even though the provincials would still have to pay the remaining Townshend tax of three pence on each pound.

Everywhere in North America North's move met stiff resistance. Merchants accused the ministry of giving the East India Company and its agents a monopoly of the local tea market which would be followed in time by other monopolies in the American trade. More frightening to Americans was the constitutional threat; they were vulnerable already since the taxed herb had been purchased in America after 1770. Now, if they consumed even more of the dutied drink, they would implicitly admit the authority of Parliament to tax them. In fact, they saw in Lord North's undertaking a cynical endeavor to get them to "barter liberty for luxury." Consignees in New York, Philadelphia, and Charleston—like the stamp tax collectors earlier—were persuaded to resign their commissions. The outcome was different in Boston, where Governor Hutchinson backed the consignees and refused to let the tea ships return to England without first unloading their cargo.

When the "Mohawks" performed the task of unloading, Parliament's response was one of unparalleled severity. It passed the Coercive Acts in order to bring rebellious Massachusetts to its knees—by closing the port of Boston, altering the structure of government in the colony, allowing British officials and soldiers accused of capital offenses to be tried in England or, to avoid a hostile local jury, in a colony other than the one where the offense had occurred, and providing for the quartering of troops once more in the town of Boston. Massachusetts and the twelve other colonies did not take the verdict lying down.

Pertinent Literature

Labaree, Benjamin W. *The Boston Tea Party.* New York: Oxford University Press, 1964.

Benjamin Labaree has written the only comprehensive study of the Boston Tea Party. Almost universally praised by scholarly reviewers, it seems destined to stand for some time as the basic work in its field. Why had the subject of the Boston Tea Party stimulated no monograph of significance before the publication of Labaree's book in 1964? The explanation for this scholarly disinterest probably lies in the fact that the Boston Tea Party was merely a single event, and until recent years most historians saw the American Revolution as the result of impersonal and inexorable forces deeply rooted in the colonial background. The performance of the "Mohawks" at the Boston wharf marked no significant turn in imperial relations; for according to this older view, the colonists were already on the march to achieve independence. With or without the Coercive Acts that followed the tea incident, revolution was inevitable.

Labaree, in contrast, belongs to a younger generation of investigators who have emphasized immediate issues and specific actions instead of long-range determinants as causes of the rupture in imperial relations. Labaree begins by describing the tea trade in the colonies, centered in the ports of Boston, New York, and Philadelphia.

Americans were heavy tea drinkers, and by 1767 tea was outranked only by woolens, linens, and ironware among Great Britain's major exports to the American colonies. Concerning smuggling, the author shows it to have been especially widespread in the Middle colonies, the illegal trade in tea there far exceeding the East India Company's legitimate traffic in the 1770's. He is skeptical of the colonists' assertion, repeated by historians, that the East India Company's reduction of tea prices would necessarily have enabled it to undersell smuggled tea. He joins other present-day historians in underscoring the colonists' genuine feeling about the illegality of Parliamentary taxation and the loss of constitutional rights, a theme that takes precedence over the once-fashionable notion that the Americans were mainly concerned with protecting their pocketbooks.

Labaree contends persuasively that a single act of violence on December 16, 1773, significantly altered the course of history. Had the tea consignees at Boston along with Governor Hutchinson acquiesced in patriot demands, as happened at Philadelphia and New York, the weeks and months ahead might have produced very different results. He poses an equally intriguing question: if the Tea Party had taken place at Philadelphia or New York, would Parliament have responded less harshly? No American city was cast in so bad a light in the eyes of Englishmen as Boston, long notorious for its disrespect and abuse of stamp officials, customs collectors, and redcoats. Labaree follows with a point that can be well documented: many British imagined that the Bostonians, forever fomenting disturbances and steeped in heresies, were also unpopular throughout the colonies. As the author says, "This assumption was a fatal misunderstanding, for it led the Parliament to believe that the town could be punished without arousing the sympathy of the other colonists."

There is an excellent account of the Parliamentary maneuvering that led to the Coercive Acts. Few Englishmen in public life were courageous enough to buck the winds of revenge and counsel moderation. The depths of British exasperation are revealed in the willingness of the normally mild-mannered Lord Dartmouth to favor a policy of coercion in 1774. Even Colonel Isaac Barré, an eloquent defender of America in the Stamp Act crisis, agreed that Boston deserved punishment. The one consideration, says Labaree, was how severe the retribution should be. If North's program was moderate compared to several private suggestions and some proposals outlined in the newspapers, it nevertheless blew up a storm in America.

Labaree considers that, "granted an enlightened colonial policy on the part of Great Britain, American aspirations to self-government might well have been achieved within a revised imperial structure." Whether this was possible, considering the nature of British politics and recognized constitutional development may well be doubted. But few would deny, after reading this well-researched volume, that specific actions in America and England during 1773-1774 had a profound impact upon the fortunes of the British Empire.

Schlesinger, Arthur M., Sr. *The Colonial Merchants and the American Revolution, 1763-1776.* New York: Columbia University Press, 1918.

An interpretation of the tea crisis strikingly different from Labaree's appears in this book by Arthur M. Schlesinger, Sr., a distinguished scholar whose many books and articles were written over a period of more than forty years. The thesis of this detailed and heavily documented volume is that before the tea episode "the struggle with Parliament had been, in large part, inspired and guided by the mercantile class for trade reforms." To achieve their objectives, the merchants had allied themselves "with their natural enemies in society"—workingmen, artisans, and radical reformers "who dreamed of a semi-independent American nation or something better. . . ." But the Boston Tea Party and the Americans' angry response to the Coercive Acts shocked the conservative mercantile aristocrats into silence. Radical elements seized control of the movement for American rights and propelled the colonists to independence against the wishes of a sizable element of the mercantile community. Class conflict in America and a general rejection of the patriots' sincerity in evoking constitutional principles are both explicit and implicit in Schlesinger's book. Whatever the merits of Schlesinger's study, a mine of information on trade and other subjects, it represents a point of view that is mostly unattractive to the current generation of American historians. At the time of its appearance in the Progressive era, however, it stood in the mainstream of American historical perspective. — *R.D.H.*

Additional Recommended Reading

Brant, Irving. *James Madison: The Virginia Revolutionist.* Indianapolis: Bobbs-Merrill Company, Inc., 1941. Provides one of the best accounts of the tea crisis in Virginia.

Sutherland, Lucy S. *The East India Company in Eighteenth-Century Politics.* New York: Oxford University Press, 1952. A major piece of historical scholarship, this work stresses the growth and importance of the relationship between the East India Company and the British government in the second half of the century, though it has little to offer directly on American affairs.

Cary, John. *Joseph Warren: Physician, Politician, Patriot.* Urbana: University of Illinois Press, 1961. A concise biography of a patriot leader who performed his most important public service between the tea crisis and his death at Bunker Hill.

Jensen, Arthur L. *The Maritime Commerce of Colonial Philadelphia.* Madison: The State Historical Society of Wisconsin, 1963. Jensen claims (contrary to Schlesinger) that Pennsylvania merchants did not lead the revolutionary movement, and that they opposed Parliamentary taxation on principle.

Donoughue, Bernard. *British Politics and the American Revolution: The Path to War, 1773-1775.* New York: St. Martin's Press, 1964. An account of events between the Tea Party and Lexington, written with a sure hand but with little fresh interpretation.

CONVENING OF THE FIRST CONTINENTAL CONGRESS

Type of event: Political: American protest against British colonial policies
Time: September 5-October 26, 1774
Locale: Philadelphia, Pennsylvania

Principal personages:

PEYTON RANDOLPH (1721-1775), Speaker of the Virginia House of Burgesses and President of the First Continental Congress

SAMUEL ADAMS (1722-1803), early advocate of intercolonial assemblages

JOHN ADAMS (1735-1826), author of the congressional resolution denying the right of Parliament to tax or legislate for the colonies

JOSEPH GALLOWAY (1729?-1803), conservative member of the Congress and author of the Plan of Union to ensure American rights within the framework of the British Empire

ALEXANDER MCDOUGALL (1731?-1786), patriot who persuaded New York to send delegates committed to a nonimportation agreement

Summary of Event

On September 6, 1774, representatives from all the thirteen American colonies, except far-off and thinly settled Georgia, assembled at Carpenter's Hall in Philadelphia to begin the business of the First Continental Congress. The significance which Americans attached to the meeting is revealed in the quality of the men chosen to attend: Peyton Randolph, George Washington, Patrick Henry, and Richard Henry Lee of Virginia; John and Samuel Adams of Massachusetts; John and Edward Rutledge of South Carolina; John Jay of New York; Roger Sherman of Connecticut; and John Dickinson and Joseph Galloway of Pennsylvania. "There is in the Congress," noted John Adams in his diary, "a collection of the greatest men upon this Continent in point of abilities, virtues, and fortunes." The greatest potential, as Adams recognized, belonged not to the

old and well-tried politicians but to younger men. The future lay with men such as John Adams, George Washington, and John Jay, who first took the measure of one another during the September and October deliberations in the Quaker City.

The cause of Massachusetts became the cause of America; chastisement of one colony, as in the Coercive Acts aimed at Massachusetts, could lead to the punishment of all unless the colonies stood together. South Carolina, among the last to hear of Massachusetts' fate, was the first outside New England to send direct aid, dispatching a shipment of rice for the beleaguered Bostonians. Suspicion of Parliament's motives increased after the early summer of 1774 when, with remarkably poor timing, that body passed the Quebec Act, giving the former Canadian province a civil government without a representative assembly and allowing Quebec's Catholic majority special privileges relative to their faith. Thoughtful Americans recognized the need to coördinate their efforts to bring about a redress of grievances. With the steadily growing acceptance of the idea of an intercolonial congress, Massachusetts led the way in June, issuing a call for a convention of deputies to be held in Philadelphia.

Proof of the mood of Congress to stand resolutely for American rights came early in the proceedings when the delegates overwhelmingly endorsed the Suffolk Resolves. Adopted earlier by Massachusetts' Suffolk County, these resolutions denounced the Coercive Acts as unconstitutional, urged the people to prepare militarily, and called for an immediate end of trade with the British Empire. In Philadelphia there was informal talk about setting up a continental army if the crisis deepened, and Charles Lee, a former British officer, showed some of the dignitaries a plan he had drafted for organizing colonial regiments. It is scarcely surprising, given Congress' adamant position on the Suffolk Resolves, that the voices of conservatism and extreme caution were few in number, and that they failed to obtain the adoption of Joseph Galloway's Plan of Union, designed to create a distinct American government within the structure of the Empire to deal with affairs which concerned more than a single colony.

The subject of commercial retaliation, which had been important in bringing about the Congress, took most of the delegates' time. Congress on September 27 adopted a resolution banning importations from Great Britain after December 1, 1774. Three days later the delegates voted to stop exportation to the various parts of the Empire, beginning September 10, 1775, provided that America's grievances were not redressed by that date. Congress' program of economic coercion, known as the Continental Association, bound the colonies to participate and created enforcement procedures.

From the outset the congressmen had set for themselves a second main objective, a review of their relationship with Great Britain. Since Parliament had refused to recognize their repeated attempts to distinguish between taxation and legislation regulating trade for the benefit of the Empire but not for revenue, many Americans felt they had no choice but to conclude that Parliament had no control over them at all. Jefferson expressed the thinking of many of his countrymen in 1774; his pamphlet, *Summary View,* referred to the King as the "Chief Magistrate" of the Empire and denied the authority of Parliament to legislate for the colonies in any case whatsoever. Some of the congressmen, however, were reluctant to repudiate Parliament completely. The result was a compromise resolution stating that by consent, not by right, Parliament might regulate commerce in the interest of all.

In addition to providing for another intercolonial meeting the next spring, Congress, before adjourning on October 26, dispatched a series of declarations and addresses to the King, to the people of Great Britain, and to the citizens of America. The delegates called for a return to the relationship they had enjoyed with the Mother Country in the years prior to 1763 and asked for a repeal or withdrawal of policies and laws, beginning with the decision to keep an army in America and concluding with the Coercive Acts. In Great Britain the appeals of Congress fell largely on deaf ears. As early as November 18, 1774, King George III informed his Prime Minister, Lord Frederick North (Earl of Guilford), that "the New England governments are in a state of rebellion, blows must decide whether they are to be subject to this country or independent."

Pertinent Literature

Boyd, Julian P. *Anglo-American Union: Joseph Galloway's Plans to Preserve the British Empire, 1774-1788.* Philadelphia: University of Pennsylvania Press, 1941.

By 1774 even men of the most conservative temperament and philosophy could not visualize a British-American settlement which failed to make fundamental alterations in the imperial relationship. But they faced a dilemma: how could the revered principle of Parliamentary supremacy be saved in view of patriot demands for virtual autonomy? The problem as seen through the eyes of one man, Joseph Galloway, forms the subject of Julian P. Boyd's scholarly and readable volume. Perhaps no one of Galloway's generation on either side of the Atlantic sacrificed more or labored harder in behalf of a compromise solution, declares the author. Boyd treats the issue within the context of the history of American federalism, which extends back to the New England Confederation of 1643 and includes a multitude of proposals for colonial union put forth by such men as William and Thomas Penn, Daniel Coxe, George Clinton, Richard Peters, and, of course, Benjamin Franklin, whose scheme at the outset of the French and Indian War appears to have influenced the shaping of Galloway's initial plan.

Boyd demonstrates that Galloway's background offers no simple explanation for his particular brand of political philosophy. Born in 1731 of a prosperous middle class family, Galloway studied law, married into wealth, and won election to the Pennsylvania Assembly, where, as a member of Franklin's anti-Proprietary party, he served as Speaker from 1765 to 1774. Galloway became affluent, but so also did such resolute patriots as George Washington and Robert Morris. Although his legal training inclined him to follow the British Constitution regardless of events, it must be noted that James Wilson, Thomas Jefferson, and John Adams were also lawyers but in time cast that constitution aside. Friendship and political association were usually preëminent considerations, so why did Galloway part company with Franklin, whose protégé and friend he had been for over two decades? Historians have yet to devise an adequate formula for determining the loyalties of men caught up in the crisis of the mid-1770's.

Galloway's first and most important plan of union, in 1774, called for the establishment of a Grand Council in America, along with a President-General appointed by the Crown. This council, composed of representatives from all the colonies, would have all the "rights, liberties, and privileges" of the House of Commons. Though its acts would require Parliamentary approval, the council would also enjoy a veto over Parliament's measures relating to the colonies. Galloway's plan of union would have been a radical proposal at an earlier time, but had it been adopted in a previous decade, American aspirations and needs might well have been met for many years within the framework of the Empire. Even in 1774 at the First Continental Congress, Galloway's plan attracted the support of able men, including James Duane, John Jay, and Edward Rutledge. However, a majority voted to table the motion for adoption of the plan and ordered it expunged from the official minutes. Boyd nevertheless believes that, had Galloway been less openly pro-British and more astute in dealing with ardent patriots, such as John Adams and Richard Henry Lee, he might have won over enough congressmen to achieve his objective. "It is perhaps not too much to say," Boyd surmises, "that [Galloway] was the chief instrument in bringing about his own defeat."

The final two chapters of the volume trace Galloway's continued efforts to bring about a satisfactory constitutional adjustment between the Mother Country and her protesting colonies. In London Galloway penned at least six additional plans of union between 1779 and 1788, all doomed to failure by the outcome of the Revolutionary War. Bitter and angry, not only because of the course America pursued but also because of Great Britain's military ineptness and its treatment of the Loyalists, Galloway, as Boyd points out, had tried to take the middle road and had found that in revolution there is seldom a place for the compromiser, who usually wins "the enmity of both and seldom the gratitude of either."

Nelson, William H. *The American Tory.* New York: Oxford University Press, 1962.

Those Americans who refused to go along with the American Revolution were abused by their contemporaries in America and in Great Britain and were later neglected by historians. Nearly a hundred years passed before a serious writer endeavored to prove that they were less than diabolical. With a few exceptions, such as Julian Boyd's *Anglo-American Union,* only a scattering of monographs and biographies sought to probe deeply into the thought of the Loyalists or the composition of royal support. Moreover, seldom were the Loyalists, called Tories by their contemporaries, allowed to state their own case. The complete writings of Jonathan Boucher, Daniel Leonard, and Joseph Galloway have not been reprinted since the eighteenth century. Fortunately, the 1960's witnessed a renewed interest in the Tories. The year 1961 saw the publication for the first time of Peter Oliver's *Origin and Progress of the American Rebellion,* by a former Chief Justice of the Massachusetts Superior Court, who put together his history while exiled in England.

In 1961 there also appeared a balanced monographic treatment of the Loyalists, William H. Nelson's *The American Tory,* which cast aside a host of long-held generalizations about the King's friends. According to Nelson, no longer can one confidently accept John Adams' statistics of one-third neutralists, one-third patriots, and one-third Loyalists; nor can flat assumptions of loyalties properly be made on the basis of back country and tidewater, artisan and merchant, or independent-minded Protestant and Anglican. Nelson is aware that serious research on the Loyalists is perhaps just beginning, but he makes a tentative judgment that Loyalists were "a third, and the revolutionists two-thirds of the politically active population of the colonies." One of the most discerning points of the book concerns the loyalism of cultural and religious minorities. After granting that many British-born settlers automatically saw no choice but to stay with the homeland, Nelson states that the Tories were normally more numerous among the non-British colonists. He finds one explanation to be that the minorities believed that Great Britain would safeguard their position from the cultural aggression of the dominant Anglo-Americans. Although it was not true for Catholics and Jews, it did apply to most other religious groups: Anglicans and many Baptists in Congregational New England, numerous Presbyterians in the Episcopal South, and most Quakers and German Pietists everywhere.

As for the Tory intellectuals, the Galloways and the Bouchers, Nelson believes that the consequence of their silencing and banishment was not so much social or political as it was philosophical; that their inherent conservatism failed to reveal itself in America after the Revolution, and part of the spectrum of the Old World's philosophy of government and society passed outside the American perspective. In fact, their failure to influence their countrymen indicated that already there was "an alarming uniformity of outlook in America." In that society, says Nelson, the Tory cast of mind had no place. — *R.D.H.*

Additional Recommended Reading

Adams, Randolph G. *Political Ideas of the American Revolution.* Durham: Trinity College Press, 1922. Recent research has made part of this volume out of date, but it is still excellent for a study of the constitutional thinking of Americans in the year of the First Continental Congress.

Burnett, Edmund C. *The Continental Congress.* New York: The Macmillan Company, 1941. The first three chapters of this massively detailed book are relevant to the events of 1774.

Meigs, Cornelia L. *The Violent Men: A Study of Human Relations in the First American Congress.* New York: The Macmillan Company, 1949. A fast-paced narrative of the years 1774-1776.

Oliver, Peter. *Peter Oliver's Origin and Progress of the American Rebellion: A Tory View.* Edited by Douglass Adair and John A. Schutz. San Marino, California: Huntington Library, 1961. Oliver, like most other Tory writers, describes the Revolution as the work of a minority of demagogues who aroused and coerced the people by "every low and dirty art."

Brown, Wallace. *The King's Friends: The Composition and Motives of the American Loyalist Claimants.* Providence: Brown University Press, 1965. Brown examines the Loyalists who between 1777 and 1790 placed claims with the British government for losses suffered in America.

BATTLE OF LEXINGTON AND CONCORD

Type of event: Military: First military action of the American Revolution
Time: April 19, 1775
Locale: Lexington and Concord, Massachusetts

Principal personages:

WILLIAM LEGGE, SECOND EARL OF DARTMOUTH (1731-1801), Secretary of State for the colonies who sent out the order to use force in Massachusetts

GEORGE III (GEORGE WILLIAM FREDERICK) (1738-1820), King of Great Britain who favored a position of no compromise in dealing with the colonists

GENERAL THOMAS GAGE (1721-1787), Governor of Massachusetts and Commander in Chief of British forces in North America

LIEUTENANT COLONEL FRANCIS SMITH (fl. 1775), headed the royal detachment sent to Concord

MAJOR JOHN PITCAIRN (1722-1775), Smith's second in command

PAUL REVERE (1735-1818), silversmith-engraver and active patriot who, together with William Dawes and Samuel Prescott, aroused the Massachusetts countryside

CAPTAIN JOHN PARKER (1729-1775), veteran militia officer who commanded the minuteman company on Lexington green

Summary of Event

In the early morning hours of April 19, 1775, Captain John Parker, forty-five year old veteran of the French and Indian War, stood with his single company of minutemen on the village green at Lexington. Several hours had passed since Paul Revere's word of an approaching column of redcoats had brought them tumbling out of their beds. Now a messenger reported that the royal troops were almost within sight. Earlier the minutemen and their neighbors had adopted a resolution that the presence of a British Army in their province constituted an infringement upon their "natural, constitutional, chartered rights." They had pledged their "estates and every thing dear in life, yea and life itself" if necessary in opposing the Coercive Acts. Hopelessly outnumbered, Parker kept his men on the green and away from the nearby road the British would follow to the next town of Concord. But if the captain of minutemen intended their presence to serve only a symbolic purpose, an expression of their displeasure at the redcoats' intrusion, British Major Pitcairn nevertheless turned and led his advance companies onto the green. In the confusion of regulars surging forward and minutemen hastily falling back, firing began. The Americans were quickly driven from the field, leaving eight dead and ten wounded. Lexington was hardly a

251

battle, and yet a war had begun. The United States was born in an act of violence, lasting but fifteen to twenty minutes.

British troops had returned to Boston following the Tea Party and the Coercive Acts. With them came a new Governor of Massachusetts, General Thomas Gage, long-time military Commander in Chief in North America. In retaliation, the Massachusetts Assembly, now calling itself the Provincial Congress and sitting as an extralegal body, took control of the militia, appointed general officers, and ordered the organizing of one-fourth of all the militia into minute companies. Massachusetts' firm resolution to fight if pressed was duplicated throughout New England, as well as in the Middle colonies and in far-off Virginia, where, on March 9, the Virginia convention sat transfixed by the eloquence of Patrick Henry: "The war is inevitable. . . . The war is actually begun. . . . Our brethren are already in the field! Why stand here idle?" The potentially explosive situation was heightened by the struggle over gunpowder in the colonies. In London the ministry imposed an embargo on the shipment of munitions to America, except for quantities headed for Gage's army. Armed clashes were narrowly averted in Rhode Island, New Hampshire, and Virginia, as patriots and British authorities sought to monopolize the critically short amounts of powder. The capture or destruction of the Massachusetts Provincial Congress' military stores was the assignment of Lieutenant Colonel Francis Smith as he headed down the silent country road that ran through Lexington and on to Concord on the night of April 18, 1775.

Long before reaching Lexington, Smith realized that his assignment was known to the patriots, whose church bells and signal guns were audible to the marchers. Consequently, Smith dispatched Major John Pitcairn ahead with six companies to occupy the bridges over the Concord river, at the same time that he wisely sent a courier to ask General Gage for reinforcements. After routing the Lexington minutemen, Pitcairn continued on the additional five miles to Concord, entering the village at eight o'clock in the morning. The patriots had managed to cart away part of their supplies. When the British had burned several gun carriages and destroyed flour, they set out about noon on their return journey.

The sixteen miles back to Boston were a nightmare for Smith and Pitcairn. The scarlet column proved an inviting target for the swarms of militia and minute companies that had converged on Concord and Lexington. From trees, rocks, and stone walls they kept up a steady fire. Smith's force may well have escaped annihilation only because at Lexington they received a reinforcement of nine hundred men under General Hugh Earl Percy. Even so, the combined column might have been destroyed had the efforts of the various American detachments been coördinated. As it was, the wild, unorthodox battle continued until the British reached Charleston, across the harbor from Boston, where dusk and the protecting guns of the Royal Navy brought an end to the mauling.

British losses came to 73 killed, 174 wounded, and 26 missing, while American casualties in all categories totaled 93. The colonists remained to besiege the enemy in Boston. The *New-*

port *Mercury* described the day's events as the beginning of "the *American Civil War,* which will hereafter fill an important page in History."

Pertinent Literature

Alden, John R. *General Gage in America: Being Principally a History of His Role in the American Revolution.* Baton Rouge: Louisiana State University Press, 1948.

In this well-written study, the first biography of Thomas Gage, John R. Alden illuminates the administration of the British Army in North America between the conclusion of the Seven Years' War and the early months of the American Revolution. Although some of the author's findings have been slightly modified in recent works by Bernhard Knollenberg and John Shy, Alden's *Gage* remains an exceedingly valuable contribution, and it is unequalled in its treatment of the British decision to use armed force against Massachusetts in the spring of 1775.

Gage emerges in Alden's pages as a prudent man, sound and judicious, seldom imaginative, and never brilliant. Talent and performance hardly guaranteed a successful military career in Gage's day. A younger son of Sussex nobility, he possessed the status and influence so essential for advancement in Britain's class-conscious army of the eighteenth century. Gage's military record, almost from beginning to end, was carved in America, where, initially, he saw extended duty in the campaigns of the Seven Years' War. Then for three years Gage governed the Montreal district and afterward received the supreme command of all British forces in North America. Alden views his subject as a competent administrator, conscious of detail and alert to ways of managing the army efficiently and economically. Moreover, Gage "was modest, decent, and just," and "better

suited for the supreme command in America in terms of personality than any other available high army officer."

Although Gage approved of Britain's controversial American program after 1763, he was no tyrant. Recognizing the ministry's responsibility for formulating policy, including the civil authority's control of the military, he avoided acting on his own to enforce unpopular laws with troops. Alden shows that, after the Coercive Acts, Gage lost favor in London because of his caution. In letter after letter, commencing in the fall of 1774, he informed the ministry that New England, supported by Americans to the south, would take up arms if pressed, that New England alone would take possibly two years to subdue, and only then if heavy reinforcements were forthcoming. Gage, veteran of twenty years' service in America, uttered truths unpalatable to his countrymen who were exasperated by the Tea Party and other incidents of defiance.

If Gage was reluctant to precipitate an armed conflict without additional regiments, then why did he send Smith's column to Concord? Alden is the historian to provide us with the full story. Displeased with Gage's unwillingness to deal harshly with the patriots and contemplating his removal, the cabinet, acting through Lord Dartmouth, sent the General a "Secret" dispatch, ordering him to employ coercion against the Massachusetts patriots and to arrest the leaders of the Provincial Congress. It was for this reason that Gage acted to seize the munitions at Concord, although he decided against the arrest of a few leaders, who would undoubtedly be replaced by equally zealous Whigs. Gage had warned his superiors of the hornet's nest in Massachusetts, but now he received the blame for the outcome of Lexington and Concord and for the heavy British losses at the Battle of Bunker Hill on June 17, the latter event triggering his recall. Gage's successors as Commander in Chief in America may have excelled him in talents; but, as Alden concludes, he was returned to England for the wrong reasons—to serve as a scapegoat for the mistakes of his political superiors who, only too late, recognized the truth in the repeated warnings of Thomas Gage.

French, Allen. *The Day of Concord and Lexington: Nineteenth of April, 1775.* Boston: Little, Brown, and Company, 1925.

The late Allen French, a son of Concord and a patrician historian of distinction, devoted years to the examination of the early phases of the War of Independence, especially those aspects relating to his beloved New England. Between 1925 and 1942 he wrote *The Day of Concord and Lexington; The Taking of Ticonderoga; General Gage's Informers; The First Year of the American Revolution;* and *Historic Concord.* French, writing between World War I and World War II, was sadly aware that military history was out of fashion, replaced in part by historical determinism that found great events the result of impersonal forces. It was French's intention to return the hero to his proper niche in history and to fix responsibility for successes and failures among human beings, the "perplexed Gage, steadfast Warren, honest Pitcairn, earnest Emerson, gallant Percy, clumsy but dogged Heath."

Nowhere did French succeed more admirably than in *The Day of Concord and Lexington,* an oft-told tale that he repeated with verve and new interpretations of "ancient subject matter." French is clearly more interested in analysis than narration. He moves skillfully through the maze of conflicting personal accounts, recognizing that men on both sides who wrote immediately after the battle did so in the flush of excitement and extreme partisanship, just as those who recorded memoirs years later were unintentionally guilty of straying from the truth.

Several of the author's points are worth repeating. He feels that historians have exaggerated the prowess of the New England minutemen and militia with firearms. If every American had inflicted one serious wound on an enemy, he observes, none of the redcoats would have escaped. But their failure to halt the retreating column is also explained by the shortage of powder among the Americans and by the limitations of the musket, their chief weapon, which would scarcely fire over sixty yards. He notes, contrary to legend (and to recent popular writers since his book appeared) that the rifle, with its much longer range, was a weapon almost unknown in New England. Other myths are eliminated, one that Gage's American-born wife warned the patriots of the intended raid on Concord, and another, that Samuel Adams prompted Captain

John Parker to oppose the British on Lexington green. French is mildly critical of William Heath, the only Massachusetts general officer on the field of battle, for failing to coördinate the various provincial companies and for not erecting roadblocks to obstruct the British retreat, although he concedes that Heath had no staff and that most of the men were "too raw" for much concerted activity.

Upon reading *The Day of Concord and Lexington,* one should consult the relevant portions of *General Gage's In-* *formers,* based on pertinent new source material discovered in England and brought to this country by William L. Clements, who subsequently established a library bearing his name at the University of Michigan. In the latter study French casts further light on the origins of the skirmish at Lexington and on the fight at the Concord Bridge. French's writings, read in conjunction with Alden's *General Gage,* provide the reader with full and judicious accounts of the background and events of April 19, 1775. — *R.D.H.*

Additional Recommended Reading

Murdock, Harold. *The Nineteenth of April, 1775: Concord and Lexington.* Boston: Houghton Mifflin, Co., 1923. Murdock sweeps away a good deal of myth and misinformation in this analytical book.

Curtis, Edward E. *The Organization of the British Army in the American Revolution.* New Haven: Yale University Press, 1926. Curtis shows what kind of an army opposed the colonists in Massachusetts and elsewhere.

Forbes, Esther. *Paul Revere and the World He Lived In.* Boston: Houghton Mifflin Co., 1942. This sprightly biography, winner of the Pulitzer Prize, takes a life and times approach.

Ward, Christopher. *The War of the Revolution.* 2 vols. Edited by John R. Alden. New York: The Macmillan Company, 1952. This is the best of the multivolumed military histories of the Revolution. It contains a spirited account of Lexington and Concord.

Tourtellot, Arthur B. *William Diamond's Drum: The Beginning of the War of the American Revolution.* New York: Doubleday, and Co., Inc., 1959. This is a sound account of the opening battles of the Revolutionary War that concludes with the creation of the Continental Army.

CONVENING OF THE SECOND CONTINENTAL CONGRESS

Type of event: Political: opposition to British Imperial program
Time: May 10-August 2, 1775
Locale: Philadelphia, Pennsylvania

Principal personages:
JOHN HANCOCK (1737-1793), delegate from Massachusetts and first President of the Second Continental Congress
GEORGE WASHINGTON (1732-1799), delegate from Virginia who was appointed Commander in Chief of the Continental Army
JOHN ADAMS (1735-1826), delegate from Massachusetts who urged the election of Washington
BENJAMIN FRANKLIN (1706-1790), delegate from Pennsylvania, a congressman experienced in military affairs
THOMAS JEFFERSON (1743-1826), delegate from Virginia and coauthor of the "Declaration of Causes of Taking up Arms"

Summary of Event

The Second Continental Congress began its deliberations at the State House in Philadelphia on May 10, 1775. It was, like the First Continental Congress, an extralegal body—until the ratification of the Articles of Confederation some years later. But it continued to meet throughout the Revolutionary War, exercising whatever authority the colony-states permitted. Although it was weak in terms of legal jurisdiction and state pressures, and lacked material resources for waging war, the amazing thing about the Second Continental Congress is that it accomplished as much as it did. Out of a bond forged by a common threat from Great Britain, a bond often frustrated by local politicians more interested in state sovereignty than wartime efficiency, there emerged a cluster of American political leaders, nationalists who echoed the plea of New York's John Jay that the "Union depends

much upon breaking down provincial Conventions."

An extraordinary task faced the delegates who came to Philadelphia from all the colonies except Georgia, which was not represented until the second session of the Congress held that fall. While the First Continental Congress had hammered out agreements on constitutional principles, the Second Continental Congress had to unite for military action. Fortunately, the new Congress contained men of distinction. John Hancock became its President. There were familiar faces from the preceding year: among others, the Adams' cousins of Massachusetts, George Washington and Richard Henry Lee of Virginia, Edmund Rutledge of South Carolina, John Jay of New York, and John Dickinson of Pennsylvania. They were joined by talented newcomers, such as the youthful Thomas Jefferson, the venerable Benjamin Franklin, and the scholarly James Wilson of Pennsylvania. Although realizing that the chances of securing an amicable reconciliation might suffer if the delegates involved themselves in the confrontation between New England and General Gage's redcoats, Congress was in no mood to turn the other cheek. In their "Declaration of Causes of Taking up Arms," the legislators solemnly announced that the American people had two choices: submission to tyranny, or resistance by force. They preferred the latter. The colonies, moreover, looked to Congress for advice and direction. Connecticut asked what should be done with munitions captured at Ticonderoga and Crown Point. New York inquired whether it should resist a landing by British troops. Massachusetts sought approval for establishing a civil government and urged Congress to assume responsibility for the New England forces besieging Boston. "Such a vast Multitude of Objects, civil, political, commercial and military, press and crowd upon us so fast, that we know not what to do first," exclaimed John Adams.

Congress nevertheless moved resolutely to put America in a state of defense, calling upon the colonies to prepare themselves, and voting to take charge of the New England troops outside Boston. In selecting a commanding general, Congress rejected Massachusetts' ranking officer, General Artemas Ward, as well as John Hancock, both of whom desired the post. It was "absolutely Necessary in point of prudence," wrote Eliphalet Dyer of Connecticut, "to pick a non-New Englander to head the Continental army; it removes all jealousies [and] . . .

more firmly Cements the Southern to the Northern" colonies. One important reason for the subsequent appointment of George Washington as Commander in Chief was to demonstrate to Americans everywhere that the war transcended the interests of a particular section, a step that would arouse support for the military effort in the middle and southern parts of America. Washington, bearing the proper regional credentials, also hailed from the "right" colony, prosperous and populous Virginia. Equally or more important, Washington possessed certain qualities as a man, a patriot, and a soldier requisite for the high office bestowed upon him. Congress, in picking a ranking general, had taken an accurate measure of its man. Aware of Congress' limitations and cognizant of state jealousies, he remained unflinchingly deferential to the civil authority. Washington was a rare combination of soldier and statesman who understood, however maddening it might be at times, that this was a peculiar kind of coalition war. It is doubtful whether his accomplishments could have been equaled by any other general officer appointed at the time: men, such as Major Generals Artemas Ward, Charles Lee, Philip Schuyler, and Israel Putnam; and Brigadier Generals Seth Pomeroy, William Heath, John Thomas, David Wooster, Joseph Spencer, John Sullivan, Nathanael Greene, and Richard Montgomery.

The first session of the Second Continental Congress came to an end on August 2, with the legislators agreeing to reconvene six weeks later. The delegates had accomplished much in less than three months. Besides calling the colonies to defensive preparations, adopting an army, providing for its regulation, and appointing its general officers, they had taken steps to issue paper money, encourage limited foreign trade, and, along with other matters, bolster the militias. Congress was no longer a temporary council of American dignitaries sitting to articulate constitutional doctrines and draft remonstrances; it was the central government of a people at war, and a revolutionary body in the fullest sense.

Pertinent Literature

Burnett, Edmund C. *The Continental Congress.* New York: The Macmillan Company, 1941.

Edmund C. Burnett was superbly qualified to write the first detailed, scholarly book about the Continental Congress. He had previously devoted nearly twenty years to the task of collecting and editing, in eight volumes, the *Letters of Members of the Continental Congress,* one of the four or five most valuable documentary collections of the Revolutionary era. The author's approach is chronological rather than topical, his purpose to "throw upon the screen the living and moving Congress." Burnett did not live to write a projected companion volume that would have treated the Congress as "architect and builder" of lasting political precedents. But it was his contention that, whereas the Declaration of Independence and the Federal Constitution had been examined in terms of their contributions to our national beginnings, the Continental Congress, though also contributing signally to the growth of nationhood, had been sadly neglected.

Congress, as Burnett is at pains to point out, was never truly continental. It never represented more than thirteen colony-states. No members came from the British mainland provinces of East Florida, West Florida, Nova Scotia, or Quebec, nor from Bermuda or the other Crown possessions in the West Indies. Only in the case of Quebec did the Congress make a strenuous effort to broaden the area of rebellion; but the defeat of patriot General Richard Montgomery on the banks of the St. Lawrence river ended this threat to Great Britain. Actually, "the Congress" was that body's official designation, although it was commonly spoken of as "the Continental Congress," and Burnett has chosen to follow the popular usage of the time.

Burnett stoutly dissents from the view of such historians as C. H. Van Tyne that Congress was scarcely more than a council of ambassadors or a debating society from the several states. It was once fashionable to maintain that the states were more important than Congress in conducting the war. It is true that some states sent diplomatic agents abroad and attempted to borrow money in Europe, that Continental soldiers were organized on the basis of state lines, that the militias were indispensable at crucial periods, and that local authorities disciplined the loyalists and directed most activities behind the lines. Furthermore, the delegates not infrequently acted in response to specific instructions from the states that sent them to Philadelphia. Admirers of Washington and advocates of states' rights have usually been active in criticizing Congress and picturing it as virtually impotent before the all-powerful and legally sovereign states.

Although the author considers that past writers have exaggerated the weaknesses and frailties of Congress, he acknowledges the mistakes of the lawmakers. They at times interfered in Washington's military planning, they made serious errors in the selection of general officers, and they displayed naïveté in handling foreign affairs. He notes that eventually the quality of its membership declined. Washington led the army; Franklin, John Adams, John Jay, and Henry Laurens took up diplomatic stations abroad; Thomas Jefferson became Governor of Virginia. Some men chosen to serve in Congress declined or attended sporadically. Congress, in short, was a congeries of delegates coming and going, few remaining the long periods necessary to keep abreast of the country's needs and obligations. In one instance, however, Bur-

nett's criticism has been invalidated by more recent scholarship: the so-called "Conway Cabal" of 1777-1778, an alleged conspiracy in the army and in Congress to remove Washington in favor of Horatio Gates, has been consigned to the rubbish heap of historical myths.

The sum total of Congress' achievements, as Burnett's study reveals, far exceeded its failures. Congress appointed Washington Commander in Chief, declared the independence of the United States, established the Navy and Marine Corps, formed a diplomatic service, negotiated foreign treaties, organized a postal service, issued currency, borrowed money, and drafted the Articles of Confederation. The best yardstick of its success is that Congress accomplished its ultimate assignment: its soldiers won the war and its diplomats won the peace at Paris. Indeed, it was Congress, not the states, that occupied the "central stage" of the American Revolution.

Alden, John R. *The American Revolution, 1775-1783.* New York: Harper & Row Publishers, 1954.

The trend to write sympathetically of the Continental Congress' perplexing problems, as well as to emphasize its positive record, is reflected in the work of John R. Alden, one of the leading authorities on the American Revolution, whose book is a volume in Harper & Row's *New American Nation* series. While the author of the study of the American Revolution in Harper's original *American Nation* series which appeared in 1905, referred to Congress as "merely the central office of a continental signal system," Alden believes that "too little credit has usually been given to the faithful in Congress who

struggled in adversity."

If the caliber of the membership declined with the passing years, the assemblage nevertheless contained many men of "talent, integrity, and energy." Drawing partly upon the research of Bernhard Knollenberg, Alden argues convincingly that evidence of a plot against Washington has not come to light. No historian has yet proved that a single congressman pushed for the elevation of Horatio Gates. Washington's bitterest detractor, Dr. Benjamin Rush, who did favor Gates, was no longer a member of Congress, and the only known persistent critic within its meeting halls was James Lovell of Massachusetts, who may well have shared Rush's sentiments.

Alden's revisionist outlook can also be seen in his treatment of Congress' management of finances. A familiar theme of nineteenth century writers was the Revolutionaries' gross mismanagement of economic affairs. Engaged in a battle for sound dollars against silverites and other inflationists, contemporaries of the Gilded Age depicted the monetary policies of the patriots as disastrous, leading to general disorder on the home front and to the near destruction of the Continental Army. Perhaps the presence of fiat money and managed economies in recent times has made it easier for a fresh assessment. We now know that paper money was usually a successful method of obtaining revenue in the Colonial Period for provincial governments without resources and a stable system of public finance. Hence, the Continental Congress turned to an old and generally satisfactory mode of acquiring revenue.

In the American Revolution, as Alden states, the Congressmen had no illusions about the possible pitfalls. Whatever the results, Congress had no choice, lacking as it did the power to tax and to compel contributions from the states. Clearly paper money was indispensable, and Alden suggests that it might have held its face value reasonably well had the states coöperated by ceasing their own issues.

Alden's book stands as one of our most balanced, up-to-date general histories of the American Revolution.
— *R.D.H.*

Additional Recommended Reading

French, Allen. *The First Year of the American Revolution.* Boston: Houghton Mifflin Co., 1934. Lengthy, well-documented, and carefully written, this excellent work includes extended treatment of the activities of Congress.

Knollenberg, Bernhard. *Washington and the Revolution, a Reappraisal: Gates, Conway and the Continental Congress.* New York: The Macmillan Company, 1940. A revisionist book of importance, critical of Washington, favorable to Horatio Gates and Congress, and opposed to the view that a "Conway Cabal" existed.

Jensen, Merrill. *The Articles of Confederation: An Interpretation of the Social-Constitutional History of the American Revolution, 1774-1781.* Madison: University of Wisconsin Press, 1940. Concerned with the social, economic, and political divisions in Congress.

Montross, Lynn. *The Reluctant Rebels: The Story of the Continental Congress. 1774-1789.* New York: Harper & Row Publishers, 1950. Popular history, but filled with lively quotations and sharply etched characterizations.

Ferguson, E. James. *The Power of the Purse: A History of American Public Finance, 1776-1790.* Chapel Hill: University of North Carolina Press, 1961. The best treatment of Congress' management of economic affairs, although some of its conclusions have been challenged.

DECLARATION OF INDEPENDENCE

Type of event: Constitutional: justification for severing the repressive ties of empire
Time: June 7-July 4, 1776
Locale: Philadelphia, Pennsylvania

Principal personages:

THOMAS PAINE (1737-1809), English-born colonist whose pamphlet *Common Sense* helped to crystallize thought toward independence

RICHARD HENRY LEE (1732-1794), Virginia delegate who presented in the Continental Congress the initial resolution for independence

THOMAS JEFFERSON (1743-1826), Virginia delegate and principal author of the Declaration of Independence

BENJAMIN FRANKLIN (1706-1790), Pennsylvania delegate who made helpful contributions

JOHN ADAMS (1735-1826), Massachusetts delegate who also gave useful assistance

Summary of Event

In the opening months of 1776 the colonists faced a momentous and fundamental decision. Should they content themselves with a return of British authority as it existed prior to 1763, or should they irrevocably sever all political ties with, and dependence upon, the Mother Country? Since Great Britain was unwilling to give them that choice, offering instead only abject surrender to Parliamentary sovereignty, Americans in increasing numbers concluded that complete independence, not merely autonomy within the Empire, must be their goal. Many of the undecided were won over to defiance of the Crown as a result of Parliament's Prohibitory Act, which called for a naval blockade of the colonies, the seizure of American goods on the high seas, and the dragooning of captured provincial seamen into the royal navy. For many colonists news of the British Ministry's decision to employ German mercenaries for use in America was the last straw. The requirements of the struggle itself lent weight to the idea of complete separation. Men would not do battle wholeheartedly for vaguely defined purposes, nor would the French or Spanish aid deemed essential to military success be forthcoming if the colonies fought merely for a greater freedom within the Empire.

In January, 1776, these colonial issues were the subject of Thomas Paine's *Common Sense*. Though it may be doubted that Paine's widely read pamphlet was the determining factor in creating the break and though he advanced no new arguments, he expressed cogent and compelling reasons why a free America should pursue its own destiny. Although Americans of almost every persuasion were already disputing the right of Parliament to rule over the colonies, there remained among the colonists a strong attach-

261

ment to the British Crown and to the present King, George III. Monarchy in general, and the Hanoverian King in particular, received scathing denunciation from Paine, who asserted that kings were frauds imposed upon people capable of governing themselves. George III, Paine reasoned, was no exception and had engaged in oppressive acts which had destroyed every claim upon American loyalties. Paine held that the break should come immediately while Americans were in arms and sensitive to their liberties. Independence, he argued, was inevitable for a wealthy, expanding continent which could not long be tied to a small and distant island.

One by one the Southern and New England colonial assemblies authorized their delegates to the Continental Congress, meeting in Philadelphia, to vote for independence. There on June 7, 1776, Richard Henry Lee, obeying instructions from Virginia, introduced a resolution declaring the colonies independent. Temporarily, the Middle colonies hesitated to make such a drastic decision, causing a delay in acting on the matter; but on July 2, with only New York abstaining, the vote was twelve to nothing in favor of Lee's resolution declaring that the colonies were "free and independent states." Anticipating the outcome, Congress had earlier formed a committee composed of Thomas Jefferson, John Adams, Benjamin Franklin, Robert R. Livingston, and Roger Sherman, to prepare a statement concerning independence. The now famous document was drafted by Jefferson with some assistance from Adams and Franklin. Congress, after first making some revisions, adopted it on July 4.

The purpose of the Declaration of Independence was not to change the legal status of America; on July 2 Congress had voted to sever the colonies from the Empire. The intent of Jefferson and his colleagues was rather to explain and justify the action of Congress in terms meaningful to Americans and Europeans alike. In doing so Jefferson drew heavily upon the general cluster of ideas associated with the eighteenth century political philosophy movement known as the Enlightenment. Besides a preface and a conclusion, the Declaration of Independence consists of a statement of the right of revolution based upon the philosophy of natural rights, a list of grievances against the King, and an account of the colonists' inability to obtain within the structure of the Empire redress of grievances.

Some modern scholars consider the barrage of accusations heaped upon the King to be lacking in dignity and significance in relation to the rest of the document. They point out that George III was a strict constitutionalist whose conduct in the political arena was in accord with the practices and traditions of the earlier Hanoverian monarchs. Moreover, most of the programs and policies held to be reprehensible by the colonists hardly originated in the mind of the King. Still, it is true that George III favored a rigid policy of government, and that he consistently turned a deaf ear to the remonstrances from the American assemblies and congresses. To counter the public mood of the times it was essential for Jefferson to lay America's troubles at the feet of the King. Since the time of the First Continental Congress in 1774, patriot leaders had denied that there was any legitimate Parliamentary authority to cast off; it was a lingering loyalty to the Crown which held many to the Empire.

The enduring qualities of the Declaration of Independence transcend the Anglo-American conflict. The statement that "all men are created equal"—that they have certain inalienable rights under God that governments may not destroy—inspired men in that day just as it has moved people here and abroad in all times since. The force that sparked the emergence of this noble document was the burning desire of its supporters to be free to shape their own destiny. The message conveyed has left a lasting imprint on the conscience of the world.

Pertinent Literature

Becker, Carl L. *The Declaration of Independence: A Study in the History of Political Ideas.* 2nd ed. New York: Harcourt, Brace & World, Inc., 1941.

Carl Becker's scholarly interests were far-ranging. A professor of European history at Cornell University, he probably wrote more in the field of American history than he did in his own teaching specialty. His most famous book, hailed as a classic from its first appearance, is *The Declaration of Independence.* Although Becker is primarily concerned with the history of political ideas, he devotes two of his six chapters to a study of the drafting of the Declaration of Independence and to the document's literary qualities. The critics, as Becker admitted in the 1941 preface to the second edition, held that the inclusion of such material was not relevant to the main theme. Even so, the chapters in question made worthwhile contributions to an understanding of the Declaration of Independence. Becker, a splendid stylist himself, was admirably equipped to describe Jefferson's "peculiar felicity of expression," as John Adams spoke of it, the clear and concise paragraphs so devoid of verbiage and trivia. Becker's account of the evolution of the text has now been superseded by that of Julian Boyd, who recently discovered part of an original draft of the Declaration of Independence. Becker, who analyzed Jefferson's clean copy, known to historians as the "rough draft," had admitted the possibility of the existence of an earlier draft.

The core of Becker's book concerns the philosophy embodied in the Declaration of Independence and its relationship to the "political and intellectual history of its time." Since the violent overturning of long-recognized political authority was virtually unprecedented in the eighteenth century colonial systems, Becker believes that the patriots' paramount objective was to justify to the world their act of separation. "The Declaration of Independence," he writes, "was essentially an attempt to prove that rebellion was not the proper word for what they were doing." They needed, besides their serious grievances, a theory which not only allowed violent change but which even in certain instances made it respectable. This requirement necessitated extracting the controversy from its British setting and placing it on a different level, that of the rights of men rather than of the rights of British subjects, for the latter would have no philosophic appeal to mankind. As Jefferson said later, this assignment did not require "originality of principles or sentiments." The natural rights tenet, forming the heart of the crucial second paragraph of the Declaration of Independence, was a part of the mental outlook of countless Americans and Europeans who believed in a "natural order" of things, designed by God but discoverable by humans through the use of reason. The laws of this "natural order," once understood, provided a gauge by which to judge officials and institutions.

Jefferson, as Becker reminds us, follows closely the reasoning of John Locke's second treatise on government, which was designed to enable the English Whigs to make their upheaval of 1688 a "Glorious Revolution." The author is willing to accept Jefferson's word that the Virginian did not consciously copy from Locke. Although Jefferson undoubtedly had read the English philosopher, the ideas in the Declaration of Independence were clearly related to the situation of the American colonies, and Becker traces the twists and turns of the contract theory of government, and the right and even the duty of citizens to overthrow

the authority of monarchy which violated the contract, through centuries of European history.

Predictably, scholars of one generation revise the conclusions of their predecessors. It is claimed that Becker overemphasized the impact of Locke upon American Revolutionary thinkers. Or it may be more accurate to say that he neglected other English writers, the nonconformists and dissenters whom Caroline Robbins has portrayed in *The Eighteenth Century Commonwealthman:* Trenchard, Gordon, Burgh, Priestly, Price, and others. A further caveat comes from historians who have demonstrated that the colonists, in opposing all forms of Parliamentary taxation, followed a more consistent line than Becker realized. A recent charge is that Becker was interested in ideas only as tools or vehicles employed in securing objectives. He is said to have been little concerned with the intrinsic quality of thought or the seriousness with which men took ideas. Notwithstanding the merits of the revisionists' arguments, Becker's *The Declaration of Independence* seems likely to remain one of the penetrating studies of the American Revolution.

Bailyn, Bernard. *The Ideological Origins of the American Revolution.* Cambridge: Harvard University Press, 1967.

Bailyn's smoothly written, tightly organized book is an elaboration of his lengthy introduction to *Pamphlets of the American Revolution, 1750-1776,* the first volume of a projected four-volume undertaking. Reviewers have almost universally acclaimed Bailyn's effort as intellectual history at its finest, a highly successful attempt to evaluate the American mind, to determine what the colonists believed and why, and to

examine their reasoned constitutional thought as well as their emotionally based ideas. Bailyn suggests that examination of the pamphlet literature of the time is the most feasible single means for determining the intellectual character of the American Revolution, because pamphlets, not newspapers, were the most common medium for the communication of ideas in the eighteenth century. Each pamphlet, of ten to fifty pages and five to twenty-five thousand words in length, was inexpensive and easy to produce.

The author is convinced that the patriots took their ideas seriously and literally; their ideas were not window dressing or camouflage to conceal real motives and aspirations. The recurrence of inflammatory expressions, such as "slavery," "corruption," and "conspiracy," indicates to Bailyn that these sentiments were penned in earnest and are not to be dismissed as propaganda. The leaders of the American Revolution were genuinely convinced that in England a deliberate policy of government was aimed at depriving them of their liberties. Bailyn shows that the fear was not only widespread but that an apprehension of plots and cabals was deeply rooted in the colonists' British heritage. If the Americans were not in fact confronted with conspiratorial designs, they nevertheless responded with vehement opposition to unpopular ministerial measures which, taken together, seemed to constitute a program designed to enslave the New World portion of the British Empire.

Bailyn's reading of the pamphlet literature reinforces his view of the Revolution as "an ideological-constitutional struggle and not primarily a controversy between social groups undertaken to force changes in the organization of society." This does not mean that Bailyn sees the American Revolution as nothing but a conservative phenomenon, which is now a popular interpretation. He finds that the Americans' intellectual exercises in the decade before 1776 produced "a radical idealization and rationalization" of their one hundred and fifty years of development. The combination of American thought and American experience "endowed the Revolution with its peculiar force and made of it a transforming event." A vital part of that transformation was the realization by the patriots that they were builders of a new day in human affairs. The details were to be filled in at a later time, but they had faith that the overall design would be effected. Thus ideas from a variety of sources, from antiquity, from Locke, from the Continental Enlightenment, from the English nonconformists, vibrated with life and meaning when applied to new issues and events. These ideas assume meanings often unintended, even unrealized, by those who initially employed them. So it was, for instance, with the institution of chattel slavery, which some Americans, in pursuing the logic of Revolutionary thought, had brought under heavy attack by 1776.

A brief summary cannot do justice to this sophisticated book which, with skill and erudition, stresses the complexity of its subject; but few studies, it is safe to conclude, have better demonstrated the power of ideas in shaping history. — *R.D.H.*

Additional Recommended Reading

Hazelton, John H. *The Declaration of Independence: Its History.* New York: Dodd, Mead & Company, 1906. For a detailed, day-by-day account of events in the Congress in 1776, Hazelton's book continues to be exceedingly useful.

Boyd, Julian P. *The Declaration of Independence.* Princeton: Princeton University Press, 1945. Containing significant new material, Boyd's monograph would seem to have the final word on the evolution of the text of the Declaration of Independence.

Dumbauld, Edward. *The Declaration of Independence and What It Means Today.* Norman: University of Oklahoma Press, 1950. The most authoritative investigation of the historical origins of many of Jefferson's phrases in the Declaration of Independence.

Rossiter, Clinton. *Seedtime of the Republic.* New York: Harcourt, Brace & World, Inc., 1953. Concerned with the origins of the traditions of liberty in the colonies, Rossiter's readable and stimulating narrative on American political thinking is excellent.

Robbins, Caroline. *The Eighteenth-Century Commonwealthman: Studies in the Transmission, Development, and Circumstances of English Liberal Thought from the Restoration of Charles II Until the War with the Thirteen Colonies.* Cambridge: Harvard University Press, 1959. In this important volume Caroline Robbins rescues from obscurity many of the English dissenting and nonconformist intellectuals. By studying the influence of the commonwealth men on American thought Bailyn and others have taken up where she left off.

Hawke, David. *A Transaction of Freemen.* New York: Charles Scribner's Sons, 1964. A new and sound history of the Declaration of Independence, embracing the latest scholarship.

FIRST TEST OF A SUBMARINE IN WARFARE

Type of event: Military: beginning of undersea warfare
Time: September 6, 1776
Locale: New York

Principal personages:
> DAVID BUSHNELL (1742?-1824), inventor of the first submarine used under combat conditions
> DR. BENJAMIN GALE (1715-1790), friend of Bushnell who assisted him
> JONATHAN TRUMBULL (1710-1785), Governor of Connecticut
> ISRAEL PUTNAM (1718-1790), Major General of the Continental Army who coöperated in Bushnell's endeavor
> EZRA LEE (fl. 1775-1776), Sergeant in a Connecticut regiment of the Continental Army who piloted the first combat submarine attack in history

Summary of Event

David Bushnell, a graduate of Yale College, was known in his native Connecticut for his inventive mind. While on his father's farm he had developed a harrow with flexible teeth which farmers could use in the stony New England fields without constantly breaking the teeth. As a college student he became interested in the possibilities of exploding kegs of black powder under water. Traditional theories of the time held that such an explosion would not work because the water would dissipate its force. Through experiment, Bushnell proved that this theory was wrong and developed the forerunner of the naval mine.

With the advent of the American Revolution, Bushnell decided that his mine would be useful against the blockading British fleet, but he needed an accurate method of placing his explosives under a ship's keel without being seen by naval gunners. Bushnell's solution was a submarine vessel called the *Turtle.* The *Turtle* was built in Say-brook, Connecticut, by Bushnell and his brother with the assistance of Dr. Benjamin Gale. No accurate drawings of the submarine exist, but its inventor wrote that it "bore some resemblance to two upper tortoise shells of equal size joined together. . . ." Made of carefully fitted, caulked oak timbers, Bushnell's craft was driven by a screw propeller, the first one ever used to power a ship. The contraption included a short primitive "snorkel" through which the one-man crew could obtain fresh air. The tube was equipped with valves that automatically closed when the submarine submerged to greater depths. The operator navigated the vessel by looking through a glass conning tower and by checking his compass and depth gauge which were illuminated by fox fire.

Through the influence of Governor Jonathan Trumbull of Connecticut in late 1775, Bushnell demonstrated the *Turtle* for Major General Israel Putnam of the new Continental Army.

267

Putnam was impressed and secured government financing for further development of the submarine. The army wanted to use the submersible to break the British blockade of Boston, but the British squadron departed before Bushnell could fully assemble the ballast pumps.

The next opportunity to strike at the British fleet was in 1776 at New York City. The *Turtle* was hauled overland and launched in the harbor. At first Bushnell's brother was to have navigated the submarine, but a prolonged illness incapacitated him. General Putnam provided three volunteers and one of them, Sergeant Ezra Lee, was trained to navigate the vessel. On the night of September 6, 1776, Lee slipped into the *Turtle* and guided it under the sixty-four-gun H.M.S. *Eagle,* the British flagship.

Lee was supposed to attach an explosive charge to the flagship by screwing it to the hull. But each time he attempted to twist the bit into the metal of the ship, it would not engage and slipped aside. Because of the great exertion necessary to accomplish the task, Lee barely had time to attempt to attach the explosive before he had used up all the oxygen inside the submarine. This lack of air forced him to withdraw, partially surface, and obtain fresh air through the submarine's snorkel. The endeavor was terminated by Lee's exhaustion, the tide's running out, and the appearance of the first light of dawn. On his way back to the New York docks, Lee released the keg of powder, which drifted harmlessly into the bay and exploded.

Lee made several other attempts to destroy British ships in New York harbor, but all were unsuccessful. When the British advanced up the Hudson river in October, 1776, Bushnell placed his invention aboard a small sloop. A British warship sank the sloop as it fled up the river in an effort to avoid capture. Although Bushnell reportedly recovered his submarine from the depths, its actual fate remains unknown. After the loss of the *Turtle,* Governor Trumbull had Bushnell commissioned as an officer in the Sappers and Miners Corps of the Continental Army, and Bushnell served during the remainder of the war as a demolition expert. After the American Revolution, the reticent inventor moved to Georgia where he practiced medicine, taught school, and died in obscurity in 1826.

Although David Bushnell's submarine failed to sink any enemy vessels, he was responsible for several notable achievements. He was the first to prove that gunpowder could explode underwater with sufficient force to disable and sink a surface ship. He also developed floating and submerged mines and invented the first practical submarine. In so doing, Bushnell solved such basic engineering and nautical problems as these: constructing a watertight and pressure-proof hull with vertical and horizontal propulsion mechanisms; achieving vertical stability and steering control; and developing the means of using variable ballast systems.

Bushnell's inventions were rapidly improved upon by other Americans. Robert Fulton developed his own submarine, the *Nautilus,* in France in 1799. Six feet wide and twenty feet long, it could sail on the surface like a normal ship and dive like a modern submarine. It used compressed air and could cruise underwater for four to six hours at a speed of four and a half knots. Fulton also invented a primitive automatic torpedo and experimented with firing cannon underwater. Both Great Britain and France refused to utilize his inventions, even though a target ship was successfully sunk in a British demonstration off Deal, England, in 1805. Fulton received a small grant from Congress to experiment further with submarines, but his work on steamboats absorbed his energies until his death in 1815.

Both Bushnell's and Fulton's underwater explosives were used during the American Civil War. Civil War naval personnel used to place a charge of powder at the end of a long pole, thrust it beneath the enemy ship, and explode the charge. This "spar torpedo," as it was called, was used by the C.S.S. *Hunley,* a Confederate submarine, to sink the U.S.S. *Housatonic* in Charleston Harbor in 1864, the first sinking of a surface ship by a submarine in combat.

Named after its inventor, H. L. Hunley, the Confederate submarine was a cigar-shaped vessel about twenty-five feet long. It had a nine-man crew who powered the ship by turning a crank-shaft connected to its propeller. A candle illuminated the navigator's controls, and sputtering of its flame warned the crew when oxygen was running low. Accidents caused the loss of part or all of several crews by drowning before the *Hunley* finally sank the *Housatonic* with a spar torpedo. Unfortunately the explosion also destroyed the Confederate vessel.

After the Civil War, Americans continued to take the lead in submarine development with the work of Philip Holland in the later decades of the nineteenth century. The "Holland Boat" was the forerunner of the modern submarine. It was run by a gasoline engine on the surface and propelled by batteries when submerged. Holland was instrumental in organizing the Electric Boat Company, which was one of the pioneers in building mass-produced undersea craft at the dawn of the twentieth century. By 1900, Bushnell's invention had become a success and, with the advent of World War I, a new deadly dimension was added to naval warfare. The submarine had come of age.

Pertinent Literature

Abbot, Henry L. *Beginning of Modern Submarine Warfare.* Edited by Frank Anderson. Hamden, Connecticut: Shoe String Press, 1966.

Little reliable information exists on either David Bushnell or the *Turtle.* Bushnell is one of the interesting men in history who accomplished something significant yet failed to be completely successful, and he is all but forgotten except by the most avid of naval historians. One of these scholars is Frank Anderson, who has reproduced and edited for modern readers a collection of pertinent documents on the *Turtle.* These papers were first published in 1881 by Henry L. Abbot and contain a wealth of earlier accounts, letters, and descriptions of the *Turtle,* its inventor Bushnell, and its first operator in combat, Sergeant Ezra Lee.

An incomplete table of contents forces the reader to refer to the index at the back of the volume, a liability if one is not already familiar with the history of the *Turtle*. The edition is organized into sections on "Personal Biography," "Preliminary Preparations," "Description of the *Turtle*," "Operations in New York Harbor, near New London, and in the Delaware River," and a series of conclusions.

The "Personal Biography" section contains an account of Bushnell's early life, his military career, and his later life in Georgia. It includes a letter dated September 26, 1785, from George Washington to Thomas Jefferson in which the General states that he had had little faith in Bushnell's device when he first learned of it during the Revolution, but because the inventor was "recommended by Governor Trumbull and other respectable characters," such as General Putnam, he had provided government money for further research on it. "I then thought, and still think, that it was an effort of genius," concluded Washington.

The second section on "Preliminary Preparations" contains numerous letters from Dr. Benjamin Gale, who wrote to Silas Deane about the difficulty Bushnell was having lighting the interior of his submarine in order that the pilot could read the compass and depth gauges. Gale asked Deane to contact Benjamin Franklin about possible light sources that could be used to replace fox fire. Franklin, a noted scientist, knew of no other source of light that would use less oxygen, and Bushnell was forced to await the spring of 1776 for new sources of fox fire before making further experiments.

A lengthy description of the *Turtle* and the various operations carried out with it in New York Harbor is followed by accounts of Bushnell's experiments in New London with naval mines and his launching of powder kegs against the British fleet in the Delaware. These kegs were charged to explode on contact with a solid object. Their use resulted in the so-called "Battle of the Kegs" in December, 1777, and January, 1778, during which terrified British sailors desperately and successfully shot at and blew up the kegs before they reached the anchored fleet.

Anderson closes his edition with his own account of Bushnell and the *Turtle,* and an extensive bibliography. Many of the books listed are old, which makes this volume an invaluable collection of sources to the modern reader.

In addition to his compilation of the Abbot volume, Anderson has prepared a comprehensive list of books dealing with all phases of submarine history, including volumes written in foreign languages. Entitled *Submarines, Submariners, and Submarining* (Hamden, Connecticut: Shoe String Press, 1963), this list is recommended to those interested in pursuing the topic of undersea warfare.

Coggins, Jack. *Ships and Seamen of the American Revolution.* Harrisburg, Pennsylvania: Stackpole Books, 1969.

One of the most intriguing volumes available on the naval aspects of the American Revolution is this work published by the Stackpole Books, a firm that publishes many fine works on all phases of military history. Coggins has written a colorful, well-illustrated book on the vessels, crews, weapons, gear, and basic tactics used in the numerous naval engagements of the Revolutionary War.

Coggins examines the poor state of the British fleet in 1775. Long accustomed to supremacy on the high seas, the British had become overconfident and allowed their fleet to deteriorate over the years. Yet, they were able to blockade the Atlantic Coast and fight a world-wide war against the French, Spanish, and Dutch, all of whom used the American conflict as an excuse to exact revenge on England for their losses in earlier wars. This vast engagement caused the British navy to overextend itself and led to the French victory off the coast of Virginia in 1781, as well as the British capitulation to General Washington at Yorktown.

Except at the end, American cities were effectively blockaded by the royal navy for the duration of the war, which led the Americans, who were revolutionaries in politics, to become revolutionaries in naval tactics as well by using floating mines and the first submarine. Although these fearful "Yankee tricks" caused the British sailors many discomforting moments, they failed to break the blockade.

Coggins devotes an entire chapter to the "Tale of the *Turtle*," a well-illustrated account of the first submarine attack in naval history. Most nineteenth century accounts assert that the *Turtle's* attack failed because Sergeant Lee could not engage the screw that would hold the explosive package under the ship. Anderson, following Bushnell's account, tends to believe that the real problem was Lee's inexperience in handling the *Turtle*. Coggins asserts that both factors contributed to failure of the mission. — *W.L.R.*

Additional Recommended Reading

Allen, Gardner W. *A Naval History of the American Revolution.* New York: Russell and Russell, 1962. 2 vols. Originally published in 1913, this classic on the Revolutionary War at sea contains references to Bushnell and the *Turtle* in the first volume.

Thoms, Herbert. *Doctors of Yale College, 1702-1815: And the Founding of the Medical Institution.* Hamden, Connecticut: Shoe String Press, 1960. Deals with Bushnell because he was a graduate of Yale and at one time practiced medicine.

Bishop, Farnham. *The Story of the Submarine.* New York: Appleton-Century-Crofts, Inc., 1943. This volume, first published in 1916, revised in 1929, and enlarged in 1943, includes references to the *Turtle* and a photograph of a portrait of Ezra Lee.

Parsons, W. Barclay. *Robert Fulton and the Submarine.* New York: Columbia University Press, 1922. Although Fulton's *Nautilus* is mentioned in several biographies, they are dated works which lack the definitive nature of this volume.

Jones, Virgil C. *The Civil War at Sea.* 3 Vols. New York: Holt, Rinehart and Winston, Inc., 1963. Jones devotes a chapter to the C.S.S. *Hunley,* "the peripatetic coffin," in his third volume, *The Final Effort, 1863-1865.*

Cable, Frank T. *The Birth and Development of the American Submarine.* New York: Harper & Row Publishers, 1924. Cable, the captain of the crew that tested the U.S.S. *Holland,* gives valuable information on submarines at the beginning of the twentieth century.

FOUNDING OF SAN FRANCISCO

Type of event: Socio-political: Spanish desire to thwart further Russian exploration along the Pacific Coast
Time: September 17, 1776
Locale: San Francisco, California

Principal personages:

JUAN RODRÍGUEZ CABRILLO (?-1543), first European to explore the California coast

SEBASTIAN RODRIGUES DE CERMEÑON (fl. 1595), Spanish seaman whose ship ran aground in an area he named San Francisco (now Point Reyes) in 1595

JOSÉ DE GÁLVEZ (1729-1787), *visitador* general for the King of Spain, who ordered the settlement of California

GASPAR DE PORTOLÁ (1723?-?1784), commanding officer of the colony at San Diego, who explored the San Francisco Bay area in 1769

JUNÍPERO SERRA (1713-1784), president of the Franciscan missionaries sent to California, who did much to insure the permanence of Spanish settlement by constructing missions

PEDRO FAGES (fl. 1772), Spanish soldier who conducted the second exploration of the San Francisco Bay area and discovered the Sacramento river in 1772

JUAN BAUTISTA DE ANZA (1735-1788), frontiersman from Tubac (Arizona) who opened the first land route to California from Mexico in 1774 and brought the first settlers to San Francisco in 1776

JUAN MANUEL DE AYALA (fl. 1775), leader of the first naval exploration of San Francisco and San Pablo Bays

ALFRÉRÉZ JOSÉ JOAQUIN MORAGA (fl. 1776), founder of the presidio of San Francisco in 1776

FRANCISCO PALÓU (1722?-?1789), Franciscan priest who established the mission of San Francisco on Laguna de los Dolores in 1776

Summary of Event

Before the first permanent settlement of Alta California in 1769, all that the Spanish knew of the territory was derived from the reports of several sea expeditions made along the coast in the sixteenth century. The most important was that of Juan Rodríguez Cabrillo in 1542. Cabrillo sailed northward from Mexico, charting the locations of San Diego, the Channel Islands, San Pedro, and Point Conception. Although he died in January, 1543, his journey was continued by Bartolomé Ferrelo, his second-in-command, northward to the Rogue river area in Oregon. The expedition failed to sight either Monterey or San Francisco Bays. Some time later, the English sailor Sir Francis Drake pillaged the Spanish settlements along the Pacific Coast in his journey around the world. Drake landed temporarily under the arm of Point Reyes at the bay that bears his name today. Other explorations of the California Coast were made by Francisco Gali (1584) and Sebastián Vizcaíno (1602-1603). They failed to note any new land-forms not seen by Cabrillo, although Vizcaíno did find Monterey Bay.

After these initial efforts, Spanish interest in California subsided until 1769 when the Visitador General of New Spain, José de Gálvez, ordered Captain Gaspar de Portolá to colonize San Diego. Gálvez was especially concerned with the interest shown in Alta California by the Russians who were advancing southward from Alaska. Three expeditions were assembled to plant the new colony. The first was led by Captain Fernando Jávier Rivera y Moncado by land up the Baja California Peninsula, followed by a second expedition under Portolá. Accompanying Portolá was Father Junípero Serra, president of the Franciscan missions in the Californias, who would supervise the religious instruction of the local Indians. A third party went by sea, commanded by Captain Juan Peréz, an experienced Pacific navigator.

The land parties arrived before the sea expedition and, after establishing the mission and presidio, or fort, of San Diego, Portolá took some of the soldiers northward to search for San Francisco. The Bay of San Francisco had been named by a shipwrecked navigator, Sebastian Rodriguez de Cermeñon, in 1595. The bay referred to by Rodriguez, however, was Drake's Bay below Point Reyes, not the Golden Gate area. The Spanish did not yet know of the large inland harbor between Monterey Bay and Point Reyes until Portolá saw it from the land side in 1769.

When Portolá returned to San Diego he found the colony near starvation because Peréz had not yet arrived by sea with extra supplies. Disappointed at not being able to reach Rodriguez's "San Francisco," and fearing that Peréz was lost at sea, Portolá resolved to terminate the colony and return to Mexico. Only at the insistence of Father Serra did Portolá wait until Peréz and the supply ships finally arrived. Portolá was soon replaced as Military Commandant by Lieutenant Pedro Fages who also tried to reach Point Reyes by land in 1772. After exploring the entire bay area eastward to the Sacramento river, he gave up the attempt. Although they failed to find San Francisco Bay, the Spanish had established by 1773 a presidio and mission at Monterey, and four other missions between Monterey and San Diego.

In 1774, the Viceroy of Mexico, Antónío Mariá Bucareli, decided that the prosperity of the new settlements depended upon opening up a land route between Mexico and California. To accomplish this task, Bucareli turned to Captain Juan Bautista de Anza. Anza was the Spanish Commandant of Tubac, in present-day Arizona. Unlike most Iberian explorers and colonizers, he was an experienced frontiersman and Indian fighter who knew the deserts and mountains of the Southwest intimately. Anza opened a land route to California that same year.

273

While Anza was breaking the trail from Sonora to California, San Francisco was explored by Rivera, who had helped to found San Diego, and Lieutenant Juan Manuel de Ayala. Rivera retraced the route taken by Fages in 1772. A year later (1775), Ayala made the first expedition around the bay area by ship, concluding that Spain now controlled the best harbor on the entire Pacific Coast, and that it would be senseless to ignore it for Drake's Bay to the north.

In 1775, Anza made a second expedition from Mexico to California, this time bringing with him about 250 colonists who were to settle San Francisco. The party advanced up the Santa Cruz river through Tucson to the Gila river. Then Anza turned westward and crossed the Colorado near Yuma. In California, Anza was temporarily diverted from his goal by an Indian uprising near San Diego. After relieving the besieged presidio, Anza's party continued to Monterey.

Leaving his colonists at Monterey, Anza and some soldiers scouted the San Francisco area in 1776, following Fages' old routes. The actual founding of the presidio of San Francisco was left to Anza's second-in-command, Alférez José Joaquin Moraga, who established the fort on September 17, 1776. Moraga presided over a large cere-

mony attended by 150 persons, including four priests who said Mass. Nearly one month later, the Franciscans, led by Father Francisco Palóu, established the mission of San Francisco de Asis on the Laguna de los Dolores, some distance south of the presidio.

The presidio was a square fort with three sides made from the adobe walls of the headquarters, barracks, and storehouses. The fourth wall was a log palisade which enclosed a parade ground 120 yards square. The old presidio was constructed of adobe of poor quality which caused the fort to deteriorate rapidly. A lack of skilled workmen prevented the crumbling walls from being repaired. Because of the harsh weather, many early commandants urged that it be abandoned, but the government considered its location to be too important, so the presidio remained and still stands today.

Father Palóu's church also made slow progress. Conversions of the local Indians were hard to obtain: there were thirty-five by 1778, nine hundred by 1791. The cornerstone for the mission was not laid until 1782, and the priests used a temporary structure until 1791 when the mission was completed. It still stands today, having survived intact the famous San Francisco earthquake of 1906, surrounded by the magnificent city which it spawned.

Pertinent Literature

Bolton, Herbert E. *Outpost of Empire: The Story of the Founding of San Francisco.* New York: Alfred A. Knopf, Inc., 1931.

Although Herbert E. Bolton died in 1953, he is still considered the outstanding authority on the history of the Spanish Empire in the United States. Bolton was one of the first Americans

to research extensively the archives in Seville and Mexico City for new information on the early history of America under Spanish rule. He not only searched the dusty archives for material, but he also went into the field and personally retraced the routes used by the early *conquistadores* to explore northward from Mexico.

Bolton's vivid style of writing makes history live in the reader's mind. His book is a moving tale about the travail, adventures, and spirit involved in establishing the most advanced outpost in Alta California to secure the rich Spanish territories and mines to the south from possible foreign invasion. Originally published as the first volume of Bolton's five-volume *Anza's California Expeditions* (Berkeley: University of California Press, 1930), *Outpost of Empire* was so well received that it was republished as a separate volume in 1931.

The founding of San Francisco is a story involving two actual events. First, Anza had to explore and develop a land route from Mexico to California that would give the Spanish a reliable communication with their northern colony. Second, he had to establish the presidio at San Francisco to thwart any designs the Russians might have as they extended their control along the Pacific Coast southward from Alaska. Anza was both an explorer and a colonizer, and his success in the two ventures marks him as a man of superior qualities of leadership. Of the 240 persons who traveled with Anza to colonize San Francisco, only one died (a

woman during childbirth). This enviable record is even more impressive considering that Anza's party made the sixteen-hundred-mile journey across hot, rough desert terrain and over snow-covered mountains.

Bolton compares Anza's accomplishments with the Lewis and Clark expedition made thirty years later. Like Lewis and Clark, Anza's first expedition marked the trail to a new land. But Anza's accomplishments surpass those of Lewis and Clark who never had to establish a colony hundreds of miles from their home base only one year after their initial exploration. The founding of San Francisco places Anza among the foremost frontier leaders of American history. He inspired his followers to herculean tasks requiring iron discipline. So great was their admiration for their leader, that Anza's colonists wept in sorrow when he left them at Monterey.

Outpost of Empire is not a biography of Anza; it covers only one episode of his life on the Spanish frontier. It is, however, the best volume available on the founding of San Francisco. Those who find themselves wanting more detailed information on the San Francisco colony should consult the other volumes of *Anza's California Expeditions* where a wealth of primary material is available.

Berger, John A. *The Franciscan Missions of California.* Garden City: Doubleday and Company, 1948.

Berger sees the settlement of California mainly in the light of Spanish desire to Christianize the Indians, although he recognizes that the prime reason was strategic; that is, to deny the area to any other colonial power.

To assist this ambitious religious project, the Pious Fund was established. This fund consisted of monetary donations given by various wealthy persons in Mexico to defray the costs of missionary work. At first, each benefactor invested his money in his own way, paying the yearly interest to the Church. Later, the monies were put into the hands of an administrator who invested the funds and paid the Church directly each year. The fund was also used to stimulate more secular exploration and settlement in Alta California in 1769 and 1774-1775.

The Franciscans established twenty-one missions in California, each about forty miles (one day's travel) from the next, and connected by the famous *El Camino Real,* The Royal Road. The missions served not only the religious needs of their congregations, but also acted as roadside inns that housed any weary traveler who desired lodging for the night. *Vaqueros,* skilled dispatch riders between the missions, could cover up to 125 miles a day, the distance between San Diego and San Ga-

briel. They accomplished this feat by riding with a small herd of horses, switching mounts (without stopping) whenever the one they were riding tired. When the Americans arrived in the mid-nineteenth century, *El Camino Real* was still the only good road in the territory.

Berger discusses briefly the Indians of California, and the society and culture established among them by the missionaries. In addition, the author covers the life and career of Father Junípero Serra, the man responsible, in large part, for the success of early California. Berger then devotes one chapter to the history of each mission, all of which are illustrated with pictures. This volume is recommended to the general reader on its own merit and also as a guide to the colorful missions of California. — *W.L.R.*

Additional Recommended Reading

Chapman, Charles E. *The Founding of Spanish California: The Northwestward Expansion of New Spain, 1687-1783.* New York: The Macmillan Company, 1916. A comprehensive book on the Spanish colonial settlements which remains the standard work in its field.

Holmes, Maurice G. *From New Spain by Sea to the Californias, 1519-1668.* Glendale, California: Arthur H. Clark Company, 1963. Concentrating on the earliest explorations of the California Coast, Holmes emphasizes Spain's inability to extend effectively its empire northward.

Bancroft, Hubert H. *History of California, 1542-1800.* Vol. XVIII: *The Works of Hubert Howe Bancroft.* 39 vols. New York: McGraw-Hill Book Co., 1967. Originally published in 1884, historians still consider Bancroft's detailed study to be valuable reading.

Palóu, Francisco. *Francisco Palóu's Life and Apostolic Labors of the Venerable Father, Junípero Serra.* Translated and annotated by Maynard J. Geiger. Washington: Academy of American Franciscan History, 1955. Palóu accompanied Serra to California, and wrote a sympathetic biography of his mentor in 1787. Geiger's edition contains numerous explanatory notes identifying terms, places, and persons involved in the settlement of California.

Repplier, Agnes. *Junípero Serra: Pioneer Colonist of California.* Garden City: Doubleday and Company, 1933. Repplier's volume is an interesting, more modern account of Serra's life and work.

Cleland, Robert Glass. *From Wilderness to Empire: A History of California, 1542-1900.* Chs. 1-6. New York: Alfred A. Knopf, Inc., 1947. A noted historian of the West, Cleland relates the fascinating story of the discovery and settlement of California.

BATTLES OF SARATOGA

Type of event: Military: defeat of British scheme to split the colonies
Time: July-October, 1777
Locale: Upper New York state

Principal personages:

LORD GEORGE GERMAIN (GEORGE SACKVILLE GERMAIN, VISCOUNT SACKVILLE) (1716-1785), Secretary of State for the colonies 1775-1782, who virtually directed the war in America

GENERAL JOHN BURGOYNE (1722-1792), British Commander of expedition from Canada who surrendered his army at Saratoga

LIEUTENANT GENERAL SIR WILLIAM HOWE (1729-1814), Commander in Chief of British forces in America who led the British invasion of Pennsylvania

LIEUTENANT GENERAL SIR HENRY CLINTON (1738?-1795), Commander of British New York garrison who succeeded Howe as Commander in Chief in 1778

MAJOR GENERAL HORATIO GATES (1728?-1806), British Army officer who took the side of the colonists at the outbreak of the Revolutionary War and who was in command of Fort Ticonderoga 1776-1777

BRIGADIER GENERAL BENEDICT ARNOLD (1741-1801), American Army officer who joined with Colonel Daniel Morgan in repulsing the British in the Battles of Saratoga

Summary of Event

The British campaign of 1777, which culminated in the defeat at Saratoga, was designed to cut the United States in two and prepare the way for final victory by Great Britain. The plan involved three separate and independent commands. One, under General John Burgoyne, was to move down from Canada along the Lake Champlain-Hudson Waterway to Albany, thereby separating New England from the middle and southern parts of America. A second, under Lieutenant General Sir William Howe, was to proceed from New York and seize Philadelphia. A third force, left behind by Howe under Lieutenant General Sir Henry Clinton, was authorized to make a diversion up the Hudson to help Burgoyne; but given his limited resources and commitments in the New York area, Clinton was hardly in a position to give Burgoyne meaningful aid. Lord George Germain, Secretary of State for the colonies, could have imposed a measure of coöperation on the operations of the three commanders, but not until it was too late did he attempt to do so.

By the time Germain notified Howe to coördinate his activities with those of Burgoyne, Sir William was at sea and headed for Philadelphia. Howe, after more than a month on the water, disembarked his army not on the Dela-

277

ware river, the shortest route to his objective, but on the upper reaches of Chesapeake Bay some fifty-seven miles from Philadelphia. Washington, astonished upon discovering that Howe was not going to support Burgoyne, hurried southward and interposed his troops between those of the enemy and the American capital. At the Battle of Brandywine on September 11, 1777, Washington was outflanked and defeated, losing about a thousand men killed and wounded compared to half as many casualties for Howe. The British then occupied the Quaker city, only to find that Washington still had gunsmoke in his nostrils. The American General made a night assault on Howe's garrison at Germantown, seven miles from Philadelphia, on October 3, 1777. There he was again repulsed, with the opposing armies suffering losses similar to those at Brandywine. Washington then went into winter quarters at Valley Forge.

In the meantime, the Burgoyne campaign had also begun auspiciously. The British army from Canada had overrun Fort Ticonderoga and several smaller American posts, drawing to within forty miles of Albany by the end of July. At this point, however, the American northern army, weak and dispirited by reversals and internal dissension, was revitalized. It received a new commander, Major General Horatio Gates, a popular officer and a skillful organizer. Gates soon received the services of Brigadier General Benedict Arnold, a splendid combat officer, and Colonel Daniel Morgan, who headed a corps of frontier riflemen experienced in the ways of the forests.

Now it was Burgoyne who ran into serious trouble. He had already overex-tended his supply lines from Canada, and many of his carts and wagons had broken down on the rough wilderness trails. A wing of his army advancing through the Mohawk Valley under Colonel Barry St. Leger had been defeated near Oriskany, and one of his flanking parties had been repulsed near Bennington. Moreover, his Indian scouts were so terrorized by the harassing activities of Morgan's riflemen that most of them deserted. Even so, Burgoyne, a reckless gambler, pushed on—into the face of Gates' growing northern army that was entrenched on Bemis Heights, a densely wooded area north of Stillwater. There in front of the American position were fought the two so-called Battles of Saratoga, or Battles of Freeman's Farm. In the first, on September 19, Burgoyne tried unsuccessfully to envelop or break through the patriot left wing. In the second, on October 7, Burgoyne made a reconnaissance in force to probe the American lines. Burgoyne's detachment was badly mauled, and the main British entrenchments were twice stormed. In the two engagements British losses were twelve hundred men, more than twice those of their opponents.

Burgoyne's resources were virtually exhausted. His army, bruised and battered by the enemy and the wilderness environment, was no longer a fighting machine. Nor could he receive effective aid from the small force that Clinton dispatched up the Hudson. With his army completely surrounded and escape impossible, Burgoyne laid down his arms on October 17 at the village of Saratoga. So ended, for all practical purposes, Great Britain's campaign to bring the war to an end in 1777. Careless planning, highlighted by a lack of coöperation among British generals, had resulted in disaster at Saratoga, an event that led France to enter the war on the side of America.

Pertinent Literature

Anderson, Troyer S. *The Command of the Howe Brothers During the American Revolution.* New York: Oxford University Press, 1936.

"It is the purpose of this study," declares Troyer Anderson, "to discover to what extent the British command, as exercised by Lord Richard and Sir William Howe, contributed to the final defeat of Great Britain" in the War of American Independence. To Anderson, the first three years (1775-1778) were crucial to Great Britain; for after the entrance of France and Spain into the war, Great Britain was engaged in a world-wide conflict in which the American theater of operations no longer occupied the center of the stage. Much would depend upon the performance of the Howes, Sir William Howe and his older brother Richard (Earl Howe), who between 1776 and 1778 were the British Supreme Military and Naval Commanders in America.

Before the appearance of Anderson's book, historians often expressed two different but equally unflattering opinions of the Howes: either the brothers failed to crack the American rebellion because of incompetence, or they secretly favored the patriot cause. Admittedly, Sir William did not immediately pursue Washington's forces following his victories in New York in 1776 and in Pennsylvania in 1777. However, an eighteenth century army was an imperfect military machine. It was often poorly supplied and maintained, and it required long periods to reorganize and reëquip itself after a major battle. Moreover, its officers adhered to the slow, conventional tactics and strategy of the day. Exceptions, such as the brilliant James Wolfe, were rare.

As to the charge that the Howes were pro-American, it is true that the brothers were Whiggish in their politics. Though they had been Members of Parliament, they had not been associated with the British government's harsh American policy of the last dozen years. The brothers had reason to think kindly of New England, where their older brother, George Augustus, had been a popular officer in the French and Indian War. When George Augustus Howe was killed at Ticonderoga, the General Court of Massachusetts appropriated money to erect a monument to his memory in Westminster Abbey. But these facts do not prove that the Howes were deliberately easy on the American patriots. It must be remembered that they had their service reputations to uphold, regardless of personal regrets over a civil war in the Empire.

In arguing these points in defense of the Howes, Anderson, a sympathetic biographer, builds a strong case. Yet the subject is not closed concerning the Howes' attitude toward the rebellion. A more recent scholar, Ira Gruber, marshals considerable evidence to show that the Vice-Admiral, at least, did not press the naval aspects of the war with all the vigor that the Ministry desired. As for the Lieutenant General, there is little direct evidence; certainly he claimed to be doing his best in the field. Unfortunately for the historian, both the Howes were reserved, taciturn men who seldom if ever put their inner thoughts on paper.

If, as Gruber claims, the Howes in 1776 had held high hopes of persuading the Americans to put down their arms (they had also been appointed peace commissioners), they were definitely aware by the beginning of the following year that the Americans were resolved to fight for independence and that it would be difficult if not impossible for Great Britain to achieve total military victory. Both Anderson and Gruber agree that in 1777 extreme pessimism characterized the outlook of the Vice-Admiral and the Lieutenant General. This attitude of mind no doubt helps to explain the complete lack of interest on the part of William Howe concerning the Burgoyne expedition.

Anderson reminds us that no phase of the command of the Howe brothers produced more hostile criticism than their part in the Burgoyne disaster. Here the author makes a substantial contribution to knowledge by demolishing the long-held notion that Lieutenant General Howe had positive orders, which reached him in ample time, to proceed up the Hudson river to unite with Burgoyne. Interestingly enough, Burgoyne felt he needed no assistance from Howe. More important is the fact that Lord Germain, the Colonial Secretary, allowed several months to elapse before he even mentioned to Howe that he should coöperate with Burgoyne; but even then, Howe was given permission to complete his Pennsylvania campaign before he extended some help to Burgoyne. Germain had been vague; and as has been noted, the message did not reach Sir William until he was sailing for Pennsylvania.

Although Sir William Howe may be absolved of any disobedience to orders, his conduct remains something of a mystery. Anderson suggests that his general pessimism and his desire to return home influenced his attitude. Taking Philadelphia would not be a dangerous undertaking; but as Anderson shows, it offered few advantages either, since the mere possession of cities was insufficient to bring impressive results. The Vice-Admiral, truly an able man, never really had a chance to display his talents, if indeed he desired to use them against America at all. For Sir William, the opportunities were there but he failed to exploit them. As Anderson concludes, "the situation demanded a great man: Sir William Howe was just a competent man."

Nickerson, Hoffman. *The Turning Point of the Revolution: Or, Burgoyne in America.* 2 Vols. Boston: Houghton Mifflin Co., 1928.

It is surprising, given the significance of the campaign of 1777, that there is no recent study of the Battles of Saratoga of first-rate quality. The best comprehensive one-volume narrative of the subject remains Nickerson's *Turning Point of the Revolution,* published in 1928. A retired army colonel and author of various books on warfare, Nickerson writes with clarity, vigor, and an eye for interesting detail. There are clever sketches of the major participants in the drama along the Hudson river: the rakish "Gentleman Johnny" Burgoyne, who brought his mistress and an assortment of fine clothing and wines on his wilderness journey; the short, ruddy-faced Gates, who schemed to gain command of the Northern Department from the proud New York aristocrat, Philip Schuyler; the fiery, opinionated, former apothecary, Benedict Arnold, who was loyal to Schuyler and distrusted Gates; and the tall, muscular backwoodsman, Daniel Morgan, who dressed in hunting garb and assembled his frontier riflemen by blowing a "turkey-call." Nickerson also shows us the bewildering array of supernumeraries that were a part of every eighteenth century army: the women, children, dogs, and sutlers. He draws heavily upon the delightful memoir of Baroness Frederika von Riedesel, who, with her three small children, braved the wilderness to be with her soldier-husband.

Although Nickerson's treatment of British planning and strategy has been superseded by the work of Anderson and others, the author's handling of the American leaders is still considered to be sound and judicious. While personally disliking Gates, Nickerson concedes the wisdom of Gates' strategy of letting Burgoyne exhaust himself by thrashing about in the wilds of upper New York, rather than making a stand prematurely and fighting a decisive battle. In the quarrel between Gates and Arnold, however, Nickerson sympathizes with Arnold, and he points out that Gates' admirers have attempted to deny Arnold any credit for the victory—to the point of claiming that Arnold was not even present at the first Saratoga battle. All things considered, Nickerson's volume remains a valuable study, but a new monograph on the subject is much needed. — *R.D.H.*

Additional Recommended Reading

Wallace, Willard M. *Traitorous Hero: Life and Fortunes of Benedict Arnold.* New York: Harper & Row Publishers, 1954. A brilliant biography of Arnold that recognizes both his strengths and weaknesses.

Higginbotham, Don. *Daniel Morgan: Revolutionary Rifleman.* Chapel Hill: University of North Carolina Press, 1961. Stresses the importance of guerrilla operations in wearing down Burgoyne before the Saratoga battles.

Mackesy, Piers G. *The War for America, 1775-1783.* Cambridge: Harvard University Press, 1964. Unlike most recent writers, Mackesy is sympathetic to Germain, and places most of the blame for the Saratoga disaster on the generals in America.

Willcox, William B. *Portrait of a General: Sir Henry Clinton in the War of Independence.* New York: Alfred A. Knopf, Inc., 1964. Offers the best account of Clinton's role in the campaign and is most unflattering to Germain.

Billias, George A., ed. *George Washington's Opponents: British Generals and Admirals in the American Revolution.* New York: William Morrow & Co., Inc., 1969. Essays on British generals and admirals who fought in the Revolutionary War. Ira Gruber's contribution on Sir William Howe is recommended.

CONCLUSION OF FRANCO-AMERICAN TREATIES

Type of event: Diplomatic: desire of both America and France to defeat Great Britain
Time: February 6, 1778
Locale: Paris

Principal personages:

LOUIS XVI (1754-1793), King of France 1774-1792

COMTE DE VERGENNES (CHARLES GRAVIER) (1717-1787), French Minister of Foreign Affairs

PIERRE AUGUSTIN CARON DE BEAUMARCHAIS (1732-1799), playwright and French secret agent whose bogus company Roderique Hortalez supplied the patriots with military stores

CONDE DE FLORIDABLANCA (JOSÉ MOÑINO Y REDONDO) (1728-1808), Prime Minister of Spain and Minister of Foreign Affairs

BENJAMIN FRANKLIN (1706-1790),

SILAS DEANE (1737-1789), and

ARTHUR LEE (1740-1792), American commissioners at the French court

Summary of Event

The American Revolutionaries did not believe that their War of Independence would go unnoticed by the outside world. In 1763, the balance of power in Europe had swung decisively toward Great Britain largely because of its defeat of France and Spain in the Western hemisphere. But Americans and Europeans agreed that the scales would remain tipped in favor of the island kingdom only so long as it retained its New World possessions. At first colonial writers warned that the Bourbon monarchies might attempt to seize several of George III's American provinces while his house was divided against itself; that such storm warnings might offer the most compelling reasons for the colonies and the Mother Country to patch up their quarrel. Later, as the imperial crisis deepened, American opinion of the Catholic states gradually shifted from fear to the

hope that they would assist America in case of war with Great Britain. That change of sentiment was one of the radical features of the American Revolution. Bred on a hatred of Catholicism and political absolutism associated especially with France, American publicists for decades had shrilled for the permanent removal of the French peril from North America. By a twist of fate, however, the elimination of France from Canada in 1763 meant that France was no longer the threat of old. France and its ally Spain were now more tolerable from afar than in the day when the *fleur-de-lis* loomed over the back door of the mainland settlements.

The need for foreign assistance, so ably expressed in Paine's *Common Sense,* was a powerful catalyst for independence. Anticipating the final break, Congress in March, 1776, dis-

282

patched Silas Deane to Paris to purchase military stores and to explore the possibilities of a commercial alliance. Even before Deane's arrival, French leaders decided to provide the patriots with covert aid. The Anglo-American war gave France the long-awaited opportunity to gain revenge for its humiliation in 1763. However, the Comte de Vergennes, French Minister of Foreign Affairs, was cautious and prudent, a tough-minded career diplomat, no messenger of Enlightenment idealism. Fearful of American defeat or a compromise settlement between the colonies and Great Britain, Vergennes plotted a judicious course until the picture cleared. The attitude of Spain, which feared an independent America as a threat to its overseas dominions, also served to restrain Vergennes and his countrymen. Nevertheless, the year 1777 marked France's increasing commitment to the American patriots. The growing stream of supplies bought with royal funds or taken surreptitiously from military arsenals, the opening of French ports to rebel privateers and warships, the procession of French officers bound for Washington's army, the unremitting pressures of Silas Deane and the more subtle blandishments of his colleague, Benjamin Franklin, all combined to move France toward the patriot's orbit. News of the British capitulation of General Burgoyne at Saratoga in October, 1777, dispelled any lingering doubts as to the patriots' ability to continue the struggle. Vergennes now feared that the American victory might give rise to a spirit of conciliation in Great Britain, leading to some form of reunion between the English-speaking peoples on opposite sides of the Atlantic. The French Min-

ister of Foreign Affairs notified Franklin and his fellow commissioners that the government of Louis XVI was ready to make formal ties with the United States.

For both parties the famous Franco-American alliance was the child of necessity. If the patriots in the beginning hoped for massive French aid and the entrance of the Bourbon nation into the war, they wanted only a strictly temporary relationship; too intimate a formal connection meant becoming involved in the future strife of the Old World, whose peoples mirrored a society and way of life incompatible with free, republican institutions. While the patriots offered only a commercial treaty to France, Vergennes successfully demanded more: a "conditional and defensive alliance." The French Minister of Foreign Affairs and his royal master were not enthusiastic about revolution against kings. Their willingness to recognize the United States of America and to sign the treaties on February 6, 1778, with the infant nation was based upon a desire to humiliate France's ancient foe. The Treaty of Amity and Commerce contained most of the proposals made by Congress for liberalization of trade along principles foreign to mercantilism. The Treaty of Alliance stipulated that, in case of war between Great Britain and France, which the two treaties made inevitable, neither America nor France would make peace without the approval of the other. France renounced forever any claims to British territory on the continent of North America and agreed to recognize America's right to any such territory seized by patriot armies. The two nations also guaranteed each other's territorial boundaries in the New World as they would be drawn at the end of hostilities.

Great Britain's international difficulties continued to mount after hostilities opened with France in the summer of 1778. The next year Spain entered the fray after securing a promise from Vergennes to continue hostilities until Gibraltar was regained. Even though Spain did not join the Franco-American alliance, the United States through

its tie with France found itself committed to fight until Gibraltar fell to Spain. In 1780, Anglo-Dutch commercial friction brought the Netherlands into the war. Great Britain was by then also confronted by the League of Armed Neutrality, organized by several non-belligerent nations in protest against British practices of search and seizure on the high seas. Unlike earlier wars of the century, Great Britain was isolated both diplomatically and militarily.

Pertinent Literature

Bemis, Samuel Flagg. *The Diplomacy of the American Revolution.* New York: Appleton-Century-Crofts, Inc., 1935.

A popular notion, venerated by time and close Franco-American ties, has it that sentiments of liberal idealism motived France in coming to the aid of the revolting British colonies. For years it was said that our great debt to France had never been paid. General John J. Pershing was long reputed to have solemnly declared on visiting the tomb of a Revolutionary War hero in France, "Lafayette, we are here!" The remark seemed appropriate, even though it was really made by Colonel Charles E. Staunton, for the attitude of France was supposedly represented by the youthful marquis, who in his memoirs portrayed himself as having come to America because of his love of liberty and the rights of man. Such an interpretation of French conduct was never held by Franklin and the other diplomats who endeavored to advance the American cause in Europe. How then do we account for the myth of French altruism concerning the American Revolution? Anti-British sentiment, coupled with the assumption that the enemies of Great Britain were

the devotees of America, provides much of the answer. Richard B. Morris has recently illuminated the perpetuation of the myth by the editors of the diplomatic documents of the period. Both the first and second editors of the American Revolutionary diplomatic materials, Jared Sparks and Francis Wharton, by faulty technical procedures and pro-French sympathies, retarded the development of a balanced picture of the thinking and actions of the participants in the drama. The same faults marred the work of Henri Doniol, whose multitomed documentary covers the French side of the story.

Nevertheless, a band of iconoclastic scholars, if not the general public, has recognized for the past half century that Benjamin Franklin, who captivated France with his democratic dress, simple manners, and rustic witticisms, who seemed the personification of an America embodying Enlightenment ideals, did not single-handedly convert the court at Versailles to a philosophical interest in American independence. In 1916, Edward S. Cor-

284

win's *French Policy and the American Alliance of 1778* asserted that France was moved chiefly by a desire to regain its prestige in Europe at the expense of an old and bitter foe. Later historians continued to chisel away at the old façade. Louis Gottschalk, for instance, demonstrated that the nineteen-year-old Lafayette embarked for America thirsting for glory and hating the British, his liberalism being of a later vintage; and Frances Acomb revealed that by no means all the philosophers in the Paris salons gave their hearts and minds to America.

Bemis' *Diplomacy of the American Revolution* appeared before all the revisionists' works had been published. Even so, the author has written what is still the most accurate and balanced survey of his subject. Bemis investigates the whole panorama of European diplomacy and international politics, besides probing the aspirations and policies of the United States. Since France held the key to American success abroad, Bemis stresses the prostration of that country in 1763 and its consuming ambition to redress the balance of power, although that ambition did not include a revival of colonial interests on the continent of North America. He finds no proof to sustain the contention of several historians that France had ceded Canada rather than Guadeloupe to Great Britain in order to free the British colonies from the need for protection against an alien power along the northern border. But both the Comte de Choiseul, French Minister of Foreign Affairs in the 1760's, and Vergennes, who occupied the same post later, believed that the cession of Canada fostered an independent spirit in the British colonies, and both followed closely the rising discontent in America. According to Bemis, Vergennes' American policy is found to rest "on the most cold-blooded calculations of eighteenth-century diplomacy, weighted in the chill balance of power." Realistic considerations also governed the conduct of Spain, the Netherlands, and the nations forming the League of Armed Neutrality.

Although few of Bemis' major conclusions have been challenged, one diplomatic historian has expressed sharp criticism on at least two points. Whether Bemis is correct that Saratoga was the event that shoved France over the brink of war, or whether, as Richard Van Alstyne argues, the formidable buildup of French naval power in the West Indies before Saratoga demonstrates that Louis XVI's government was already preparing to intervene, must remain open questions pending further investigation. Nor is it clear that Bemis exaggerates the role of the British secret service in apprising the royal cabinet of France's growing involvement with America, as charged by Van Alstyne, who contends that this allegedly confidential information was common knowledge in London social and political circles.

We are not concerned here with the final installments of Bemis' book, which cover the treaty of peace. Though still valuable, they are less comprehensive than Richard B. Morris' new and exhaustive *The Peacemakers.*

Conclusion of Franco-American Treaties

Gilbert, Felix. *To the Farewell Address: Ideas of Early American Foreign Policy.* Princeton: Princeton University Press, 1961.

After declaring their independence, the thirteen colonies became the United States and assumed the direction of their external affairs, a function that Great Britain had formerly exercised for them. Not surprisingly, they had given little systematic thought to the management and formulation of foreign policy. "It was to Europe," writes Felix Gilbert, "that the American leaders in 1776 had to turn for instruction about the traditions and nature of diplomacy." But the process was critical and selective rather than imitative. In the spirit of the Enlightenment, the leaders of the new nation voiced approval of the concept of natural law and the use of reason in determining relations between sovereign states, in the same way that they denounced the balance of power system as productive of rivalries, wars, and the disruption of commerce. If Americans feared entangling alliances, they were not isolationists but took a world view, declares the author. The colonial background also played a hand in fashioning foreign policy, at least indirectly, for the revolutionists were conditioned by their experiences in the British mercantile system and by their limited trade contacts with the outside world. Gilbert argues convincingly that influential Americans believed foreign relations should be confined primarily to commerce. As Paine's *Common Sense* expressed it, "Our plan is commerce," the true interest of his countrymen being "to steer clear of European contentions." Thus by 1776 the American Revolution had added to its objectives a campaign for commercial freedom, and, with the simultaneous publication of Adam Smith's *Wealth of Nations,* it heralded the decline of mercantilism and the emancipation of trade.

Congress in 1776 drew up a proposed "Model Treaty" for its commissioners in Paris to submit to France. After noting that the document was limited to commercial inducements, which Congress was willing to extend to other nations as well, Gilbert continues: "What is astounding is how little the Americans were willing to offer. Political and military coöperation with France was to be avoided even if France should enter the war against England." If it was hardly common for a state struggling for its very survival to dictate terms to a world power, one has to remember the great value then placed upon the trade of the non-European areas of the globe. Even so, commercial considerations alone did not move the French government, and the eventual Franco-American alliance of 1778 showed that Americans had to sacrifice temporarily certain principles to obtain the full support of France. But American opinion on the subjects of commercial freedom and entangling alliances survived the war and found expression in Washington's Farewell Address. — *R.D.H.*

Additional Recommended Reading

Corwin, Edward S. *French Policy and the American Alliance of 1778.* Princeton: Princeton University Press, 1916. Takes a revisionist and a realistic look at the motives of France in supporting the American Revolution.

Savelle, Max. "America and the Balance of Power, 1713-1778," in Richard B. Morris' *The Era of the American Revolution.* New York: Columbia University Press, 1939. A study of American thinking on the role of the New World in the rivalries of the European powers.

Gottschalk, Louis. *Lafayette Comes to America.* Chicago: University of Chicago Press, 1935. This first installment of Gottschalk's multivolume biography tears away much of the myth surrounding Lafayette and also reveals attitudes of the French Court toward America.

Acomb, Frances. *Anglophobia in France, 1763-1789.* Durham: Duke University Press, 1950. This slender monograph reveals the complexity and diversity of French liberal thought.

Morris, Richard B. *The American Revolution Reconsidered.* New York: Harper & Row Publishers, 1967. Explores certain misconceptions about the diplomatic history of the Revolution.

Varg, Paul A. *Foreign Policies of the Founding Fathers.* East Lansing: Michigan State University Press, 1963. A provocative book that deals with the relationship between commerce and foreign policy.

Van Alstyne, Richard. *Empire and Independence: The International History of the American Revolution.* New York: John Wiley and Sons, 1965. A controversial book which departs from accepted interpretations at many points.

ADOPTION OF THE ARTICLES OF CONFEDERATION

Type of event: Constitutional: desire to create a permanent American union
Time: March 1, 1781
Locale: Philadelphia, Pennsylvania

Principal personages:

JOHN DICKINSON (1732-1808), principal author of the first draft of the Articles of Confederation

DR. THOMAS BURKE (1747?-1783), North Carolina delegate who won acceptance for Article 2, a strong statement in favor of states' rights and limited government

THOMAS JEFFERSON (1743-1826), who led Virginia into ceding most of its Western lands to the Confederation

THOMAS JOHNSON (1732-1819), and

CHARLES CARROLL (1737-1832), and

SAMUEL CHASE (1741-1811), prominent Maryland patriots

CHEVALIER DE LA LUZERNE (fl. 1781), French envoy to the United States

Summary of Event

The American experience with nationalism ran counter to recent developments leading to nationhood in Africa and Asia. National feeling scarcely existed in our colonial period; it certainly did not produce a revolution aimed at unified independence. Slowly, almost imperceptibly, Americans' sense of oneness grew in the course of standing together in opposition to Great Britain's post-1763 imperial program. As Americans traveled the long road to 1776 and became more aware of their shared principles and traditions, they began to think simultaneously of independence and union. Since the independent states must be an independent nation as well, the revolutionists turned immediately to the task of creating a confederacy.

In June, 1776, while Thomas Jefferson and his committee worked at a statement to justify independence, a second committee—with one representative from each colony—toiled to present the forthcoming United States with its first written constitution. Constitution-making is never an easy assignment, even when men generally share a common body of political thought.

Nearly five years elapsed before all agreements and compromises at the congressional and state levels could be reached. The exigencies of the war slowed the process as Congress grappled with enlistments, supplies, finances, and foreign aid; as the lawmakers twice fled, to Baltimore and to York, Pennsylvania, to escape capture; and as the state governments were similarly distracted. But there were also political clashes in and out of Congress about the contents of the proposed document. Historians have differed sharply over the nature of the struggles. Some contend that they were ideological in substance between so-

288

called radicals and conservatives; others see rivalries between the small and large states as the real divisive factors. Few scholars deny that the conflicts over questions of local versus central authority, whatever else may be said about them, were conditioned by the colonists' previous experience with remote, impersonal control from London. Nor should it be forgotten that the framing of a constitution for a continent—or participation in government above the colony level—was an experience largely foreign to Americans.

Although the committee report, of which John Dickinson was the main architect, was placed before Congress as early as July 12, 1776, it foundered on the questions of administering the West, and of apportioning representation and financial burdens among the states. Most delegates favored a loose confederation as opposed to a highly centralized national government. Sometimes explicitly, but more often implicitly, it seemed to many that the Dickinson draft left too much authority in the hands of Congress. Finally, in November, 1777, Congress voted its approval of a constitution for the United States—the Articles of Confederation—and submitted it to the states to accept or reject. Under the articles, the Congress continued as the only branch of the central government. Each state was still to have one vote to cast, regardless of population, by delegates selected by the legislatures. A simple majority of states assembled decided issues, except for specified matters that required the consent of nine. Each state alone could tax itself or regulate its commerce, although each was to contribute its share of money (based upon improved lands) to the up-

keep of the Confederation. Each state claiming territory in the Trans-Appalachian region was to keep its possessions instead of turning them over to the United States. Individually, the states were to retain their "sovereignty, freedom and independence, and every power, jurisdiction, and right," not specifically granted Congress. In turn, Congress' authority covered making war and peace, making military and naval appointments, requisitioning men and money from the states, sending out and receiving ambassadors, negotiating treaties and alliances, settling Indian relations, managing postal affairs, coining money, deciding weights and measures, and settling disputes between states.

The Articles of Confederation vested momentous responsibilities in Congress without giving it the authority to discharge those responsibilities. Without the ability to tax or regulate trade, Congress could only hope—lacking as it did powers of enforcement—that the states would meet their assigned requisitions and cooperate in other vital areas. Even so, some states were reluctant to give their consent to the articles, questioning this or that jurisdiction assigned to the central government. But by 1779, all except Maryland had given an affirmative response. Although Maryland's motives were probably deplorable, that state's refusal led to a fair and significant settlement of the Western lands problem. Colonial charters had given all the states below the Potomac, along with Connecticut and Massachusetts, land grants extending westward to the Pacific Ocean. Many people from the "landless" states felt that regions beyond the settled areas should be turned over to the Confederation so that some states would not enter the union with distinct natural advantages over others. Also, they maintained, the West would eventually be won through the combined military efforts of all.

If Maryland land speculators (who hoped to fare better from Congress than from the Commonwealth of Virginia in having prewar claims recognized) had exercised a decisive role in their state's refusal to ratify, their stand did not invalidate the reasoning of other men who demanded an equitable solution to the Western lands problem. To break the impasse, Congress reversed itself and now recommended that the "landed" states relinquish generous portions of their transmontane territories. Virginia, with vast claims, held the key, and, prompted by Thomas Jefferson, that state, on January 2, 1781, offered the Confederation its rights to all

lands north of the Ohio river. Equally important and far-reaching were Virginia's stipulations (ultimately accepted) that speculators' claims be cancelled and that new states be created and admitted to the union on terms of equality with the original thirteen. New York also responded, abandoning its tenuous claims, as Connecticut abandoned its more solid ones. In time, the remaining "landed" states followed suit.

Maryland, which had requested French naval protection, was prodded into ratification by the French envoy, the Chevalier de la Luzerne, and on March 1, 1781, Congress announced the formal creation of a "perpetual" union. Time was to show whether the Articles of Confederation were wholly adequate for the needs of the new nation, but a step, at least, had been taken in the right direction.

Pertinent Literature

Jensen, Merrill. *The Articles of Confederation: An Interpretation of the Social Constitutional History of the American Revolution, 1774-1781.* Madison: University of Wisconsin Press, 1940.

Jensen, Merrill. *The New Nation: A History of the United States During the Confederation, 1781-1789.* Madison: University of Wisconsin Press, 1950.

By focusing attention through his own research on the previously neglected Confederation period, Merrill Jensen has earned for himself a permanent niche in the historiography of the American Revolutionary era. Prior to the studies of Jensen, the Confederation had been examined negatively and incidentally in terms of the alleged weaknesses of the articles and of the supposedly dismal condition of the country in the 1780's. The "critical period," as historian John Fiske described it, was brought to an end and the country saved from chaos and col-

lapse by the Federal Constitution. Besides rejecting such a simplistic explanation of events, Jensen sees the articles as far more than a narrow, arid story of institutional history. The subject, in his hands, becomes a means of illuminating further the nature of the American Revolution and the society that produced it. Jensen believes, as did several historians of the Progressive era, that the American Revolution brought to the surface deep antagonisms in eighteenth century American society. Carl Becker's *History of Political Parties in the Province of New York,*

1760-1776(1909), maintained that New York politics came to revolve around two questions: home rule from Great Britain, and who among the Americans should rule at home. The existence of serious social and economic divisions among Americans was also the conclusion of Arthur M. Schlesinger's *Colonial Merchants and the American Revolution* (1918). Without these tensions, there would presumably have been no need for a democratic upheaval during the Revolution, the kind described by John F. Jameson in *The American Revolution Considered as a Social Movement* (1926). The abolition of primogeniture and entail, the lowering of property qualifications for voting, and the disestablishment of the Church of England all bore witness to the Revolution's liberal upthrust.

In the *Articles of Confederation,* appropriately subtitled *An Interpretation of the Social Constitutional History of the American Revolution, 1774-1781,* Jensen probes deeper into the conflicts among the patriots. After treating the struggles for control within the various colonies, he examines the continuation of the strife as it spilled over into the Continental Congress. Broadly speaking, there were two contending groups, though for the most part each side lacked formal organization, and members occasionally shifted sides. Jensen's so-called "conservatives," initially reluctant to break the British connection completely, became revolutionists decidedly cautious in regard to internal affairs, desiring to leave the colonial political and economic structure unchanged in the independent states. Their opponents, whom Jensen calls "radicals," soon committed themselves to independence, and while they did

not all hold the same opinions, many hoped to make the Revolution a movement for widespread democratic reform. The most significant, clear-cut division between the parties was over the nature of the central government for the thirteen states. The two fundamental problems that emerged in drafting the Articles of Confederation concerned the division of authority between central and local governments and whether ultimate authority, or sovereignty, should rest with the individual states or with the Confederation government. Jensen believes that in writing both the state constitutions and the articles that the radicals triumphed. Self-rule as proclaimed in the state constitutions was reflected in the loose organization of the Confederation that prevented the central government from infringing upon local rights. Indeed, the most-quoted phrase in the book asserts that the articles were "the constitutional expression of the philosophy of the Declaration of Independence."

In a real sense one may say of the radicals, as does Jensen, that the Revolution was "their war." In fact, it was their Revolution, while the conservatives were the outsiders, the movement's stepchildren. How the articles fared after implementation and why they failed to endure, representing as they did the mainstream of Revolutionary thought and practice, are the subject of Jensen's second major scholarly undertaking: *The New Nation* (1950), a history of the United States in the 1780's. This book is invaluable, literally a mine of information about the Confederation years, regardless of whether or not one accepts its point of view. Jensen concludes that the "critical period" was not critical at all in the generally accepted sense. It was critical in that the conservatives, the same old reluctant revolutionaries of 1776, were out to engineer their own counterrevolution. Frustrated by, and disdainful of, the democracy unleashed by the Revolution, they worked to create a powerful central government that would play the conservative, stabilizing role previously exercised by Great Britain. In their campaign to gain the up-per hand, the conservatives (called "nationalists" in this work) exaggerated the seriousness of the country's problems—foreign commerce, internal economic affairs, and tariff wars between the states—while they ignored or minimized the Confederation's solid achievements, such as organizing the West and creating a useful governmental bureaucracy. The articles did not fail, argues Jensen; rather, they were abolished on the verge of success.

Brown, Robert E. *Middle-Class Democracy and the Revolution in Massachusetts, 1691-1780.* Ithaca: Cornell University Press, 1955.

Since the early 1950's the Becker-Schlesinger-Jameson-Jensen interpretation of the Revolution has been under constant attack. It has been claimed that these so-called Progressive historians overestimated the inequalities in colonial life. American society, in fact, presented increasing opportunities for the common man. Land was relatively cheap; the suffrage was widespread; feudalistic land laws, such as primogeniture and entail, were often circumvented or ignored; and the established church had lost much of its authority and scarcely posed a threat to the mushrooming dissenting sects. According to the Progressives, the "internal revolution" that swept away these feudalistic institutions after 1776 was not a revolution at all. For these structures, already decayed, were generally felled without great fanfare. If, then, there were no issues in colonial society to produce deep divisions within the patriot camp, what happened to the hitherto accepted "radical" and "conservative" political groupings? Differences between Americans were minimized or lost their ideological character. The state constitutions and the Articles of Confederation were not the work of any one political segment but represented the contributions of both radicals and conservatives. Thus continuity and consensus stand out as recent themes in scholarly interpretations of the American Revolution. To the revisionists, it is anything but fashionable to depict the movement for the federal Constitution as a counterrevolution.

In the vanguard of the recent revisionists is Robert E. Brown, author of several controversial books, who has attempted to demonstrate that the pre-Revolutionary society of Massachusetts was democratic in character. In *Middle-Class Democracy and the Revolution in Massachusetts,* Brown finds no class conflict. After examining statistics for towns which he considers representative, he concludes that the overwhelming majority of free white males had the right of the franchise long before Lexington and Concord. There was, he claims, no unrest in the back country directed against Boston and other coastal areas, for the Western farmers were as fully represented in the legislature as the Eastern mercantile people. Brown believes that in still other ways, especially in religion and education, Massachusetts was a democratic society. "Men who belonged to other churches did not pay taxes to the Congregational church; education and political office were open to those who were not Congregationalists." It was the Crown's effort to restrain this democracy that drove Massachusetts to rebellion. The Revolution in Massachusetts, as viewed by Brown, was fought to maintain the existing freedoms and the contemporary social order. "It was not, as we have often assumed, a dual revolution in which Americans won their independence from the British on one hand, and in which unenfranchised and underprivileged lower classes wrested democratic rights from a privileged aristocracy on the other." Indeed, the Massachusetts State Constitution of 1780 was the "logical consequence" of an entrenched "middle-class society."

In spite of the criticism levelled at Jensen and his predecessors, no comprehensive interpretation has emerged to replace the neat Progressive framework. More detailed state studies are needed and some phases of the Confederation years call for further investigation. Brown has been challenged on his statistical method of determining property ownership and voting rights; and certain writers, though not unsympathetic to some of Brown's conclusions, question his use of the term "democracy" to describe the eighteenth century social and political scene. Doubtless no simplistic, symmetrical interpretation will ever satisfactorily cover all the fascinating aspects of the American Revolution, but the significance of that formative era will continue to stimulate intensive study and not a little historical debate. — *R.D.H.*

Additional Recommended Reading

Becker, Carl L. *The History of Political Parties in the Province of New York, 1760-1776.* Madison: University of Wisconsin Press, 1909. The classic Progressive expression of the origins and nature of the American Revolution without suggesting directly that New York was typical.

Jameson, J. Franklin. *The American Revolution Considered as a Social Movement.* Princeton: Princeton University Press, 1926. Stimulating and suggestive, though the degree of immediate change produced by the Revolution may be exaggerated.

Douglass, Elisha P. *Rebels and Democrats: The Struggle for Equal Political Rights and Majority Rule During the American Revolution.* Chapel Hill: University of North Carolina Press, 1955. Demonstrates that the fortunes of the pre-Revolutionary ruling class varied from state to state.

Brown, Robert E. and B. Katherine Brown. *Virginia, 1705-1786: Democracy or Aristocracy?* East Lansing: Michigan State University Press, 1964. The Browns believe that in Virginia, as in Massachusetts, the colonists fought to preserve rather than to change their social structure.

Main, Jackson T. *The Social Structure of Revolutionary America.* Princeton: Princeton University Press, 1965. Sees the era as one of relatively little social change, although few Americans were frozen in a lower-class status.

SURRENDER OF CORNWALLIS AT YORKTOWN

Type of event: Military: termination of British attempts to subdue the colonies
Time: October 19, 1781
Locale: Yorktown, Virginia

Principal personages:
LIEUTENANT GENERAL SIR HENRY CLINTON (1738?-1795),
British Commander in Chief in America 1778-1781
MAJOR GENERAL LORD CHARLES CORNWALLIS (1738-1805),
ranking British General in the South
BRIGADIER GENERAL COMTE DE ROCHAMBEAU (JEAN BAPTISTE DONATIEN DE VIMEUR) (1725-1807), Commander of
French land forces at Yorktown
GEORGE WASHINGTON (1732-1799), Commander in Chief of
the Continental Army
MAJOR GENERAL BENJAMIN LINCOLN (1733-1810), American
officer who accepted the British surrender at Yorktown
MAJOR GENERAL NATHANAEL GREENE (1742-1786), Commander of the American Southern Department

Summary of Event

The surrender of Lord Cornwallis in 1781 at Yorktown made immortal the name of that sleepy village at the tip of a Virginia peninsula. The roots of the Yorktown debacle are to be found in a train of events which followed the decision of the Ministry in London in 1778 to shift the focus of the war to the region below the Potomac. French intervention and failure to win in the North led to the British campaign in the South. Although such a campaign would see royal military forces dispersed from Manhattan to the Floridas, the policy-makers at Whitehall based their decision on two crucial assumptions: first, that the Southern Loyalists were exceedingly numerous, and second, that on the sea Great Britain could maintain naval superiority against its Bourbon enemies.

Even though the Loyalists were not so numerous as anticipated, and a British garrison at Savannah almost fell to French Admiral d'Estaing in October, 1779, when he caught the British fleet napping, the basic assumptions in London were never altered. Indeed, the war in the south went extremely well for the home government until 1781. Georgia fell in 1779 and South Carolina in 1780. In major actions in the latter state, at Charleston on May 12, 1780, and at Camden on August 16, 1780, two American armies were eliminated, the first captured, the second destroyed. In the dark days of autumn, 1780, the Continental Congress entrusted to Major General Nathanael Greene, an ex-Quaker from Rhode Island, the task of rallying the scattered and dispirited American forces. His antagonist was Major General Lord Charles Cornwallis, who headed the British field army when Lieutenant General Sir Henry Clinton returned to

New York. Cornwallis showed none of the caution or timidity which many of the British senior officers had shown during the American Revolution. Determined to overrun North Carolina, and hopefully Virginia as well, he refused to allow the annihilation of two of his detached units, at King's Mountain on October 7, 1780, and at Cowpens on January 17, 1781, to dampen his ambitions. Nor did the failure of the Loyalists, whose numbers he exaggerated, alter his thinking. Greene, a master of harassment tactics, severely mauled still more of Cornwallis' irreplaceable redcoats at Guilford Court House, North Carolina, on March 15, 1781. In April, Greene and Cornwallis went opposite ways—Greene south to pick off British outposts in South Carolina, Cornwallis north to invade Virginia.

Greene's brilliant campaign eventually cleared the enemy from all points except Charleston, South Carolina, and Savannah, Georgia, but Cornwallis, far from his supply depots, took the road to disaster. Although Clinton had favored the establishment of a naval base on the Chesapeake and had sent turncoat Brigadier General Benedict Arnold to Virginia on a raiding expedition, he had been more concerned about the welfare of British interests in the lower South. Consequently, he had instructed his restless subordinate to undertake nothing that might endanger "the tranquility of South Carolina." But after limping to Wilmington, North Carolina, to rest his troops, Cornwallis wrote to Clinton, who previously had been in the dark as to Cornwallis' whereabouts, that "a serious attempt upon Virginia . . . would tend to the security of South Carolina and ultimately to the submission of North Carolina." On May 20 Cornwallis joined Arnold at Petersburg, Virginia, and assumed direction of the combined force of seventy-two hundred men. Apprehensive about the possible arrival of a French fleet in the Chesapeake, Clinton disapproved of Cornwallis' abandoning South Carolina and voiced reluctance at turning Virginia into a prime military theater. Clinton, an able strategist but an insecure Commander in Chief, failed to deal decisively with Cornwallis, a personal rival who, he feared, might be appointed to succeed him at any moment. Cornwallis, meanwhile, idled away vital weeks skirmishing in the Old Dominion before retiring to Yorktown in the late summer to erect fortifications.

In New York Clinton fretted, and Washington awaited a large French fleet. Approximately five thousand French troops under Brigadier General Comte de Rochambeau were already at Newport, Rhode Island, but the Comte de Barras' escorting ships had been quickly blockaded inside the harbor by a superior British squadron. Finally, word came of Admiral de Grasse's sailing from France to the West Indies with plans to detach part of his fleet later to assist a mainland campaign. Though Washington preferred to attack New York City, after hearing on August 14 that de Grasse was bound for the Chesapeake, he recognized that his better prospect would be to trap Cornwallis. Accordingly, Washington and Rochambeau hurried southward with seven thousand men, while Barras, loaded with the siege guns for the allied armies, slipped out of Newport. It was scarcely the British Navy's finest hour; not only had the navy permitted

295

Barras to elude the Newport blockade, but the West Indian squadron also had been equally lax, because Admiral Sir George Rodney had assumed erroneously that de Grasse would not sail to the Virginia Coast with his entire fleet of twenty-eight ships. Rodney consequently sent only fourteen vessels northward under Admiral Sir Samuel Hood, who united with the seven ships of Admiral Sir Thomas Graves at New York. Unaware of de Grasse's strength, Graves hastened down the coast and met the French Admiral at the mouth of Chesapeake Bay on September 5. The ensuing contest was indecisive, but Graves felt compelled to return to New York. The fate of Cornwallis at Yorktown was then all but sealed.

Franco-American land operations began on September 7, when soldiers carried by de Grasse and Lafayette's Americans took up positions on the land side of Yorktown. By September 28, after the arrival of Washington and Rochambeau, the entire allied force was in siege position. It numbered more than sixteen thousand men, about half of it French and half American. Once the first parallel was opened and allied siege guns were emplaced, the firing was incessant, forcing the British to withdraw to their inner fortifications. On October 17, when Cornwallis asked for terms, the allies demanded complete surrender. Two days later his seven thousand scarlet-uniformed veterans marched out between rows of white-coated Frenchmen and ill-clad Americans and stacked their arms, while the British bands played "The World Turned Upside Down." News of Yorktown convinced responsible leaders on both sides of the Atlantic that Great Britain's American empire had been permanently rent asunder.

Pertinent Literature

Willcox, William B. *Portrait of a General: Sir Henry Clinton in the War of Independence.* New York: Alfred A. Knopf, Inc., 1964.

There is scarcely a surfeit of reliable biographies of British political and military leaders active during the American Revolution. George III, Lord North, Lord George Germain, and Lord Sandwich all need further scrutiny, as do the generals and admirals, the Howe brothers, Burgoyne, Cornwallis, and Arbuthnot. Monographs on British strategy have also appeared all too infrequently. Fortunately the situation seems to be changing. The year 1964 witnessed the publication of four notable books on the British side of the conflict. Three of these works cover the Southern campaign, each with a different focus. Willcox's is the fourth, and it may be compared with Piers Mackesy's *The War for America, 1775-1783.*

Mackesy writes comprehensively of British strategy and leadership in a war which eventually assumed worldwide dimensions. He maintains that the military effort of Lord North's Ministry must be examined within the context of eighteenth century political and administrative machinery. Mackesy, looking sympathetically upon Great Britain's task of crushing the rebellion, may well be influenced by the post-World War II difficulties of France, the United States, and other Western nations in undertaking military action in distant parts of the world where conventional strategy, tactics, and logistics are thwarted by geography and the unpredictable actions of the local inhabitants. Great Britain's task, according to Mackesy, was unparalleled in the past and was not attempted again, relatively speaking, until the twentieth century. Furthermore, with the widening of the struggle in 1778-1779, Great Britain for the first time "faced what she had always dreaded and averted, a coalition of maritime enemies undistracted by war in Europe."

Willcox has written a biography with a pronounced life-and-times approach. Long considered the leading American scholar on British aspects of the conflict, he has contributed many articles and essays on the subject. Clinton's Revolutionary War role as Deputy Commander in Chief from 1776 to 1778 and Supreme Commander from 1778 to 1782 inevitably involved the author in the manifold British problems of transportation, supply, and civil-military relations. The overall conclusions of Willcox are almost diametrically opposed to those of Mackesy. Willcox believes that Great Britain should have won quickly and decisively. With a professional army pitted against disparate colonial forces, with an advantage of naval preponderance and for three years uncontested control of American waters, the British squandered time and opportunity before the Bourbons entered the fray. Whatever the creaky machinery

and the distances involved, Willcox contends that Great Britain's primary deficiency was in the quality of its leaders, political and military. Clinton is by no means absolved of blame, but he is faulted no more than Sir William Howe, Cornwallis, and Colonial Secretary Germain, the London Minister chiefly responsible for coördinating the military effort. Clinton's greatest deficiency was his inability—explained partly by Willcox in psychological terms—to take his sound plans and put them into action; his well-executed conquest of Charleston in 1780 was a striking exception to his characteristic indecision as Commander in Chief. Although Willcox readily acknowledges Sir Henry's shortcomings in the South, especially in launching a campaign which dispersed his forces, he is more critical of Rodney and is devastating toward Cornwallis, who ignored his responsibilities in South Carolina and placed his army in the position of being dependent for its safety upon sea power.

Probably Willcox's most controversial conclusion, challenged by other authorities, is that the British, by a blockade in home waters, could have choked off French naval operations in the American theater. Certainly a meaningful explanation of the British cabinet's failure to establish a blockade of the French Coast was never made. Had this been done, it may be presumed that Cornwallis would never have received his *coup de grace* at Yorktown.

Smith, Paul H. *Loyalists and Redcoats.* Chapel Hill: University of North Carolina Press, 1965.

Paul H. Smith's thesis, that Great Britain blundered badly in dealing with the Tories, reflects an old and orthodox

point of view. Rarely, however, has the story been told so fully or so well. Throughout most of the war the opinion was held in London that the majority of Americans remained loyal to the Crown. Before 1778, His Majesty's ministers and generals made small effort to cultivate this supposed provincial support because they believed that the rebels could be subdued without it. The disaster at Saratoga and the entry of the Bourbons into the struggle prompted Whitehall to go to the opposite extreme. With fewer regiments available for American service and with enemy forces augmented, the assistance of the Tories was deemed to be essential, especially for garrison and police duties. Smith believes that "the most important factor in the reorientation of British strategy" after 1778 "was a renewal of interest in the military support of the southern Loyalists." Years of neglect and fear of Whig retaliation, however, made the Tories, whose numbers were always grossly overestimated, reluctant to rally to the standard. Even when they took the field, they usually received treatment inferior to that of the regulars. As Smith says, the government "offered the provincials a second-rate status in the army which they often found more disconcerting than gratifying." Yet the so-called Loyalist strategy continued to dominate London thinking about the Southern theater, and Germain never ceased to wax enthusiastic over the slumbering Tory strength which awaited only the presence of royal troops to be aroused. Long before Yorktown, Clinton and even Cornwallis had learned the truth of the Loyalist chimera.

Had the British made a serious effort to organize, train, and protect the Tories early in the war, the outcome of the conflict might have been different. This suggestion, however, is one of the imponderables of the time, and Smith wisely refrains from futile speculation. However, such Loyalist units as Tarleton's legion and Ferguson's frontier militia excelled in the kind of Southern guerrilla warfare in which regulars were extremely deficient. A British scholar, the late Eric Robson, declared that in the wilderness terrain of America any one of these far-ranging mobile units was almost as valuable as a complete army. In any case, there can be no disagreement with Smith's concluding comments: "In dealing with the Loyalists, Britain made two palpable errors: she turned to them for assistance much too late, and then relied upon them much too completely." — *R.D.H.*

Additional Recommended Reading

Johnston, Henry P. *The Yorktown Campaign and the Surrender of Cornwallis, 1781.* New York: Harper Brothers, 1881. Though now superseded to a large extent, this book was formerly the standard work on the subject.

Gottschalk, Louis. *Lafayette and the Close of the American Revolution.* Chicago: University of Chicago Press, 1942. Provides an excellent detailed account of the campaign in Virginia.

Freeman, Douglas Southall. *George Washington.* Vol. V: *Victory with the Help of France.* New York: Charles Scribner's Sons, 1952. In this volume of his stately biography of Washington, Freeman carries his hero through the climactic end of the war and offers an analysis of Washington's military leadership.

Mackesy, Piers G. *The War for America, 1775-1783.* Cambridge: Harvard University Press, 1964. An indispensable work, written from the standpoint of the British government and its military and naval leaders directing a complex war fought around the world.

Treacy, Mildred F. *Prelude to Yorktown: The Southern Campaign of Nathanael Greene.* Chapel Hill: University of North Carolina Press, 1965. A splendidly written book which provides valuable insights into Nathanael Greene's first campaign in the south.

NEGOTIATION OF THE TREATY OF PARIS

Type of event: Diplomatic: recognition of the former British colonies in America as an independent nation.
Time: September 3, 1783
Locale: Paris

Principal personages:
COMTE DE VERGENNES (CHARLES GRAVIER) (1717-1787), French Minister of Foreign Affairs 1774-1787
GÉRARD DE RAYNEVAL (1746-1812), Vergennes' secretary and diplomatic courier
CONDE DE ARANDA (PEDRO PABLA ABARCA Y BOLEA) (1718-1799), Spanish ambassador to France
EARL OF SHELBURNE (WILLIAM PETTY, MARQUIS OF LANSDOWNE) (1737-1805), Prime Minister of Great Britain 1782-1783
RICHARD OSWALD (1705-1784), Shelburne's agent in Paris
JOHN JAY (1745-1829), and
BENJAMIN FRANKLIN (1706-1790), and
JOHN ADAMS (1735-1826), American commissioners chiefly responsible for negotiating the peace

Summary of Event

Winning the war did not necessarily mean winning the peace for the United States. Formal recognition of the independence of the new nation had to be gained from Great Britain, as did agreements on boundaries and fishing rights off Newfoundland and Nova Scotia. Americans could look forward to altruistic generosity from neither friend nor foe. France, which was in league with Spain, hesitated at pushing American interests against the wishes of its Bourbon ally, which objected to any new rising empire in the Western hemisphere. If Great Britain might seem conciliatory toward America, its motives would be dictated by a desire to weaken the Franco-American alliance. On the other hand, as events were to show, Great Britain and France were not unwilling to work together surreptitiously to limit the territorial aspirations of the United States when it proved to be in the interest of either power. Fortunately, the American diplomats were a match for their French and English counterparts. Of the Americans appointed to negotiate a peace, Thomas Jefferson did not serve because of the fatal illness of his wife, and Henry Laurens was a prisoner in the Tower of London during the crucial period of the peacemaking. Two of the other appointees were on previous assignments, John Jay at Madrid and John Adams at the Hague, and did not reach Paris until after Benjamin Franklin had begun discussions.

In London, Lord North (Frederick North, Earl of Guilford) had been Tory Prime Minister during the war but he had allowed King George III to dictate government policy. The revolt and loss of the American colonies led to his resignation in 1782, and the Earl of Rockingham (Charles Watson-Wentworth) succeeded him with a cabinet of Whigs. The Home Secretary was the Earl of Shelburne, who was given responsibility for dealing with the United States and who later the same year became Prime Minister himself. Shelburne sent to Paris a Scottish merchant named Richard Oswald, an old friend of Franklin, to start conversations aimed at luring the venerable commissioner away from France. Oswald argued that the former British colonies in America could gain more by dealing separately with the Mother Country, but while Franklin revealed a willingness to speak with the British representatives, he remained firmly committed to the French alliance. He did, however, assure Oswald that a generous peace would go far toward rebuilding ties between the English-speaking nations. When Lord Rockingham died and Shelburne became Prime Minister, the latter was reluctant to concede total independence to the former colonies. Jay joined Franklin in Paris in August, 1782, and expressed his deep suspicion of French intentions, believing that the Comte de Vergennes, French Minister of Foreign Affairs, favored the ambitions of Spain in the disputed Trans-Appalachian region. The Conde de Aranda, Spanish ambassador to France, informed Jay of the unwillingness of Charles III, Bourbon King of Spain, to recognize America's western claims to all lands to the east bank of the Mississippi river north of latitude 31° north and free navigation of the entire river. Subsequently, Aranda and Gérard de Rayneval,

Vergennes' secretary and diplomatic courier, proposed that the region between the Great Lakes and the Ohio river remain in British hands and that much of the Southwest should become a Spanish protectorate. When he learned that Rayneval had slipped away to London, Jay suspected that the Bourbons might negotiate with Britain at America's expense.

Led by Jay, who personally took the initiative, the American commissioners assured Shelburne of their willingness to deal directly with the British if London would only change Oswald's instructions to permit him to negotiate openly with the representatives of the United States, an implicit recognition of American sovereignty which Great Britain had hitherto refused to acknowledge. Shelburne responded eagerly, believing that the patriots could be separated from France. Franklin was disappointed at not gaining Canada, but the boundaries agreed upon in the preliminary treaty met America's legitimate aspirations in the northwest and southwest, the new nation was given access to the Canadian fisheries, and British forces were to be evacuated from American soil. In return, the congressional commissioners agreed to validate prewar debts owed to British subjects and to "recommend" to the states that they return confiscated Loyalist property.

The preliminary articles, signed on November 30, 1782, without the advice or consent of Vergennes, did not violate the letter of the Franco-American alliance, for the treaty was not to go into effect until France and Great Britain had come to terms. What the commissioners had violated, happily for the United States, were the instructions given by Congress in June, 1781, that they do nothing without the knowledge and consent of France. Indeed, at that time, Congress had even withdrawn as a *sine qua non* the Mississippi river as the nation's western boundary, ordering its commissioners to insist only upon independence. The commission-ers' coup enabled Vergennes, never really eager to keep fighting until Spain recovered Gibraltar, to persuade Charles III's ministers to settle for the Floridas and Minorca. The final treaties were signed at Paris on September 3, 1783. The United States had entered the community of nations.

Pertinent Literature

Morris, Richard B. *The Peacemakers: The Great Powers and American Independence.* New York: Harper & Row Publishers, 1965.

After signing the preliminary peace in November, 1782, John Adams wrote in his diary that at a future day he, "or some other who can do it better," should collect and publish the records of the remarkable negotiations that ended the Revolutionary War and brought diplomatic recognition to the infant Republic. Experiencing rough handling from Old World statesmen, the American commissioners had traversed a thicket of intrigues, double-dealings, and cynicisms in the plush courts of Europe. "Undisciplined as we were," recorded Adams, "we were better tacticians than was imagined." To this day many of the relevant materials remain unpublished, residing in the diplomatic archives at Washington, London, Paris, Madrid, the Hague, Vienna, Stockholm, Lisbon, and elsewhere. Even so, Richard B. Morris, in preparing *The Peacemakers,* has examined a large number of the manuscript sources in America and Europe. The result is the first comprehensive, fully documented book on the peacemaking of 1782-1783. Rather than traditional diplomatic history, which often fails to transcend "the sententious tolling of dispatches," Morris is concerned with the aims and aspirations of the various belligerents and neutrals, the geopolitical factors, and the social and economic forces that shaped their actions. He is, however, far from being a rigid determinist, for his book is most of all the story of the twenty-nine men who acted out the drama on the panoramic European stage: "an extraordinary band of vibrant, subtle, prideful, and complex human beings, who tried to bend, or shape, or stretch, but, most of all, to dominate their world according to the set of national interests to which they were devoted."

But it is chiefly the American peace-makers who draw Morris' admiration and attention. The patriot commission-ers were on their own, having been undercut by France in their own Continental Congress and finding none of the European powers willing at first to accept their terms for peace. In the final scene, the Americans won because they persevered: they were the only diplomats with firm objectives from which they refused to budge, notwithstanding threats, cajolery, or the other sinister sides of eighteenth century diplomacy. The hero of the book is undoubtedly John Jay, the conservative, serious-minded New Yorker to whom the British secret service paid grudging tribute by terming him "obstinate," "indefatigable," and "dogmatical." Morris shows that Jay was uncompromising on the Mississippi river question, and from the first he demanded the right of New Englanders to the Atlantic fisheries; previous writers had sometimes given foremost credit on the latter point to the New Englander John Adams.

The author dwells at length upon what he considers to be certain myths that have beclouded our thinking. One is that France was more faithful to the alliance than the American commissioners. In dissenting, Morris maintains that twice within a year of the Franco-American pact Vergennes broke the spirit if not the letter of the treaties with America. By the secret accord of Aranjuez, which brought Spain into the fray, France promised the empire of Castile a share of the fisheries and pledged to continue the war until Spain won Gibraltar.

Morris strongly applauds Jay for going behind Vergennes' back and treating seriously with the British in 1782. Even if Vergennes were personally committed to all the objectives of the patriots (and he was not), the French Minister of Foreign Affairs was not the sole voice of policy-making at Versailles. In 1780, the Prime Minister of France (Comte Jean Frédéric Phélippeaux Maurepas) and the Minister of Finance (Jacques Necker) had sent out peace feelers to Lord North in London. Generally, "the appeasers," as Morris calls them, would have settled for splitting the United States, giving to Great Britain those areas then occupied by George III's armies. In time, Vergennes also would have accepted a truce, writes Morris, if the proposal had come from outside mediators. But British intransigence, together with a stern warning from Adams, led Vergennes to give up his idea of a peace conference sponsored by Austria and Russia. Another myth of the peacemaking, according to Morris, is that if the American commissioners had dropped their demands for recognition from Great Britain prior to peace talks, they would have fared better than they did in the preliminary treaty of November, 1782. But Shelburne himself was adamant about what Great Britain would concede to America. The Rayneval mission and the other factors that impelled Jay to take the initiative are treated in detail, including Jay's well-founded apprehension that France would not stand behind America in its quest of the fisheries and the Trans-Appalachian West. Seldom has American diplomacy been so audacious, never so successful. "Neophytes in the arts of secret diplomacy," concludes Morris, "they were the peers of their Old World counterparts at the finish."

Stourzh, Gerald. *Benjamin Franklin and American Foreign Policy.* Chicago: University of Chicago Press, 1954.

Gerald Stourzh's purpose is "to analyze systematically the principles of Franklin's approach to foreign policy by probing into his actions as well as into his expressions of opinion concerning international politics." He holds that the stereotype of the "pragmatic" and "opportunistic" Franklin has been overdrawn, that the Pennsylvanian's thought on international politics is more systematic and consistent than generally recognized.

As a colonial writer and leader, Franklin appreciated the concept of power for what it would accomplish. A colonial union, as he advocated in 1754, would have given America greater strength and protection. Power, too, played a hand in the outcome of the imperial rivalries between 1689 and 1763. An advocate of British-American continental expansion, a prophet of the future Westward movement in American history, he saw the removal of France as a means of fulfilling the former colonies' destiny while the departure of the *fleur-de-lis* would eliminate the likelihood of future conflicts. Franklin, even before the word "independence" entered his vocabulary, had developed his concept of foreign policy, according to Stourzh, "based on his all-powerful desire of living space for a rapidly increasing people." It provided a striking contrast to eighteenth century diplomacy that cavalierly ignored peoples and nationalities in favor of dynastic and balance of power considerations. Worried about the possibilities of entangling alliances, Franklin before 1778 seems to have preferred no more of a formal tie with France than a commercial treaty.

If Franklin under duress had to face up to a political involvement in the Treaty of Alliance in 1778, did his personal reservations about such involvements disappear afterward, as John Adams claimed? Did the distinguished philosopher-scientist, unlike Adams and Jay, go to excess in his gratitude to France and neglect America's vital interests? Rejecting this interpretation, the author compares the diplomatic methods of Franklin and Adams, the former a practitioner of "subtle suasion," the latter an advocate of "constant direct pressure" and "the policy of the big stick." The tactful Franklin, a genuine moralist in Stourzh's opinion, felt that it was proper not only to express gratitude for French support, but also that such sentiments were also to America's immediate interest. Franklin, more than Adams, was aware of France's continued fear of an Anglo-American reconciliation. The building of French trust and confidence was uppermost in Franklin's mind, although he was never deluded by notions of disinterested generosity on the part of Louis XVI's courtiers. In fact, Franklin, whose instructions after 1781 were "to proceed only under the full confidence and advice of the French Minister [Vergennes]," was the first American commissioner to disobey orders when they appeared to conflict with the vital concerns of the United States. In April, 1782, he had confidentially suggested to Oswald, Shelburne's representative at Paris, the cession of Canada, which Vergennes desired to remain in British hands. Eventually, of course, Jay did become the moving force behind direct talks with Great Britain, but it was at a time when Franklin fell ill. Although conceding that Franklin did not share Jay's suspicions of de Rayneval's trip to London, and that Jay dispatched his own emissary to London without Franklin's knowledge, Stourzh stresses that Franklin subsequently concurred in Jay's actions and contributed valuable advice in mapping subsequent procedures; even Adams, scarcely a Franklin enthusiast, testified to his colleague's usefulness. Franklin gave up his designs on Canada, his "diplomatic hobbyhorse," which had fitted into his expansionist designs for an expanding American population, but so did Jay and Adams. For the Mississippi river boundary was the issue of paramount importance. That in itself, remarks Stourzh, represented "a concession on the part of England which stunned America's allies." Always aware of the "national interest," a term he himself employed, Franklin, in Stourzh's pages, emerges as a more consistent and constructive foreign policy maker than many historians have been willing to concede. — *R.D.H.*

Additional Recommended Reading

Bemis, Samuel Flagg. *The Hussey-Cumberland Mission and American Independence: An Essay in the Diplomacy of the American Revolution.* Princeton: Princeton University Press, 1931. Examines dealings behind the scenes between Great Britain and Spain designed to bring an end to the war.

Darling, Arthur B. *Our Rising Empire, 1763-1803.* New Haven: Yale University Press, 1940. In analyzing early American expansion, Darling contributes sound chapters on the peacemaking.

Harlow, Vincent T. *The Founding of the Second British Empire, 1763-1793.* 2 vols. New York: Barnes and Noble, Inc., 1952. Describes the impact of the loss of the North American colonies upon Great Britain.

Christie, Ian R. *The End of North's Ministry, 1780-1782.* New York: St. Martin's Press, 1958. An excellent study dealing with this important period.

De Madariaga, Isabel. *Britain, Russia, and the Armed Neutrality of 1780.* New Haven: Yale University Press, 1962. A study of Anglo-Russian relations together with a fresh account of Russia's role in the League of Armed Neutrality.

Smith, Page. *John Adams.* 2 vols. Garden City: Doubleday & Company, Inc., 1962. Discusses in detail Adams' diplomatic activities.

ADOPTION OF THE ORDINANCE OF 1785

Type of event: Legal: legislation regulating the sale of the public domain
Time: May 20, 1785
Locale: New York

Principal personages:

THOMAS JEFFERSON (1743-1826), of Virginia, leading member of the Confederation Congress committee which drafted the report upon which the Ordinance of 1785 was based

THOMAS HUTCHINS (1730-1789), congressional geographer, who surveyed the first eleven ranges of the Ohio country

MANASSEH CUTLER (1742-1823), skillful lobbyist for the Ohio Company of Associates

GENERAL RUFUS PUTNAM (1738-1824), who was involved in the Ohio Company of Associates

WINTHROP SARGENT (1753-1820), who was involved in the Ohio Company of Associates and later became Secretary of the Northwest Territory

JOHN CLEVES SYMMES (1742-1814), who organized the Symmes Purchase

WILLIAM DUER (1747-1799), secretary of the Confederation's Board of the Treasury, who was involved in the Scioto Company

Summary of Event

By 1779, twelve of the thirteen American States, engaged at that time in the Revolutionary War, had ratified the Articles of Confederation. The recalcitrant state, Maryland, ostensibly refused to ratify the document until the states with land claims in the West ceded those lands to the new government. Pressure from the landless states and the exigencies of the war finally compelled the landed states, particularly New York and Virginia, to cede their Western claims to the Revolutionary government. Maryland then ratified the Articles of Confederation early in 1781, and the Confederation government came into existence as the owner of a vast public domain. Although little was done by that govern-ment to dispose of these lands during the war, Congress did pass, in October, 1780, an act declaring its intent to sell the public lands and to create states out of the new territories.

After the Treaty of Paris had been signed in 1783, the Confederation Congress turned to the formulation of a national land policy. To implement the intentions expressed in the Act of 1780, three problems had to be met. First, security against the Indians was necessary before the new lands could be established, and some measure of success in this direction was achieved with General Anthony Wayne's victory at the Battle of Fallen Timbers. Second, some procedure had to be devised for the political organization of the new regions, and this problem was resolved with the Northwest Ordinance in 1787. Third, a system for the survey and sale of the lands had to be established, and this was the purpose of the Ordinance of 1785.

The debate over disposal of the public domain brought into view two divergent approaches which persisted into the nineteenth century. There were those who desired rapid settlement of the land and who, therefore, favored a policy which would attract settlers by the cheapness of the land. Others, moved by a variety of motives, advocated less liberal terms to settlers. Some of these were concerned about the grave financial situation of the government. The Articles of Confederation did not provide the government with an independent and reliable source of revenue. Proceeds from the sale of public lands might alleviate this situation. Some from Eastern (tidewater) areas feared that the rapid growth of the West would quickly diminish the political power of the older states. Others, interested in the possibilities of land speculation, looked upon liberal policies as dangerous competition.

There was also disagreement as to the method of land disposal. Two basic forms were available. One was the New England practice of township settlement which provided for concentrated patterns of ownership, security in communities, and such community institutions as schools and churches. This was the more systematic of the two forms available. The other method, generally referred to as the Southern, resulted in dispersed settlement with each individual staking out a claim to hitherto unsettled lands. In the New England plan, survey preceded sale and the possibility of conflicting claims was considerably lessened.

The matter was debated through 1784 and 1785 and, when the Ordinance of 1785 was passed, it appeared to incorporate the basic features of the New England practice. The principle that survey should precede sale was adopted, as the act provided for rectangular surveys which divided the land into townships of six square miles. Townships were divided into tracts of 640 acres, or sections, which were to be sold at public auction for a minimum price of one dollar an acre. In each township, one lot was set aside for the support of public schools and four for the Federal government. A provision giving similar support for religion was narrowly defeated.

This ordinance with its minimal purchase requirement of 640 acres and its prohibition against indiscriminate settlement seemed to favor the needs of speculators more than bona fide settlers. There were few individuals of the type willing to carve a farm out of the wilderness in an area open to Indian attack that had $640 in cash. Moreover, the disposition of the men who moved west was to settle where they lit, regardless of surveys which, in any event, were unable to keep up with settlement during the nineteenth century.

Congress itself, in its desperate need for ready money, compromised the intent of the act by disposing of vast tracts of land to private land companies for purposes of sale to settlers at a profit. The most famous of these companies was the Ohio Company of Associates. In 1787, Congress agreed to sell to this group one and a half million acres of land and another three and a half million acres to the Scioto Company. This latter speculative venture included many of the most important men in Congress, and their inclusion in the speculation made possible the passage of the Ohio Company grant. Also in 1787, the Symmes Purchase of two million acres was made at about sixty-six cents per acre.

The Confederation government did not realize much money from these sales, nor did these sales greatly stimulate settlement. Conditions were too precarious in the Ohio country. The Land Act of 1796 which raised the minimum price to two dollars an acre did not do much to advance settlement. The change to a more liberal policy began with the Harrison Land Act of 1800.

Pertinent Literature

Treat, Payson Jackson. *The National Land System, 1785-1820.* New York: E. B. Treat & Company, 1910.

Faced with a number of perplexing problems after ratifying the Treaty of Paris on September 3, 1783, the Confederation Congress acted most successfully on the matter of what to do with the nation's western lands. After those seven states having western land claims relinquished them, decisions had to be made on how to acquire treaties of cession with the Indians, to govern the new settlements growing up in the West, and to dispose of the unoccupied lands. Treat, in his study of the national land system, is concerned with the methods of land disposition employed by the government from 1785 to 1820. In the preface Treat states his intention "to show how the national public lands passed into private ownership." The author achieves his goal with clarity and precision. Despite its age, Treat's work remains one of the better books on the early application of the Ordinance of 1785.

Feelings that the western lands were fought for in common, and were therefore to be held in common, abounded both before and after the Revolution. Treat believes the seeds for a national land system were planted in these revolutionary calls for a "common estate." More importantly, Congress, even before the war ended, saw in a vast public domain the best possible source of badly needed revenues. Furthermore, if development of the West were left to Congress, bounties promised to soldiers during the Revolution could be satisfied. Fears of losing position and population to states with large western land claims would be alleviated among those states not having such claims. Congress answered the question of what to do with the western lands by adopting the Ordinance of 1785, which initiated the rectangular survey system in the United States. Except for the large tracts held out by Virginia and Connecticut as military reserves, Congress acquired by 1786 all of the Northwest, composed of the present states of Ohio, Illinois, Indiana, Michigan, and Wisconsin. Of the remaining states claiming western lands, Georgia held out the longest, not surrendering her claims to the federal government until 1802.

The future of America's western lands rested in the application of the rectangular survey system. In the middle chapters, the reader is introduced to the steps first taken under the Articles of Confederation and then under the federal Constitution to dispose of the public domain. Small success was recorded before the closing decade of the eighteenth century. At first, congressional stipulations that a settler had to buy an entire section of land (640 acres) at a dollar an acre prevented all but a few from taking advantage of the new land system. In the place of the individual pioneers large land speculating companies became active. The Ohio Company of Associates obtained a massive land grant from Congress through the use of shrewd and persuasive lobbyists who managed to include in their schemes certain influential members of the Congress, among them, William Duer, secretary of the Board of the Treasury. Besides the sale of land to companies and individuals, Congress also awarded land grants for military service, schools and colleges; state health aslyums; and numerous public buildings. Before 1820, Congress also made special grants of land; for example, land was set aside on several occasions for Canadian refugees and Christianized Indians.

The last chapter of this book is an excellent summary of the relationship between the operation of the Ordinance of 1785 and the progress of Western settlement prior to 1820. Although Treat recognizes the advantages the rectangular survey system ultimately brought to the states, settlers, and even the speculators with its accurate surveys, sound deeds, and relatively cheap lands, he does not ignore the frustrations it could provide, the most nagging of which were the delay while the Indians were treated with and the land boundary lines marked off. Settlers frequently refused to wait for these and took to squatting on the best lands hoping to secure preëmption rights. More often than not, however, more time and money was wasted in removing the intruders, while opening of the land offices was further delayed. Another way of avoiding these delays happened when many settlers headed for Kentucky or Tennessee where the Ordinance of 1785 did not apply.

Nonetheless, Treat tells us, by 1820, the Ordinance of 1785 had been successfully tested. Despite minor shortcomings, by that time the surveys and land offices had proceeded beyond the Mississippi. Moreover, by 1820 discussions on preëmption were gaining ground in Congress and the Land Law of 1796 reduced the amount of land a settler had to buy from 640 to 320 acres. This was further reduced in 1820 when settlers were able to purchase an eighty-acre farm for a hundred dollars. The real problems encountered by the government in disposing of the public domain were not over its curacy as provided for under the Ordinance of 1785 but over the terms of its sale. The government wanted a source of revenue, while the pioneer wanted free land or the nearest thing to it that he could get. The Ordinance of 1785 was an important event in American history because it established "a national land system," on the basis of opening the West to settlement.

309

Adoption of the Ordinance of 1785

Pattison, William D. *Beginnings of the American Rectangular Land Survey System, 1784-1800.* Chicago: University of Chicago Press, 1957.

Based upon exhaustive research, this book offers the reader a wealth of factual material on the system of rectangular surveying in the United States to 1800. The book is divided into three parts: the first considers the basis in law for the rectangular survey system; the second details the survey of the first seven ranges; and the third examines the private surveys of 1787 and the later surveys carried out by the federal government until 1800. Choosing not to go into the politics of the Ordinance of 1785 or of its application, Pattison's book is a "chronicle and analysis" of public land surveying under the 1785 ordinance.

In 1784 the Committee on Public Lands headed by Thomas Jefferson drew up the first proposals for the survey and sale of the nation's western lands. According to the committee's plan, the western lands were to be divided into hundreds and parcelled out in squares measuring ten geographical miles on each side. Though Jefferson is usually credited with working out the 1784 ordinance, much of his thinking on the matter was influenced by the ideas of Hugh Williamson, a delegate to Congress from North Carolina and a member of Jefferson's committee. Williamson made his suggestions to Jefferson hoping that a more uniform and controlled land system might replace the Southern method of "indiscriminate location." Although Williamson was well versed in mathematics, an historian of sorts, and a inveterate astronomical observer, Pattison points out that his ideas on a base ten land system were not original. Evi-

dently the system was long known in Europe. Pattison cites evidence that takes dividing land into squares back to the Roman period. Williamson was not familiar with the Roman land system, but he was with the Dutch, who also surveyed their lands into sections of one square mile. It was from the Dutch system that Williamson borrowed, but there existed closer precedents. The northeastern colonies used the square as the foundation for new towns and townships. Pattison informs us that the "hundred" was used as frequently as the township to indicate land surveys. Even the idea of breaking up the land into units of ten was not without local precedent. In 1765 Colonel Henry Bouquet, an officer of the British regular army, advanced a plan for garrisoning the Pennsylvania frontier that called for a hundred families to develop and defend tracts one mile square.

The Land Ordinance of 1784 was not adopted. The Congressional Committee on Land, of which Jefferson was chairman, reported a new plan, and the Ordinance of 1785, which was based upon this report, was adopted. This law rejected the southern system of indiscriminate location of tracts and adopted that of survey before location. It also dropped the hundred and the decimal system of subdivision as well as the geographical, or nautical, mile. Instead the township of six miles square, which was generally similar to that used in New England, was adopted. The use of natural boundaries, as was often permitted in New England, was not allowed. All boundaries were to be arbitrarily surveyed. An early provision to reserve a square mile in each township for the support of religion was later dropped.

Once the ordinance was adopted, Congress was eager to have some of the land surveyed and put on the market. It sent Indian commissioners to treat with the Northwest tribes for lands west of Pennsylvania, and it ordered the first surveys to be made. By April, 1787, four ranges were laid out west of Pennsylvania and north of the Ohio river. These surveys were not very accurate. Many of the township lines did not close. The total cost of the surveys of the first seven ranges was fifteen thousand dollars. The first and only sale of land in the seven ranges under the Ordinance of 1785 was held in New York City in the fall of 1787. It produced a little more than $100,000, and less than a third of the land offered for sale was taken. The average price was $1.26 an acre. Most of the land purchased was right on the Ohio river or near it. Later sales of land in the seven ranges did not take place until 1796 when a new land law was passed. — *J.G.C.*

Additional Recommended Reading

Robbins, Roy M. *Our Landed Heritage: The Public Domain, 1776-1936.* New York: Peter Smith Publisher, Inc., 1962. A general survey of land laws and their application.

Hibbard, Benjamin H. *A History of the Public Land Policies.* New York: Peter Smith Publisher, Inc., 1960. Another good survey work which includes a summary of the story of the adoption and implementation of the Ordinance of 1785.

Harris, Marshall D. *Origin of the Land Tenure System in the United States.* Westport, Conn.: Greenwood Reprint Corp., 1953. Evaluates the influence of colonial precedents on the Ordinance of 1785.

Donaldson, Thomas. *The Public Domain: Its History with Statistics.* New York: Johnson Reprint Corp., 1970. This large work contains a great deal of important documentary information on the survey and disposition of the public lands.

Pattison, William D. "The Survey of the Seven Ranges," in *Ohio Historical Quarterly,* LXVIII (April, 1959). Demonstrates that the slowness with which these surveys were executed stimulated the organization of the Ohio Company Associates, a private company which purchased a large tract of land just west of the seven ranges.

BEGINNINGS OF STATE UNIVERSITIES

Type of event: Cultural: commitment to public support for higher education
Time: 1785 ff.
Locale: The South and the Midwest

Principal personages:
THOMAS JEFFERSON (1743-1826), third President of the United States and founder of the University of Virginia
ABRAHAM BALDWIN (1754-1807), state legislator, lawyer, and author of the charter of the University of Georgia
MANASSEH CUTLER (1742-1823), clergyman and lobbyist before Congress for the Ohio Company
JOHN MARSHALL (1755-1835), Chief Justice of the United States and author of the opinion rendered in the Dartmouth College Case

Summary of Event

For most Americans, state universities may be defined as publicly supported and controlled non-sectarian, degree-granting institutions of higher learning, designed to discover, conserve, and disseminate knowledge. The concept, if not the realization, is at least as old as the Republic. In 1779 Thomas Jefferson proposed a comprehensive educational plan, part of which involved converting his *alma mater,* William and Mary College, into the State University of Virginia. Even earlier, North Carolina's founding fathers drafted a constitution which authorized the creation of one or more publicly controlled and endowed universities for that state. They also barred clergymen from holding office in the general assembly. Although neither Jefferson nor the Carolinians succeeded in the 1770's, their schemes to create state universities reflected the strongly republican and secular sentiments prevalent among many of America's revolutionary leaders. They also illustrated the firm conviction of

many public men that no self-governing people could long endure without making provision for an informed electorate and an educated leadership.

The first state universities created in the original thirteen states were concentrated in the South, where only one of the nine sectarian colleges founded in the colonial period was located. Under the leadership of a recent immigrant from Connecticut, Abraham Baldwin, Georgia chartered her state university in 1785, although the institution did not admit students until 1801. By that time, North and South Carolina also boasted state universities. Created in 1789, the University of North Carolina began classes at Chapel Hill in January, 1795. South Carolina's legislature acted in 1801 and the state university opened its doors four years later. Maryland, Virginia, and Delaware followed Georgia and the Carolinas in chartering state universities but, of these, only Jefferson's carefully planned institution at Charlottesville, Virginia, operated without interruption or significant change in legal status before the Civil War.

Among the new states added to the Union before 1861, at least a dozen of them chartered state universities, largely as a result of the westward movement and federal largesse. In 1787, lobbying for a group of New England land speculators organized as the Ohio Company of Associates, Massachusetts-born clergyman Manasseh Cutler persuaded Congress to award two free townships to the land company for the purpose of creating a university. Otherwise, Cutler argued, New Englanders would not emigrate. From these grants came Ohio University (1802) and, after another land sale, Miami University at Oxford (1809). By the outbreak of the Civil War, the land grant pattern set by Congress in Ohio had been applied to twenty-one of the twenty-four states admitted to the Union following ratification of the Constitution.

American state universities did not develop without a struggle. Early advocates of state-supported, non-sectarian education, despite their initial successes in the South and on the frontier, made almost no headway where denominational schools were well entrenched or where, as in Massachusetts and Connecticut, separation of church and state did not occur until well into the nineteenth century. In any case, by the time Thomas Jefferson had left the Executive Mansion in 1809, the strongly secular spirit regarding higher education, so widespread immediately following the Revolution, had largely disappeared in a wave of evangelicalism that has been called the second "Great Awakening."

Another obstacle to the early establishment of state universities was the Dartmouth College Case decision of 1819. In 1816 the New Hampshire legislature, influenced by the results of a recent election, sought to bring Dartmouth College, a Congregational institution founded in 1769, under state control. The Board of Trustees sued to retain the college's charter as a private institution, but the New Hampshire high court upheld the state law. Undaunted, the board appealed to the United States Supreme Court. In a precedent-setting opinion Chief Justice John Marshall reversed the lower court, holding that a charter granted to a private corporation constituted a contract, and a contract, under Article I, Section 10 of the Constitution, could not be impaired by the action of a state. Dartmouth College, therefore, was immune from legislative tampering. More important, the Dartmouth decision killed efforts in other states to make public universities out of private colleges. It also unleashed what one authority on higher education has called a Protestant counter-reformation; that is, it spurred the creation of innumerable inferior denominational colleges, all secure in the knowledge that their charters, once obtained, placed them beyond state control.

America's first state universities, never very well-supported from public funds, came under increasing attack after the War of 1812. While sectarians accused them of "godless atheism," an upwardly mobile electorate suspected them of promoting aristocratic privilege at the expense of the common man. Timid legislators responded predictably. They either refused to support state universities altogether, diverted university funds to the common schools, or parcelled out meager resources among a host of inferior denominational colleges. In some instances, lawmakers blunted popular criticism by naming representatives of the most powerful sects to state university faculties or boards of trustees. The net effect was that true state universities were almost stifled in their infancy. Not until the Civil War would they begin to break free from the crippling effects of sectarianism, local boosterism, political demagoguery, and niggardly legislative appropriations. By that time new forces were active in American society. The Industrial Revolution and the political coming of age of the middle and lower classes combined to bring about a concerted drive for what contemporaries called a more "practical education," one which would stress the agricultural and mechanical arts so necessary to a progressive and developing materialist society.

Pertinent Literature

Rudolph, Frederick. *The American College and University: A History.* New York: Alfred A. Knopf, Inc., 1962.

There is no single volume extant which deals specifically or adequately with the history of state universities in America. Interested readers, therefore, must seek out books devoted to particular institutions, or they must resort to general histories of higher education, works which treat both public and private, sectarian and secular institutions, if they would learn something about the beginnings of state universities. A highly satisfactory volume of the latter type is Frederick Rudolph's *The American College and University: A History.*

Rudolph begins by disclaiming any attempt at having composed a definitive work on this broad subject. He has, however, produced an interpretive account, weaving the story of higher education skillfully into the fabric of American social and intellectual history. In a chapter devoted to the colonial period, Rudolph explains that America's first colleges, whatever they may have become, were not designed for the masses. Planned as elite training grounds for future civil and religious leaders, they naturally had some effect in molding colonial society. But in time their influence was largely eclipsed by other factors present in the environment. Frontier conditions, natural abundance, a reverence for individual effort, and a hostility to privilege convinced most upwardly mobile Americans that four years devoted to Latin or Greek was a sheer waste of time. It is no accident, remarks Rudolph, that of the two men who best characterized the eighteenth century, one, Benjamin Franklin, symbolized the self-made man in social and economic terms, and the other, Jonathan Edwards, appealed to his audiences because of his mysticism and his vivid portrayals of hell, not because of his intellectual prowess.

In succeeding chapters, Rudolph deals with the democratizing effects of the American Revolution on society and higher education. For a brief period, culminating with the election of Jefferson to the Presidency in 1800, Americans manifested their pro-French, republican, and anti-sectarian sentiments by adding French studies to

314

the curriculum, separating church and state by law, and attempting to impose state control over existing denominational colleges. The first state universities were a product of this era.

The secular spirit spawned by the American Revolution and the French Alliance soon passed. In the first decades of the nineteenth century a wave of religious revivalism swept the country, particularly the frontier regions, and as a result a great many colleges were founded by competing denominational groups. The enthusiasm with which these struggling institutions were begun was typical of the era. So, too, was their propensity to fail. Some seven hundred came and went before the Civil War. Americans, remarks Rudolph, created colleges the same way they built canals and prospected for gold: with unshakable faith that no enterprise in this land of endless progress could do anything but prosper.

Professor Rudolph carries the story of American higher education into the 1960's. With unusual clarity and skill he explains how Jacksonian Democracy, the Civil War, the rise of science and industry, Progressivism, two World Wars, and a major depression affected American colleges and universities. He also discusses in detail how the colleges responded to the challenges of each generation for educational reform. The demand for scientific education, the elective movement, the development of coeducation and graduate education, the general education movement, the controversy between those who favored specialized education and the supporters of the liberal arts—all are given due consideration in Rudolph's well-balanced history. Finally, for those who seek additional information or a more detailed treatment of a particular topic or institution, the author has included a splendid bibliographical essay.

Brubacher, John S. and Willis Rudy. *Higher Education in Transition: A History of American Colleges and Universities, 1636-1968.* New York: Harper & Row Publishers, 1968.

Another recently published history of American education is the volume by Brubacher and Rudy. First published in 1958, the work was revised and enlarged because of the vast amount of new material published on higher education in recent years. This book is less artfully written than Rudolph's and, if the reader is relatively unfamiliar with American history, is more difficult to follow. The volume is organized topically rather than chronologically and is much narrower in focus than Rudolph's study; but those readers especially interested in the history of state universities will find an entire chapter devoted to the subject.

Brubacher and Rudy define the term "university" as an educational institution of large size affording "instruction of an advanced nature in all the main branches of learning." None of America's earliest universities, public or private, truly fitted that description, if only because they did not give instruction advanced enough to qualify as university work. Neither were America's first state universities truly "public." Their boards of control were often self-perpetuating and their income, what there was of it, usually came from tuition, lotteries, or an endowment fund derived from the sale of public land. Regular appropriations by state legislatures did not become commonplace until after the Civil War.

Brubacher and Rudy consider Thomas Jefferson's university at Charlottesville, Virginia, to be America's "first real state university" because, from the very beginning, it gave more advanced instruction than existing colleges, it allowed students to elect courses and to specialize, its charter made its board responsible to the state, and finally, its creator did all in his power to make and keep it a secular institution. Jefferson did not achieve everything he hoped for at the university. Nevertheless, Brubacher and Rudy believe the institution had a significant influence on higher education not only in the South, but also in New England, at Harvard and Brown; and in the Midwest, at Michigan. Rudolph disagrees, claiming that the University of Virginia plan was not widely copied in the antebellum period because it was too novel and too expensive. Educational reformers around the country were aware of the experimental program at Charlottesville, but when state universities of the modern type finally developed, they were modeled after institutions in the Midwest like the University of Michigan, founded in 1831. Not until after 1865 would Jefferson's ideas on university organization and the elective system be resurrected. By that time advocates of scientific and industrial education found his proposals very effective arguments in their fight to liberalize the essentially classical undergraduate program. — *G.M.R.*

Additional Recommended Reading

Tewksbury, Donald G. *The Founding of American Colleges and Universities Before the Civil War with Particular Reference to the Religious Influences Bearing upon the College Movement.* Hamden, Connecticut: Archon Books, 1965. First issued in 1932 as part of a long series published by Teachers College of Columbia University, Tewksbury's book was reprinted in its original form in 1965. It is still valuable, particularly because of its extensive use of maps and tables.

Hofstadter, Richard and Walter P. Metzger. *The Development of Academic Freedom in the United States.* New York: Columbia University Press, 1955. This volume, much broader in scope than the title indicates, is highly critical of the destructive effects wrought by Jacksonian democracy on the quality of American colleges and universities in the nineteenth century.

Conant, James B. *Thomas Jefferson and the Development of American Public Education.* Berkeley: University of California Press, 1962. Conant, a former president of Harvard University, uses Thomas Jefferson's eighteenth century education proposals with great effect to present his own conviction that selective scholarship schemes are the best means of achieving upward social mobility in twentieth century American society.

Crane, Theodore R. *The Colleges and the Public, 1787-1862.* New York: Teachers College, Columbia University Press, 1963. In an essay prefacing a collection of documents on American higher education, the author contends that debates among reform-minded scholars in the Northeast and experiments at Harvard, Brown, and Union Colleges ultimately had more to do with shaping American higher education than did Jefferson's work at the University of Virginia.

Coulter, E. Merton. *College Life in the Old South.* New York: The Macmillan Company, 1928. Coulter's book, typical of many devoted to a single institution by professionally trained historians since the 1920's, describes curriculum, teaching, administration, and student life at the University of Georgia during the first seventy years of its existence.

ADOPTION OF VIRGINIA STATUTE OF RELIGIOUS LIBERTY

Type of event: Politico-religious: separation of the church and the state in a key state of the United States
Time: January 16, 1786
Locale: Richmond, Virginia

Principal personages:

ROGER WILLIAMS (1603?-1683), founder of Rhode Island and an early advocate of separation of the church and the state

ISAAC BACKUS (1724-1806), Baptist leader of the fight for the disestablishment of religion in Massachusetts

PATRICK HENRY (1736-1799), leader of the effort in the Virginia legislature to enact the General Assessment bill for the public support of Christian churches

THOMAS JEFFERSON (1743-1826), author of the "Bill for Establishing Religious Freedom"

JAMES MADISON (1751-1836), leader of the fight in the Virginia legislature to enact Jefferson's bill

Summary of Event

The adoption by the State of Virginia of the Statute of Religious Liberty was a pivotal episode in the long struggle for separation of church and state in America. The American colonies had inherited, through England, an organic concept of society which was predominant in the Middle Ages and which had survived the Protestant Reformation; there the church and the state had been ideally regarded as parts of a greater and divinely sanctioned social order, and owed mutual support to each other. While the Puritans and other sects emigrated partly to practice their particular faiths without molestation, few were committed to genuine religious freedom. The legal toleration of all Christians in Maryland and Pennsylvania, and the complete toleration offered in Rhode Island, were exceptional in the seventeenth century. While in the later colonial period toler-

ation of dissenting sects was often a practical necessity, connections between the church and the state persisted. The Church of England was legally established in the Southern colonies, and Protestant churches were supported by public funds in most of New England. Non-Protestants remained under civil disabilities in some states until well into the nineteenth century.

The period of the American Revolution, however, accelerated a long-term evolution to a concept of society in which political and religious life existed in separate compartments and in which religion withdrew, theoretically, into the private sphere of activity. Part of the impetus behind the separation of church and state was itself religious. Some originally radical Protestant sects were early committed to separation, either because of their own experi-

318

ence with persecution, or out of more abstract considerations. Some agreed with Roger Williams that a church could only be corrupted by connection with the state. The Baptists were particularly energetic advocates of their separation. Isaac Backus, Baptist leader of the fight for religious disestablishment in Massachusetts, has been characterized as the leading American advocate of religious liberty after Williams. In addition to these strains within American Protestantism, Enlightenment ideas emphasizing the sanctity of individual conscience were influential, most notably among Thomas Jefferson and other leaders of the disestablishment struggle in Virginia. Perhaps the overriding factor in deciding the general issue in the United States, however, was the practical consideration that the extreme multiplicity of sects in the country meant that in the long run the establishment of any one of them, or even of a combination, was not politically feasible.

The American Revolution, bringing new state constitutions and the withdrawal of British support for the Anglican establishment, provided an occasion for the reform of relationships between church and state. Virginia's action in the period following the Declaration of Independence was particularly significant. One of the several largest and most important states in the new republic, and the seat of the most deeply rooted of the Anglican establishments, Virginia took the lead in moving toward religious liberty and the complete separation of church and state. Only Rhode Island, which despite its beginnings had barred non-Protestants from citizenship in the late colonial period, offered comparable liberty among the original states.

Revolutionary Virginia inherited a strongly antiestablishment sentiment, marked historically by disputes over clerical salaries and the long struggle by Baptists and Presbyterians against Anglican domination. The Declaration of Rights, adopted by the Virginia legislature three weeks before the Declaration of Independence, asserted that "all men are equally entitled to the free exercise of religion, according to the dictates of conscience. . . ." James Madison had suggested this liberal phrasing in preference to a more narrow statement of religious "toleration." Later in 1776, penalties against those of dissenting religious persuasion were repealed, and dissenters were exempted from contributing to the support of the still-established Church of England. In 1779, the legislature moved in the direction of disestablishment by discontinuing the payment of salaries to clergy of the Church of England in Virginia.

The conclusive debates in Virginia took place in 1784-1785. Patrick Henry led a move in the legislature to establish a general assessment for the support of Christian worship, which would in effect have substituted for the Anglican establishment a more general Christian establishment. Initially passed in November, 1784, this General Assessment Bill was sharply attacked by Madison, and defeated on its final reading in October, 1785. Madison followed up this victory by securing a vote on the "Bill for Establishing Religious Freedom," proposed by Thomas Jefferson and originally introduced in the legislature in 1779. It was adopted, and became law as the Statute of Religious Liberty in January, 1786.

319

With a preamble asserting that God had "created the mind free" and that attempts to coerce it "tend only to beget habits of hypocrisy and meanness, and are a departure from the plan of the Holy Author of our religion," Jefferson's statute provided "that no man shall be compelled to frequent or support any religious worship, place or ministry whatsoever, nor shall be enforced, restrained, molested, or burthened in his body or goods, nor otherwise suffer on account of his religious opinions or belief. . . ." There remained some vestigial connections between the church and the state, but their separation had been completed by 1802.

Few other states immediately followed Virginia's lead. Officeholders under many of the original state constitutions were required to be believers in God, Christians, or even Protestants. It was not until 1818 that Connecticut did away with compulsory public support of churches, and not until 1833 was a similar establishment completely eliminated in Massachusetts. The First Amendment to the federal Constitution, which prohibited religious establishment or infringement of religious liberty on the national level, helped to commend the example of Virginia to its sister states.

Pertinent Literature

Greene, Evarts B. *Religion and the State: The Making and Testing of an American Tradition.* Ithaca: Cornell University Press, 1941, reprinted 1959.

Evarts B. Greene offers a concise historical survey of the separation of the church and the state in the United States. Emphasizing that early relationships between the two institutions reflected the successful transplantation of European assumptions, Greene traces their progressive adaptations to American conditions. His discussion is sensitive to the remaining complexity of relations between church and state, and although he wrote before the most recent Supreme Court decisions on the subject, it seems unlikely that these opinions would substantially have changed his interpretation. The significance of the Virginia Statute of Religious Liberty emerges here in the long perspective of national history.

Greene devotes particular attention to the Revolutionary period, when political and religious issues were closely intertwined, and American concepts of civil and religious freedom were often closely associated. In late colonial times, the author points out, religious equality was "something to be applied within the limits of Protestant Christianity"; the Quebec Act of 1774, for instance, which granted religious rights to the Roman Catholic Church in Canada, was viewed by the first Continental Congress as a grave parliamentary threat to the "ancient free Protestant colonies." The Revolutionary War itself, however, brought significant changes in such attitudes, partly because doctrines concerning natural rights, as opposed to religious discrimination, were circulating freely, and partly because of the expediency of appealing for aid from Canadian and European Catholics. Yet as Greene points out, the authors of the first state constitutions clearly did not propose that government be neutral in matters of religion, and they generally assumed the existence of a Protestant, or at least a Christian, consensus.

Why, within this halfway house of religious liberty, did Virginia assume a position of leadership toward true separation of church and state? The very strength of the Anglican establishment prior to the American Revolution, Greene suggests, helped to force the issue. Although many of the clergy had sided with the rebels, some of the more prominent of them had remained Loyalists. More fundamental was the legacy of popular resentment over establishment claims, manifested in such episodes as the "Parson's Case" (or "Cause") of 1763. In that dispute over clerical salaries, Patrick Henry had successfully argued against the position taken by the British government, and had helped to associate the Church of England with royal "tyranny." In Virginia, as in other colonies, the Great Awakening had stimulated the rise of popular sects, particularly those of the Presbyterians and Baptists, who comprised a large dissenting element fearful of the power of the Establishment. Furthermore, the Whig leadership in Virginia more than in other colonies was tinctured with Deist and anticlerical thought.

Although the Church of England had already lost much of its privileged position during the American Revolution and was too weak to resist disestablishment, Greene makes it clear that the complete separation of church and state, though virtually accomplished in 1786, remained a matter for serious debate. The "General Assessment" plan represented the views of many who believed that the state should support religion, even if it supported no particular denomination exclusively. Some, including Henry himself, were concerned over the apparent decline of religion and morality, and doubted that voluntary religious contributions would be adequate. The radical decision, in the context of the times, was to reject even a generalized association of church and state.

Greene describes the eventual adoption by the other States of Virginia's solution to the ancient problem, but he is aware that no perfect answer has been found. Alexis de Tocqueville, he recalls, found an intimate and essential connection between democracy and religion in America. While such an association might be compatible with formal separation, there remained always the possibility of conflict between claims of the state and claims of religious conscience.

Marnell, William H. *The First Amendment: The History of Religious Freedom in America.* New York: Doubleday and Company, 1964.

Covering much the same territory as Greene, William H. Marnell writes from a later, and in some respects a more anxious, vantage point. His history of religious freedom reflects concern over recent Supreme Court decisions on the relation between church and state, and is in part an attempt to subject these decisions to historical scrutiny. Marnell's study is scholarly rather than polemical, however, and he intelligently helps to place present issues in perspective with the Virginia Statute of Religious Liberty, the First Amendment to the Constitution, and other episodes in the history of religious freedom. It is useful also for its relatively extended treatment of the medieval and Reformation background of the conflict between church and state, without which the evolution of the American solution to the problem is incomprehensible.

Marnell believes that modern judicial interpretation has distorted the historic meaning of separation of church and state. The "establishment of religion," which such separation was meant to preclude, he argues, had a precise definition in the eighteenth century; it meant not the mere political protection or encouragement of religion, but the creation of an established church as "an integral part of the state," and receiving from the state "support appropriate to its nature as an integral part." Separation of church and state as defined in the First Amendment, Marnell believes, was far from implying indifference toward religion; indeed, it reflected a general determination to safeguard the diversity of American churches within the framework of the new federal union.

Marnell views the Virginia Statute of Religious Liberty as a logical recognition of the drastically weakened position of the Anglican establishment. Madison and Jefferson simply "put into legislation what the impact of events in Virginia had put into practice." Even at that, the author points out, the Virginia debate belies the popular notion of the founding fathers

as unanimously opposed to religious establishment, for among those who favored the "general assessment" plan for public support of Christian churches were George Washington, Richard Henry Lee, Patrick Henry, and John Marshall. Marnell interprets the Statute of Religious Liberty itself as an "equation" involving three factors: the church, the state, and the individual. While protecting the individual from civil or legal disadvantage on account of religion, "it did not attempt to define the relations between Church and State except in terms of the individual."

The author's present concern is that the Supreme Court has abandoned this concept of the separation of church and state in favor of a doctrine of "strict and lofty neutrality" which may actually tend to establish the rule of the minority in religious matters. The no-establishment clause of the First Amendment, he warns, may come into conflict with the free-exercise clause; to hold the requirement of prayer in public schools to be an establishment of religion, for instance, may involve denying people the free exercise of religion within public institutions. Marnell's position on these contemporary issues necessarily colors his view of their historical background, and provides a sharply defined interpretive scheme for the evolution of relations between church and state in Virginia and the nation. — *M.D.C.*

Additional Recommended Reading

Eckenrode, Hamilton J. *Separation of Church and State in Virginia: A Study in the Development of the Revolution.* Richmond, Virginia: Department of Archives and History, 1910. Eckenrode's study of the Revolutionary Period remains a basic monographic treatment, and a source of information not readily obtainable elsewhere.

Humphrey, Edward F. *Nationalism and Religion in America, 1774-1789.* New York:

Russell & Russell, 1924, reprinted 1965. Humphrey treats separately the major American churches in their relations with government before turning to the more general themes of separation of church and state.

Cobb, Sanford H. *The Rise of Religious Liberty in America: A History.* New York: The Macmillan Company, 1902. Concerned predominantly with the Colonial period, Cobb's study presents disestablishment in Virginia and other states as the denouement of a long and hard-fought struggle.

Stokes, Anson P. and Leo Pfeffer. *Church and State in the United States.* Revised one-volume ed. New York: Harper & Row Publishers, 1964. A full and well-researched survey of the subject from the seventeenth century to the present, giving particular attention to legal issues and court decisions.

Meyer, Jacob C. *Church and State in Massachusetts from 1740 to 1833: A Chapter in the History of the Development of Individual Freedom.* Cleveland: Western Reserve University, 1930. As Massachusetts was the last state to do away with religious establishment, Meyer's history of the protracted struggle in that commonwealth provides interesting contrast to Virginia.

Howe, Mark De Wolfe. *The Garden and the Wilderness: Religion and Government in American Constitutional History.* Chicago: University of Chicago Press, 1965. The garden, in a metaphor of Roger Williams, is the church, and the wilderness is the world; in the lectures which make up this volume, Howe demonstrates an urbane grasp of the historical complexities of their relationship.

PASSAGE OF THE NORTHWEST ORDINANCE

Type of event: Legal: legislation providing for the political organization of the public domain
Time: July 13, 1787
Locale: New York

Principal personages:

ARTHUR ST. CLAIR (1736?-1818), President of the Confederation Congress in 1787 and first Governor of the Northwest Territory 1787-1802

TIMOTHY PICKERING (1745-1829), of Massachusetts, who was opposed to a liberal policy regarding the West

Summary of Event

In March, 1784, the Congress of the Confederation accepted the cession of lands Virginia had claimed west of the Appalachian Mountains. A congressional committee headed by Thomas Jefferson, delegate from Virginia, then took steps to provide for the political organization of the vast area south of the Great Lakes, west of the Appalachians, and east of the Mississippi river. The committee's task was to draft legislation for the disposal of the land as well as for the government of its settlers. The proposal of Jefferson's committee met the approval of Congress as the Ordinance of 1784.

The Ordinance of 1784 divided the West into eighteen districts. Each district would be admitted to the Union as a state when its population equaled that of the least populous of the original states. In the meantime, when the population of a district reached twenty thousand it might write a constitution and send a delegate to Congress. As Jefferson envisaged it, as many as ten new states might be carved from the new lands, many of them provided with mellifluous classical names. In Jefferson's oriognal version, slavery was to be excluded after 1800, but this was stricken from the ordinance when it was adopted in 1784. The Ordinance of 1784 was to become effective once all Western lands claimed by the states had been ceded to the government. Before the states ceded their lands, however, a new ordinance was adopted which superseded that of 1784.

The Ordinance of 1787, known as the Northwest Ordinance, was passed according to the historian Merrill Jenson, at the insistence of land speculators who opposed the liberality of the Ordinance of 1784. The new ordinance did indeed slow down the process by which a territory might become a state, but it also added certain important features and provided for the more orderly creation of new states. While the Northwest Ordinance may have been less liberal than its predecessor, it was not undemocratic.

The Northwest Ordinance was drafted to provide political control over the territory north of the Ohio river. To do so, the legislation provided that the whole Northwest region was to be governed temporarily as a single territory, administered by a Governor, a secretary, and three judges appointed by Congress. When the population of the territory reached five thousand free, adult, male inhabitants, the citizens might elect representatives to a territorial assembly. Property qualifications for voting were established but they were small. The general assembly was to choose ten men, all of whom owned at least five hundred acres, from whom Congress would choose five men to serve as the upper house of the legislature. The Governor would continue to be selected by Congress and have an absolute veto over all legislation.

The territory was to be divided into not fewer than three nor more than five districts. Whenever the population of one of the districts reached sixty thousand free inhabitants, it was to be allowed to draft a constitution and submit it to Congress, which would then, if the Constitution guaranteed a republican form of government, pass an enabling act admitting the district into the Union as a state on an equal basis with those states already in the Union.

The ordinance also guaranteed certain basic rights to citizens who might move into the new lands. A bill of rights provided for freedom of religion, guaranteed the benefits of writs of *habeas corpus* and the right of trial by jury, bail, and general process of law. The third article read: "Religion, morality, *and knowledge being necessary to good* government and the happiness of mankind, Schools and the means of education shall forever be encouraged. The utmost good faith shall always be observed towards the Indians." The first of these moral injunctions was implemented as the inhabitants obtained the means to do so. The second, regard-

ing the Indians, has still to be achieved. The fourth article established the basis for relations between the general government and the territories and states which might be formed from them. The article provided for equitable taxation and the free navigation of the waters leading into the Mississippi and St. Lawrence rivers.

The sixth article was epoch-making. It read: "There shall be neither Slavery nor involuntary Servitude in the said territory otherwise than in the punishment of crimes, whereof the party shall have been duly convicted. . . ." This determined that the society that developed north of the Ohio river would be free. No such provision was written into the act establishing the Southwest Territory in 1790.

The pattern established by the Northwest Ordinance was more or less followed in the later admission of states into the Union. Some, such as Texas and California, came in without a territorial period. Others, such as Michigan, caused trouble because of boundary disputes with neighboring states. As for the Ohio country, Arthur St. Clair, President of the Confederation Congress in 1787, was appointed first Governor of the territory; Indiana Territory was organized in 1803, the same year in which Ohio entered the Union, but entered as a state in 1816 as did Illinois in 1818, Michigan in 1837, and Wisconsin in 1848. The ordinance proved to be the crowning legislative achievement of the otherwise lackluster Confederation government. But even while Congress was debating the Northwest Ordinance, another debate was occurring in Philadelphia.

Pertinent Literature

Philbrick, Francis S. *The Rise of the West, 1754-1830.* New American Nation series. New York: Harper & Row Publishers, 1965.

This work, by a distinguished legal scholar is one of the volumes of the *New American Nation* series. It is a treatment of the legal, political, and social development of the Trans-Appalachian West in the period immediately preceding the Revolution through the beginning of the Jacksonian era. As might be expected from the work of a legal scholar, the book emphasizes political and diplomatic developments in the West. The discussion of the Ordinance of 1787 is essentially legalistic. Philbrick agrees with historians like Merrill Jensen in stressing the conservative nature of the ordinance. Comparing Jefferson's 1784 Ordinance with that enacted in 1787, Philbrick calls the earlier document "remarkably democratic." The Ordinance of 1787, on the other hand, "achieved, as respects merely government, the reëstablishment in the West of the very colonial system from which the Eastern states had just escaped. In repealing Jefferson's ordinance they in effect repealed the Revolution for others than themselves." Jensen and Philbrick agree on seeing the latter document as one piece of evidence of the conservative reaction against what many Eastern leaders saw as the "excesses" of the revolutionary period. Philbrick describes the very pronounced prejudices of the leading Eastern spokesmen in Congress against Western settlers in general. Philbrick's discussion, however, does not dwell on the selfish interests of land speculators; rather it traces the legislative development of the act and specifically the work of the man who drafted the final

ordinance, Nathan Dane of Massachusetts. In this volume, Philbrick borrows freely from his earlier and more extensive work on the legal and constitutional history of the territory northwest of the Ohio—a 475-page "Introduction" to *The Laws of Illinois Territory 1809-1818 (Collections* of the Illinois State Historical Library. Volume XXV, Law Series, Volume V), edited by Francis S. Philbrick, Illinois State Historical Library, Springfield, Illinois, 1950.

Although the Ordinance of 1787 was the product of a committee, Dane made two important personal contributions to the final document. The first was a provision which prohibited the territorial legislatures from impairing the obligation of contracts, a provision strikingly like a similar prohibition on state power which would appear in the Constitution then being drafted in Philadelphia. The second personal contribution of Dane was the establishment of the inheritance laws of the territory along the "liberal" lines of those of the state of Massachusetts. Dane was also the man who moved on the floor of Congress to add to the ordinance a provision barring slavery from the territory. Thus, ironically, the conservative Easterners and their fellow representatives from the slave states were responsible for inserting into the document that far-reaching antislavery provision which even the more "democratic" Jeffersonian Ordinance of 1784 did not contain. Philbrick portrays Dane as a conservative, but gives him credit for a fundamental faith in feder-

326

alism and personal liberties which indicated that he "could tolerate social democracy."

Philbrick suggests the possibility that the two bodies, the Congress and the Constitutional Convention, which had met in the summer of 1787, might have been in contact on some major issues. Evidence that such contacts meaningfully affected the ordinance or the Constitution as it emerged from the convention in Philadelphia is largely circumstantial. The possibility, however, intrigued the great constitutional thinker John C. Calhoun. As a fundamental constituent of the Constitution, he once suggested in an argument about slavery that the South accepted the antislavery provision of the ordinance only in order to secure the constitutional provision for the rendition of escaped slaves, (reported in Richard Current's *John C. Calhoun*, New York, 1963).

A recent historian has undertaken the most extensive inquiry into this problem. Staughton Lynd in "The Compromise of 1787," published in his *Class Conflict, Slavery, and the United States Constitution* (New York: Bobbs-Merrill Company, Inc., 1967), argues that in fact, the two bodies worked out the first of the great sectional compromises over slavery that kept the peace and union between North and South until 1861. The antislavery provisions of the ordinance, the reduction of the number of states to be carved out of the territory from the ten proposed by Jefferson, and the constitutional provisions for slave rendition, along with the three-fifths clause on representation, were all involved in the sectional compromise. The Southerners gave freedom to the Northwest Territory but they expected compensation by a greater rate of growth for the Southern states in general and in the territories south of the Ohio which were open to slavery. It was by no means clear in the year 1787 that the center of population and growth would be in the Northern states. The Southern states hoped for dominance of the House of Representatives through the three-fifths clause and controlled growth of Northern strength in the Senate by limiting the number of free states to be formed from the Northwest Territory. Much of Lynd's evidence is only circumstantial, and he may have overestimated the strength of proslavery and antislavery feeling in both the Congress and the convention, but his article is learned and closely argued. Among the first acts of the new Congress under the Constitution was the reënactment of the Ordinance of 1787, a recognition of its fundamental nature for territorial government in the Northwest. Without reading the sentiments of men who were to fashion sectional compromises a generation or two later into evidence, there still remains the fascinating problem of the coöperation and collaboration of the men in New York and in Philadelphia that summer of 1787.

Jensen, Merrill. *The New Nation: A History of the United States During the Confederation, 1781-1789.* New York: Alfred A. Knopf, Inc., 1950.

The proponents of ratification of the Constitution in 1787 painted a dark picture of American progress under the Articles of Confederation. They won the partisan argument and their views have generally been accepted by most historians. Perhaps the classic statement of the nationalist view that the Constitution was an absolute necessity to restore social and economic order to the country was John Fiske's *The Critical Period of American History.* Jensen describes the work as "a book of vast influence but of no value as either history or example." His reëxamination of the period suggests that many of the problems of the United States in this period are actually common to most post-war situations and were not unduly exacerbated by the weakness of the central government. Furthermore, among the defenders of the articles against a "national" government, there were men who wanted to strengthen the Congress without tipping the balance of power too strongly towards central authority. Finally, he argues that the Confederation government gave to the new government under the Constitution two institutions virtually indispensable for its own development. One was a federal bureaucracy, which though small was expert and experienced; the other was a national domain, ordered and organized for development.

The Ordinance of 1787 was the final statement on organization of the national domain from the Confederation government. It represented a need felt in the Congress for greater federal direction and supervision of the development of the West. Reconsideration and repeal of Jefferson's Ordinance of 1784 arose, according to Jensen, "from the fear of Westerners and the danger of Indian war," and "was given urgency by the Ohio Company," a group of speculators in Western lands with influence in the Congress. Settlers were moving into the territory, and their lawlessness aroused intense Eastern prejudices against them. The Congress wanted orderly, and profitable, exploitation of the Western lands, both for members of Congress with personal interests in land companies, and, more importantly, for the liquidation of the national debt. These interests met in the provisions for greater federal control over the settlers than had been provided by the Ordinance of 1784, in the protection of property rights by the new ordinance, and in congressional action to protect the interests of the Ohio Company. The "democratic" Jeffersonian Ordinance "was abolished in 1787 by the land speculators and their supporters who wanted congressional control of the West so that their interests could be protected from the actions of the settlers."

There is only a slight mention of the antislavery provision of the ordinance; however, even the discussion of the document itself is only a small part of a work whose primary concern is an attempt to revise the conventional view of the history of the United States in those crucial if not "critical" years. As important as it was, even the Northwest Ordinance was only the last congressional determination on the issue of Western land which had absorbed the attention of the Congress from its inception. Perhaps in spite of the motives of some of its proponents, the Ordinance of 1787 provided a workable balance between local self-government and federal supervision in the early stages of settlement which was the model for future expansion. — *G.J.C.*

Additional Recommended Reading

Fiske, John. *The Critical Period of American History, 1783-1789.* Boston: Houghton Mifflin Co., 1888. Until recently, this work represented the standard interpretation of the Confederation period.

James, James A. *The Life of George Rogers Clark.* Chicago: University of Chicago Press, 1928. The subject of this biography figured largely in the history of the Northwest during the Revolutionary War decade.

Abernethy, Thomas P. *From Frontier to Plantation in Tennessee: A Study in Frontier Democracy.* Chapel Hill: University of North Carolina Press, 1932. The problems of conquering a frontier are dealt with in this volume.

Harris, Marshall D. *Origin of the Land Tenure System in the United States.* Ames: Iowa State College Press, 1953. This standard work covers the colonial period clearly and in detail.

Wright, Benjamin F. *Consensus and Continuity, 1776-1787.* Boston: Boston University Press, 1958. One of the most significant analyses of American attitudes and goals during the formative period of the Republic.

Barrett, Jay A. *Evolution of the Ordinance of 1787, with an Account of the Earlier Plans for the Government of the Northwest Territory. First American Frontier* series. New York: Arno Press and *The New York Times,* 1971. Originally published in April, 1891. Uses contemporary diaries, letters of correspondence, the *Journals of Congress,* and various monographic studies to provide a detailed look at the "evolution" of the Northwest Ordinance.

Ogg, Frederic A. *The Old Northwest: A Chronicle of the Ohio Valley and Beyond.* Vol. XIX: *The Chronicles of America* series. New Haven: Yale University Press, 1919. Ogg's book is a general survey, unfortunately without footnotes, of the years from 1760 to 1849.

ADOPTION OF THE CONSTITUTION

Type of event: Constitutional: definition of the power and duties of the United States and its citizens

Time: September 17, 1787

Locale: Philadelphia

Principal personages:

GEORGE WASHINGTON (1732-1799), presiding officer at Constitutional Convention

ALEXANDER HAMILTON (1757-1804), strong advocate for abandoning the Articles of Confederation and adopting a new constitution

WILLIAM PATERSON (1745-1806), sponsor of the so-called New Jersey Plan which favored a weak central government

JAMES WILSON (1742-1798), prominent lawyer who contributed considerably to the writing of the Constitution

JAMES MADISON (1751-1836), probably the most active delegate, who kept a detailed record of the proceedings

Summary of Event

By the middle 1780's, much dissatisfaction with government under the Articles of Confederation became evident. Many men prominent in American political life—George Washington, Thomas Jefferson, John Jay, Alexander Hamilton, and Noah Webster among others—in papers, letters, and conversations were critical of the functioning of the Confederation Congress. And some agreement was being reached concerning basic defects in the articles themselves. Specifically criticized was Congress' lack of power to tax, to regulate interstate commerce, and to force the states into more effective coöperation with the central government. All efforts to amend the Articles of Confederation were doomed to failure because amendments required unanimous approval by the states. It became evident to most concerned persons that the desired changes might best be accomplished by abandoning the articles and writing a new constitution.

A meeting between delegates of Virginia and Maryland in March, 1785, gave impetus to this plan. The two states managed to work out an agreement involving commercial regulations on the Potomac river. The success of their meeting brought forth from Virginia a call for another meeting at Annapolis, Maryland, in the following year to discuss additional common problems. Nine states were invited, but only five sent delegates. The most important result of this convention at Annapolis was the publication of a report, probably drafted by Alexander Hamilton, that called for a convention to assemble in May, 1787, in Philadelphia to remedy the defects of the government then in existence. Copies of the report were sent to all states with a request that delegates be appointed and sent to Philadelphia.

Every state except Rhode Island sent

delegates, although some came late and others left early. In all, seventy-four men were appointed as delegates, fifty-five attended at one time or another, and thirty-nine signed the final document. George Washington was appointed presiding officer—a significant appointment because of his prestige and popularity. In the minds of most American citizens, any convention presided over by so great a man had to produce some good results. The presence of Benjamin Franklin was also significant. Although enfeebled by old age, his great reputation added importance and dignity to the convention. Alexander Hamilton, one of the earliest advocates of the creation of a stronger government, was also in attendance, but his effectiveness was seriously curtailed by his fellow delegates from New York, who cast the state vote for the continuation of the Articles of Confederation.

The most active delegates in favor of establishing a stronger federal government were James Madison and George Mason from Virginia; James Wilson and Gouverneur Morris from Pennsylvania; John Dickinson from Delaware; John Rutledge and Charles Pinckney from South Carolina; and Oliver Ellsworth from Connecticut. There were differences of opinion among these leaders, especially concerning the power of the states in the new framework. Nevertheless, they agreed that a stronger form of union was necessary. The more active and important leaders among those who would have been satisfied to merely amend the Articles of Confederation were Roger Sherman from Connecticut, William Paterson from New Jersey, Elbridge Gerry from Massachusetts, and Luther Martin from Maryland.

The convention first met on May 25. Electing a presiding officer and adopting rules occupied the first few days. On May 29, the Virginia delegation proposed a series of resolutions that occupied the convention's attention for weeks. This so-called Virginia Plan, drafted largely by Madison and introduced by Edmund Randolph, proposed several changes. The most important among the proposals was the one that called for the convention to adopt a wholly new constitution rather than attempt to revise the Articles of Confederation. In opposition to this proposal (in fact in opposition to the entire "Virginia Plan") William Paterson, from New Jersey—who represented the so-called smaller states of New York, Maryland, Connecticut, and Delaware—introduced a series of resolutions sometimes referred to as the "New Jersey Plan." The two plans were debated simultaneously, and eventually a majority of the states voted to sustain Randolph's proposal for a new constitution that would provide a strong national government.

Other aspects of both plans were continually debated throughout the hot summer months, and largely by compromise and concession a new constitution was forged. One of the great concerns of the small states that feared loss of power and authority to the national government was that they would be consistently outvoted in the legislature if representation in the legislature were according to population. The compromise reached was to allow representation in the House according to population, but to give each state two senators regardless of population. As an added safeguard, every bill had to pass both houses of Congress and be signed by the President.

While this was one of the major compromises of the convention it was by no means the only one. The office of Chief Executive, the length of his term, the electoral procedure, the judicial system, the process of amendment, slavery and the slave trade, and many other issues produced differences of opinion and necessitated compromise. It would not be a gross exaggeration to state that the final draft of the Constitution was one huge compromise, not perfect by any means but acceptable to most of the delegates because, as Benjamin Franklin said: "We can expect no better."

Although a total of thirty-nine delegates signed the Constitution, several notable delegates refused to do so. Prominent among the dissenters were Edmund Randolph, George Mason, and Luther Martin. Nevertheless the document was declared adopted "by unanimous consent of the states present" and was sent out to the states for ratification.

Pertinent Literature

Mitchell, Broadus and Louise P. Mitchell. *A Biography of the Constitution of the United States: Its Origin, Formation, Adoption, Interpretation.* New York: Oxford University Press, 1964.

Broadus and Louise Mitchell have produced an unusual book, described by the authors themselves as the life story of the Constitution. It begins with a brief account of the government under the Articles of Confederation, showing the need for a stronger government. They then proceed to the calling of the Constitutional Convention, the debates, the writing of the Constitution, its adoption by the Constitutional Convention, the ratification by the states, and the addition of the amendments. The final third of the book is devoted to interpreting the Constitution through the nineteenth and twentieth centuries, the theme being that the Constitution is whatever the Supreme Court says it is.

A long chapter entitled "The Constitution is constructed" provides an excellent study of the workings of the Constitutional Convention. The authors lead the reader step by step through the tangled debates of the convention with sufficient detail and a minimum of confusion. The authors show how hurdles were surmounted and extreme positions were usually brought within reach of one another. Much credit for conciliation is given to Benjamin Franklin, Oliver Ellsworth, and William Samuel Johnson of Connecticut.

In another fine chapter, "Champions and Critics," the Mitchells take up the ratification struggle. They credit George Washington as the most influential person in securing ratification by the states. They believe that the average person was ignorant of the provisions in the Constitution and was unable to judge the document on its merits. But if Washington advised acceptance, the people were ready to accept.

Nevertheless, strong opposition to the adoption of the Constitution was led by certain prominent men in some areas. Luther Martin, Patrick Henry,

Samuel Adams, John Hancock, and George Clinton all had serious doubts about the wisdom of ratifying the new Constitution. Had these men, and others like them, remained opposed, ratification might have been prevented in several key states.

The authors selected Virginia, Massachusetts, and New York as key states deserving special attention in the ratification struggle. Without participation of these three states it was doubtful whether the new government could begin to function. The Mitchells provide an accurate and thorough account of the effort put forth by the defenders of the Constitution to persuade, cajole, or force the opposition to concede. Point by point, objections were answered and opponents were won over. Even so, the outcome of the debate was long in doubt and the final ballot was extremely close.

Rutland, Robert A. *The Ordeal of the Constitution: The Antifederalists and the Ratification Struggle of 1787-1788.* Norman: University of Oklahoma Press, 1965.

This scholarly work gives a detailed account of the unsuccessful attempt of the Anti-Federalists to prevent the ratification of the Constitution in 1787 and 1788. Although the contest in each of the states is touched on, special attention is given to the key states of Pennsylvania, New York, Massachusetts, and Virginia. It was commonly agreed that ratification by these states would lead to ratification by the rest. In every state there was a group determined to prevent ratification, and in the country as a whole there were certainly as many citizens opposed to ratification as there were in favor of it. Yet the Constitution was ratified; the Federalists had their way and the Anti-Federalists went down in bitter defeat. Rutland reaches the conclusion that the Anti-Federalists failed because they lacked "coördination" and were "without a definite counter proposal, and without unified leadership." He also notes that ninety percent of the newspapers and an almost equally high percentage of the influential upper classes supported ratification. These conclusions are supported with adequate data. Many well-known names were found among the Anti-Federalists, such as Governor George Clinton of New York; Elbridge Gerry and Sam Adams of Massachusetts; Richard Henry Lee, George Mason, and Patrick Henry of Virginia; and Samuel Chase and Luther Martin of Maryland, to name only a few. It is still a fair statement, however, that the Anti-Federalists had no outstanding leader. Only Willie Jones of North Carolina and Patrick Henry came close to providing any effective leadership; all of the others for one reason or another failed to gain a following. Rutland also maintains that the Anti-Federalists were disorganized. In spite of some similarity of ideas and goals among them, such as demand for a bill of rights, fear of tyranny and government by remote control, and hope for a second constitutional convention, the Anti-Federalists were able neither to consolidate their efforts nor sustain an offensive. Commenting on their defeat in Massachusetts, one of their Federalist opponents said: "There was not a single character capable of uniting their wills or directing their measures—they had no plan whatever.

333

They looked no farther than to put a negative on the Constitution and return home." Rutland suggests that the ratification struggle provides another historical example of a well-organized minority overcoming a disorganized majority.

It is of some interest to note that although the Anti-Federalists were outmaneuvered, outdebated, and outvoted, many of their fears were justified and many of their predictions have come true. Luther Martin, for example, feared the growth of federal power and the corresponding weakening of the powers of the states, and Robert Yates of New York predicted that the general welfare clause would be used to infringe upon the authority of the states. A sizeable number of Anti-Federalists showed concern over the powers of taxation granted to the national government. Likewise, John Sullivan expressed alarm over the possibility that a Jew, a Turk, or a Roman Catholic might become President of the United States.

Although Rutland seldom cites secondary works, it is obvious that he is familiar with works about this general period. The sources he has relied on most heavily are printed collections of letters, papers and documents, and unpublished manuscript materials. Although his conclusions may not be startling or revolutionary, his material is fresh and well presented; and the book is a noteworthy contribution to the literature of the Federalist and Anti-Federalist dispute. — *E.J.M.*

Additional Recommended Reading

Hockett, Homer C. *The Constitutional History of the United States.* Vol. I. New York: The Macmillan Company, 1939. Several chapters in this well-written and well-documented book are devoted to the formation, adoption, and ratification of the Constitution.

Swisher, Carl B. *American Constitutional Development.* Cambridge: Houghton-Mifflin Co., 1943. A standard, well-respected constitutional history of the United States.

U.S. House Document number 206. *The United States Constitution.* G.P.O., June 29, 1961. A useful annotated copy of the Constitution, including twenty-three amendments and the amendments accepted by Congress but never ratified by the states.

Jensen, Merrill. *The Making of the American Constitution.* Princeton: Van Nostrand Company, Inc., 1964. A brief but excellent account of the creation of the Constitution, beginning with the colonial background and concluding with ratification by the states.

Beard, Charles A. *An Economic Interpretation of the Constitution of the United States.* New York: The Macmillan Company, 1913. Advances the thesis that the framers of the Constitution were not so much motivated by patriotic reasons as they were by the selfish desire to establish a stronger union in order to preserve their own money and property interests.

Brown, Robert E. *Charles Beard and the Constitution.* Princeton: Princeton University Press, 1956. A reaction to, and a refutation of, the Beard thesis.

Farrand, Max. *The Records of the Federal Convention of 1787.* 4 vols. New Haven, Conn.: Yale University Press, 1966. The definitive set of primary source documents for the convention.

PUBLICATION OF *THE FEDERALIST*

Type of event: Political: series of essays on constitutional government
Time: October, 1787-May, 1788
Locale: New York City

Principal personages:

ALEXANDER HAMILTON (1757-1804), lawyer, member of Congress under the Articles of Confederation, member of the Constitutional Convention, author of more than half the essays in *The Federalist*

JOHN JAY (1745-1829), lawyer, member of the First and Second Continental Congresses, member of Congress under the Articles of Confederation, Secretary of Foreign Affairs under the Articles of Confederation, author of five of *The Federalist* essays

JAMES MADISON (1751-1836), member of the Constitutional Convention and principal author of the Constitution, author or co-author of probably twenty of the essays in *The Federalist*

Summary of Event

The Federalist comprises a series of eighty-five essays published anonymously by Alexander Hamilton, John Jay, and James Madison between October, 1787, and May, 1788, urging ratification of the United States Constitution. That constitution, drafted by the Philadelphia Convention of 1787, sought to increase the power of the national government at the expense of the state governments. The national debate over ratification began almost immediately after the Philadelphia Convention sent the proposed constitution to Congress on September 10 and its contents became known. Before the document could take effect, it had to be ratified by specially elected conventions in at least nine of the thirteen states, and throughout the nation critics of the Constitution (Anti-Federalists) battled its supporters (Federalists) in campaigns to elect men to the state conventions. The debate was particularly tense in New York, which was sharply divided over the Constitution. New York City and the surrounding areas were strongly Federal but the rural upstate areas were strongly Anti-Federal as was the state's popular and powerful Governor, George Clinton.

Late in September, 1787, the *New York Journal* began printing a series of Anti-Federal essays by "Cato" (who may have been Governor Clinton). In order to refute these and other Anti-Federal tracts, Alexander Hamilton and John Jay, two of New York's most prominent Federalists, agreed to write a series of newspaper essays under the name "Publius." The first (*The Federalist No. 1*), written by Hamilton, appeared in the *New York Independent Journal* on October 27, and in it Hamilton outlined the purpose of the entire series. The essays would explain the necessity of the union for "political prosperity," the "insufficiency of the present Confederation to preserve that Union," the need for a more "energetic" government than that which existed under the Articles of Confederation, the "conformity of the proposed constitution to the true principles of republican government," and the security that the Constitution would provide "to liberty and to property."

John Jay wrote the next four installments before ill health forced him to quit. In November, James Madison, who was in New York representing Virginia in Congress, took Jay's place and between them, Madison and Hamilton produced all but one of the remaining eighty essays; Jay wrote *No. 64.*

Madison's first contribution to the series, *The Federalist No. 10,* is the most famous of all the essays. In it he discussed the origins of parties, or "factions" (as he called them), and he argued that they sprang inevitably from "the unequal distribution of property." "Those who hold, and those who are without property," he continued, "have ever formed distinct interests in society." In any nation, "a landed interest, a manufacturing interest, a mercantile interest, a monied interest," and "many lesser interests, grow up of necessity" and divide people into "different classes. . . ." Some Anti-Federalists had argued that the nation was much too large and too diverse to be governed effectively by a powerful central government without sacrificing people's liberties and freedoms in the process, but in *The Federalist No. 10,* Madison used his ideas about factions to reverse their argument. The nation's size, he wrote, and the great variety of its people and their interests were sources of strength, not weakness.

There were so many different groups (or factions), so many different interests that would be represented in the new government, that no one faction, no one group, no lone demagogue could ever capture control of the national government. Far from inviting tyranny, he argued, the nation's size and diversity when coupled with the federal republican form of government proposed by the Constitution would provide a strong check *against* tyranny.

Addressed to "the People of the State of New York," *The Federalist* essays were intended primarily as New York ratification campaign tracts, but they were also reprinted by newspapers in other states and cities, particularly in Philadelphia and Boston. Hamilton had the first thirty-six numbers published as a book in March, 1788, and some of these books were sent to Virginia where they arrived in time to be useful to Federalists at the Virginia ratifying convention. A second volume, containing the remaining forty-nine essays appeared the following May.

It is hard to estimate the impact of *The Federalist* on the campaign to ratify the Constitution even in New York, much less nationally. Certainly the articles were not as successful as their authors hoped, for New York voters sent twice as many opponents of the Constitution to the New York ratifying convention as they sent supporters. By the time the convention balloted, however, ten states had already ratified, and New York did so too on July 26, 1788, by a narrow three-vote margin. But it is unlikely that *The Federalist* contributed much to the result.

Whether or not the essays in *The Federalist* were effective political tracts in 1788, they have long been considered important keys to understanding the intentions of the members of the Philadelphia Convention. Historians and even Supreme Court justices have studied the papers as a guide to "the intent of the framers," even though they were written as election tracts, and in spite of the fact that one author (Jay) did not attend the Philadelphia Convention, another (Hamilton) played a very small role there and was himself dissatisfied with the Constitution, and the third (Madison) came to have serious doubts about the meaning of the Constitution and the kind of government it created within a few years after he wrote his essays for *The Federalist.*

The reputation of *The Federalist* has grown steadily since 1788. The work has been widely republished around the world in several languages and is regularly reprinted in the United States. The essays have been brought into many public political debates since 1789, particularly during times of constitutional crisis, such as the states' rights debates that preceded the Civil War, the public discussion over the constitutionality of President Franklin Roosevelt's New Deal policies, and the more recent debate over states' rights and civil liberties in the 1950's.

Apart from its partisan political value, past and present, many historians and political scientists consider *The Federalist* to be the best existing defense of federal republicanism in general and of the American Constitution in particular, and it is undeniably among the foremost works of political science ever produced in the United States.

Pertinent Literature

De Pauw, Linda G. *The Eleventh Pillar: New York State and the Federal Constitution.* Ithaca: Cornell University Press, 1966.

Linda De Pauw's *The Eleventh Pillar* is a history of ratification in New York that provides a good basis for understanding the political context in which *The Federalist* was written. Many historians treat *The Federalist* as a national document; that is, as a series of eighty-five articles written for a national audience and which had a national impact at the time they were published. De Pauw, however, suggests the opposite. She argues convincingly that the essays were local campaign tracts, aimed primarily, if not exclusively, at New York state residents, and she suggests that they had little impact on the outcome of the ratification campaign even there. *The Federalist* essays were printed extensively in the New York City newspapers, but much less frequently beyond the city limits; and if circulation is a measure of political impact, then Anti-Federal tracts such as Richard Henry Lee's *Letters from the Federal Farmer* were probably more effective. Only five hundred copies of the first volume of *The Federalist* were printed and distributed, but Lee's essays, collected into a pamphlet, sold in the thousands.

Beyond New York State, De Pauw points out, *The Federalist* did not circulate widely at all, in spite of the fact that many historians say that it did. In five of the thirteen states (New Jersey, Delaware, North Carolina, South Ca-

337

rolina, and Georgia) no newspaper republications of any of the papers have survived.

De Pauw also points out that however brilliant the essays may be as exercises in political science and the theory and practice of a federal republican government, they were badly designed as political propaganda. They were much too long, much too scholarly, and there were too many of them to appeal to a popular audience—or as one sympathetic critic put it at the time, they were "not well calculated for the common people."

De Pauw argues that *The Federalist* missed the main point of the dispute between New York Federalists and Anti-Federalists over the Constitution. Madison, Hamilton, and Jay assumed their opponents rejected the very idea of a stronger national government, and consequently many of the essays were aimed at establishing the urgent need for such a government. Most New York Anti-Federalists, however, did not reject the notion of a strengthened central government. What concerned them was the need to guarantee that personal freedoms and individual liberty would be secure under the new Constitution, that individual rights would not be carelessly lost in the process of strengthening the government. Consequently, says De Pauw, "Publius" spent most of his time belaboring a point that both Federalists and Anti-Federalists in New York conceded— the need for a strengthened national government. In fact, says De Pauw, in arguing so forcefully for the Constitution, *The Federalist* may have increased opposition to it since some of the papers inflamed, rather than calmed, Anti-Federalist fears about the unchecked power of a central government. *The Federalist No. 9,* for example, written by Hamilton, explained at length how the new order under the Constitution might be used to suppress insurrections like Shays' Rebellion—a revolt of western Massachusetts farmers against high taxes and strict debtor laws during the winter of 1786-1787. The essay awoke traditional Englishmen's fears of a permanent peacetime standing army—fears that had deep roots in English history and in the American revolutionary experience in particular, since the stationing of English troops in the colonies in time of peace was one of the major complaints the colonists leveled against England.

Dietze, Gottfried. *The Federalist: A Classic on Federalism and Free Government.* Baltimore: The Johns Hopkins University Press, 1960.

Unlike Linda De Pauw, Gottfried Dietze examines *The Federalist* more as essays in political science than as campaign tracts or propaganda; he is more concerned with their contribution to Western political thought than in their short-run impact on the ratification campaign. Also in contrast to De Pauw, Dietze argues that the protection of individual liberties and personal freedoms is the main theme of the essays. In fact, the idea that a federal form of government provides strong protection for the individual against the abuses of government was the most important contribution Hamilton, Madison, and Jay made to Western political thought. Federations and federated governments of one sort or another had existed since ancient times, and the three authors were well aware of them. In fact, they studied them in order to understand better the benefits of Federalism and its weaknesses. But the purpose of earlier attempts at Federalism was, says Dietze, to guarantee stability, security, and protection from foreign invasion. Few men in history before Hamilton, Madison, and Jay argued that a federal form of government is uniquely suited to the protection of individual liberties from the oppressions of government.

Dietze by no means ignores the political context in which the papers were written. His book includes two chapters that discuss their historical setting, and he examines at some length the practical experience of the three authors and the way it shaped their thinking and writing. He points out, for example, that Jay's service as a diplomat made him extremely conscious of the need for national unity, particularly in foreign affairs. Thus it shaped and strengthened his nationalism, while Madison's more limited experience as a Virginia legislator and member of Congress made him more aware of the nation's regional differences and less of an ardent nationalist than either Jay or Hamilton. Madison's sharp awareness of just how diverse a nation the United States was is best illustrated by *The Federalist No. 10.*

The particular strength of Dietze's book is that it discusses the way many different influences joined together to guide the authors of *The Federalist.* If their experiences in the American Revolution, and under the Articles of Confederation, made them wary of placing too much power in the hands of the people, their study of history led them to exactly the same conclusions. Their practical experience reinforced what they learned from their research into ancient and modern governments, and their research in turn supported the lessons they drew from experience.

Dietze's book examines the continuing impact of *The Federalist* as well as its origins. He notes that it guided the establishment of several federal governments and the writing of many constitutions during the nineteenth century, particularly in Latin America. He concludes, finally, that the United States today has drifted far away from the kind of government Hamilton, Madison, and Jay recommended. American political thought has strayed far from their healthy skepticism about the dangers of an unchecked government of the majority. The nation, warns Dietze, has lost sight of the need to protect the individual from the encroachments of government, and in particular from the dangers of a tyrannical majority. In short, he concludes that much of the wisdom of *The Federalist* has been, if not rejected, at least forgotten. — *R.A.B.*

Additional Recommended Reading

Cooke, Jacob E., ed. *The Federalist.* Middletown: Wesleyan University Press, 1961. The most dependable recent edition of *The Federalist.* The text of each essay is carefully annotated to explain vague references that might be unclear to modern readers.

Kenyon, Cecelia M., ed. *The Antifederalists.* Indianapolis: Bobbs-Merrill, Co., Inc., 1966. A collection of essays that offers a good selection of the kinds of arguments *The Federalist* was written to refute.

Publication of The Federalist

Miller, John C. *Alexander Hamilton: Portrait in Paradox.* New York: Harper & Row Publishers, 1959. A political biography of the major author of *The Federalist.*

Brant, Irving. *James Madison: Father of the Constitution, 1787-1800.* Indianapolis: Bobbs-Merrill, 1950. Part of a six-volume biography of Madison, this book deals at length with his role at the Constitutional Convention and his efforts to win ratification.

Rutland, Robert A. *The Ordeal of the Constitution: The Antifederalists and the Ratification Struggle of 1787-1788.* Norman: University of Oklahoma Press, 1965. Provides good background for understanding the national context in which *The Federalist* was written.

340

INAUGURATION OF GEORGE WASHINGTON AS FIRST PRESIDENT

Type of event: Constitutional: installation of the first President of the United States
Time: April 30, 1789
Locale: Federal Hall, New York City

Principal personages:
> GEORGE WASHINGTON (1732-1799), first President of the United States 1789-1797
> JOHN ADAMS (1735-1826), Vice-President of the United States under Washington
> ROBERT R. LIVINGSTON (1746-1813), Chancellor of the State of New York, who administered the oath of office
> SAMUEL OTIS (fl.1789), Secretary of the Senate, who held the Bible

Summary of Event

Early on the afternoon of April 30, 1789, George Washington took the oath of office of President of the United States as prescribed by the new Constitution. Standing on a small portico at Federal Hall, New York City, Washington repeated the solemn words administered by Robert Livingston, Chancellor of the State of New York, and then added his own suffix: "So help me God." Bending forward, the first President of the United States kissed the Bible held for him by Samuel Otis, Secretary of the Senate. Livingston then declared, "It is done!" and turning to the multitudes on the rooftops, in the street, and at the windows of Broad and Wall Streets below, he shouted: "Long live George Washington, President of the United States." The crowd roared back, "God bless our President," and the flag was jubilantly raised to the cupola of the great hall while gun salutes and church bells resounded.

The fifty-seven-year-old Washington took office in a newly formed nation of four million citizens living in thirteen states. He came to the Presidency without previous experience in any public executive position other than that of Commander in Chief of the Continental Army. Yet Washington provided the fledgling nation with a simple dignity—the soul and air of a hero-leader. Earnest and sincere, he evoked memories of the victorious American Revolution, and offered unity and confidence to the citizens in their new government. As such, he had been unanimously chosen by the Electoral College under the new Constitution.

The anxieties of war, his labor for the Constitution, his desire for retirement from public life, and his love for his family and his home at Mount Vernon made Washington's decision to accept the presidency a difficult one. He wrote: "My movements to the chair of government will be accompanied by feelings not unlike those of a culprit who is going to the place of his execution, so unwilling am I, in the evening of a life nearly consumed in public

341

cares, to quit a peaceful abode for an ocean of difficulties, without that competency of political skill, abilities and inclination which is necessary to manage the helm."

Thus it was with mixed emotions that Washington set out for New York on April 16, 1789. Acclamations met him on each stage of his journey. In Alexandria, Georgetown, Baltimore, Wilmington, and Philadelphia grateful citizens welcomed their acknowledged leader who traveled by carriage, horseback, and flotilla. One week before his inauguration, Washington arrived at the end of Wall Street by barge from Elizabeth Town Point, New Jersey, to be met by thousands of cheering New Yorkers, a great display of boats and festooned ships, and the loud roar of cannon.

Washington represented for the people who cheered him the last great hope for unity. Wearied by the Revolution and its aftermath, the young nation looked to the new Constitution for the leadership which would set its government in motion and make it endure.

That Washington keenly felt the need for unity was apparent in his inaugural address. After taking the oath of office, the new President entered the Senate Chamber where both houses of Congress and various dignitaries took seats. On the canopied dais with the President were Vice-President John Adams, Chancellor Livingston, and New York Governor George Clinton. President Washington modestly delivered the well-fashioned phrases of his maiden address. In his opening remarks he spoke of his inner conflict, his consciousness of his "inferior endow-

ments," and his lack of experience "in the duties of civil administration." He paid homage to God whose provident hand had guided the people through their struggles and deliberation. Recognizing his duty under the Constitution to make recommendations to Congress, he expressed his trust that the legislators would rise above "local pledges or . . . attachments" and "petty animosities." In the only specific suggestion of the address, Washington urged Congress to quell "inquietude" by deciding to what extent it would advocate Constitutional amendments. He expressed confidence in Congress' ultimate wisdom in "pursuit of the public good." Washington concluded on the theme of unity, trusting that God had "been pleased to favor the American people, with opportunities for deliberating in perfect tranquillity, and dispositions for deciding with unparalleled unanimity on a form of government for the security of their Union and the advancement of their happiness; so his divine blessing may be equally conspicuous in the enlarged views, the temperate consultations and the wise measures on which the success of this Government must depend."

From Federal Hall the President walked triumphantly with Congressmen and guests through streets lined with militia to services at St. Paul's Chapel. That day, Washington believed, was the consummation of the Revolution. The "experiment should have a fair trial," and the new President "would lose the last drop of his blood in support of it." Thus Washington and the American people set out on a venture of hope and trust.

Pertinent Literature

Freeman, Douglas Southall. *George Washington: A Biography*. Vol. VI: *Patriot and President*. New York: Charles Scribner's Sons, 1954.

Douglas Southall Freeman, author of four volumes on Robert E. Lee, three volumes on Lee's lieutenants, and many more, wrote his final words in this book. Freeman died within a few hours after completing the draft of the final chapter in the sixth volume of what was to have been a seven-volume biography of Washington. Two associates of Freeman's, John Alexander Carroll and Mary Wells Ashworth, completed the final volume in 1957. The work is exhaustive. Freeman's attention to detail and his devotion to history for history's sake render this biography definitive. The writing style is masterful, well-paced, and dramatic. These seven volumes should stand for some time to come as the standard biography of Washington.

Freeman devotes considerable attention in Volume VI to Washington's inauguration. He shares Washington's belief that the Constitution was a momentous achievement which saved the new nation from chaos and disintegration. Thus the origins of the new experiment are important. Freeman emphasizes Washington's reluctance to undertake the presidency. The decision once made, however, Freeman's Washington carries out his expected role as no one else could have done. The inaugural event nevertheless had drama. Freeman recaptures the tenuous nature of the moment. At the center of the stage is Washington. He is grand enough to inspire awe for his office and government. He is unpretentious enough to befit the leader of a republic. Thus Freeman displays the essential enigma of Washington in describing the inauguration. The President is both heroic and human. Washington on the day of his inauguration wore stockings of the finest imported silk but a plain brown suit manufactured in Connecticut. Thus in Freeman's eyes, Washington is both charismatic and common at the same time.

These interpretations are well woven into the narrative which dominates Freeman's work. The richness of detail is the product of copious research combined with ingenious technique. For example, Freeman calculates the time that the inauguration took, based upon an average reading speed of one hundred words per minute and the number of words in Washington's address. The book is a detailed, interpretive study of Washington by a biographer at home with his subject.

Miller, John C. *The Federalist Era, 1789-1801*. *New American Nation* series. New York: Harper & Row Publishers, 1960.

The Federalist Era is a volume in the prestigious *New American Nation* series, and John C. Miller is well-qualified to write it. The book deals with the period of Federalist ascendancy in American politics, the Washington and John Adams Administrations. It is a balanced, judicious summary of the origins of the United States government under the Constitution.

Miller does not regard Washington as being especially adroit politically.

Yet Washington is ever the leader, always in command of the situation. He, to some extent like the other Federalists, misgauged the basically democratic sentiments of the American people, but Washington was scrupulous about his use of power and in sympathy with both the spirit and the letter of the new Constitution.

The inauguration of Washington is given only a few pages in Miller's summary, but Miller captures the mood of expectancy and concern surrounding the event. He emphasizes Washington's agitation and embarrassment as well as the petty problems dwelt upon by lesser men. For example, Miller writes in detail about the controversy as to how the President should be addressed. Vice-President John Adams and others insisted that Washington have a title, such as "His Elective Highness." The new President, however, saw the squabble over title as a threat to his popularity and the essentials of a republican form of government. Thus Washington adopted "Mister President" or "President," and allowed the "monarchists" to fume in private.

Miller holds that however tenuous was the "Great Experiment," Washington's "renown, prestige, and ability offered the best guarantee of its success." Thus Washington stood above the hordes of office-seekers who plagued him and the pettiness of officeholders who often embarrassed him. Miller presents the first President as an aloof yet austere leader who maintained his dignity by keeping people "at arm's length." Washington adopted an elaborate set of rules governing "official society" and adorned simple republican institutions with enough pomp to alarm the more doctrinaire democrats. But Miller's Washington remains a plain man whose regality of person and presidential "style" lent much needed substance to the new government. — *E.M.T.*

Additional Recommended Reading

Stephenson, G. W. and W. H. Dunn. *George Washington.* 2 vols. New York: Oxford University Press, 1940. A good brief biography of Washington.

Cunliffe, Marcus. *George Washington: Man and Monument.* Boston: Little, Brown, and Company, 1958. Cunliffe is less sympathetic toward Washington than most biographers, which makes reading of this work necessary for a well-rounded view of the first President.

Chinard, Gilbert. *Honest John Adams.* Boston: Little, Brown, and Company, 1933. The standard biography of the first Vice-President.

Schachner, Nathan. *The Founding Fathers.* New York: G. P. Putnam's Sons, 1954. A good sympathetic summary of the Federalist Administration.

Dos Passos, John. *The Men Who Made the Nation.* New York: Doubleday and Company, Inc., 1957. Essentially a popular rather than a scholarly work.

PASSAGE OF THE JUDICIARY ACT

Type of event: Legal: establishment of the Federal Court System
Time: September 24, 1789
Locale: New York City

Principal personages:

GEORGE WASHINGTON (1732-1799), first President of the United States 1789-1797

JOHN JAY (1745-1829), of New York, first Chief Justice of the United States 1789-1795

OLIVER ELLSWORTH (1745-1807), United States Senator from Connecticut, second Chief Justice of the United States 1796-1799

JOHN RUTLEDGE (1739-1800), of South Carolina, acting Chief Justice of the United States whose nomination the Senate refused to confirm

JAMES WILSON (1742-1798), of Pennsylvania, Associate Justice of the United States 1789-1798

Summary of Event

The Constitution of the United States created the basic framework for a government. It remained for the First Congress, meeting in New York in April, 1789, to implement the document. Few Congresses have been of greater importance than the first. Virtually every act set a precedent. The vagueness of the Constitution added to the significance of congressional activity. The document contained many vague clauses and unanswered questions regarding the powers and responsibilities of the various branches of the federal government. These so-called "Silences of the Constitution" left Congress with much discretionary power and included the power of removal of the President, executive power over foreign affairs, the extent of the treaty-making power, and the problem of judicial authority.

The Constitution, in Article III, Sections 1 and 2, provided for an independent judiciary to consist of a Supreme Court and inferior courts. The general jurisdiction of the court system was defined in Section 2. The Constitution did not deal with the question of judicial review—the power of the federal courts to determine the constitutionality of both federal and state legislation. Nor did the Constitution address itself to the responsibility of the federal courts to interpret the meaning of the Constitution.

In the Philadelphia Convention it appears that most members agreed that the judiciary should possess the power to determine the constitutionality of legislation but that they did not intend that the courts should have the power to interpret the document. Neither question was settled with any certainty and much was left to the discretion of Congress.

The members of the First Congress were uncertain as to the proper relationship between the federal courts which they were to create and the al-

345

ready functioning state systems. Even though most of the Congressmen had been ardent supporters of ratification of the Constitution, and therefore nationalist in sentiment, they were fearful that too powerful a federal judiciary would invade the rights of the states. The Judiciary Act of 1789 was a compromise between those who desired a truly national court system and those fearful for the integrity of the state courts.

The Judiciary Act created a Supreme Court, three circuit courts, thirteen district courts, and the office of Attorney General. The state courts were given a limited concurrent jurisdiction with the national courts; that is, cases arising under the Constitution, laws, and treaties of the United States were first heard in the state courts. But the nationalists achieved a significant victory in providing, in Section 25 of the Judiciary Act, for appeals from the state courts to federal courts in all instances where it could be shown that the state courts had failed to give full recognition to the United States Constitution, federal laws, or treaties to which the United States was a party—these three constituting the supreme law of the land according to the Constitution. This appellate jurisdiction implied the power of the federal courts to review the constitutionality of state and federal legislation. In later years a great controversy arose over the constitutionality of Section 25 of the Judiciary Act.

The influence and prestige of the Supreme Court grew slowly during the first decade of its existence. Precedents were established which defined the powers of the Court and its relationship with other branches of the government. In one instance, President George Washington requested that the Court advise him concerning certain questions of international law. The Court declined to involve itself in extrajudicial or nonjudicial matters. This firmly established the separate and independent existence of the Supreme Court.

In certain decisions, the Supreme Court did assume the power of judicial review. In *Ware* v. *Hylton* (1796) the Supreme Court invalidated a Virginia statute sequestering the pre-Revolutionary War debts of British creditors. These debts were guaranteed by the Treaty of Paris, made in 1783. According to the Constitution, treaties were part of the supreme law of the land and therefore superior to state laws. In *Hylton* v. *United States* (1796), upholding a Virginia law taxing carriages, the Court not only applied the power of judicial review, but in deciding whether this tax was direct or indirect, the Court interpreted the Constitution. The lower federal courts were also involved in reviewing state laws.

The decision in the case of *Ware* v. *Hylton* aroused considerable opposition to the Supreme Court from the Republican Party, which accused the Court of being pro-British. Even more serious opposition was engendered by the decision in *Chisholm* v. *Georgia* (1793). In that case, two citizens of South Carolina, as agents for a British subject, brought suit in the Supreme Court for the recovery of confiscated property. The Court found in favor of the British creditor. Opponents of this decision immediately launched a campaign to curtail the power of the Supreme Court. The result was the Eleventh Amendment, ratified in 1798, which denied to the Court the authority to decide cases "commenced or prosecuted against one of the United States by Citizens of another State, or by Citizens or Subjects of any Foreign State." States could not be brought into federal courts to be sued without their consent.

In spite of the Eleventh Amendment the Supreme Court was firmly established by 1800. The Supreme Court, under the dynamic leadership of Chief Justice John Marshall of Virginia, survived an attack of the Republican Party on its independence during the Jefferson Administration and became the most effective force for nationalism in the federal government.

Pertinent Literature

Haines, Charles G. *The Role of the Supreme Court in American Government and Politics, 1789-1835.* Berkeley: University of California Press, 1944.

This exhaustive study of the role of the Supreme Court in the development of the American nation during its formative years is especially concerned with pointing out those areas in which the Court played a political role and influenced political evolution. The author recognizes as a fundamental principle that judges, in interpreting and applying the Constitution, both at the state and federal levels, "must of necessity participate in the process of legislation." To insist, as some constitutional historians and jurists do, that judges must always avoid interfering with political processes is to insist that judges stop functioning.

Haines maintains that the Supreme Court has been an important political agency from the time of its establishment to the present. The first two Presidents, George Washington and John Adams, started the trend of constitutional development along party lines with their appointment of Federalists to judicial offices under both the first and second Judiciary Acts, the second being a reorganizing act passed in 1801 and repealed by the Republicans in 1802. It is obvious to the author that the Federalists used the courts to put into effect their political doctrines of judicial review of legislation, national supremacy over states' rights, and the protection of property from disturbing legislative attack. All this was accomplished under the direction of Chief Justice John Marshall, who molded constitutional law to fit his own political principles.

The political designs of the Federalists did not succeed without challenge by the partisans of states' rights and localism. Moreover, localists were able to associate their attack on the Court with democracy while accusing the Federalists of aristocratic tendencies. The Federalists were successful in warding off the attacks of the Jeffersonians during the period of Marshall's Chief Justiceship. Marshall's brand of "judicial nationalism," although partially diluted by his successor, Roger B. Taney of Maryland, won ultimate acceptance. Moreover, with appointment to the bench of Justices in sympathy with the Jacksonians, the Court quickly regained its prestige and captured a measure of popularity. "The impression was gaining ground that the Supreme Court was a protecting agency that would stand between the people and their governments and in its interpretation and application of the

Constitution would carry out the people's will."

Warren, Charles. "New Light on the History of the Federal Judiciary Act of 1789," in *Harvard Law Review,* XXXVII, No. 1 (November, 1923), 49-132.

Professor Charles Warren's analysis of the background of the passage of the Judiciary Act of 1789 is the most thorough examination of that subject in print. Warren was able to uncover original drafts and amendments of the judiciary bill hidden away in the attic and cellar of the Capitol. Relying on these and on contemporary accounts, he was able to reconstruct the legislative history of the bill. It is his thesis that if the history of the passage of the bill had been known to the generations that followed, it is very probable that certain fundamental Supreme Court decisions would have been different. This is especially true since many of the framers of the act had served in the Constitutional Convention or had participated in the formulation of the Bill of Rights.

Warren points out that the Judiciary Act, as finally passed, was a compromise measure. "Its provisions completely satisfied no one, though they pleased the Anti-Federalists more than the Federalists." The final form of the act was also dependent upon the fate of the sundry amendments to the judiciary article of the Constitution which were being debated in Congress at the very same time. The relationship between the Judiciary Act and the amendments, which were later to emerge as the Bill of Rights, was so close that the act was not signed by President Washington until September 24, 1789, the same day that Congress finally agreed on the final form of the amendments to the Constitution which

were to be submitted to the States.

Four vital changes which were made in the draft of the bill were examined in depth by Professor Warren. He believes his analysis proves that United States district and circuit courts were intended to have jurisdiction over common law crimes, and not only over crimes specifically defined by Congress. Second, the author holds that the jurisdiction of the circuit courts in controversies between citizens of different states was made far more restrictive than the draft bill intended. Third, he feels it is surprising that the draft bill did not contain the much litigated Section 34 of the act, which states that "the laws of the several States, except where the Constitution, treaties or statutes of the United States shall otherwise require or provide, shall be regarded as rules of decision in trials at common law in the Courts of the United States, in cases where they apply." This, he demonstrates, was added as a Senate amendment. Fourth, he writes that it is of even greater significance that the word "laws" in Section 34 was intended to include the common law of the State as well as its statute law. The greater part of the essay was devoted to a discussion of these four points.

Although the prevailing sentiment in modern times has been that the Judiciary Act of 1789 was one of the most important and satisfactory acts ever passed by Congress, Warren points out that "such was not the opinion of this statute during the first fifty years after its passage." Yet, despite some *caveats* with the way in which the act has been interpreted, he believes that it has worked well. Its greatest shortcoming, he thinks, was the framers' "neglect to make any provisions regarding jurisdiction as to corporations." Furthermore, it is averred that the act as first passed was superior to the act as it was later amended. For example, he thinks that it might be advisable to return to the original Judiciary Act and thus cut down on the jurisdiction of the inferior federal courts. Likewise, he recommends that "cases arising under the Federal laws and Constitution might now be left to come to the Supreme Court of the United States through the State Courts," instead of having to pass through the federal courts. He also suggests that "it might be wise to return to the original practice of making many Federal statutes enforceable by the State Courts," and thereby help relieve the congestion of the dockets. Professor Warren closes his essay by stating: "It is in its bearing on these phases of the law of Federal jurisdiction that a close study of the Judiciary Act of 1789 is worth the while of all students of our peculiar Federal system." — *J.G.C.*

Additional Recommended Reading

Brown, William G. *The Life of Oliver Ellsworth.* New York: The Macmillan Company, 1905. The only biography of a powerful Federalist leader who was United States Senator from Connecticut and Chief Justice of the United States.

Corwin, Edward S. *The Doctrine of Judicial Review.* Princeton: Princeton University Press, 1914. A classic study, by one of the foremost students of the Constitution, of the intent of the Founding Fathers regarding judicial review.

Warren, Charles. *The Supreme Court in United States History.* 3 vols. Boston: Little, Brown, and Company, 1923. The best scholarly work on the evolution of the Court.

Haines, Charles G. *The American Doctrine of Judicial Supremacy.* 2nd ed. Berkeley: University of California Press, 1932. The author finds the origins of judicial review in various European theoretical concepts and in the working of the colonial courts; he then traces its evolution and significance in the United States.

Barry, Richard H. *Mister Rutledge of South Carolina.* New York: Duell, Sloan and Pierce, 1942. Rutledge was a major figure in the Revolutionary War, a wealthy planter, a powerful factor in South Carolina politics, and for a short time Chief Justice of the United States.

McCloskey, Robert G. *The American Supreme Court.* Chicago: The University of Chicago Press, 1960. An excellent historical synthesis of the Supreme Court as it exercised the power of judicial review.

Smith, Charles P. *James Wilson: Founding Father, 1742-1798.* Chapel Hill: University of North Carolina Press, 1956. The biography of a man who was important in shaping the Constitution, and who, as an Associate Justice of the United States, played an important role in the defense of national supremacy in the early days of the Court's existence.

EMERGENCE OF THE FIRST POLITICAL PARTIES

Type of event: Political: development of American form of representative government
Time: 1790's
Locale: Philadelphia, Pennsylvania

Principal personages:

GEORGE WASHINGTON (1732-1799), first President of the United States 1789-1797

ALEXANDER HAMILTON (1757-1804), Secretary of the Treasury 1789-1795

THOMAS JEFFERSON (1743-1826), Secretary of State 1790-1793, Vice-President 1797-1801, President 1801-1809

JOHN ADAMS (1735-1826), Vice-President 1789-1797, President 1797-1801

ALBERT GALLATIN (1761-1849), Congressman from Pennsylvania and Republican leader

JAMES MADISON (1751-1836), Congressman from Virginia and Republican leader, President 1809-1817

TIMOTHY PICKERING (1745-1829), Secretary of State under Washington and Adams 1795-1800

FISHER AMES (1758-1808), Congressman from Massachusetts and Federalist leader

JOHN BECKLEY (fl. 1799), Republican organizer and leader in Pennsylvania

AARON BURR (1756-1836), Republican organizer in New York, Vice-President 1801-1805

Summary of Event

The Founding Fathers did not anticipate the development of political parties in the United States, and the Constitution made no provision for them. James Madison, in writing *The Federalist No. 10,* discussed factions (parties) in detail and considered them to be a disease in the body politic. Madison feared the rise of factions, stating: "When a majority is included in a faction, the form of popular government . . . enables it to sacrifice to its ruling passion or interest both the public good and the rights of other citizens." He clearly believed that parties were sources of turbulence, oppression, and corruption. Madison argued that one of the blessings of the Constitution would be its applicability to the control of factions. He believed that a federal and representative form of government operating in a country of vast size would make it impossible for permanent majorities to form. Ironically, within four years, Madison became the congressional leader of one of the two political parties contending for power in the United States.

Parties arose in the United States in response to the economic and foreign policies of the Washington Administration. By the end of the debate over

350

Jay's Treaty, parties were operating. In tracing their origin it is necessary to begin with the debate over ratification of the Constitution.

Although there are certain exceptions, the men who supported ratification of the Constitution generally became Federalists, and those who opposed the Constitution became Republicans. The most important exception was Madison himself, the "father of the Constitution," and also a founder of the Republican Party. Patrick Henry, who opposed the Constitution, became a firm Federalist during the Washington Administration. For the most part, Washington appointed men who had strongly advocated ratification, while congressional support for Washington's programs derived from the same source.

The debates over Hamilton's economic programs provided the first serious indication that a strong and vocal opposition existed in Congress. The nucleus for a party was to be found in this opposition, composed mainly of men from the South. Madison opposed the funding of the national debt, the assumption by the federal government of the states' war debts, and the creation of a national bank for two reasons: the legislation favored the North more than the South; and since the power to charter the Bank was not one of the enumerated powers of Congress in the Constitution, it was therefore unconstitutional. Madison and others were able to unite their sectional fears with strict construction of the Constitution into a general states' rights philosophy which became the ideological arm of the Republican Party. But at this stage of development, while factions existed in Congress supporting or opposing

Hamilton's program, parties in a national sense did not exist.

Further progress in the organization of parties at the national level and the growth of support at the local level came basically from two causes: implementation and funding Hamilton's program; and divisions arising from the outbreak of the French Revolution and the French Revolutionary wars.

Paying off the national debt placed an enormous burden on the nation, requiring a tax policy which caused complaints. In particular, the excise tax on whiskey sparked a small uprising in western Pennsylvania. Troops were sent in to crush the rioting, men were arrested, and popular indignation drew many into opposition to Washington's Administration. The government was criticized as oppressing the poor to aid the rich. These domestic tensions were coupled with differences that appeared as the French Revolution emerged in Europe and soon plunged the Continent into war. Americans, while basically neutral, openly expressed preferences for either the French or the British.

Many Americans immediately experienced a psychological association with the idealism of the French Revolution. Others, more conservative, looked to Great Britain as the last bulwark between stability and order and the turbulence of the democratic masses. Hamilton, for example, was outspoken in his preference for Great Britain and his abhorrence of the French Revolution. Jefferson, on the other hand, was openly pro-French in sympathy. The coincidence of his opposition to Hamilton's economic policies, of his attitudes towards the French Revolution, and of his sectional

351

residence, was striking. New Englanders were generally pro-British and pro-Hamilton. Southerners were generally pro-French and anti-Hamilton. In the Middle states, where sectional feeling was less strong, the division was often East-West rather than North-South. Men from western Pennsylvania, such as Albert Gallatin, fell into the anti-Administration ranks, as did western New Yorkers, while the seaboard was pro-administration. The divisions were much less clear-cut, however, in the Middle states than in the South or in New England.

Jay's Treaty was the catalyst of party formation. All the elements were present. A momentous issue was necessary for the bonding. The reaction to the treaty was sharp and violent. Widespread opposition appeared at both national and local levels. The debate raged in the year prior to the Presidential election. Washington's decision to step down provided the opportunity for men opposed to his administration to gather their forces in an effort to replace those in power. Opposition to the great Washington was dangerous and almost impossible, but John Adams presented no such problems. In 1796, Thomas Jefferson, running as a Republican, contested with Adams for the nation's first position. Parties were formed but, as the next four years would prove, their permanency was not guaranteed. A two-party system was not yet customary, and there were men in power who preferred the existence of a single party—the party to which they belonged.

Pertinent Literature

Cunningham, Noble E., Jr. *The Jeffersonian Republicans: The Formation of Party Organization, 1789-1801.* Chapel Hill: University of North Carolina Press for the Institute of Early American History and Culture, 1957.

In this study of the formation of the Republican Party from 1789 to 1801, Noble Cunningham, using a methodology which stresses party machinery and procedures, has helped pioneer a new method of studying the history of political parties. What Cunningham proposes to do, and largely does, is to study the formation of the Party's machinery from its nebulous beginnings in the congressional opposition to Hamilton's financial program through its development into a mature and responsible party by the Election of 1800. To show this development, Cunningham uses a chronological organization which notes the changes in leadership, nomination, election, and other party procedures which occurred during the period he is considering. After detailing this development of party machinery, he is able to formulate some important new conclusions concerning its development.

Parties first appeared, Cunningham contends, in the Second Congress (1791-1792), when a rather consistent cleavage in congressional voting patterns became evident for the first time. The election of 1792 revealed the very rudimentary level of these parties, however, because nominations were outside their control and campaigning was still handled by a candidate's personal following. In 1793 popular associations which were Republican in character began to emerge, and though they lasted only a short time, the same year saw the beginning of James Madison's congressional leadership of the Republican faction. Cunningham states that in three years, Madison laid the groundwork for party organization. By the Election of 1796, the Republicans attempted a congressional caucus to nominate a vice-president, and several state party tickets were framed at these party meetings; nominations were becoming a party and not a personal matter. Despite setbacks during the Adams Administration, the Republicans under Vice-President Jefferson began early to prepare for the 1800 election. They developed party machinery in the states, and their congressional caucus nominating Jefferson and Burr was successful. They established partisan newspapers and made use of such procedures as the canvass and actual electioneering. They even presented a platform—varying its emphasis to appeal to each area of the electorate. Clearly, their party machinery had developed greatly since 1796, and the fact that Jefferson and Burr tied in the voting attests to the responsibility and discipline the Republicans had achieved by 1800.

After presenting this narrative of Republican organizational development, Cunningham arrives at several new and related conclusions concerning the formation of the party. He contends that the Republican Party was a new entity, springing from the divisions in Congress. It was a product of national politics and was not the outgrowth of a confederation of state parties as some historians have suggested. Furthermore, this party growth was a process of gradual development, not a sudden joining of existing state parties. Cunningham stresses the importance of party development beginning on a national level; it was here that the early signs of party development were most noticeable. Parties began by endorsing congressional candidates, and later they were able to support state candidates. The Congressmen were the first real party men, and their caucuses and "conventions" were the first real party meetings. Thus, for Cunningham, the Republican Party was a national party first—and only after gaining national development did it expand to the state and local levels.

Insofar as criticism can be leveled at Cunningham's work, perhaps the most significant is that of Stephen G. Kurtz in the *William and Mary Quarterly.* Kurtz questions the validity of using the early roll calls to show factional cleavages in Congress, and he feels that the discipline achieved by the Republicans in 1800 was not caused by party machinery as Cunningham suggests, but by the bitterness which the Republicans felt toward the "highhanded Federalist measures" of the Adams Administration. Generally, however, Cunningham's book is regarded as an essential work in the study of the development of political parties.

Chambers, William N. *Political Parties in a New Nation: The American Experience, 1776-1809.* New York: Oxford University Press, 1963.

One of the most significant developments of the past several decades has been the rise of new nations in various parts of the world, each of which has arisen out of a colonial past of some duration. In seeking to find political stability and identity, these underdeveloped countries have frequently attempted to organize their political structures along the lines of the more advanced Western nations. Typically the constitutions of these countries provide for a two-house legislature or parliament, an executive responsible to both the legislature and the electorate, and a party system. Chambers, in studying the origin of parties in the United States, seeks to discover some general truths concerning the nature of party formation which might be useful in understanding the difficulties facing the emergent nations of the world. Chambers considers the United States as the first modern emergent nation and the parties which developed as forming the first party system in the modern world.

Chambers defines political parties as "broadly based social structures that perform crucial political functions in a regularized manner." He discovers that according to this definition, parties existed in the United States before they did in Great Britain despite Great Britain's longer tradition of representative government. While there were many obstacles to party formation in the United States—cultural pluralism, lack of precedent, doubts about the wisdom of parties, and state-oriented politics—political leaders in the United States were faced with a growing electorate. Parties proved convenient devices to deal with the electorate.

American parties developed out of factions during the 1790's in response to opposition to the policies of Alexander Hamilton and over foreign policy issues. The Federalists were the first to form due to the coherent program offered by Hamilton. The Republicans, while their origins may be traced to attitudes about the Constitu-

tion, were little more than a congressional faction until the French Revolutionary wars injected world politics into the political arena. Chambers concludes that it was Jay's Treaty that transformed a Republican movement into a Republican Party. In the debate over that treaty, the Republicans achieved a remarkable degree of party unity, as did the Federalists. The treaty was debated both in and out of Congress in intensely partisan terms.

The party of Jefferson was, as Chambers describes it, a new political engine, the first of its kind in modern history. The Republican outlook, or party line, developed in terms of leaders acting on, and interacting with, their following. In this sense the Republicans went far beyond the Federalists who were less interested in popular political participation than in manipulating and molding the views of a passive electorate.

Chambers judges the maturity of the American party structure by measuring it according to several general party functions: (1) nominating candidates, (2) electioneering, (3) shaping opinion, (4) mediating among groups to find a formula for agreement and party unity, (5) managing the government, and (6) providing a connection between the branches of government. The Republicans came close to fulfilling these functions as they passed from opposition to power. In the Election of 1796 both parties nominated candidates, but the Republicans (even though they lost) were more energetic in electioneering and shaping opinion. Chambers sees the activity of Republicans in Pennsylvania as particularly mature and skillful.

The United States, unlike many contemporary emergent nations, was possessed of several advantages which hastened party development. The American social structure was more individualistic, less aristocratic, and more egalitarian. Suffrage in the United States was extensive. The United States had a high and rising standard of living and education. These factors called forth a new kind of politician to organize political society. The most efficient method was a party system. — *J.G.C.*

Additional Recommended Reading

Brant, Irving. *James Madison: Father of the Constitution, 1787-1800.* 6 vols. Indianapolis: The Bobbs-Merrill Company, 1950. In this portion of his six-volume work on Madison, Brant treats Madison's role in the Constitutional Convention and then follows his career as he became the founder of a political party.

Brown, Stuart G. *The First Republicans: Political Philosophy and Public Policy in the Party of Jefferson and Madison.* Syracuse: Syracuse University Press, 1954. An interesting but short attempt to relate Jeffersonian theory and practice.

Binkley, Wilfred E. *American Political Parties: Their Natural History.* 4th ed., enlarged. New York: Alfred A. Knopf, Inc., 1962. A chronological account of the development of political parties from the Federalists to contemporary Republicans and Democrats.

McCormick, Richard P. *The Second American Party System: Party Formation in the Jacksonian Era.* Chapel Hill: University of North Carolina Press, 1966. McCormick investigates, in a state-by-state analysis, the period of party formation following the disintegration of the first system which evolved in the 1790's.

White, Leonard D. *The Federalists: A Study in Administrative History.* New York: The Macmillan Company, 1948. White believes that the Federalists made many positive contributions to the development of our early governmental structure.

ISSUANCE OF ALEXANDER HAMILTON'S *REPORT ON PUBLIC CREDIT*

Type of event: Political: assumption of the public debt
Time: January-August, 1790
Locale: Philadelphia

Principal personages:

GEORGE WASHINGTON (1732-1799), first President of the United States 1789-1797

ALEXANDER HAMILTON (1757-1804), Secretary of the Treasury 1789-1795

JAMES MADISON (1751-1836), Congressman from Virginia

THOMAS JEFFERSON (1743-1826), Secretary of State 1790-1793

ROBERT MORRIS (1734-1806), Congressman from Pennsylvania, financier and speculator

WILLIAM DUER (1747-1799), Assistant Secretary of the Treasury

FISHER AMES (1758-1808), Congressman from Massachusetts

JAMES JACKSON (fl. 1790), Congressman from Georgia

Summary of Event

On September 21, 1789, the House of Representatives of the First Congress of the United States passed a resolution instructing the Secretary of the Treasury to "prepare a proper plan for the support of the Public Credit." Shouldering this responsibility and opportunity, Secretary of the Treasury Alexander Hamilton submitted his plan in January, 1790. The *Report on Public Credit* touched off a vigorous congressional debate and, as the opposition to the legislative recommendations contained in the report became clear, the first faint outlines of a two-party system became apparent.

The *Report on Public Credit* was the first of three classic reports emanating from the fertile mind of Hamilton. In December, 1790, he submitted his *Report on a National Bank*, followed one year later by the *Report on Manufactures*. Taken together, the reports outlined a comprehensive system of economic nationalism.

Of the three reports, the *Report on Public Credit* was most significant. It was crucial that the new government take steps to secure the debt contracted since the Revolutionary War, which amounted, according to Hamilton's calculations, to seventy-seven million dollars. This included a state debt of twenty-five million dollars and interest in arrears of over fourteen million dollars. The funding and assumption of this enormous amount would serve several purposes, according to Hamilton. If the debt were gathered together as the sole responsibility of the federal government, the credit of the nation would be restored at home and abroad. As capital came out of hiding, interest rates would be lowered. With lower interest rates, investments in land, commerce, and industry would increase, and capital would multiply along with wages and jobs. In addition, Hamilton anticipated that his policy would secure the allegiance of the monied classes to the federal government. All that would then be required was a national bank to provide internal control of finances and national programs to stimulate commerce and industry within the nation. With such things accomplished, Hamilton theorized, economic dominance would soon pass from Great Britain to the United States —as indeed it did, but not for another one hundred and twenty years.

Hamilton's credit proposals ran into immediate opposition in Congress. Leading the opposition was Hamilton's former comrade in arms, James Madison of Virginia. There was no opposition to the funding and assumption of the foreign debt amounting to $11,700,000. It was also agreed that the debt contracted by the Continental Congress and Confederation should be assumed and funded. But there was considerable debate over Hamilton's proposal to pay off the holders of this debt at its full specie value. There had been much speculation in this debt, and by 1790 few of the original owners retained any portion of the securities. Speculators had purchased the debt at greatly depreciated prices, and, if Hamilton's proposal was carried, they stood to turn a monumental profit on their investment. Soon members of Congress, such as Madison, believed that some portion of this windfall should go to the original owners. The Secretary of the Treasury rejected this idea, arguing that such discrimination violated the rights of fair purchase and was equivalent to a breach of the public faith. Hamilton had his way.

Hamilton's plan for the assumption of states' debts encountered even more strenuous opposition. The South was especially hostile because many of the Southern states had made substantial progress in meeting their financial obligations. New England was favorable and owed the largest portion of the states' collective debt. Southerners charged that a large portion of the unpaid debt of the Southern states was in the hands of the Northerners. For the states of Virginia, North Carolina, and South Carolina, it has been estimated that nonresident owners, largely Northern, held fifty-three percent of the total combined debt. Not only would the South pay more than its proper share, Madison argued, but the actual payments would also be largely in the North.

Such was the opposition that Hamilton's measures suffered four successive defeats in Congress. Hamilton seemed to be checked. But then occurred one of the classic political deals of American history. Hamilton made an arrangement with Thomas Jefferson, Secretary of State, whereby Hamilton agreed to support a national capital on the Potomac river. Jefferson in turn promised to use his influence to secure Madison's support of the Funding and Assumption Bill. Jefferson succeeded, and the two Virginians managed to influence enough Southern Congressmen to allow the enactment, by a narrow margin, of Hamilton's proposal into legislation. The nation had shouldered a great burden. The government was compelled to expend eighty percent of its annual revenues to service the debt. Payment of the interest alone consumed over forty percent of the national revenue.

The arrangement between Hamilton and the two Virginians was the last significant act of coöperation between them. Thereafter, Jefferson and Madison drifted farther away from the Washington Administration. Within a year, Jefferson and Hamilton were engaged in a debate without hope of compromise over the constitutionality of the First Bank of the United States. The French Revolution and the question of the proper relationship of the United States to the First French Republic widened the division, which became an unbridgeable gulf with the outbreak of the Anglo-French War of 1793. While both men cherished visions of the future greatness of the United States, the substance of this greatness and the means by which it would be achieved constituted a difference between the two men that they believed irreconcilable.

Pertinent Literature

Beard, Charles A. *Economic Origins of Jeffersonian Democracy.* New York: The Macmillan Company, 1915.

This study is, in a sense, a sequel to the author's highly controversial *An Economic Interpretation of the Constitution of the United States* (New York: The Macmillan Company, 1913 and 1935). In this study of the framing of the Constitution, Beard maintains that the security-holding members of the Philadelphia Convention created a document designed to protect personal property. Having done so, the Founding Fathers foisted their idea of a constitution upon an unsuspecting public in which large numbers of men were disfranchised by various undemocratic suffrage qualifications. The Constitution was the result of a conspiracy. Beard's economic orientation necessarily leads him to the assumption that Hamilton's measures were implicit in the Constitution and that the Constitution did not really go into effect until the economic measures "which its adoption implied were put upon the statute books and carried into execution."

Beard's study is centered around the theme that the Federalists, representing commercial capitalism and composed largely of men who had supported the Constitution, engaged in a basically economic struggle with the Republicans, representing agrarian interests and composed of men who had generally opposed ratification. Needless to say, the "father of the Constitution," James Madison, was an exception to this general rule, as was Patrick Henry. In short, the struggle was one in which the financial, commercial, and industrial classes were pitted against the agricultural classes. The former were dominant in the North and the latter in the South. Thus, the sectional division was a factor of basically economic differences between the sections.

Hamilton's economic program was designed to produce immediate benefits to holders of public securities and to capitalists in general. His measures contained a distinct bid to the financial, commercial, and manufacturing classes to give their confidence and support to the government in return for a policy calculated to advance their interests. The agrarian forces resisted this class legislation by attacking the whole process of capitalistic inflation and expansion. Their spokesmen were seeking a just discharge of the debt, not the augmentation of fluid capital already concentrated in the urban areas of the North. Representative James Jackson of Georgia was unable to see how the people would benefit by taxing themselves to maintain a large funded debt. The agrarian party marshaled similar arguments against the Bank and Federalist tax measures. In a chapter on the economics of Jay's Treaty, Beard sees obvious economic interests in the desire of capitalists to reach a settlement with Great Britain.

Beard does not equate the agrarian party with democracy. The leadership of the agrarians, including Jefferson, was generally suspicious of too much power lodged in the majority. But even if this were so, the planter aristocrats, in opposing the use of the central government for the benefit of capitalist groups in the North, were forwarding the interests of the agrarian masses. Jefferson and his followers appealed directly to those masses whose response carried Jefferson to power in 1800. "The wonder is," concludes Beard, "that the small compact group of capitalists were able to hold the reins of power for so long a period in a country predominantly agrarian." The "wonder" would have been less had Beard considered the possibility that Federalist successes in diplomacy and in stabilizing the economy of the nation produced certain tangible benefits to the farmer. When these benefits became negligible because of increased taxes to support a military establishment during a time of peace, enough voters switched parties to carry Jefferson to the Presidency in 1800.

Mitchell, Broadus. *Alexander Hamilton.* Vol. I: *Youth to Maturity, 1755-1788.* New York: The Macmillan Company, 1957.

Mitchell, Broadus. *Alexander Hamilton.* Vol. II: *The National Adventure, 1788-1804.* New York: The Macmillan Company, 1962.

These volumes give an account of Hamilton's life from his West Indian birth through his fatal duel at Weehawken, New Jersey, in 1804. There is no doubt where Mitchell stands in assessing the net worth of his subject, whom he describes as "an architect of the new nation." There is no doubt that Hamilton was indeed a major, if not the major, influence in the early days of the American Republic.

It is difficult to write about a man of such brilliance, industry, and ambition with complete objectivity. The problem is compounded in Hamilton's case because of his constant involvement in affairs of state during the Washington and Adams Administrations. Hamilton is one of the most controversial figures in American history. His case has been treated harshly by American historians who, for the most part, appear to be the partisans of Jeffersonianism. In spite of his protests, Mitchell does take sides. But it is refreshing to have a Hamiltonian of such talent in the lists.

Hamilton's career is classic in the American drama. It is a story of rags to fame, if not riches. Hamilton was as much the self-made man as Abraham Lincoln or Andrew Jackson. His presence in New York as a student at King's College (later Columbia University) during the exciting days immediately preceding the American Revolution was fortuitous. But Hamilton proceeded to exploit the opportunity by involving himself totally in the patriot cause. After that, his advance was rapid, aided as it was by his close association with General Washington. Hamilton shared the frustrating years of war with Washington and experienced a taste of glory by storming a British redoubt at Yorktown.

Hamilton, as a chief critic of the Confederation government, was also one of its most serious representatives in Congress. Whatever task he undertook was completed with vigor and skill. Mitchell believes that his ideas about government and finance had crystalized by this time and only awaited the opportunity to be put into effect. This chance presented itself with his appointment as Secretary of the Treasury under Washington and under the new Constitution which Hamilton almost single-handedly carried through to ratification in New York by moral and oratorical force.

Mitchell deals with Hamilton's economic program as Secretary of the Treasury at length in the first eight chapters of the second volume of his biography. He emphasizes that Hamilton's program was based on "his confidence in the future growth of the economy of the country." He declares that, despite what many scholars have written, Hamilton "was not a special pleader for the rich, constructing American institutions for the salvage and advancement of their claims. His only client was the whole country. . . . he sought stability and system in which a young nation could mature." Hamilton's plans were the product of

a great deal of study and preparation and were based in no small part on British laws and practices. Mitchell not only discusses these plans fully, but he also gives a detailed account of their passage through Congress.

Although Mitchell is completely in sympathy with Hamilton's economic program, he treats some of his other activities less favorably. He is, for example, critical of Hamilton for his "calamitous" attack on President John Adams in 1800. Hamilton had worked against Adams in 1796. During the next four years, Hamilton's opposition grew as Adams refused to pursue what Hamilton considered to be the proper policy toward France and defense. By 1800, Hamilton was ready to engage in a scheme to unseat Adams through the manipulation of the votes of Federalist electors. Hamilton so lost his sense of proportion that he played directly into the hands of Jefferson and his party. The capstone of Hamilton's temporary imbalance was a scathing attack on Adams in his "Letter from Alexander Hamilton concerning the Public Conduct and Character of John Adams, Esq. President of the United States" (Philadelphia, 1800). The Federalists, already suffering from unpopularity as a result of their tax policies and the Alien and Sedition Acts, were irreparably split by Hamilton's actions. Jefferson came to power in 1800 but only after Hamilton had thrown his weight into the Jeffersonian camp in the congressional vote on the Presidency following the tie in electoral votes between Aaron Burr and Jefferson.

If there was one man whom Hamilton distrusted more than Jefferson, it was Burr. This distrust and opposition to the devious Burr propelled Hamilton to his meeting with Burr and to his death. Mitchell's biography is the most comprehensive we have on Hamilton, but we can be certain that it will not be the last. — *J.G.C.*

Additional Recommended Reading

Maclay, William. *Journal of William Maclay: United States Senator from Pennsylvania, 1789-1791.* Edited by E. S. Maclay. New York: D. Appleton and Company, 1890, reprinted 1927. A vivid though biased account by a participant concerning the machinations of the Hamiltonian faction.

Lodge, Henry Cabot, ed. *The Works of Alexander Hamilton.* 9 vols. New York: G. P. Putnam's Sons, 1885-1886. Hamilton's three reports are given in volumes two and three.

Bowers, Claude G. *Jefferson and Hamilton, the Struggle for Democracy in America.* Boston: Houghton Mifflin Co., 1925. An exciting but pro-Jefferson version of the party struggles of the 1790's, reflecting an effort by a liberal Democrat to find his roots in Jeffersonianism.

Schachner, Nathan. *Alexander Hamilton: A Biography.* New York: Appleton-Century-Crofts, 1946. Still the best one-volume biography of Hamilton.

Miller, John C. *Alexander Hamilton and the Growth of the New Nation.* Originally published as: *Alexander Hamilton, Portrait in Paradox.* New York: Harper & Row Publishers, 1955. A biography by one of the foremost scholars of the period which discusses Hamilton's economic policy sympathetically and in some detail.

Miller, John C. *The Federalist Era, 1789-1801.* New York: Harper & Row Publishers, 1960. A balanced account of the United States during the 1790's.

Charles, Joseph. *The Origins of the American Party System.* Williamsburg, Virginia: The Institute of Early American History and Culture, 1956. Sees political parties rising out of reaction to Hamilton's financial program and Jay's Treaty.

Cunningham, Noble E., Jr. *The Jeffersonian Republicans: The Formation of a Party Organization, 1789-1801.* Chapel Hill: University of North Carolina Press, 1957. Traces the efforts of many men besides Jefferson and Madison which resulted in the organization of the Republican Party.

Rossiter, Clinton. *Alexander Hamilton and the Constitution.* New York: Harcourt, Brace & World, Inc., 1965. Views Hamilton as the major force in putting the Constitution to work and credits Hamilton with projecting the form which the United States was to assume.

ERECTION OF SLATER'S SPINNING MILL AT PAWTUCKET

Type of event: Economic: beginning of United States industrialization
Time: 1790
Locale: Pawtucket, Rhode Island

Principal personages:
SAMUEL SLATER (1768-1835), English mechanic who built the first successful cotton spinning mill in America
RICHARD ARKWRIGHT (1732-1792), English inventor and developer of the methods of modern textile manufacturing
JEDEDIAH STRUTT (1726-1797), English textile manufacturer, former partner of Arkwright, in whose mills Slater learned the Arkwright system
MOSES BROWN (1738-1836), Rhode Island merchant who employed Slater to build Arkwright machinery in the United States

Summary of Event

On December 20, 1790, the waters of the Blackstone river surging through Sargeant's Trench in the tiny village of Pawtucket, Rhode Island, began to turn a water wheel outside Ezekiel Carpenter's clothier shop. Inside the building a small but anxious gathering watched intently as the wheel started to transmit power to America's first successful textile machinery built on the Arkwright pattern. After a few difficulties, the operation became an unqualified success. The foundations of a great American industry were established.

The background to this important event can be traced to September 1, 1789, when twenty-one-year-old Samuel Slater, a former apprentice in Jedediah Strutt's textile mills of Derbyshire, England, announced that he was going to seek his fortune 134 miles away in London. Actually his ultimate destination was America, where he thought that his skills might enable him to rise higher than he could in England. He brought with him something of tremendous potential value to the infant nation: ideas for the construction of textile manufacturing machinery based on the work of Richard Arkwright. America was about to enter the age of industrialization.

Secrecy was essential, for the English wished to preserve their monopoly of modern textile manufacturing and they refused to allow plans or models of industrial machinery to leave the country; they also prohibited the emigration of skilled workers who might build such machinery abroad. So according to legend, Slater sailed from London wearing the clothing and affecting the manner of a Derbyshire farmer, part of his natural environment; but in his mind Slater carried encyclopedic knowledge of the Arkwright machinery which he intended to reproduce in the New World.

The young man's background and

362

training made the plan realistic. Born near Belper in 1768, Samuel Slater grew up near the banks of the Derwent, a river which powered the world's first water-driven spinning mill. The year after Slater's birth, Arkwright received a patent for his famous "water frame," a machine for spinning thread which was driven by water power. This invention accompanied those of other pioneers in textile technology, such as James Hargreaves, Samuel Crompton, and John Kay. Arkwright went further, however, in combining under one roof the various processes involved in making thread. Arkwright built his first spinning mill in 1769, but needing capital for further development, he went into partnership with Jedediah Strutt, a wealthy manufacturer of stockings. In 1771 the partners built the first water-powered spinning mill on the banks of the Derwent, and they constructed another mill at Belper in 1776 before the partnership was dissolved. Strutt took over direction of the mills, and Samuel Slater was apprenticed to work for him in 1783.

Slater not only worked with the Arkwright machinery, but during his seven-year apprenticeship undertook increasingly important duties, so that by the time he finished, he had mastered the system. It was, however, problematical whether or not he could reproduce the machinery entirely from memory.

Slater landed in New York on November 18, 1789; within a few days he accepted employment with the New York Manufacturing Company in lower Manhattan, but he was soon disillusioned with this operation and sought out Moses Brown, a Rhode Island Quaker who had been experimenting for some years without success to mechanize textile production. An exchange of letters brought Slater to Providence in January, 1790, when he inspected Brown and Almy's plant at Pawtucket. The young immigrant advised the Quaker and his associate that their machinery was unworkable and would have to be abandoned. A working agreement was reached whereby Slater, laboring in the wood shop of Sylvanus Brown behind shuttered windows, reproduced the Arkwright machinery. Brown cut the wooden parts and David Wilkinson did the metal work, assisted by Pliny Earle, a Quaker from Leicester, Massachusetts, who made the hand cards, and an elderly Negro named Samuel Brunius Jenks. By December, 1790, the Slater-Arkwright machinery was installed in Ezekiel Carpenter's shop and Slater had become a partner in the firm.

The machinery worked, and the fortunes of the partners began to grow. It was impossible to prevent the machinery from being copied, and in fact no attempt was made to stop the dissemination of the ideas being used. Slater's own first attempt was replaced in 1793 by the famous Old Slater Mill, placed twenty rods up the Blackstone river. Slater himself branched out into other textile manufacturing ventures, and by 1827 he held no less than thirteen separate partnerships throughout New England.

By 1815, there were 165 cotton mills in New England, all working to full capacity. America had entered into the age of industrialization, and Samuel Slater's contribution fully justified the title bestowed upon him by President Andrew Jackson in 1883: "Father of American Manufactures."

Pertinent Literature

White, George S. *Memoir of Samuel Slater: The Father of American Manufactures.* New York: Augustus M. Kelley, Publisher, 1967.

The United States of the 1830's was a young nation on the move, reaching out to claim a continent and becoming fully conscious of its strengths and opportunities. Led during the first half of the decade by Andrew Jackson, an intense Anglophobe and ardent nationalist, the country was fired with a spirit of national exuberance which extolled past accomplishments and confidently anticipated a glorious future. George S. White's *Memoir of Samuel Slater,* originally published by the author in 1836, exudes the spirit of this period of gestation.

This book is the standard source of factual information used by later authors to describe the career of Samuel Slater. It derives much of its value and fascination, however, from the fact that it is far more than a mere chronicle of the great manufacturer's career. White, as a literate contemporary, provides an insight into the age. Because of the attitude which is implicit in his writing, one can sense America's lust for industry in the late eighteenth and early nineteenth centuries, and its overwhelming pride in those individuals who helped to attain this goal. In addition, the author had the advantage of personal friendship and long discussions with Slater, as well as conversations, interviews, or correspondence with a wide range of Slater's friends and associates. In writing the *Memoir* shortly after Slater's death, White assembled and preserved much general information and personal detail about his subject that would otherwise have been lost. Finally, the author includes a wide selection of Slater's correspondence and many documents concerning his life and career.

Like many early nineteenth century books, the style and organization of White's volume may seem quaint to twentieth century readers. The author has a tendency to wander from topic to topic without clear transitions or appearing to conform to any consistent pattern, and he devotes a good deal of time and space to personal observations and moral homilies. The tone throughout is extremely respectful, if not laudatory, toward Samuel Slater and his achievements.

White begins with a description of the background of the textile industry and the pre-Slater state of manufacturers in the United States. He then discusses Slater's decision to come to the New World. Citing conversations with Slater, the author says that his decision to emigrate was well planned and reached long before the actual departure. Slater was attracted by newspaper advertisements and other information offering rewards for skilled mechanics who would come to the United States. He then successfully sought greater duties and opportunities for education in Jedediah Strutt's English operations in order to prepare for the challenging tasks awaiting when he would reach America.

The author describes early American textile manufacturing and efforts to introduce the Arkwright system in this country, and then tells of Slater's initial encounter with Moses Brown and his disappointment upon first viewing the old Quaker's textile machinery, which was later abandoned as unworkable. Much of this material is based on conversations between White and Brown. After describing the success of the first efforts in Pawtucket, White chronicles the rise of the cotton textile industry. He credits Slater with the spread of the industry and points out that most of the factories built between 1790 and 1809 were constructed and operated by men who had been trained under Slater. Among the most valuable portions of the book are White's descriptions of several small New England textile towns. There are also descriptions of early nineteenth century textile equipment, manufacturing operations, and managerial policies and practices.

White's book, now published by Augustus M. Kelley, is the standard source for students interested not only in Samuel Slater but also in the rise of the American textile industry.

Cameron, E. H. *Samuel Slater, Father of American Manufactures.* Portland, Maine: The Bond Wheelwright Company, 1960.

Samuel Slater was not among the many contributors to American development who died without acclaim from their contemporaries only to be lauded by later generations. Recognized in his lifetime by his peers and fellow citizens, Slater derived great financial rewards from his part in founding the United States textile industry. Scarcely a textbook survey of American history or a standard reference work fails to grant Slater much of the credit for the foundations of American industrial development. It is therefore surprising that E. H. Cameron's biography of Slater is the only published twentieth century study of this famous industrial pioneer.

Cameron's work makes no major contribution to the history of American industry or technology, and it adds little additional luster to Samuel Slater's reputation. Poorly organized, the book cannot be compared favorably with other volumes treating economic and technological history in a popular style.

Serious students will not be pleased at the volume's shortcomings. At the outset, Cameron acknowledges his debt to a great-grandson of Samuel Slater who apparently spent much of his time and money in efforts to honor his ancestor's accomplishments. The uncritical approach and laudatory tone of this biography raise the question of whether the author's objectivity was unduly influenced by his contact with Slater's great-grandson.

Furthermore, Cameron fails to place his subject in perspective, both in his own time and in the general development of American industry. While extravagantly praising Slater as an industrial pioneer, efficient entrepreneur, and just employer, Cameron does not compare Slater with other persons of similar talents both in this country and in England. Such comparisons would have helped significantly in the effort to determine Slater's true importance. Surprisingly, little attention is focused on the personal side of Samuel Slater—his boyhood in England, his training under Jedediah Strutt, and his family life and relationships in this country—all matters which might have shed light on Slater's drives, methods, and accomplishments.

As a tool for further study of Samuel

Slater and the birth of American industrialization, this volume has its weaknesses. There is a total absence of footnotes, no index, and only a rudimentary bibliography. The author furnishes no real indication of the extent of his research, although he does acknowledge heavy dependence on an unpublished Slater biography written by Dr. Frederick Lewton, and on George S. White's *Memoir of Samuel Slater,* originally published in 1836. — *J.E.F.*

Additional Recommended Reading

Thompson, Mack. *Moses Brown: Reluctant Reformer.* Chapel Hill: University of North Carolina Press, 1962. Contains a chapter on the Pawtucket story, with emphasis on Moses Brown.

Ware, Caroline F. *The Early New England Cotton Manufacturer.* Boston: Houghton Mifflin Co., 1924. The standard account of the early textile industry, with the Slater material based on George S. White's work.

Hedges, James B. *The Browns of Providence Plantations.* Vol. II: *The Nineteenth Century.* Providence: Brown University Press, 1968. Contains a chapter on the origins and development of cotton manufacturing.

Bagnall, William R. *The Textile Industries of the United States.* Vol. I: *1639-1810.* Cambridge, Massachusetts: H. O. Houghton & Company, 1893. Reprinted, New York: Augustus M. Kelley, Publishers, 1967. An old but standard source on the history of the textile industry.

RATIFICATION OF THE BILL OF RIGHTS

Type of event: Constitutional: necessity of stating individual rights
Time: 1791
Locale: The United States

Principal personages:

GEORGE MASON (1725-1792), Virginia delegate to the Constitutional Convention, and an early advocate of a bill of rights

JAMES WILSON (1742-1798), Federalist who saw no need for a bill of rights

JAMES MADISON (1751-1836), Federalist and a staunch supporter of the Constitution who guided amendments through Congress

ELBRIDGE GERRY (1744-1814), from Massachusetts, who demanded a bill of rights

RICHARD HENRY LEE (1732-1794), from Virginia, whose writings advocated a bill of rights

Summary of Event

The first ten amendments to the United States Constitution are known as the Bill of Rights. These amendments were added two years after the adoption of the Constitution because of demand from prominent people in the states. Their omission from the original document was not a mistake or an oversight. No such list of rights or privileges was included in the original Constitution because majority opinion held that it was unnecessary to guarantee rights that were already commonly accepted and in most cases were already guaranteed by the various state constitutions.

However, when the Constitution was approved by the Constitutional Convention in Philadelphia in 1787 and sent to the states for ratification, a movement to append a bill of rights was immediately evident. Richard Henry Lee, George Mason, Patrick Henry, Elbridge Gerry, and many other prominent state leaders announced opposition to the ratification of the Constitution because it contained no bill of rights. There is no doubt that the Anti-Federalists, who opposed ratification of the Constitution, objected to several different parts of the document. They chose, however, to concentrate their attack on the absence of a bill of rights. They correctly reasoned that this issue would bring them popular support.

As the various state conventions met to discuss ratification of the Constitution, it became apparent that the Anti-Federalists had gathered support for their demands for a bill of rights. The Federalists, who staunchly supported the Constitution, began to show concern and worry. James Madison from Virginia, Alexander Hamilton from New York, James Wilson from Pennsylvania, Roger Sherman from Connecticut, and many other Federalist leaders stepped up their campaign for a quick ratification. Better organized

367

than the Anti-Federalists and equipped with power and persuasive arguments favoring ratification, Federalists in all states put party machinery into operation and worked hard to promote their cause. A study of the ratification struggle state by state shows that the Federalists prevailed, but the demand for some kind of a bill of rights remained strong.

Pennsylvania, the second state to ratify the Constitution, did so by a vote of forty-six to twenty-three. However, twenty-one of the twenty-three opponents met afterwards and drew up a manifesto demanding the addition of a bill of rights. In Massachusetts a close vote favoring ratification was preceded by a heated debate on the bill of rights question. A compromise was reached by which the state's ratification was accompanied by a recommendation for the addition of a bill of rights. Ratification in Virginia (eighty-nine to seventy-nine) and in New York (thirty to twenty-seven) passed by narrow margins, and both states sent with their ratifications strong demands for changes in the Constitution that would protect personal liberties. Several other states followed this pattern, and by the time the Constitution was ratified, it was admitted by all but a few die-hard Federalists that a bill of rights would have to be adopted.

Though a Federalist in 1788 and a strong supporter of the Constitution from the beginning, James Madison was at first only lukewarm toward a bill of rights, but he assumed leadership of the Anti-Federalists who were determined that the First Congress should produce a bill of rights.

The House of Representatives assembled early in April, 1789, and soon turned its attention to the problem of raising money for the operation of the new government. But Madison announced that he would introduce the subject of amendments before the congressional session ended, which he did early in June. A wide variety of opinions was expressed concerning the manner in which a bill of rights could be incorporated into the Constitution. Some suggested that the body of the Constitution be amended in different places in order to weave a bill of rights into the original document. Others preferred a declaration of rights as a preface. Still others thought one big amendment would solve the problem. Finally, after lengthy debate, it was agreed to place the Bill of Rights in a series of amendments. There followed more discussion concerning the subject matter of the amendments. In September, 1789, a conference committee composed of three Senators and three Congressmen worked out a compromise agreement consisting of twelve amendments. The Senate and the House of Representatives both passed these amendments and sent them to the President to be presented to the states for ratification. Two of the twelve amendments were rejected by the states, but the other ten were ratified by the necessary three-fourths of the states by December 15, 1791. In March, 1792, Secretary of State Thomas Jefferson announced to the Governors that these amendments, now known as the Bill of Rights, were in effect.

Pertinent Literature

Rutland, Robert A. *Birth of the Bill of Rights, 1776-1791.* Chapel Hill: University of North Carolina Press, 1955.

This volume is the complete story of the creation of the Bill of Rights, beginning with the British and colonial background during the seventeenth and eighteenth centuries and concluding with the ratification by the states in 1791. The intervening chapters provide a fine treatment and analysis of such antecedents as the Declaration of Rights promulgated by the Second Continental Congress, the Virginia Declaration of Rights, and other bills of rights adopted by various colonies or states. The author clearly demonstrates the fact that the several colonies were developing intellectually along similar lines. By the time of the American Revolution, the American colonists, regardless of the colony in which they resided, were able to reach some agreement concerning the nature and extent of their rights. Such a consensus was an important unifying factor in the struggle for American independence. Rutland also points out the significant fact that preparation of a written bill of rights became an important facet of the American political tradition.

In discussing personal freedom in the new Republic, the author takes up the problem of the Loyalists during the Revolutionary War and shows that a bill of rights is of no great value if its provisions are ignored. Loyalists sometimes were denied liberties for which the patriots themselves were fighting. Personal rights, according to James Madison, were violated "by overbearing majorities in every state," and Jefferson commented that "the Declaration of Rights is like all other human blessings alloyed with some inconveniences."

Rutland also discusses the issue of religious freedom, which caused more discussion and legislative action than any other. And he takes up the equally difficult topics of trial by jury and freedom of the press. His discussion points up the fact that, prior to the adoption of the Constitution, personal rights were guaranteed by the states rather than by any central government. He also demonstrates the difficulty of defining the extent of personal rights in specific cases. Where, for instance, does freedom of speech end and verbal abuse begin?

The second half of this intriguing volume deals with the debates in the Constitutional Convention and the opposition to the Constitution because no bill of rights was included, the subsequent demand for a bill of rights, and the preparation and adoption of the first ten amendments. Rutland demonstrates the validity of his thesis that the federal Bill of Rights represents the "sum total of American experience and experimentation with civil liberty."

Mitchell, Broadus and Louise P. Mitchell. *A Biography of the Constitution of the United States: Its Origin, Formation, Adoption, Interpretation.* New York: Oxford University Press, 1964.

In the section of their book dealing with the first ten amendments, or the Bill of Rights, Broadus and Louise Mitchell contend that any such statement of rights was deliberately left out of the original document. The framers of the Constitution believed such a statement to be unnecessary because no new rights were being conferred. The people already had all these rights and more, and in most cases they were protected in them by state constitutions.

The authors also present the view that there was popular demand for a bill of rights as soon as the people in the states became aware of the fact that the Constitution had been drawn up without any specific guarantee of their rights and liberties. Much credit is given to James Madison for satisfying this popular demand and pushing the amendments through Congress.

Because of the authors' premise that the people demanded a bill of rights, the conclusion is easily reached that the states would ratify the amendments as soon as they were given the chance. Therefore little space is given to action by the states, and attention is centered on the attitude of the members of the Senate and House of Representatives. A short but good account of the debate in Congress is given. As in the case of the Constitution itself, the Bill of Rights was agreed upon because of the willingness of intelligent men to compromise their differing viewpoints. — *E.J.M.*

Additional Recommended Reading

Weinberger, Andrew D. *Freedom and Protection: The Bill of Rights.* San Francisco: Chandler Publishing Company, 1962. The author of this small book takes a broader view of the Bill of Rights than most writers. He includes in the Bill of Rights the first ten amendments, amendments thirteen, fourteen, fifteen, and nineteen, and those parts of the original Constitution that deal with personal liberty.

U.S. House Document number 206. *The United States Constitution.* G.P.O., June 29, 1961. A useful copy of the Constitution with the twenty-three amendments which had been adopted by 1961 and with the amendments accepted by Congress but never ratified by the states.

Jensen, Merrill. *The Making of the American Constitution.* Princeton, New Jersey: Van Nostrand Company, Inc., 1964. Includes a section on the Bill of Rights and a copy of the Virginia amendments of June 27, 1788, which show the kind of rights being demanded by the states.

WHITNEY INVENTS THE COTTON GIN

Type of event: Technological: innovation for cotton manufacturing
Time: 1793
Locale: Georgia

Principal personages:
ELI WHITNEY (1765-1825), American inventor of the cotton gin
JAMES WATT (1736-1819), Scottish inventor of the steam engine
SAMUEL CROMPTON (1753-1827), English inventor of the spinning mule
JAMES HARGREAVES (?-1778), English inventor of the spinning jenny
SIR RICHARD ARKWRIGHT (1732-1792), English inventor of the water frame for spinning cotton
EDMUND CARTWRIGHT (1743-1823), English inventor of the power loom
EDMUND RUFFIN (1794-1865), Virginia advocate of scientific farming
J. D. B. DEBOW (1820-1867), editor of *DeBow's Review* in New Orleans and apostle of Southern diversification

Summary of Event

The invention of the cotton gin by Eli Whitney was one of a series of significant technological innovations made during the eighteenth century which revolutionized methods of production and habits of consumption throughout Europe and the United States. Whitney's contrivance did for the cotton planter what Arkwright, Hargreaves, and Crompton had done for the cotton manufacturer in Great Britain. The cumulative result of the water frame, the spinning jenny, and the mule was to increase the demand in England for raw cotton, and the cotton gin made it possible for American planters to meet that demand. The application of steam to these machines greatly increased the output of yarn and cloth, thus serving to intensify the demands made upon the American planters. The growth of the cotton in-dustry in the United States was a major force in the rapid economic development of the nation, and much credit for this fact must go to the invention of the cotton gin.

The period of greatest growth followed hard upon the coming of peace in 1815. Cotton production in the United States rose from 364,000 bales in 1815, of which eighty-two percent was exported, to 4,861,000 bales in 1860, of which seventy-seven percent was exported. By 1860, Great Britain was consuming one quarter of the entire United States crop. Cotton was also the leading domestic export of the United States. In 1860, the total value of United States exports reached $334 million. Cotton formed fifty-seven percent of this total. If to this figure is added the value of exports of other Southern staples, notably tobacco, sugar, and rice, the contribution of the South to the nation's export trade approached sixty-five percent. In spite of these impressive statistics, Southerners complained that the fruits of their labor were gathered by other sections of the country.

To a large degree this charge was accurate. Southern planters sold their crops abroad or to the Northeastern states. The market was erratic, varying according to demand and supply; it was sensitive to international incidents, and almost impossible to predict. Communications were slow. Planters shipped according to one set of prices only to find a different set operative when their cargoes arrived in port. Risks at sea were great. The costs of shipment were large and paid in the form of commissions to agents of the planters. These men, called factors, handled every detail of the shipment in addition to making purchases for, and offering credits to, the planters.

These disabilities were common to all the participants of the staple trade. But they fell with greater impact, especially after 1830, on the older cotton producing regions along the South Atlantic coast. There, constant plantings without attention to soil conservation reduced yields per acre while increasing costs of production per unit of crop. South Carolina planters found it extremely difficult to compete with those from Mississippi's lush and virgin lands. Economic stagnation and nullification inevitably followed. Another result was an effort on the part of some farsighted Southerners to stimulate economic diversification in the region. Men, such as J. D. B. DeBow of New Orleans and Edmund Ruffin of Virginia, preached the virtues of scientific agriculture, industrialization, and transportation improvements.

The dramatic growth of the cotton plantation was, of course, more than a matter of production statistics and marketing problems. It was the story of great movements of population into the lush lands of the lower Mississippi River Valley. It was the story of the master and the slave. To some historians, particularly those from the South, it was the story of the evolution of a culture distinct from that of other regions. Most historians, including those who deny the concept of cultural distinctiveness, agree that according to most economic indices the South was in a manifestly inferior position, perhaps in a colonial position, relative to the North by the 1850's. Most would also agree that the institution of slavery was a major cause of this inferiority.

The North was not an industrial section in 1860, although strong beginnings had been made in some parts. The North was basically agrarian but was more industrialized than the South. This meant that the North offered more nonagricultural opportunities for economic advancement. The agricultural sector in the North was based on the small farm. In the South, small farmers found it increasingly difficult to compete with the plantation. The size of individual land holdings increased markedly in the South after 1840 while farms became smaller in the North. The population of the North was compact while the plantation system dispersed population in the South resulting in a retarded Southern town and city development. Fewer urban areas meant less adequate commercial and banking facilities, which in turn meant a slow rate of capital formation and presented difficulties to those wishing to diversify or undertake transportation improvement. Fewer inducements were available to attract skilled labor, and the fear of competing with slaves was also an obstacle. The scattered population retarded the development of public schools. The people of the South, less mobile than those in the North, were thrown back on themselves. The master and the slave only had each other. The psychological consequences of this introversion are only now coming under serious scrutiny.

The effect of all these factors was to make the South economically weaker than the North, although the South was integrated in the budding national economy. The South was neither distinct nor unique, but as pressures on, and criticism of, the South accumulated, Southerners created the myth of their cultural uniqueness. This invention was of more moment than Eli Whitney's.

Pertinent Literature

Green, Constance M. *Eli Whitney and the Birth of American Technology*. Boston: Little, Brown, and Company, 1956.

Eli Whitney is portrayed as one of the first of American industrialists, an inventor possessing both practical and theoretical genius. Throughout this study the author emphasizes the difficulties of manufacturing during the early days of the nation. Early entrepreneurs lacked adequate capital. Every venture was a risk. There existed no domestic market but only a number of unconnected local markets. Factory owners were always hampered by shortages of labor, which in turn put a premium upon the development of labor-saving machinery. Through the ingenuity of men, such as Whitney, Simon North, Oliver Evans, and Samuel Slater, the United States by the 1850's had achieved a degree of mechanization, standardization, and mass production that surprised competent foreign observers.

Eli Whitney's great contributions were the invention of the cotton gin and the development of the principle of interchangeable parts. The latter, intrinsic to the growth of a modern industrial system, is considered the more important of his two achievements.

Whitney's genius did not bring him the financial rewards he expected. The gin was of such great general utility that the South refused to allow anyone a monopoly of production of the machine. As a result there was much pirating. Whitney's problems with the gin and the patent struggles he engaged in affected his thinking during his industrial career. He was willing to improve the efficiency of his shop only if it did not threaten his security. He conceived the design of a musket-barrel-turning machine but did not build it for fear that competitors would use it to entice away his trained workmen.

Whitney's business abilities were not outstanding. He was primarily interested in the mechanics and efficiency of production. But in those early days, the entrepreneur had to be his own chief engineer, foreman, salesman, and public relations expert. It was only in the latter part of the nineteenth century that industrial specialization, as we know it today, became common on the industrial front.

373

Craven, Avery O. *Soil Exhaustion as a Factor in the Agricultural History of Virginia and Maryland, 1606-1860.* Urbana: University of Illinois Press, 1925.

This study of the tobacco regions of Virginia and Maryland rejects the normal account of soil exhaustion as something strictly Southern, or as a phenomenon to be explained solely in terms of the exhausting qualities of tobacco or the inefficiencies of slave labor. While recognizing that to a large extent the cultivator and his methods stand out as the determining forces in the problem of soil fertility, Craven also describes how the location of markets, the activities of governments, and strictly geographical factors can produce soil exhaustion.

In carrying his story from colonial times to the Civil War, Craven demonstrates how problems accumulate, intensify, and bring disaster to the farmer, who is then forced to migrate or reform his agricultural methods. During the colonial period the planters of Virginia and Maryland faced many difficulties, among which were the single crop, the labor system, the methods of cultivation, the burdens of government regulations and duties, and the high costs of indirect marketing and buying. All these forces tended in a single direction. Planters were forced to procure the largest return from the soil in the shortest space of time. The result was great stretches of worn-out and abandoned lands. When tobacco migrated to the West, the story was repeated.

To Craven, such a process of agriculture explained much of Southern life. An abundance of land was required and expansion became a normal way of life. The growth from small to large units and the movement from old to new regions were characteristics that marked not only Virginia and Maryland but also much of the South at later dates. Success apparently meant expansion. The concomitant growth of slavery accelerated the growth of great estates, and the large planter assumed an even more dominant position in society.

While Craven's study details the process of agricultural degeneration, it also depicts efforts at agricultural reform beginning after the War of 1812. Although reformers, such as George Washington, James Madison, and Thomas Jefferson, were active prior to that period, they ran counter to the general backward drift. Even in the so-called reform period, the percentage that took up reform was never great. But the reformers were more numerous and better organized. Agricultural societies sprang up and agricultural newspapers, such as John Skinner's *The American Farmer* of Baltimore, Maryland, became agents of reform. The great figure in reform was Edmund Ruffin of Virginia, who undertook publication of the *Farmer's Register* in 1833.

By the 1850's, Craven can point to noticeable improvement in the agriculture of both Virginia and Maryland. An important factor in this improvement was the adoption of Peruvian guano as a fertilizer. For the most part, the improvement was inseparable from the adoption of general farming which had been made possible by the growth of markets and improved transportation facilities. Baltimore, for instance, grew into a great grain center and cap-

374

tured the Brazilian trade. Baltimore, of course, had been instrumental in promoting the Baltimore and Ohio Railroad and the Baltimore and Susquehannah Railroad, as well as the Chesapeake and Ohio Canal.

With the coming of general farming, the old advantage of size disappeared.

Emigrants from the North began to move into the upper South and the interests of Virginia and Maryland were drawn northward at the very time that sectional animosities started to crescendo. Much of the improvement was tragically ruined by the Civil War. — *J.G.C.*

Additional Recommended Reading

Olmsted, Frederick L. *The Cotton Kingdom.* New York: Alfred A. Knopf Inc., 1953. Originally published under three separate titles between 1856 and 1860, this account remains one of the best of a large number of descriptions of the South and slavery written by travelers to the South.

Phillips, Ulrich B. *American Negro Slavery: A Survey of the Supply, Employment, and Control of Negro Labor as Determined by the Plantation Regime.* New York: D. Appleton and Company, 1918. Long the traditional account of slavery, this work has more recently been qualified in the conclusions to be drawn from the data. Phillips pioneered in the accumulation and investigation of manuscript sources in this field.

Gray, Lewis C. *History of Agriculture in the Southern United States to 1860.* 2 vols. Washington, D.C.: Carnegie Institution of Washington, 1933. This study, the most comprehensive available, is based on wide research into primary and statistical sources.

Robert, Joseph C. *The Tobacco Kingdom: Plantation, Market, and Factory in Virginia and North Carolina, 1800-1860.* Durham: Duke University Press, 1938. A detailed history of the crop from first planting to manufacturer.

Hidy, Ralph W. *The House of Baring in American Trade and Finance: English Merchant Bankers at Work, 1763-1861. Harvard Studies in Business History,* XIV. Cambridge: Harvard University Press, 1949. Hidy has written a rewarding account of the details of the Anglo-American trade including the Southern staples, as conducted by a prominent English commercial house through its agents and correspondents in America.

Sitterson, J. Carlyle. *Sugar Country: The Cane Sugar Industry in the South, 1753-1950.* Lexington: University of Kentucky Press, 1953. The standard account of the sugar cane industry, which is especially useful for insights into the sugar plantation in Louisiana.

Stampp, Kenneth M. *The Peculiar Institution: Slavery in the Ante-Bellum South.* New York: Alfred A. Knopf, Inc., 1956. Historians generally consider that this work contains the best overall analysis of slavery in its physical, social, and economic setting.

Smith, Alfred G., Jr. *Economic Readjustment of an Old Cotton State: South Carolina, 1820-1860.* Columbia: University of South Carolina Press, 1958. An excellent study of the difficulties faced by the state in its efforts to diversify its economy.

North, Douglass C. *The Economic Growth of the United States, 1790-1860.* Englewood Cliffs, New Jersey: Prentice-Hall, Inc., 1961. The book successfully attempts to reach a general understanding of the forces involved in the economic development of the United States.

Genovese, Eugene D. *The Political Economy of Slavery.* New York: Pantheon Books, 1965. In looking to slavery as the source of the South's woes, Genovese apparently returns, with the element of class consciousness superimposed on the thesis, to the original interpretation of Phillips.

THE WHISKEY REBELLION

Type of event: Political: agrarian protest against excise tax on whiskey
Time: 1794
Locale: Western Pennsylvania

Principal personages:

GEORGE WASHINGTON (1732-1799), first President of the
United States 1789-1797

ALEXANDER HAMILTON (1757-1804), Secretary of the Treasury

THOMAS MIFFLIN (1744-1800), Governor of Pennsylvania

ALBERT GALLATIN (1761-1849), member of Pennsylvania Assembly

DAVID BRADFORD (fl. 1794), anti-excise leader in Pennsylvania
who fled to Louisiana to escape arrest

JAMES MARSHALL (fl. 1794), anti-excise leader in Pennsylvania

THOMAS MCKEAN (1734-1817), Republican who was elected
Governor of Pennsylvania in 1799

Summary of Event

One of the most pressing and difficult problems faced by the Washington Administration was that of guaranteeing the loyalty of the West to the Union. This was largely a matter of security and defense against the resident Indian nations and their European allies. Prior to Jay's Treaty with Great Britain and Pinckney's Treaty with Spain, much of the Ohio and the Mississippi River Valleys were claimed or occupied by Great Britain and Spain. Settlers in this vast region were threatened by constant Indian wars against which the federal government appeared to be impotent. Settlement was thus retarded, Western dissatisfaction was aggravated, and foreign powers sought by various means to cause the separation of the American West from the United States.

Part of the Western problem was economic. Western farmers were required by the economics of transportation costs to ship their bulky produce down the river systems to the Gulf of Mexico. Overland freight rates were prohibitive. If the western portions of the nation were to advance economically, not only would the federal government have to exert itself militarily against the Indians, but it would have to secure free navigation on the Mississippi river as far as the mouth of the river.

The economic program of Alexander Hamilton, Secretary of the Treasury, which in its major parts provided for the funding and assumption of the federal and state Revolutionary War debts, further compounded the problem. Hamilton successfully steered his program through Congress in the face of stiff Southern opposition. The federal debt was guaranteed, but means had to be found to insure the annual payment of the enormous debt contracted by the new government. Various taxes were established on the advice of the Secretary of the Treasury, but the one which aroused immediate opposition in Congress, and stimulated considerable Western discontent between 1792 and 1794, was the excise tax on distilled whiskey.

Whiskey was a major export product in the West, especially in western Pennsylvania. Farmers found it almost impossible to export bulk grain to market because of the difficulties of transportation. Grain then had to be converted into a form less bulky and more valuable in proportion to its weight. One such form was livestock which was driven to market, but this, too, was an arduous and risky business; another form, less difficult, was the conversion of grain into distilled spirits. Whiskey could be carried profitably from the western regions to markets in the East. But the profit margin was gravely endangered by the excise tax passed in 1791. Moreover, the tax discriminated against the West, because whiskey was worth twice as much per gallon in the East as in the West. Western resentments were also aroused by the appointment of tax collectors by the federal government—the forerunners of the "Revenuers" who were hated so bitterly by the hill people later. Westerners resented this interference in their economic life and were particularly antagonistic toward the snooping and prying of the excise agents. Men in the West placed no special trust or faith in the central government, located as it was in the East, and representing in the minds of many Westerners a danger to local freedoms.

The excise on whiskey passed Congress without much trouble but met with an adverse reception in the West. Meetings were held in Western Pennsylvania in 1791 and 1792 to express

this opposition. Some damage was caused, and President Washington was moved to issue a proclamation which warned against obstruction of the law. Disturbances also occurred in North and South Carolina. But agitation tapered off in 1793, and it appeared for a time that the problem had dissolved. However, the storm broke in the summer of 1794.

Western dissatisfaction with the course of the federal government reached a peak in 1794-1795. Federal efforts to pacify the Indians had been checked by Indian military victories. British and Spanish influence over the tribes seemed stronger than ever. The United States seemed no closer to securing the evacuation of the British from the Northwest or free navigation on the Mississippi river. Life was hard in the West and the burden of taxation seemed almost unbearable. The crisis in western Pennsylvania occurred when the federal government demanded that men who had failed to comply with the provisions of the Excise Act be taken to Philadelphia for trial. In July, 1794, an armed mob attacked and burned the home of the excise inspector of Allegheny County, Pennsylvania. This act of defiance was followed in August by a mass meeting at Braddock's Field and a march to Pittsburgh.

President Washington, acting upon reports from state and federal authorities in Pennsylvania, moved swiftly to quell the disturbances. After a Presidential proclamation failed to restore order, the President called upon several states to furnish the federal government with twelve thousand men. Hamilton was placed in command. The immense army marched toward the forks of the Ohio. Hamilton's hopes of military fame were frustrated, for the army found no opposition. Westerners suddenly discovered that discretion was the better part of valor, and the whiskey rebels were nowhere in evidence. The army met only with loyal citizens of the United States. A few arrests were made. Two men were convicted of high treason, but both were pardoned by the President.

Washington had demonstrated the ability of the federal government to act with dispatch to maintain law and order. The action also succeeded in securing western Pennsylvania to the Republican Party in 1796, in spite of Washington's diplomatic successes of 1795 and the defeat of the Indians at the Battle of Fallen Timbers in the same month as the Whiskey Rebellion.

Pertinent Literature

Link, Eugene P. *Democratic-Republican Societies, 1790-1800.* New York: Columbia University Press, 1942.

The Republican Party was the organized result of widespread dissatisfaction with the domestic and foreign policies of the Washington Administration. Hamilton's economic programs of Funding and Assumption, the National Bank, taxation to pay the enlarged national debt, and protection to manufacturers, coupled with the ineptness of America's foreign policy on the one hand, and the apparently pro-British stance of the Washington Administration on the other, created a large enough body of practical issues to call into being an organized opposition. At first the opposition was centered in Congress and led by a solid core of Southern politicians. Before this factional opposition could be transformed into a political party, it was necessary to open channels of communication between the national leadership and the grass roots as well as to find intersectional support. One of the major vehicles in marshalling grass-roots sentiment throughout the nation against the Washington Administration is the subject of this monograph.

The Democratic-Republican socie-

ties appeared in 1793-1794. They were organized in various localities around the nation, and according to Link they were committed to the protection and spread of democratic government. The membership of the societies believed that democratic self-government was threatened by the forces of wealth and aristocracy which apparently controlled the Washington Administration. Hamilton served to symbolize in his policies and attitudes the fearsome alliance of wealth, privilege, and political power. To combat this conservative force which threatened to turn the United States from the democratic path chosen in 1776, local leaders called the societies into being.

Link maintains, in what some historians feel to be too polemical and doctrinaire a manner, that the societies, or clubs, galvanized public opinion against the Federalists by reducing the various concrete issues facing the public to their ideological common denominator. The author of the monograph "tells how farmers, artisans, tradesmen, and sailors, among others, in the spirit of '76, rolled up mass opposition to the anti-democratic tendencies of the period." The path to the organization of the Republican Party was smoothed by the clubs.

Link deals with the purposes, membership, ideology, and achievements of the clubs. They were obviously local movements without contact with a central body of any kind. The strength of any one society depended solely upon its local image. But the Federalists recognized the political importance of the clubs by launching attacks upon them at various times and places. The Federalist newspapers criticized the clubs as anarchistic and atheistic, among other things. President Washington inveighed against the clubs in the days following the Whiskey Rebellion and again in his Farewell Address. These attacks did some harm in isolated areas, but by then the Republican Party was functioning and Thomas Jefferson had taken over the leadership. Again during the period immediately following the publication of the XYZ dispatches, the Democratic societies retreated before the assault of an enraged public. Frequently the clubs dropped their names, adopted another form of organization, or used the town meeting as their rostrum. During this period of war fever, the clubs persisted in opposing war with France.

The clubs served many purposes. Link points out their usefulness in attracting unknown citizens to active participation in politics. They manufactured propaganda, discussed candidates for office, watched carefully the performance of incumbents, studied the science of government, and served as social clubs in frontier areas. For these reasons alone the clubs are worthy of study.

Baldwin, Leland D. *Whiskey Rebels: The Story of a Frontier Uprising.* Pittsburgh: University of Pittsburgh Press, 1939.

Professor Baldwin begins this monograph by painting a broad picture of the four-county area around Pittsburgh. He discusses the religion, nationality, education and economic condition of the people and concludes that in the 1790's "John Buckskin" had come close to creating a perfect democracy. Yet he rejects the idea that there was complete agreement in thought among men in western Pennsylvania especially when it came to armed resistance to the national government.

Among Westeners he thinks only tax collectors and inspectors favored the excise on spirituous liquors. The "Neville connection," headed by General John Neville and his son Presley, wealthy Westeners entrusted with enforcing the excise, led the move to suppress the insurrection. Baldwin maintains that Pittsburgh wanted to avoid violence. Albert Gallatin of Pittsburgh was one of the most prominent leaders in this faction. Another was Hugh Henry Brakenridge, a Princeton-trained printer and attorney. If anyone stands out as Baldwin's hero it is Brakenridge whose *Incidents of the Insurrection* (1795) was quoted liberally. The large German minority stood aloof from the rebellion, and the Presbyterian church, the largest sect in the region, actively opposed it. Indeed, he argues that "the official position of the church was the most decisive factor in the outcome of the insurrection."

Professor Baldwin pays scant attention to Alexander Hamilton's maneuvering to pass the Assumption Act which necessitated the excise on whiskey. Nor does he dwell on the reaction to the tax from other liquor-producing regions. He thinks the Democratic societies were used to coördinate the resistance, but little time is spent discussing the make up or activities of these groups. It was popularity seekers like David Bradford and hotheads and irresponsible men, like David Hamilton, Benjamin Parkinson, John Holcroft, and James Marshall, whom Baldwin cites as being most responsible for the uprising. Yet even though the Monongahela country thought the federal excise of 1791 was galling, he argues that it was not so much the tax itself that stirred the people toward rebellion, for from 1684 until 1791 Pennsylvania was never without an excise on liquor. It was the stipulation in the 1791 law that excise cases were to be tried in Philadelphia, some three hundred miles distant, that set the West aflame.

The various mass meetings held by the whiskey rebels are related in detail, as are the unsuccessful activities of the commissioners sent by President Washington and Governor Thomas Mifflin of Pennsylvania to heal the problems in the West. The author also describes the march of the 15,000 militiamen sent under the command of Governor Henry Lee, accompanied by Alexander Hamilton, to quell the insurrection. Having encountered no resistance in the West, the army marched away in November 1794, less than three weeks after its arrival. With it trudged prisoners who were eventually to stand trial in Philadelphia. The study ends with a discussion of the trial and eventual release of the accused men.

Professor Baldwin concludes by suggesting that the Jeffersonian Republicans gained most from the Monongahela troubles. He thinks that the Whiskey Rebellion was much like the Regulator movement and the Populist revolt and that it was but "one of the signposts that marked the cleavage amidst the people, particularly between the agrarians and the rising industrial and mercantile class." — *J. G. C.*

Additional Recommended Reading

Fox, Dixon R. *The Decline of Aristocracy in the Politics of New York.* New York: Columbia University Press, 1919. The standard account of the democratization of politics in New York during the early national period.

Gilpatrick, Delbert H. *Jeffersonian Democracy in North Carolina, 1789-1816.* New York: Columbia University Press, 1931. A narrative of the decline of Federalism and the rise of Republicanism in early North Carolina.

Ferguson, Russell J. *Early Western Pennsylvania Politics.* Pittsburgh: University of Pittsburgh Press, 1938. Describes Pennsylvania politics and party development.

Fee, Walter R. *The Transition from Aristocracy to Democracy in New Jersey, 1789-1829.* Somerset, New Jersey: Somerset Press, Inc., 1933. This book points out that a generally democratic attitude prevailed in New Jersey prior to the advent of President Jackson.

Brunhouse, Robert L. *The Counter-Revolution in Pennsylvania, 1776-1790.* Harrisburg: The Pennsylvania Historical and Museum Commission, 1942. This book tells the tale of the effort, ultimately successful, to discard the liberal state constitution of 1776.

The Whiskey Rebellion

Wallace, Paul A. *The Muhlenbergs of Pennsylvania.* Philadelphia: University of Pennsylvania Press, 1943. A good study of a Pennsylvania family of considerable political importance.

Tinkcom, Harry M. *The Republicans and Federalists in Pennsylvania, 1790-1801: A Study in National Stimulus and Local Response.* Harrisburg: Pennsylvania Historical and Museum Commission, 1950. A very good detailed study of politics in Pennsylvania.

BATTLE OF FALLEN TIMBERS

Type of event: Military: defeat of Indians attempting to hold Americans south of the Ohio river
Time: August 20, 1794
Locale: Northwestern Ohio

Principal personages:

GEORGE WASHINGTON (1732-1799), first President of the United States 1789-1797

HENRY KNOX (1750-1806), Secretary of War

BRIGADIER GENERAL JOSIAH HARMAR (1753-1813), who commanded the first unsuccessful campaign against the Wabash-Maumee Indians in 1790

ARTHUR ST. CLAIR (1736?-1818), Governor of the Northwest Territory 1787-1802, who as Major General of federal troops commanded the disastrous second campaign against the Wabash-Maumee Indians

MAJOR GENERAL ANTHONY WAYNE ("MAD ANTHONY") (1745-1796), Commander of the Legion of the United States 1792-1795, whom Washington and Knox carefully selected in 1792 to command the successful third campaign against the Wabash-Maumee Indians

JOSEPH BRANT (THAYENDANEGEA) (1742-1807), Mohawk chief and leading advocate in the 1780's of a defensive confederacy between the Six Nations of the Iroquois of New York and the predominantly Algonquian tribes living west of the Ohio river and around the Great Lakes

ALEXANDER MCKEE (fl. 1790-1796), superintendent of Indian Affairs at Detroit for the British Indian Department, who advised and supplied the Indians before, during, and after the American campaigns

MATTHEW ELLIOTT (fl. 1790-1796), assistant agent of Indian Affairs at Detroit for the British Indian Department 1790-1796

Summary of Event

Great Britain recognized American sovereignty over the territory north of the Ohio river in the Treaty of Paris of 1783. As individual states relinquished their titles to the area, it became part of the national domain, to be surveyed and sold according to the Ordinance of 1785, and governed and formed into new states according to the Northwest Ordinance of 1787. Meanwhile, the Confederation government pressured the Indians to cede their territorial claims.

The Indians of the Old Northwest had not been included in Anglo-American negotiations for peace and terri-

383

tory, even though the area had been guaranteed to them by the Treaty of Fort Stanwix of 1768. They were now unwilling to submit to American sovereignty if that meant that they would lose actual possession of the land. But the Confederation government maintained that the Indians had forfeited their land rights by supporting the British during the Revolution. It managed to dictate another Treaty of Fort Stanwix to the Iroquois in 1784, the Treaty of Fort McIntosh to the Chippewa, Delaware, Ottawa, and Wyandot in 1785, and the Treaty of Fort Finney to the Shawnee in 1786, forcing them to surrender their claims to the eastern and southern portions of present-day Ohio. Subsequently, multitribal councils declared these cessions invalid, arguing that separate tribes could not, and should not, be forced to cede territorial possession without the consent of all the tribes in the nascent northwestern Indian confederacy, which the Indians were trying to form into a viable instrument of resistance. In January, 1789, new treaties signed at Fort Harmar with some of the tribes reaffirmed previous cessions, but the Indians subsequently disavowed these treaties as well.

In response to the Confederation government's aggressive policy toward the incursions of white squatters and toward raids by Kentuckians against their villages, Indian bands attacked squatters and government surveyors, harassed pioneers migrating down the Ohio river, and raided parts of Kentucky. In 1788 and 1789, following the passage of the Northwest Ordinance, the Indians attacked the new white settlements at and around Marietta and Losantiville (later Cincinnati), am-bushed army detachments, and stepped up their raids into Kentucky.

President George Washington and Secretary of War Henry Knox, who had come to office in the spring of 1789 under the new federal Constitution, decided to attempt what the Confederation government had been unable to do for lack of funds and a sizable army. In 1790 they approved plans for a campaign to defeat hostile warriors and destroy their centers of resistance, the villages along the Wabash, Auglaize, and Maumee rivers. Leaving Fort Washington at Cincinnati on September 30, Brigadier General Josiah Harmar slowly marched the main force of about 1,130 militia and 320 regulars northward through the wilderness. In October he destroyed several villages along the Maumee river, but in three subsequent engagements with Indian warriors, detached portions of his army lost more than two hundred men. The campaign was a failure and it united the Western tribes. Major General Arthur St. Clair, Governor of the Northwest Territory, led the next expedition. It was a national disaster. On November 4, 1791, about one hundred miles north of Fort Washington, the Indians surprised his army in camp, killing 650 and wounding 270.

Indian confidence soared. In negotiations in 1793 at Lower Sandusky, the Chippewa, Delaware, Miami, Ottawa, Potawatomi, Shawnee, Wyandot, and other Western tribes insisted on the reëstablishment of the Ohio river boundary. The Iroquois were prepared to cede eastern Ohio, but the Americans were unwilling to relinquish their hold on southern and eastern Ohio.

Washington and Knox had expected

diplomatic failure. In 1792 and 1793 Major General Anthony Wayne (known as "Mad Anthony") organized another army, the Legion of the United States, first at Pittsburgh and later at Cincinnati. His force was better trained than Harmar's or St. Clair's; it was harshly disciplined; there was a greater proportion of regulars to militia; supply preparations were sounder; and friendly Indian scouts were recruited. Wayne started north in October, 1793, after receiving news of the failure of negotiations. Ordered by Knox to avoid a winter campaign, however, Wayne halted six miles north of Fort Jefferson, built Fort Greenville, and encamped for the winter. In December his troops built Fort Recovery on the site of St. Clair's defeat.

With British encouragement and assistance the Indians began to gather at the junction of the Auglaize and Maumee rivers in the spring of 1794. By June at least fifteen hundred warriors were in the field. The British advised them to avoid battle and instead to increase their attacks on vulnerable American supply trains moving up the chain of forts from Fort Washington. On June 30 and July 1, however, they vainly assaulted Fort Recovery, suffering their first setback in years.

Wayne's army of thirty-five hundred men began its advance on July 28, stopped at the junction of the Auglaize and Maumee rivers to build Fort Defiance, resumed the march up the Maumee river, and then halted on August 18, about ten miles below the British Fort Miami. Nearby, about thirteen hundred warriors, principally of the Delaware, Miami, Ottawa, Shawnee, and Wyandot tribes, awaited his attack at a spot strewn with trees felled by a tornado years before. Expecting the attack to come the next day, they began their customary prebattle fasting. But Wayne did not advance until August 20, by which time many of the Indians had gone to Fort Miami for provisions, leaving only about five hundred warriors to face the Legion of the United States. The Americans outflanked the Indian line, charged, and after a brief, hard fight, drove the warriors from the field. Some fled to Fort Miami, but the British closed their gates. The Legion of the United States lost 133 men and the Indians about fifty, including several principal warriors. Wayne then laid waste to Indian crops, supplies, and villages along the Maumee river, threatening the Indians with starvation.

Wayne had clearly demonstrated American power. On August 3, 1795, the defeated Indian confederacy signed Wayne's Treaty of Fort Greenville, giving the United States southern and eastern Ohio and a strip of southeastern Indiana.

Pertinent Literature

Downes, Randolph C. *Council Fires on the Upper Ohio: A Narrative of Indian Affairs in the Upper Ohio Valley Until 1795.* Pittsburgh: University of Pittsburgh Press, 1940.

Randolph Downes' carefully researched and well-written narrative is a rich source of information about the complex events on the Ohio frontier in the 1780's and the 1790's, and it conveys better than most "frontier histories" the tragedy of the conflict between the red men and whites. To a large extent historians of the American West have written about the Indians summarily and unsympathetically. As Jack D. Forbes observed in an article entitled "The Indian in the West," in *Arizona and the West,* Vol. I (Autumn 1959), many historians have adopted the white pioneer's point of view, depicting the Indian only as a savage obstacle to the inevitable and desirable expansion of a morally and technologically superior white civilization. They have, for example, stressed the sufferings of the "democratic" and "individualistic" pioneers and the problems of their government in extending the frontier, but have ignored those of the "warlike" Indians in defending their land. They have diligently noted Indian massacres but have disregarded white atrocities and injustices, and the disastrous impact of white culture upon Indian culture.

Council Fires on the Upper Ohio is exceptional because Downes' attempts to tell the story of the conquest of the Ohio Valley from the Indian's point of view, which he feels is necessary for a true interpretation of the event. He does not pass judgment on the comparative merits of white and Indian ways of life, but simply takes the position that Indian culture was a distinct phenomenon which the Indians believed was worth defending. His narrative focuses on the Delaware and Shawnee tribes from their arrival in the upper Ohio River Valley in the early eighteenth century, through their struggle with the French and the British, to their defeat at the Battle of Fallen Timbers. The Indians emerge from the story not as savage opponents of civilization but as victims of it. They were caught in the web of British,

French, and American rivalry for control of the continent, and, mainly through the workings of the fur trade, they were to a large extent dependent on the technologically superior whites for clothing, tools, and weapons. The ultimate threat was the advance of the white farming frontier. It was incompatible with their way of life, based as it was on hunting and rudimentary agriculture.

After the Revolutionary War, Indian leaders of the various northwestern tribes believed that their best hope of preserving the Ohio river boundary was to confederate and present a unified stance against the American government. But unity was difficult to achieve. The proximity of some tribes to the frontier made them more vulnerable than others to American retaliation and consequently more susceptible to American diplomatic pressures. Militarily the Indians were no match for the Americans, whose raids against crops and villages could disrupt their economy and inflict crippling casualties. Aware of Indian weaknesses, the Confederation government pursued a policy of "divide and conquer"; it insisted on dealing with tribes individually. At Fort Stanwix, Fort McIntosh, Fort Finney, and Fort Harmar, Downes explains, it used the threat of force to intimidate those warriors present into signing away territory.

History books often make it appear as though the Indians, in subsequently disavowing these treaties, were guilty of violating sacred agreements solemnly made. This assumption of Indian treaty-violation, in addition to the emphasis given to Indian reprisals during the 1780's, has the effect of justifying the indiscriminate raids of Kentuckians throughout the 1780's and the expeditions of Harmar, St. Clair, and Wayne in the 1790's. But Downes points out, without justifying them, that only certain Indian bands of some tribes resorted to reprisals, and that these were fundamentally a response to the intrusions of squatters, the raids of Kentuckians, and the aggressive diplomatic policy of the Confederation government.

Horsman, Reginald. *Matthew Elliott, British Indian Agent: A Study of British Indian Policy in the Old Northwest.* Detroit: Wayne State University Press, 1964.

Reginald Horsman has written several articles and books on American, British, and Indian relations. In this biography of Matthew Elliott he synthesizes many of his findings and offers a concentrated view of British and Indian activities in the Old Northwest from about 1760 to 1814. As fur trader, farmer, and Indian agent at Detroit, Elliott was intimately involved in the events leading to the Battle of Fallen Timbers.

Some historians have accused the British, and particularly British fur traders, of fanning Indian hostility to American expansion into war. According to Horsman's account, the role of the British in helping to bring on war was more complex and less calculating. Independently of their government, he finds, some fur traders did encourage the Indians to resist American expansion, to distrust American overtures, and to believe that the British army would fight with them against the Americans. The British government, on the other hand, wanted to preserve peace on the frontier because it believed that a general Indian-American war would endanger Canada and the fur trade, and it tried to avoid making firm promises of military support to the Indians.

But Horsman argues that despite the British government's desire for peace, its policy and the behavior of its agents had the effect of strengthening the Indians' will and ability to resist American pressures. Regarding the maintenance of good relations with the Indians as essential to its own interests, the British government assured the Indian tribes in 1783 that they were still the sole proprietors of the territory. During the 1780's and 1790's the Indian Department supplied them with food, clothing, and weapons, encouraged Indian efforts to confederate, and gave advice on diplomatic and military matters. Moreover, the British refusal to withdraw from Mackinac, Detroit, and Niagara—posts within territory it had officially ceded to the United States —led the Indians to trust in British military support and underrate American strength. There is also reason to suspect that Matthew Elliott and Alexander McKee, who as superintendent and assistant agent of Indian Affairs at Detroit for the British Indian Department attended the Indian-American negotiations in 1793, encouraged the Western tribes to insist on the Ohio river boundary. Joseph Brant (Thayendanegea), a Mohawk chief, representing the New York Iroquois, accused McKee of undermining his attempts to persuade the western tribes to relinquish eastern Ohio. But McKee's influence, if Brant was correct, may not have mattered much at the negotiations after all. The victorious

western tribes were not eager to com- Americans were not satisfied with
promise on American terms, and the Brant's concession. — *J.K.*

Additional Recommended Reading

Callahan, North. *Henry Knox: General Washington's General.* New York: Holt, Rinehart & Winston, Inc., 1958. Based largely on primary sources, this is a recent biography of Knox. In the chapter entitled "The Indian Troubles," Callahan tries to explain how Knox first recommended against an Indian campaign for humanitarian reasons, then recommended a punitive expedition, and finally played a major role in defeating the Indians.

Hagan, William T. *American Indians.* Chicago: University of Chicago Press, 1961. One of the Chicago *History of American Civilization* series, this brief, fairly sympathetic general history of the Indians stresses the American government's policies toward them.

Horsman, Reginald. *The Frontier in the Formative Years, 1783-1815.* New York: Holt, Rinehart & Winston, Inc., 1970. Written for the publisher's *Histories of the American Frontier* series, Horsman's book is based on original research and provides a detailed summary of American, British, Indian, and Spanish policies and problems on the frontier.

Jacobs, James R. *The Beginning of the United States Army, 1783-1812.* Princeton: Princeton University Press, 1947. Jacobs' scholarly book, written with an anti-Indian bias, is the standard history of the vicissitudes of the army in less vigorous campaigns. It contains a detailed account of the early Indian campaigns, an explanation of the unique organization of the Legion of the United States, and a discussion of how Wayne won the title "Father of the Regular Army."

Prucha, Francis P. *The Sword of the Republic: The United States Army on the Frontier, 1783-1846.* New York: The Macmillan Company, 1969. Part of the *Macmillan Wars of the United States* series, Prucha's well-researched book is broader in scope than Jacobs' work. Prucha offers the thesis that "army men . . . were agents of empire, who made possible the development of the American republic throughout the land it now enjoys."

Risch, Erna. *Quartermaster Support of the Army: A History of the Corps, 1775-1939.* Washington: Quartermaster Historians Office, 1962. Risch's general history of army supply, making full use of archival sources, provides information not available elsewhere on the logistical problems that Harmar, St. Clair, and Wayne faced in the wilderness, resulting mainly from lack of funds, contractors' failures, winter campaigning, and Indian harassment.

NEGOTIATION OF JAY'S TREATY

Type of event: Diplomatic: negotiations improving relations between Great Britain and the United States
Time: 1794-1795
Locale: Philadelphia, Pennsylvania; and London, England

Principal personages:

GEORGE WASHINGTON (1732-1799), first President of the United States 1789-1797

ALEXANDER HAMILTON (1757-1804), Secretary of the Treasury 1789-1795

THOMAS JEFFERSON (1743-1826), Secretary of State 1790-1793

JAMES MADISON (1751-1836), anti-administration leader in the House of Representatives

JOHN JAY (1745-1829), Chief Justice of the Supreme Court and Envoy Extraordinary to the British government 1789-1795

JAMES MONROE (1758-1831), American Minister to France during Jay's negotiations

WILLIAM PITT, THE YOUNGER (1759-1806), Prime Minister of Great Britain 1783-1801

WILLIAM WYNDHAM GRENVILLE (BARON GRENVILLE) (1759-1834), Foreign Secretary of Great Britain 1791-1801

GEORGE HAMMOND (fl. 1794-1795), British Minister to the United States

Summary of Event

By the Treaty of Paris in 1783, Great Britain recognized the independence of the United States. The United States now had to make that independence meaningful and permanent. For the next three decades the new nation struggled to maintain its integrity by achieving security against the hostile forces which surrounded it both on the north and the south. America's southern boundary was in dispute with Spain; the British were ensconced in Canada and refused to evacuate posts in the Northwest Territory which the Treaty of Paris recognized as American. In 1793, the European powers went to war to put down the subversive doctrines evolving from the French Revolution and, later, the military ambitions of Napoleon Bonaparte. The war between France and the rest of Europe continued, with only a brief intermission from 1793 to 1815, and the United States was buffeted first by one belligerent and then by the other. The treaty negotiated by John Jay of New York is an episode in the struggle of the United States to "secure the blessings of liberty" promised by the Constitution.

Anglo-American relations bordered on the tempestuous from 1783 onward. There were many outstanding problems, a number of which stemmed from the apparent unwillingness of either power to abide by the Treaty of

389

Paris. There were difficulties over boundaries and over the fishing rights of Americans along the Grand Banks.

The United States and Great Britain found themselves competing in commercial affairs. In an effort to secure the carrying trade for British vessels, Great Britain prohibited American vessels from carrying goods to British colonial ports. At the same time, Great Britain enjoyed a virtual monopoly of the American market for manufactured goods. Americans attempted to substitute the French market. Soon it became evident that Great Britain could best supply credit and merchandise to the United States. Many Americans deeply resented their economic subservience to Great Britain. The Washington Administration only with difficulty prevented the passage of commercial legislation designed to retaliate against alleged British discriminatory practices.

When war between France and Great Britain broke out in 1793, new grievances were rapidly added to the old, and relations between Great Britain and the United States took a rapid turn for the worse. The position of the United States as the major maritime neutral was critical. There was also residual hostility toward Great Britain in contrast to a generally favorable attitude toward France, our ex-comrade-in-arms.

The British rapidly gained mastery of the oceans, which theoretically isolated the French West Indies. These islands could no longer trade with France in French ships. Into this vacuum flowed the merchant fleet of the United States, which gained great profits from this trade. The British realized that traffic in American ships

negated to a certain degree their naval supremacy. In November, 1793, a British Order in Council ordered British naval commanders to seize all neutral vessels trading with the French islands. So suddenly was this order implemented that some 250 American ships were seized and about half of them condemned to be sold as lawful prizes. This action alienated some of the best friends Great Britain had in the United States. James Madison, the Congressman from Virginia, led a vigorous campaign to pass retaliatory legislation. Alexander Hamilton, Secretary of the Treasury, fought off this effort successfully, with President Washington's blessing. To blunt the edge of Madison's attack, John Jay was dispatched as Envoy Extraordinary to the British government. Washington apparently believed that war was inevitable unless Jay returned with an acceptable settlement.

The treaty which Jay brought back proved to be barely acceptable. According to Henry Adams, "There has been no time since 1810 when the United States would have hesitated to prefer war rather than peace on such terms." It provided for the British to surrender the posts which they held on American soil in the Northwest by June, 1796; and for the creation of joint commissions to settle the claims of British citizens for unpaid pre-revolutionary American debts, to settle the claims of Americans for the illegal seizures of their ships, and to determine the disputed boundary between Maine and Canada. The rest of the treaty dealt with commercial matters, and was to be in force for twelve years. It stated that the most favored national principle was to operate between the United

States and the United Kingdom. American vessels were to have the same privileges as British in both Great Britain and the East Indies. American trading rights with the British West Indies were so restricted, however, that the United States struck out that part of the treaty. The agreement included a definition of contraband, but it said nothing on the important matters of the rights of visit and search and impressment.

When the terms of the treaty became known, after ratification by the Senate in a strictly sectional vote (North for, South against), a furious debate raged. The Republicans charged the Washington Administration with selling the nation out to the British. Effigies of John Jay were burned throughout the country. Political pamphleteers and journalists entered the fray. Washington, disappointed by the treaty, signed it because he believed its acceptance the only alternative to war. Only an intense effort by the Washington Administration prevented the Republicans in the House of Representatives from defeating the treaty by refusing to appropriate the funds necessary to its implementation.

The effects of this treaty were momentous. Most importantly, it kept the peace between the United States and Great Britain. It also induced Spain to conclude a treaty which was very favorable to the United States, and it prepared the way for the large-scale settlement of the Northwest. The fight over the treaty completed the organization of the opposition Republican Party, which antagonism to the Hamiltonian program had initiated. The Federalists were weakened and divided. Washington's invulnerability to political attack was breached. The restraining influence of the British on the Indians along the northwestern frontier was withdrawn. Most significantly, the French First Republic was incensed at this apparent repudiation by the United States of the Franco-American Treaty of 1778. While relations with Great Britain improved temporarily, the United States and France drifted apart. This rift between the only republican governments in the world culminated in an undeclared war and proved to be the dominant issue during the administration of President John Adams.

Pertinent Literature

Bemis, Samuel Flagg. *Jay's Treaty: A Study in Commerce and Diplomacy.* 2nd ed. New Haven: Yale University Press, 1962.

The author, one of the outstanding authorities on American diplomatic history, deals with more than the negotiation of Jay's Treaty in this volume. It is, among other things, the story of an emergent nation—the United States—and its first critical confrontation with what was then the world's most powerful country—Great Britain. More particularly, Bemis critically analyzes the role of the first Secretary of the Treasury in the formation of foreign policy for the new nation. It is a judiciously written work, although diplomatic historians continue to dispute Bemis' conclusions regarding Hamilton's overall influence.

The work is organized into three relatively self-contained units: Anglo-American relations from 1783 to 1792;

the impact of the French Revolutionary Wars on Anglo-American relations, 1793-1794; and the response of the American government and its domestic opponents to the British challenge. Each section leads naturally to the other, and the whole toward the culmination in Jay's Treaty and the author's assessment of the success of the United States in meeting its first great crisis in foreign affairs.

During the Confederation period and up to the Anglo-French War, relations between the United States and Great Britain were focused upon basically commercial matters. The United States, stripped of the commercial advantages it had enjoyed while a member of the British Empire, was not only denied a share of the lucrative trade with the British West Indies but also compelled to accept the continued presence of British troops south of the Great Lakes. There the British maintained control over the Indians and had a virtual monopoly over the fur trade. Elements in the American government that wished to retaliate against Great Britain were prevented from doing so by the Washington Administration, ably led by Hamilton, who even then conducted much of the nation's foreign policy by circumventing the Secretary of State, Thomas Jefferson. Hamilton at all times wished to accommodate Great Britain and to avoid tension whenever possible.

Conditions changed radically when France and Great Britain went to war. There was much pro-French sentiment latent in the United States as a result of France's aid to the rebellious colonies from 1778 to 1783, and many Americans viewed the French Revolution as a sequel to the American struggle for independence and liberty. The growing anti-British faction in Congress sought to exploit the situation in Congress, and it appeared that it would succeed when news reached the United States of the wholesale seizures of American vessels by the British in the Caribbean Sea.

Hamilton, who sincerely believed that war with Great Britain would prostrate the new government, recommended to President Washington that a special peace envoy be sent to Great Britain. Hamilton himself declined the honor of serving in this capacity, and John Jay was chosen. According to Bemis, Hamilton was running the foreign affairs of the nation. The results of this arrangement were significant. Hamilton conveyed to the British Minister to the United States, George Hammond, the impression that the United States wished compromise and had no intentions of exerting pressure on Great Britain. Bemis concludes therefore that Jay was never in any position to negotiate a favorable treaty for the United States. Hamilton had undermined the American position before Jay even left the country.

Bemis is negative in his evaluation of Jay's work. The United States accepted the British definition of neutral rights howsoever the British defined those rights at any given time. Moreover, the so-called concessions granted to the United States as part of Great Britain's agreement to evacuate the Northwest and to ease off in its seizure of American shipping had been decided before Jay's mission became known. A serious failure on Jay's part was his inability to secure an article protecting Americans from impressment.

Hamilton, according to the author,

was primarily responsible for Jay's Treaty and therefore should bear the blame for its failure. Jay is criticized for completely surrendering to the British position, but given Hamilton's interference, he could have accomplished little in any event. Bemis concludes, however, that although the articles in the treaty were not to America's advantage, the United States was fortunate to obtain a treaty at all. The very fact that the British negotiated with the United States as an equal compensated to some degree for the general inadequacy of the treaty's provisions.

DeConde, Alexander. *Entangling Alliance: Politics and Diplomacy Under George Washington.* Durham, North Carolina: Duke University Press, 1958.

The participation of France in the Revolutionary War is generally agreed to have been the most important contributing factor in America's successful struggle for independence. During the following decade, the two nations enjoyed amicable relations. With the coming of the French Revolution in 1789, Americans were confident that the French were on the verge of writing a new chapter in the story of man's progress toward liberty and enlightenment. The French did indeed write a new chapter, but it was not in the book which Americans had in mind and the results were not those which Americans had reckoned with. By 1798-1799 the two powers were engaged in an undeclared naval war which threatened to break out into a formal war. The author of this study investigates the causes for this deterioration of relations with France through the end of the Washington Administration.

DeConde defines two major issues in the Washington era—Hamilton's politico-economic policies, and problems arising from the wars of the French Revolution. In both cases, the domestic impact was paramount. The Hamiltonian program created factions in Congress and anti-administration feelings in the country. The second issue, foreign affairs, brought the factions and public opinion together in a formally organized political party, the object of which was to replace the Federalists in power. The deterioration of Franco-American relations was as much the result of internal struggles for power as the result of French policy toward the United States. In the first stages of this development, which culminated during the Adams Administration, the dominating figure was Hamilton.

DeConde is correct in emphasizing the fact that the permanence of the Franco-American alliance depended upon the strengthening of commercial ties between the two nations. It was obvious by the mid-1780's that trade with France was less profitable and less necessary than trade with Great Britain. French concessions and British discrimination did not change the position. Hamilton therefore put no stock in the alliance. When the Anglo-French war broke out, Hamilton was ready to scrap the alliance and to bend American neutrality in a pro-British direction. Jefferson and Madison, more favorable to the French, opposed Hamilton's attitude. The consequence of Hamilton's policies, Jay's Treaty, was considered by France and its friends in America, to be a repudiation of American neutrality and an insult to the French Republic. But Hamilton reigned supreme in Washington's cabinet.

The French had not endeared themselves to Washington and his supporters during the period immediately following the outbreak of war in 1793. Representatives from the French Revolutionary government to the United States had a penchant for intervening in the domestic affairs of the United States. At first aimed mostly against the British and their Spanish allies, the intervention soon took on a political hue as the French aligned themselves with the anti-administration faction. One French representative, Citizen Edmond Genet, acted so high-handedly that the President was compelled to demand his recall. But his successors were no different; all interfered in domestic politics, and all came down on the Republican side.

In 1796, the French representative, Pierre Adet, intervened in the Presidential election. He conjured up the possibility of war with France if John Adams were elected. The net result was probably to the advantage of Adams, whose followers dramatized this blatant effort by a foreigner to determine the course of American politics. The victory of Adams presaged no improvement in Franco-American relations.

DeConde's most controversial statements concern the role of Hamilton in determining the foreign policy of the United States. To DeConde, Washington's policy was Hamilton's policy. Washington was essentially the tool of Hamilton and necessary to the latter because of his prestige. Thus, the famous "Farewell Address" was a partisan pronouncement expressive of Hamilton's philosophy and designed for political purposes. While it is rather difficult to accept such views without serious qualification, they reflect the controversy that still rages around Alexander Hamilton and his place in American history. — *J.G.C.*

Additional Recommended Reading

Wood, G. C. *Congressional Control of Foreign Relations During the American Revolution, 1774-1789.* Allentown, Pennsylvania: H. R. Hass & Co., 1919. The author traces the origins of American foreign policy back to the Continental Congress.

Bemis, Samuel Flagg and Robert H. Ferrell, eds. *The American Secretaries of State and Their Diplomacy, 1776-1925.* 10 vols. New York: Alfred A. Knopf, Inc., and Cooper Square Publishers, 1927-1965. This outstanding collection studies the work of each Secretary of State from Robert Livingston to James F. Byrnes.

Thomas, Charles M. *American Neutrality in 1793: A Study in Cabinet Government.* New York: Columbia University Press, 1931. A study of the contribution of Washington's cabinet in the evolution of the American concept of neutrality.

Burt, Alfred L. *The United States, Great Britain, and British North America from the Revolution to the Establishment of Peace After the War of 1812.* New Haven: Yale University Press, 1940. One of the most suggestive studies of Anglo-American relations, especially revealing about British objectives.

Freeman, Douglas Southall. *George Washington.* Vol. VII: *First in Peace.* 7 vols. New York: Charles A. Scribner's Sons, 1948-1957. This monumental study, the last volume of which was completed by two of Freeman's research assistants, covers the period from

1793 to 1799.

Perkins, Bradford. *The First Rapprochement: England and the United States, 1795-1805.* Philadelphia: University of Pennsylvania Press, 1953. This work, the first of two volumes dealing with Anglo-American relations to 1815, emphasizes the relatively peaceful course of relations during the decade covered.

NEGOTIATION OF PINCKNEY'S TREATY

Type of event: Diplomatic: boundary settlement between Spain and the United States
Time: October 27, 1795
Locale: Spain

Principal personages:

GEORGE WASHINGTON (1732-1799), first President of the United States 1789-1797

THOMAS PINCKNEY (1750-1828), Minister to Great Britain and Envoy Extraordinary to Spain

MANUEL DE GODOY (Manuel de Godoy y Alvarez de Faria) (1767-1851), Minister who directed both negotiations with the United States

BARÓN FRANCISCO LUIS HÉCTOR DE CARONDOLET (? 1748-1807), Spanish Governor of Louisiana 1795-1797, hostile to American expansion

JAMES WILKINSON (1757-1825), Major-General in United States Army who received payments from Spain to incite disunion in the West

JOHN SEVIER (1745-1815), pioneer and speculator, governor of the abortive state of "Franklin"

WILLIAM BLOUNT (1749-1800), land speculator, United States Senator from Tennessee, and leader of the Blount Conspiracy

WILLIAM SHORT (fl.1795), joint Commissioner Plenipotentiary to negotiate a treaty with Spain

DON DIEGO DE GARDOQUI (fl.1795), Spanish Minister to the United States who negotiated with the United States on the question of trade between the United States and Spain and the navigation of the Mississippi river

Summary of Event

One of the most pressing diplomatic problems facing the United States after 1783 was Spanish occupation of, and claims to, a large portion of the southern and southwestern United States. The Spanish had enjoyed undisputed possession since 1763 of the territory that had been French Louisiana. They had also regained Florida in 1783, temporarily taken over by Great Britain between 1763 and 1783. Spanish power rested solidly along the entire Gulf Coast of North and Central America, both banks of the Mississippi river from its mouth to a point midway between present-day Baton Rouge, Louisiana, and Natchez, Mississippi, and the west bank of the river north to the Missouri river and west to the Pacific Ocean. In addition to these vast holdings, the Spanish claimed by right of conquest during the American Revolution a large portion of the present-day states of Alabama, Mississippi, and Tennessee. In other words, Spain held or claimed both banks of the Mississippi from its mouth to the mouth of the Ohio river and east to the western slopes of the Appalachian Mountains. It was in this disputed territory and on the Mississippi river that American expansion ran into Spanish power.

The United States received the right to navigate the Mississippi to its mouth in the Treaty of Paris in 1783. Spain, not a party to this treaty, refused to accede, and closed the Mississippi to all but Spanish commerce. American settlers crossing the Appalachians were also pressing against Spanish claims east of the river. The Spanish, as did the English in the North, utilized Indian antagonism toward American expansion to thwart the westward movement of the United States. At the same time, the Spanish intermittently schemed with dissident Western Americans, dissatisfied with Western policies of the federal government, in an effort to stimulate the separation of the West from the new republic. The Spanish were kept in a constant state of agitation because of the aggressive, lawless nature of American frontiersmen. The frontiersmen, for their part, threatened the Spanish with invasion because of Spain's closure of the Mississippi river and Spanish support of Indian raids on American settlements. The Washington Administration was sensitive to the threat of Western separation. The federal government recognized that the right to free navigation of the river was an absolute necessity to the West, since the river was the only economically feasible route to market. The federal government was also under pressure by Western speculative interests whose landholdings suffered in value as a result of Spanish-supported Indian attacks.

Little progress was made in solving the disputes until 1794. Until that time Western intrigues, Spanish fears of a Franco-American invasion, and Indian wars were recurrent themes along the southern border. The Spanish attempted, with the aid of the American Major-General James Wilkinson, and others, to stimulate disunion in the West. The Spanish, to woo the West, opened up trade on the Mississippi to Americans on payment of a fifteen percent duty. This somewhat mollified the West but failed to stimulate serious separatist movements. Then, in 1794-1795, the French Revolutionary Wars brought relations to a crisis. In this instance the wars provided the United States with the opportunity of achieving a striking diplomatic victory.

Spain had joined with Great Britain in the war against the French First Republic. In 1794-1795, the war turned against Spain, which then began to look for a way out. In 1794, before Spain made its decision relative to the war, it indicated willingness to negotiate with the United States. Washington dispatched Thomas Pinckney, Minister to Great Britain, as Envoy Extraordinary and Minister Plenipotentiary to Madrid. Pinckney arrived in 1795. The delay worked to America's advantage, because by then Spain's military position had so deteriorated that it had decided to make a separate peace with France. Spain was also apprehensive concerning Jay's mission to Great Britain. Spain, about to deceive Great Britain, wished to protect itself against anticipated British retaliation. The Jay negotiations indicated to Spain that a possible Anglo-American *rapprochement* was about to take place, and that a joint attack on Spain's overseas empire might cement such an alliance.

Pinckney was able to capitalize on Spain's fears in negotiating the Treaty of San Lorenzo, signed on October 27, 1795. The Spanish conceded point after point, while the United States gave up virtually nothing in return. Spain recognized American sovereignty to the east bank of the Mississippi north of the 31st parallel; granted permission to Americans to navigate the river; established a place to deposit American goods for transfer to ocean-going vessels; and recognized the American definition of neutral rights. Both powers promised to restrain the Indians. This was a tacit admission by Spain that it had incited them in the past. The United States did not promise to restrain the westward-pressing frontiersmen.

The Spanish implementation of the treaty came slowly. But once again Spain's unfavorable situation in Europe aided the United States. Spain pulled out of the disastrous war with the French First Republic in the secret Treaty of Basel in 1795. The following year, in the secret Treaty of San Ildefonso, Spain plunged into an equally disastrous war as an ally of the French against Great Britain.

For the second time the possibility of an Anglo-American alliance against Spain compelled Spain to placate the United States. The Treaty of San Lorenzo was executed in full by 1798. In negotiating the Treaty of Greenville (1795) with the Indians, Jay's Treaty, and Pinckney's Treaty, the Washington Administration had achieved much in the field of diplomacy. At least the West was secured to the Union.

Pertinent Literature

Whitaker, Arthur P. *The Spanish-American Frontier, 1783-1795: The Westward Movement and the Spanish Retreat in the Mississippi Valley.* Boston: Houghton Mifflin Co., 1927.

Whitaker, Arthur P. *The Mississippi Question, 1795-1803: A Study in Trade, Politics, and Diplomacy.* New York: Appleton-Century-Crofts, 1934.

The Americans, both as British colonists and citizens of the United States, faced the power of Spain along the southern frontier from the colonization of South Carolina in the 1660's to the conclusion of the Transcontinental Treaty of 1819, (Adams-Onís Treaty). Between 1700 and 1763, the *fleur-de-lis* of Bourbon France represented a third power in the South to whose possessions Spain fell heir in 1763. In 1783 a new force, the United States, appeared along the frontier while possessions of an older power, Great Britain, passed into the hands of a still older power, Spain. The Spanish-American conflict, which is the theme of Whitaker's two volumes, was a direct outgrowth of the American Revolution which gave birth to an energetic republic. Spain was flung across the path of America's continental growth. To Whitaker, the destiny of the Mississippi River Valley was at stake. In these volumes, Whitaker traces the causes and consequences of the Spanish-American confrontation.

It is obvious at once that Spain, a declining power soon to be involved in a series of incredibly disastrous wars, did not stand a chance against the natural movement of Americans westward and southwestward. For a time, until 1793-1794, Spanish seapower precluded the unilateral conquest of Spanish Louisiana and the Floridas by the United States. But the developing foreign policy of John Jay during the Confederation and George Washington and Thomas Jefferson in subsequent years would count on time, population growth, and the inevitable European crises to force Spain into complete surrender.

These are the factors which led not only to Pinckney's Treaty of 1795, but also to the retrocession of Louisiana to Napoleonic France in 1800 and to the purchase of Louisiana by the United States in 1803. Time and numbers combined during the years 1783-1803 to create an American economic empire in the Mississippi River Valley. Louisiana was an economic burden to Spain, as it had been to France. As American control of the trade and commerce of the valley matured, in spite of Spain's strategic location athwart the river, Spain became more receptive to French demands for a retrocession of the colony. Spain unloaded Louisiana on France. European exigencies and the failure of Napoleon to pacify Santo Domingo made Louisiana valueless to Napoleon. Napoleon swiftly unloaded Louisiana, for a price, on the United States.

Whitaker's volumes are especially revealing concerning the various political, economic, and international pressures exerted on the disputants. The United States faced the unceasing demands of the West to resolve the Mississippi river question on favorable terms. Land speculators, such as John

Sevier, Governor of the state of "Franklin" in North Carolina, James Robertson, leader of a group in the Nashville area, and William Blount, politician, Senator from Tennessee, and leader of the Blount Conspiracy against Spanish Louisiana, agitated both governments. Their schemes for settlement frightened the Spanish who used the Indians against the settlers. This incited Western retaliation, stirred up Western indignation against Spain, and aroused impatience with the apparent weakness of the Union. The speculators attempted to exploit this turmoil by forcing the issue between Spain and the United States. Not only did the success of their speculative ventures depend upon the free use of the Mississippi but also Spain, in extending its territorial claims northward to the Tennessee river, preëmpted the sites most desired by the speculators.

Such was the situation when the French government beheaded Louis XVI, precipitating a general European war which played directly into the hands of the United States. Spain was at war with France until 1795 and with Great Britain between 1796 and 1801.

Whitaker considers that the Treaty of San Lorenzo was a momentous surrender for Spain. He also charges that American diplomacy was singularly incompetent in that the United States failed to use Jay's mission to England to squeeze greater concessions out of Spain. Whitaker dismisses the contention that the Spanish were ignorant of the contents of Jay's Treaty, which Samuel Flagg Bemis in *Pinckney's Treaty: A Study of America's Advantages from Europe's Distress* uses to explain the favorable terms of Pinckney's Treaty. Rather, according to Whitaker, the Spanish surrendered out of fear of British vengeance. American neutrality, considered to be indispensable by the Spanish, was purchased through the treaty.

The Treaty of San Lorenzo, in Whitaker's view, admitted the failure of Spanish policy on the east bank of the Mississippi and involved a tacit admission of failure on the west bank as well. Although Spain retained Louisiana, which served as a buffer between the aggressive Americans and Spain's lucrative Mexican possessions, the authority and power of Spain in the Mississippi River Valley deteriorated rapidly. Louisiana was a parasitic colony. In retroceding the colony to France, Spain shrewdly planned to let France pay the cost of Louisiana's defense, which was Mexico's defense as well. To Whitaker, the Treaty of San Ildefonso in 1800, whereby Spain retroceded Louisiana to France, was the fitting complement of Pinckney's Treaty.

Bemis, Samuel Flagg. *Pinckney's Treaty. A Study of America's Advantages from Europe's Distress.* Baltimore: The Johns Hopkins University Press, 1926. Rev. Ed., New Haven: Yale University Press, 1960.

On October 27, 1795, an elite yet patriotic South Carolinian, Thomas Pinckney, and Manuel de Godoy, Spain's new *Principe de la Paz* and Queen Maria Luisa's comely young lover, affixed their signatures and seals to a twenty-three article treaty between their respective nations at San Lorenzo, the autumnal residence of the Spanish Court. This document which, among other things, recognized the southern boundary of the United States as the 31st parallel and gave Americans the right to navigate the Mississippi river to its mouth, was one of a series of spectacular diplomatic triumphs won in the eighteenth and nineteenth centuries by the infant republic that had so recently fought its way out of the British womb. According to Samuel Flagg Bemis, these successes came about not because of the abilities of men, such as Franklin, Jefferson, or Monroe, but as the results of "a fortuitous and nonrecurring geopolitical situation in the world." This situation made possible American independence and the liberation of her Western ter-

ritories. It also carried the country through the War of 1812, and enabled it to engage in a costly civil war with no real outside interference. Composed of America's naturally protected geographical position, Canada's status as a "linchpin" for Anglo-American solidarity, and, especially, turmoil or "distress" on the European Continent, this condition gave the United States a "free security" that has been as significant in its development as the "free land" of the frontier. Bemis maintains that the Treaty of San Lorenzo, popularly known as Pinckney's Treaty, would never have been written or ratified had it not been for Europe's troubled political affairs. Indeed, as the subtitle of his much heralded *Pinckney's Treaty* asserts, the compact was an American advantage gained from Europe's distress.

As with so many diplomatic maneuvers, the story of Pinckney's mission to Madrid, his negotiations with de Godoy, and the eventual pact they signed is relatively simple in comparison to an account of the protracted and perpetually frustrating arbitrations of the preceding twelve years. Consequently, Bemis dedicates the bulk of this study to setting the stage for the great event in the fall of 1795, and, true to his thesis, most of this is an account of Europe's mounting distress.

After the War for American Independence, Spain owned all of Florida and Louisiana,, and she refused to recognize the 31st parallel as the new Confederacy's southern border or to allow Americans to navigate the Mississippi through her territory. Realizing that literally thousands of pioneers had migrated west of the Appalachians and that these people demanded free use of the river and potentially threatened Spanish holdings, in October, 1784, the Count of Floridablanca, King Charles' Foreign Minister, dispatched Don Diego de Gardoqui to the United States to discuss the questions of the river, the boundary, and future commercial relations between the two nations. For nearly five years de Gardoqui negotiated with John Jay and other governmental leaders, but neither side would modify its position enough for an agreement to be reached.

During this time, James Wilkinson, John Sevier, and other opportunistic and disgruntled Westerners initiated conspiracies to separate their section from the United States, declare its independence, and place it under the protection of the Spanish Empire in order to secure navigation rights. De Gardoqui's government encouraged these intrigues on the assumption that it possibly could by-pass the Continental Congress and still achieve its diplomatic goals. However, most of those who settled Kentucky and Tennessee opted for the Union and its new Constitution. When King Charles' envoy returned home there was no reason to believe that one of the world's oldest monarchies would grant rights to an unstable republic for no tangible reason or that that republic would change its position.

Negotiations ended until Thomas Jefferson became Secretary of State in 1790. He had been in Europe for the past six years and firmly believed Continental quarrels would work to America's advantage. Because it feared an Anglo-American combination against its holdings in the Western Hemisphere, in December, 1791, Spain informed the United States of its willingness to reopen talks. The Washington Administration sent William Short, perhaps this country's first professional diplomat, to join William Carmichael, the U. S. *chargé d'affaires* in the Spanish capital, a man of questionable character. Short arrived on February 1, 1793, the same day France declared war on Britain. A month later Spain too came under the Gallic gun, and, shortly thereafter, found itself in an alliance with England—an alliance that removed any Anglo-American threat in Louisiana and Florida.

About this same time, Manuel de Godoy took over Spain's Foreign Office, and designated none other than Diego de Gardoqui to deal with the two American envoys. Ridiculing their claims, de Gardoqui needlessly prolonged negotiation, and nothing happened until November, when, in a surprise move, the Spanish offered to accede to all American demands on the condition that the two nations would form an alliance. Uneasy with the Anglo compact, Spain wanted to insure its possessions in America, and, late in

1794, when news arrived that John Jay had concluded an agreement in London, the Castilian Court frantically desired friendship—in writing—with the United States. The awful uncertainty of not knowing the provisions of Jay's Treaty made this seem all the more urgent.

When a disposition favorable to American interests seemed so imminent, William Short, who had done more than anyone else to intensify Spanish fears and bring that nation into accord, received a dispatch stating that Thomas Pinckney had been named the new Envoy Extraordinary and Commissioner Plenipotentiary for the settlement of matters of navigation, boundary, and commerce. This was a hard blow for Short who had visions of moving to a higher position in the foreign service, but he stayed on to help Pinckney finalize the treaty, only to resign his post soon after.

This is Bemis' version of how Pinckney's Treaty came into existence. Whether or not one accepts his thesis that this compact was the result of European distress and that the precipitating factors in its origin were the Jay Treaty, Spain's ignorance of its provisions, and the fear of what it might entail for its holdings in the new world, this book must be regarded as a near classic. Not only does it make use of the extensive holdings of both Spanish and American archives, many of which never had been exploited by historians before, but its author wrote it in an enticing style that brings all the intricate diplomatic machinations to life. *Pinckney's Treaty* is truly a brilliant achievement in American historiography. — *J.G.C.*

Additional Recommended Reading

Hayden, Ralston. *The Senate and Treaties, 1789-1817: The Development of the Treaty-Making Functions of the United States Senate During Their Formative Period.* New York: The Macmillan Company, 1920. This work details one of the most important functions of the Senate during this period of global war: its treaty-making power which gave it a direct role in foreign affairs.

Jacobs, James R. *Tarnished Warrior: Major-General James Wilkinson.* New York: The Macmillan Company, 1938. This biography of the controversial Wilkinson describes how he was apparently intriguing for the Spanish and on the Spanish payroll while on duty with the United States Army.

Burson, Caroline M. *The Stewardship of Don Estaban Miro, 1782-1792.* New Orleans: American Printing Company, Ltd., 1940. Miro, Governor of Spanish Louisiana, was actively engaged in preventing American expansion southward and in fomenting Western separatism.

Darling, Arthur B. *Our Rising Empire, 1763-1803.* New Haven: Yale University Press, 1940. A readable synthesis of American diplomatic history from the French Alliance of 1778 to the Louisiana Purchase.

Schachner, Nathan. *The Founding Fathers.* New York: G. P. Putnam's Sons, 1954. One of the best general histories of the Federalist period.

De Conde, Alexander. *Entangling Alliances: Politics and Diplomacy Under George Washington.* Durham, North Carolina: Duke University Press, 1958. An important modern study.

PUBLICATION OF
WASHINGTON'S FAREWELL ADDRESS

Type of event: Intellectual: statement of principles for guiding the new nation
Time: September 19, 1796
Locale: Philadelphia, Pennsylvania

Principal personages:

GEORGE WASHINGTON (1732-1799), President of the United States 1789-1797

ALEXANDER HAMILTON (1757-1804), Secretary of the Treasury 1789-1795; principal adviser to Washington; helped write the Farewell Address

JAMES MADISON (1751-1836), leading Federalist; prepared a Farewell Address for Washington in 1792

PIERRE ADET (fl. c.1796), French Minister to the United States in 1796

THOMAS JEFFERSON (1743-1826), leading Anti-Federalist; former Secretary of State and elected President in 1800

JOHN ADAMS (1735-1826), Vice-President of the United States

TIMOTHY PICKERING (1745-1829), Federalist Secretary of State in 1796

JOHN JAY (1745-1829), Federalist who negotiated unpopular agreement (Jay's Treaty) with Great Britain in 1794

CITIZEN EDMOND GENÊT (1763-1834), French Minister to the United States who in 1793 attempted to recruit for the French Revolution while in the United States

Summary of Event

On September 19, 1796, Claypoole's *American Daily Advertiser,* a Philadelphia newspaper, published the valedictory remarks of outgoing President George Washington. The speech, which Washington did not read before Congress, promptly became known as Washington's Farewell Address. It is considered, along with the Declaration of Independence, the Constitution, and the Monroe Doctrine, one of the classic statements of American political philosophy.

Four years earlier, when Washington had thought seriously of retiring from office, James Madison had prepared a final address for him. In 1796, however, Washington asked Alexander Hamilton, his closest adviser and a leading Federalist theorist, for assistance in writing a final political testament. Historians differ over the nature of Washington's contribution, but it is generally agreed today that the Farewell Address represents the joint labor of Hamilton and Washington. It embodies ideas to which Washington had long subscribed, but is written in an elegant fashion which was Hamilton's special talent.

Washington's Address has been remembered as a classic statement of

American foreign policy, and rightly so, but the address concerned mostly domestic problems, not foreign affairs. In particular, Washington feared that sectionalism and extreme party spirit might wreck the national unity of the nation. Washington had entered office when there were no identifiable political parties. By 1796, however, he had witnessed the formation of opposing factions, a development he felt boded ill for the future. The "baneful effects of the spirit of party generally," he warned, "opens the door to foreign influence and corruption." It is clear that Washington was particularly upset about the formation of organized opposition to the policies of his administration, in particular Thomas Jefferson's Anti-Federalists. His Farewell Address was intended in part as a campaign document which would explain the necessity of a Federalist victory in 1796.

Washington's remarks about a suitable foreign policy for the United States have come to be known as his "Great Rule of Conduct." His general comments were based on recent severe problems in Franco-American relations. In 1778 the United States had concluded a Treaty of Amity and Commerce with France. After the French Revolution began in 1789, France demanded American assistance—just as the French king had provided the colonies during their revolution against the British king. Washington instead issued a proclamation of neutrality and supported a treaty (Jay's Treaty) quite favorable to France's bitter enemy, England. As a Federalist, Washington saw no reason to support revolution in France. Jefferson and the Anti-Federalists charged that Washington had an obligation to support revolution in France because of the Treaty of 1778. The arrival of a French Minister, Citizen Edmond Genêt, in 1793, initially produced a wave of popular support for the French Revolution. For a time Genet even actively recruited soldiers for the Revolution.

Thus when Washington, in his address, warned "against the insidious wiles of foreign influence . . . [to which] the jealousy of a free people ought to be *constantly* awake," his readers knew it was France which had in mind. And when the President, in the most oft-quoted passage from the address, suggested that "the great rule of conduct for us in regard to foreign nations is, in extending our commercial relations to have with them as little *political* connection as possible," he justified his decision that the United States should not honor its obligation to France. The dispassionate tone of his remarks may obscure their unmistakably Federalist bias from the unwary modern reader. Washington considered some political alliances, such as the Jay Treaty, to be legitimate: "So far as we have already formed engagements let them be fulfilled with perfect good faith." The 1778 treaty with France was another matter: "Here let us stop."

If the Farewell Address spoke to political passions of the moment, it also seemed to offer advice about the future. And it is here that the ambiguous language of the address has caused so much confusion. Washington wanted both commercial relations ("liberal intercourse") and political isolation. Though such a goal may seem desirable, the United States has never been able to avoid political involvement with other countries when it gains commercial ties. Washington did not rule out all political alliances, nor did he say that political alliances would never become a necessity in the future. And yet he did seem to support a policy of isolation by advocating virtual separation of the interests of the United States from those of Europe. The ambiguity of the Farewell Address, widely considered a statement of political isolation as recently as 1940-1941 in political debates over foreign policy, has led one scholar to conclude that "the words are . . . inherently unclear, and yet, with certain predispositions in the interpreter, sufficiently suggestive to give the illusion of clarity to interpreters from the most diverse schools of thought." Because of this, it is best to think of the Farewell Address less as a guide to future conduct than a document addressed to the American people in 1796, and to realize that Washington's concern was as much to bring about Federalist victory in the upcoming election as it was to suggest a guide to foreign policy for the nation for the next two centuries.

Pertinent Literature

Kaufman, Burton Ira. *Washington's Farewell Address: The View From the Twentieth Century.* Chicago: Quadrangle Books, 1969.

Burton Ira Kaufman has produced a useful collection of excerpts from some of the major books and articles written about the Farewell Address. First he includes the address itself, required reading since the words themselves have caused so much confusion. Then he includes a selection of essays which suggest how the Farewell Address was used to justify American expansion into the Philippines in 1899, or American participation in the League of Nations in 1919, or a declaration of war against Adolf Hitler in 1941.

He also includes an article of his own in which he expands the ideas of William Appleman Williams concerning the relationship between mercantilist theory and the Farewell Address. Williams has never written extensively about the Farewell Address itself, so Kaufman, after giving credit to the source of his inspiration, explains the economic expansionist ideas to which Washington subscribed. Kaufman suggests that Washington's interest in trade reflected his longtime enthusiasm for westward American expansion and his feeling that the United States might replace Europe as a major world power. Isolation did not mean a nonexpansionist foreign policy, but the United States' refusal to send an army to Europe. Because Washington so clearly desired expansion based on trade, particularly with Latin America, Kaufman concludes that after 1796 "one of the great distortions in American history began. An apostle of empire was transformed into an architect of isolationism." Surely Kaufman has overstated his case, but his article suggests an important aspect of Federalist thought (the desire for western lands and the commercial policy culminating in Jay's Treaty) which has not been kept in mind by those who believe that the Farewell Address demands this nation's strict isolation from the rest of the world.

405

Along with Kaufman's book, the reader interested in the historiography of the Farewell Address should consult Arthur A. Markowitz's "Washington's Farewell and the Historians: A Critical Review," *Pennsylvania Maga-* *zine of History and Biography* (April, 1970). It contains a clear and thorough discussion of such matters as authorship, meaning, and changing interpretations of Washington's "Great Rule."

Gilbert, Felix. *To the Farewell Address: Ideas of American Foreign Policy.* Princeton: Princeton University Press, 1961.

Felix Gilbert has written a valuable discussion of the intellectual origins of the Farewell Address. His concern is not to apply the words of Washington in some twentieth century context; rather to explain, as his title indicates, the manner in which the Farewell Address represents the culmination of American eighteenth century political beliefs. Much of this book is background—not just of the Farewell Address, but of American political beliefs about foreign policy in general.

Gilbert explains which parts of the address came from Hamilton and demonstrates why Washington's words have been termed the valedictory of Federalism. He shows ways in which various numbers of *The Federalist* make explicit what was purposely left unsaid in the Farewell Address. For instance, Gilbert suggests that the statement in *The Federalist No. 11* that the United States should " 'aim at an ascendant in the system of American affairs' revealed Hamilton's full thought. Because Washington hardly would have liked this open announcement of an aggressive imperialist program, Hamilton refrained from expressing this idea explicitly in the Farewell Address."

Gilbert places great emphasis on Hamilton's success in transforming the original words of Washington into an eighteenth century political testament.

He demonstrates the European origins of many ideas in the address. He states, for instance, that the French *philosophes* (especially the Physiocrats) taught that power politics and state policy based on the teachings of Machiavelli were wrong. Washington's address, based in part on the ideas of the Physiocrats, contained, Gilbert emphasizes, a blend of idealism and realism.

Although some of the conclusions seem unconvincing, *To the Farewell Address* provides by far the most satisfactory account of the European origins of Federalist thought about foreign policy. At the same time, Gilbert has presented a careful argument for the importance of the Farewell Address as a statement of foreign policy, not merely a campaign document for the election of 1796.

Along with Gilbert, the leading discussion of the Farewell Address as a statement of foreign policy is Samuel Flagg Bemis' "Washington's Farewell Address: A Foreign Policy of Independence," *American Historical Review* (January, 1934). Bemis does not discuss European intellectual influences on the thought of Hamilton and Washington, but he does state forcefully that Washington intended to let France, in particular, know that America would not tolerate "foreign meddling in our own intimate domestic concerns." To Bemis this was clearly

a warning to Europe, not a statement   in the coming election. — *D.H.C.*
designed to further the Federalist cause

Additional Recommended Reading

De Conde, Alexander. "Washington's Farewell, the French Alliance, and the Election of 1796," in *Mississippi Valley Historical Review*, XLIII (March, 1957), 641-58. Argues that the Farewell Address was written by Hamilton, and was merely "political propaganda" intended to ensure a Federalist victory in 1796. DeConde's thesis is expanded in his *Entangling Alliance: Diplomacy and Politics Under George Washington* (1958).

Paltsits, Victor Hugo, ed. *Washington's Farewell Address, In Facsimile, with Transliterations of All the Drafts of Washington, Madison, and Hamilton.* New York: Public Library, 1935. The title suggests the contents; Paltsits argues that the Farewell Address was a joint project of Washington and Hamilton.

Weinberg, Albert K. "Washington's 'Great Rule' in Its Historical Evolution," in Eric F. Goddman, ed., *Historiography and Urbanization: Essays in American History in Honor of W. Stull Holt.* Baltimore: The Johns Hopkins University Press, 1941. Pp. 109-138. A careful treatment of Washington's Address as an evolving aspect of American political folklore.

Williams, William A. "The Age of Mercantilism: An Interpretation of the American Political Economy to 1828," reprinted in Williams', *The Shaping of American Diplomacy.* 2d ed. Chicago: Rand McNally & Company, 1970. 2 vols. A brilliant article which suggests the importance of mercantilist thought in shaping Washington's Federalist policies.

Kaplan, Lawrence S. *Colonies into Nation: American Diplomacy, 1763-1801. American Diplomatic History* series. New York: Macmillan and Co., 1972. A good recent survey of diplomatic events which helps explain the background of foreign policy statements in the Farewell Address.

Miller, John C. *Alexander Hamilton: Portrait in Paradox.* New York: Harper & Row Publishers, 1959. The best biography of Hamilton—but one which does not argue that Washington had nothing to do with writing the Farewell Address.

THE XYZ AFFAIR

Type of event: Diplomatic: attempt of French agents to bribe an American diplomatic mission
Time: 1797-1800
Locale: Paris, France; Philadelphia, Pennsylvania; Federal City (Washington, D.C.)

Principal personages:
JOHN ADAMS (1735-1826), Second President of the United States 1797-1801
TIMOTHY PICKERING (1745-1829), Secretary of State 1795-1800
ALEXANDER HAMILTON (1757-1804), Federalist Party chieftain
ELBRIDGE GERRY (1744-1814), Massachusetts Republican, member of Adams' first mission to France
WILLIAM VANS MURRAY (fl. 1800), Federalist Minister to the Hague, member of Adams' second mission to France
CHARLES MAURICE DE TALLEYRAND-PÉRIGORD (PRINCE DE BÉNÉVENT) (1754-1838), French Minister of Foreign Affairs under the Directory and the Consulate

Summary of Event

The Presidency of John Adams of Massachusetts was not a happy one. Adams inherited all the problems of Washington but none of his prestige. Franco-American relations were now inextricably entangled with domestic politics, and relations with the French First Republic progressively worsened. Adams also faced dissension within his own party. Not all Federalists were satisfied when he was chosen as Washington's successor. Alexander Hamilton was known to have opposed Adams and would do so again in 1800. Adams did not help himself by retaining the Washington cabinet, composed as it was of men with no particular loyalty to the new President. The overriding issue was the question of war or peace with France, but hardly less critical was the question of Adams' ability to control his own administration.

In the eyes of the French govern-ment the United States, in signing the Jay Treaty, had repudiated the Franco-American alliance of 1778. The French charged that the acceptance of the treaty was an unneutral act inasmuch as the United States had obviously accepted the British definition of neutral rights at sea. The French decided to break off normal relations with the United States. To give force to this action, the French subjected American vessels on the high seas to the same indignities so recently experienced at the hands of the British. In the year following July, 1796, the Secretary of State, Timothy Pickering of Massachusetts, reported that the French had seized 316 American vessels.

In an effort to forestall a complete break between the two nations, President Adams sent a three-man delegation to negotiate with the French. At the time of the mission there was no recognized American representative in France because the French had refused to receive Charles Cotesworth Pinckney (brother of Thomas), whom Washington had sent to France as the successor to James Monroe. Adams chose two distinguished Americans—Elbridge Gerry, a Massachusetts Republican, and John Marshall, a Virginia Federalist—to join with Charles C. Pinckney in presenting the American position to the French government. The three Americans were in Paris by October, 1797.

While Adams and the Federalists were determined to avoid war if at all possible, Adams called upon Congress to look to the defenses of the nation. Bills were introduced calling for the enlargement of the regular army, the creation of a provisional army of fifteen thousand men, the construction of three new frigates for the navy, and tax measures to pay for the preparedness program. The program ran into stiff opposition. The Republicans accused Adams and his party of warmongering and succeeded in defeating the army and tax bills.

The three Americans in Paris made no progress in their negotiations during several weeks in the city. Then when the Americans were convinced that their mission was a failure, three representatives (the notorious Messrs. X, Y, and Z) from Talleyrand (Charles Maurice de Talleyrand-Périgord), the French Minister of Foreign Affairs, approached them with certain demands as prerequisites to negotiation. President Adams was to apologize for certain statements in his last message to Congress; and the United States was to pay a sum of 1,200,000 livres and make a loan of thirty-two million florins to the French, which was simply a demand for a bribe. The Americans with no instructions relative to the payment of such a huge sum of money could do nothing but refuse. Pinckney and Marshall, convinced of the futility of remaining in France, took their departure while Gerry lingered on in Paris in the hope of achieving something. He was soon recalled.

When news of this attempt by the French to dishonor the name of the United States was made public, Americans of virtually all political persuasions were united in condemning the insolence of the French. There were demands that the United States take immediate steps to defend its integrity. Some called for war; most shouted the slogan, "Millions for defense but not one cent for tribute." Congress declared that the treaties of alliance and friendship of 1778 with France were void and authorized public and private vessels of the United States to capture French armed ships on the high seas. The United States and France were dangerously close to war. In the spring of 1798, Congress created a Department of the Navy and appropriated funds to build warships. Preparations were made to raise an army of fifteen thousand men. During the next two years an undeclared war, or Half-War, as Adams called it, was waged against France. By 1800, the United States Navy with the aid of hundreds of privateers had successfully cleared American waters of French cruisers and had even carried the naval warfare into the seas surrounding the French West Indies.

President Adams soon found himself in a difficult position. He was rapidly losing control of his own administration. Alexander Hamilton seemed to have more influence with Congress and the Cabinet than the President. Adams, a good New Englander, was basically opposed to the creation of a large standing army. He emphasized the navy as America's first line of defense. Hamilton and his supporters pushed army legislation through Congress. The army was to be commanded by Washington, but until he actually took the field, Hamilton was to be in charge. Adams opposed Hamilton but could do nothing since Washington made it clear that he would accept command only on his own terms. Adams, finally recognizing that his Cabinet was disloyal, ultimately forced the resignations of Pickering and James McHenry, Secretary of War. Adams also learned that the French government was then willing to negotiate seriously. With war fever high among certain Federalists, Adams opted for peace. Without consultation with his Cabinet or the Federalist leadership, Adams submitted the name of an envoy to France.

This action precipitated a split in the Federalist Party. Adams did succeed in reopening negotiations with the French, although he was forced to accept a commission of three Federalists rather than the one individual he had nominated. By the time that the three commissioners reached France, Napoleon was First Consul. The settlement reached in the Convention of 1800 provided for the mutual abrogation of the Franco-American treaties of 1778, but that the United States was to receive no indemnity for the French seizures of American merchant shipping. Although not entirely satisfactory to the United States, the agreement did end the undeclared war. The peace was popular with most Americans but the rift which it caused between the supporters of the President and those of Hamilton seriously injured Adams' chances of reëlection in 1800.

Pertinent Literature

Kurtz, Stephen G. *The Presidency of John Adams: The Collapse of Federalism, 1795-1800.* Philadelphia: University of Pennsylvania Press, 1957.

This study begins with the election of 1796 and concludes with the election of 1800. The Presidential aspirants remain the same. Adams, elected in 1796 by three electoral votes, went down to defeat in 1800, losing by eight electoral votes. Kurtz attempts to discover the reasons for the fall of Federalism. In doing so, he concentrates largely on the role of the newly formed political parties, the performance of the party leadership in meeting the issues of the day, and the impact of these issues on the general electorate. Since the study deals with a period when foreign affairs dominated the attention of politicians, and presumably the voters, the focus of the book is on Franco-American relations.

Kurtz is essentially in sympathy with John Adams. He recognizes the almost impossible task that faced this capable man. Obviously, Kurtz believes that Adams has suffered at the hands of most historians, not because of his ineptness, but largely because his administration was sandwiched between those of Washington and Jefferson. Kurtz does brilliantly in producing a balanced evaluation of the Presidency of John Adams.

Adams was engaged in three major struggles during his four years in office. Two were political and the third was diplomatic and military. As President, Adams was at least the nominal leader of the Federalist Party. As such it was his responsibility to maintain party unity against attacks from the opposition, which were to be expected. But Adams' leadership was challenged not only by the Republicans but also by dissident groups within the Federalist Party. Led by Alexander Hamilton and supported by members of Adams' Cabinet, this group attempted, according to Kurtz, to drive the President into a war with France. Adams found himself being accused by the Republicans of militarism and warmongering whenever he presented preparedness measures to Congress. Adams also was bitterly criticized by the so-called "High Federalist" faction of Hamilton and Pickering for not asking Congress for a declaration of war against France.

As President of the United States, Adams was the chief diplomatic officer of the nation and Commander in Chief of the armed forces. It was his responsibility to defend the nation against aggression by the most expedient means available. Once the French rebuffed the three man mission to France in the XYZ Affair, Adams "unleashed" the infant American Navy against the nation's enemies. The navy made a good showing and had taken the offensive by

1799-1800. This success convinced the French that little was to be gained by continuing the naval struggle. Word reached Adams that the French were willing to negotiate in an honorable manner.

By 1799 it was apparent to many, including the President, that Americans were tired of the war. The tax burden was heavy as a result of the buildup in naval strength, and the expenditures connected with recruitment of the fifteen thousand man army that the Federalist Party had, at least on paper, created. Adams had not supported the army measure, but Hamilton and his supporters had driven it through Congress. At the same time, the Federalists had passed the Alien and Sedition Acts, which were rapidly turned against them, politically, by the adroit Republican Party. Adams realized that certain elements within his party were opposed to renewed negotiations with the French. But Adams, possessing greater sensitivity to public opinion than these High Federalists, also realized that the country desired peace. Adams faced an election in 1800, which he was very anxious to win. If he continued the aggressive policies of the past, however, he was likely to split his own party.

Adams at last came out for peace by nominating a representative to the French nation. Not only did Adams prefer peace to war, but he also believed that such a policy was the only way to break the control of Hamilton and his faction. It was a calculated political risk. Kurtz points out that this decision did not damage Adams in the election of 1800. Adams actually made a stronger showing than in 1796. More

411

significantly, Kurtz maintains, the move for peace removed much of the difference between Jefferson and Adams. In defeating the militarist ele-ments in Federalism, Adams inaugurated the return to responsible government.

DeConde, Alexander. *The Quasi-War: The Politics and Diplomacy of the Undeclared War with France, 1797-1801.* New York: Charles Scribner's Sons, 1966.

This recent study of the naval war with the French and of the efforts of both the French and American governments to resolve their difficulties without loss of face, is especially valuable for understanding the French position. DeConde is interested in both the politics of the Adams Administration, dominated as it was by the crisis with France, and the diplomatic negotiations which resulted in an amicable settlement. DeConde attempts to explain why peace resulted instead of war.

There are two major threads running through the study; one revolves around President Adams and his developing policy toward the French, and the other concerns itself with the general policy of successive French governments toward the United States. DeConde emphasizes the fact that neither government at any time shut and locked the door to negotiation. Regardless of the truculent attitude of Adams and the bitterness which the French government felt toward the Jay Treaty, both sides preferred peace to war. As the story develops it becomes apparent that it was the French desire for peace that was decisive.

DeConde offers an interesting analysis of the shifting attitude of President Adams. When news of the XYZ Affair reached him, Adams apparently preferred war to peace. Through the summer of 1798 Adams would have accepted with joy a declaration of war by Congress. Adams reacted in this way because of his belief that the French wanted to fight. But as the news filtered in to the President from sources in Europe to the effect that the French wished to reopen negotiations and did not want war, Adams' attitude changed. He began to drift away from the belligerent policy advocated by the High Federalists, whom DeConde, not always successfully, associates with Hamilton. Chief among such men were William Vans Murray, Minister to the Hague; Elbridge Gerry, one of the three American diplomats involved in the XYZ Affair who remained in Paris after Marshall and Pinckney departed; and John Quincy Adams, the President's son and the Minister to Prussia. These ministers convinced the President that the French desire for peace was sincere. The weight of this evidence convinced Adams to reopen negotiations. The result of this decision completed the split in the Federalist Party. Adams, during this period of decision, was confronted not only by French aggression but also by the attempts of Hamilton and his associates to control American policy. Adams' decision for peace thwarted this scheme.

Adams was enabled to make this decision due to the forbearance of the French. The High Federalists believed that America's energetic and efficient response to French aggression on the high seas would result in a French declaration of war. But the French had nothing to gain from war with the United States. The Minister of Foreign Affairs, the wily Talleyrand, though willing to damage American commerce, was unwilling to push the United States into war. He and the French Directory, as well as Napoleon Bonaparte, who followed the Directory into power and became First Consul in December, 1799, feared that war with America would drive the United States into a British alliance, cause the loss of French colonies, and prevent French reoccupation of Louisiana. At the very moment that American policy was most aggressive, the French became most conciliatory. Talleyrand convinced Gerry, Vans Murray, and others of the French desire to negotiate.

Adams was soon convinced, and a new mission to France was appointed.

The new commission to France arrived after Bonaparte had seized control. Again the Americans were faced with Talleyrand. This time the negotiations resulted in a settlement acceptable to both nations. The United States in the Convention of 1800 (Treaty of Mortefontaine) agreed to drop the question of French indemnities for damages to American shipping while the French recognized that the treaties of 1778 were no longer in operation. The United States in effect purchased French acquiescence to the abrogation of the embarrassing alliance of 1778.
— *J.G.C.*

Additional Recommended Reading

Hazen, Charles D. *Contemporary American Opinion of the French Revolution.* Baltimore: The Johns Hopkins University Press, 1897. The author analyzes American attitudes through the eyes of Jefferson and Gouverneur Morris of Pennsylvania, and explains the growing opposition in the United States to the Revolution.

Bond, Beverly W., Jr. *The Monroe Mission to France, 1794-1796.* Baltimore: The Johns Hopkins University Press, 1907. The story of Monroe's ministerial career in France and of his recall by Washington.

Allen, Gay Wilson. *Our Naval War with France.* Boston: Houghton Mifflin Co., 1909. Narrates the story of the naval war in some detail and also discusses the spoliation claims dispute based on incidents occurring after the Convention of 1800.

Chinard, Gilbert. *Honest John Adams.* Boston: Little, Brown, and Company, 1933. Still an excellent one-volume biography of Adams.

Hyneman, Charles S. *The First American Neutrality: A Study of the American Understanding of Neutral Obligations During the Years, 1792-1815.* Urbana: University of Illinois Press, 1934. A comprehensive account of America's efforts to defend its neutrality during the French Revolutionary and Napoleonic wars.

Dauer, Manning J. *The Adams Federalists.* Baltimore: The Johns Hopkins University Press, 1953. Dauer recounts the story of Adams' efforts to control his administration and tries to categorize Federalists into pro and anti-Adams factions.

413

PASSAGE OF THE ALIEN AND SEDITION ACTS

Type of event: Legal: legislation aimed at suppressing alien and domestic subversives
Time: June-July, 1798
Locale: Philadelphia, Pennsylvania

Principal personages:
JOHN ADAMS (1735-1826), second President of the United States 1797-1801
THOMAS JEFFERSON (1743-1826), Vice-President of the United States, author of the Kentucky Resolutions
JAMES MADISON (1751-1826), Republican leader in Virginia, author of the Virginia Resolutions
TIMOTHY PICKERING (1745-1829), Secretary of State, chief enforcement officer of the Alien and Sedition Acts
MATTHEW LYON (1750-1822), Republican Congressman from Vermont who was prosecuted under the Sedition Act
HARRISON GRAY OTIS (1765-1848), Federalist Senator from Massachusetts, one of the chief architects of the Alien and Sedition Acts
ALBERT GALLATIN (1761-1849), Republican Congressman from Pennsylvania, leader in debate against the Alien and Sedition Acts
WILLIAM DUANE (1760-1835), Republican editor of the Philadelphia *Aurora,* who was prosecuted under the Sedition Act

Summary of Event

News of the XYZ Affair descended upon the American people and their representatives in Congress like a thunderbolt. It galvanized the government into action on the high seas; it helped unite the American people against the French just as the initial news of British seizures had united them against Great Britain; it seriously weakened the infant Republican Party which was associated with Francophilism; and it firmly entrenched the Federalists in power. Even President John Adams, for a time, seemed to relish the thought of leading the United States against its newest antagonist. Fortunately for the nation, Adams regained his sense of moderation in time to prevent a catas-trophe. The same cannot be said of certain elements of the Federalist Party which exploited the explosive situation to strike out at their political opponents.

The Federalist Party, or at least the old guard, deeply resented gains made by the opposition. Indeed it is not too extravagant to say that they resented the very existence of the opposition. The High Federalists were by no means committed to a two-party system based on the legitimacy of a loyal opposition. With the Republican tide at low ebb, these Federalists intended to strike a killing blow at two sources of Republican strength: the immigrant vote and the control of public opinion through the use (and abuse) of the press. In this tactic the Federalists demonstrated an acute awareness of the impact of the press on the growth of political parties. This knowledge was not to be used to build up the Federalist press but to destroy the Republican press.

Many Federalists had a long history of antiforeign sentiment. With the United States on the verge of war with France, the Federalists were apprehensive over the loyalty of the thousands of French West Indian refugees who had flocked into the United States in an effort to escape the revolutionary ferment and the "Terror." What made matters worse was that the refugees who ultimately became American citizens generally aligned themselves with the Republicans. Much the same was true of the Irish who supported anyone in opposition to the English. To deal with such potential subversives, foreign and domestic, the Federalist-controlled Congress passed a series of four acts, known as the Alien and Sedition Acts.

Two of the acts dealt with aliens. The Alien Enemies Act gave the President the power to deport suspected aliens if war had been officially declared; the Alien Act gave the President similar authority during peacetime. Neither act was enforced. The third bill, the Naturalization Act, struck at the immigrant vote. Previously, aliens could become naturalized citizens in five years. The new act raised the probationary period to fourteen years. The most notorious of the four was the Sedition Act, entitled an "Act for the Punishment of Certain Crimes."

The Sedition Act punished by heavy fines and imprisonment all those found guilty of writing, publishing, or speaking against the federal government. Although the Sedition Act was a definite improvement over the English laws of seditious libel in making truth a defense and giving the jury the responsibility of deciding the fact of libel, the fact remains that its intent was the repression of political opposition and the annoying Republican press. Under the law, suits were initiated against the editors of eight major opposition presses. The principal target was the Philadelphia *Aurora,* long a thorn in the side of the Federalists, whose editor William Duane was prosecuted under the act.

Republican opposition to these laws was immediate. Thomas Jefferson, the Vice-President, believed that the Alien Acts were destined to be used against such leading Republicans as the Swissborn Albert Gallatin, the Congressman from Pennsylvania. All Republicans were convinced that the Sedition Act was designed to destroy them as an organized political party. The vote in the House was strictly along sectionalparty lines. The bill passed by a vote of forty-four to forty-one with only two votes for passage coming from south of the Potomac river.

From the Federalist point of view, the acts were completely unsuccessful in suppressing the opposition. They were resented by many, and it soon became obvious to even those who first supported them that they were completely unnecessary as well as ineffective. The handful of "subversives" prosecuted under the Sedition Act hardly compensated for the fact that the Republicans now had another campaign issue. Jefferson, through the Kentucky legislature, and Madison, through the Virginia legislature, penned immediate responses to the implications of the Alien and Sedition Acts. These statements, known as the Virginia and Kentucky Resolutions, aroused little enthusiasm at the time but did serve to point out not only some of the basic principles of the Republican Party but also some striking differences between two streams of thought within the party.

Both resolutions maintained that the Constitution was a compact between sovereign states which granted to the federal government certain narrowly defined powers while retaining all other unenumerated powers. The states created the Constitution and hence had the power to decide when the federal government had overstepped its proper bounds. Jefferson in the Kentucky Resolutions went much further than Madison in assigning to the states the power to nullify a federal law—to declare it inoperable and void within the boundaries of a state. South Carolina was to do so in 1832 when it nullified the Tariff of 1828. The resolutions had no immediate effect, but they had spelled out the theoretical position which those advocating states' rights could and did ultimately take.

The Alien and Sedition Acts took their place among a growing list of grievances aimed at the Federalist Party. The Alien Act expired in 1800 and the Sedition Act in the following year. The Naturalization Act was repealed by the Republicans in 1802. Their only tangible effect was to contribute to the defeat of Federalism in 1800. But the mood which led to their passage was to return in later days.

Pertinent Literature

Miller, John C. *Crisis in Freedom: The Alien and Sedition Acts.* Boston: Little, Brown, and Company, 1951.

One of the most severe challenges to American civil liberties in the nation's history occurred when the United States was little more than a decade old. John C. Miller's *Crisis in Freedom* is an inquiry into the origins and milieu in which the Alien and Sedition Acts were passed by Congress in 1798. The author details their effects with a thoroughly Jeffersonian eye. It is his thesis that the Alien and Sedition Acts failed utterly to accomplish the ends for which they were designed, and ironically, that the acts came to precisely the opposite end their sponsors had in mind.

The last decade of the eighteenth century in America witnessed the emergence of two political factions, which owed much of their identity to their opinions on foreign developments. The predominant faction, the Federalists, looked to Great Britain as a bulwark against the rampant "Jacobinism" of revolutionary France, which was in turn defended by the Democrat-Republicans. The source of this antipathy was, purportedly, the recent treatment of American diplomats to France in the celebrated "XYZ Affair," in which French agents attempted to exact a bribe from the Americans in return for French willingness to negotiate outstanding differences with the United States. Doubtless, animosity existed between these political factions well before the XYZ Affair, but this incident served as a focus for Federalist resentment against the Democrat-Republicans. Partisan newspapers railed at each other and opposition political figures in the most intemperate manner. The Federalists, seized by ill-founded fears of a Jacobin uprising in the United States, resolved to use its majority position in the Congress to rid the country of recent immigrants (who always, it seemed, were of the "Jacobin" variety), and to suppress the Democrat-Republican press, whose attacks were daily exhorting the people to resist the Federal government and defending the precepts of the French revolution.

Miller contends that the Federalists were deluding themselves about the potency of the Democrats. For the most part, he asserts, the Federalists had a loyal press; the Democratic exceptions did make it seem to iron-clad Federalists, however, that the Jacobins had already seized most of the presses of America as a preface to insurrection. Moreover, the Federalists had the executive branch; with this advantage, they could control the mails, and award government printing contracts to favored newspapers, thus subventing their presses with public monies. Finally, the recent indiscretion committed by the French Foreign Minister, Talleyrand, in the XYZ Affair gave the Federalists proof of French immorality. Isolated incidents, some so innocuous as the raising of a maypole, provided the majority faction with additional means of attacking the Democrats.

Each of the four acts passed during the summer of 1798 was intended to silence Democrat opposition in some manner. The Naturalization Act raised the citizenship waiting-period from five to fourteen years, but since the states also had powers to grant citizenship, the law's effect was counterbalanced. The Alien Act, which allowed Presidential discretion to deport seditious aliens, was never applied, and expired quietly. The Alien Enemies Act was passed in contemplation of war with France; it, too, died a natural death. The most pernicious of the laws, the Sedition Act, was brought into action, but with minimal results. Only fifteen persons were indicted and of those, ten actually went to jail. More often than not, those who went to jail continued writing the same polemics which put them in jail in the first place. Thus, while orthodox Federalists insisted that the country was overrun with Jacobins, they had a most difficult time in producing them for trial.

The Federalist witch-hunting was checked even more when Talleyrand, the French foreign minister, made a number of conciliatory moves toward the United States after 1798, and when the British victory over the Napoleonic fleet in Egypt spiked the assertion that a French invasion was imminent. At home, sympathy for persecuted Democratic editors caused the West and the South to close ranks against the Federalists, and doubtless played a role in the passage of the Kentucky and Virginia Resolutions, which challenged the constitutionality of the Alien and Sedition Acts. The ultimate result of the Federalists' paranoia was the triumph of the Democrat-Republicans at the polls when Thomas Jefferson was voted into the Presidency in 1800.

Author Miller obviously files a brief in behalf of Jeffersonianism and free press here. There is an element of present-mindedness in this work, discernible if one considers the time in which it was written. Miller infuses the book with a certain wit, which makes it rather pleasant reading. The footnotes and bibliographic data are adequate; but the author often quotes directly from secondary sources, a practice which does little to aid a scholarly reader.

Smith, James M. *Freedom's Fetters: The Alien and Sedition Laws and American Civil Liberties.* Ithaca: Cornell University Press, 1956.

In April, 1798, the *New York Gazette,* reacting to the news of the XYZ Affair, solemnly instructed its readers that: "To be lukewarm after reading the horrid scenes [reported in the XYZ dispatches] . . . is to be criminal—and the man who does not warmly reprobate the conduct of the French must have a soul black enough to be *fit* for *treasons, strategems* and *spoils.*" Similar feelings were expressed in Federalist newspapers across the nation. The Federalist Party, seizing the main chance presented by this universal denunciation of France, attempted not only to stimulate patriotic ardor but to crush their political opposition. In so doing the Federalists came dangerously near to destroying freedom of the press and freedom of speech. Smith's intention in this study is "to discover why a society which generally agreed on the necessity of state and federal bills of rights should have differed so violently on the meaning of those guarantees."

Much of Smith's work is based on the assumption that there were basic differences between the Federalists and Republicans concerning the democratic heritage of the American Revolution. The Alien and Sedition Acts demonstrate that the Federalists were not yet fully willing to accept the obligations that representative government places on the shoulders of those in power; namely, to accept the possibility of being legally displaced by a recognized and legal opposition. The Republicans for their part were the champions of popular government, civil liberties, and the right of a minority to transform itself into a majority through constitutional means.

Smith traces the origin and legislative history of the four bills composing the Alien and Sedition Acts. Throughout this portion of the book, Smith consistently maintains the unconstitutionality of three of the acts: the two dealing with Aliens and the Sedition Act. Smith also asserts that by 1798 liberty of the press was accepted as an inviolable civil right by most Americans. The very fact that Americans embarked upon an experiment in representative government implied acceptance of such a right. But the Federalists, particularly in enacting the Sedition Act, would have reduced the limits of speech and press to those in England before the American Revolution and thus negated any advance made since then.

The Federalist Party committed a strategic error in trying to force the Alien and Sedition Acts upon the American people. They were founded on the already discarded belief that the government was the master of the people. They were founded on the rejected idea that the responsibility of government resided in the hands of a chosen few. The Federalists identified their administration with the government and that government with the Constitution. Thus, any criticism of their administration was the equivalent of an attempt to overthrow the Constitution. In their minds the only Americans were Federalists. It is obvious to Smith as he analyzes the election of 1800 that Americans did not agree.

Smith places great emphasis on the impact of the Alien and Sedition Acts on the election of 1800. The victory of Jefferson indicates to Smith that the people rejected not only the Acts themselves but the "party which tried to protect itself behind the Sedition Law." The election of Jefferson in 1800 represented a double gain for Americans: it placed the government in the hands of men responsive to public opinion and committed to democratic government, and it strengthened the American tradition of civil liberties. — *J.G.C.*

Additional Recommended Reading

Childs, Francis S. *French Refugee Life in the United States, 1790-1800: An American Chapter of the French Revolution.* Baltimore: The Johns Hopkins University Press, 1940. A fine analysis of French exiles, their activities in the United States, and the reasons why no Franco-American group arose from this experience.

Levy, Leonard W. *Freedom of Speech and Press in Early American History: Legacy of Suppression.* Cambridge: The Belknap Press, 1960. Levy traces the ideological origins of the First Amendment to the Constitution and concludes that it was not meant to wipe out the common law of seditious libel.

Levy, Leonard W. *Jefferson and Civil Liberties: The Darker Side.* Cambridge, Massachusetts: The Belknap Press, 1963. Levy concludes that the reputation of Jefferson as a civil libertarian is basically unwarranted.

Malone, Dumas. *Jefferson and the Ordeal of Liberty.* Boston: Little, Brown, and Company, 1962. This book, the third volume of Malone's *Jefferson and His Time,* covers the critical period 1792 to 1800.

THE SECOND AWAKENING AND FRONTIER RELIGIOUS REVIVAL

Type of event: Religious: reawakening of certain inherent Protestant tendencies, caused by alarm over religious demoralization
Time: 1800-1830's
Locale: The United States generally, but particularly in the West

Principal personages:
> JAMES MCGREADY (1758?-1817), Presbyterian minister, leader of the revival in Kentucky
> FRANCIS ASBURY (1745-1816), Methodist bishop who did much to establish the circuit system in America
> CHARLES GRANDISON FINNEY (1792-1875), leading evangelist who helped to create the style of modern revivalism
> TIMOTHY DWIGHT (1752-1817), president of Yale College and champion of a refurbished Congregationalism
> NATHANIEL WILLIAM TAYLOR (1786-1858), member of the Yale Divinity School who taught a modified Calvinism
> JOHN HUMPHREY NOYES (1811-1886), founder of the Oneida Community in New York
> WILLIAM MILLER (1782-1849), Adventist who preached the imminent end of the world

Summary of Event

The upsurge of religious feeling which began at the end of the eighteenth century constituted one of several such major revivals in American history. Designated the "Second Awakening" in reference to the "Great Awakening" of the 1730's and 1740's, the revival of 1800 followed a period of relative religious laxity. The Protestant clergy complained of the decay of morality, particularly in the West where access to organized religion was difficult. The spread of Deism, not entirely an elite doctrine in the United States, was viewed as a dangerous threat by orthodox believers.

By the late 1790's, stirrings of revived religious consciousness were apparent in all regions of the United States. Timothy Dwight, who became President of Yale in 1795, did much to restore that college as a citadel of Congregationalist orthodoxy. The Presbyterian colleges of Hampden-Sidney and Washington in Virginia had already experienced renewed religious concern, and would provide a significant part of that denomination's evangelical leadership during the Second Awakening. Western New York, which became one of the most fertile areas of spiritual zeal, knew the winter of 1799-1800 as the time of the "Great Revival." The most spectacular of the early manifestations, however, came on the Western frontier. James McGready, a Presbyterian minister, played the leading role in bringing about the Logan County, or Cumberland, revival in Kentucky, which culminated in 1800, and helped to spark revivalism throughout the West. The Cane Ridge, Kentucky, camp meeting, which attracted between ten and twenty-five thousand people in the following year, has been described as the largest and most emotional revival of early American history.

The Second Awakening affected all the major Protestant denominations, although the more evangelical among them gained the most in strength. The Congregationalists and Presbyterians contributed some of the outstanding revivalists, but their participation in the more emotional phases of the revival was inhibited by their more staid Calvinist traditions. Working together in their Western endeavors, the two sects sanctioned only "rational" revivalism, a stand which was rejected by such schismatic groups as the "Stonite" or "New Light Presbyterian" Church. Quantitatively, Baptists and Methodists dominated the Second Awakening, being in particular the leaders of frontier revivalism. The Methodists were most successful in the West. Methodism combined the advantages of a free will theology and a centralized ecclesiastical organization. Less bound by tradition than the more conservative denominations, it readily embraced new methods. The itineracy system, which had been adapted to America by Francis Asbury, was a major key to Methodist success. Circuit-riding preachers, directed by the church, energetically brought the gospel to scattered settlements. The Methodists, moreover, enthusiastically adopted the system of protracted outdoor revival services known as "camp meetings." Indeed, by 1825 the camp meeting had become "almost exclu-sively a Methodist institution."

Methodist acceptance of the doctrine that men have free will to attain salvation was in accord with a general shift of theological emphasis within American Protestantism in the early nineteenth century. Calvinist sects, including Congregationalists, Presbyterians, and certain Baptists, had traditionally adhered to the doctrine of predestination, and in the early phase of the Second Awakening predestinarian Calvinism and free will "Arminianism" were preached side by side. But after 1810, Calvinism was modified by such theologians as Timothy Dwight and Nathaniel William Taylor, and later the revivalist Charles Grandison Finney took the lead in establishing what was clearly an Arminian brand of evangelism within the traditionally Calvinist sector of American Protestantism. The ascendancy of Arminianism appears to have reflected the social and political climate of the country. Although historians have found affinities between Calvinist revivalism and political radicalism in the eighteenth century, by the Jacksonian period the message of free will seemed to many the spiritual counterpart of manhood suffrage and laissez-faire.

The Second Awakening saw changes not only in evangelical doctrine but also in tone and method. The concept of the ministerial office shifted from that of pastor to that of soul-winner. At his most successful the soul-winner became a professional mass evangelist, such as Finney, who did much to create the style of modern revivalism represented subsequently by Dwight L. Moody, Billy Sunday, and Billy Graham. With Finney also, the preoccupation with theology exemplified in the

Great Awakening by Jonathan Edwards, began to yield to a more one-sided concern with religious experience; revivalism purveyed increasingly a simple religion of the heart.

The tide of religious feeling had begun to ebb by the early 1830's, but the social effects of the Second Awakening were pervasive and lasting, giving rise to the establishment of denominational schools and colleges. It also provided a major impetus to social reform. Despite the inherent revivalistic concern with individual salvation, and the reluctance with which evangelists such as Finney embraced social causes, Finney's own "post millennialism" involved the belief that the world could be made better in preparation for the Second Coming of Christ. The anti-slavery movement was the most important of the reform causes with roots in the revival.

Pertinent Literature

Johnson, Charles A. *The Frontier Camp Meeting: Religion's Harvest Time.* Dallas: Southern Methodist University Press, 1955.

The camp meeting, as Charles A. Johnson makes clear, was a socially important as well as a highly colorful aspect of the Second Awakening. Confining himself to the Trans-Allegheny West between 1800 and 1840, Johnson gives a sympathetic but scholarly appraisal of this preëminently frontier institution. He sets out to correct the often distorted image of the camp meeting, and, quoting frequently from contemporary accounts, he endeavors to recreate the atmosphere of the backwoods revival of the early nineteenth century.

Johnson accepts a traditional picture of the pre-Awakening West as largely demoralized and spiritually destitute, characterized more by debauchery, brawling, and superstition than by any pristine natural virtue. Deism, hardly less reprehensible from the orthodox standpoint, was apparently a movement of major proportions in Kentucky. The ground is thus prepared for the author's portrayal of the camp meeting as one of the most successful of the "weapons forged by the West in its struggle against lawlessness and immorality. . . ."

The camp meeting, Johnson points out, has been controversial from its inception. Exalted by its champions as the work of God, it was condemned by the more conservative as an occasion for religious hysteria. Historians have been inclined to place a pejorative emphasis on the spectacular and emotional aspects of the camp meeting, while being less alive to its broader social significance. The author sees the camp meeting as a reasonable frontier institution reflecting the distinctive religious attitudes of the American pioneer; following H. Richard Niebuhr, Johnson views these attitudes as the products of the frontiersman's "bold nature in revolt against society's restraints, and the leveling influence of poverty." Religion which made room for emotional fervor, emphasized personal spiritual experience, and played down abstract doctrine and ritual was the result; it was amply accommodated by the camp meeting.

Johnson describes the camp meeting

in graphic detail. The early meetings, held typically in forest clearings with no protection against the elements, were more impressive for their lack of artificiality. Beyond rows of benches segregated for the sexes, and the speaker's stand candlelit for night meetings, were arrayed rows of tents and wagons. Food was cooked over family campfires, and often shared, for the meeting was a rare opportunity to socialize. In both North and South, Negroes often set up separate camps and held their own services, sometimes joining with the whites when both races reached a certain level of enthusiasm.

The author emphasizes that the frontier camp meeting was not a static institution, but underwent significant evolution during its half-century of prominence. "Tumultuous almost beyond comprehension" in their early manifestations, camp meetings tended later to become more sedate. Local revivals had always run through cycles of emotional beginnings, institutionalization, and gradual decline; eventually this experience was generalized. The early days of the Second Awakening, furthermore, had a notable non-denominational character, marked by large "General Camp Meetings," at which Presbyterian, Methodist, and Baptist ministers preached side by side. After the first few years of the 1800's, however, the more usual pattern of denominational rivalry reappeared. Although its great days were past by 1840, Johnson concludes that the mass enthusiasm of frontier camp meetings left a lasting imprint on American society.

Cross, Whitney R. *The Burned-Over District: The Social and Intellectual History of Enthusiastic Religion in Western New York, 1800-1850.* Ithaca: Cornell University Press, 1950.

The spectacular manifestations of the Second Awakening in frontier areas such as Kentucky have sometimes obscured religious phenomena in other sections which, if less explicitly emotional, were at least as profound. Whitney R. Cross calls attention to the part of New York State west of the Catskill and Adirondack Mountains, which in the first half of the nineteenth century was so seared by the fires of religious zeal that it was known as the "Burned-Over District."

His microcosmic approach permits Cross to examine the district in close detail and to delineate the social and religious factors which combined to make it a fertile spiritual seedbed. Quantitative methods are used to demonstrate the relationship of revivalism to economic maturity, education, and other social characteristics. The author emphasizes the predominantly New England origins of the population of the Burned-Over District. New Englanders had moved west in large numbers after 1790, the emigration being as much one of communities as of individuals. The district thus inherited the moral intensity that characterized Yankee culture, while the period of migration coincided with the general religious resurgence. "Emotional religion was thus a congenital characteristic, present at birth and developed throughout the youth of the section."

While much of the energy generated by the Second Awakening stayed within orthodox channels, the Burned-Over District was extraordinarily prolific in the production of religious and social experiments. Cross discusses, for instance, the origins of Mormonism, which was not a frontier phenomenon in inception; it arose in western New York after the pioneering period. Cross shows that Joseph Smith (whose family moved to the district from Vermont when he was ten) was a product of the westward-moving Yankee culture, and notes that the *Book of Mormon* unmistakably bears the marks of contemporary composition in the region.

Religious fervor spilled over into social "benevolence," often in the belief that to reform society was to approach the prophesied millennium. Sabbath-observance, "temperance," antislavery, and a number of other causes drew sustenance from New York millennialism, with such lasting results that "neither the causes of the Civil War nor the origins of national prohibition, to cite only two prominent examples, can be thoroughly understood without reference to the Burned-Over District." The extreme of millennialist reform was the phenomenon of "Ultraism," radical both in its reliance on the guidance of the Holy Ghost, and in its impatience to bring about the transformation of society. Cross views Ultraism as a type of radical democracy, in spirit "complementary to the Jacksonian brand." He points out that the Ultraists were extreme egalitarians, intending to convert all sinners and to achieve ultimate equality with the advent of the millennium.

Reaching its peak about 1836, according to Cross, Ultraism disintegrated along with Jacksonianism. The Ultraist spirit tended to diverge along two paths, one seeking by a fundamentalist route a supernaturally wrought millennium, the other leading toward a this-worldly Utopia. Symptomatic of the latter approach were numerous attempts to establish Fourierist "phalanxes" and other socialistic communities. Most representative of the history of the Burned-Over District, Cross indicates, was the Oneida Community organized by John Humphrey Noyes in the 1840's. Unlike the Fourierist and Owenite communities, Oneida was primarily a religious experiment, intended to realize a "total communism under God." The Oneida colonists were perfectionists in the antinomian tradition, believing themselves released by their sinlessness from literal obedience to Scripture, even to the point of practicing a sexual communism. The fundamentalist route to perfection, on the other hand, led to the Adventist movement of William Miller, which expected the world to end in 1844. Adventism, Cross emphasizes, was only an extreme manifestation of the millennialist tendencies of American Protestantism at this time.

While concluding that the religious radicals were weakened by "their exaggerated concern for the individual soul," as well as by their weakness for panaceas, Cross points out that many Ultraists were absorbed into the antislavery movement. Outgrowing Ultraist individualism, they helped, furthermore, to change the emphasis of abolition from the personal sinfulness of slavery to an attempt to "reconstitute this world" through reform. The Second Awakening in the Burned-Over District was pervasive and multifarious in its results. — *M.D.C.*

The Second Awakening and Frontier Religious Revival

Additional Recommended Reading

Sweet, William W. *Revivalism in America: Its Origin, Growth, and Decline.* New York: Charles Scribner's Sons, 1945. Sweet, a prolific writer on American religion, here traces the revival tradition through the Great Awakening and the Second Awakening.

Cleveland, Catherine C. *The Great Revival in the West, 1797-1805.* Gloucester, Mass.: Peter Smith Publisher, Inc., 1959. First published in 1916, this remains a substantial account of the highly emotional early phase of the revival, with due attention to the social, economic, and psychological factors involved.

Posey, Walter B. *Frontier Mission: A History of Religion West of the Southern Appalachians to 1861.* Lexington: University of Kentucky Press, 1966. Posey considers southwestern revivalism in a wider context which includes specific treatment of Negroes and Indians, Roman Catholic expansion in the West, and slavery as a religious problem.

Smith, Timothy L. *Revivalism and Social Reform: American Protestantism on the Eve of the Civil War.* New York: Harper & Row Publishers, 1957. Although primarily concerned with the 1840's and 1850's, Smith's work is extremely useful in unraveling the theological and denominational distinctions of nineteenth century American Protestantism, as well as in tracing the revival spirit in the antislavery and other reform movements.

Weisberger, Bernard A. *They Gathered at the River: The Story of the Great Revivalists and Their Impact upon Religion in America.* Boston: Little, Brown, and Company, 1958. Weisberger's readable and scholarly survey of an American tradition gives special attention to Finney in the period of the Second Awakening.

McLoughlin, William G., Jr. *Modern Revivalism: Charles Grandison Finney to Billy Graham.* New York: Ronald Press, 1959. McLoughlin in this substantial interpretive study finds that evangelism became a tribalistic "national religion," eventually tied to political conservatism, economic laissez-faire, and social conformity. Finney, the author believes, unwittingly helped to push it in this direction.

ELECTION OF JEFFERSON TO THE PRESIDENCY IN 1800

Type of event: Political: Presidential election
Time: 1800
Locale: The United States

Principal personages:

THOMAS JEFFERSON (1743-1826), presidential candidate in 1800 and third President of the United States 1801-1809

JOHN ADAMS (1735-1826), second President of the United States 1797-1801

AARON BURR (1756-1836), vice-presidential candidate in 1800 and Republican leader in New York

ALEXANDER HAMILTON (1757-1804), Federalist leader in New York

JAMES A. BAYARD (1767-1815), Federalist Representative to Congress from Delaware

CHARLES COTESWORTH PINCKNEY (1746-1825), Federalist vice-presidential candidate in 1800

Summary of Event

The Presidential campaign of 1800 pitted President John Adams against Vice-President Jefferson, an old adversary and an older friend. Adams had won over Jefferson in 1796 by the slim margin of three electoral votes. New England seemed to be solidly Federalist and the South seemed to be solidly Republican. The critical states were Pennsylvania and New York. Jefferson had carried Pennsylvania in 1796; he hoped to maintain his position there and he also hoped to win New York to his side. South Carolina was also an important state, for the Federalists enjoyed strong support there.

Relations with France dominated the Adams Administration. The Federalists were able to parlay American indignation over the XYZ Affair into strong political support for their program. Many Federalists, including Adams for a time in 1798-1799, were willing to declare war or force a decla-

ration of war from France. The High Federalists realized that their continued popularity depended on maintaining public opinion at a high emotional level against the French. For a time, in 1799, it seemed that the Republicans, damned by their opponents as pro-French, were out of the running in 1800. But as the popular mood changed, as the war fever declined, as opposition to the military program and taxes increased, and as Adams himself became less aggressive, Republican chances proportionately improved. When the President suddenly decided to send a new peace mission to France, the High Federalists realized that they were doomed. Peace was now the major theme. The Republicans had all along been committed to peace.

Adams' peace policy split the Federalist Party. Alexander Hamilton attacked the President directly and

426

schemed to replace him. The Republicans, united behind Jefferson, applied themselves diligently to capturing the critical states of New York and Pennsylvania. As the outcome proved, the Republicans were more efficiently organized than the Federalists.

In New York, Aaron Burr was the Republican leader and Hamilton directed the opposition. At stake was the composition of the state legislature. Whichever party captured this body would control the twelve electoral votes cast by New York. Burr completely outmaneuvered Hamilton, and the Republicans captured a majority in the Lower House, thus giving them a majority of one in the combined vote of both Houses. This defeat deflated the hopes of the Federalists. The Republicans then staved off an energetic Federalist campaign in South Carolina and brought Jefferson home the victor by eight electoral votes. This margin was not particularly impressive, but it did represent a significant shift of party strength in the crucial Middle states. The Republican Party did not penetrate New England, but John Adams did improve his position in some Southern states. President Adams, in spite of a serious split in his own party, looked stronger in 1800 than he had in 1796.

The Federalist Party had a second opportunity to prevent the election of the "atheistic, Jacobinic, democratic" Jefferson. In 1800 the electors did not distinguish between the President and the Vice-President in casting their votes. The man who received the highest number of votes became President, and the runner-up became Vice-President. In a display of party unity, each Republican elector cast a vote for Jefferson and a vote for Burr, the vice-presidential candidate on the Republican ticket. The resulting tie meant that the decision would be made in the House of Representatives with each state casting one vote. A sufficient number of Federalists preferred Burr so as to make Jefferson's election dubious.

Hamilton, whose dislike of the devious Burr later caused the famous duel in which Hamilton lost his life, preferred and supported Jefferson in the House. But the Federalist Party ignored Hamilton's advice in the hope that a prolonged contest would damage the Republican Party and perhaps postpone the transfer of power. The Federalists also sought some guarantees from both candidates regarding their plans for the future. But neither Jefferson nor Burr would commit himself. Finally after thirty-five ballots, James Bayard, the lone Representative from Delaware, decided to switch his vote, and thus his state's support, to Jefferson. This made the ninth and decisive vote for Jefferson. The nation finally, on February 17, 1801, had a President-elect.

Jefferson considered the election of 1800 "as real a revolution in the principles of our government as that of 1776 was in form." Jefferson's view was supported by some Federalists. Many High Federalists were positive that Jefferson would lead the nation into chaos and anarchy. But Jefferson, in his inaugural address, spoke of conciliation and moderation rather than revolution.

The most concrete issue separating Adams from Jefferson's policy toward France evaporated when Adams came out for peace. Jefferson, in later days, charged Adams with monarchist and antirepublican tendencies. There was little substance to those charges. Jefferson did articulate a greater confidence in popular government than Adams, and the former was more suspicious of centralist tendencies in government. But both men were nationalists, devoted to representative government, determined to disengage America from European politics, and convinced of the future greatness of the Republic. In 1800, while Adams did lose to Jefferson, he also defeated the High Federalists in his own party. In so doing, Adams closed the already narrow gap between himself and Jefferson.

Pertinent Literature

Channing, Edward. *The Jeffersonian System, 1801-1811.* Vol. XII: *The American Nation: A History.* New York: Harper & Brothers, 1906.

Channing's survey of the administration of Thomas Jefferson and the first years under Madison is a volume in the old *American Nation* series, edited by Albert Bushnell Hart. This series was one of the first attempts by the historical profession to create a multi-volume synthesis of American history for American colleges and universities. The same publisher has been bringing out for the last decade a *New American Nation* series with much of the same purpose as the first, but produced by a later generation of professional historians. Channing declares in the introduction to this volume that he is indebted to the earlier work of Henry Adams on the administrations of Jefferson and Madison. His study, however, goes beyond Adams for sources and retains value even in the light of the publication of more recent works on Jefferson's Presidency. A major portion of this book is devoted to foreign matters—that combination of events which led the United States to the Louisiana Purchase and eventually toward war with Britain. The first two chapters, however, deal with the domestic events of the first years of the Jefferson Administration—those years which were to have seen the implementation of a "Jeffersonian Revolution."

The "revolution" that ensued, according to Channing, was moderate indeed. Jefferson did move against the Judiciary by securing and repealing the Circuit Court Act of 1801 and later by the impeachment of Justice Samuel Chase. He also moved toward greater economy in government and away from some of the formality that his predecessors had created for the office of Chief Executive. A number of Federalist officeholders, though not enough for some of his supporters, were removed. Altogether, however, Channing sees only a moderate change in the governmental system. He ascribes that moderation chiefly to two things. First, Jefferson discovered that opposition to the party in power gives a political leader greater freedom than he enjoys upon assuming the responsibilities of office. As President, Jefferson had a different perspective from the one he had as opposition party leader. Second, his Republican Party needed to build its strength in New England, and thus could not afford to alienate completely the people of that strongly Federalist section. Channing asserts that the Republican Party in power was the South in power, and that section needed alliances with Northern factions to hold power. The Jeffersonian and the Virginia-Pennsylvania-New York alignment was in danger of being seriously weakened by the machinations of Jefferson's Vice-President, Aaron Burr, in his home state of New York, and the Pennsylvania Republicans were wracked by factionalism.

Much has been made of the inconsistency between the declared political principles of the Republicans and their actual conduct in office. The outstanding example of this inconsistency was Jefferson's purchase of Louisiana. Generally applauded as one of the greatest acts of his administration, it has also been pointed to as an example of what happened to those principles of strict construction of the Constitution which were supposed to have been enthroned in the "revolution of 1800." In that act, Jefferson used a very advanced and liberal construction of his powers as President, and indeed of the powers of the national government. Channing simply says, ". . . the Jeffersonian theory of strict construction was abandoned in the house of its friends." In-

consistent with Republican principles, too, was the Ohio Admission Enabling Act of 1802, which provided for continued federal ownership of ungranted land within the area and thereby established a precedent for all the public land states. The provisions of that law which granted land to Ohio for specific educational or internal improvement purposes set a pattern which can be contrasted rather sharply with the Jeffersonians' avowed sovereignty of the individual states and a limited role for the federal government.

Channing does not belabor these points, however, and in general seems to applaud the moderation and the conciliatory spirit which marked Jefferson's Administration. The election of Jefferson, he finds, did not so much bring about a revolution as it affected a temporary arrest of forces for the centralization of power that had developed in the preceding years. The "revolution," the "rise of the common man," that many seem to see in the election of Jefferson is largely ignored by Channing and perhaps rightly so—for however great a social change may have occurred, there simply was not a drastic political change.

Malone, Dumas. *Jefferson and His Time.* Vol. III: *Jefferson and the Ordeal of Liberty.* Boston: Little, Brown, and Company, 1962.

This is the third volume in Dumas Malone's multivolume biography of Thomas Jefferson which carries the overall title *Jefferson and His Time*. Malone is the greatest scholar of Jeffersonian America and his study ranks as the definitive biography of Jefferson. However, each volume in the series stands as a unit in itself and may be read with value not only as biography but also for information on Virginia

and national politics, as well as agriculture, science, and society. The first two volumes in the set carry Jefferson through his earlier career in Virginia and national politics and his diplomatic service as Minister to France. This volume picks up Jefferson in 1793 when he first contemplated resigning as Secretary of State and carries the biographical narrative through Jefferson's election as President in February,

1801.

Except for Jefferson's last year as Governor of Virginia during the Revolutionary War, 1793 became the most trying and discouraging year he spent in public life. Jefferson longed to retire and return to Monticello, yet Washington urged him to stay on as Secretary of State, and he remained out of his sense of duty. The democratic movement in Europe assumed a violent character, and Jefferson spent much of this year formulating American policy toward that troubled area. Though Jefferson sympathized with the French in their struggle against Britain, he worked with Washington to establish a policy of "fair neutrality." Malone emphasizes that Washington gave Jefferson a good deal of latitude in handling the nation's foreign policy. This subject, however, was not the work of Jefferson alone, but rather of several men working under the direction of the Secretary of State.

Early in 1794 Jefferson resigned as Secretary of State and returned to Monticello where he spent the next three years. Malone describes in some detail Jefferson's family life and his agricultural experiments during those years. Prior to 1796 Jefferson offered little direct service to the Republican Party. He reluctantly acquiesced in his election to the Vice-Presidency in 1796, but by the summer of 1797 he had assumed the reins of Republican Party power.

In a sense the contest for the Presidency in 1800 began in 1798 with the Federalist sponsored Alien and Sedition Acts, designed among other things to strike at the Republican Party by limiting its enlistment of new immigrants and silencing its criticism of the Adams Administration. Jefferson turned to the state governments for weapons against the Alien and Sedition Acts. As Malone describes it, Jefferson in effect performed a holding action designed to protect the rights of minorities and individuals. In his protests, especially in the Kentucky Resolutions which he authored, Jefferson took the most extreme states' rights position of his life. His intent was not to enlarge state power at the expense of federal power, but to safeguard individual freedom.

The election of 1800, despite its verbal scurrility, never became a national election. Although the Federalists controlled the national government, the Republicans controlled a majority of the state governments in an age when Presidential electors were selected by the legislatures. During the November federal elections, both Republican candidates—Burr and Jefferson—received an equal number of electoral votes. The Republicans also won control of the House of Representatives but the newly elected Congress would not take office until December, 1801. Since Burr and Jefferson tied, the choice between the two men was constitutionally delegated proceeded to the House of Representatives. The majority of the state delegations of the old House which was still sitting was Federalist. In general, Representatives from the Republican states mainly in the South and West supported Jefferson, while those from the Federalist states of the Northeast supported Burr; but those from Vermont and Maryland were split. As a result the House was deadlocked for thirty-five ballots. Finally, however, on the thirty-sixth ballot, Federalists from Vermont and Maryland abstained, giving those states to Jefferson. Two additional states abstained, leaving Burr only the votes of four New England states, and giving Jefferson the election. Thus with Jefferson, the Republican Party leader on his way to the Executive Mansion, and his party in control of Congress, the "Jeffersonian Revolution" was accomplished. — *J.G.C.*

Additional Recommended Reading

Schachner, Nathan. *Thomas Jefferson: A Biography.* 2 vols. Toronto: William Collins & Co., Ltd., 1951. A competent biography of Jefferson by a writer familiar with the period.

White, Leonard D. *The Jeffersonians: A Study in Administrative History, 1801-1829.* New York: The Macmillan Company, 1951. As in his study of the Federalists, White is concerned with the Republican contribution, in both theory and practice, to the administration of the government.

Wiltse, Charles M. *The Jeffersonian Tradition in American Democracy.* New York: Hill and Wang, Inc., 1935; reissued 1960. Wiltse seeks to isolate the contributions of Jefferson to the development of democratic thought in America.

Wiltse, Charles M. *The New Nation: 1800-1845.* New York: Hill and Wang, Inc., 1961. An interesting overview of the history of the United States during this period, emphasizing the clash between nationalism and sectionalism.

Peterson, Merrill D. *The Jeffersonian Image in the American Mind.* New York: Oxford University Press, 1960. This study seeks to show how American political parties have sought to associate themselves with the Jeffersonian heritage.

Cunningham, Noble E., Jr. *The Jeffersonian Republicans in Power: Party Operations, 1801-1809.* Chapel Hill: The University of North Carolina Press, 1963. The author, following up an earlier study of the Jeffersonians in opposition, continues into the period of Republican ascendancy.

Peterson, Merrill D. *Thomas Jefferson and the New Nation: A Biography.* New York: Oxford University Press, 1970. This thousand-page work, considered by many to be the definitive one-volume biography, details the life of Jefferson in a refreshing style.

Smelser, Marshal. *The Democratic Republic, 1801-1815.* New York: Harper & Row Publishers, 1968. This volume in the *New American Nation* series is the counterpart of the Channing volume in the original *American Nation* series. Smelser describes Jefferson as a great defender of civil liberty whose election in 1800 was the result of the "counterattack of theologically conservative farmers against the Federalists' contempt for America's sunburned agricultural drudges."

Adams, Henry. *History of the United States of America During the Administrations of Jefferson and Madison.* 9 vols. New York: Charles Scribner's Sons, 1889-1891. This monumental old work stands as a major source on the history of the period.

ESTABLISHMENT OF THE UNITED STATES MILITARY ACADEMY

Type of event: Military: necessity for training future military leaders
Time: March 16, 1802
Locale: West Point, New York

Principal personages:

JOHN ADAMS (1735-1826), second President of the United States 1797-1801

MAJOR LOUIS DE TOUSARD (fl. nineteenth century), army officer who made significant recommendations for a national military academy

ALEXANDER HAMILTON (1757-1804), leading proponent of a military academy

HENRY KNOX (1750-1806), General George Washington's chief of artillery and the first Secretary of War

GENERAL DOUGLAS MACARTHUR (1880-1964), Superintendent of the United States Military Academy from 1919 to 1922

THOMAS JEFFERSON (1743-1826), third President of the United States 1801-1809

JAMES MCHENRY (1753-1816), Secretary of War under President John Adams

SYLVANUS THAYER (1785-1872), Superintendent of the United States Military Academy from 1817 to 1833

GEORGE WASHINGTON (1732-1799), first President of the United States 1789-1797 and a long time, persistent advocate of a military academy

Summary of Event

Even after emerging victorious from the Revolutionary War, the United States faced hostile forces from all directions. Monarchical European countries to the east were eager for the American experiment in democracy to collapse. Indians menaced settlement and further advancement in the American West. British Canada occupied the territory to the north and Spain to the south and southwest. The new nation obviously needed a system of national defense. Yet many, if not most, Americans feared an aristocracy as the most formidable threat to their democracy; Aristocracies, they believed, had their roots in standing armies. What the United States needed, many Americans agreed, was an army of citizen-soldiers led by a trained officer corps. These officers, who would come from many segments of society, would be trained in a military academy, but that academy would be controlled by civilians.

One of the first advocates of a military academy was Colonel Henry Knox, George Washington's Chief of Artillery and the first Secretary of War.

In 1783, Washington himself called for the establishment of "academies, one or more, for the instruction of the art military." No action was taken, and by 1785 the army had dwindled to less than one hundred officers and men. In 1790, the government purchased the fort of West Point on the Hudson river for $11,085, at a time when the United States seemed to be once again on the brink of becoming involved in war. France, America's ally, was at war with Great Britain and Spain, and it was apparent that the United States would have to bolster its national defenses in order to remain neutral. On May 7, 1794, Congress authorized an increase in the Corps of Artillerists and Engineers at West Point. It also established the rank of cadet for junior officers assigned to West Point to be trained in the arts of war. With other duties absorbing most of their time, however, they received little training. Less than two years later, a new commander, Lieutenant Colonel Stephen Rochefontaine, was ordered to West Point by the War Department with instructions to begin training the cadets. The war in Europe continued to mount and with it came pressures not only to enlarge the army drastically but also to found a military academy. On July 16, 1798, Congress empowered President John Adams to appoint four teachers for the purpose of instructing the cadets and young officers in the Corps of Artillerists and Engineers, but no qualified teachers could be found.

At this juncture, after years of failure, Alexander Hamilton informed the Secretary of War, James McHenry, that the United States needed a system of military education, including a school at West Point, another for artillerists and engineers, a third for cavalry and infantry, and a fourth for the navy. Students would attend West Point for two years and would then spend two more years at one of the other schools. Washington echoed this sentiment, writing shortly before his death that "The Establishment of an Institution of this kind . . . has ever been considered by me as an Object of primary importance to this Country." McHenry received further advice in the form of a memorandum prepared by Louis de Tousard, a major in the First Regiment of Artillerists and Engineers. In January, 1800, McHenry consolidated the recommendations of Hamilton and Major Tousard; President Adams, in turn, sent this plan to Congress. Congress again did nothing, chiefly because of the lingering fear that a trained corps of officers would threaten democracy.

What finally provided the impetus for the establishment of the United States Military Academy was something other than a concern for the state of the nation's defense. It was the desire for a national university, one that would substitute an emphasis on science for that on the classics. Thomas Jefferson was a leading advocate of more empirical courses in higher education; and when he became President in 1801, he believed that a military academy could fill this role and might also be supported by those who would oppose the idea of a national university. On March 16, 1802, Congress authorized Jefferson's ideas by passing legislation which enabled the President to establish a Corps of Engineers which "shall be stationed at West Point . . .

and shall constitute a military academy." After years of efforts by Knox, Washington, Hamilton, and others, a law had finally been enacted which acknowledged the need for such a civilian-controlled academy emphasizing training in the military arts.

Pertinent Literature

Ambrose, Stephen E. *Duty, Honor, Country: A History of West Point.* Baltimore: The Johns Hopkins University Press, 1966.

Several writers and historians have told the story of the origins of the United States Military Academy, though none has done it so skillfully as Stephen E. Ambrose. After recounting West Point's origins in the late eighteenth and early nineteenth centuries, the author gives a standard periodization of its history. Following its founding the Academy entered its "Golden Age, 1840-1860," a period during which it was the best engineering college in the country. West Point, Ambrose writes, "would prosper or not according to the abilities of its ranking officer," and its superintendent during the formative years from 1817 to 1833 was Sylvanus Thayer. "The methods and techniques he introduced are, for the most part, in effect today, the course of studies he outlined is essentially the same, his disciplinary measures are the basis of those in use today, while his aims and goals are those of the present West Point. He was the 'Father of the Military Academy.'" Thayer not only devised many of the enduring qualities of the academy, but he also had the strength of character to see that they were instituted. Dignified, intelligent, dressed faultlessly in the uniform of the professional soldier, living in solitude and "with perfect neatness, order and comfort, in all his arrangements," and absolutely punctual, Thayer made his mark on the Academy and its cadets. "He never married," Ambrose notes. "The Academy was his only love."

The cadets during Thayer's tenure and up to the Civil War made a significant contribution to American national development. Perhaps better than any civilian college, West Point taught its students to live and work with machines, and it was graduates of West Point who built much of the nation's transportation system of canals and railroads. They also held important positions in business, education, and government. After the Civil War, however, there was a period of "stagnation," as alumni and faculty resisted change. The academy fell behind the civilian colleges and universities, which were undergoing a rapid transformation in such things as curricula and graduate study.

Only when General Douglas MacArthur became Superintendent in 1919 did the academy begin to show progress again. Ambrose describes these years and the reforms which MacArthur carried out. "MacArthur rescued the Academy in a time of crisis. . . ." The country and its military needs had changed. America "no longer required a public institution for civil engineers; it did need a cadre of professional soldiers able to lead civilian soldiers in war involving the large masses of society. . . ." MacArthur had to overcome the conservatism of alumni and the academic board. When he left in 1922 it seemed that he had failed. "But that was not really so," Ambrose notes. "MacArthur had brought a new spirit to the Academy, a willingness to experiment, to break with tradition, to question everything, that could never be shut out." His ideas were accepted eventually. Other progressive minded superintendents, such as General Maxwell Taylor, followed, and the academy is now a modern institution. Its advanced curriculum includes such courses as atomic and nuclear physics, comparative literature, comparative foreign governments, international relations, law, and thermodynamics.

In this entertaining book, Ambrose also tells anecdotes about some cadets who "simply refused to conform to the West Point mold." Among these were James McNeill Whistler, who became a famous artist, and the writer Edgar Allan Poe. Other aspects of cadet life, such as hazing, football, the introduction of Negroes into the academy, and scandals, are recounted in this study. Photographs and a comprehensive bibliography of both published and unpublished materials also add to its value.

West Point is a unique institution, being national in scope and having been established and regulated by the federal government. Ambrose has skillfully told the history of the Academy, placing the story of its origins and development within the context of American politics, social attitudes, and higher education.

DuPuy, Ernest R. *Men of West Point: The First 150 Years of the United States Military Academy.* New York: William Sloane Associates, 1951.

Ernest DuPuy's sesquicentennial tribute to the United States Military Academy is not simply a compendium of the accomplishments of the Academy's alumni. Nor is it a history of West Point. It is a narrative, written with color and verve, of the roles played in the development and defense of the nation by some four hundred West Point men. The book deals with commanding generals and junior officers who have been heroic in battle, and also with alumni who have made their mark as civilians. Sometimes romantic, obscuring the faults of some men while exaggerating the greatness of others, it is nevertheless an interesting study of how ideals inculcated at West Point continue to influence the lives and actions of its graduates.

"This narrative," DuPuy writes, "is an attempt to show, against the background of our national history and of national crises in war and peace, the part played therein by certain graduates of the United States Military Academy." The author's "final criterion of selection has been: 'Did this man's deed contribute significantly to the good of the nation, to its growth and its maintenance?' " Some of the more interesting parts of this book deal with America's military heroes, including Grant, Lee, Jackson, Sherman, Pershing, MacArthur, Eisenhower, Bradley, Wainright, and Clark. There is perhaps a disproportionate emphasis on World War II, that being the subject of almost one half of the book, and this deëmphasizes such events as the role of West Point in the Indian wars.

In showing what made leaders of

certain West Point graduates, DuPuy also tells a great deal about the academy itself and what it stands for. Many if not most of its graduates, the author believes, have followed an honorable code of behavior even as the weapons and conditions of war have changed. The honor system, for example, is a "code unique in the history of education," for it "permits two roommates to take exactly the same examination on two different days, yet prevents the earlier examinee from discussing this experience in any manner whatsoever with the man yet to take the test." This enduring code he attributes not only to Sylvanus Thayer but also to Dennis Hart Mahan, the "architect of captains" and father of the famous naval historian and theorist. — *W.M.T.*

Additional Recommended Reading

Forman, Sidney. *West Point: A History of the United States Military Academy.* New York: Columbia University Press, 1950. A history of West Point from its beginnings as a fortification on the Hudson river to its transition into a military academy.

Jacobs, James R. *The Beginning of the United States Army, 1783-1812.* Princeton: Princeton University Press, 1947. Focuses on the early role of the army in defending the Western frontier from Indians and foreign powers, and tells of the military leadership of Generals Harmar, St. Clair, Wayne, and Wilkinson.

MacArthur, General Douglas. *Reminisences.* New York: McGraw-Hill Book Company, 1964. The autobiography of a man whose extraordinary and controversial public career was to some extent bound up with his early work at West Point.

Maher, Marty. *Bringing Up the Brass: My 55 years at West Point.* New York: David MaKay Co., Inc., 1951. Maher, who served as an enlisted man at West Point for over half a century, has recalled his experiences in a colorful memoir.

Masland, John W. and Laurence I. Radway. *Soldiers and Scholars: Military Education and National Policy.* Princeton: Princeton University Press, 1957. Analyzes the entire structure of American military education, including the service academies and the Reserve Officer Training Corps in civilian colleges and universities.

Weigley, Russell F. *History of the United States Army.* New York: The Macmillan Company, 1967. A comprehensive one-volume history of the army that is encyclopaedic in scope and detail.

SUPREME COURT'S FIRST EXERCISE OF THE RIGHT OF JUDICIAL REVIEW
(*Marbury* v. *Madison*)

Type of event: Legal: establishment of the principle of judicial review as a function of the Supreme Court
Time: February 24, 1803
Locale: Washington, D.C.

Principal personages:

WILLIAM MARBURY (1761?-1835), the man appointed Justice of the Peace by President Adams whose commission Madison refused to deliver

JAMES MADISON (1751-1836), Secretary of State, ordered by President Jefferson to withhold Marbury's commission

JOHN MARSHALL (1755-1835), Chief Justice of the United States 1801-1835

JOHN ADAMS (1735-1826), second President of the United States 1797-1801

THOMAS JEFFERSON (1743-1826), third President 1801-1809

Summary of Event

To John Adams in 1801, the transfer of Presidential power to Thomas Jefferson signaled a virtual revolution in American political life. The Jeffersonian Republican Party represented to Adams and the Federalists not just a different political party which had opposed their stewardship of the federal government, but it represented the enemy of that government. The campaign of 1800 had been marked by almost hysterical appeals on both sides. The Federalists had identified themselves with government under the Constitution; the Republicans seemed to call for a radical change in the nature of that government. As the inauguration of Jefferson neared, the Federalists feared that their work of over a decade in establishing a strong, viable government under the Constitution was in jeopardy, for Jefferson was sweeping into office a Republican Congress. The one branch of government that the Republicans would not control was the Judiciary, and in its last days, the Adams Administration moved in several different ways to secure that last bastion of defense of the constitutional order as they envisioned it. Congress authorized, and Adams appointed, sixteen new circuit judges to relieve Supreme Court justices from circuit duty and also to strengthen the Federalist complexion of the federal bench. Adams appointed and the Senate quickly confirmed his Secretary of State, John Marshall, to the vacant Chief Justiceship, while Congress reduced the size of the Supreme Court from six to five members upon the occasion of the next vacancy, thus presenting Jefferson with a Court headed by a political enemy with a membership he might not be able to affect before the end of his term. The Congress also authorized the appointment of up to fifty Justices of the Peace by Adams for the District of Columbia. Their appointments had been approved by the Senate, but Adams and his Secretary of State (Marshall was still acting in that capacity) did not have all the commissions delivered before the expiration of Adams' term on March 4, 1801. William Marbury, one of Adams' appointees, sued before the Supreme Court in December, 1801, for a writ of mandamus to Jefferson's Secretary of State, James Madison, for the delivery of his commission. On assuming the Presidency, Jefferson had apparently ordered the commissions destroyed. He had drawn up a slightly different list of new Justices of the Peace, replacing that of Adams, and had not included the name of Marbury.

Jefferson and his party had not failed to note the last-minute efforts of Adams and his Federalist Party to "pack" the judiciary. Jefferson and his party leaders in Congress expected a confrontation with the judicial branch. In 1802, the Republican Congress repealed the Circuit Court Act of 1801, thus removing sixteen sitting judges from their seats. This repeal was considered to be unconstitutional by many, especially Federalists, but no judge raised the issue in a court of law. To prevent immediate adjudication if one did, the Congress passed a law setting the next meeting of the Supreme Court for February, 1803. No attack on the Repeal Act was made, but Marbury again demanded an order from the Supreme Court, under section thirteen of the Judiciary Act of 1789, to the Secretary of State to perform his duty under

the law and to deliver the commission to Marbury.

Jefferson's Administration virtually ignored the Court process. The President resented the notion of judicial interference in what he considered strictly an executive matter—the appointment process. Marshall, on the other hand, seemed eager to assert for the Court a strong and vigorous role in government as the guardian of the Constitution, a function which he believed could not be left to the Republicans. The unanimous decision of the Court asserted that role, but at the cost of Marbury's commission. In giving the Court's opinion, Marshall reversed the usual order and discussed Marbury's right to his commission as a Justice of the Peace before he considered the Court's jurisdiction in the case. In a rebuke to the President, he declared that Marbury indeed had a right to the commission which should be delivered to him, but that Marbury could not obtain a writ of mandamus from the Supreme Court ordering its delivery, because the Court did not have the power to issue such a writ. Section thirteen of the Judiciary Act of 1789, which had added authority to the original jurisdiction of the Court, was void because it violated Article III of the Constitution. In describing the powers of the Supreme Court as a court of first instance, Marshall found no mention in Article III of the authority to issue writs of mandamus.

Many subsequent students of the Constitution have held that Marshall could have interpreted Article III differently and could have accepted the power of Congress to add to the original jurisdiction of the court as he could subtract from its appellate jurisdiction.

By taking the action he did, Marshall was able to assert sweeping power of the Court to declare acts of Congress unconstitutional, while in the instant case, he essentially satisfied Jefferson by refusing to order the President to do something which he manifestly did not want to do.

The rule of the Court in *Marbury* v. *Madison* has been cited on countless occasions by the federal courts since 1803. To support his position that the Supreme Court could invalidate laws of Congress, Marshall relied heavily on the arguments of Alexander Hamilton supporting the doctrines of judicial review as set forth in *The Federalist No. 78*. The argument was simple. It is the duty of judges, where there is doubt, to say what the law in a particular case is. The Constitution is the supreme law. If, therefore, in the consideration of a case, the Supreme Court finds a conflict between the law as passed by Congress and the supreme law as stated in the Constitution, it must, under its constitutional oath, apply the supreme law. At times even Jefferson and his adherents had taken this position. They, for example, had chided earlier federal judges for not declaring the Alien and Sedition Acts of 1798 unconstitutional for violating the First Amendment to the Constitution.

Jefferson was placed in a somewhat difficult position by the Marbury case. The Court had rebuked him, but it had desisted from ordering him to deliver Marbury's commission; it had claimed for itself a sweeping power, but had exercised this power in favor of the immediate desires of the President.

Although it would not exercise this power again for a half century, Marshall had succeeded in securing for the Court a preëminent position in the interpretation of the Constitution. From then until now it has been the decision of the Supreme Court in cases brought before it which have been the definitive statement of the meaning of the Constitution for the courts, the Congress, and the President.

Pertinent Literature

Corwin, Edward S. *The Doctrine of Judicial Review: Its Legal and Historical Basis and Other Essays.* Princeton: Princeton University Press, 1914.

Corwin, Edward S. *Court Over Constitution: A Study of Judicial Review as an Instrument of Popular Government.* Princeton: Princeton University Press, 1938.

Corwin was a legal scholar rather than a historian of the Supreme Court. His interest in the doctrine of judicial review was more as to its use in the general American political framework than in its place in the development of the Supreme Court. Corwin, influenced heavily by the theories of "sociological jurisprudence" as they grew in the first decades of this century, goes beyond the strictly legal reasoning of Marshall and his defenders to a discussion of the making of that real law through which government acts on people within a political framework.

Marshall asserted, as have judges and others before and since *Marbury* v. *Madison,* that it was the peculiar province of judges to say what the law is, to be the final interpreters of the Constitution as the supreme law of the land. Corwin examines that assertion and its origins, both in the American experience in colonial and early national times and in its English background. While the right of judicial review was invariably asserted in seventeenth century England, the development in that nation since then has been in the direction of a virtually omnipotent legislature. The American experience has been very different, for here the courts on both the state and federal levels have for many reasons asserted a greater role in saying what the law is. The federal system, with its apportionment of powers between state and federal government, has given rise to much litigation over which power belongs to which government. The provisions of the Constitution itself, and especially its prohibitions of various kinds of governmental actions, have required much judicial interpretation.

The evidence strongly suggests that some kind of judicial review was intended by the framers of the Constitution, but it is unclear as to where the final determination of what the law is should belong. Chief Justice Marshall himself was not sure of the finality of his decision in *Marbury* v. *Madison.* He expressed the fear that Jefferson and his Republican majorities in Congress might very well impeach and harass the members of the Court, and in their place install a friendly majority who would overrule his decision.

Corwin's essay in his *Doctrine of Judicial Review,* and the general discussions in his later work, *Court over Constitution,* were essentially the same positions. The latter work is heavily colored, however, by the recent attempt of President Franklin Roosevelt to assert political power over the Su-

preme Court in his 1937 court packing plan. In 1918, Corwin argued that the opponents of judicial review within the Progressive movement had little to complain of concerning the courts, as they seemed to be moving in the direction of accepting progressive legislation. By 1938, Corwin was not defending the importance of the distinction between "discovering" the law and "making" the law—the former a power asserted by judges, the latter a function of legislatures. The two functions, he believed, were both part of the political process. They differed more in form than in substance. In *Marbury* v. *Madison,* Marshall made a choice in the way he interpreted Article III of the Constitution. The words of the Constitution in that case do not, nor will they often, ordain a clear course of action for judges any more than they do for legislatures or executives. Article III was susceptible of being interpreted in such a way as to leave section thirteen of the Judiciary Act of 1789 valid. Federal judges have generally followed the rule that when an act of Congress *can* be construed as constitutional, it will be, giving the Congress the benefit of the doubt in the absence of clear indications that the power of Congress has been misused. Marshall claimed, as have judges since, that their function is almost mechanical; they merely measure the statute against the Constitution, and if they cannot find constitutional authority, they must void the law. Corwin and others in the tradition of legal realism point out that the processes of reasoning, the values, and the political feelings of judges necessarily make their task more than mechanical and involve them in a process which is practically political. In discovering law, they necessarily make law. Judicial review, then, while a useful and often a beneficent device, is essentially no more sacred than any other.

Warren, Charles. *The Supreme Court in United States History.* Vol. I: *1789-1821.* Boston: Little, Brown, and Company, 1923.

This first volume of three is one of the standard histories of the Supreme Court. Two chapters focus on the confrontation between the Federalist Judiciary and the Republican President, with the latter chapter specifically discussing the case of *Marbury* v. *Madison.* Warren examines closely the political issues separating Marshall and Jefferson and the essentially political nature of the case, but he treats the outcome of that case as a great triumph in American law for the valuable contribution of Marshall to the assertion of the right of judicial review by the high tribunal.

According to Warren, the doctrine of judicial review of acts of Congress was largely accepted as a constitutional doctrine before 1803. Both defenders and opponents of the Constitution during the ratification process pointed to the Judiciary as the guardian of the limitations on the powers of the nation as well as of the states included in that document. The Court itself had considered the constitutionality of a federal carriage tax in 1797, and had decided that such a tax did not violate the limited constitutional prohibition on direct taxes. Jeffersonian opponents of the Alien and Sedition Acts of 1798 were highly critical of federal judges for enforcing that legislation rather than declaring it in violation of provisions of the Bill of Rights. Even the decision in *Marbury* v. *Madison* did not cause much unfavorable comment on the power of the Supreme Court to review federal legislation; most critical comment centered on Marshall's *obiter dictum* in the beginning of the decision where he rebuked Jefferson for failing to deliver to Marbury his commission. In the year before *Marbury* v. *Madison,* however, there had arisen a powerful attack on the powers of the judicial branch, and especially its power to control congressional legislation. It arose from political reasons and died down when the urgency of political events themselves died away.

The Republican Congress under Jefferson's leadership had responded to what it considered a purely partisan Circuit Court Act of 1801 by simply repealing the act, thereby depriving the judges of their offices in 1802. This issue was the one which many expected to cause a confrontation between the Court and the other two branches of government. The attacks on judicial review were part of the preparation by Congress for its side of the debate if the Supreme Court should declare the 1802 act unconstitutional, as many expected it would. As it turned out, not one of the judges challenged the repeal act, and Marshall was at that time unable to assert the power of judicial review, as he probably would have done against a partisan attack on the Judiciary. According to Warren, he welcomed the opportunity to assert a vigorous role for the Supreme Court by declaring its primacy on constitutional matters in a minor case where he was able to decide in favor of his old political enemy in the Executive Mansion. Marshall seems clearly to have looked for an opportunity to assert judicial independence; Warren agrees with Corwin that Marshall was not forced merely by logic to his invalidation of section thirteen of the Judiciary Act of 1789. By doing so, however, he suc- ceeded in reducing legislative power by invalidating an act which, he claimed, unconstitutionally added to the power of the Supreme Court. The opinion of Marshall and of Hamilton that a government of limited powers must include judicial review was to prevail. — *E.J.M.*

Additional Recommended Reading

Beveridge, Albert J. *The Life of John Marshall.* Vol IV: *Conflict and Construction, 1800-1815.* Boston: Houghton Mifflin Company, 1919. The four-volume biography of the Chief Justice by a distinguished attorney and a former United States Senator is considered by most historians to be one of the finest biographies ever written by an American about an American.

Haines, Charles G. *The American Doctrine of Judicial Supremacy.* Los Angeles: University of California Press, 1932. A classic in its field, this seven-hundred-page volume discusses the roots of judicial review and the case of *Marbury* v. *Madison* in a scholarly and detailed manner.

McLaughlin, Andrew C. *A Constitutional History of the United States.* New York: D. Appleton-Century-Crofts, 1935. A complete history of constitutional development in the United States from its pre-revolutionary antecedents to the 1930's, this volume by one of the giants in the field gives a complete coverage of *Marbury* v. *Madison.*

McCloskey, Robert G. *The American Supreme Court. Chicago History of American Civilization* series. Chicago: University of Chicago Press, 1960. Discussion of *Marbury* v. *Madison* is somewhat shorter than those mentioned above, but it is well written and researched.

Kelly, Alfred H. and Winfred A. Harbison. *The American Constitution: Its Origins and Development.* New York: W. W. Norton Company, Inc., 1970. An up to date and scholarly treatment of the American Constitution and those cases which were instrumental in its development.

Garraty, John A., ed. *Quarrels That Have Shaped the Constitution.* New York: Harper & Row Publishers, 1962 and Colophon paperback. One of the essays in this volume gives a concise and readable account of this important decision.

THE LOUISIANA PURCHASE

Type of event: Political: purchase of territory that opened the Far West to United States expansion
Time: 1803
Locale: The Trans-Mississippi West

Principal personages:

RENÉ ROBERT CAVELIER, SIEUR DE LA SALLE (1643-1687), French explorer of Louisiana who claimed the area for France and named it

THOMAS JEFFERSON (1743-1826), third President of the United States 1801-1809 who was responsible for the purchase of Louisiana

JAMES MADISON (1751-1836), Jefferson's Secretary of State who gave directions for the purchase negotiations 1801-1809

ROBERT R. LIVINGSTON (1746-1813), United States Minister to France who conducted most of the negotiations for the purchase

JAMES MONROE (1758-1831), Envoy Extraordinary and Minister Plenipotentiary whom Jefferson sent to Paris to assist Livingston in negotiating for the purchase

JUAN VENTURA MORALES (fl. 1803), Spanish Intendant of Louisiana at New Orleans who suspended the right of deposit for American goods at New Orleans thereby making evident the critical need for a secure American access to the mouth of the Mississippi river

NAPOLEON I (BONAPARTE) (1769-1821), First Consul of France who decided to sell Louisiana to the United States

TOUSSAINT L'OUVERTURE (1743-1803), leader of the slave rebellion in Santo Domingo whose success in defeating French efforts to recover control of the island led to Napoleon's decision to sell Louisiana

MARQUIS FRANÇOIS DE BARBÉ-MARBOIS (1745-1837), Napoleon's Minister of Finance who negotiated the sale of Louisiana to the United States for the French government

Summary of Event

The first Europeans to explore Louisiana were the Spanish in the sixteenth century, but they failed to occupy the area effectively. In 1682 the French Explorer, Robert Cavelier, Sieur de la Salle, claimed the region for France and named it in honor of King Louis XIV. Louisiana remained French territory until the end of the Seven Years' War in 1763, when France ceded it to Spain in return for her help in the war against England and to compensate Spain for the loss of the Floridas. In the late 1790's France began to plan to rebuild her empire in the Western hemisphere, and by the

443

secret Treaty of San Ildefonso of October 1, 1800, Spain ceded Louisiana back to France.

Reports of the transfer of Louisiana, and perhaps even the Floridas, from Spain to France began to reach the United States in the spring of 1801. The Jefferson Administration viewed this transfer with some alarm because a powerful and aggressive Napoleonic France in control of the mouth of the Mississippi river would constitute a much graver threat to American rights on that vital artery of communication than did weak and declining Spain's presence there. When reports of the transfer continued to reach Washington, Secretary of State James Madison instructed Robert R. Livingston, the United States Minister to Paris, to investigate them. Should they prove to be true, Livingston was to try to acquire the Floridas, or West Florida at least, if they were part of the cession; if they had not been ceded to France, the United States would try to obtain them from Spain. Livingston learned that France had acquired Louisiana and New Orleans, but not the Floridas; his discussions with the French government were otherwise inconclusive.

When negotiations were at this stage, on October 16, 1802, the Spanish Intendant of Louisiana at New Orleans, Juan Ventura Morales, issued a proclamation withdrawing the right of Americans to deposit goods at New Orleans as had been provided for by the Pinckney Treaty with Spain of 1795. This decision meant that American goods brought down the Mississippi river could no longer be unloaded at New Orleans to be reloaded aboard ocean-going vessels for shipment to the East Coast or to foreign ports. The Americans blamed the French for this decision even though France had in fact not yet taken possession of Louisiana.

When news of the suspension of the right of deposit at New Orleans reached the Westerners who depended upon the Mississippi river and the use of the port of New Orleans as their commercial lifeline, they were greatly aroused, as were their spokesmen in Congress. There was a real possibility that the Westerners might march on New Orleans and seize it.

In response to their demands for action to protect American rights on the Mississippi and at New Orleans, President Jefferson sent James Monroe as Envoy Extraordinary and Minister Plenipotentiary to France to help Livingston in the negotiations with the French government. Livingston and Monroe were still to try to acquire at most only New Orleans and the Floridas, should they belong to France, and the right of the free navigation of the Mississippi river.

Napoleon's plans for the restoration of the French Empire in America depended upon the subjugation of the slaves on the West Indian island of Santo Domingo who were in revolt under the leadership of Toussaint L'Ouverture. The sugar, coffee, indigo, and cotton produced on this island were very important to the French economy, and if it could not be kept under French control, Louisiana would be of little value to Napoleon. At the end of 1802, despite the expenditure of many lives and enormous sums of money, the blacks were far from subdued and the island was in ruins. Napoleon decided to abandon Santo Domingo, and since Louisiana was to have been mainly a granary and supply region for that island, it would be of little value to France. Napoleon, therefore, decided to sell Louisiana to the United States. Other reasons for his decision were: he had determined to resume war against Great Britain and during those hostilities Great Britain might well take Louisiana away from him; he could forestall the formation of an alliance between the United States and Great Britain, and instead help to build up in the United States a possible rival to Great Britain which would help to block her expansion; he could avert a war in the future with an expanding United States; and he would need money to resume the war.

On April 11, 1803, Napoleon ordered his minister of finance, the Marquis de Barbé-Marbois, to negotiate the sale of Louisiana to the United States. Although they had no authorization to purchase Louisiana, Livingston and Monroe entered into the negotiations and, after some haggling as to price, came to terms. The negotiations were completed by May 9, but the treaty and two conventions comprising the agreement were all dated April 30. By their terms, the United States acquired Louisiana, including New Orleans, but with its boundaries otherwise vaguely defined. In return, the United States was to pay approximately $15,000,000,

and the inhabitants of Louisiana were to be incorporated into the United States and were to be accorded all the rights of American citizens.

Although Jefferson had some grave doubts about the constitutionality of the purchase, since the Constitution did not expressly grant the President or Congress the power to acquire foreign territory, he approved it. The Senate ratified the agreements on October 20, and the President proclaimed them in effect the next day. The lower part of the territory was transferred from Spain to France on November 30, 1803, and from France to the United States on December 20. Upper Louisiana was transferred from Spain to France on March 9, 1804, and to the United States the following day.

The acquisition of Louisiana virtually doubled the territorial extent of the United States, giving almost limitless room for expansion, and it made possible the later expansion to the Pacific Ocean. It set a precedent for acquiring foreign territory and peoples by treaty, and it improved feelings of nationalism in the people and largely ended the secessionist intrigues in the West. The new territory also provided a place to which the Indians living east of the Mississippi could be removed in the ensuing four decades.

Pertinent Literature

Adams, Henry. *History of the United States of America During the Administrations of Jefferson and Madison.* Vol. II. New York: Charles Scribner's Sons, 1898.

Henry Adams' deservedly praised multivolume *History of the United States During the Administrations of Jefferson and Madison* has long stood as the standard treatment of the period

against which all later works are measured. As befits a descendant of the second and sixth Presidents, Adams' work is magisterial in tone. Few historians today write with such ability or such an assumption of authority as he did.

The Louisiana Purchase, the problems it solved, and the problems it caused are the major subjects of this volume in the series. The first chapter and part of the second trace the European and colonial background of Napoleon's decision to part with Louisiana; the second and third chart and examine the course of Franco-American negotiations. In chapters four and five, Adams discusses, with almost undisguised glee, the problems of Jefferson and his supporters in reconciling with their particularistic philosophy and attachment to a "strict construction" of the Constitution accommodate to this unprecedented accomplishment. Adams could find only one Jeffersonian Republican who strove for consistency in his attachment to principles, and that Republican was John Quincy Adams.

President Jefferson instructed Robert Livingston to obtain for the United States from France the "island of New Orleans." Jefferson and his party were particularly open to the aspirations of those people in the West who felt access to the *entrepôt* at New Orleans, then in the hands of Spain but soon to be handed over to France, was necessary to their economic growth and prosperity. Traffic down the Mississippi had for too long, according to these Westerners, been subject to fickle Spanish authorities, and transfer to France could make the situation worse. Livingston was more successful than he had hoped to be. Suddenly the French negotiators began to talk seriously about the cession of New Orleans and additionally the whole of the trans-Mississippi territory. The American accepted the offer, but bargained over the cost, not knowing, according to Adams, that delay might have jeopardized the contract which Napoleon had decided upon against the opposition of many of his closest advisers. However, the deal was finally struck. James Monroe had arrived as a special emissary from the President, and both he and Livingston signed for the United States. Adams calls the Louisiana Purchase "the greatest diplomatic success recorded in American history."

The United States was the beneficiary of a series of events, over many of which it had no control. It was the decision of the First Consul of France, Napoleon Bonaparte, to sell the whole of Louisiana, not the aim of American diplomacy. Napoleon did not present the treaty to the French legislature, as he was required to do under the constitution, since it would have met great opposition, even from two of his brothers. He chose to ignore the advice even of Talleyrand and elected to abandon his American empire, an act for which "no true Frenchman forgave" the First Consul. There were many reasons why Napoleon acted as he did. He was preparing for war and needed funds, but he could have obtained a larger price for Louisiana from Spain. Essentially, Napoleon sold Louisiana to rid France of the memory of his colonial defeats, particularly the humiliation of Haiti's successful stand against his armies. Adams writes of the debt the United States owes to 500,000 "Haytian negroes," and of Napoleon's wish to "wipe from her [France's] memory the record of his failures . . . and bury it forever from the sight of France in the bosom of the only government which could absorb and conceal it." The price he received for Louisiana was spent "to the last centime" for war with Great Britain.

The American government was almost stunned with the success of its negotiators. Most of the credit due to the American side belonged to Livingston, but, as Adams maintains, "Virginia was all-powerful," and much of the credit fell to Jefferson's Virginia protegé, James Monroe. Their success put Jefferson into a quandary. He personally doubted the constitutionality of adding such a vast territory to the United States merely by treaty and privately drafted a constitutional amendment to legalize the work of his commissioners. Most of the other Republicans, even the most vociferous partisans of the Kentucky and Virginia Resolutions of 1798, managed to rationalize away their theoretical constitutional objections and applauded the acquisition of this magnificent territory. They saw it as an end to the Spanish-French threat to the Mississippi River Valley. Adams may overemphasize the distance the Republicans had

to depart from their principles to accept the Louisiana Purchase. There is more than a little of the Massachusetts-Virginia rivalry in the discussion of the constitutional difficulties. Adams may be less than fair to the philosophy of the Jeffersonians—who, after all, formulated the Kentucky and Virginia Resolutions in response to the Alien and Sedition Acts—when he declares that by accepting broad national powers to purchase Louisiana "the essential point was that for the first time in the national history, all parties agreed in admitting that the government could govern."

The addition of this great territory transformed the American republic and the party of Jefferson, not merely enlarged them. Although Adams was unable to remove himself and his family pride completely from his narrative, his work transcends that narrow outlook. Few studies produced in the last years of the nineteenth century have stood up so well to the tests of the professionalizing of history.

Lyon, E. Wilson. *Louisiana in French Diplomacy, 1759-1804*. Norman: University of Oklahoma Press, 1934.

Lyon, E. Wilson. *The Man Who Sold Louisiana: The Career of François Barbé-Marbois*. Norman: University of Oklahoma Press, 1942.

As most of the studies of Louisiana and the Louisiana Purchase have been written from an American point of view, Professor Lyon has consciously set out to tell that story from a European and specifically French standpoint. His bibliography reveals extensive work in French archives, and the work itself is enriched by copious quotes from the primary sources. The focus of his work is the role of Louisiana as a tool of French di-

plomacy in the half-century from the Seven Years' War through the rise of Napoleon and the final end of French hegemony in that part of North America. Roughly the second half of the book is devoted to the series of events which led immediately to the sale of Louisiana to the United States.

Lyon indicates in his bibliography in a note on Henry Adams' *History of the United States During the Administrations of Jefferson and Madison* that, although Adams' work has generally stood well over the years, recent scholarship gives him reason to modify some of Adams' findings, especially the motives that led Napoleon to decide to sell Louisiana to the United States. The major modification that Lyon makes in explaining Napoleon's motivations seems to be the laying of more emphasis on Napoleon's desire to placate the United States and to gain its friendship, or at least neutrality, as he prepared for war against Great Britain. After signing the treaty Napoleon announced, "I have just given England a maritime rival that sooner or later will lay low her pride." According to Lyons the motives of a man as complex as Napoleon were more complicated than that statement would indicate. He wished a United States strong enough to provide a rival to Great Britain on the sea, but he expected the Louisiana Purchase to weaken the United States as a hemispheric, continental power by the centrifugal effect he expected it to have on the Western and Eastern states. Napoleon had abandoned his dreams of an American empire, sketched by Lyon in Chapter V, but had no desire to help create a great power which could dominate the Western hemisphere. Both Adams and Lyon minimize Napoleon's desire merely for funds; they both see a decision made by Napoleon in 1802-1803 to assert French power essentially on land and in Europe, though Lyon asserts that Napoleon never abandoned hopes for empire in the Orient. Both historians see the Santo Domingo fiasco as a trigger to Napoleon's decision to abandon America. Lyon follows Adams almost exactly when he attributes part of Napoleon's decision to his desire to "cover up the lamentable failure in the Caribbean." Expecting war with the British, his colonial policy in Santo Domingo a humiliation, Napoleon saw Louisiana as a relatively small price to pay for American friendship or at least American abstention from an alliance with Great Britain. Given that alliance, Louisiana would have been lost in any case.

For both Lyon and Adams, the crucial figure in the history of the purchase was Napoleon. American requests were, by comparison at least, modest, but he gave away an empire. In the diplomacy of the period even the acquisitiveness shown by the United States for New Orleans and the Floridas was not viewed as modest ambition by Spain or for a long time by France. Persistent American attention to the Mississippi question, spurred as it was by the demands of the Western settlers, made Louisiana the important pawn it became in the hands of Napoleon. American policy was magnificently successful; Napoleon, it turned out, was little more than a decade away from Saint Helena.

Professor Lyon's biography of François Barbé-Marbois has a title that is a little misleading. Barbé was the French participant in the negotiations with Livingston and Madison, but he was following the directives of the First Consul. As Minister of Finance he was charged with responsibility for France's fiscal condition. As negotiator of the Louisiana Purchase he was moderately successful in improving that condition, gaining more for France than Napoleon had at first insisted on. Beyond that his major contribution was probably his history of the negotiations, which provides, as Lyon indicates in his general study of *Louisiana in French Diplomacy,* the only information available on Napoleon's decisions in early April, 1803, which were crucial days for the decision to sell the territory. Barbé-Marbois himself was a French bureaucrat who served successive French governments from the *ancien régime* through the Orleans Monarchy. As a young man he had served in the infant American nation. He was known as a friend of the country and was regarded as a man with strong republican feelings. He was primarily, however, a supremely efficient servant of the state. Lyon denies that he was an opportunist and describes events which indicated he was capable of courage in defense of convictions. Like the histories of other "moderate" men, his story of accommodation, matched with real ability in his chosen field of public administration, may tell us as much about an age as stories of the men who contested the tides of public affairs. — *J.L.L.*

Additional Recommended Reading

Whitaker, Arthur P. *The Mississippi Question, 1795-1803: A Study in Trade, Politics, and Diplomacy.* New York: D. Appleton-Century Co., 1934. Contains an excellent account of the background and negotiation of the Louisiana Purchase.

Fletcher, Mildred S. "Louisiana as a Factor in French Diplomacy from 1763 to 1800," *Mississippi Valley Historical Review,* XVII (December, 1930). Describes the efforts of France to effect the retrocession of Louisiana from Spain to France.

LaFargue, André, "The Louisiana Purchase: The French Viewpoint," in *Louisiana Historical Quarterly,* XXIII (January, 1940). LaFargue takes the position that the cession of Louisiana to the United States benefited France.

James, James A. "Louisiana as a Factor in American Diplomacy, 1795-1800," in *Mississippi Valley Historical Review,* I (June, 1914). James traces the growth of American interest in Louisiana.

Brooks, Philip C. "Spain's Farewell to Louisiana, 1803-1821," in *Mississippi Valley Historical Review,* XXVII (June, 1940). Examines the early years of Louisiana under American control.

LEWIS AND CLARK EXPEDITION

Type of event: Scientific: exploration of the Far West
Time: 1804-1806
Locale: Trans-Mississippi West

Principal personages:
THOMAS JEFFERSON (1743-1826), third President of the United States 1801-1809
MERIWETHER LEWIS (1774-1809), co-leader of the expedition
WILLIAM CLARK (1770-1838), co-leader of the expedition
GEORGE DROUILLARD (fl. early nineteenth century) expert half-Indian hunter and interpreter for the expedition
SACAJAWEA (1787?-1812), Shoshoni squaw whose presence with the expedition facilitated making the Rocky Mountain portage

Summary of Event

Meriwether Lewis and William Clark with their companions were the first white men to cross the western half of North America within the present limits of the United States. Their exploration was the concluding act in the long and fruitless search for a water route through the continent—a Northwest Passage—that had begun soon after Columbus discovered the New World.

The author of the exploration was Thomas Jefferson, the third President of the United States. He had first thought of such an undertaking about the time the United States achieved independence in 1783, and during the succeeding decade he twice tried unsuccessfully to have a transcontinental exploring party sent out. Not until he assumed the Presidency in 1801, however, was Jefferson in a position to have his plan implemented.

On January 18, 1803, the President asked Congress for authorization and for an appropriation of $2,500 to send a military expedition to explore along the Missouri river to its source in the Rocky Mountains, and then down the nearest westward-flowing stream to the Pacific. Jefferson gave two purposes for the proposed mission: to prepare the way for the extension of the American fur trade to the tribes throughout the area to be explored; and to advance geographical knowledge of the continent.

When he sent his message to Congress, none of the territory Jefferson wanted to be explored lay within the United States. The area between the Mississippi river and the Rocky Mountains, called Louisiana, belonged to France, while the Pacific Northwest was claimed by Great Britain, Spain, and Russia, as well as by the United States. While he was maturing his plans for the transcontinental exploring expedition, however, the President was also conducting negotiations with the government of Napoleon Bonaparte, which resulted in the purchase of Louisiana from France by a treaty signed on May 2, though antedated to

450

April 30, 1803. Thus, in ascending the Missouri the expedition would be exploring American territory, while, by completing the journey to the Pacific Ocean, it would be strengthening the United States claim to the region beyond the mountains.

To command the expedition, Jefferson chose his private secretary, Captain Meriwether Lewis. He, with the President's concurrence, then invited his old friend William Clark to be its coleader.

After making initial preparations in the East, Lewis traveled to Wood River, Illinois, opposite the mouth of the Missouri river. Clark and several recruits joined him on the way down the Ohio river. Lewis and Clark spent the winter of 1803-1804 at Camp Wood River recruiting and training their men, gathering additional supplies and equipment, and collecting information about the Missouri from traders and boatmen. The permanent party as finally organized included twenty-seven young, unmarried soldiers; a half-breed hunter and interpreter named George Drouillard; and Clark's Negro slave, York. In addition, a corporal and five privates with several French boatmen were to accompany the expedition during the first season, and then return with its records and scientific specimens.

The Corps of Discovery began its historic journey on May 14, 1804. It started up the Missouri in a fifty-five foot keelboat and two pirogues, or dugout canoes. Averaging about fifteen miles a day, by the end of October it reached the villages of the Mandan and Minnetaree Indians near the mouth of the Knife river in present-day North Dakota. There the explorers built a log fort and went into winter quarters.

During the long, frigid winter at Fort Mandan, Lewis and Clark made copious notes in their journals, drew maps of their route, and counseled with numerous Indian visitors. From the Minnetarees, especially, they obtained invaluable information about the course of the Missouri river and the country through which it ran. The contributions of these and other Indians to the success of the exploration cannot be exaggerated.

On April 7, 1805, the expedition resumed its journey. The party now numbered only thirty-three persons. It included, besides the permanent detachment, an interpreter named Charbonneau, his young Shoshoni squaw Sacajawea, and her papoose. Passing through country never before visited by white men, by August 17, the expedition reached the navigable limits of the Missouri river. With Sacajawea's help, Lewis and Clark purchased horses from Indians who lived nearby and began the portage of the Rocky Mountains. After crossing the mountains, the explorers descended the Clearwater, Snake, and Columbia rivers to the Pacific, where they arrived in mid-November.

After wintering at Fort Clapsop (named for a neighboring tribe) on the banks of the present Lewis and Clark river on the south side of the Columbia river, the explorers started for home on March 23, 1806. Enroute they divided temporarily in present Montana. Lewis and a small party explored Marias river, while Clark and the rest of the men descended the Yellowstone river. Reuniting below the mouth of the Yellowstone, they hurried on down the Missouri and arrived in St. Louis on September 23, 1806.

The Lewis and Clark Expedition had accomplished its mission with remarkable success. During more than twenty-eight months it had covered over eight thousand miles. On the entire journey, only one man, Sergeant Charles Floyd, lost his life, probably of a ruptured appendix. Although having met thousands of Indians, the explorers had only one violent encounter with them. This violence occurred while Lewis was high up the Marias river, and it resulted in the death of two Indians. The total expense of the undertaking, including the special congressional appropriation of $2,500, was something less than $40,000. At this small cost Lewis and Clark and their companions took the first giant step in opening the Trans-Mississippi West to the American people. Their achievement has well been called the most perfect of its kind in the history of the world.

Pertinent Literature

Bakeless, John. *Lewis and Clark: Partners in Discovery.* New York: William Morrow, 1947.

This book is the only reliable biography of both Lewis and Clark. Its main emphasis is on the Lewis and Clark Expedition. The account of the lives of the two men before that event is designed in no small part to show their special qualifications to lead the expedition. Jefferson knew both men and their families. All were Virginians. Young Lewis had been a neighbor of Jefferson, and Jefferson was an admirer of Clark's older brother, George Rogers Clark, the hero of the American Revolution in the West. William had left Virginia when he was only fourteen years old, however, when his family had moved to Kentucky.

As young men, both Lewis and Clark acquired considerable experience as army officers serving on the frontier. Before he was twenty, Clark participated in campaigns against the Indians living north of the Ohio river. In 1794, he took part in Major General Anthony Wayne's campaign against the Indians living along the Maumee river in northwest Ohio, which culminated in the red men's defeat in the famous Battle of Fallen Timbers. A few months later, Clark was in command of a select rifle company to which Lewis was assigned for a short time. It was presumably then that the two men became close friends. In 1796, Clark resigned his commission and returned to Kentucky to manage his father's plantation. Lewis, however, remained in the army. In 1801, he became Jefferson's private secretary but retained his military rank.

It was while serving as the President's secretary that Lewis, with Jefferson, planned the transcontinental explorations which Jefferson had so long wanted to see carried out. In all probability, before Congress even passed the legislation appropriating $2,500 to help defray the cost of the expedition, Lewis had begun to prepare for it. Not only did he obtain scientific instruments, arms, munitions, supplies, and equipment, but he also received rudimentary instruction in natural science and other useful subjects from members of the faculty of the University of Pennsylvania. Bakeless describes these preparations in some detail. He then follows Lewis from Washington to Pittsburgh by wagon, and from there down the Ohio river and up the Mississippi by keelboat to Wood River, Illinois. During the five months that they were encamped there, Lewis and Clark recruited most of the party, trained and disciplined them, and made all other preparations for their journey.

After describing these events, Bakeless gives a lengthy account of the expedition itself. This magnificent adventure story is based upon the extant journals kept by the two captains and by a few of their men on the historic tour. Upon their return, the explorers were handsomely rewarded for their services. In addition to receiving grants of land, Lewis was appointed Governor of the Territory of Louisiana, while Clark was made the territory's principal Indian agent and Brigadier General of its militia.

Lewis's career as Governor of Louisiana was short, for he died in October, 1809, but Clark lived for twenty-nine more years. Bakeless devotes only one short chapter to this long period. In 1813, Clark became the Governor of Missouri Territory (as Louisiana had been renamed the year before), and he remained the territory's Chief Executive until Missouri was admitted to the Union in 1821. Congress then created the post of Superintendent of Indian Affairs at St. Louis, to which Clark was appointed in 1822, holding this office until his death in 1838. As Indian agent, Territorial Governor, and Superintendent of Indian Affairs, Clark administered the United States' relations with the tribes west of the Mississippi and some of them east of the river for more than three decades. By the standards of his own time, he treated the red men with great humanity and sympathy. Few men in American history were regarded with as much affection and respect by the Indians as their "red-headed father" in St. Louis. The basis for this relationship was laid in no small part by Clark's contacts and experiences with the Indians during the Lewis and Clark Expedition.

Dillon, Richard. *Meriwether Lewis: A Biography.* New York: Coward-McCann, 1965.

Lewis has been called "undoubtedly the greatest pathfinder this country has ever known." Dillon's biography is the only modern full-length study of Lewis. His account of the explorer's life is more complete than Bakeless' and is based upon some new material. It, like Bakeless' book, deals mainly with the Lewis and Clark Expedition. For information concerning this epic event the author relies heavily on a few basic works, such as Reuben G. Thwaites' *Original Journals of the Lewis and Clark Expedition* and Donald Jackson's *Letters of the Lewis and Clark*

Expedition.

Lewis is a minor tragic hero of American history. Most of his short life was successful and relatively happy, but its end was marked with failure and catastrophe. Although his father died when he was only five years old, Lewis spent a carefree childhood and youth in Virginia and, for a short time, in Georgia. Entering the military service as a militia private in 1794, he was a captain in the 1st U.S. Infantry Regiment by the end of 1800. Early the following year, President-elect Jefferson invited the young officer to become his private secretary, and two years later named him commander of a transcontinental exploring expedition.

Although on the exploring tour itself Lewis and Clark acted as equals, the federal government considered Lewis to be the expedition's Commander and always treated him as such. While Clark's position of inferiority in rank and status in the eyes of the administration in Washington disappointed and irritated him, his relations with Lewis on the expedition and subsequently were, without exception, excellent. There is no record of the two men's ever having had a serious disagreement. This happy relationship was all the more unusual in view of the fact that the two men's personalities were entirely different. Lewis was inclined to be moody, introverted, and somewhat antisocial, while Clark was open, eventempered, and gregarious. Both during the expedition and afterwards, Clark was more successful than his companion in dealing with red men and whites. As a reading of their journals reveals, however, Lewis was the more literate and intellectual of the two explorers.

Although he won undying fame as the official leader of the Lewis and Clark Expedition, Lewis' life after that historic event was largely one of frustrated hopes and unfulfilled expectations. His plans to publish his own and Clark's journals of the expedition came to naught. He failed in his avowed desire to find a wife. His performance in the role of Governor of Louisiana Territory was so disappointing that there was good reason to doubt that he would have been reappointed for a second term had he lived out the first. Temperamentally unsuited to the demands of the office, Lewis became unpopular with many of the inhabitants of the territory and fell under severe criticism from his superiors in Washington. It was while on his way to the capital in the fall of 1809 to explain some of his acts as Governor and to renew his efforts to secure the publication of the journals of the expedition that Lewis died a mysterious and violent death at the age of thirty-five. The evidence as to whether he was murdered or committed suicide is inconclusive. In view of the uncertainty, Dillon holds his subject to be innocent of suicide. Clark, however, apparently believed that his friend killed himself, and so did Jefferson, at least for a time.

Dillon's biography is generally accurate and contains few flaws. It is likely to remain the standard life of Lewis.
— *J.L.L.*

Additional Recommended Reading

De Voto, Bernard. *The Journals of Lewis and Clark.* Boston: Houghton Mifflin Co., 1953. A useful one-volume condensation of the *Original Journals of the Lewis and Clark Expedition,* edited by Reuben G. Thwaites in eight volumes.

Biddle, Nicholas. *History of the Expedition Under the Command of Captains Lewis and Clark.* 2 vols. Philadelphia: J. B. Lippincott Co., 1961. Prepared by Biddle, a young Philadelphia lawyer, between 1810 and 1814, this work is based mainly upon the journals of Lewis and Clark.

Salisbury, Albert and Jane Salisbury. *Two Captains West.* Seattle: Superior Publishing Co., 1950. Designed for the layman, this volume contains a description of the Lewis and Clark trail with maps and photographs.

Lewis and Clark Expedition

Mirsky, Jeannette. *The Westward Crossings.* New York: Alfred A. Knopf, Inc., 1946. The last section of this book contains a brief account of the Lewis and Clark Expedition.

Gass, Patrick. *A Journal of the Voyages and Travels of a Corps of Discovery.* Minneapolis: Ross and Haines, Inc., 1958. Heavily edited by David McKeehan, a schoolteacher, this diary kept by a sergeant on the Lewis and Clark Expedition first appeared in 1807.

Cutright, Paul R. *Lewis and Clark: Pioneering Naturalists.* Urbana: University of Illinois Press, 1969. An interesting discussion of the scientific contributions of the Lewis and Clark Expedition.

THE TWELFTH AMENDMENT

Type of event: Constitutional: amendment designed to simplify procedure for electing the President and Vice-President
Time: September 25, 1804
Locale: Washington, D.C.

Principal personages:

JOHN ADAMS (1735-1826), second President of the United States 1797-1801

THOMAS JEFFERSON (1743-1826), third President of the United States 1801-1809

THOMAS PINCKNEY (1750-1828), unsuccessful vice-presidential candidate in 1796

AARON BURR (1756-1836), Vice-President of the United States 1801-1805

JOHN TAYLOR (1753-1824), Senator from Virginia, advocate of the Twelfth Amendment

JAMES MADISON (1751-1836), Secretary of State in 1804

Summary of Event

The Twelfth Amendment to the United States Constitution was necessitated by a basic flaw in the original document. Article II section 1 of the Constitution established a most complicated and confusing procedure for electing the President and Vice-President. According to this procedure the election was to be determined by the vote of an electoral college composed of electors from each of the states. Each state was entitled to the same number of electors as it had representatives in Congress. These electors, appointed in whatever manner the individual state legislatures chose, were to vote for two persons, presumably one for President and the other for Vice-President, though the ballots were not so labeled. The person receiving the highest number of votes, provided he received a majority of the electoral votes possible, was elected President. The person having the next highest number of votes

was elected Vice-President.

If the electoral voting resulted in a tie, the House of Representatives was to meet to choose one of the two candidates for President. If no candidate received a majority of electoral votes, the House of Representatives was to meet in order to select the President from the five candidates who received the most electoral votes. In similar situations the Senate was to decide the Vice-Presidency.

The vote in the House of Representatives was to be taken by states, with each state having a single vote. This procedure was written into the Constitution to protect the rights of the smaller states. In the final balloting in the House, they would be equal to the larger states.

It was presumed at the time of the writing of the Constitution that many worthy candidates would receive votes from the various electors and that sel-

456

dom, if ever, would anyone receive a majority of the electoral vote. The electoral college was intended to serve only as a nominating procedure to provide five good men for consideration by the House. The Founding Fathers did not anticipate the development of political parties. But political parties were forming in the 1790's, and the election of 1796 found Federalist John Adams from Massachusetts opposed by Republican Thomas Jefferson from Virginia. Adams won the election, but his running mate, Thomas Pinckney from South Carolina, finished in third place, nine votes behind Jefferson. This unusual election resulted in a situation where presidential rivals, representing different political parties, were forced to serve four years together as President and Vice-President.

A different but equally awkward result came out of the electoral balloting in 1800. In this election, Jefferson and his vice-presidential running mate, Aaron Burr from New York, received the same number of votes. This election went into the House of Representatives where Federalist opposition to Jefferson was strong. Although it was common knowledge that the electors who voted for Jefferson and Burr intended to place Jefferson in the top position, many diehard Federalists were determined to thwart their intentions and to put Burr into the Presidency. Moderate Federalists, influenced by Burr's home-state rival Alexander Hamilton, finally tipped the scales in favor of Jefferson. The Virginian was elected on the thirty-sixth ballot, dangerously close to Inauguration Day.

The somewhat bizarre results of the elections of 1796 and 1800 brought forth a demand for a change in the electoral system. John Taylor and other Jeffersonian Republicans prepared a series of resolutions suggesting an appropriate amendment to the Constitution. The resolutions were introduced into Congress where support from several states was immediately evident. The major objection to changes in the electoral college came from smaller states and from the Federalists. The smaller states feared that their role in Presidential elections might be diminished if the electoral college were abandoned. The Federalists merely hoped to disrupt or confuse the election of 1804. After much debate, agreement was finally reached in Congress in December, 1803. An amendment was written and was sent to the states for ratification. Within a year the necessary number of states, thirteen out of seventeen, had ratified the amendment. On September 25, 1804, Secretary of State James Madison announced the adoption of the Twelfth Amendment in time for the election of 1804.

Although the Twelfth Amendment did not abolish the electoral college or radically change the method of electing the President and Vice-President, it did remedy some basic defects. Separate ballots were provided for the election of President and Vice-President, thus preventing the problem of 1796. Provision was also made for the Vice-President to take over as acting President if the House should delay too long in selecting a President which almost occurred after the election of 1800. When no candidate received a majority vote in the electoral college, the House of Representatives was to choose a President from the three candidates who received the most votes, rather than from five. Equality among the states was maintained when Presidential or Vice-Presidential elections went into the House or the Senate. Other parts of the original Constitution remained intact.

Pertinent Literature

House, Lolabel. *A Study of the Twelfth Amendment of the Constitution of the United States*. Philadelphia: privately printed, 1901.

This sixty-three page monograph effectively outlines the genesis of the Constitutional Amendment that came in the wake of one of the young Republic's most vexing crises. It opens by briefly summarizing the plans of Thomas Paine, Pelatiah Webster, Noah Webster, and James Madison to strengthen the Executive under the Articles of Confederation, and then it follows the reasoning of the delegates to the Philadelphia Convention as they drafted the Second Article of the Constitution. After reviewing the weaknesses inherent in the new system of selecting the nation's chief magistrate that led to such a spectacular climax in the election of 1800, the author traces the development of the amendment that allowed electors to designate their votes for President and Vice-President, and she points out the most important political consequences of it.

From its first days, the Continental Congress tried to fill the Executive vacuum in the Articles of Confederation by creating committees and boards to enforce its resolutions. However, none of these bodies ever functioned effectively. After the Revolution, Congress created a new committee, composed of one delegate from each state, that was to sit between legislative sessions and to provide at least a semblance of governmental continuity. Such a council met at Annapolis in the summer of 1784, but it had virtually no power; its members bickered with one another and complained about the heat, and it soon disbanded.

Most of those in attendance at the Federal Convention of 1787 realized that the nation needed a new form of Executive administration, but few agreed on how the head of state should be elected, or how long he should serve. Debates were long and often confusing, as issues arose, died, and came to life again. House surveys the arguments of Edmund Randolph, Roger Sherman, Gouverneur Morris, James Wilson, and others. She maintains that the final solution ignored the inevitability of party influence, and that it was a compromise between forces that desired the supremacy of the Legislature and those in favor of a strong Executive.

Because of George Washington's overwhelming personality, the first two elections did little to test the efficacy of the new formula for electing Presidents. However, struggles for the Vice-Presidency, especially in 1796 and 1800, demonstrated that as long as electors could not specify their choice for the first two offices, there would be a potential crisis every four years. Consequently, in 1796, 1797, 1798, and 1800, Congress considered amendments that provided for the designation of votes for President and Vice-President, but they attracted only sporadic attention. What is significant about these early attempts to alter the supreme charter is that they were Federalist programs, even though the eventual Twelfth Amendment was a Republican Party measure.

After the House of Representatives decided in 1801 that Thomas Jefferson, and not Aaron Burr, would be the third President, Republicans reintroduced a resolution to reform the Constitution's Second Article. Throughout both sessions of the Seventh Congress, Federalists successfully opposed it as a partisan issue, but Jefferson's Party captured the majority in the next Congress, and the proposed amendment passed. By September 25, 1804, all but three states had ratified the new amendment, and it became the law of the land.

As House correctly contends, the enormous consequence of the Twelfth Amendment was that it modified one of the basic concepts of the Constitution by legalizing party government. By 1800 political parties had matured into opposing armies, and this measure wrote new reality into the nation's paramount ordinance. No longer would it be possible for a President and Vice-President to come from different coalitions, unless, of course, the House and Senate had to determine the outcome of an election.

More of an essay than a book, this study goes into little detail on any of the points it makes. However, it stands as a solid resumé of the events that culminated in the Twelfth Amendment, and its author based it upon research into the most important available documents on her subject. The most surprising thing about this work is that it has not been reprinted or anthologized, as it surely deserves to be.

Wilmerding, Lucius, Jr. *The Electoral College.* New Brunswick: Rutgers University Press, 1958.

Wilmerding's book is one of the best accounts of the electoral college available. Although a relatively small work, it covers the historical development of the electoral system in some detail. The author explains how and why such a system for selecting a President was agreed on in the first place. His well chosen quotations from the Founding Fathers show that there was disagreement concerning the merits of the system from the beginning. The major objection to the electoral procedure was that the voice of the people would only remotely be reflected by the election results. However, arguments in favor of the electoral college prevailed. Advocates of this system argued that the electoral procedure, while not perfect, was the best known method of selecting a good President and an equally good Vice-President.

Wilmerding next discusses the controversial elections of 1796 and 1800 and the subsequent adoption of the Twelfth Amendment. He is most critical of the original method and of the Twelfth Amendment. The second half of his book is devoted to various electoral college reforms that have been proposed from time to time. He leaves little doubt that he would like to see the present electoral system abandoned in favor of one or another of the reforms he discusses. — *E.J.M.*

The Twelfth Amendment

Additional Recommended Reading

Swisher, Carl B. *American Constitutional Development.* Boston: Houghton-Mifflin Co., 1943. Professor Swisher's work, which has long been recognized as an outstanding contribution to the field of constitutional history, contains a chapter on the early Presidency which includes useful information concerning the adoption of the Twelfth Amendment.

Hockett, Homer C. *The Constitutional History of the United States.* Vol. I. New York: The Macmillan Company, 1939. This well-written and well-documented book contains pertinent information regarding the demand for and the adoption of the Twelfth Amendment.

Roseboom, Eugene H. *A Short History of Presidential Elections.* New York: Collier Books, 1967. In this brief but useful account of Presidential elections from George Washington to Lyndon Baines Johnson, the elections of 1796 and 1800, which pointed up the need for a change in the electoral procedure, are clearly explained.

Schachner, Nathan. *Thomas Jefferson: A Biography.* Vol. II. New York: Appleton-Century-Crofts, 1951. Reveals the behind-the-scenes maneuvering of both Federalists and Republicans in 1800, and shows the obvious need for a change in the electoral procedure.

BURR'S CONSPIRACY

Type of event: Political: Aaron Burr's desire to regain his political fortunes
Time: 1805-1807
Locale: Western frontier of the United States

Principal personages:

AARON BURR (1756-1836), former Vice-President 1801-1805 and principal participant in Burr's conspiracy

JAMES WILKINSON (1757-1825), Commanding General of the United States Army and co-conspirator with Burr, who reported to President Thomas Jefferson a plot to dismember the Union

HARMAN BLENNERHASSETT (1765-1831), Irish immigrant and co-conspirator with Burr

ANTHONY MERRY (fl. 1805-1807), British Minister to the United States from whom Burr solicited financial and military assistance

MARQUIS OF CASO YRUJO (fl. 1805-1807), Spanish Minister to the United States from whom Burr solicited financial aid

THOMAS JEFFERSON (1743-1826), third President of the United States 1801-1809 who pressed charges of treason against Burr

JOHN MARSHALL (1755-1835), Chief Justice of the United States and presiding judge at Burr's trial

Summary of Event

Burr's conspiracy involved an alleged attempt in 1806 by former Vice-President Aaron Burr to separate the Western states from the remainder of the Union, or to conquer the Spanish possessions of Texas and northern Mexico, or possibly to do both. While it is clear that Burr planned some kind of military expedition in the West, there were so many different contemporary versions of what he had in mind that his real intentions remain shrouded in mystery even today.

Until his election as Vice-President in 1800, Burr enjoyed a successful political career. Ambitious, crafty, and elegant in manner, he managed in 1800 to secure the election of enough Republicans to the New York state legislature to ensure that that state's crucial twelve electoral votes would go to Thomas Jefferson in the fall. As a reward, he was given the second position on the Republican ticket. When the electoral votes were counted, it was found that Burr had received as many votes as Jefferson. The election had thus to be decided in the Federalist-controlled House of Representatives. Although some of the Federalist representatives preferred Burr to Jefferson, Hamilton favored the Virginian. Burr himself remained silent, apparently willing to accept the Presidency even though he knew that his party had intended him to be Vice-President. Finally, after thirty-five ballots, some Federalists switched their votes from

461

Burr to Jefferson, who was elected. For his attempt to thwart the will of his party, Burr incurred the wrath of the new President, who gave New York state's patronage to Burr's arch political rival, George Clinton. In 1804, Burr ran for Governor of New York against Clinton but was soundly defeated. Angered during the campaign by disparaging remarks made by Hamilton, Burr fought a duel and mortally wounded his old enemy. News of Hamilton's death led to public outrage against Burr which put an end to his political career.

Discredited and indicted for murder, Burr fled to Philadelphia to escape arrest. There he met with James Wilkinson, the principal participant in the unsuccessful attempts of the 1780's to separate Kentucky and Tennessee from the Union and now Commanding General of the Army. It was during their meeting that Burr's conspiracy was born. What the two men discussed is not entirely clear, but they seemed to have laid plans to conquer Texas and northern Mexico; they might also have discussed separation of the Western country from the remainder of the United States. Apparently to further his plans, Burr persuaded Jefferson to appoint Wilkinson to the office of Governor of the Territory of Louisiana.

At the expiration of his term as Vice-President in 1805, Burr met with Anthony Merry, the British Minister to the United States, and offered to detach Louisiana from the United States for one-half-million dollars and a British fleet in the Gulf of Mexico. Although Merry was interested in Burr's scheme, his superiors in London showed no interest in furthering American secessionism.

Following his interview with the British Minister, Burr proceeded to the West where he recruited volunteers for an expedition against Spanish territory. Reaching New Orleans, he made contact with the Mexican Associates, a group of Creoles (native-born Americans of French or Spanish descent) whose purpose was the conquest of Mexico. He even gained the support of the Catholic bishop of the city for an expedition against Mexico. It is not clear, however, whether Mexico was his real or his only objective, for in the following months he sought unsuccessfully to solicit financial aid from the Spanish minister to the United States, the Marquis of Caso Yrujo, in order to dismember the Union and establish an independent Western confederacy.

In the summer of 1806, Burr returned to the West where he continued to recruit volunteers for a military expedition down the Mississippi river planned for the late fall. One of his most loyal recruits was an Irish immigrant, Harman Blennerhassett, who owned an island in the Ohio river, near present-day Parkersburg, West Virginia, where he collected men and supplies for the expedition. Unfortunately for the plotters, the activities on Blennerhassett's island awakened the suspicions of the Governor of Ohio. In a lightning raid, the state militia seized most of Blennerhassett's supplies. Escaping with only one boat, Blennerhassett joined Burr, who had established headquarters at the mouth of the Cumberland river. In December, with a force of only nine boats and sixty men, they started down the Ohio river towards the Mississippi river and New Orleans, explaining their purpose as one of colonization in the Red River

Country.

During most of this time, Burr had worked closely with Wilkinson, who was expected to supply Burr with troops when he arrived in New Orleans. Unknown to Burr, however, Wilkinson had decided several months earlier that Burr's plans could not succeed. In order to save his own career and even appear as savior of the Union, Wilkinson informed Jefferson of a widespread scheme to dismember the United States. At the same time, he declared martial law in Louisiana and ordered the arrest of several individuals who were supposedly implicated in the plot.

Although Jefferson had heard rumors previously about Burr's conspiracy, he had hesitated in taking action, preferring to wait until Burr committed an overt criminal act. He responded to Wilkinson's messages, however, by ordering the arrest of anyone conspiring to attack Spanish territory. Burr had already reached Natchez when he learned of the President's order. Attempting to flee to Spanish Florida, he was arrested near Mobile and brought back to Richmond for trial on charges of conspiring to commit treason by trying to dismember the Union.

Burr's trial turned into a contest between Jefferson, who was bent on convicting Burr more, it has been said, for his treason to his party than to his country, and the presiding judge, Chief Justice John Marshall, a staunch Federalist and the inveterate foe of the President. Almost as much at issue in the trial as the charges against Burr were Jefferson's determination to discredit Marshall and the Chief Justice's determination to maintain the independence of the Judiciary and to embarrass the Chief Executive.

As presiding Justice, Marshall narrowly interpreted the clause in the Constitution which states that no one can be found guilty of treason unless there are two witnesses to the same "overt act" against the United States. Intention to divide the Union, Marshall stated, did not constitute an overt act. Under such a strict interpretation of the Constitution, the government had no case, and Burr was found not guilty of treason. He was also indicted on the charge of committing a high misdemeanor by planning to commit an act of war against a power with whom the United States maintained peaceful relations. This charge was dropped, however, when the government was unable to prove that Burr's expedition had been military or had been directed against Spanish territory.

Upon his release, Burr went to Europe where he spent the next four years before returning to New York and taking up the practice of law. His co-conspirator Wilkinson was investigated by Congress and court-martialed by the army, but he was cleared and retained his command. Although there is little doubt that both men were guilty of plotting either to attack Mexico or to divide the Union, or both, Marshall's strict interpretation of the Constitution was a major victory for individual liberty. It removed treason from the realm of politics and preserved the right of Americans to voice opposition to the government without fear of retaliation. In the struggle between the Executive and Judicial branches of the government, each successfully maintained its independence of the other.

Burr's Conspiracy

Pertinent Literature

McCaleb, Walter F. *The Aaron Burr Conspiracy: With a New Light on Aaron Burr.* Expanded edition with an introduction by Charles A. Beard. New York: Wilson-Erickson, Inc., 1936.

Walter F. McCaleb's volume has long stood as the standard work defending Aaron Burr against charges of treason and conspiracy. He argues that Burr was not guilty of conspiring to dismember the West or of planning an attack to capture Washington, D.C. and plunder the nation's capital. McCaleb implies, however, that Burr was guilty of indiscretion and of a "consummate piece of imposture" when he intrigued with the British and Spanish ministers to the United States. He maintains that Burr thought he could dupe the representatives of these two European powers and use their hatred for the American Republic to secure funds to finance a filibustering expedition against the Spanish colony of Mexico. Burr hoped to recoup his political fortunes through military exploits. McCaleb states that Burr was guilty, at the most, of a misdemeanor for conspiring to invade the Spanish domain. Burr is seen not as an adventurer bent on establishing an empire for himself at the expense of Spain, but as an early believer in Manifest Destiny who hoped to see Anglo-Saxon liberty spread to the benighted peoples of Latin America. Burr's downfall came not only because he misrepresented his real plans, but also because he held ideas whose time had not yet arrived.

Although most of McCaleb's narrative is devoted to a study of the period between 1805 and 1807, he does briefly trace aspects of Burr's career both before and after these tragic years. The author characterizes Burr as a distinguished patriot, orator, organizer, lawyer, and soldier, and as "easily one of the two most brilliant men of his day." McCaleb commends Burr for being one of the first politicians to appreciate the importance of party organization. He also asserts that Burr was "probably the first feminist in the United States," because of the care which he took with the education and up-bringing of his daughter, Theodosia. Little mention is made of Burr's split with Jefferson, the Hamilton duel, or his activities after the conspiracy trial.

McCaleb's research is thorough, and he quotes at length from a variety of primary sources to prove Burr innocent. He claims that Anthony Merry and the Marquis of Caso Yrujo, the British and Spanish ministers, probably thought Burr was indeed committing treason, but this in itself is not enough to prove Burr guilty. Many Westerners were also misinformed about his real intentions, especially since President Jefferson's proclamation against Burr convinced substantial numbers of them of Burr's guilt. McCaleb insists that there was no possibility of a successful secession of the West. To support his position he uses the testimony of prominent Westerners who knew Burr and argues that the West was perhaps the most loyal section of the country, especially when the actions of New England during the War of 1812 are considered. If the West were to have taken up arms, McCaleb maintains, it would only have been against Spain.

While McCaleb tries to rehabilitate Aaron Burr's reputation, he does not hesitate to assault Thomas Jefferson's or General James Wilkinson's. He writes that Jefferson used everything from innuendo to bribery to unjustly convict Burr of treason. Much space is devoted to a description of General Wilkinson's connection with Burr. McCaleb accuses Wilkinson of duplicity and states that the general betrayed Burr "to strike a compromise with the Spaniards, and to drive his own criminal ends with an impetuosity and finesse which were only too successful." The machinations of both Jefferson and Wilkinson in Burr's arrest and trial are discussed at length. McCaleb also traces closely the positions of Chief Justice John Marshall and of Luther Martin, Burr's chief defense counsel, at the Richmond trial.

In conclusion, it should be said that even though the author develops a strong case, it is not entirely convincing. The contradictions in testimony which he cites tend to raise doubts about Burr's single-minded altruism or candor. Walter F. McCaleb's volume, first published in 1903, however, must still be considered whenever the Burr conspiracy is examined.

Abernethy, Thomas P. *The Burr Conspiracy.* New York: Oxford University Press, 1954.

Challenging McCaleb's contention that Aaron Burr was innocent of trying to dismember the Union, Thomas Perkins Abernethy, one of the most respected historians of the early American West, assumes throughout his work that Burr was guilty as charged at his Richmond trial. Indeed, he argues that the plot of the former Vice-President was almost as momentous as the acquisition of Louisiana, and that, next to the Civil War, it potentially posed the greatest threat to the preservation of the Union in the nation's history.

Using hitherto unexplored primary materials, Abernethy depicts Burr and James Wilkinson (whose complicity in Burr's schemes the author establishes to his own satisfaction) as having been the authors of not one but a number of different plots, including a plan to attack the city of Washington. He notes throughout his work, moreover, that Burr's schemes found favor not merely with the frontiersmen of the West but with influential personages throughout the country who were ready to coöperate in their execution. In marked contrast to the sense of national unity emphasized by McCaleb, Abernethy leaves the reader wondering how the country was able to survive, given the fragility of national sentiment which existed at the turn of the nineteenth century.

But Abernethy no more establishes his case against Burr than McCaleb proves his in defense of the former Vice-President. The web of intrigue which the author describes leaves one uncertain whether Burr took his proposal to dismember the Union more seriously than his plot to invade Mexico. Moreover, Abernethy relies heavily on the testimony of government witnesses, many of whom were later impeached for giving false testimony. The result is the fullest treatment of the Burr conspiracy that has been written, but one which leaves the reader still undecided as to Burr's real plans. — *B.K.*

Burr's Conspiracy

Additional Recommended Reading

Parton, James. *The Life and Times of Aaron Burr.* 2 vols. Boston: Houghton Mifflin Co., 1892. This, the first major biography of Burr, asserts that he planned to establish an empire out of lands conquered from Spain, but denies that he intended to lead the Western states into secession.

Adams, Henry. *History of the United States of America During the Administrations of Jefferson and Madison.* 9 vols. New York: Charles Scribner's Sons, 1889-1891. Volumes V and VI on the administration of Thomas Jefferson accuse Burr, in the author's usual masterful style, of conspiring to dismember the Union. Adams' version of the Burr Conspiracy gained wide acceptance until the publication of Walter McCaleb's study of the conspiracy.

Beveridge, Albert J. *The Life of John Marshall.* 4 vols. Boston: Houghton Mifflin Co., 1919. Written by a distinguished historian and United States Senator, these volumes vindicate Burr of planning to dismember the Union, and defend Chief Justice Marshall for his narrow constitutional interpretation of treason. Beveridge closely follows McCaleb's argument.

Wandell, Samuel H. and Meade Minnigerode. *Aaron Burr.* 2 vols. New York: G. P. Putnam and Sons, 1925. A well-written and lively study of Burr based on solid scholarship, which makes a valiant and mainly successful attempt at impartiality in its assessment of Burr's career. The authors, however, find Burr innocent of the charge of treason.

Schachner, Nathan. *Aaron Burr: A Biography.* New York: F. A. Stokes Co., 1937. A work based on exhaustive research by a well-known scholar of the Federalist era which, nevertheless, is marred by Schachner's tendency to accept whatever Burr claimed as true.

PIKE'S EXPLORATION OF THE SOUTHWEST

Type of event: Military: expedition to explore part of the area acquired by the Louisiana Purchase
Time: July 15, 1806-July 1, 1807
Locale: The greater Southwest

Principal personages:

JAMES WILKINSON (1757-1825), Commanding General of the Western Army of the United States, who ordered Pike to make his explorations

ZEBULON MONTGOMERY PIKE (1779-1813), young army lieutenant who led the exploration

DON FACUNDO MELGARES (fl. 1806), Spanish lieutenant who led a counterexpedition to intercept Pike's

DR. JOHN HAMILTON ROBINSON (fl. 1806), Pike's civilian companion whose arrival in Santa Fe disclosed Pike's presence in New Mexico

Summary of Event

On July 15, 1806, Lieutenant Zebulon Montgomery Pike of the Western Army of the United States set out from St. Louis with a party of twenty-two men with orders to explore the headwaters of the Arkansas and Red rivers. His plan was to ascend the Arkansas river, cross over to the Red river, and then descend that river to its junction with the Mississippi river. With the boundary line between the United States and Spanish territory in the Southwest as yet undetermined, the farther west he moved the more likely he was to encounter trouble. Pike had returned from a successful exploration to the upper Mississippi river, where he had negotiated land concessions from the Sioux and protested the presence of British fur posts in the Minnesota region. On this second, or Southwestern, expedition Pike's first concern was to negotiate peace between the Osage and Pawnee Indians. He ascended the Mis-

souri and Osage rivers to the Osage villages, where he obtained horses, and then moved on to the Pawnee villages on the Republican river. There he found the Indians ready to resist his advance westward because they had recently been visited by a much more impressive Spanish expedition sent out to intercept the Americans. Don Facundo Melgares, leading a force of six hundred men and driving two thousand horses and mules, had distributed Spanish flags and medals among the Pawnees, captured American traders in the region, and urged the Indians to turn back all Americans who tried to head farther west. By a stroke of good fortune, Pike had moved so slowly that he had avoided an encounter with the superior Spanish detachment. With a display of force the Americans intimidated the Pawnees, then pressed on to the Big Bend of the Arkansas river, where six men descended the river in

467

two canoes fashioned of cottonwood logs and buffalo skins and returned to the United States.

Following the return route of Melgares, Pike's trail led up the Arkansas river. In November, 1806, Pike's party sighted the Rockies for the first time. From an encampment on the present site of Pueblo, Colorado, Pike and three companions set out to climb the peak now bearing his name. He did not complete the ascent, but he wrote about this massive pinnacle of the Rockies, establishing his identification with it to this day. During the next two months he explored the Colorado country, hunting in vain for the headwaters of the Red river, and finally went into camp at the Royal Gorge, or Grand Canyon of the Arkansas.

Leaving two men in a log shelter at this camp to guard the exhausted horses and a portion of the expedition's baggage, Pike with his few remaining men, headed south over the snowy Sangre de Cristo Mountains and across the San Luis Valley to the Rio Grande river, which Pike later said he thought was the Red river. There the small party of explorers built a stockade. The weather was bitterly cold during this February journey, and the men waged a grim struggle with hunger. Although he was apparently uncertain as to where he was, Pike alleged that he was in fact still on United States soil.

From the encampment on the Rio Grande, the enigmatic Dr. John H. Robinson, a civilian who had joined the expedition some time after its departure, set out for Santa Fe professedly with a commission to collect a debt for a friend in Illinois. Robinson's arrival in Santa Fe made known Pike's presence in Spanish territory.

On February 26, 1807, one hundred Spanish troops appeared, took Pike and his men prisoner, and escorted them to the New Mexican Capital. The Spanish were uncertain whether the explorers' presence was accidental or purposeful, and they were perplexed about what should be done with Pike and his men. Pike's maps and papers were seized, and their contents convinced the Spanish that he was on a spying mission. His party was escorted to Chihuahua City and detained there for several months until a decision was made to deport the group to the United States. Under escort, the Americans were taken by way of San Antonio, Texas, to Natchitoches, on the Louisiana border, and there turned over to United States troops on July 1, 1807.

From the time he left Santa Fe, Pike took voluminous notes on the country through which he passed and concealed them skillfully to make certain that they would not be confiscated. Although he failed to carry out his assignment to locate the headwaters and descend the Red river, he incorporated the information he had obtained in a report published in 1810, thereby adding to American knowledge of the Southwest. Pike gained national fame as a result of the publication; editions also appeared in French, German, and Dutch.

Pike was such a keen observer that when he returned to the United States he was able to provide precise figures on the number and types of troops stationed in the northern provinces of Mexico, as well as information concerning the character and personality of the Spanish military officers. In addition to this intelligence, Pike declared that the Great Plains were "sandy deserts" similar to those in Africa. Thus he originated the so-called "Great American Desert" myth. Finally, he pointed out in great detail the potential trade to be had with Santa Fe.

Pertinent Literature

Hollon, W. Eugene. *The Lost Pathfinder, Zebulon Montgomery Pike.* Norman: University of Oklahoma Press, 1949.

This is a full-length biography of Pike. Through meticulous research Hollon establishes the birthplace of Pike in New Jersey and ably presents the known facts of Pike's life prior to his coming under the influence of James Wilkinson, Commanding General of the Western Army of the United States. Considerable attention is given to the relationship between Wilkinson and Pike. Historical conjecture has linked Aaron Burr, the third Vice-President of the United States, with Wilkinson and, in turn, with Pike, in a conspiracy against the Spanish in the Southwest to further their own ambitions. Pike's conduct could be interpreted as evidence to support the conspiracy charge. His letters to Wilkinson referred to the possible military approaches to Santa Fe. When Spanish soldiers came upon his stockade near Taos, on the Rio Conejos, a branch of the upper Rio Grande river, they offered to escort him to the sources of the Red river, his declared objective, but he was not interested. Finally, the fact that Dr. Robinson joined the expedition some time after its departure, ostensibly to collect debts in Santa Fe, indicates to Hollon that the town was intended to be the expedition's destination. Earlier scholars had suggested that by June, 1806, Wilkinson had decided to abandon Burr, and that he therefore sent Robinson to make peace with the Spanish. Presumably, Pike and his men were hostages to insure Wilkinson's good faith and at the same time to act as spies. Wilkinson supposedly notified the Spanish agents in Natchez of Pike's expedition in order to make certain that they would contact his secret emissary, Robinson, before a border clash occurred. After his capture Pike was reunited with Dr. Robinson, entertained by the Spanish authorities, and given an unparalleled opportunity to observe and collect strategic information about northern Mexico.

Although sympathetic to Pike, Hollon examines with critical judgment the evidence relative to the "conspiracy theory." He argues that Pike had no part in Wilkinson's intrigue with Burr and that Pike's unwavering defense of Wilkinson was simply the result of misplaced loyalty. To many, this interpretation is not wholly satisfying. Unfortunately for Pike's reputation, his personal papers were burned in 1890, and evidence is not available either to exonerate or to convict him of treasonable conduct. The issue over the charge of conspiracy is still subject to debate among historians. The events of Pike's Southwestern expedition are presented with discernment in this biography. More important, the interrelationships and the impact of this exploration upon Pike's later career are made clear.

Pike's Exploration of the Southwest

Pike, Zebulon Montgomery. *Journals, with Letters and Related Documents.* Edited by Donald Jackson. Norman: University of Oklahoma Press, 1966.

This edition of the records of the Pike expeditions, the first to appear in over seventy years, is exceptionally valuable, because Jackson used the manuscript rather than the published versions of Pike's explorations. Moreover, he has had access to the Pike documents which were confiscated at the time Pike was taken into custody in Santa Fe. These documents were not returned to the United States until 1910. Particularly valuable are the translated Spanish correspondence bearing on the Southwestern excursion and Pike's rough sketch maps. Jackson insists there is no clear evidence of Pike's implication in the Burr-Wilkinson schemes. At the same time, the author acknowledges that there is no doubt that Wilkinson expected Pike to accomplish more than the discovery of river sources, and that the young lieutenant knew what was expected. Jackson explains Pike's continuing loyalty to Wilkinson as that of a military career officer who was determined to suc-

ceed. Dr. Robinson is pictured as a free-lance adventurer rather than Wilkinson's emissary. Pike emerges as a patriotic officer who kept his eyes open for the benefit of his country.

The material in this volume suggests, however, that Pike was an inept and vain commander, awkward, somewhat inarticulate, and humorless, but at the same time conscientious and dedicated. He was capable of enduring sustained hardship, was an excellent hunter, and took pride in his ability to compete on equal terms with the Indians. Jackson concludes that Pike should be ranked as an explorer, not merely a traveler. The author is reserved in his judgment concerning the importance of Pike's maps, although others think the maps justify Pike's recognition as one of the great contributors to the acquisition of geographical knowledge of the United States. At no time, however, did he demonstrate the exceptional capacity of Meriwether Lewis or William Clark. — *W.T.J.*

Additional Recommended Reading

Coues, Elliott, ed. *The Expeditions of Zebulon Montgomery Pike.* 3 vols. New York: Francis P. Harper, 1895. For many years these volumes were accepted as the standard account of Pike's expedition to the headwaters of the Mississippi river and into the Southwest. The earliest edition of Conrad in 1810 was disorganized and it garbled Pike's material. Thomas Rees in the London edition of 1911 attempted to incorporate into the daily journals material which had been contained in appendixes of the earlier edition. Coues retained the original form in his work, but he rearranged the order, added chapter headings, and wrote a new preface with a memoir of Pike.

Pike, Zebulon M. *Zebulon Pike's Arkansas Journal.* Edited by Stephen H. Hart and Archer B. Hulbert. Westport, Conn.: Greenwood Press, Inc., 1972. This reprint of a 1932 edition of Pike's *Journal* provides yet another published account of Pike's exploratory ventures.

FIRST SUCCESSFUL VOYAGE OF THE *CLERMONT*

Type of event: Technological: application of steam power to water transportation
Time: 1807
Locale: Hudson river

Principal personages:
ROBERT FULTON (1765-1815), builder of the *Clermont*
JOHN FITCH (1743-1798), builder who constructed a number of steamboats between 1785 and 1788
OLIVER EVANS (1755-1819), engineer who developed the high-pressure steam engine
ROBERT R. LIVINGSTON (1746-1813), who coöperated with Fulton in developing and exploiting the steamboat
NICHOLAS J. ROOSEVELT (1767-1854), who coöperated with Fulton and Livingston in their venture
HENRY MILLER SHREVE (1785-1851), who developed the flat-bottomed steamboat for use on Western waters

Summary of Event

Robert Fulton constructed the first successful steamboat to ply the internal waterways of the United States. His ship, the *Clermont,* sailed from New York City on August 17, 1807, and arrived in Albany thirty-two hours later. It was a momentous occasion for the United States. Steam applied to transportation opened up new opportunities for economic advance in freeing man from a total dependence upon the vagaries of wind and weather which had restricted his waterborne mobility since the days of the first sailing vessel. It would be but a short time before steam was applied to ocean-going navigation and to land transport.

As with most inventions, that of the steamboat was not the work of any one man or of any one nation. While Fulton's name will always be associated with its evolution, Fulton was only the last in a series of individuals inspired to apply steam power to transporta-

tion. Basically, the steam engine was the work of the Scottish engineer James Watt. It was the firm of Boulton and Watt which supplied the engine for the *Clermont.* The low-pressure engine furnished was not really a suitable type for a steamboat because of the large size of the engine that would be required in order to produce the necessary power. In 1787, an American, Oliver Evans, inventor of a steam-powered automatic flour mill, designed the high-pressure engine which became standard on American steamboats. Another American, John Fitch, constructed the first steam-powered vessel in the United States in 1787. It did not prove to be practical at that time. Nor was the steamboat launched by James Rumsey on the Potomac river in 1787. Fulton's was the first practical steamboat.

It is difficult to measure satisfactorily the ramifying influences of Fulton's achievement. By the 1820's and

471

1830's, the internal waterways of the United States were crowded with steamboats of various shapes and sizes. Steamboat men took their vessels up rivers that appear to be creeks by today's standards. It was no great feat in the 1820's to navigate the Sangamon river in Illinois or, in the 1850's, the Kaw river in Kansas. With the opening of the Erie Canal in 1825, connecting Buffalo and Albany, and the Welland Canal in 1833, connecting Lake Erie with Lake Ontario, the steamboat age came to the Great Lakes. Steamboats were used in the coasting trade all along the Atlantic and Gulf Coasts of the nation and, in 1819, the *Savannah* made the first steamboat crossing of the Atlantic. The decision of the Supreme Court in *Gibbons* v. *Ogden* (1824) freed internal transportation, especially steamboating, from the restraints of state sponsored monopolies.

The steamboat had its most striking impact economically and technologically. The steamboat created, especially in the West, a new industry. Towns, such as Louisville, Pittsburgh, and Cincinnati, became centers of technology, and supplied most of the steam engines used on Western waters. Steamboat construction was a major industry and created a host of subsidiary industries which supplemented and supplied the shipyards. Construction reached a peak in the 1850's. The low life expectancy of these vessels, caused by accidents of various kinds, supplied an undesirable stimulus to construction.

Steamboats speeded up the commerce of the United States and ex- panded the trade areas of towns and cities located along navigable waterways. The steamboat brought prosperity to such places by making them centers of distribution for the surrounding countryside. It is true that the steamboats, operating on natural waterways, were at the mercy of unfavorable climatic conditions, such as freezing temperatures and low water, and they were limited in routes that could be navigated. But they did extend the market areas of towns. St. Louis, for example, utilized the steamboat to develop markets in a region that included the entire Mississippi and Ohio River Valleys as well as the country through which the Cumberland and Tennessee rivers flowed. Steamboats made feasible extensive up-river trade which was especially important in the development of New Orleans as an entrepôt serving the entire Mississippi Valley. New Orleans engaged in an extensive trade with Cincinnati, Louisville, St. Louis, and other river cities. Much of the produce arriving at and leaving New Orleans came and went on steamboats.

The low-slung vessels bellowing smoke were, in many cases, floating palaces around which a whole river mythology arose. The riverboat gambler, the riverboat pilot who knew every twist, turn, snag, and sandbar, the heroic captain willing to sacrifice his vessel rather than be beaten in a race, the black stevedores singing on the levees, the painted ladies who plied their trade among the silks and velvets of plush staterooms—all these and more gave the steamboat a permanent place in American tradition.

Pertinent Literature

Baldwin, Leland D. *The Keelboat Age on Western Waters.* Pittsburgh: University of Pittsburgh Press, 1941.

While the steamboat dominated the river trade of the United States after the 1820's, it did not entirely replace older river vessels. The several hundreds of thousands of tons of steamboat shipping operating on the nation's waterways had to be constantly on the lookout for sailing craft and an odd assortment of flatboats and keelboats left over from the early days of the nation. This was especially true on the Mississippi river and the waters which fed that river.

The flatboats and keelboats carried a fair amount of tonnage to New Orleans until the Civil War. Vermillion County, Indiana, for instance, loaded between two hundred and two hundred fifty flatboats annually in the 1840's. An unknown number of flatboats from Indiana to the Ohio and the Mississippi rivers sold their goods north of New Orleans. The fact that flatboat arrivals at New Orleans dropped from 2,792 in 1847 to 547 in 1857 must not be taken to mean that such conveyances were eliminated.

According to Leland D. Baldwin, the keelboat probably came into general use on the Western rivers soon after the Revolutionary War. In chronicling the history of these crafts, Baldwin tells a delightful and important story. These craft and the men who operated them form an important part of the history of the West. The keel and flatboats performed an important economic function since, prior to the advent of the steamboat, they carried most of the produce shipped to major markets from distant production cen-

ters. Farmers living ten to fifteen miles from a navigable stream could conceivably market their crops by utilizing flatboats or keelboats. Farmers in south central New York did navigate the Susquehanna river to Baltimore's grain market. And in the Old Northwest, farmers did navigate the tributary streams of the Ohio river and make the journey to New Orleans. Abraham Lincoln was one of the thousands to make such a trip.

Much of the navigational information used by the river pilots was derived from the practical experience of keelboatmen and flatboatmen. And the men who operated these vessels were themselves legendary. Mike Fink, the most famous of all the boatmen, was a mighty drinker who loved to boast that he could "out-run, out-hop, out-jump, throw down, drag out, and lick any man in the country." He was a champion marksman and a renowned strongman, truly "half-horse, half-alligator." Men such as Mike Fink make up an important part of American folklore.

The keelboat itself was generally from forty to eighty feet long with a shallow keel and from seven to ten feet in beam. On the trip downstream, it went with the current and was guided by a steersman with a long sweep oar. Keelboats with their narrow beam and shallow draft were the only vessels capable of upstream traffic. This was extremely difficult. Staying close to shore in order to take advantage of backwater, the members of the crew propelled the craft against the current by poling.

It generally took a keelboat over two months to make the trip from New Orleans to Cincinnati.

The trip, whether up or downstream, was filled with danger. In the early days, the hazards of the river, with its shifting sandbanks and treacherous snags, were exacerbated by Indians and river pirates. A widely known center of river piracy was Cave-in-Rock on the Illinois shore of the Ohio river, twenty miles below Shawneetown. Although less dramatic than pirates, the rivers themselves were the most dangerous opponents of the hardy boatmen. The accident rate was extremely high, and many lives and much property were lost on the Western rivers through unrecorded accidents. Nevertheless, the traffic continued throughout the antebellum period and especially on those streams which were not navigable for steamboats.

Hunter, Louis C. *Steamboats on the Western Rivers: An Economic and Technological History.* Cambridge: Harvard University Press, 1949.

This study of the steamboat and its economic and technological impact in America may be viewed as a model of its kind. Not only does Hunter cover the ground with great thoroughness, but he also brings a perspective to the study which allows the student of economic history to assess accurately the role of the steamboat in the life of Americans.

The steamboat and steamboating have always held a certain fascination for Americans which makers of myth and legend have exploited in draping the steamboat in the cloth of romance. Hunter attempts to separate fact from fiction in his account of this significant development in American economic history. There was more to the steamboat era than dramatic races and legendary roustabouts on the wharves. There was more to steamboating than accidents, although there were many such tragedies.

Steamboats came to the Western rivers in the decades surrounding the War of 1812. By 1820 these vessels were fully established on the major waterways of the West and had a fairly complete monopoly of passenger service and up-river freight. Although the steamboat never did monopolize the downstream freight or totally replace older forms of transportation from north to south, it did play an important role in carrying the produce of the West to coastal markets. By the 1830's, steamboats had penetrated most of the navigable rivers of the West and entered a period of rapid expansion.

Hunter is concerned with the total economic and technological impact of these vessels. Not only did steamboats speed up trade and contribute to the development of river cities, such as New Orleans and St. Louis, but they also had a lasting impact on technological development. The steamboat, according to the author, both structurally and mechanically represented the period of transition from a technology of wood to one of iron and steel. During the antebellum period, experiments from iron-hulled vessels were carried on, frequently with the support of the federal government. Mechanically, Hunter points out, the steamboat hastened the transition from the familiar art of woodworking to the shaping of "iron within narrow limits of tolerance by hand and machine tools." The steamboat also stimulated the development of the high-pressure engine which became standard equipment on Western vessels. Oliver Evans was crucial in this phase of technology. The rapid increase in the number of steamboats on the rivers stimulated the growth of a sophisticated steam engine industry as well as repair shops. Hunter maintains that the steamboat was more important in the general growth of the machine-tool industry and repair facilities than the railroad.

The impact of steamboating on the organization of transportation industries receives skillful treatment in this volume. Hunter asserts that steamboating during its heyday was preëminently the field of small-scale enterprise. The typical entrepreneur was the small operator who owned a single steamboat or owned parts of several steamboats. There was, however, packet and line service on a scheduled basis between closely related river ports. The Pitts-

burgh and Louisville line operated twelve vessels in the middle 1830's. Competition was close with so many operators in the field and this had the effect of keeping freight rates at relatively low levels although there is some evidence that rates rose during the 1850's, in spite of increasing competition from the railroads.

Other facets of steamboating are covered with authority by Hunter. He deals with steamboat labor, passenger traffic, varieties of freight, the hazards of the trade, and the movement for regulation by the federal government. The story is carried in detail through the Civil War and the swift decline of steamboats which was coincident with the rapid growth of railroads in the nation. But while population, industry, and trade were concentrated along the trunk lines of the river system, steamboats played a vital role in the economic life of the West and of the nation. — *J.G.C.*

Additional Recommended Reading

Twain, Mark (pseud.). *Life on the Mississippi.* Boston: J. R. Osgood and Company, 1883. A classic account of steamboating on the Mississippi river by the most famous of all riverboat pilots.

Gould, E. W. *Fifty Years on the Mississippi; Or, Gould's History of River Navigation.* St. Louis: Nixon, Jones Printing Company, 1889. New edition 1951. This volume contains much information useful to students of transportation history.

Hartsough, M. L. *From Canoe to Steel Barges on the Upper Mississippi.* Minneapolis: University of Minnesota Press, 1934. The author deals with the role of river and lake transportation from the period of Anglo-French competition for furs to the development of the Messabi iron range.

Tyler, David B. *Steam Conquers the Atlantic.* New York: D. Appleton-Century Company, 1939. A study of the substitution of steam for sail in Atlantic commerce.

Havighurst, Walter. *Voices on the River: The Story of the Mississippi Waterways.* New York: The Macmillan Company, 1964. A popular account of transportation on the nation's major river system.

Havighurst, Walter. *The Long Ships Passing.* New York: The Macmillan Co., 1942. A popular account of steamboating on the Great Lakes.

CHARTERING OF THE AMERICAN FUR COMPANY

Type of event: Economic: creation of the first American monopoly
Time: April 6, 1808
Locale: Albany, New York

Principal personages:

JOHN JACOB ASTOR (1763-1848), New York fur trader and merchant prince, organizer and principal stockholder of the American Fur Company

RAMSEY CROOKS (1787-1859), Astor's chief assistant in the Western fur trade and president of the American Fur Company during its final days

WILSON PRICE HUNT (fl. 1808), leader of the overland expedition to Astoria in 1811-1812

ROBERT STUART (1785-1848), one of Astor's lieutenants in the fur trade

Summary of Event

On April 6, 1808, the American Fur Company was chartered by the New York State Legislature for a period of twenty-five years. The capital stock of the company was not to exceed one million dollars until two years had passed, and thereafter it was not to exceed two million dollars. The sole stockholder was John Jacob Astor, who, in 1783, had come to this country at the age of twenty-one as an impoverished German immigrant. After serving as an assistant to a fur merchant in New York City, Astor entered the business on his own account in 1786 and soon began to trade with China and the Far East. By the early nineteenth century he had become one of America's richest and most powerful men. By 1808, inspired by the Louisiana Purchase and the possibilities of the fur business in that vast internal area, Astor decided to challenge Canada's North West Company and the Michilimackinac Company, which were tapping the fur trade of the United States.

Astor envisioned American control of the fur trade in the mountain regions of the Northwest extending to the Pacific Coast. He dreamed of developing the fur trade from the Pacific coast to China and the Orient. The furs would be taken to the Orient and traded for spices, silks, and teas which in turn would be shipped to the United States to complete the Pacific "triangular trade." Astor's scheme called for a huge company with trading posts along the shores of the Great Lakes and the Columbia and Missouri rivers. First, however, Astor had to consolidate his holdings and obtain new capital, hopefully with governmental approval. He therefore engineered the chartering of the American Fur Company in 1808 and the creation two years later of the Pacific Fur Company, controlling both companies and interchanging their resources so that they were virtually indistinguishable.

Once Astor had established the

476

Pacific Fur Company he made plans to dispatch two parties to the Columbia river. One party arrived by sea at the mouth of the Columbia in March, 1811. Work promptly began on a post called Astoria on the lower Columbia river. The second party, commanded by Wilson Price Hunt, departed overland from St. Louis in March, 1811. This group experienced terrible hardships along the way and the few who survived did not reach their objective until February, 1812. The Astorians were beginning to win their struggle for survival and had established trade with local Indians when they were foiled by the outbreak of war between the United States and Great Britain. In 1813 Astor, who feared a British seizure of his Columbia river post, elected to sell the project to the rival North West Company. Astor dissolved the Pacific Fur Company and abandoned his plans in the Pacific Northwest. His activities, however, had contributed greatly to knowledge of the region, and he had incidentally helped to establish the American claim to the Oregon territory.

The War of 1812 also affected Astor's considerable operations in the East. In 1811 the American Fur Company had merged with the North West and Michilimackinac companies to form the South West Fur Company, which was to confine its activities to the Great Lakes south of the Canadian border. Though interrupted by the war, the operation thrived later and in 1817 Astor was able to buy out his partners. He established the Northern Department of the American Fur

Company with headquarters at Michilimackinac, and as Congress excluded foreign traders from United States territory the same year, Astor had achieved a monopoly of the fur trade in the Great Lakes region.

He then moved to gain control of trade in the Upper Missouri region. In 1817 he arranged a working agreement with powerful firms in St. Louis to set up the Western Department of the American Fur Company. In 1822, Congress abolished government-operated trading posts for Indians, the so-called "factory system," which had operated since 1796 but which Astor succeeded in annulling by using his considerable political influence.

Agents of the American Fur Company extended their sphere of influence in the Upper Missouri region, crushing opposition ruthlessly. In 1827 Astor absorbed his greatest competitor, the Columbia Fur Company, and operated between the Upper Mississippi and the Upper Missouri as the Upper Missouri Outfit. By 1828, the American Fur Company enjoyed a monopoly of the United States fur trade.

At the peak of his fortunes, Astor retired and his company split. One group included some ten stockholders of the Northern Department headed by Ramsey Crooks, Astor's chief assistant, and it assumed the name of the American Fur company, becoming one of the first great American trusts. It broke up in 1834 when the fur trade began to decline. Furs were becoming scarce as the colorful trappers and mountain men were swept aside by the onrushing tide of civilization.

477

Pertinent Literature

Lavender, David. *The Fist in the Wilderness.* Garden City: Doubleday and Co., Inc., 1964.

David Lavender, a popular scholarly writer of Western history, has written this account of the American Fur Company from the point of view of Ramsey Crooks, who was one of Astor's early associates. Extensive research of both primary and secondary sources is revealed in explanatory and bibliographical notes.

Lavender is the first writer to spotlight Crooks as the innovating force behind the company's policies and operations. While giving him more credit than other scholars for the American Fur Company's accomplishments, Lavender is less critical of the techniques used to ensure monopolization of the fur trade.

Starting with an account of Crooks' activities in the Great Lakes fur trade with the British, Lavender sketches the early conflicts between Great Britain and the United States for control of trading activities. The relationship between Crooks and Astor was frequently stormy; Lavender sees Crooks as the daring and impetuous innovator, with Astor as the negotiator of government favors who had to curb Crooks' excesses.

Lavender's account of the rise of the American Fur Company is detailed and vivid; he emphasizes the personalities involved, the picturesque aspects of the American West, and the schemes and intrigues of frontier life. His writing portrays colorful trappers and traders, daring young entrepreneurs, Indians in gaudy finery, French *voyageurs,* government officials, and soldiers doing their duty. He describes in detail the Eastern counting houses, warehouses, and offices; the frontier posts and camps; and Montreal, Michilimackinac, St. Louis, and Prairie du Chien.

Lavender tells of the American Fur Company's disastrous attempt to leap the continent with the establishment of Astoria, its development and exploitation of the Great Lakes trade, and finally its reluctant entry into trading in the Upper Missouri region as the result of prodding by Crooks. Other personalities come alive, especially the hot-tempered Robert Stuart, one of Astor's lieutenants who frequently clashed with Astor and Crooks over trading policies and practices.

In describing the decline of the American Fur Company, Lavender suggests that Crooks' inordinate desire to monopolize the American fur trade led him to overextend his grasp. In absorbing new individuals and additional companies, and allowing them freedom to operate, the original leaders lost effective control of the business. "The monster's own size was its undoing. To get what he wanted Crooks had surrendered control of local affairs." The firm was no longer manageable.

There is an old tale that the aging Astor decided to liquidate his fur trade assets when he saw a silk topper on a trip to Paris in 1832 and realized that the beaver hat was doomed. Lavender rejects this reason for Astor's withdrawal from the company, and suggests that steadily declining fur prices and the loss of his former drive pushed the old man from the business. "Silk did not drive Astor from the trade. Age and illness did that."

After extensive protracted negotiations, Crooks purchased the American Fur Company from Astor in 1834 and made plans for further ruthless dealings. He was active in the small-skin trade during the 1830's when raccoon caps became popular in European circles, and the venerable firm survived the depression of 1837-1838. Continued competition with other traders, however, and the declining fortunes of the trade itself forced the company to suspend payments on September 10, 1842. Crooks eventually managed to pay off the debts and opened a small commission house in New York dealing in pelts. His death came peacefully in 1859 at the age of seventy-two. His life had encompassed the rise and decline of the American fur trade's glory days, and of its greatest institution, the American Fur Company.

Porter, Kenneth W. *John Jacob Astor, Business Man.* 2 vols. Cambridge: Harvard University Press, 1931. Reprinted by Russell & Russell, 1966.

This biography of one of America's most famous and successful early merchants originally appeared in 1931 as the first publication in the *Harvard Studies in Business History.* It is a comprehensive study of all aspects of Astor's life, not merely his business career, though it does emphasize economic matters.

Copiously documented, the author's treatment is based on exhaustive research. Porter has used most of the extant Astor materials available, including those in Harvard's Baker Library, but he has had to contend with a difficulty typical of business history: in the early 1870's and again in the 1880's, Astor's descendants ordered the bulk of his papers destroyed. Nevertheless Porter has managed to construct an excellent account of the origins, development, and day-to-day operation of Astor's economic empire from extensive manuscript sources, letter books, government reports, and other materials in many depositories not only in this country but also in Canada and England. The result is a standard source of reference for later scholars and writers, such as Lavender who have drawn their own conclusions from this basic material.

Actually in his treatment of the American Fur Company Porter differs from later scholars who, for example, rationalize the company's sale of liquor to the Indians by saying that it was necessary in order to compete with other traders; Porter condemns Astor for not applying his energies and influence toward securing effective prohibition of the Indian liquor traffic by both Canadians and Americans. The company's harsh and often penurious treatment of its own agents, *engagés,* and *voyageurs* is also criticized strongly. Porter makes no effort to gloss over the sharp practices used by Astor and his cohorts in driving out or absorbing competitors as they built their monopoly for the American Fur Company.

Yet Porter concedes that Astor started his own career in circumstances as humble as those of his victims, and that his rise was a result of his superior organizational ability. Furthermore, Astor, when judged by the standards of competitors, "occupied higher ground." Astor's strong point, the au-

479

thor concludes, was not the daring thrust nor the startling innovation. "Few of Astor's enterprises were marked by a pioneering spirit." Rather, "he excelled in profiting by the successes and failures both of others and of himself." — *J.E.F.*

Additional Recommended Reading

Phillips, Paul C. *The Fur Trade.* 2 vols. Norman: University of Oklahoma Press, 1961. A massive history of the North American fur trade from the beginning of the seventeenth century to the middle of the nineteenth, written for scholars, with Astor playing a leading role in the second volume.

Chittenden, Hiram M. *The American Fur Trade of the Far West.* 3 vols. New York: F. P. Harper, 1902 and later editions. A classic account, though it ignores the trade of the Southwest.

De Voto, Bernard. *Across the Wide Missouri.* Boston: Houghton Mifflin Co., 1947. An epic account of the peak years and decline of the Rocky Mountain fur trade written by one of America's great storytellers.

Terrell, John U. *The Six Turnings: Changes in the American West, 1806-1834.* Glendale, California: The Arthur H. Clark Company, 1968. A brief popular account of significant events in the development of the American West, with emphasis on the fur trade and focus on Astor.

Terrell, John U. *Furs by Astor.* New York: William Morrow and Company, 1963. A popular account based on Kenneth Wiggins Porter's *John Jacob Astor, Business Man.*

Cleland, Robert Glass. *This Reckless Breed of Men: The Trappers and Fur Traders of the Southwest.* New York: Alfred A. Knopf, Inc., 1950. An excellent supplement to the Chittenden volumes.

APPEARANCE OF THE KNICKERBOCKER SCHOOL

Type of event: Literary: influence upon nineteenth century American literature of a group of writers
Time: c. 1809-1840
Locale: New York City, New York

Principal personages:
WASHINGTON IRVING (1783-1859), writer, and author of *Diedrich Knickerbocker's A History of New York from the Beginnings of the World to the End of the Dutch Dynasty*
JAMES KIRKE PAULDING (1778-1860), novelist and poet
FRITZ-GREENE HALLECK (1790-1867), poet
JAMES FENIMORE COOPER (1789-1851), novelist
WILLIAM CULLEN BRYANT (1794-1878), poet and critic

Summary of Event

The Knickerbockers consisted of a number of American writers—notably, Washington Irving, James Kirke Paulding, Fritz-Greene Halleck, William Cullen Bryant, and James Fenimore Cooper—who gathered in and around New York City during the first four decades of the nineteenth century. They were not formally organized, and their careers and interests led them in diverse directions; thus, they represent a literary "school" only in a very loose sense. Nevertheless, they all took part, at least for a time, in a literary tradition which developed in New York under the primary influence of Irving, whose fictional narrator of *Diedrich Knickerbocker's A History of New York from the Beginnings of the World to the End of the Dutch Dynasty* (1809) provides the name for the group.

The origins of the Knickerbockers may be traced to a club of young men to which Irving and Paulding belonged, the "Lads of Kilkenny." Their meetings in "Cockloft Hall" became the basis for the collaboration of Irving, his brother William, and Paul-

ding in *Salmagundi* (1807-1808), a periodical commenting on the New York scene in a witty, satiric style patterned after that of the English essayists Addison, Steele, and Goldsmith. Irving followed in 1809 with his famous treatment of the early Dutch settlement of New York, *Diedrich Knickerbocker's A History of New York*. The Knickerbocker name itself, applied to the antiquarian Diedrich, is that of a prominent Dutch family in New York, one of whose scions had been elected to Congress a few years earlier. After 1809, however, the name became inextricably linked with Irving and his cohorts in their roles as satiric chroniclers of the local scene.

Irving was soon to leave behind the vogue he had inspired. In 1815 he began a seventeen-year stay in Europe. After his return to America, he made a tour of the West and settled for a time at his "Sunnyside" estate on the Hudson river before leaving again for Europe to serve as Minister to Spain from 1842 to 1846.

Paulding combined his literary production with a career in naval administration. Interested in the establishment of a national literary tradition, he satirized the tyrannical influence of Great Britain upon American history in *The Diverting History of John Bull and Brother Jonathan* (1812). In 1819 he published a second series of *Salmagundi,* seeking without much success to revive the earlier tradition. Other works by Paulding, including *The Backwoodsman* (1818) and *Westward Ho!* (1832), reflect his interest in the life and legends of the American frontier.

Halleck came to New York from Connecticut in 1811. The works which best link him with the Knickerbocker tradition are *Fanny* (1821), a poetic satire on social life in New York, and *The Croaker* (1819), a series of satirical poems written in collaboration with his close friend, Joseph Rodman Drake, a New York physician who died in 1820 at the age of twenty-five.

James Fenimore Cooper came to New York City in 1822. Like his good friend Paulding, Cooper was interested in the potential for fiction in the American frontier. He wrote the first of the Leatherstocking novels, *The Pioneers,* in New York in 1823. Cooper also enjoyed the Knickerbocker style of city life and was the founder of a club—The Bread and Cheese—in 1824. He went to Europe in 1826, however, and when he returned seven years later, he continued his writing career at the family home in Cooperstown.

Some of the minor writers associated with the Knickerbocker group include Samuel Woodworth, John Howard Payne, Robert C. Sands, and Nathaniel P. Willis. One significant by-product of the Knickerbocker vogue was a magazine, *The Knickerbocker* (1833-1865),

edited from 1834 to 1861 by Lewis Gaylord Clark, a friend of Irving. Most of the Knickerbockers, as well as other leading authors of the times, were contributors. Irving was under contract as a regular writer for the magazine from 1839-1841.

In a preface to the 1848 edition of *Diedrich Knickerbocker's History of New York,* Irving observed that his narrator's name had become a "household word" in New York. As a rallying cry for New York authors, however, the name had long since outlived its usefulness. By the 1840's the most prominent members of the group were gone from New York City. Halleck had returned to Connecticut, Cooper to Cooperstown, and several of the others, including Irving, Paulding, and Willis, had settled up the Hudson river. In the meantime American literature was outgrowing the stylistic conventions of the Knickerbocker tradition, and other writers, such as Emerson, Whittier, Longfellow, and Hawthorne, were at work establishing New England as the new center of American letters.

While the Knickerbockers did not make a profound impression upon American literature comparable to that of their fellow New Yorkers Herman Melville and Walt Whitman, they were, nevertheless, influential in several ways: they gave young authors in the New York area a sense of camaraderie and a literary tradition; they were a strong force in nineteenth century literary style, helping to maintain until the Civil War what Stanley T. Williams *(Life of Irving,* I, xiv) terms "the cult of elegance"; and some of their writings helped to popularize American literary subjects and foster the nation's cultural life.

Pertinent Literature

Brooks, Van Wyck. *The World of Washington Irving.* New York: E. P. Dutton and Co., Inc., 1944.

The World of Washington Irving is a panoramic view of the American literary scene preliminary to what Van Wyck Brooks terms "the flowering of New England" (a phrase he had used as the title of an earlier work). Brooks interprets the period of American literature from 1800 to 1840 through a series of sketches representing each area where writing Americans could be found: Philadelphia, New York, New England, the South and Southwest, the West, and Europe.

Each chapter focuses upon a central figure—ranging from Irving, Poe, and Cooper to Audubon, Jefferson, and N. P. Willis—as an influence upon, or representative of, his particular time and place. Irving is not introduced until Chapter VII, "William Dunlap and His Circle," where he is included among the young writers in New York gathered about Dunlap, the prominent playwright and director. From this perspective Brooks relates how Irving first attracted public attention by dis-

cussing the New York theater in his "Jonathan Oldstyle" essays published in his brother's newspaper.

Irving reappears in Chapters IX, XIV, and XVI, "Washington Irving in England," "Irving and Cooper Abroad," and "The West: 1830-1840." Brooks thus interprets the "world" of Irving as one drawn by the polarities of Europe on the one side and the American frontier on the other. Irving's difficulty in dealing effectively with these opposing influences in his life was, as Brooks points out, indicative of the transitional times.

The World of Washington Irving has many characteristics that the literary scholar would consider weaknesses. It is loosely organized, overly generalized, and sparsely documented. For a general audience, however, it is a useful introduction to the literary activity in each part of America, especially New York, during the era of the Knickerbockers.

Williams, Stanley T. *The Life of Washington Irving.* 2 vols. New York: Oxford Press, 1935.

This definitive biography of Irving is an indispensable resource for any study of Irving and his circle. The first volume, consisting of fifteen chapters, follows Irving's life through 1829, fourteen years into his seventeen-year sojourn in Europe. The second volume contains the final twelve chapters, an appendix, and index. Both volumes are illustrated and extensively documented.

In Chapters II-VI, Williams traces the first phase of Irving's writing

career: the Knickerbocker period, through the "Jonathan Oldstyle" letters, the collaboration of *Salmagundi,* and the culmination in *Diedrich Knickerbocker's A History of New York.* Despite this early literary use of the American scene, Williams proceeds to interpret Irving as basically uninterested in the nineteenth century movement to found a native American literature. Instead, in his long residence abroad, Irving chose to remain under the spell of British tradition and cultivated, with his "obsolete, sweet rhetoric," an audience both in England and America "which rejoiced in 'elegance' of sentence and paragraph."

The image of Irving which emerges from *The Life of Washington Irving* is that of a limited literary talent, effectively catering to the taste of the times and mirroring a general American sense of cultural deficiency and dependency upon Europe. But Williams also shows that Irving was a man of many aspects and had American interests as well. It is, after all, chiefly for his use of American materials—in *Diedrich Knickerbocker's A History of New York,* "Rip Van Winkle," and "The Legend of Sleepy Hollow"—that Irving is remembered today. — *C.E.M.*

Additional Recommended Reading

Adkins, Nelson F. *Fitz-Greene Halleck: An Early Knickerbocker Wit and Poet.* New Haven: Yale University Press, 1930. This biography includes bibliographies and uncollected letters and poems of Halleck.

Hedges, William L. *Washington Irving: An American Study, 1802-1832.* Baltimore: The Johns Hopkins University Press, 1965. A critical study of Irving concentrating on the New York and European phases of his career.

Herold, Amos L. *James Kirke Paulding: Versatile American.* New York: Columbia University Press, 1926. This brief biography contains a Paulding bibliography.

Pochmann, Henry A., ed. *Washington Irving: Representative Selections.* New York: American Book Company, 1934. A convenient one-volume selection of Irving's work; Pochmann is preparing a new complete edition of Irving.

Long, Orie W. *Literary Pioneers.* New York: Gordon Press, 1935. A standard work which treats the Knickerbocker School and places it in its historic context.

JUDICIAL RECOGNITION OF THE DOCTRINE OF THE SANCTITY OF CONTRACTS
(*Fletcher v. Peck*)

Type of event: Legal: expansion of the idea of the sanctity of contracts as expressed in the Constitution
Time: March 16, 1810
Locale: Washington, D.C.

Principal personages:

JOHN MARSHALL (1755-1835), Chief Justice of the United States

JOHN RANDOLPH (1773-1833), who opposed the idea of the United States paying investors in the Yazoo lands

JOHN PECK (fl. nineteenth century), of Boston, who sold a small tract of the Yazoo lands

ROBERT FLETCHER (fl. nineteenth century), of Amherst, New Hampshire, who purchased the lands and then demanded a refund which Peck refused to grant

LUTHER MARTIN (1748?-1826), member of the Constitutional Convention, and attorney for Peck

JOHN QUINCY ADAMS (1767-1848), son of President John Adams and future President of the United States, who represented Peck

GIDEON GRANGER (1767-1822), Postmaster General under Jefferson who advocated legislation to permit the United States to reimburse investors in the Yazoo lands

Summary of Event

While it is axiomatic that many of the cases from which great constitutional principles are derived have sordid backgrounds, few if any have come out of such a comic opera background of corruption as *Fletcher* v. *Peck.*

On January 7, 1795, the Georgia Legislature passed a bill permitting the sale of some thirty-five million acres of fertile, well-watered land for five hundred thousand dollars payable over a five-year period. The purchasers were four land companies which had been formed to speculate in Western lands. The fact that the state of Georgia did not have clear title to the lands appar-

ently did not bother the legislature because, with one exception, every member of the legislature had been bribed. Nor did the problem of the title appear to inhibit the Governor of the state who signed the legislation into law. To be sure, the action was not without some benefits to the state. It needed the money, and the problem of wresting the title to the land from the Indian tribes through action by the federal government now became the concern of the speculators. Moreover, the state had sold a slightly smaller tract to other speculators six years earlier with the same clouded title and on inferior

485

terms, and the electorate of the state had not been disturbed. In the interval, however, Eli Whitney had invented the cotton gin. Now these lands would be in great demand for the production of cotton, given the elimination of the Indian menace. Moreover, the gross dishonesty of the whole transaction upset many conscientious citizens. As a consequence, in 1796, a new legislature was elected with every member pledged to vote for the repeal of the act of sale. Accordingly, on February 13, the Rescinding Act was passed. So strong was the feeling in the state that a formal ceremony was held on the steps of the State House during which the initial bill was formally burned.

Quick as the Georgia reaction to undo the fraudulent deal had been, it had not come in time to prevent the sale of certain of the lands to "innocent" third parties. It was over the titles of the latter that the legal and political battles took place.

The land companies, moreover, did not consider the second act as valid, and they continued to sell the land. Most of the purchasers lived in the Middle Atlantic and New England states, and they were greatly concerned as to the validity of their purchases. To defend their purchases, the New England-Mississippi Company had been formed to protect the rights of investors. This company sought an opinion from Alexander Hamilton concerning the legality of its land claims. Hamilton did not attempt to investigate the question of Georgia's title to the land, but stated in a pamphlet published in 1796 that if the title was valid, then the Rescinding Act was void and in his opinion the courts would so rule. Thus, armed with an opinion from one of the

country's most distinguished public servants, the company continued to offer its lands to both prospective settlers and speculators.

During the time that the New England-Mississippi Company was selling its lands, a proposal was made to Congress, with the full backing of the Jefferson Administration, that the United States should enter into an arrangement by which Georgia would cede her claims to the lands in question to the federal government in return for compensation. In addition, the federal government would handle the claims to the area of the several Indian tribes and the Spanish government. This proposal became law. The report of the commissioners whom Jefferson appointed to study the problem proposed that five million acres of the lands be retained and the proceeds from their sale be used to indemnify the Yazoo land purchasers. Although the claims of the speculators, in the commissioners' opinion, could "not be supported," they proposed the indemnity for them to insure "the tranquility of those who may hereafter inhabit the territory," and stated that the federal government should find it "expedient to enter into a compromise on reasonable terms." This move was, however, to cause a political fight of major proportions. When the commissioners' proposal reached the House floor, it was attacked by a wildly indignant John Randolph, who was determined to defeat it by any means possible. Randolph's motives were partly ideological and partly emotional. He had been in Georgia when the Rescinding Act had been passed and had been present at the burning ceremony; he undoubtedly felt that he understood the depths of the popular opposition to the grant in Georgia. His contention was simply that Georgia had no initial right to make the sale, that the sale was so firmly rooted in fraud and corruption as to make it invalid, and that it was legally impossible to sell a third purchaser a better title. Randolph was opposed in the House by Gideon Granger, the Postmaster General, who was lobbying with his considerable ability in favor of the measure. After four days of intensive debate, Randolph's eloquence won and the measure was defeated. The supporters of the legislation brought up the measure each year for several years only to be defeated each time. Eventually, following the implicit advice given earlier by Alexander Hamilton, the purchasers sought relief through the courts.

The "friendly" suit of *Fletcher* v. *Peck* originated with the sale by Peck (of Massachusetts) to Fletcher (of New Hampshire) of fifteen thousand acres of Yazoo land, and it was Fletcher's intention to test the legality of his purchase. Because the litigants lived in different states, the case was heard in the federal courts. When, in October, 1807, Justice William Cushing of the Supreme Court, acting in his capacity as a Circuit Judge, found for Peck, the case was appealed to the Supreme Court. Luther Martin, attorney for Peck, contended that the several states were free, sovereign, and independent entities, and that "the sovereignty of

each, not of the whole, was the principle of the Revolution." Consequently, the federal courts had no jurisdiction in the matter. John Quincy Adams, later replaced by Joseph Story, the future Supreme Court Justice, based his case on Hamilton's old opinion that the grant was a contract, and under Article I, Section 10 of the Constitution it could not be rescinded.

Following Hamilton's arguments fairly closely, Chief Justice Marshall in the majority opinion held that the original act of sale had not exceeded the powers of the Georgia Legislature. He refused to look beyond the record, or to go into the issue of the initial fraud. While agreeing that one legislature can change the enactments of another earlier body, Marshall noted that "if an act be done under a law, a succeeding legislature cannot undo it," and that finally, a grant was a contract under the meaning of the Constitution. The Court's decision was the first step in the legal process of defining the constitutional provision concerning the "obligation of contract." It laid the foundation for the law of public contracts.

Although the speculators had won in the courts, they were not to secure a congressional, or monetary, victory until 1814, when Congress, after John Randolph's failure to win reëlection passed an appropriation of five million dollars to buy up their now untarnished titles.

Pertinent Literature

Beveridge, Albert J. *The Life of John Marshall.* Vol. IV: *Conflict and Construction, 1800-1815.* Boston: Houghton Mifflin Co., 1919.

The fourth volume of this monumental study of the Chief Justice covers in detail the political and legal background of this case. Albert J. Beveridge, former United States Senator from Indiana, devotes almost sixty pages to the most complete discussion of the case that has appeared until recently.

Beveridge, using source material available when he wrote, begins his story with a well-documented discussion of the background of bribery that occurred in the capital when the Georgia Legislature first began its debate on the land grant legislation. He follows the first piece of legislation as it successfully passed both houses of the legislature, its passage smoothed by money and promises of land, to its veto by the governor on the grounds that it was not the right time to sell the land, that the price was too small, that too little of the land was reserved for Georgians, and that it created a monopoly. The author then traces the passage of the second land grant bill which was designed to meet the objections of the Governor.

He notes the beginning of opposition to the measure, but suggests correctly that it was not until the invention of the cotton gin that the land suddenly became valuable and the citizens of the state began to realize the value of the grant. In several magnificently written pages, Beveridge conveys the depth of the feelings of the population towards those legislators who had voted for the bill, and he sketches the pomp and ceremony with which the offending law was publicly burned following its repeal. The messenger of the House, he writes, announced in a loud voice on the steps of the state capitol: "God save the State!! And long preserve her rights!! And may every attempt to injure them perish as these corrupt acts now do !!!!"

From Georgia, Beveridge takes the reader to New England, which was the center of speculation in these lands and the center of the agitation to have the Rescinding Act declared unconstitutional, or at least to have the money of the investors refunded. In sure, clear strokes the author follows the attempts of these individuals, who included some of the most distinguished men in the new nation, to persuade Congress to honor their claims, and he describes John Randolph's successful fight in the House to stop the legislation there, even at the risk of splitting the Jeffersonian coalition.

From this defeat, Beveridge follows the story as it shifts to the judicial arena. He leads the reader through the complexities of the legal battle with a sure skill that makes the most obscure points of law understandable. He also explains clearly the significance of the case and its ramifications.

The principal fault that historians have found with this biography is that Beveridge's obvious admiration for his subject has resulted in lack of objectivity in his interpretation. While this complaint is generally valid, it should be pointed out that in his discussion of this case he does press hard on the Chief Justice on two points. Beveridge duly notes that Marshall had more than a passing interest in the principle of law at stake here, because his brother had a case then pending in the Virginia Court of Appeals involving roughly the same legal principle. Thus, in Beveridge's words, "No man in America, therefore, could have followed with deeper anxiety the Yazoo controversy than did John Marshall." Beveridge also gently faults his hero for not noting that the case was collusive

488

because both parties to the controversy wanted the same decision. Justice William Johnson, in a concurring opinion, noted that there appeared to him "to be strong evidence, upon the face of it, of being a mere feigned case." He did not, however, pursue the matter further.

Beveridge concludes his treatment of the subject with a brief discussion of the speculators' final successful attempts to be indemnified following the absorption of the land into the public domain.

McGrath, C. Peter. *Yazoo: Law and Politics in the New Republic, the Case of Fletcher vs. Peck.* Providence: Brown University Press, 1966.

Professor McGrath has not only written an admirable account of a most interesting court case, but has, in many ways, produced a monograph which can be used as a model for the litigation of a constitutional issue. McGrath discusses the matter from three distinct but connected points of reference. In the early chapters, he places the case and its principals in their proper socio-economic setting, thereby making it into more than a dry legal squabble. At the same time, he discusses its implications with regard to national politics and sees it as one of the earliest examples of an attempt by a well-organized pressure group to influence the Supreme Court as well as the legislative and executive branches of the national government.

McGrath identifies the initial pro-Yazoo sentiment at the national level with the Federalist Party. Its adherents opposed repeal of the land grant because it interfered with private property rights. Furthermore, they did not feel that legislatures could make the acts of earlier ones unconstitutional because that procedure was the special province of the courts. As an avowedly nationalist party, they had no qualms about the federal courts' declaring a state law unconstitutional. There was also the fact that most of the Yazoo claimants were New Englanders of

wealth and substance, the sort of people from whom the Federalist Party drew most of its strength. The Republicans, the opposition party, felt that the legislature's act of repeal was a legitimate expression of the popular will of a "sovereign independent state"; moreover, following the reasoning behind the Kentucky and Virginia Resolutions, they were convinced that a state legislature could void unjust legislation at both the state and national levels. And since the Republicans drew the bulk of their strength from south of the Mason-Dixon Line, they were not prone to worry a great deal about the financial well-being of their northern opponents. Yet, as McGrath points out, the Federalist Party steadily declined, its adherents shifted their allegiance, and the Republicans began to concern themselves more with the problems of the New Englanders. This change led, in turn, to an increase in tension between the northern and southern wings of the Republican Party and eventually forced the national leadership to commit itself to some sort of partial compensation for the speculators.

In some of his most enlightening pages, the author discusses the Yazooists in the role of a pressure group organized to win its claims against the government. He traces their efforts to lobby relief legislation through Congress. When they were defeated, he shows how they acted to bring the matter into the federal courts. Their supporters were then able to use the favorable *Fletcher* v. *Peck* decision to great advantage in the congressional debates of relief bills.

In his concluding chapter, "Fletcher v. Peck and American Constitutional Law," McGrath traces the significance of the case as it concerns contracts and the law. He argues that from the case came three important conclusions which "become dogma in the subsequent cases": (1) both public grants and private contracts are covered by the contract clause of the federal constitution; (2) by implication, private property and its concerns enjoy a paramount position in the Court's scale of priorities; (3) the courts have a positive duty to set aside state legislation "tampering with either private or public contracts." The book concludes with approximately eighty pages of appendixes designed to "provide the interested reader with a more thorough background to the Yazoo lands controversy by reprinting its major documents." This feature is valuable because the items reprinted, with the exception of the decision itself, are not easily obtainable. — *G.L.S.*

Additional Recommended Reading

Adams, Henry. *History of the United States of America During the Administrations of Jefferson and Madison.* Vol. II. New York: Charles Scribner's Sons, 1909. A classic history of the period by the grandson of one of the attorneys involved, which discusses the case in its political and constitutional settings.

Hunting, Warren B. *The Obligation of Contracts Clause of the United States Constitution.* Baltimore: The Johns Hopkins University Press, 1919. A study containing a technical discussion of an important phase of American constitutional history and giving detailed coverage to *Fletcher* v. *Peck.*

Wright, Benjamin F., Jr. *The Contract Clause of the Constitution.* Cambridge: Harvard University Press, 1938. A more recent and detailed study of the contract clause than Hunting's and broader in scope.

Haines, Charles G. *The Role of the Supreme Court in American Government and Politics, 1789-1835.* Berkeley: University of California Press, 1944. The definitive study of the Supreme Court during its formative period; it gives adequate coverage to *Fletcher* v. *Peck,* and places it in the framework of the development of the Supreme Court.

Corwin, Edward S. *John Marshall and the Constitution.* New Haven: Yale University Press, 1919. A brief but authoritative treatment of the subject.

CONSTRUCTION OF THE NATIONAL ROAD

Type of event: Technological: development of national transportation system
Time: 1811-1819
Locale: Cumberland, Maryland, to Wheeling, Virginia

Principal personages:

ALBERT GALLATIN (1761-1849), Secretary of the Treasury and author of a report on roads and canals

THOMAS JEFFERSON (1743-1826), third President of the United States 1801-1809, who signed the bill authorizing construction of the road

EBENEZER ZANE (1747-1812), pioneer road builder in America who laid out Zane's Trace

DAVID SHRIVER, JR. (fl. nineteenth century), first superintendent appointed by Congress to supervise construction of the road

Summary of Event

The Congress of the United States passed a bill in 1806 authorizing the construction of a road from Cumberland, Maryland, to Ohio. Much difficulty occurred in trying to determine the precise route which the proposed road was to take. But by 1811 the jealousies of competing localities and states had been compromised sufficiently to allow for the first contracts. The road reached Wheeling in 1818; it was 130 miles long and cost, on the average, thirteen thousand dollars per mile. This was the famous National or Cumberland Road. Its major purpose was to provide transportation facilities between the growing West and an East which yearned to establish regular commercial relations with the West.

The National Road, upon reaching the Ohio river, became one of the major trade routes to the West. Large numbers of travelers left testimony to the economic importance of the road. Goods from Baltimore could now reach the Ohio river via wagon at a considerable savings in freight. The road gave Baltimore, for a time, a definite advantage over its major competitor to the north, Philadelphia. That town was to feel increasingly pressed by its competitors, for in 1817 the State of New York authorized the construction of the Erie Canal. Thus both Baltimore and New York City would be directly linked to the West. To maintain its commercial position, Philadelphia, with the aid of Pennsylvania, launched its own system of internal improvements in the direction of Pittsburgh.

Enormous quantities of goods and large numbers of people passed over the road. Cattle from the Ohio River Valley, Monongahela flour, and spirituous liquors passed over the road to market. Taverns and grazing stations sprang up along the road to serve the wagoners, drovers, and immigrants who moved along the route. Wheeling boomed, as did some of the towns located along the National Road. It served its purpose, and it appeared to be a harbinger of future federal efforts to link sections of the nation together.

Albert Gallatin, Secretary of the Treasury under President Thomas Jefferson, submitted to Congress in 1808 what came to be regarded as a classic report on the transportation needs of the nation. Gallatin recommended that the central government expend some twenty million dollars in developing a comprehensive and national transportation network. He was well aware that private or state capital, without the active financial aid of the federal government, could not accomplish such a vast undertaking. The National Road seemed to indicate that Gallatin's projected system had taken the first momentous step. It was a successful first step. It also proved to be the last, for many Americans were not convinced that the federal government had the constitutional authority to finance and to build internal improvements. The constitutional barrier proved to be an obstacle that could not be overcome. The states were thrown back on their own resources and the federal government repudiated its responsibilities in this critical area.

Two specific issues, one arising during the Presidency of James Madison and the other during that of James Monroe, doomed the federal government to a passive and nondirective role in meeting the nation's transportation requirements.

The logistical problems of the War of 1812 and the rapid movement of population into the West aroused considerable support for federal activity in internal improvements. To meet the demand both of citizens and of national security, John C. Calhoun, Representative from South Carolina, introduced the Bonus Bill into Congress in 1817. This bill was designed to provide a permanent fund for the construction of internal improvements, and it passed both Houses of Congress. President Madison, who had publicly called for such a system, nevertheless vetoed the bill on strict constructionist grounds. He argued that the Constitution was one of enumerated powers; that federal activity in internal improvements was not one of those powers; and that to justify such activity under the "general welfare" clause was to make the government the judge of its own powers. Madison maintained that a constitutional amendment was required before the government could operate in the area of internal improvements. Five years later, President Monroe vetoed a bill authorizing repair of the National Road which would be financed by the collection of tolls. The general tenor of his veto message was similar to Madison's. These vetoes and rising sectional antagonisms put an end to the hopes of many that the federal government would provide leadership and support in transportation.

Although in 1824 Congress passed the General Survey Act enabling the President to plot out a comprehensive system of roads and canals, the battle was already lost. Nothing came of this legislation. The federal government, thereafter, confined itself to the granting of alternate sections of public lands along the route of intended canals and railroads. New York, as early as 1815, had anticipated this outcome and proceeded to construct the Erie Canal with state funds. State funds and private capital, both domestic and foreign, provided the financial support required to construct the canals and railroads that eventually bound the nation together.

Pertinent Literature

Jordan, Philip D. *The National Road.* Indianapolis: The Bobbs-Merrill Company, 1948.

This volume is a solidly researched and well-balanced survey of not only the origins and construction of the pike that took thousands of land-hungry pioneers west of the Alleghenies, but also of the multi-faceted social, political, and economic impact of the highway from Cumberland, Maryland to Vandalia, Illinois on the young nation and its frontier.

Jordan opens his narrative with two chapters describing early trails along the route that would become the National Road. The first was Nemacolin's Wilderness Path. In the winter of 1753, Christopher Gist, its discoverer, led young Major George Washington from Will's Creek, near Cumberland, to the mouth of the Monongahela river with a letter from Virginia's Governor Robert Dinwiddie ordering any Frenchmen there to leave. This journey convinced Washington of the need for an adequate road between the Eastern seaboard and the frontier. General Edward Braddock hacked out the other early corridor across the mountains in June, 1755, when he led British troops from Fort Cumberland to Fort Duquesne and disaster. It basically followed the same course as Nemacolin's Path, but Braddock's men bent their backs and swung sharp axes to make it twelve feet wide.

From Gist's trail and Braddock's road, the author turns to a brief analysis of the life and activities of Ebenezer Zane, the founder of Wheeling and the first significant promoter of a federally sponsored thoroughfare into the West. Before Zane died in 1812 he saw much of what he had advocated materialize. Under the guidance of energetic men like Thomas Worthington, Ohio had become a state, and the enabling act for its admission into the union contained a provision for a road to be financed by the sale of public lands.

Although Congress passed the enabling act for Ohio statehood in April, 1802, it was not until 1806 that Josias Thompson began surveying the route of the road that was to stretch from Cumberland into Ohio. Actual construction did not begin for another five years. Burdened with almost insurmountable obstacles, David Shriver, Jr., the first superintendent of building, pushed ahead foot by foot. Stone crushing, tree falling, ditch digging, and grading all had to be done by hand, and at prices that were astronomical in the context of their times. By December, 1813, only ten miles had been completed, and the trace did not reach Wheeling until 1818. In 1825 Congress appropriated funds for further westward expansion of the pike, but, again, progress was painfully slow.

Together with the multitude of problems encountered by laborers, foremen, and coördinators, Jordan emphasizes the additional dilemmas involving maintenance and repair of sections of roadway that already had been "finished." Road building was an infant

493

science in the 1820's, and it comes as no surprise that great lengths of the highway easily succumbed to the elements. Mile upon mile had to be resurfaced, and this required more and more money.

Congress had been divided over the question of the National Road's constitutionality since Ohio entered the union, but, as its costs mounted and as debates over internal improvements intensified, the highway to the frontier became a major political issue. Jordan summarizes the arguments employed by both sides, quotes key figures in the imbroglio, and points out how the nation split sectionally over this matter. The ultimate settlement of the battle saw the road fall into the hands of the states where it would remain for many years to come.

The National Road was more than a pioneer trail and a political issue. By offering a means whereby commerce as well as people could traverse the mountains and move into the rich interior, it fostered the growth of cities, such as Hagerstown, Wheeling, Zanesville, and Columbus. Taverns, stage lines, general stores, warehouses, and many other businesses sprang up all along it. Hundreds of speculators and "new breeds of men" like the "land admirals" (stage line operators) emerged to take advantage of economic opportunities it created. Politicians, peddlers, re-

formers, gamblers, theatrical companies, and circuses traveled the road's rough miles to break the isolation of back country farmers.

Jordan examines life in the remote hinterland of the National Road in penetrating chapters on folklore, legends, and the hardships endured by those who attempted to make new homes in the bountiful yet brutal Western lands. He correctly maintains that settlers seldom were the hale and hearty creatures that populate romantic fiction, and that sickness and death were their almost constant companions.

To illustrate all of these points, the author cites a host of contemporary newspapers, diaries, travel accounts, promotional tracts, and government publications. He superbly exploits the writings of Europeans and Easterners who rode in stages that were like "dice cups" and came into contact with the unpredictably independent "root-hog-or-die" frontiersmen along the trace to Wheeling and beyond. To round out his biography of this "highway of hope," Jordan follows its emergence into what is known today as U. S. Highway 40.

Written in a style that captures the drama of its story, this book is well illustrated with twenty-five half tone photographs, and it contains an excellent bibliography.

Hulbert, Archer B. *The Cumberland Road.* Vol. X: *Historic Highways of America.* 16 vols. Cleveland: Arthur H. Clark Company, 1902-1905.

The Cumberland Road is the tenth volume of Archer Butler Hulbert's *Historic Highways of America,* and it complements the earlier numbers in the series. Although proceeding from the premise that this nation's first inter-

state highway fostered the rapid growth of the West, and thereby helped to consolidate the Union, this study fails to delineate exactly how this was accomplished. Instead, it peripherally discusses the genesis and construction of the road, its use as a mail route, and the taverns that dotted the landscape along it. Somewhat more comprehensively, the book elucidates the operation and control of the thoroughfare in Pennsylvania and Ohio, and the stage and freight lines that did business on it. These accounts are supported by voluminous, and often unnecessary, quotations. In fact, almost a fourth of the volume is composed of quotations and large parts of the work resemble a documentary history.

Hulbert opens his narrative by asserting that increases in the population of present-day Ohio, Indiana, and Illinois caused the federal government to undertake this first great internal improvement with the object of creating a link between navigable Eastern waterways and the Ohio River. Section seven of the enabling act for Ohio statehood provided for land sales to finance such a road. Four years later, on March 29, 1806, President Thomas Jefferson signed "An Act to Regulate the Laying Out and Making a Road From Cumberland, in the State of Maryland, to the State of Ohio." This act authorized the President to appoint "three discreet and disinterested citizens" to oversee the venture. It also set specifications for the road and appropriated $30,000 to initiate surveying. Less than a year later, Jefferson's three commissioners estimated that the highway would cost $6000 per mile, exclusive of bridges, but, in the end, the actual cost averaged $9,745 per mile between Cumberland and Uniontown, and $13,000 for the rest of the distance.

Money was only one of the problems. Permission had to be secured from the legislatures of the states through which the road would pass

before labor gangs could turn the first shovel full of earth. Pennsylvania's lawmakers hesitated and finally approved only on the condition that the route pass through Washington and Uniontown. A great controversy also raged between Steubenville and Wheeling over which was vied to be the western terminus of the road. These difficulties delayed completion of the project until 1818. Perhaps more important in slowing the work were the incredible physical difficulties which the contractors had to face, but Hulbert treats these very lightly. After quoting the laws of 1802 and 1806 that sanctioned the enterprise, he simply says that the government let no contracts until 1811, and that the road did not enter Wheeling for seven more years.

Although the author recognizes that by the early 1820's the National Road had been a political and constitutional issue, his analysis of this subject is very superficial. He identifies President James Monroe's position on the matter, quotes Harriet Martineau's *Society in America* on the question of internal improvements, and points out that those who championed the highway argued that there was no question of its constitutionality because it was to carry United States troops and mail, but nothing more.

Although claiming that the most important function of the road and the principal basis of the government's right to build and maintain it was to serve as a postal road, the chapter outlining the pike's role in the postal service is way short. It describes the Great Eastern, Great Western, and Express Mails carried on the road, and quotes schedules to prove that letters and newspapers moved over it surprisingly fast, at least on paper. The author contends that any slowness in the service resulted from inefficient processing rather than trouble on the trail. While he points to taverns as striking features of life along the trace, Hulbert does little more than list their names, describing them as eating and drinking emporiums and havens for weary travelers.

The strongest sections of the book deal with the maintenance of the road after it came under the control of the states, and the passenger and freight lines that operated on it. Largely confining his remarks to Pennsylvania and Ohio, Hulbert summarizes the methods used to collect tolls and keep the thoroughfare in good repair. To minimize damage to the stone surface, states encouraged the use of wide tires, and they imposed penalties for vandalism, riding on unfinished portions, allowing wagons to stand overnight, and locking wheels, except on ice. Traffic always was heavy, and tariffs paid by drovers, drivers, and horsemen amounted to large sums. However, it cost even more to keep the highway in top condition. It never supported itself.

The National Stage Company, the Ohio National Stage Company, Neil, Moore, and Company, and a host of smaller concerns remitted a major share of these tolls to operate vehicles with names like "Jewess," "Ivanhoe," and "Sultana." Troy coach drivers and their counterparts in the freight business constituted a new breed of men, and the road engendered them. Hulbert describes these flamboyant teamsters and much of their equipment in a very thorough manner.

This rather old book is still a major source of information on the building and early use of the national road. — *J. G. C.*

Additional Recommended Reading

Seabright, Thomas B. *The Old Pike, A History of the National Road.* Uniontown, Pennsylvania: privately printed, 1894. Although written in an anecdotal manner, the book is a useful compendium of information on the Cumberland Road.

Young, Jerimiah S. *A Political and Constitutional Study of the Cumberland Road.* Chicago: The University of Chicago Press, 1907. The author concentrates on the development of congressional attitudes toward and the debate over internal improvements.

Gephart, William F. *Transportation and Industrial Development in the Middle West.* Vol. XXXIV: *Studies in History, Economics, and Public Law.* New York: Columbia University Press, 1909. This work attempts to correlate transportation improvement and industrial development within the larger context suggested by the general title for the series.

Dunbar, Seymour. *History of Travel in America.* 4 vols. Indianapolis: Bobbs-Merrill Company, 1915. This series serves as a useful narrative history of travel from the most primitive forms to the most complex, and contains many relevant illustrations and maps.

Ambler, Charles H. *A History of Transportation in the Ohio Valley.* Glendale, California: The Arthur H. Clark Company, 1932. Beginning with the keel and flat boats, the author traces the changing forms of river transportation into the twentieth century and emphasizes the continued importance of riverways in the industrial development of a region.

Heath, M. Sydney. *Constructive Liberalism: The Role of the State in Economic Develop-*

ment in Georgia to 1860. Cambridge: Harvard University Press, 1954. Although the federal government played a passive role in many sectors of the economy before the Civil War, Heath demonstrates that state governments such as Georgia assumed important responsibilities in the field of transportation.

BATTLE OF TIPPECANOE

Type of event: Military: savage Indian fighting which helped to bring on the War of 1812
Time: November 7, 1811
Locale: Northwestern Indiana

Principal personages:
WILLIAM HENRY HARRISON (1773-1841), Governor of the Indiana Territory and later, ninth President of the United States 1841
TENSKWATAWA, "THE PROPHET" (1768?-1834), Shawnee Indian medicine man and religious leader known as "The Prophet"
TECUMSEH (1768?-1813), brother of the Prophet (possibly his twin), political and military leader of the Indian tribes of the Northwest

Summary of Event

About 4 A.M. on November 7, 1811, a faint rustling behind a thicket of willows caught the attention of a sentinel in William Henry Harrison's encampment three-quarters of a mile west of Prophetstown, near the confluence of the Tippecanoe and Wabash rivers in present-day northwestern Indiana. Summoning a companion, and warning him that there were Indians in the vicinity, the sentinel listened intently for a moment until the whir of an arrow pierced the early morning air and sent the two men scurrying back to camp. A fearsome yell roused Harrison and his soldiers from their sleep. Within seconds the forest and nearby river bottoms echoed with the sounds of savage screams, musket and rifle fire, shouted curses and commands, and the cries of frightened, wounded, and dying men and animals.

Two hours later, all was again relatively calm. Harrison's force surveyed its position and discovered some 188 casualties, of whom sixty-three were dead or dying. The Indians, who had been driven back into the swamps and river bottoms, had left behind thirty-eight corpses. Such were the immediate results of the widely-heralded Battle of Tippecanoe, which has been considered by many historians to have been of fundamental importance in breaking Tecumseh's plan for a Western Indian confederation; speeding the outbreak of the War of 1812; and contributing to the election of William Henry Harrison to the American Presidency in 1840.

In broad terms, the clash at Tippecanoe was the inevitable result of two vastly different civilizations struggling for domination of the North American continent. In a more immediate sense, the conflict stemmed from the differing drives, personalities, and objectives of two significant Western leaders: the great Shawnee chieftain, Tecumseh, and the aspiring politician and military man, William Henry Harrison, Governor of Indiana Territory.

The clash at Tippecanoe was a single episode in the long series of confrontations between red men and whites going back to the early days of European

498

colonization in North America. Conflict rather than coöperation between the races was the rule, and Tippecanoe represents one of the last stands east of the Mississippi river for the Indians as they were pushed farther and farther west by the encroachments of white civilization and institutions.

For the Indians, Tippecanoe was one round in a long struggle in which they were poorly matched against the land-hungry and grasping white frontiersmen. They were dependent on the whites for arms and ammunition among other needs, many had been weakened by addiction to alcohol obtained from frontier bootleggers, and they lacked organization and unity of purpose. Tecumseh, political and military leader of the Indian tribes of the Northwest, and his brother, "the Prophet," sought to overcome these weaknesses by calling on their people to reject the white man's culture, reassert their independence, and unite to drive the whites back across the Ohio.

Despite the Indians' defeat at Tippecanoe, the idea of confederation continued until Tecumseh, allied with the British in the War of 1812, was killed at the Battle of the Thames River, across Lake Erie on Canadian soil in October, 1813. The red man had resisted white aggrandizement for a quarter of a century, but it was Tippecanoe that brought the Prophet's career into eclipse. He was never again trusted by his brother, and he drifted into obscurity.

Harrison's later career was largely built around the conflict at Tippecanoe. He was an ambitious man who extracted every ounce of glory that could be gained from his success in the battle. His version of the episode depicted the policies of the United States government toward the Indians as enlightened and compassionate. American settlers were admittedly encroaching on Indian lands, but those lands were legitimately acquired through treaties with the old village chiefs. Furthermore, the Americans were making efforts to uplift and civilize the red men. If the Indians, particularly Tecumseh and "the Prophet," resisted these policies and the inevitable American expansion, then it was because of their savage nature or, still worse, the result of British influence.

Harrison's views were not universally accepted by his own people, who heatedly debated everything about the Battle of Tippecanoe, but Harrison was so widely accepted that as "Hero of Tippecanoe" he was given the opportunity of winning more military honors during the War of 1812, and he parlayed his military reputation into political offices, culminating in his election to the Presidency.

The impact of the Battle of Tippecanoe on public sentiment was more important in linking it to the War of 1812 than the actual outcome. Feelings between the United States and Great Britain were running high in 1811, and tempers were close to the breaking point. Many Americans believed, with some justification, that the British were stirring up trouble among the Indian tribes. The discovery of British arms at the Battle of Tippecanoe was widely accepted as proof of a British-Indian conspiracy which threatened American security and violated the rights of the United States as a sovereign nation. The fact that the British had actually attempted to restrain Tecumseh and the Prophet was either unknown or ignored. The important fact is that many Americans were highly incensed by the Battle of Tippecanoe; that bad feeling became part of the package of western grievances and ambitions which helped to trigger the War of 1812.

Pertinent Literature

Tucker, Glen. *Tecumseh, Vision of Glory.* Indianapolis: Bobbs-Merrill Company, Inc., 1956.

One of the most dynamic individuals in the annals of American history was Tecumseh, the great Shawnee chieftain whose dream of a vast Indian confederation and resistance to American settlement in the Old Northwest provided part of the background for the Battle of Tippecanoe and the outbreak of general hostilities in the War of 1812. Physically cast in a heroic mold, Tecumseh was a six-foot, bronze, lithe, and muscular man with a magnificent head and a commanding presence. Coupled with his abilities as a linguist, military strategist, and diplomat, Tecumseh's appearance and mental capacity combined to produce a figure of great proportions, certainly the outstanding leader of the American Indians of his time, and the equal of any white luminary of the period. In *Tecumseh, Vision of Glory,* Glenn Tucker has rescued his subject from the shadows of historical oblivion, and in a fast-moving, colorfully-written, and sympathetic narrative finally has given him a richly-deserved share of the limelight.

Tucker is not a professional historian, and his book does not feature the documentation one would expect in a scholarly study. Nevertheless, it is clear that the author has carefully used most of the relevant sources, primary and secondary, and he furnishes a short bibliographical note and a lengthy formal bibliography. Any deficiencies in this area are offset by the skill with which Tucker writes as he develops Tecumseh's story from the perspective of the red man.

This book makes no pretense at being an "objective" study. It views the Americans and William Henry Harrison as the aggressors in the Indian-white conflict for control of the Old Northwest. Tucker thus supplies a healthy counterbalance to works which view Harrison as a hero, all Indians as "savages," the Battle of Tippecanoe as a glorious American victory, and Indian military successes as "massacres." As the author ably demonstrates, an objective witness might well be impressed or appalled by the savagery on both sides in the conflicts between Indians and whites, and the alleged superiority of the white civilization which was destined to replace that of the red men is apparent only from the point of view of contemporary whites.

Tecumseh's hatred for the advance of the "long-knives" and their settlements is easily understood in view of his personal experiences. Born in Ohio, the son of a Shawnee chieftain and a mother who nursed a deep hatred of white civilization, the young boy was profoundly affected by the tragic events of Lord Dunmore's War in 1774. His people were forced to surrender their rights south of the Ohio river in order to protect their settlements in Ohio. When, shortly thereafter, Tecumseh's father was murdered by a band of whites, the young lad swore revenge against the race whose members had perpetrated the crime. The young man's feelings of hatred were soon reinforced by the senseless murder of the Shawnee chief, Cornstalk, under whom Tecumseh's father served.

Tecumseh fought against the Americans in the Revolution, learning the tactics of guerrilla warfare from the Shawnee chief, Blackfish. He then spent several years as a marauder, finally emerging in the 1790's as a Shawnee chieftain. As Tecumseh matured and gained experience, his concept of a great Indian confederation, or state, began to evolve as the only means of halting the constant encroachments of white settlers on Indian lands, often in utter disregard of earlier treaties and agreements. Concurrently, Tecumseh's brother, "the Prophet," began to develop the outlines of his puritanical religious philosophy, an Indian manifestation of the Great Awakening. As the one-eyed Prophet's following began to grow, religion and politics gradually merged behind the two brothers. They proposed to lead their people toward a return to the golden age of Indian civilization by urging them to turn their backs on white culture, institutions, and vices, and to offer stiff resistance to the spread of white settlements.

The Shawnee brothers had embarked upon a collision course with the expanding American nation, and the explosive situation finally culminated in the clash at Tippecanoe. In discussing the immediate background of the battle, Tucker argues that the British, rather than encouraging and prodding the red men toward the confrontation, actually strove to restrain and temper Tecumseh's compulsive urge to attack the Americans. In Tucker's analysis, it seems clear that Harrison was responsible for deciding to provoke warfare against the Indians, and that he took advantage of Tecumseh's absence when he was seeking allies in the South by moving to destroy the settlement at Prophetstown. Tucker is specific in assessing responsibility for the encounter at Tippecanoe. "He was *the* aggressor," says the author, referring to Harrison and his campaign up the Wabash. Furthermore, "the Prophet was as anxious to avoid conflict in his brother's absence as Harrison was eager to provoke it." Finally, Tucker charges that once the battle was concluded, Harrison's energies were devoted to defending his actions through a campaign of self-glorification that transformed an insignificant skirmish into a major and momentous triumph. In this way, says Tucker, Tippecanoe, which was "a minor engagement that settled little or nothing," in time "loomed up as one of the decisive battles of American history."

Goebel, Dorothy B. *William Henry Harrison: A Political Biography.* Vol. XIV: *The Indiana Historical Collections.* Indianapolis: The Historical Bureau of The Indiana Library and Historical Department, 1926.

Harrison was one of the major protagonists of the Indian conflicts in the West which contributed to the outbreak of the War of 1812. He achieved his first military glory as the victor at the Battle of Tippecanoe. Harrison later used his military reputation and association with the West to win a brief residence in the White House by means of the oft-described "Tippecanoe and

Tyler too" campaign of 1840. Later generations of Americans, particularly those reared in the areas most affected by Harrison's activities, have generally regarded the General as a regional and national hero, a man who secured vast areas of the Middle West from the "savage" red men and then went on to national glory.

Since he died after only one month in office, Harrison left almost no mark on the American Presidency, and his fame, therefore, rests almost entirely on his military reputation and Western activities. However, recent scholars have resurrected some of the charges leveled against him by Harrison's contemporaries, who viewed even these more significant aspects of the General's career rather critically. Since this is a relatively recent trend, perhaps stimulated in part by the last decade's interest in the history and problems of minority groups, including American Indians, it is interesting to note that Goebel's book, published almost forty-five years ago, is highly critical of Harrison's Indian policies as well as his military preparations before the heralded Battle of Tippecanoe.

Goebel's work is generally regarded as the standard Harrison biography, although some scholars prefer Freeman Cleaves' *Old Tippecanoe*. As the subtitle indicates, Goebel's study has a strong political emphasis. However, the author carefully traces her subject's family background, his decision to embark upon a military career, and the subsequent development of that career in the Old Northwest Territory. Harrison was an aide-de-camp during "Mad Anthony" Wayne's 1794 campaign against the Miamis which culminated in the victorious Battle of Fallen Tim-

bers, and he continued to serve in that capacity as Wayne negotiated the Treaty of Greenville. Harrison thus learned at first hand conditions in the West, the nature of frontier warfare, and the protocol and procedures of Indian diplomacy.

Harrison rose to the rank of captain in the army after winning General Wayne's praise in the Fallen Timbers campaign. He then retired from military service in 1798, apparently feeling that Wayne's victory and treaty had calmed the Indian troubles for a time and thereby ending his opportunities for rapid military advancement. Following in the Harrison family tradition, the twenty-five year old William Henry entered politics, receiving in 1798 a commission as secretary of the Northwest Territory. From this position he was elected as the territory's delegate in Congress, where he exhibited a great natural interest in public land policies, which were, of course, of great importance to the Northwest Territory. In May, 1800, Harrison received an appointment as Governor of the newly-created Territory of Indiana. It was during his tenure in this office that he achieved fame as the hero of Tippecanoe.

Harrison, as a Territorial Governor, served as *ex officio* Superintendent of Indian Affairs, reporting to the Secretary of War, who was responsible for general supervision of such matters. In discussing Harrison's Indian policy, Goebel argues that frontier disturbances and conflicts with the red men came about not so much because of British instigation, as Harrison charged, as from the harsh treatment of the Indians by American settlers who had a seemingly unquenchable rapacity for Western lands. This hunger for land was reflected in President Thomas Jefferson's instructions to Harrison, who, the author admits, carried out the Chief Executive's orders of rapid land acquisition "with a generous enthusiasm." Beginning with the Treaty of Fort Wayne in 1803, Harrison initiated a three-year program of acquiring Indian lands north of the Ohio, followed by a similar period of attempting to contain the growing surge of Indian resentment which brought sporadic raids against isolated settlers and the threat of general Indian warfare. The situation grew increasingly grave in direct relationship to the rise of the twin Shawnee brothers, Tecumseh and the Prophet, with their ideal of an Indian confederation. When Harrison purchased an additional two and one-half million acres of Indian lands at Fort Wayne in September, 1809, the situation became serious, and Tecumseh warned that he would not submit to the surrender of the lands.

With the frontier in a state of agitation, Harrison became convinced that the Indian settlement at Prophetstown on the upper Wabash river must be destroyed in order to safeguard the whites. After being restrained by his superiors, Harrison finally received permission to move against the town in August, 1811 while Tecumseh was in the South seeking support for his confederation. In late September, Harrison moved up the Wabash. His army reached the vicinity of Prophetstown on November 6. The Indian surprise attack and ensuing battle came during the early morning hours on the following day.

The selection of Harrison's campsite and his failure to take adequate precautions against a surprise attack were deficiencies criticized by many contemporaries, and Goebel generally concedes that such charges were justified. She describes the General's attitude during the battle as "admirable," though the total effect of the campaign was worthless. "The Battle of Tippecanoe, contrary to expectations that it would make the frontiers safe, increased the immediate danger to the settlers," she concludes. "With the declaration of war on England in June, 1812, a new chapter was begun in relations with the Indians; but the preface had been written at Tippecanoe in 1811, or at Fort Wayne in 1809." — *J.E.F.*

Additional Recommended Reading

Green, James A. *William Henry Harrison, His Life and Times.* Richmond, Virginia: Garrett and Massie, Inc., 1941. A popular account which is laudatory and sees the Battle of Tippecanoe as a "great victory" of our "splendid and heroic past."

Klinck, Carl F. *Tecumseh, Fact and Fiction in Early Records.* Englewood Cliffs: Prentice-Hall, Inc., 1961. Documents illustrating Tecumseh's life with editorial notes leading the reader to pertinent literature about Indian warfare in the late eighteenth and early nineteenth centuries.

Cleaves, Freeman. *Old Tippecanoe: William Henry Harrison and His Time.* New York: Charles Scribner's Sons, 1939. A major Harrison biography containing a colorful and detailed account of the Battle of Tippecanoe.

Dangerfield, George. *The Era of Good Feelings.* New York: Harcourt, Brace & World, Inc., 1952. This Pulitzer and Bancroft Prize-winning study contains an excellent chapter on the Battle of Tippecanoe, placing it in the general background of the War of 1812.

THE WAR OF 1812

Type of event: Military: challenge to the national sovereignty of the United States
Time: June 18, 1812-December 24, 1814
Locale: The United States and Europe

Principal personages:

THOMAS JEFFERSON (1743-1826), third President of the United
States 1801-1809, who adopted a policy of economic coercion
against Great Britain

JAMES MADISON (1751-1836), fourth President of the United
States 1809-1817, who declared war against Great Britain

HENRY CLAY (1777-1852), Speaker of the House of Representatives in the Twelfth Congress and leader of the War Hawks

NAPOLEON I (BONAPARTE) (1769-1821), Emperor of the
French 1804-1815, who issued the Berlin and Milan Decrees

GEORGE ERSKINE (fl. nineteenth century), British Minister to
the United States, who was recalled after the Erskine Agreement was made

GEORGE CANNING (1770-1827), Foreign Secretary of Great
Britain, who followed a hard line toward the United States

Summary of Event

The War of 1812 was a result of the Napoleonic Wars in Europe during the first decade of the nineteenth century. Ever since war had first broken out between France and Great Britain in 1793, the United States had tried, with some success, to follow a policy of neutrality toward both belligerents, avoiding a struggle with Great Britain by Jay's Treaty of 1794 and ending a war crisis with France in 1800 by the Convention of Mortefontaine.

In 1805, however, the Napoleonic War took a new turn, placing American neutrality on a precarious basis. With Napoleon dominating the European continent and the British controlling the seas, the struggle turned into an economic squeeze with the United States in the middle.

In an attempt to starve the other into submission, each side began to harass and seize American shipping. By the Order in Council of 1806, Great Britain decreed a paper blockade of the European coast from Denmark to Brittany and required American shipping to be searched for contraband. France countered with the Berlin Decree which authorized the seizure of any ship going to England before coming to a Continental port. When Great Britain responded by issuing a second Order in Council requiring neutral vessels destined for a Continental port to stop first in England, Napoleon issued the Milan Decree, ordering the seizure of any neutral vessel which submitted to British search.

Because the British dominated the seas, their restrictions on American shipping were more serious than those of France. Moreover, the British practice of impressing seamen under the American flag whom they claimed were deserters from the Royal Navy was an affront to the nation's honor and a challenge to its sovereignty. As a result, war almost erupted with Great Britain in the spring of 1807 when the British seamen from H.M.S. *Leopard* boarded the U.S.S. *Chesapeake,* after firing a broadside, and seized alleged deserters on board. Outraged, President Thomas Jefferson barred British ships from American waters and obtained another embargo confining all American shipping to port. By thus withholding needed supplies from the belligerents, he hoped to gain their recognition of American neutrality.

The embargo was the first of a series of economic, coercive measures adopted by the United States in an attempt to avoid war. Because the embargo seriously depressed the economy, which was dependent on export trade, it was replaced in 1809 by the Non-Intercourse Act which cut off shipping with Great Britain and France only. This measure was replaced the following year by Macon's Bill Number Two, restoring complete freedom of trade but providing that in case one of the belligerent nations should recognize America's neutral rights, nonintercourse would be revived against the others. When Napoleon pretended to revoke the Berlin and Milan decrees, President James Madison revived the policy of nonintercourse against Great Britain.

Despite United States efforts at economic coercion, the British refused to change their maritime policies. In 1809, an agreement was worked out between the British Minister to the United States, George Erskine, and Secretary of State James Madison whereby Great Britain would abandon its orders in council and the United States would suspend nonintercourse. But Erskine was recalled from his post by George Canning, the Foreign Secretary of Great Britain, who pursued a hard line towards the United States. As a result of this diplomatic fiasco, relations between Great Britain and the United States deteriorated further, each side feeling that it had been deceived by the other.

The failure of the Erskine agreement placed the United States firmly on the road to war. In 1810, a new Congress was elected which, when it took office at the end of 1811, brought into positions of leadership a group of young Republicans who were impatient with pacific responses to humiliation abroad. Angered by the British challenge on the seas to their country's sovereignty, these "War Hawks," as they were known, were also incensed by news of secret British aid to the Indians in the Northwest. Naming Henry Clay as Speaker of the House, they passed a series of resolutions to increase the army and the navy, and to arm the militia. In April, 1812, the Madison Administration boosted war sentiment in Congress by requesting a thirty day embargo on American shipping as a prelude to war. Finally, in June Madison asked Congress to declare war against Great Britain. In a close vote which revealed sharp opposition to war, especially in the Northeast, Congress responded affirmatively.

Meanwhile in Great Britain opposition to the orders in council had mounted sharply, and two days before war was declared, the British government announced its intention to repeal them. Even so, Madison refused to end the struggle as long as the issue of impressment remained unresolved.

The war itself proved indecisive. Neither side was able to inflict a mortal blow on the other. The United States was able to control the Northern Great Lakes and Northwest for most of the war, but its strategy of invading upper Canada proved a dismal failure. An army under General Solomon Van Rensselear was forced to surrender to the British in 1812, and while the United States did invade Canada the following year, burning the capital of York and defeating a combined Indian and British force at the Battle of Thames, American forces never established real control over Canadian soil. Moreover, although the navy won several skirmishes with the British in 1812, most notably the sinking of the H.M.S. *Guerriere* by the U.S.S. *Constitution,* the British were able to drive most American shipping off the seas.

The British strategy of launching a three-pronged attack against the United States also proved unsuccessful. In 1814, a British armada entered Chesapeake Bay and, in retaliation for the burning of York, burned Washington, D.C. However, the British force failed in its second objective of taking Baltimore, despite an all-night bombardment of Fort McHenry in Baltimore Harbor. A second British drive across northern New York was repulsed at Plattsburg, while a third British force suffered a major defeat at the Battle of New Orleans as it tried to secure control of the Mississippi river. Ironically this most bitter struggle of the war took place two weeks after peace had been concluded in Europe between the belligerent powers.

Pertinent Literature

Perkins, Bradford. *Prologue to War: England and the United States, 1805-1812.* Berkeley: University of California Press, 1961.

There have been numerous interpretations of the causes of the War of 1812. Noting that President Monroe stressed maritime questions in his war message to Congress, early writers of the war interpreted these as its primary cause. Their interpretation was later challenged, however, by other historians who emphasized the influence of the frontier and the largely negative vote from the seaboard areas in response to Monroe's request for war, which they contrasted to the widespread support his call received from Western Congressmen, particularly from the War Hawks. To explain this frontier support they pointed to the West's desire to drive the British from Canada, and the Southern ambition to conquer Florida. In both cases they argued that war was the pretext which these sections used in fulfilling their objective. This expansionist interpretation of the War of 1812 had its most definitive expression in Julius Pratt's *Expansionists of 1812,* which remains a classic even today.

More recently, historians have been turning away from the expansionist interpretation of the war. They question why certain states, such as Pennsylvania, which had no fear of Indians and did not desire Florida, voted in favor of war. They are also unclear as to why the Indian question became politically vocal only after 1810. Finally, they challenge the contention that there was a general desire in the South to seize Florida. Instead they return once more to the maritime issues raised by President Monroe in his war message. But they place these issues in the larger context of national honor, which, they argue, was the real cause of the war and which united all sections of the country (with the exception of a few New England diehards) against Great Britain. It is such an interpretation that Bradford Perkins presents in *Prologue to War.*

Stressing such intangible factors in bringing on the war as national pride, sensitivity, and frustration, Perkins looks at the causes of the War of 1812 from both sides of the Atlantic. He states that the friction between the two countries came about from the fact that Great Britain was fighting for survival against Napoleon, while the United States chose to remain neutral and expected to be treated as such by both Great Britain and France. In order to keep its navy manned, however, Great Britain found it necessary to enlist men forcibly from American ships, and in order to deprive Napoleon of needed goods, was forced to blockade the Continent, giving concessions to no one, not even neutrals.

Americans were very sensitive about questions of national honor. They saw impressment and trade restrictions as snubs by the arrogant British and as an insult to their newly acquired independence. Great Britain, on the other hand, was anxious to contain Napoleon and could see no reason why the United States should object to its practices. Indeed, the British government believed that the blockade by the Royal Navy was not only protecting its own freedom, but protecting America's freedom as well. The countries could find no middle ground on which to settle these differences, and thus finally drifted into war.

The major point of contention between the two countries, Perkins believes, was the order in council which set up the blockade of Europe. In trying to lift the blockade and to prevent war, the United States enacted an embargo which was meant to hit Great Britain where it hurt most, in the pocketbook. In the end this caused more dissatisfaction at home than it did in England. In order to get the embargo lifted, the British tried various concessions short of entirely removing the blockade. Canning and Perceval thus tried to buy American coöperation by passing a new order in council which would give favors to American ships breaking the Embargo Act. Canning's gestures of concession failed, however, because the United States wanted complete freedom of the seas. By the time that the orders in council were lifted, war had already been declared.

Challenging the expansionist interpretation of the war, the author indicates that the War Hawks were never a majority in Congress, but the Congress was just simply kicked into war by British stubbornness. He also points out that the acquisition of Canada was not a major goal of the war, but its possible annexation was only a means to end the war quickly.

Perkins believes that the two Republican Presidents, Jefferson and Madison, had to bear much of the responsibility for the war. He argues that they often committed the United States to seek absolute rights with inadequate weapons. The justice of American demands, he admits, was undeniable, but the two men did not realize that justice was not a weapon and that compromise was necessary to avoid conflict. Instead, they expected warring nations to face collateral problems the same way as did the neutral United States. Unlike Washington and Adams they did not keep objectives and means in harmony.

Perkins argues his case forcefully and well, relying heavily on manuscripts from both the United States and England.

White, Patrick. *A Nation on Trial: America and the War of 1812.* New York: John Wiley & Sons, 1965.

This work is an excellent short account of the War of 1812. Professor White devotes one chapter of his work to the military history of the struggle, but his primary emphasis is on the diplomacy leading to war and on the negotiations which brought a final settlement to the struggle. White's thesis is simple and clear. The European conflict threatened the very existence of the United States, and the new republic went to war to preserve her national sovereignty. In a real sense, then, the conflict represented a struggle for its independence by the United States. While the war proved to be a standoff militarily and diplomatically from the point of view of the United States, it represented a milestone. Hereafter the new nation's sovereignty was assured.

The author's stress on national sovereignty as the primary cause of the War of 1812 is similar to Perkins' emphasis on the intangibles of national pride, sensitivity, and frustration. Like Perkins, he also relegates frontier grievances to minor importance as a cause. Congressional proposals for a conquest of Canada, he argues, were made out of military considerations rather than for the purpose of territorial expansion. He also dismisses the importance of Indian unrest, which he blames more on Americans who were encroaching on Indian lands than on British efforts to unite the Indians.

More important than Western grievances were the maritime questions of neutral rights and impressment. Violations of American neutrality on the seas, particularly with respect to impressment, were a slap at American sovereignty which Americans felt could not go unchallenged. On the other hand, England could not give up impressment without threatening her naval supremacy over France. The ultimate result was war.

Despite the tone of inevitability present in White's remarks on the causes of the war, the author is harsh in his judgment of American political leaders. He criticizes Jefferson for his policy of economic coercion, which, he says, failed to resolve any of the old problems facing the nation and created new ones for Jefferson's successor, Madison. He suggests strongly that Jefferson should have been more conciliatory in his attitude towards Great Britain, particularly with respect to impressment. As for Madison, he accuses him of a serious lack of leadership both before and during the war.

This lack of able leadership severely hampered the American war effort. Yet the new nation ultimately proved her determination and ability to maintain her national sovereignty. Here, in the author's view, is found the real significance of the struggle. — *E.M.T.*

Additional Recommended Reading

Brant, Irving. *James Madison: The President, 1809-1812.* Indianapolis: Bobbs-Merrill, Company, Inc., 1956. An attempt by Madison's principal biographer to refurbish the fourth President's reputation. Brant blames the apparent unwillingness of the British to modify their orders in council.

Burt, Alfred L. *The United States, Great Britain and British North America from the Revolution to the Establishment of Peace After the War of 1812.* New Haven: Yale University Press, 1940. A highly respected history of British-American relations 1783-1814, emphasizing maritime rights as the principal cause of the War of 1812.

Coles, Harry L. *The War of 1812.* Chicago: University of Chicago Press, 1965. A well-documented account of the military side of the War of 1812, with chapters on the causes of the war and the conclusion of peace.

Horsman, Reginald. *The Causes of the War of 1812.* New York: A. S. Barnes and Company, 1962. A somewhat repetitive study of the causes of the War of 1812 whose interpretation of the war is similar to that of Perkins and White.

Mahan, Alfred T. *Sea Power and Its Relations to the War of 1812.* London: S. Low, Marston and Company, Ltd., 1905. An important work by a leading advocate of a strong navy, who stresses the importance of impressment and the orders in council in bringing on war.

Mahon, John K. *The War of 1812.* Gainesville: University of Florida Press, 1972. An excellent comprehensive history of all aspects of the war.

NEW HARMONY, INDIANA, AND THE COMMUNITARIAN MOVEMENT

Type of event: Sociological: early attempts at coöperative living
Time: 1814-1830
Locale: New Harmony, Indiana

Principal personages:
GEORGE RAPP (1757-1847), founder of the Rappites and first owner of New Harmony
ROBERT OWEN (1771-1858), British industrialist, second owner of New Harmony
WILLIAM MACLURE (1763-1840), intellectual and partner of Robert Owen
ROBERT DALE OWEN (1801-1877), son of Robert Owen, radical freethinker, and later United States Congressman and Senator

Summary of Event

New Harmony, Indiana, founded in 1814, was a small village located on the banks of the Wabash river in the southwestern part of the state. Its chief historical importance rests in the fact that it was the site of two experiments in communal living in the first part of the nineteenth century which reflected an important phase of American social and cultural history during the pre-Civil War period. The town was founded by George Rapp, a German pietistic believer in communal life who sought a place in the American West where he might implement in detail his social theories. Rapp, having already developed a flourishing settlement of German immigrants like himself in Pennsylvania, sought a new abode that would be more spacious and closer to river transportation for the many goods his followers were producing for sale to the outside world. In the spring of 1814, he purchased over twenty-four thousand acres of rich alluvial land near the Wabash river south of Vincennes, then the capital of the Indiana territory.

The hamlet of Harmonie, so named by Rapp after the town they were abandoning in Pennsylvania, flowered and prospered under the guiding hand of the industrious Germans. Within a few short years the colony had placed under cultivation hundreds of acres of rich Indiana bottomlands that included large fruit orchards and an extensive grape vineyard as well as the usual farmlands. In addition, they created an extensive system of small manufactures including a grist-mill, a tannery, a center for weaving, a distillery, and a cotton gin. The Rappites sold their products from farm and factory throughout the entire area and shipped quantities of goods by keelboat and flatboat down the Ohio and Mississippi rivers to New Orleans.

The social practices of the community were as interesting as their economic life was successful. Rapp ruled with an iron hand, his decisions serving as the infallible guide to daily action within the town. Celibacy of both sexes

511

was practised, men and women living in separate dormitories constructed soon after the town was established. Regular churchgoing at the two churches in Harmonie, a flourishing school system, and weekly social activities, lectures, and intellectual discussions made life in the town busy and stimulating.

In 1824, the Rappites decided to move their colony back to Pennsylvania. The reasons for this decision are not fully clear, but early in that year Rapp sent agents to England who sought out prospective buyers of the communal property in Indiana. Robert Owen, the famous philanthropist, social reformer, and textile manufacturer, showed immediate interest in the site, viewing it as an opportunity to acquire a ready made place to implement his personal theories for reform of society. The terms of sale were arranged early in 1825, while Owen was on a personal inspection tour of the lands in Indiana. Thereafter the name of the town changed to New Harmony, by which it is best known in the history books and to students of the communitarian movement in America.

Owen was a powerful propagandist—a man with a mission to bring reform, theoretical and practical, to the world. He wrote and traveled widely to disseminate his ideas; the purchase of New Harmony gave him a "laboratory" in which to experiment very concretely with these theories. Within a relatively short time following the announcement of the transfer of ownership to Owen, people interested in participating in the new experiment in community living began to arrive in New Harmony. Hampered by overcrowding and by groups of people with a diversity of intentions and points of view, from the beginning the New Harmony experiment struggled to keep afloat. Lacking the cohesiveness of the Germans who had preceded them, Owen and his supporters never experienced the economic success that had been accorded the Rappites. Only the commitment of Owen's considerable personal fortune to the enterprise prevented the operation from going under quickly. At the same time, however, a substantive community life developed at New Harmony under the leadership of Owen and his sons, especially William and Robert Dale. For a time widely recognized intellectual leaders, such as William Maclure, a famous geologist and philanthropist, and Thomas Say, curator of the American Philosophical Society, lived at New Harmony and participated enthusiastically in the bustling life of the experimental community.

After 1830 Robert Owen turned his attention to other reform projects. He had lost much of his fortune in financing the social experiment in Indiana and, perhaps understandably, his interest declined as debts piled up and small groups broke off from the main community of reformers. The reformist spirit symbolized by Owen continued in New Harmony long after the Welsh philanthropist personally abandoned his project. Experimental efforts in public education initiated by Maclure, and the continued residence in New Harmony throughout the 1830's and 1840's of various sons of the founder, served to remind the outside world of the significant heritage demanding basic changes in society that was emanating from this obscure village on the edge of the civilized world.

New Harmony, both under Rapp and during the time of Robert Owen and his followers, was technically a community of social equals. A primitive form of socialism was attempted there under Owen's leadership, although it never functioned successfully. But this backwoods settlement was symbolic of efforts in many other parts of America in the pre-Civil War era to establish small egalitarian communities which were to serve as beacon lights of reform for all of American society, and, indeed, for the Western world in general. The leading historian of this "communitarian" movement has identified almost one hundred of these small reformist societies that were established between 1825 and 1860, chiefly in the Midwest. New Harmony, then, clearly serves as a prototype for the entire movement. Communitarianism was collectivistic by nature, opposed to revolution, yet impatient with gradualism. The purpose of the small experimental community was, first, to implement apparently incompatible aims—to achieve immediate, root-and-branch reform by gradual, nonrevolutionary means. A second purpose was to serve as a model of peaceable change for the larger world. Microcosms of society could undergo drastic alterations and then the rest of society could be depended upon to imitate these models, somewhat more slowly over a period of time, in achieving widespread and desirable social reform.

These two communitarian experiments at New Harmony also reflected the broad historical development of the communitarian ideal. It had its origins in the religious ideology of the radical Protestant sects that appeared at the time of the Reformation—attitudes that were transferred to the United States in the colonial and early national periods by immigrants much like George Rapp and his band of followers from Würtemberg, Germany. By the second quarter of the nineteenth century, however, the communitarian ideal was becoming rapidly secularized. Robert Owen, an atheist, symbolized this second phase in the development of the movement. Those attracted to New Harmony during his régime almost without exception were vitally interested in the social regeneration of mankind, but saw no need to connect this concern to specific religious doctrines.

The communitarian ideal received the widespread attention it did in the four decades prior to the Civil War for a variety of reasons. The rapid Westward expansion of the frontier during this period left the entire social structure of the country somewhat in flux. This movement seemed to give a special thrust to the work of social reformers, since their efforts might well serve as the basic institutional framework for the nation's foreseeable future as plastic institutions matured into permanence and the frontier era passed into history. The work of the communitarians also seemed attractive because alternative methods of social reform now were thought to be at a dead end. Rampant individualism seemed incapable of answering the need for some sort of collective action to deal with the ills of the nineteenth century. Remembering the bloodlettings of the period from 1789 to 1815 in Europe, observers suggested that revolution had revealed itself to be a dangerous two-edged sword. Moreover, the problems created by industrialization seemed already to have moved beyond gradualism as a means of solving them. Drastic reform was necessary, but drastic reform without revolution. The communitarian approach seemed a model solution to the dilemmas posed by these attitudes. It was voluntaristic, genuinely experimental, involved deliberate planning and rational choice, and was nonrevolutionary. All these characteristics were immensely appealing to reformers throughout the Western world in the first half of the nineteenth century.

These tendencies, and others, provided a special appeal to Americans during the same period. Faith in the idea that men can remake their institutions by reasoned choice seemed normal, for that is what Americans had done during the period of constitution-making. The communitarians' belief in social harmony, not class warfare, was also a deeply held American attitude. The experimentation of the communitarians found a ready response in a nation of tinkerers—a nation that was

thought in itself to be an experiment. Perhaps most important, the group procedure that was at the heart of the communitarian effort reflected a tendency that has revealed itself in many areas of American thought and activity. Perhaps as a product of the frontier experience and a deeply revered democratic tradition, the United States has always placed great stress upon the development of voluntary associations. From the Mayflower Compact to the establishment of the Tennessee Valley Authority and the encouragement of grass-roots "community action" programs in more recent times, the belief in voluntary associations has asserted itself in American life. The communitarian movement neatly fits into such an ideological framework. Thus one comes to understand something of the larger historical and intellectual context of which New Harmony, first under a German, George Rapp, and then under the influence of an Englishman, Robert Owen, was a part.

Pertinent Literature

Wilson, William E. *The Angel and the Serpent: The Story of New Harmony.* Bloomington: Indiana University Press, 1964.

A popularized account, lacking scholarly references and footnotes, the book nevertheless shows evidence of extensive research and provides the reader with the necessary chronological outline of the history of New Harmony from its beginnings in 1814 to the present. Especially valuable are the discussions of the earliest days of New Harmony, during the tenure of the Rappites, and the author's comments on developments in New Harmony after Robert Owen abandoned the pro-

ject for other interests in the 1830's. Wilson is generally favorable in his attitudes toward the reformers who built and maintained the town, but he lacks the broad perspective of a trained historian. This means he views the history of New Harmony too narrowly, never placing specific events occurring in Indiana in the larger ideological and institutional setting of American social and cultural history of the first half of the nineteenth century.

New Harmony, Indiana, and the Communitarian Movement

Bestor, Arthur E. *Backwoods Utopias: The Sectarian and Owenite Phases of Communitarian Socialism in America, 1663-1829.* Philadelphia: University of Pennsylvania Press, 1950.

All of the weaknesses of Wilson's volume are avoided in this superb study of New Harmony and the communitarian movement published a decade and a half prior to Wilson's work. Bestor seeks to place the communitarian movement in America in the broadest possible cultural setting. The title is somewhat misleading, since Bestor pays special attention to Robert Owen's work at New Harmony as a case study of the larger communal movement, and thus loses some of the comprehensive analysis suggested by the title. About half the book deals with developments at New Harmony. Nevertheless, the full intellectual and cultural setting of Owenite socialism is set forth. Particularly valuable is an appendix listing all known utopian communal groups established prior to 1860 in the United States. Bestor also offers a detailed analysis of Owen's thoughts concerning communitarianism, a topic largely ignored by Wilson. Bestor is not especially pleased with Owen's theories regarding their realism and practicability. He demonstrates that the utopian reformer's vagueness concerning the details of land ownership in his project in Indiana assured the failure of that social experiment almost as soon as it was launched. Nevertheless, in many instances, the analysis is sympathetic. Most important, Bestor's delineation of the complex intellectual traditions which lay behind utopian communal thought in the nineteenth century, and the relation of these traditions to general intellectual movements in both Europe and America is a highly illuminating exercise for anyone who desires to understand the full historical significance of the story of New Harmony, Indiana.

Harrison, John F. *Quest for the New Moral World: Robert Owen and the Owenites in Britain and America.* New York: Charles Scribner's Sons, 1969.

Harrison's focus is upon Owenism as a social and intellectual movement, not on the communitarian tradition *per se.* Thus it is not as fully related to the issues discussed here as is Bestor's study. Nevertheless, it is by all odds the most comprehensive analysis of Owen's ideas and the institutions fostered by those ideas in the context of nineteenth century history that has yet appeared. Of special significance is Harrison's use of comparative analysis. He seeks to explain how Owenism could appeal both in England and America, where social and cultural contexts were different. He concludes that the Owenite reformist philosophy made the impact it did because the social structures in both England and the United States were in a state of extreme flux during the first half of the nineteenth century, although for differing reasons—because of industrialism in England and because of movement west into vast, unpopulated areas in the United States. Also useful is Harrison's connection of Owenism with the important Anglo-American intellectual tradition of millennialism, with the philanthropic impulse in both countries, and with the rapidly developing working class movements that were affecting both England and the United States during the second quarter of the nineteenth century. — *J.F.*

Additional Recommended Reading

Leopold, Richard W. *Robert Dale Owen: A Biography.* Cambridge: Harvard University Press, 1940. The standard biography of one of Robert Owen's sons who lived in New Harmony for a number of years and eventually became an American citizen.

Lockwood, George B. *The New Harmony Movement.* New York: Appleton-Century-Crofts, Inc., 1905. An old yet useful work fully covering the history and sociological implications of the New Harmony movement.

Owen, Robert D. *Threading My Way: Twenty-Seven Years of Autobiography.* New York: G. W. Carleton, 1874. Contains firsthand reminiscences of a key participant in New Harmony during its early years.

Tyler, Alice Felt. *Freedom's Ferment: Phases of American Social History from the Revolution to the Outbreak of the Civil War.* Minneapolis: University of Minnesota Press, 1944. Though somewhat out of date, this comprehensive narrative of the socio-cultural context in which the communitarian movement grew remains a standard account.

THE HARTFORD CONVENTION

Type of event: Political: dissatisfaction over the War of 1812
Time: December 15, 1814-January 5, 1815
Locale: Hartford, Connecticut

Principal personages:
JAMES MADISON (1751-1836), fourth President of the United States 1809-1817
HARRISON GRAY OTIS (1765-1848), Massachusetts Federalist who conceived the idea of a New England convention
CALEB STRONG (1745-1819), Governor of Massachusetts and leader of the Federalist opposition to the Madison Administration's war policy
GEORGE CABOT (1752-1823), Massachusetts Federalist
JOHN (JACK) LOWELL (1769-1840), radical member of the extremist faction in the Federalist Party

Summary of Event

The War of 1812 had never been popular among New England Federalists; they called it "Mr. Madison's War." New Englanders as a whole recoiled from the war of conquest preached by Southerners and Westerners, and Federalists were eager to find fault with the Republicans' conduct of the war. By the fall of 1814, sectional and political feelings about the war had reached alarming proportions. The American invasions of Canada had been abortive. British troops had burned Washington in August, 1814. The British Army occupied eastern Maine, and enemy ships hovered about the New England coast. The Madison Administration collected war taxes and militia units in New England, but it appeared that a disproportionately small share of money and men were allotted to the defense of that section. New Englanders believed that they were carrying the dual burdens of defending themselves and also supporting the war effort of an incompetent national administration which showed no concern for them. Moreover, the bad situation threatened to become worse; Congress appeared to be ready to enact a national conscription act which presumably would remove even more of New England's defenders. The American commissioners at Ghent in Belgium were making no progress toward a negotiated peace; nor were they likely to do so as long as the British enjoyed military success. New England, with good reason, was alarmed.

Fear and frustration showed plainly in the results of the elections of 1814. The Federalists gained large majorities in both state and national offices, and the party leadership interpreted its success as a mandate for action against "Mr. Madison's War." The activities of Governor Caleb Strong of Massachusetts demonstrated how extreme such action might become. In November, 1814, Strong offered thinly veiled

517

hints of a separate peace and an alliance to General Sir John Sherbrooke, the British Governor of Nova Scotia. Strong's overtures to the enemy came to nothing, but they served as an index of the desperation which infected Strong's section and his party.

This same mood of desperation moved Strong to call the Massachusetts General Court, or legislature, into special session in October, 1814. It responded to the crisis by calling for a convention of delegates from the New England states to meet at Hartford, Connecticut, on December 15. According to Harrison Gray Otis, the acknowledged author of the convention plan, the delegates were to discuss ways and means of sectional defense and to take steps to revise the United States Constitution to accord with sectional interests.

Three of the five New England states heeded Massachusetts' call. The legislatures of Connecticut and Rhode Island joined the Bay state in selecting delegations. Vermont and New Hampshire took no official action, but delegates chosen by local and county conventions in those states attended the Hartford sessions. Twenty-six men took part in the convention, and for the most part they were of a moderate temper. Extremists, such as Jack Lowell and Timothy Pickering, took no part in the proceedings and privately bewailed the convention's lack of "bold and ardent men." Well aware that a firm but fine line separated political opposition from treason in wartime, the Hartford delegates sought to play a positive, not negative, role.

The Hartford Convention, when assembled and organized, conducted most of its business in committees.

George Cabot, the leader of the Massachusetts delegation who had explained that one of his objectives was to prevent "hot-heads from getting into mischief," was probably instrumental in stacking the committees with moderate men. Otis was apparently the guiding spirit of the committees and the author of the report adopted by the convention on January 3, 1815.

Otis' report, the product of the Hartford Convention, began by stating the mission of the convention, which was to provide for concerted sectional defense and to propose repairs to the Constitution. The report then discussed at length the circumstances which gave rise to the convention. It focused upon the disaffection of extremists, and although it opposed radical solutions, such as dissolving the Union, it plainly implied that the Union was in peril. In effect it contained a mild ultimatum to the Madison Administration to listen to the convention and its moderate solutions or be prepared to face the radicals and disunion. There followed a cataloging of the sins of Republican Administrations past and present. Finally, the convention offered its solution in the form of a series of seven amendments to the Constitution providing that: (1) the "three-fifths compromise," which allowed states to count a portion of their chattel population in determining proportionate representation in Congress and the Electoral College, be abolished; (2) a two-thirds vote of both houses of Congress be required to admit new states into the Union; (3) no embargo be imposed for more than sixty days; (4) a two-thirds vote of both Houses of Congress be required to adopt declarations of war; (5) a two-thirds vote of both Houses of Congress be required to adopt declarations of commercial non-intercourse acts; (6) naturalized citizens be ineligible for federal office, elective or appointive; (7) no President might succeed himself, nor should successive Presidents be from the same state.

The work of the convention reflected a mixture of sectional complaints and political rancor. Its enemies accused the assembly of treason; yet its temper was moderate. Although the convention addressed itself to some legitimate sectional grievances, it lapsed into the rhetoric of narrow partisanship. Perhaps no man came closer to the truth than John Adams, who described the Hartford delegates as "intelligent and honest men who had lost touch with reality."

The supreme irony was that even while the convention debated, American arms won a great victory at New Orleans, and the British and Americans made peace at Ghent. By the time representatives carrying the report of the Hartford Convention arrived in Washington, the country knew that peace had come. Such circumstances blunted New England sectionalism, and the Federalist Party seemed treasonous, ludicrous, or both. Its demise was imminent.

Pertinent Literature

Morison, Samuel Eliot. *Harrison Gray Otis, 1765-1848: The Urbane Federalist.* Boston: Houghton Mifflin Co., 1969.

With this book Samuel Eliot Morison has come full circle. His first book, published in 1913, was *The Life and Letters of Harrison Gray Otis.* Since that time Morison has written dozens of books and has become one of the most distinguished historical scholars in the United States. Originally intending to produce a new edition of his now rare first book, Morison decided to produce a new study. The result is a well-written, sympathetic biography of the moving spirit behind the Hartford Convention.

Morison covers Otis' entire life. Because Otis' most remembered act on the national stage was his participation in the Hartford Convention, the biographer deals in great detail with the background, actions, and aftermath of the convention. Indeed, Morison's treatment of the Hartford Convention is the only thorough study of the subject written within the past several decades.

As a biographer, Morison presents the convention through the eyes of his subject. He adds conversational and editorial comments to enforce his view that the Hartford Convention offered a moderate solution to a potentially explosive situation. Morison places the Hartford Convention in the context of other conventions in the American political tradition and suggests that it was the lineal descendant of such assemblies as the Stamp Act Congress and the Constitutional Convention. His analysis of the membership indicates that, with few exceptions, the delegates were moderate Federalists who sought a middle ground between the aggressive nationalism of the Republicans and the secessionist schemes of the more radical Federalists. Consequently, Morison proposes that the convention was more of a safety valve for venting sectional and political emotions than it was a serious threat to the war effort or the Union. Once the delegates rejected the alternative of secession, their demands for amendments to the Constitution were likely to fall on deaf ears outside New England. The difference between New England in 1814 and the South in 1860-1861, Morison argues, was that the South was prepared to accept disunion.

Thus, in Morison's view, the Hartford Convention was the natural product of genuine grievances carried out by moderate men. Its failings were not the result of disaffection for the Union or of treason, but rather those of uncreative moderation and bad timing. Perhaps these judgments are too kind. Yet because they are based upon copious research and belong to Samuel Eliot Morison, they have and deserve great authority.

Dangerfield, George. *The Era of Good Feelings.* New York: Harcourt, Brace & World Inc., 1952.

George Dangerfield is a wide-ranging scholar whose work is characterized by thorough research, keen analysis, and a fine writing style. *The Era of Good Feelings* illustrates these qualities. The book deals with the administrations of James Monroe and John Quincy Adams, and emphasizes politics and diplomacy.

Dangerfield devotes only a few pages to the Hartford Convention while describing the background of the "Era of Good Feelings" under Monroe. He treats the convention as a decided threat to the Union— "disunion is disunion, however mildly asserted." But Dangerfield does not take the Hartford proceedings too seriously. He emphasizes the air of unreality which pervaded the period, section, and party. Asserting that "New England Federalism was less a right wing of American politics than a left wing of the British navigation system," the author suggests that the Hartford Convention was the last, weak gasp of a dying breed of men. Dangerfield shows another New Englander, John Quincy Adams, as a foil to the delegates at Hartford. Adams was in Ghent negotiating peace while the convention met. The implication in the *Era of Good Feelings* is that Adams was living in the real world, while some of his New England neighbors were groping about in an unreal world, which, if it ever existed, was well in the past. — *E.M.T.*

Additional Recommended Reading

Perkins, Bradford. *Castlereagh and Adams: England and the United States, 1812-1823.* Berkeley: University of California Press, 1964. A thorough study of Anglo-American relations during the period, treating the Hartford Convention as a mild yet potentially dangerous threat to the Union.

Horsman, Reginald. *The War of 1812.* New York: Alfred A. Knopf, Inc., 1969. A general study of the war which describes the Hartford Convention as "more petulant than revolutionary."

Coles, Harry L. *The War of 1812.* Chicago: University of Chicago Press, 1965. Regards the Hartford Convention and the Federalist opposition to the war seriously and unsympathetically.

Smelser, Marshall. *The Democratic Republic, 1801-1815.* New York: Harper & Row Publishers, 1968. The Hartford Convention is discussed briefly in this volume of the *New American Nation* series.

Adams, Henry. *History of the United States of America During the Administrations of Jefferson and Madison.* Vol. II. New York: Charles Scribner's Sons, 1891. This volume in Adams' great classic on the history of the Jefferson and Adams Administrations contains a chapter on the Hartford Convention in which Adams notes that the opinion of the public in New England was probably more radical than that of the majority in the convention.

NEGOTIATION OF THE TREATY OF GHENT

Type of event: Diplomatic: declaration of peace between Great Britain and the United States

Time: December 24, 1814

Locale: Ghent, Belgium

Principal personages:

JOHN QUINCY ADAMS (1767-1848), Republican nationalist from Massachusetts, the leading American delegate at Ghent

HENRY CLAY (1777-1852), Republican "War Hawk" from Kentucky and American delegate at Ghent

ALBERT GALLATIN (1761-1849), moderate member of the American delegation who made peace among his colleagues at Ghent

JAMES A. BAYARD (1767-1815), moderate Federalist from Delaware and American delegate at Ghent

JONATHAN RUSSELL (fl. 1814), "War Hawk" from Rhode Island and American delegate at Ghent

JAMES MADISON (1751-1836), fourth President of the United States 1809-1817

JAMES MONROE (1758-1831), United States Secretary of State 1811-1817

ROBERT STEWART (First VISCOUNT CASTLEREAGH) (1769-1822), Foreign Secretary of Great Britain

Summary of Event

Chances of a negotiated, "honorable" peace ending the War of 1812 appeared remote in the late summer of 1814. The United States had gone to war, ostensibly at least, to protect its neutral rights on the high seas. President James Madison and Secretary of State James Monroe had repeatedly stated that the recognition of such rights, and particularly an end to the practice of impressing American sailors into the British Navy, was essential to any peace settlement. The British had refused to abandon impressment whenever the Americans had demanded it, and the war continued. Militarily, the conflict had been inconclusive. Yet in the summer of 1814, the

British and their Continental Allies had defeated Napoleon; now Great Britain could turn its full attention and energies to the war with the former colonies. With France subdued and veteran troops available for duty in North America, Great Britain seemed in a position to end the war by military conquest. Moreover, the Americans were divided over "Mr. Madison's War." The Federalist Party and New England generally had opposed the war from its beginning. The Republican Administration faced the unpleasant prospects of political humiliation, or military defeat, or both, should it continue to pursue its war aims.

Such were the circumstances when

the American and British commissioners met at Ghent, Belgium, in August, 1814, to discuss peace. The British agreed to the meeting as an alternative to mediation by Alexander I, Tsar of Russia, and evinced no haste in treating with the American upstarts. Their delegation included Admiralty Lawyer Dr. William Adams, Vice-Admiral Lord Gambier, and Henry Goulburn of the Colonial Office. The five American commissioners—John Quincy Adams, Albert Gallatin, Henry Clay, James A. Bayard, and Jonathan Russell—represented a broad spectrum of backgrounds. Adams, a Massachusetts Republican and nominally the head of the delegation, was a staunch nationalist politically, but was full of personal rancor. Bayard, a Delaware Federalist, and Gallatin, a Pennsylvania Republican, were moderates, and the latter, because of his role as peacemaker among his colleagues, emerged as the functional leader of the Americans at Ghent. Clay and Russell were "War Hawks" from Kentucky and Rhode Island, respectively. The Americans often quarreled among themselves, but they stood firmly together in the face of their British counterparts.

Although the United States had always posed as the injured party in the conflict, the British, negotiating from strength, dominated the early months of the conference. They proposed the establishment of an Indian buffer state in the American Northwest and asked for a substantial cession of land along the border between Canada and the United States. The Americans refused. The British, anticipating the capture of New Orleans, then suggested that each party continue to occupy the territory it held at the conclusion of hostilities.

Again the Americans refused.

Finally, the constancy and apparent unanimity of the United States delegation bore fruit. Throughout the negotiations the British Cabinet had debated whether to conquer or conciliate the United States. Viscount Castlereagh (Robert Stewart), Foreign Secretary of Great Britain, led the way towards compromise; he foresaw greater good in Anglo-American friendship than in lasting enmity between the kindred nations. Several factors, some only vaguely relating to the American war, confirmed Castlereagh's tentative judgment. The British were having a difficult time at the Congress of Vienna with their recent allies in the wars against Napoleon. Indeed, it seemed for a time that war with Alexander's Russia was imminent. France was restive, portending Napoleon's return in 1815. At home, the British people were warweary and growing resentful of war taxation. To make matters worse, the Americans won a timely victory at Plattsburg on September 11, 1814; the architect of the victory over Napoleon, the Duke of Wellington, estimated that conquest in North America would come only at a heavy cost of men, money, and time. At this juncture, Castlereagh and the British determined to compromise with the United States.

The commissioners at Ghent still bargained hard. Yet the stakes were no longer so great. The Americans had agreed that the treaty say nothing about impressment. The British abandoned their designs on United States territory and their desire for an Indian buffer state. The British still demanded the islands in the Passamaquoddy Bay, the right of navigation on the Mississippi river, and prohibitions on Americans' rights to dry fish in Newfoundland. In the end, the participants at Ghent delegated these matters to commissions to resolve after peace had been concluded. The Americans agreed to exact no retribution or take no land from the Indians who had fought on the British side. In fact the Peace of Ghent provided for a return to the *status quo ante bellum.* The commissioners signed the treaty on Christmas Eve, 1814.

The treaty was, in itself, a victory for neither side. Yet for the Americans there was cause for rejoicing. The United States had stood firm against a "great power." Castlereagh and the British had recognized American military potential and decided to court instead of conquer. Most important, the peace which both sides wanted and needed was secure.

The War of 1812 had several important results for the United States. It gave the American people a greater feeling of national identity; it left a legacy of bad feeling between Great Britain and the United States which persisted for many years; the defeat of the Indians in the Old Northwest and Southwest helped to open those regions to settlement; the war stimulated the growth of manufactures; and it turned the American people away from foreign affairs to a primary concern for domestic matters. It has well been called the second war for independence.

Pertinent Literature

Perkins, Bradford. *Castlereagh and Adams: England and the United States, 1812-1823.* Berkeley: University of California Press, 1964.

This book is part of a three-volume study of Anglo-American diplomacy between 1795 and 1823. Perkins is a thorough researcher, and one of the strengths of his book is its extensive use of British primary sources as well as American materials. Perkins complements his copious research by a facile prose style. Although the work is not specifically about the Peace of Ghent, the diplomacy of the War of 1812 occupies more than half the book. The grand theme of Perkins' trilogy is the maturing relationship of the United States and the former Mother Country. The Peace of Ghent, Perkins suggests, was a vital part of this extended *rapprochement.*

The American commissioners went to Ghent still hoping to wring concessions from the British. For President Madison and Secretary of State Monroe the cessation of impressment by the British was a *sine qua non* for peace. Perkins recounts how the Americans soon realized that it was not they, but the British, who were in a position to make demands. Perkins traces the various positions of the two delegations on Great Britain's territorial demands and on the idea for an Indian buffer state between the United States and Canada. He emphasizes the important role played by the British Cabinet, and especially by Castlereagh, in controlling and thus weakening the freedom of action of the British commissioners, and in ultimately deciding on compromise instead of conquest. Because he believes that this latter decision was the vital one in the negotiations, Perkins devotes considerable attention to British affairs both domestic and foreign. Once the British Cabinet had determined to make peace, Perkins quickens the pace of his narrative and describes how the negotiations were concluded.

In keeping with his general theme, Perkins concludes that the treaty was more than adequate for both sides. The Americans at Ghent wisely had used the latitude allowed them by Madison and Monroe. They were not proud of the treaty, but Perkins suggests that they should have been; they had collectively solidified a position and bargained hard from a posture of relative weakness. The British had tested the strength of the new nation in the field and at the conference table, and had decided on peace. Thus Perkins concludes that "the silent treaty served America well."

Engleman, Fred L. *The Peace of Christmas Eve.* New York: Harcourt, Brace & World, Inc., 1960.

This book is intended more for the general reader than for the historical specialist, but it is nevertheless good popular history. Engleman writes well and often wittily. He has done considerable research, and his judgments are sound.

Engleman focuses upon the negotiations at Ghent, yet his scope is broad. He deals with many aspects and events of the War of 1812 as they relate to the treaty. Engleman's epilogue follows the careers of the American commissioners and Anglo-American relations well beyond 1814.

Unlike Bradford Perkins' work, which deals with the Peace of Ghent from a broad Anglo-American perspective, Engleman's book presents narrative from an almost exclusively American point of view. For example, Engleman suggests that the American victory at Plattsburg on September 11, 1814, was a significant factor in influencing the British to come to terms.

Perkins, on the other hand, treats Plattsburg as only one of a number of considerations which induced the British cabinet to seek a compromise peace. Engleman gives the American commissioners high praise for their actions at Ghent. He portrays the five Americans as the architects of the treaty because their proposal on November 10, 1814, embodied the broad essentials of the final *status quo ante bellum* settlement. Moreover, he goes on to ascribe the later good will between Britain and the United States to the work done on the treaty by the Americans.

Engleman devotes much attention to the personalities at Ghent. His sketches of the individuals and their interaction are not only lively, but they also serve to express a historical idea. Engleman emphasizes people more than institutions, and his emphasis on the five lonely Americans is refreshing. — *E.M.T.*

Additional Recommended Reading

Bemis, Samuel Flagg. *John Quincy Adams and the Foundations of American Foreign Policy.* New York: Alfred A. Knopf, Inc., 1949. A master diplomatic historian presents Adams' role at Ghent as part of a larger triumph in statecraft.

Dangerfield, George. *The Era of Good Feelings.* New York: Harcourt, Brace & World, Inc., 1952. Dangerfield treats the negotiations at Ghent in broad European perspective and regards them as contributing to the founding of American nationalism.

Burt, Alfred L. *The United States, Great Britain, and British North America from the Revolution to the Establishment of Peace After the War of 1812.* New Haven: Yale University Press, 1940. A judicious summary of Anglo-American relations in the period.

Horseman, Reginald. *The War of 1812.* New York: Alfred A. Knopf, Inc., 1969. In this general history of the war, Horseman treats the Peace of Ghent in its broader European context.

Coles, Harry L. *The War of 1812.* Chicago: University of Chicago Press, 1965. Included in this brief but incisive narrative of the war are chapters on the Peace of Ghent which provide a penetrating summary of the negotiations.

THE GREAT MIGRATION

Type of event: Sociological: expansion into the West
Time: 1815-1820
Locale: The Old Northwest, Kentucky, Tennessee, Missouri, and the Gulf Coast Plains

Summary of Event

One of the great developments in the decade which followed the end of the War of 1812 was the mass migration of tens of thousands of Americans into the country west of the Appalachian Mountains. The West, of course, was not created overnight. Even before the American Revolution, American colonists had moved into the middle and upper Ohio River Valley. In 1775, Daniel Boone and thirty axmen blazed the Wilderness Road through the Cumberland Gap and founded the Kentucky settlement of Boonesborough. Settlers could follow the Great Valley Road down the Shenandoah Valley to a connection with Boone's route and thence continue into Kentucky. To the north, routes such as Braddock's Road and Forbes' Road led to the forks of the Ohio river. By 1790 the population west of the mountains already totaled over two hundred thousand, but the movement had only begun.

A number of factors stimulated men and their families to undertake the arduous journey westward. Not the least of these were policies and programs pursued by the federal government. The Harrison Land Act of 1800, including subsequent amendments in 1804, reduced the minimum amount of land a settler could purchase to a quarter section (160 acres) and the minimum price to $1.64 an acre. The act also granted credit for four years. Under this act millions of acres of land were disposed of by the United States.

As important as a liberal land policy in encouraging westward migration in the late eighteenth century was the establishment of security along the frontier. This was effected through both diplomatic and military measures. By treaties concluded with Great Britain and Spain in 1794 and 1795, respectively, Canadian and Florida boundary settlements were made and anti-American influence among the Indians was reduced. About the same time, American military campaigns against the Indians both north and south of the Ohio river subdued the red men temporarily. The Louisiana Purchase of 1803 and the Adams-Onís Treaty in 1819 gave the United States title to the Gulf Coast west to the Sabine river, while the campaigns of the War of 1812 crushed Indian military power in the eastern Great Lakes region. With reasonable security thus obtained, the land proved more attractive to potential settlers.

Applying largely to the South, another factor which stimulated western migration was the invention of the cotton gin in 1793. This device opened up most of the land in the South to the production of upland cotton, which found its major market in the enormous textile industry that had developed in England since the beginning of the nineteenth century. Cheap, fertile land to the west and depleted land to

527

the east caused a great shift of cotton production into the Trans-Appalachian area between 1815 and 1835. A factor, applying largely to the North, which reduced the cost of travel was the construction of the Erie Canal, which was completed in 1825. And a final factor, applicable to all sections, was the invention and quick exploitation of the steamboat. By the 1820's, the rivers were so crowded with steamboats that, as one wag told it, the fish petitioned Congress for preëmption rights.

The results of these factors working simultaneously with others was the rise of a new section: the West. In 1790, about ninety-five percent of the total population resided east of the mountains; by 1820, about twenty percent was west of the mountains. Between 1790 and 1812, the Western states of Kentucky (1792), Tennessee (1796), Ohio (1803), and Louisiana (1812) were admitted to the Union. Then admissions increased rapidly: Indiana (1816), Mississippi (1817), Illinois (1818), Alabama (1819), and Missouri (1821). Michigan and Arkansas were organized into territories in 1805 and 1819, respectively. By 1820, the population was in a vast triangle with its base along the Atlantic Ocean and its apex roughly at the confluence of the Ohio and Missouri rivers with the Mississippi. Along both sides of the triangle, people were spilling over—north to the upper Great Lakes and south to the Gulf of Mexico.

This development had momentous political and economic consequences for the nation. By 1820 there were, for example, eighteen new Senators in Congress from the West. No longer could the older regions operate in tandem or in opposition to each other without regarding Western interests. The West had become a political force and Westerners were not long in taking advantage of the fact that they were being courted by both the North and the South. Politics in America took on an increasingly sectional tone after 1815 which made political parties even more important than earlier since they were the sole vehicle through which national interest could contest with sectional interest. In the period between 1815 and 1830, there was little apparent difference between the objectives and needs of the Northwest and the Southwest. With the assimilation of the Southwest into a greater and solid South by about 1830, the Old Northwest became even more politically significant.

Economically, the postwar migration of 1812 was of vast import. New land was brought into production, towns were developed, new market patterns were established, and new industries were created. The opening of the West was an incentive to further movement westward, and wave after wave passed on, bringing with them still newer needs and wants as well as the establishment of churches, schools, theaters, and prisons. Whatever was happening politically, the flow into the West of American and foreign immigrants created that mass consumer demand upon which industry could thrive and out of which the beginnings of a national economy would develop.

The Great Migration

Pertinent Literature

Caruso, John Anthony. *The Great Lakes Frontier: An Epic of the Old Northwest.* Indianapolis: Bobbs-Merrill Co., Inc., 1961.

Truly one of the more readable volumes on the Old Northwest, John Anthony Caruso's *The Great Lakes Frontier* treats the political history of the region from the explorations of the French to the admission of Wisconsin as a state. Since the study begins and ends in Wisconsin, Caruso presents his story as a full circle, beginning on the Fox river at Green Bay in 1673 and concluding nearby in the newly founded state capital of Madison in 1848. The author's main emphasis, however, is on the American period originating with the military exploits in the era of George Rogers Clark during the American Revolution.

Caruso's concentration upon Clark marks his continual theme—that of great men as movers of history. From Marquette and Jolliet, La Salle, and Clark of the earlier period through Arthur St. Clair, "Mad" Anthony Wayne, William Henry Harrison, Ninian Edwards, and Lewis Cass of the later period, Caruso emphasizes the contributions of key men in molding their environment. Also included are the red leaders, the tragic Cornplanter, the great Little Turtle, the brilliant Tecumseh, and the legendary Black Hawk, who fought bravely yet vainly to keep their land free from the curse of white civilization.

The author sees four large migrations making up the settlement of the Old Northwest. The first took place after the Revolutionary War when towns like Steubenville, Marietta, and Losantiville were established. Legend has it upon hearing that he had arrived in the latter settlement, the gout suffering Governor St. Clair boomed out, "Losantiville? . . . God damn it, change it to Cincinnati!" and so it was. But the initial movement into the area was slowed by unsure land titles and Indian hostility.

The conquest of Ohio by General Wayne and the ensuing Treaty of Greenville opened the region for whites. Prompted by state and federal land grants for Revolutionary War service, the first really big wave of settlers arrived. Under this stimulus Ohio qualified for statehood, and preliminary settlements were founded in Indiana and Illionis. The rise of Tecumseh's Indian confederation and problems with Great Britain, however, caused the migration to lag.

It was not until after the end of the War of 1812 and the death of Tecumseh at the Battle of the Thames, that the Great Migration, the third and largest influx of settlers, occurred. This event had profound effect on the Old Northwest. Following the traditional story, Caruso points out that the population in Indiana became predominantly Yankee. Buttressed by non-slaveholding Southerners, this led to the rise of antislavery sentiment. When Governor William Henry Harrison tried to walk a middle course, he was condemned by both sides. The proslavery forces, led by Jesse B. Thomas, cut Illinois off from Yankee dominated Indiana, while the antislavery forces, led by Jonathan Jennings, set up a new free state in Indiana by 1816. The admission of Illinois to statehood two years later was, according to Caruso, effected by men like Ninian Edwards to halt the growing demand for the admission of slavery to the territory to counter the growth of slaveholding Missouri across the Mississippi river. The idea was that statehood would demonstrate that growth had been achieved without slavery.

The final migration into the Old Northwest was the product of the Erie Canal and the steamboat which opened up Michigan and Wisconsin to settlers of Yankee and northern European stock after 1825. Here initial settlement was encouraged by the indefatigable

activities of Governor Lewis Cass, who organized surveys, conducted personal explorations, pacified the Indians, and induced the federal government to make large land grants in the area to veterans.

Caruso's book is an action-packed account of an exciting group of important people. It reveals the qualities of young America's leaders and the hardy common folk who civilized the Old Northwest through the Great Migration, and introduces the reader to a storehouse of information in a most readable manner.

Buley, R. Carlyle. *The Old Northwest: Pioneer Period, 1815-1840.* 2 vols. Bloomington: The Indiana Historical Society and the Indiana University Press, 1950.

In 1787, Congress passed the Northwest Ordinance which established the "Territory Northwest of the Ohio River." From this region came five future states and a part of a sixth. These states, ranging from Ohio on the east to Minnesota on the west, were an important geographic segment of the new nation. The Old Northwest linked together the Great Lakes and the St. Lawrence river to the Mississippi and Ohio basins. With the age of canal building there soon arose a complete inland water route from New York to New Orleans that was the center of domestic commerce before the Civil War.

In writing his volumes on this key period and area in American history, R. Carlyle Buley professes to have three major purposes: first, to present a balanced account of the region's social and political history, emphasizing the "dry facts" but liberally spicing the story with the drama of the times; second, to introduce the reader to the rich

contemporary literature of the period; and third, to capture some of the attitudes, beliefs, struggles, and the way of life of the era. The author has succeeded admirably in this monumental task, producing a work that is interwoven with feeling for the people and region, and one that holds the reader spellbound to the end.

If the Old Northwest was created by an act of Congress in 1787, it was assured of a perpetual place of importance in American life by the Great Migration after the War of 1812. Recognizing this, Buley begins his study with a look at the area and its attractions for the settlers, skillfully tying in local events with the national scene. The Great Migration had been preceded by the movement into Kentucky, Tennessee, and Ohio during the 1790's, justifying statehood for each of these territories by 1803. Further settlement had been delayed, however, by the disputes with England over maritime rights and control of the Northwest Indian tribes. By 1815 the recently disbanded armies, prompted by unemployment, bad harvests in the East, and the slow recovery of shipping and industry from the effects of the War of 1812, began their movement westward to seek new fortunes. They were drawn by tales of wealth, new lands, furs, timber, fertile prairies, and hoped-for freedom for social and religious differences. As the promise of the West became widely known, the trickle of migration turned into a flood. It was not important that the West did not quite live up to the romantic paradise depicted by adventurers and speculators. A little hard work would bring the settler as close to Eden as a man could expect in this lifetime.

Buley examines the types of people who went into the Northwest—quiet French-Canadians, driving Yankees, and stout farmers from the South—and their cultural differences. While recognizing that the Southerners represented a majority of the early settlers, he sees a stronger Yankee influence in the early years of the territory's history than do most historians of the region. The author also describes the alarm in the Eastern states, which feared a loss of their able-bodied men to the new West. The East often worked to expose the falsehoods about the West's riches, but to no avail. The tide of settlement was not to be stopped, and the regular admission of new states, Ohio (1803), Indiana (1816), Illinois (1818), Michigan (1837), and Wisconsin (1848), showed the inexorable march westward.

In addition to the standard political history of each territory, Buley covers a whole list of interesting problems not usually found in most works. These include land policy, the day-to-day drudgery of pioneer life, disease and cures, the social setting, trade, travel and transportation, money and banking, education, religion, science, and reforms. Each topic is set off in its own chapter, making reference easy and allowing the curious to dabble at will in specialized areas and problems. Through it all, Buley keeps his quick-moving, readable style, revealing historical facts garnished with anecdotes one would normally expect from a novelist rather than a historian.

Of special interest to the reader are the numerous illustrations. Political developments are portrayed in several maps showing how each territory was established and modified, when Indian land claims were extinguished, and the admission of each territory to statehood. Buley's, *The Old Northwest,* is a classic work that will remain a standard of scholarship for the region for years to come. — *J.G.C.*

Additional Recommended Reading

Jacobs, Wilbur R. *Wilderness Politics and Indian Gifts: The Northern Colonial Frontier, 1748-1763.* Lincoln: University of Nebraska Press, 1950. Although treating a period preceding widescale settlement, the issues dealt with in this study had much influence on later settlement patterns.

Wade, Richard C. *The Urban Frontier: The Rise of Western Cities, 1790-1830.* Cambridge: Harvard University Press, 1959. The author seeks to demonstrate that an urban frontier existed alongside and interacted with the rural frontier in fashioning the American West.

Billington, Ray A. *Westward Expansion: A History of the American Frontier.* New York:

The Macmillan Co., 1967. The best synthetic, interpretive, and narrative account of the frontier.

Turner, Frederick Jackson. *Rise of the New West, 1819-1829. The American Nation* series. New York: Harper & Row Publishers, 1968. (Reprint of 1906 edition.) A classic study by the author of the hypothesis of the significance of the frontier in American history.

Philbrick, Francis S. *The Rise of the West, 1754-1830.* New York: Harper & Row Publishers, 1968. An anti-Turnerian interpretation which emphasizes legal institutions.

Mathews, Lois K. *The Expansion of New England: The Spread of New England Settlements and Institutions to the Mississippi River, 1620-1865.* New York: Russell and Russell Publishers, 1962. (Reprint of 1909 edition.) Describes the migration of New Englanders into the Middle West.

Clark, Thomas D. *The Rampaging Frontier.* Bloomington: Indiana University Press, 1964. A highly entertaining account of life on the early midwestern frontier.

BATTLE OF NEW ORLEANS

Type of event: Military: awakening of American nationalism
Time: January 8, 1815
Locale: New Orleans, Louisiana

Principal personages:

HENRY BATHURST (THIRD EARL BATHURST) (1762-1834), British Secretary for War and the Colonies 1812-1827

ADMIRAL SIR ALEXANDER FORRESTER INGLIS COCHRANE (1758-1832), Commander of the American Station of the Royal Navy and Naval Commander of the New Orleans expedition

MAJOR GENERAL ROBERT ROSS (1766-1814), appointed British Commander of the New Orleans expedition but killed at North Point, Maryland, in 1814 before assuming command

GENERAL JOHN KEANE (fl. 1815), temporary Commander of the British Army expeditionary force after Ross' death

MAJOR GENERAL SIR EDWARD MICHAEL PAKENHAM (1778-1815), brother-in-law of the Duke of Wellington who succeeded Ross as British Commander of the New Orleans expedition and who was killed in the Battle of New Orleans

MAJOR GENERAL ANDREW JACKSON (1767-1845), Commander of the U.S. Military District Number Seven (Louisiana, Mississippi Territory, and Tennessee)

COMMANDANT DANIEL T. PATTERSON (fl. 1815), U.S. Commander of the New Orleans Naval Station

Summary of Event

For more than two years Louisiana lay on the fringe of the Southern theater of the War of 1812. The campaigns were waged in Spanish Florida where Americans seized Mobile, and in the Mississippi Territory where frontiersmen fought Creek Indians. The British blockade brought commerce to a standstill at New Orleans, but before late 1814 the war did not otherwise threaten its polyglot population. Engaged in a vast struggle with Napoleon's France, Great Britain could barely spare enough troops to defend Canada against American attack, and the British War Ministry dismissed early proposals to capture New Orleans.

Napoleon's defeat at Leipzig in October, 1813, allowed the British to begin consideration of large-scale operations against the United States. When Napoleon's abdication in April, 1814, released substantial British forces from European commitments, preparations began in earnest to tighten the blockade of the United States, to raid the Atlantic Coast, and to invade northern New York from Canada. In July, the War Ministry decided to attack New Orleans and subsequently appointed Admiral Sir Alexander Forrester Inglis

533

Cochrane and Major General Robert Ross to command the expedition. The Secretary for War, Earl Bathurst (Henry Bathurst), explained the purposes of the invasion to Ross in September—to obtain command of the mouth of the Mississippi river and deprive Trans-Appalachian Americans of their link with the sea; and to occupy a valuable land possession whose restoration would improve the terms of peace for Great Britain, or whose cession by the United States could be exacted as the price of peace. Bathurst gave Cochrane and Ross discretion to strike at New Orleans directly from the Gulf of Mexico or overland from Mobile, and he instructed Ross to aid the Creoles if they desired to reattach themselves to Spain. At the time, Cochrane and Ross were raiding the Chesapeake Bay area, but New Orleans was their next target.

Cochrane believed that Indians, slaves, and pirates who sheltered at Barataria, an island in the swamps off New Orleans, would assist a Gulf Coast invasion directed against New Orleans. Operating under orders Cochrane issued before the War Ministry's decision, his subordinates occupied Spanish Pensacola in August and began to organize and arm Indians and escaped slaves. In early September they made overtures to the Baratarians and prepared to attack Mobile, but their efforts came to nothing.

Andrew Jackson was Major General of the Tennessee militia when he defeated the Creeks at Horseshoe Bend in March, 1814, and seriously weakened their ability to continue fighting. Two months later, Jackson was appointed Federal Commander of Military District Number Seven, which included the Mobile-New Orleans area, as well as the U.S. Army in the Southwest. Fully aware of British activities, he went south in August to strengthen Mobile's defenses, to sever remaining British and Spanish connections with the Indians, and to secure the coast against invasion. In mid-September his forces defeated the British attempt on Mobile, which had been made without the Baratarians, who showed no signs of coöperating. In early November, Jackson expelled the British and Indians from Pensacola.

Ross' death near Baltimore in September dealt British fortunes another blow. The ship carrying Major General Sir Edward Michael Pakenham, Ross' successor, was slow in crossing the Atlantic. As a result, he was not with Cochrane's mighty invasion fleet when it sailed from its Jamaica rendezvous into the Gulf of Mexico in late November nor when Cochrane's sailors overcame American gunboats at the mouth of Lake Borgne on December 14. Cochrane had decided to attack New Orleans from the Gulf of Mexico by sailing through Lake Borgne.

Jackson had arrived in New Orleans on December 1 and proceeded to block all invasion approaches, but through a subordinate's negligence, one approach was left open. On December 23, the vanguard of British troops landed, advanced along unprotected Bayou Bienvenue, and emerged from the swamps on the east bank of the Mississippi, less than ten miles below the city. Jackson responded quickly. That night he attacked the British camp, inflicting large casualties and throwing the invaders off balance. When Pakenham arrived on Christmas Day, he found his army in a *cul-de-sac.* On its right were cypress swamps; on its left were two American warships and the Mississippi river; and in front Jackson's small but growing army was constructing a mud and log breastwork on the narrow plain of Chalmette, barring the way to New Orleans.

Attempting to regain the advantage, the British destroyed one of Commandant Daniel T. Patterson's ships on December 27. But in the following days they suffered serious reverses: the Americans turned back a reconnaissance-in-force on December 28, 1814, and won an artillery duel on January 1, 1815, thwarting Pakenham's attempt to breach the breastwork. The only remaining alternative was a direct assault. Pakenham developed his plan: one large column would attack the American center at the edge of the swamp; a smaller column would assault the American right; and a third would support one of the other two according to developments; a small force would attack the weak American positions across the river; and the rest of his approximately ten thousand redcoats, some of whom were veterans of the Napoleonic Wars, would form the reserve.

At daybreak on Sunday, January 8, Pakenham gave the signal to advance. Waiting for the attack was a heterogeneous collection of about five thousand defenders—Louisiana Acadians, "Anglo-Saxons," Creoles, and free men of color: Baratarians, Choctaw Indians, and French *emigrés;* Mississippi, Kentucky, and Tennessee militia; and United States Marines, regulars, and sailors. Only portions of the line were directly engaged, but the terrific fire from their artillery, muskets, and rifles cut down Pakenham's troops as they advanced through the mist across the rain-soaked field. Pakenham was killed while desperately urging his men on. Shortly afterwards, his crippled army withdrew. The partially successful attack on the west bank came too late to affect the outcome of the great assault. American casualties totaled seventy-one (of whom only about a dozen were killed), while British losses were 2,057.

Because of the apparent impregnability of Jackson's lines and a shortage of supplies, the British leaders decided to retreat. By late January, the troops were aboard their transports and the fleet sailed away to attack Fort Bowyer at Mobile. After its fall, official news of the ratification of the Treaty of Ghent reached the armies. In mid-March the fleet returned to England. In New Orleans Jackson rescinded martial law. The Battle of New Orleans, the last major battle in the War of 1812, constituted a British tragedy inasmuch as it had taken place two weeks after the Treaty of Ghent brought the war to a close. Despite the fact that the bloody engagement did not play a role in the outcome of the war, however, the Battle of New Orleans made Andrew Jackson a national hero.

Pertinent Literature

Bassett, John S. *The Life of Andrew Jackson.* New ed. New York: The Macmillan Company, 1925.

The story of the Battle of New Orleans is also the story of Andrew Jack-son. Coming after years of dismal military failure, the spectacular victory he helped to achieve contributed to the emergence of nationalistic feelings and thrust Jackson into national prominence. One of the fullest and most scholarly accounts of the Creek and New Orleans campaigns is contained in John S. Bassett's biography. First published in 1911, it is still regarded as the most judicious and, on the whole, the best biography of "Old Hickory." Jackson emerges as a capable, strong-minded, but vindictive man, who often blamed others for his own errors and who immoderately applied martial law, creating a minor constitutional crisis over civil as against military authority. Bassett notes that Jackson made some tactical mistakes, especially in neglecting the defenses of the west bank. But he acknowledges Jackson's overall military ability and comes to his defense concerning one of the most controversial aspects of his generalship in the campaign.

Contemporary critics maintained that Jackson was irresponsibly slow in seeing that New Orleans was the real point of danger on the Gulf Coast. Henry Adams repeated this theme in his influential and scholarly *History of the United States during the Administrations of Jefferson and Madison* (1889-1891). Adams argued that Jack-

son disregarded warnings of a direct attack on New Orleans in September and October, 1814, and wasted his time at Mobile preparing to seize Pensacola in order to strike at the Spanish and Indians. Then, before going to inspect the defenses of New Orleans, he foolishly stationed some of his meager forces at Mobile, where he mistakenly thought the British would land. Jackson arrived in New Orleans with barely enough time to begin preparing its defenses, and even then the British landing took him by surprise. Had it not been for Secretary of War James Monroe's earlier efforts in sending additional troops and arms to the city, Adams implies, Jackson would not have been able to defeat Pakenham. Qualifying Adams's argument, Bassett makes the following points: no one was certain where the British would land; available information indicated that Mobile was the most likely place; and while at Mobile, Jackson ordered defensive measures to be taken at New Orleans. Jackson's victory at Pensacola, moreover, finally undermined Indian confidence in the British and Spanish, and boosted the morale of American forces and of Creoles in Louisiana.

Brown, Wilburt S. *The Amphibious Campaign for West Florida and Louisiana, 1814-1815: A Critical Review of Strategy and Tactics at New Orleans.* University, Alabama: University of Alabama Press, 1969.

Wilburt S. Brown's book is one of the few devoted exclusively to the Battle of New Orleans and events directly leading up to it. It is the first book about the battle that is based on both printed and manuscript sources, and Brown is the first author to go beyond the usual narrative style to provide a

detailed, informed analysis of strategy and tactics. Not all of his conclusions will find unanimous acceptance, but his arguments are persuasive regarding the crucial points of disagreement—for example, the battle's historical significance, British aims, Cochrane's reasons for attacking New Orleans directly from the Gulf of Mexico, and the generalship of Jackson and Pakenham.

The battle occurred after British and American envoys agreed upon the Treaty of Ghent, which provided for an end to hostilities and a territorial *status quo ante bellum*. Historians, therefore, usually minimize its importance in deciding the conflicting territorial claims and aims of Great Britain, Spain, and the United States in the Old Southwest. Fred L. Engelman, in *The Peace of Christmas Eve* (1962), denies that the British ministry still entertained in January, 1815, aspirations for conquest at New Orleans to create a barrier to America's expansion. The most they hoped for was a victory to boost morale and to use as a bludgeon in case the Americans were slow or unwilling to ratify the treaty. In *Castlereagh and Adams* (1964), Bradford Perkins denies that the British ever seriously thought of conquest; Bathurst only toyed with the idea of returning Louisiana to Spain. The attack was merely a raid for burning and booty.

Brown maintains, on the contrary, that documentary sources provide strong evidence that it was British strategy and policy to capture and hold New Orleans. He adds that large reinforcements were ordered to Pakenham in January, 1815, after the envoys at Ghent signed the treaty and before the governments exchanged ratifications, indicating that the ministry still aimed for conquest in 1815. *Status quo ante bellum* need not have applied to New Orleans, for neither Great Britain nor Spain recognized the legality of the Louisiana Purchase; it is instructive, Brown notes, that Americans kept Mobile in spite of the treaty. Brown dis-

misses the oft-repeated charge that the decision to attack New Orleans was a result of Cochrane's advice, and that his advice was based on a lust for prize money. He argues that the War Ministry itself planned the campaign in the winter of 1814, and that Cochrane's subsequent advice on the subject was based more on strategic considerations than on the lure of booty. In "British Command Decisions," *Louisiana History*, Vol. VI (1965), John K. Mahon reveals that the War Ministry decided to attack New Orleans in July, 1814, not in the winter; but his findings, nevertheless, support Brown's contention that the decision was made independently of Cochrane's advice which he offered on details of the strategy, that is, on how best to approach the city.

Brown admits that Jackson was fortunate that the British did not attack New Orleans sooner, but facing the conundrum of where to concentrate his meager forces to meet a landing somewhere along the coast, he was correct, Brown holds, in fortifying Mobile and attacking Pensacola. Cochrane actually considered attacking New Orleans through Mobile, but a combination of factors led him to choose the Lake Borgne approach: shortage of provisions; lack of shallow-draft boats to navigate Gulf Coast waters between Mobile and New Orleans; Jackson's defeat of the Creeks and defense of Mobile; and his probable belief, in November that, since Jackson was at Pensacola, New Orleans was weakly defended. Ironically, the open Bayou Bienvenue route became a trap, but Pakenham, according to Brown, did everything a resourceful commander could do in such a predicament. Altogether, American luck and skill com-

bined to produce a victory that had significance for American nationalism, for
Jackson's political career, and for the

future of Florida and the West. —
J.K.

Additional Recommended Reading

Brooks, Charles B. *The Siege of New Orleans.* Seattle: University of Washington Press, 1961. Relying on printed sources only, Brooks offers a detailed and detached account of the campaign in which he avoids analysis and lets the events speak for themselves.

Fortescue, John W. *A History of the British Army, 1813-1815.* Vol. X. London: Macmillan & Company, 1920. Fortescue provides one of the fullest accounts of the British in the campaign with a pro-army, anti-navy bias, repeating Wellington's charges that Cochrane advocated the project against New Orleans for the purpose of plunder and then led the army through Lake Borgne into a trap.

De Grummond, Jane L. *The Baratarians and the Battle of New Orleans.* Baton Rouge: Louisiana State University Press, 1961. Professor De Grummond explains that Jackson reluctantly accepted the aid of Jean Lafitte's "hellish banditti" because he needed their cannon, powder, and ammunition, but she underrates Lafitte's self-interested motives in offering his services. On the battle, she takes the position that artillery and ordinary muskets played a more important role in the victory than the celebrated "Kentucky rifles."

James, Marquis. *Andrew Jackson: The Border Captain.* Indianapolis: Bobbs-Merrill, 1933. This first volume of James's two-volume biography of Jackson is as well-researched as Bassett's but is more favorable to the Old Hero, and many readers prefer his colorful, narrative style to Bassett's straightforward approach.

McConnell, Roland C. *Negro Troops of Antebellum Louisiana: A History of the Battalion of Free Men of Color.* Baton Rouge: Louisiana State University Press, 1968. McConnell's slim volume is the fullest and best documented history of this unique militia organization from its beginnings in 1729 to its official demise in 1834. Most of the book is devoted to the role of free men of color in the Battle of New Orleans.

538

CHARTERING OF THE SECOND BANK OF THE UNITED STATES

Type of event: Economic: evolution of a central banking system in the United States
Time: April, 1816
Locale: Washington, D.C., and Philadelphia

Principal personages:

JAMES MADISON (1751-1836), fourth President of the United States 1809-1817

ALBERT GALLATIN (1761-1849), Secretary of the Treasury 1801-1814

ALEXANDER JAMES DALLAS (1759-1817), Secretary of the Treasury 1814-1816

JOHN RANDOLPH (1773-1833), Congressman from Virginia

JOHN CALDWELL CALHOUN (1782-1850), Congressman from South Carolina

DANIEL WEBSTER (1782-1852), Congressman from Massachusetts

WILLIAM JONES (1760-1831), Secretary of the Navy 1813-1814, and first president of the Second Bank of the United States

LANGDON CHEVES (1776-1857), Speaker of the House of Representatives and second president of the Second Bank of the United States

NICHOLAS BIDDLE (1786-1844), director and third president of the Second Bank of the United States

STEPHEN GIRARD (1750-1831), powerful Philadelphia merchant banker and largest subscriber to the Second Bank of the United States

JOHN JACOB ASTOR (1763-1848), New York merchant who coöperated with Girard to press for the chartering of the Second Bank of the United States

JOHN MARSHALL (1755-1835), Chief Justice of the United States Supreme Court 1801-1835

Summary of Event

In April, 1816, James Madison, fourth President of the United States, signed a bill authorizing the establishment of the Second Bank of the United States. In January, 1817, the bank commenced operations in Philadelphia in the same building that had housed the First Bank of the United States.

The First Bank of the United States had failed to gain recharter in 1812 after a productive and efficient existence of twenty years. The creation of Alexander Hamilton, first Secretary of the Treasury from 1789 to 1795, it had served its purpose well under both the Federalist and the Republican Parties.

Although Thomas Jefferson, third President of the United States, had opposed the original charter in 1790, the bank had become a necessary adjunct to government by the time he assumed power in 1801. Albert Gallatin, Secretary of the Treasury from 1801 to 1814 under both Jefferson and Madison, was intelligent enough to realize that the bank was valuable to the government and was also useful as a stabilizing force in the economy. By opening new branches in various parts of the country, he extended the bank's operations.

In spite of the success of the bank in keeping currency stable, in meeting government expenses, and in preventing the drain of specie from the country, opposition was strong enough in 1812 to prevent recharter. The bank met opposition from several quarters. Republicans of strict constructionist views argued, as Jefferson had stated originally, that the bank was unconstitutional. Many of these individuals, such as John Randolph of Virginia and Henry Clay of Kentucky, feared the concentration of financial power in such a centralized institution. Others opposed recharter because of the restraints exercised by the bank on state banks. Another adverse criticism pointed to the large number of foreigners who owned stock in the bank. This may have been the most generally expressed criticism directed at the bank. Moreover, there were those, such as Samuel and Robert Smith of Baltimore, who sought to use the issue to drive Albert Gallatin from office and to embarrass the Madison Administration.

These forces successfully combined against the bank. In a critical Senate vote, Vice-President George Clinton broke a 17-17 tie on recharter with a negative vote. A critical factor in the proceedings was the failure of the President himself to enter the struggle on behalf of the bank. Madison's personal intervention would probably have broken the back of the opposition, particularly that faction which was conducting a vendetta against Gallatin.

The bank was dead. The United States soon found itself at war with Great Britain and in serious financial difficulties. During the four years following 1812, significant sentiment arose in favor of the creation of a second national bank. By 1816, with peace reëstablished, debate on the new bank had reached the critical point. Debate had in fact begun in 1814 and a bank bill had passed Congress. But President Madison had vetoed it, not because he doubted its constitutionality but because he opposed the charter provisions.

The proposed bank gained many proponents, such as Clay and John C. Calhoun, who had opposed or been lukewarm concerning recharter of the First Bank of the United States. Calhoun brought in a bill in January, 1816, and in the resulting debate it became apparent that the original advocates of a national bank, the Federalists, opposed the bill. The Republicans, originally opposed, came out in its favor. Daniel Webster led the Federalist attack while John Randolph spearheaded the opposition of the strict-constructionist Republicans. In the decisive vote, the House of Representatives passed the bill in March by a vote of 80-71. It passed the Senate in April after a spirited debate in which Rufus King of New York directed the campaign against the charter.

The Second Bank of the United States resembled the first institution in its functions although its capitalization, at thirty-five million dollars, was larger, and it was required to pay the government $1,500,000 for its franchise. It provided a depository for federal funds in every state where a branch was opened. Between 1817 and 1828, twenty-eight branches were established in the major commercial cities of the nation. It was through these branches that the Second Bank of the United States was enabled to exercise efficient control over the rapidly increasing number of state banks. The bank transferred federal funds from place to place and paid public creditors without charge to the government. The bank was authorized to issue notes which were declared to be receivable at par in all payments to the United States. In this way, the notes of the second bank acted as a national currency. The bank was also authorized to lend money, and to buy or sell bills of exchange.

The Second Bank of the United States under its first president, William Jones, ran into trouble when the nation went through a postwar boom followed by the Panic of 1819 and the subsequent depression. It is generally agreed that Jones was inefficient, and consequently the policies of the bank, instead of acting as a check on the inflationary trends apparent in 1817 and 1818, contributed to them. When the economy showed signs of strain in 1818, the bank undertook a severe policy of credit and monetary restriction. The curtailment of business aggravated the monetary stringency already felt in the economy, especially in the West and the South. Dissatisfaction with the

bank grew in those regions and reached a peak during the period from 1819 to 1823. In the meantime Jones was discredited and replaced in 1822 by Langdon Cheves of South Carolina.

Cheves probably saved the bank from disaster. Under Jones there had been not only mismanagement but also fraud. The bank had lost an estimated three million dollars. But more significantly, popular hostility was rampant. In 1817, Maryland placed a tax upon the branch office in Baltimore. In 1819, after several other states had followed the example of Maryland, Ohio and Kentucky imposed taxes of sixty thousand dollars and fifty thousand dollars, respectively, on the branches in those states. The constitutionality of these prohibitive taxes was denied in *McCulloch* v. *Maryland* and in *Osborn* v. *the Bank of the United States.*

Although these decisions saved the bank constitutionally, more was required. Cheves employed conservative banking practices and restored the institution to a sound condition. But his restrictive policies did not endear the bank to expansionist elements in society. The third president, Nicholas Biddle of Pennsylvania, took office in 1823. In pursuing a policy of measured growth, in expanding credit, and in securing a large circulation of bank notes, Biddle contributed to the revitalization of the economy. But it was Cheves who placed the bank in the financial position which made expansion and growth possible. In spite of the achievements of Cheves and Biddle, opposition and antagonism to the bank smoldered in various parts of the country. Within a decade of 1823, the bank was engaged in a fight for survival.

Chartering of the Second Bank of the United States

Pertinent Literature

Govan, Thomas P. *Nicholas Biddle: Nationalist and Public Banker, 1786-1844.* Chicago: University of Chicago Press, 1959.

Nicholas Biddle of Philadelphia became the third president of the Second Bank of the United States in January, 1823, after having served the four previous years as a government director of the institution. The bank, under the presidency of Cheves, had been struggling along with the rest of the country to pull out of the depression which struck in 1819-1820. Biddle served as president of the Second Bank of the United States and its successor in 1836, the United States Bank of Pennsylvania, until March, 1839. He resigned a few months before a great economic disaster struck the nation.

The reader of Biddle's biography by Thomas Payne Govan is forewarned in the preface of the author's pro-Biddle orientation. Govan admits his bias but justifies it by asserting that the sources allow for no other construction. Govan wishes to set the record straight and does so convincingly, except at one point. In the closing rounds of Biddle's struggle with President Jackson, it does appear that the banker went too far in pursuing his policy of contraction, and that Biddle did materially contribute to the monetary stringency which plagued the country in 1835 and 1836. The fact that the Jackson Administration also contributed to this condition does not make Biddle's action any more justifiable. But it is true that Biddle should not be judged by this act alone. He had at that time been president of the bank for thirteen years. Certainly those years form part of his record.

Biddle, according to Govan, took control of a bank whose national reputation had been damaged by its shortsighted, overly conservative and, at the same time, immoderately speculative policies between 1817 and 1823. The bank in 1823 was not exerting leadership in the American economy. It was not serving that purpose which its sponsors had envisioned. The South and the West were particularly antagonistic to the restrictive lending policies of the bank. Money was scarce, debtors were under pressure from creditors, interest rates were high, and the bank was reluctant to lend. Biddle himself agreed with the substance of these charges against the bank. He thought that the depression had been prolonged as a result of the bank's restrictive policies. He set himself to change the bank's policies.

By 1825, conditions had improved materially; Biddle's policies greatly increased credit facilities for the country's business, which in turn created more business and increased productivity. Prices remained stable while profits increased. The nation, once the bank began to issue its currency, again had a national medium of exchange.

Biddle also reëstablished an amicable relationship with the state banks. While the national bank did restrain the previously extravagant lending and note-issuing policies of local banks, the Bank of the United States also acted as a partner of local institutions in providing local credit. In addition, the federal bank was able to protect the national economy from overseas pressures which frequently caused a great drain of specie from the country. Govan concludes that Biddle did make the bank a national institution.

In the last analysis, the nationalism exhibited in Biddle's policies is the true measure of the man. He was responsible to the stockholders of this semipublic bank. But he refused to allow himself to take measures "the sole purpose of which was to increase the profits of the Bank." He was aware at all times of the responsibility of the bank to the general public. The power of the institution which he directed was great. Biddle used it with discretion and always with the aim of strengthening the national economy. It may be true that at one moment in his career, and while under increasing pressure from the Jackson Administration, Biddle lost sight of the national interest in his passion to save the bank, but his prior record should not be ignored. Least of all should he be set up as a whipping boy by partisans of Jackson.

Redlich, Fritz. *The Molding of American Banking: Men and Ideas. History of American Economy* series. Vol. 2, pt. 1. New York: Johnson Reprint Corporation, 1968.

Students of American history can point to a few seminal thinkers who have pioneered in charting the paths to historical knowledge and truth. In this group would be included explorers, such as Frederick Jackson Turner, Carl Becker, and Charles Beard. These men opened up areas of research by asking new questions and by questioning the assumed truths in historical interpretation. While some might consider it presumptuous to include Fritz Redlich in this honored group, he approaches it as closely as any American historian in recent years.

Redlich is concerned with the entrepreneur and his role in the economic development of the United States. He wishes to understand how the business leaders of the nation contributed to economic growth and who they were. The author maintains that human beings rather than anonymous forces determine the course of history; that ideas are the "driving forces back of the action of history-making men." In this volume, which concentrates on banking, Redlich also concerns himself with the impact of public men—politicians, statesmen, and similar people—on the evolution of banking in the United States, and with thinkers, the generators of ideas.

Redlich seeks to demonstrate continuity in the development of banking practices in the country. American banking in the period before 1815 was dominated by a banking theory which was based on private credit or on mercantile credit. The Bank of North America, organized in 1781, was the first mercantile bank in the country and the pioneer in the establishment of an American banking system. This institution and others founded in the East were generally possessed of local banking monopolies.

During the period from 1815 to 1840, while the old banking principles were still followed, banks undertook novel roles, and in their daily transactions they greatly expanded the types of credit instruments circulated by banks. As in earlier periods, banks were still considered to be instruments for advancing the public welfare rather than as institutions serving narrow business and commercial functions. Banks, however, were at a crossroads at this time, and more and more they came to serve strictly commercial purposes; banks were established not because capital was seeking investment but because men without capital were seeking loans. In his descriptive analysis of this trend, Redlich investigates the methods and philosophies of the men who owned and operated the banks.

In an interesting discussion, Redlich studies the fall of the First Bank of the United States and the career of its successor. He believes that the First Bank of the United States fell because it had put itself "into the commanding position of a rudimentary central bank." Men opposed to central banking led the fight against it. The Second Bank of the United States came into existence through the concerted efforts of a few businessmen—including John

Jacob Astor of New York and Stephen Girard of Philadelphia—and statesmen-politicians, such as Alexander James Dallas, Secretary of the Treasury from 1814 to 1816, and John C. Calhoun, the Congressman from South Carolina. Redlich then follows the Second Bank of the United States through its first troubled years to the administration of Biddle. He evaluates Biddle's various roles as president of a bank functioning not only as a commercial bank but also as a central bank tied to the government. Redlich's discussion of the interaction of Biddle's spheres of responsibility is one of the most rewarding sections of this study.

The reader learns why it was that the nation which nurtured central banking to relative sophistication proceeded on two different occasions to destroy its handiwork. To Redlich this represented the triumph of laissez-faire in America. — *J.G.C.*

Additional Recommended Reading

Dewey, Davis R. *State Banking Before the Civil War.* Washington, D.C.: Government Printing Office, 1910.

Dewey, Davis R. and John T. Holdsworth. *The First and Second Banks of the United States.* Washington, D.C.: Government Printing Office, 1910. These two studies, although outdated, place in perspective the interrelationships of state and central banking before 1861.

Jenks, Leland H. *The Migration of British Capital to 1875.* New York: Alfred A. Knopf, Inc., 1938. Great Britain was the major source of capital in the nineteenth century, and Jenks traces its export around the world, including the United States.

Hartz, Louis. *Economic Policy and Democratic Thought: Pennsylvania, 1776-1860.* Cambridge: Harvard University Press, 1948. Hartz studies economic policy, its implementation, and its responses to political pressures and needs.

Dangerfield, George. *The Era of Good Feelings.* New York: Harcourt, Brace & World, Inc., 1952. This volume deals primarily with the political stresses and strains of the period following the War of 1812.

Smith, Walter B. *Economic Aspects of the Second Bank of the United States.* Cambridge: Harvard University Press, 1953. Smith investigates the relation of the bank to the general economic development of the United States and critically appraises the charges leveled against the bank by its opponents.

Dorfman, Joseph. *The Economic Mind in American Civilization, 1606-1933.* 5 vols. New York: Augustus M. Kelley, Publishers, 1946, republished 1966. This work is the major treatment of the history of economic thought in America, and it is especially useful for the period in which the First and Second Banks of the United States operated.

CONSTRUCTION OF THE ERIE CANAL

Type of event: Economic: need for a direct transportation link between the Great Lakes and the Atlantic Ocean
Time: 1817-1825
Locale: New York

Principal personages:

JAMES MADISON (1751-1836), fourth President of the United States 1809-1817

DEWITT CLINTON (1769-1828), Governor of New York 1817-1821 and 1825-1828

ALBERT GALLATIN (1761-1849), Secretary of the Treasury 1801-1814

JOHN CALDWELL CALHOUN (1782-1850), Congressman from South Carolina

OLIVER EVANS (1755-1819), inventor who developed a high-pressure steam engine

Summary of Event

During the antebellum period, coastal cities in the United States engaged in strenuous competition for the commercial wealth of the expanding West. But before progress could be made in weaving the sections together into a single economic unit, difficulties had to be overcome concerning the accessibility of markets. In 1815, the Old Northwest was without convenient access to the markets of the East coast. Farmers and merchants were forced to send their products to market by way of the Ohio and Mississippi rivers to New Orleans and from there to the East Coast. Farmers in the area of Pittsburgh found it cheaper to ship their goods over this long circuitous route than to send them overland to Philadelphia or New York, a much shorter distance. Although the federal government had completed the National Road from Cumberland, Maryland, to Wheeling, Virginia, by 1817, it was uneconomical to ship bulky farm produce over this route.

The first major effort to open an economic commercial connection between the West and the East Coasts occurred with the construction between 1817 and 1825 of the 363-mile-long Erie Canal connecting Albany on the Hudson river with Buffalo on Lake Erie. Skeptics at first called the canal "Clinton's Ditch" after its most consistent advocate, Governor DeWitt Clinton of New York. But skepticism soon disappeared when the canal had a direct and cumulative effect on the nation in general and the Northwest in particular throughout the entire antebellum period.

During the first decade of its operation, the Erie Canal played a large part in the development of the south shore of Lake Erie. Areas in the northwestern part of New York, now provided with access to markets in New York

546

City, increased in population and productivity. The Genesee River Valley soon developed into a great grain-producing region. The Erie Canal supplied an all-water route to the northern portions of the Old Northwest and accelerated the populating of these regions. This growing population caused an expansion of production to meet the needs of the immigrants. They, in turn, were able to increase the amount of farm produce available for the East. Their presence also augmented the demand for the importation of eastern manufactured goods. The waterway reduced considerably the cost of freighting goods both eastward and westward.

Perhaps the most important of all the consequences of the opening of "Clinton's Wonder" was the stimulus it gave to other regions, both in the East and in the West, to emulate the success of New York by building canals of their own. The state of Ohio in the 1830's, and Indiana and Illinois somewhat later, undertook the construction of canals which joined interior areas to the Great Lakes-Erie Canal System. Ohio's canals connected Cincinnati and two other Ohio river points with Toledo and Cleveland. In Indiana, the Wabash and Erie Canal connected Toledo with Terre Haute, while in Illinois, the Illinois and Michigan Canal connected Chicago with the lush lands along the upper and middle Illinois river. As a consequence of the opening of these waterways, interior farms were opened up and production rose, for farmers now had new routes to market.

The effects of the Erie Canal in the East were equally momentous. The canal solidified the position of New York City as the greatest emporium in the nation. Other Eastern cities, such as Philadelphia and Baltimore, could not afford to sit while New York monopolized the Western trade. If they were to survive as commercial centers, they would have to develop their own connections with the West. Thus, Pennsylvania constructed a system of canals and inclined planes between Philadelphia and Pittsburgh, and followed up with the Pennsylvania Railroad. Baltimore undertook two major improvements with construction of the Baltimore and Ohio Railroad, and the Chesapeake and Ohio Canal. Farther to the north, Boston decided on a railroad and constructed one across to Albany, hoping thereby to intercept some of the Western trade.

This vigorous and deadly—for not all could be successful—competition was not without its effects on the established Mississippi river system. Cities functioning as parts of the lake system competed not only with one another but with cities which formed part of the river system. Thus, Toledo and Cleveland were engaged in commercial warfare with Cincinnati and Louisville; St. Louis, especially in the 1850's, felt the impact of the Illinois and Michigan Canal in its struggle with Chicago; and downstream, New Orleans was sensitive to any events which impinged on the trade of St. Louis, Cincinnati, and Louisville.

The railroads added a new dimension to the struggle, and their development overlapped and went beyond the era of the great canals. By the 1850's, the competition initiated by the construction of the Erie Canal had entered a new phase. A struggle involving three transportation systems and a host of cities and towns had evolved. Cities which had pinned their hopes on the canals were bypassed by the railroad. Cities bid with one another, mortgaging their future for the privilege of becoming rail hubs. Smaller towns with exalted visions of their economic potential rose and then fell, succumbing to the economic power of more dynamic and luckier competitors. The intensity of the struggle demonstrated the economic viability of the nation, and the pattern which emerged was national.

Pertinent Literature

Shaw, Ronald E. *Erie Water West: A History of the Erie Canal, 1792-1854.* Lexington: University of Kentucky Press, 1966.

There has long been a great need for a serious study of the Erie Canal, considered by many Americans at the time of its operation to be the "Eighth Wonder of the World." This volume fulfills that need as the author investigates the formulation of the idea for such a canal, its political implications, the problems of financing and constructing it, its impact on commerce and travel, and its social and cultural significance. As the folk song "Fifteen Miles on the Erie Canal" implies, there was more to the Erie Canal than merely its economic function. The canal, as did the railroad a little later, took an honored position in the folklore of the nation.

Although it is to be regretted that the author cuts off his study in 1854, when the railroads and the canals really began their period of vigorous competition, the positive features of the study more than compensate for this. Probably the most significant portions of the book deal with the genesis of the canal in the minds of far-sighted men. Governor DeWitt Clinton, who had his triumph in November, 1825, when the wedding of the waters of Lake Erie and the Atlantic Ocean was symbolized by the pouring of a keg of Lake Erie water into the Atlantic, was one of a number of dreamers. Clinton, who has been mythologized for his role in pressing for the canal, is taken to task by Shaw for being "wanting in the arts of political leadership."

The canal did become and remained to some extent involved in a good deal of political maneuvering. Buffalo fought with Black Rock for the privilege of being both the termination point and the center of transfer. Towns not located along the projected line of the main canal withheld their support in the hope of gaining subsidiary canals. Engineering difficulties stimulated political controversy. Clinton's faction fought with opponents for control of the Canal Board. The anti-Clintonians, known as Bucktails, were primarily concerned with the defeat of Clinton. Since the progress of the canal was bound up with Clinton's popularity, the Bucktails sought to secure some of the credit for the canal, while the Clintonians viewed their opponents as obstructionists. The battle cry of the Clintonians was "The Canal is in Danger."

But the canal was completed, perhaps in spite of the politicians, and did its work. The 363-mile waterway became a symbol of national accomplishment. Indeed, its construction was a marvelous feat of engineering; one need only consider, for example, the skill that went into the building of the eight-hundred-foot aqueduct which carried the canal across the Genesee river at Rochester. Towns sprouted up along its length. Men believed that the canal proved the American institutions were somehow better than those in Europe. If to such reactions and effects the economic consequences are added— the stimulation of the New York econ- omy, the rapid rise of New York City, the emulation of this effort by other cities and states both to the East and to the West, the binding together of the East and Old Northwest—then one can appreciate that the feeling of triumph in Clinton's breast as he poured that keg of inland water was not unjustified.

Taylor, George R. *The Transportation Revolution, 1815-1860.* Vol. IV: *The Economic History of the United States.* New York: Holt, Rinehart, and Winston, Inc., 1951.

This volume deals with the impact which developments in transportation had on the growth of the American economy. It is not narrowly focused on the construction and financing of roads, canals, and railroads, although these activities are dealt with adequately, but seeks to relate transportation improvements to the transformation of the economy between 1815 and 1860. Although the history of agriculture is separately dealt with by Paul W. Gates in the third volume of this series, Taylor does not ignore the relationship between transportation and agriculture, and he includes a useful bibliography.

Transportation networks are constructed in order to move people and goods. As the population increases and spreads into new areas and as productivity increases, need is expressed for the enlargement and modernization of transportation facilities. In the Eastern states from New England to Virginia the result of such demands was the construction of a whole series of canals designed to improve transportation between the up-country and tidewater. An example was the Susquehanna and Tidewater Canal which was opened to traffic in 1840 and was sponsored by Baltimore interests in order to draw the rich trade of central Pennsylvania from Philadelphia. The most famous canal, the Erie, was designed to link the Atlantic states with the Ohio River Valley. The less successful Chesapeake and Ohio had the same purpose, as did the Pennsylvania system.

In the West, the canals built in Ohio, Indiana, and Illinois were constructed in order to link the interior of those states with the river and lake networks leading to the major markets. On both the Great Lakes and Mississippi river systems, the steamboat became increasingly important during the decades following the War of 1812. Taylor includes a chapter on the impact of the steamboats on the rivers and lakes of the West and South and the bays of the East.

Taylor's study focuses upon the great effect of the railroad, and his survey deals with all its functions, as well as with such problems as obtaining state charters, selling railroad stock, private and state aid, and federal subsidies. He attempts to measure the impact of the railroad, and compares its functions with those of other modes of transportation. He is particularly concerned with the competition between railway and waterway.

Taylor is concerned not only with

internal transportation but also with the foreign trade of the United States. In discussing the advances made in ocean transportation, the author describes those factors which affected the growth of the merchant marine and which retarded the widescale adoption of the ocean-going steamship.

Much of the book centers around the great changes in manufacturing that occurred during this period. The United States took its first steps toward industrialization in the antebellum period. Growth of society, improvements in transportation, general technological advances, and relative peace made this industrialization possible. Industry also had its impact on society, on transportation, and on technology. Taylor discusses many of these points. One normally thinks of the organized labor movement as a relatively recent development. But, in fact, the first hints of industrialization called forth responses from workingmen and there was a fairly vigorous labor movement between 1835 and 1860. Similarly, ur-

banization was both cause and effect of industrialization.

Taylor maintains that a national economy developed between 1815 and 1860. Domestic commerce and industry had grown rapidly along with foreign commerce. Capital accumulation was notable. The agricultural sector had been brought within the national framework. Railroads made possible the manufacture of products in one section and their profitable sale at reasonable prices in another section. Local markets were invaded and disrupted. Great cities like New York commanded enormous monetary wealth and power.

In this expansive period of the nation's growth, the basis of the prosperity was internal. Trade between the East and West, North and South, urban and rural dwellers, farmers and manufacturers contributed to the building of a vigorous domestic economy to such a degree that foreign markets mattered little. Ease of transportation was the root cause. — *J.G.C.*

Additional Recommended Reading

McClelland, C. P. and C. C. Huntington. *History of the Ohio Canals: Their Construction, Cost, Use, and Partial Abandonment.* Columbus: Ohio State Archeological and Historical Society, 1905. A useful but outdated narrative of canal development at the state level.

Esarey, Logan. *Internal Improvements in Early Indiana. Indiana Historical Society Publications.* Vol. V. Indianapolis: Indiana Historical Society, 1912. Traces the effort of a frontier state to modernize its transportation network.

Putnam, James W. *The Illinois and Michigan Canal. A Study in Economic History.* Vol. X: *Chicago Historical Society Collections.* Chicago: Chicago Historical Society, 1918. Analyzes the impact of this significant canal on the region that it served.

Albion, Robert G. *The Rise of New York Port, 1815-1860.* New York: Charles Scribner's Sons, 1939. Evaluates the factors, including the Erie Canal, that led to the commercial leadership of New York City.

Meyer, Balthaser H. *History of Transportation in the United States Before 1860.* Washington, D.C.: Peter Smith Publishers, Inc., reprinted 1948. A reference work containing facts and information regarding all the major road, canal, and railroad developments in the nation.

Construction of the Erie Canal

Aitken, Hugh G. *The Welland Canal Company: A Study in Canadian Enterprise.* Cambridge: Harvard University Press, 1954. An exceptionally able study of Canada's efforts to develop the St. Lawrence system into a major route to market.

Goodrich, Carter. *Government Promotion of Canals and Railroads, 1800-1890.* New York: Columbia University Press, 1960. A study of federal, state, and local government aid and encouragement of internal improvements, including an enlightening analysis of state efforts.

Gates, Paul W. *The Farmer's Age: Agriculture, 1815-1860.* Vol. III: *The Economic History of the United States.* New York: Holt, Rinehart and Winston, Inc., 1960. A skillful synthesis of agricultural history with attention to the transportation needs of America's farmers.

NEGOTIATION OF THE MISSOURI COMPROMISE

Type of event: Political: admission of new states to the Union
Time: February, 1819-February, 1821
Locale: Washington, D.C.

Principal personages:

JAMES MONROE (1758-1831), fifth President of the United States 1817-1825

JAMES TALLMADGE, JR. (1778-1853), Congressman from New York

JOHN W. TAYLOR (fl. 1819), Senator from New York

RUFUS KING (1755-1827), Senator from New York

JESSE B. THOMAS (1777-1853), Congressman from Illinois

NATHANIEL MACON (1758-1837), Senator from North Carolina

THEODORE DWIGHT (1764-1846), editor of the *New York Daily Advertiser*

Summary of Event

Missouri applied for admission as a slave state early in 1819. Its application was not acceded to until February, 1821. During the interim, the nature of slavery and the expansion of slavery into the territories became the subject for a full-fledged congressional debate. It was the first time in the history of the young nation that the institution of slavery advanced to the center of the political stage.

In February, 1819, Representative James Tallmadge of New York offered an amendment to the Missouri Enabling Bill which prohibited the further introduction of slavery into the territory and provided for the gradual emancipation of slaves already in Missouri. The amendment was passed by the House of Representatives in a sectional vote and was sent to the Senate where the amendment was eliminated. The House refused its assent to the Senate action, and this act was virtually

the last of the Fifteenth Congress. The slavery issue awaited the organization of the Sixteenth Congress. It was that body which hammered out the Missouri Compromise.

The Tallmadge Amendment stirred up a hornets' nest in the South. That section was just entering upon an era of great expansion westward. The plantation system advanced to and beyond the Mississippi river. The future held out a bright promise for those engaged in the production of cotton and other Southern staples. The Tallmadge Amendment threatened this future. It also challenged the doctrine of states' rights which had become accepted doctrine throughout much of the South. Southerners also believed that Tallmadge and his supporters were leveling a moral attack on the Southern way of life. Many Southerners believed that the amendment masked an insidious plot by commercial capitalists in the

552

North to transform the South into the colony of the North. The South, then believed that it had ample reasons for opposing the amendment.

The Sixteenth Congress debated all aspects of the question from December, 1819, through March, 1820. The significance of the debate lay not so much in the fact that slavery was opposed by some in the North, but in the stance taken by Southerners in defending slavery. All the arguments which Southerners marshaled during the next thirty years in justification of the besieged institution of slavery were first aired during the Missouri debates. Slavery was defended as a positive good. No longer did Southerners admit the evil of the system but they did deplore their inability to reach a solution. In the Missouri debates, Senator Nathaniel Macon of North Carolina argued that slavery was a moral system. Senator William Smith of South Carolina agreed, turning to the Scriptures to justify the system. "Mr. President," Smith declared, "the Scriptures teach us that slavery was universally practiced among the holy fathers." Northerners, for their part, although attacking the morality of slavery indirectly, were more concerned with preventing its expansion into the new territories. This tactic was taken by Senator Rufus King of New York. He had no wish to disturb slavery in the several states but only to prevent its extension.

The compromise finally effected was proposed by Congressman Jesse B. Thomas of Illinois. The Thomas Amendment coupled the admission of Missouri as a slave state with that of Maine as a free state and prohibited the introduction of slavery into the remaining portions of the Louisiana Purchase north of latitude 36°30′ north. The bill was passed by both Houses with this amendment. But Congress and the nation were not quite finished with Missouri. A second, if less dramatic, debate occurred with the submission of Missouri's proposed constitution to the Congress.

In the proposed constitution, the Missouri Assembly was ordered to pass laws prohibiting free Negroes or mulattoes from entering the state. This prohibition was a direct repudiation of the federal Constitution's clause guaranteeing that "the citizens of each State shall be entitled to all of the privileges and immunities of citizens of the several States." The status of the free Negro in the North was at stake. Free Negroes were considered citizens in the state of Massachusetts. Were their rights to be denied? Congress temporized on this clear-cut issue and finally, under the leadership of Speaker of the House Henry Clay, passed a resolution admitting Missouri on the condition that the legislature of that state abstain from passing any laws which abrogated the privileges and immunities clause. Missouri denied that Congress had the right to bind the state in any way, and it was finally admitted to the Union. In acts passed in 1825 and 1847, Missouri passed laws designed to prohibit the immigration of free Negroes and mulattoes into the state.

The Missouri Compromise debate of 1820 was the harbinger of the great intersectional debates over the nature of the Union and the expansion of slavery which dominated the political life of the nation during the 1840's and 1850's. The congressional struggle which finally produced the Missouri Compromise brought the South into being as a self-conscious political section. The South considered itself to be on the defensive after 1820. Sectional controversy and conflict became the norm.

Pertinent Literature

Wiltse, Charles M. *John C. Calhoun.* Vol. I: *Nationalist, 1782-1828.* Indianapolis: Bobbs-Merrill, 1941-1944.

The sectional nature of politics in the United States was nowhere better reflected than in the long career of John C. Calhoun of South Carolina. According to Wiltse, Calhoun entered politics as a nationalist and died as the foremost apologist and defender of the South. He was not, however, wholly sectionalized until the eleventh hour of his long and noteworthy life. His love for the Union remained deep, and many of his actions which appear to have been motivated by sectional commitments were, according to his biographer, actually motivated by a sincere desire to preserve the Union.

The career of Calhoun represents in its apparent fluctuation one of the most pressing problems confronting the student of the early national period. How are sectional or national commitments measured? How is the historian to determine whether the position of a man at any given moment is motivated primarily by sectional or national interests? Can the two be separated? Were there any New Englanders or Southerners immune to the pulls of purely sectional interests? Probably not, but how immune must one be in order to merit inclusion in the category of nationalist?

Calhoun entered politics at the national level in 1810 and soon became associated with the group called the "War Hawks." He believed that the war with Great Britain was inevitable given the humiliation suffered by the United States at the hands of the British. He was also aware of the harm done to the Southern economy by British depredations. Was his advocacy of preparedness and war nationalist or sectionalist?

The Missouri Compromise does not adequately represent the sectional nature of American politics in the 1820's. The North was not united sufficiently to insist upon the Tallmadge Amendment. The issue of slavery was not yet of overwhelming importance. But other issues were. Issues, such as protective tariffs, internal improvements, public land policy, and national banks, were fought out and compromised on a sectional level. These patterns were of major concern to Calhoun and his contemporaries. These issues slowly but surely pushed Calhoun from a national to a sectional attitude.

It is the contention of Wiltse that Calhoun was the last of the great political leaders during the 1820's to retreat from nationalism to sectionalism. Wiltse is critical of men, such as John Quincy Adams and Henry Clay. This view is understandable given Wiltse's portrayal of the South Carolinian as taking a national stance on such controversial questions as the tariffs bills proposed after the War of 1812, the Bank of the United States and the Bonus Bill, which provided for a national system of internal improvements. Calhoun represented enlightenment in his approach to such questions. Any who opposed him, or sought to use these issues to serve other than national purposes as defined by the author must, by definition, be less enlightened, less nationalistic than Calhoun. Besides, Calhoun was ambitious for the Presidency during the 1820's and faced similar ambitions on the part of Adams, Clay, Andrew Jackson, and William H. Crawford of Georgia. It is in terms of Presidential aspirations and a depressed economy that Wiltse discusses the Missouri controversy.

Wiltse approaches sectional disputes, including Missouri, from an economic viewpoint. He sees the Missouri debates as aiding in the consolidation of two major divisions in the nation. The North recognized its dependence upon a strong central government for economic advance and thus supported protective tariffs, banks, and internal improvements. The North also sensed, without understanding, that the expansion of slavery into new territories would retard economic growth by increasing the political power of the South and by obstructing, if not containing, the regions into which industrial capitalism could expand. The South saw economic nationalism as a direct threat to slavery and resorted to a states' rights defense. The South and Calhoun, by 1830, feared for its economic system and manifested their awareness of the South's position as the minority section in the nation. It was Calhoun's self-imposed task to secure the position of the South within the Union by solving the problem of minority rights in a government of the majority. Calhoun formalized his solution in the *South Carolina Exposition and Protest* of 1828.

Moore, Glover. *The Missouri Controversy, 1819-1821.* Lexington: University of Kentucky Press, 1953.

The Missouri Compromise debates shattered the apparent equanimity of the American political scene. It brought into the open fissures in the American body politic which were to widen as the years passed. The passions and fears aroused in the debates went far beyond those which were the normal result of the political life of a new nation, recently emerged from war with the most powerful country in the world, and still uncertain as to the meaning of American nationalism. American politics, although significantly sectionalized even in 1820, still manifested an ability to achieve an accommodation among the various major regions of the country on all the most crucial issues. As of 1819 the tariff had been satisfactorily handled in Congress; internal improvements subsidized by the federal government were not yet beyond the realm of possibility in spite of the Bonus Bill Veto of 1817; Congress was in the process of changing the land laws in response to the Panic of 1817 and succeeding years of hard times; and a second Bank of the United States had been chartered. Difficulties were to arise from each of these issues. Sectional attitudes would harden. But this was not yet clear in 1820. The reaction of men from the North to the application of Missouri for admission to Congress as a slave state afforded the first warning of things to come.

Glover Moore has written the only

monographic study of the Missouri controversy. He is concerned not only with the developing debate within the Congress and the role of the various antagonists and self-appointed mediators, but also with attitudes throughout the nation. He points out, for example, that sectional attitudes within the South were hardening on economic issues. The South, willing to go along with the protective tariff of 1816, was in 1820 the chief obstacle to further tariff increases. Moreover, the protectionists were, in general, intensely anti-Southern, believing that an adequate protective policy would not be possible until the expansion of slavery and Southern political influence were checked. Moore emphasizes the connection between the apparently conflicting economies of the North and the South and the Missouri controversy. The North feared that continued slavery expansion would retard industrial and commercial progress, while the South feared economic oppression.

The significance of the Missouri debates receives considerable attention from Moore. He writes that "the Missouri Controversy was the first occasion on which all of the strands in the fabric of North-South sectionalism were brought together and paraded before the public . . . This was the first full-scale dress rehearsal . . . for the great sectional contest which was to dominate the last two decades of the antebellum period." Every item in the Northern attack on slavery and the Southern defense of its institution had been introduced in the Missouri debates. Particularly critical was the Northern attitude toward expansion. The Adams-Onís Treaty of 1819 by which the United States received Florida from Spain and repudiated its claims to Texas was affected by the Missouri debates. Moore suggests that President Monroe's willingness to part with Texas may have been prompted by Northern opposition to the acquisition of that vast potential slave territory. By the same token, the debates resulted in a crystalization of Southern attitudes toward slavery.

While the contest over Missouri "foreshadowed the sectional tension of the forties and fifties, it also provided a formula by which this tension might be kept under control." Moore argues that the 36°30' demarcation between freedom and slavery followed limitations imposed by nature. The compromise line was a most important factor in maintaining a degree of sectional harmony. Its repeal in 1854 had tragic results. — *J. G. C.*

Additional Recommended Reading

Adams, Henry. *John Randolph.* Boston: Houghton Mifflin Co., 1893. This book remains the best single account of the career of this eccentric politician from Virginia.

Trexler, Harrison A. *Slavery in Missouri, 1804-1865.* Baltimore: The Johns Hopkins University Press, 1914. Traces the growth of slavery in Missouri from the American occupation to abolition.

Brown, Everett S., ed. *The Missouri Compromise and Presidential Politics, 1820-1825, from the Letters of William Plumer, Jr.* St. Louis: Missouri Historical Society, 1926. These letters of Congressman Plumer of New Hampshire afford important insights into the political forces at work in the Missouri controversy.

Sydnor, Charles S. *The Development of Southern Sectionalism, 1819-1848.* Vol. V: *A History of the South.* Baton Rouge: Louisiana State University Press, 1948. A comprehensive account of the growth in sectional consciousness in the South.

Dangerfield, George. *The Era of Good Feelings.* New York: Harcourt, Brace & World Inc., 1952. An excellent and highly readable analysis of the political problems and issues facing the United States during the decade following the War of 1812.

NEGOTIATION OF THE ADAMS-ONÍS TREATY

Type of event: Diplomatic: demarcation of boundaries between Spanish America and the United States
Time: 1819 (became effective February 22, 1821)
Locale: Washington, D.C.

Principal personages:

JAMES MONROE (1758-1831), fifth President of the United States 1817-1825

JOHN QUINCY ADAMS (1767-1848), Secretary of State of the United States under President Monroe 1817-1825

MAJOR GENERAL ANDREW JACKSON (1767-1845), Commander of the military expedition into East Florida in 1818

JOHN CALDWELL CALHOUN (1782-1850), Secretary of War of the United States under President Monroe 1817-1825

LUIS DE ONÍS (1762-1827), Minister of Spain to the United States

FERDINAND VII (1784-1833), King of Spain 1814-1833

Summary of Event

After the Louisiana Purchase had been made in 1803, most Americans who were interested in further expansion looked to the weakly-held Spanish provinces of East and West Florida. Indeed, the initial aim of Thomas Jefferson, third President of the United States, when he opened negotiations with the French in 1801 had been to purchase East or West Florida or both, and New Orleans. Having obtained Louisiana instead, Jefferson and his successors James Madison and James Monroe worked strenuously to obtain the Floridas. American ambitions were finally satisfied by the Adams-Onís Treaty, also called the Transcontinental Treaty. Signed in Washington in 1819 and finally ratified by the United States and Spain in 1821, the treaty essentially completed territorial organization east of the Mississippi river and also defined the Spanish-American boundary from Texas to the Pacific

Ocean.

To satisfy American ambitions in acquiring Florida, various methods were used. President Jefferson claimed West Florida because it had once been an administrative division of French Louisiana; but Spain, which had a much stronger legal case, rejected this argument. Jefferson then made several attempts to gain recognition of United States claims to East and West Florida by combining offers of renouncing American claims against Spain or making an outright purchase, together with vigorous assertions that the Floridas were destined to come under United States dominion. In the years before the War of 1812, expansionists combined their demand for the seizure of Canada from Great Britain with another demand for the acquisition of Florida from Spain. Even before the outbreak of war, there had been several revolts in both Floridas, carried

558

out largely by American immigrants. While most failed, in 1810 the Americans living in that part of West Florida between the Iberville and Perdido rivers declared their independence, and later that year President Madison ordered the Governor of Orleans Territory to take possession of the territory. Its occupation was not completed, however, until 1813 while the United States was at war with Great Britain.

When peace was concluded in 1815, East Florida was still precariously in Spain's possession, but it was recognized that the Spanish regime had only two choices to avoid a shameful political abandonment of sovereignty over the region: to gain support of a European ally, or to attain some semblance of honor in the affair by winning from the United States favorable territorial concessions elsewhere in North America. Great Britain and the other European powers refused Spanish pleas for assistance, and Spain turned to the alternative adjustment of all boundary questions with the United States.

The American government, especially the brilliant Secretary of State, John Quincy Adams, was entirely willing to have discussion of the East Florida issue become the basis for the resolution of all Spanish-American boundary disputes. Adams saw in these negotiations a magnificent opportunity to extend American territorial claims to the Pacific Ocean, and to realize the dream of a continental Republic.

To this end, Adams undertook negotiations with Luis de Onís, Minister of Spain to the United States, who had been given full powers to settle outstanding differences. Onís' instructions provided that he was to transfer the Floridas to the United States in return for comparable American concession west of the Mississippi river. Thus, the theoretical issue of Florida's cession was from the outset not in dispute. Onís was also to win a promise that the United States would not give material aid to, or recognize the independence of, Spain's colonies in South America which were then in revolt. Difficulties arose over negotiating a satisfactory boundary in the West and also over the dispatch in 1818 of United States military forces into East Florida. The first problem prolonged the negotiations, but the second threatened to disrupt them entirely.

The military expedition which interrupted the Adams-Onís conversations was at first glance another in a long series of actions to punish border raids by bands of escaped Negro slaves and Seminole Indians residing in Spanish territory. This expedition, however, was commanded by Andrew Jackson, the hero of New Orleans, and the Tennessean had more in mind than a punitive raid. Like most Americans in the old Southwest, Jackson desired the forcible seizure of Spanish East Florida. Jackson's orders from Washington authorized him to penetrate Spanish territory and attack the Seminoles "unless they should shelter under a Spanish post." Jackson disregarded these orders. Crossing the border with two thousand men in mid-March, 1818, Jackson quickly defeated the Seminoles and destroyed their principal settlements. He next occupied the Spanish fort of St. Marks, raising the American flag and capturing two British subjects, Alexander Arbuthnot and Lieutenant Robert C. Ambrister. Both were court-martialed and executed; Arbuthnot, for supplying munitions to the Seminoles, and Ambrister, for inciting the Indians to war.

Jackson's zeal threatened to bring about serious international complications. Spain lodged a prompt and violent protest. The United States feared that Great Britain would use the execution of two British subjects by Americans on Spanish territory as an excuse to intervene. President Monroe's Cabinet disapproved of Jackson's activities, except for Secretary of State Adams, who strongly defended Jackson. When the British government agreed, however, that it had no grounds for interference, Spain had no choice but to return to negotiations.

After negotiations were resumed, Adams and Onís made use of the French Minister, Hyde de Neuville, to work out a compromise boundary for Texas, the point over which the talks had broken down before. Adams, who apparently desired to gain all of Texas, proposed the Colorado river as the demarcation line. Onís firmly insisted upon the Sabine river. After prolonged discussions and several proposals and counterproposals, Adams and Onís agreed near the end of 1818 upon a boundary which went up the Sabine river from its mouth and continued on to the Red river, zigzagged westward along the Red and Arkansas rivers, followed the crest of the Rockies to the 42nd parallel, and then turned west-ward to the Pacific Ocean.

On February 22, 1819, Onís and Adams signed the treaty which embodied this compromise boundary and other provisions; Spain retained Texas but gave up its claim to the Oregon country. In retrospect, the most important aspect of the treaty was that the United States became a continental power. Spain ceded to the United States all its territory east of the Mississippi river. Both nations renounced all claims for damages and injuries, although the United States agreed to assume the claims of its citizens against Spain up to a maximum of five million dollars. Adams successfully avoided any commitment regarding recognition of the Spanish colonies which were in revolt.

The final article of the treaty provided for ratification within six months. The United States Senate gave its advice and consent immediately, but certain difficulties then arose. Apart from doubt concerning the validity of land grants made in Florida by Ferdinand VII, King of Spain, during the final stage of negotiating the treaty, Ferdinand was forced in 1820 to accept a constitution under which the Cortes, the national legislature of Spain, had to approve of any cession of territory. There was a long delay, but the Adams-Onís Treaty finally became effective on February 22, 1821.

Pertinent Literature

Dangerfield, George. *The Era of Good Feelings.* New York: Harcourt, Brace & World, Inc., 1952.

This volume contains a superb interpretation of the political, economic, and social turmoil occurring in America between 1817 and 1825. It won for George Dangerfield the Pulitzer and Bancroft prizes. The era was a time of transition in many ways. Dangerfield gives emphasis to three factors which separate the "era of good feelings" (an ironic description for a period of so much conflict) from the Jeffersonian era and the age of Jackson. These three main themes are the remarkable growth of nationalist sentiment which predominated in the first years of Monroe's Presidency; the effect of the Panic of 1819 upon nationalism and political affairs; and the pressure for reform which arose in the 1820's. Dangerfield is at his best when dealing with the clash of personalities and the broad themes of political conflict, economic change, and social upheaval. This study foregoes details in favor of discussing people, ideas, and conflict; for this reason the interpretations presented are sometimes open to question.

Among the best chapters are the two which deal with the acquisition of Florida, entitled "The General" and "The Secretary." Jackson is described as the personification of the frontier hero. Dangerfield writes that Jackson "was all tenderness on the one hand, and all savagery on the other." His personal creed, as once stated for the benefit of a Spanish official, was: "An Eye for an Eye, Toothe for Toothe, and Scalp for Scalp." Jackson's actions in Florida could be easily predicted, and Dangerfield speculates about the Monroe Administration's aims in appointing such a man to lead the punitive expedition against the Seminoles. The General's execution of Ambrister and Arbuthnot is condemned on the ground that the two men, while perhaps technically guilty, "deserved more sympathy than recrimination." Jackson would have dismissed this argument.

Dangerfield's examination of Adams and of the negotiations with Onís is equally enlightening. Adams, he states, had nothing to do with Jackson's sortie into Spanish Florida until after the event, but he welcomed the effect upon the Spaniards. The most important period in the Adams-Onís talks was between July 11 and July 16, 1818, for it was then that the United States decided to press for a boundary line reaching to the Pacific Ocean. Adams first mentioned such a line on July 11. According to Dangerfield, President Monroe was willing to give up American claims to Texas and supported his Secretary of State in pressing for that "magnificent generalization," a transcontinental boundary. Adams alone would not have abandoned Texas, but the President, shocked by Jackson's deeds in Florida, demanded a conciliatory approach to Spain. Onís stubbornly opposed relinquishing the Spanish claim to Texas while bravely resisting Adams' threats and pleadings from the French Minister. The final settlement recognized Spanish control of Texas in return for ever greater concessions along the line to the Pacific. Dangerfield writes that the Adams-Onís Treaty was the Secretary of State's triumph. He had secured for the United States a continental empire.

James, Marquis. *Andrew Jackson: The Border Captain.* Indianapolis: The Bobbs-Merrill Company, 1933.

The part played by Andrew Jackson in the events which led to the Adams-Onís Treaty was clearly an important one. Old Hickory's exploits in Florida were of even greater significance for the course of American politics, for they, together with his victory over the British at New Orleans in 1814, made Jackson the foremost military hero of his day. They set him on the road to the White House and that central position in American politics which has resulted in his tenure (and that of his immediate successors, Van Buren, Harrison, Tyler, and Polk) being labelled "The Jacksonian Era." Few anticipated in 1817 that rough-talking, ruthless Andrew Jackson would attain the Presidency. At that time Major General Jackson was the famous and well-regarded Commander of the Southern Department. His command was comprised basically of militia forces. Although he was known to act intemperately and to be especially antagonistic to Indians, no one expected that Jackson would cause an international crisis in 1818.

This volume, which describes Jackson's actions in Florida and their effect on Spanish-American relations, is the first of a two-volume biography of Jackson. In it is chronicled Jackson's life from his birth in North Carolina to his resignation as Governor of the Floridas in October, 1821. Among the most important sections, certainly the most interesting is the chapter concerned with Jackson's Florida adventure and the political arguments which followed. James notes that Jackson almost missed the Florida campaign, for he decided in 1817 to resign from the army rather than to accept certain orders from the War Department which he considered insulting. Finally, President Monroe himself, anxious to retain the services of the nation's foremost military leader, intervened to arrange a compromise. Jackson received instructions to "adopt all necessary

measures" to end the Indian depredations. He at once indicated his position by proposing to ignore the War Department's order not to attack Spanish military installations. So eager was Jackson to proceed with this patriotic expedition that he personally advanced funds to equip the Tennessee troops.

The author justifies Jackson's invasion of Florida, the capture of Spanish garrisons, and, in particular, the trial and execution of Arbuthnot and Ambrister. He notes without comment Jackson's decision to enforce the sentence of death in Ambrister's case even though the military court had reconsidered its verdict and had reduced Ambrister's sentence to fifty lashes and imprisonment for one year. The consequences of these actions, however, are treated in detail. The immediate reaction of Monroe and his Cabinet was that Jackson had acted "not only without, but against his instructions; that he has committed war upon Spain." Unless these acts were disavowed, the administration might be ruined politically and might face war with Great Britain and Spain. Only Secretary of State John Quincy Adams opposed the attempt of the Monroe Administration to repudiate Jackson's actions. Adams championed Jackson not from admiration or sympathy for the Western hero but because Jackson's victories in Florida had given him decisive advantages in the negotiations with Onís. Even when Madrid threatened to end the negotiations unless Jackson's actions were disavowed and the General "suitably punished," the Secretary of State stood his ground. Interpreting the documentary record according to his own requirements, Adams argued that American activities were justified on grounds of self-defense. Adams attacked Spanish policies in Florida and rejected completely any need to defend those of Jackson. "Thus a Jacksonian spirit in the Cabinet to support Jacksonian measures in the field," writes James. One may dispute the argument that Jackson's campaign against the Spanish-sheltered Indian tribes caused Spain to cede Florida to the United States; it is clear, however, that Andrew Jackson's determination to obtain this territory was of large importance. — *T.A.W.*

Additional Recommended Reading

Brooks, Philip C. *Diplomacy and the Borderlands: The Adams-Onís Treaty of 1819*. Berkeley: University of California Press, 1939. Brooks's monograph remains the outstanding analysis of the Adams-Onís Treaty.

Whitaker, Arthur P. *The United States and the Independence of Latin America, 1800-1830*. Baltimore: The Johns Hopkins University Press, 1941. This study examines the wider context of United States involvement in the Latin-American struggle for independence.

Bemis, Samuel Flagg. *John Quincy Adams and the Foundations of American Foreign Policy*. New York: Alfred A. Knopf, Inc., 1949. A magnificent biography, Bemis' study ably describes Adams' role in the acquisition of Florida.

Perkins, Bradford. *Castlereagh and Adams: England and the United States, 1812-1823*. Berkeley: University of California Press, 1964. This study analyzes the relationship between the United States and Great Britain during the period of the Florida controversy.

Cox, Isaac J. *The West Florida Controversy, 1798-1813*. Baltimore: The Johns Hopkins University Press, 1918. Cox treats one part of the Florida question in this older but still valuable work.

JUDICIAL RECOGNITION OF THE DOCTRINE OF IMPLIED POWERS
(*McCulloch* v. *Maryland*)

Type of event: Legal: challenge by the states regarding the constitutionality of the Second Bank of the United States
Time: March 6, 1819
Locale: Washington, D.C.

Principal personages:

JOHN MARSHALL (1755-1835), Chief Justice of the United States Supreme Court 1801-1835

JAMES W. MCCULLOCH (fl. 1819), cashier in the Baltimore branch of the Second Bank of the United States

LUTHER MARTIN (1748?-1826), Attorney General of Maryland and chief counsel for Maryland in *McCulloch* v. *Maryland*

WILLIAM PINKNEY (1764-1822), counsel for McCulloch and the Second Bank of the United States in *McCulloch* v. *Maryland*

WILLIAM WIRT (1772-1834), Attorney General of the United States and counsel for the Second Bank of the United States in *McCulloch* v. *Maryland*

DANIEL WEBSTER (1782-1852), United States Senator and counsel for McCulloch and the Second Bank in the case

Summary of Event

From its inception, the Constitution of 1787 has stirred controversy as to the nature of the Union which it created and the extent of federal authority. The Civil War settled certain outstanding questions as to the nature of the Union, but a more articulate consideration of the problem was provided by the Supreme Court of the United States in 1819 in the monumental case of *McCulloch* v. *Maryland*.

The arguments surrounding the case were as old as the Constitution itself. Although the Constitutional Convention of 1787 had considered and rejected the proposal that Congress be empowered to charter corporations, a classic constitutional debate took place during the first administration of President George Washington over the question of chartering the First Bank of the United States. In their opinions written at the President's request, Secretary of the Treasury Alexander Hamilton and Secretary of State Thomas Jefferson presented diametrically opposite advice on the question of whether or not the President should approve the bill chartering the First Bank of the United States. Hamilton contended that Congress' power under the "necessary and proper" clause meant that it had power to make all laws which it considered expedient or convenient; Jefferson insisted that the clause authorized Congress to pass only those laws which were necessary to give effect to its delegated powers.

Washington took Hamilton's advice, and the bank was chartered in 1791. The charter of 1791 expired in 1811, and the adverse economic impact of the War of 1812, coupled with the abuses and irresponsibility of state-chartered banks, led to the chartering in 1816 of the Second Bank of the United States. The chartering of the First Bank of the United States had prompted a movement in favor of a constitutional amendment to restrict Congress' powers under the "necessary and proper" clause, and the chartering of the Second Bank of the United States led many states to adopt laws designed to suppress the bank's operations. The hostility toward the bank rested on a number of factors: (1) it had been regarded as a Federalist-controlled enterprise; (2) much of the stock was held by foreign investors; (3) the operations of the First Bank of the United States had tended to undercut the success of the state banks; and (4) many blamed the bleak economic conditions following the War of 1812 on the policies of the First Bank of the United States, which had operated from 1791 until 1811. Champions of the bank regarded renewal of its charter as the only hope of improving economic conditions.

In certain states, anti-bank sentiment was rampant. Indiana, Illinois, Tennessee, Georgia, North Carolina, Kentucky, Ohio, and Maryland adopted laws designed to curtail or prohibit the operation of the bank. The momentum of the anti-bank movement was encouraged by the mismanagement and fraud of the managers of the Second Bank of the United States. The growing anxiety over the deteriorating state of the economy made an appeal to the courts an attractive way of settling the question of the legitimacy of the state burdens which were being imposed on the bank's operations. This was the immediate motivation for the litigation which resulted in *McCulloch* v. *Maryland.*

An agent of the State of Maryland, John James, called on James W. McCulloch, the cashier of the Baltimore, Maryland, branch of the bank, and demanded that McCulloch comply with the state law. The Maryland law, adopted in February, 1818, required all banks chartered outside Maryland to pay a tax of one hundred dollars on all notes issued or, alternatively, to pay an annual sum of fifteen thousand dollars into the state's treasury. McCulloch refused to comply with this prohibitive state law, and upon his being prosecuted for his refusal, the Maryland courts ruled against McCulloch and in September, 1818, the case was appealed to the United States Supreme Court.

The Supreme Court heard arguments for nine days. Appearing on behalf of the bank were Attorney General William Wirt, William Pinkney, and Daniel Webster; Luther Martin, the fiery Attorney General of Maryland who had expedited the bringing of the case to the Supreme Court, Joseph Hopkinson, and Walter Jones were the lawyers appearing for Maryland.

The Supreme Court handed down its decision on March 6, 1819, only three days after completion of arguments and while there was much activity in Congress aimed at revoking the bank's charter. The opinion by Chief Justice John Marshall is regarded by most scholars as his most important pronouncement in constitutional law. The Constitution, said Marshall, established a truly national government which "is emphatically and truly a government of the people. In form and in substance it emanates from them, its powers are granted by them, and are to be exercised directly on them, and for their benefit." Much of the remainder of his opinion is an extension and application of this "national" theory of the Constitution's foundations. The judiciary, he wrote, is constitutionally required to construe Congress' enumerated powers broadly. The "necessary and proper" clause was designed to empower Congress to exercise its delegated powers by any convenient and expedient methods not prohibited by the Constitution itself. "A constitution, to contain an accurate detail of all the subdivisions of which its great powers will admit, and all of the means by which they may be carried into execution, would partake of the prolixity of a legal code, and could scarcely be embraced by the human mind. It would probably never be understood by the public. Its nature, therefore, requires, that only its great outlines should be marked, its important objects designated, and the minor ingredients which compose those objects be deduced from the nature of the objects themselves." Both the spirit and the language of the Constitution supported

this view; the framers had "omitted to use any restrictive term which might prevent its receiving a fair and just interpretation. In considering this question, then, we must never forget, that it is a constitution we are expounding." Marshall found that the "necessary and proper" clause gave rise to what we have come to call "implied powers." "Let the end be legitimate, let it be within the scope of the Constitution, and all means are appropriate, which are plainly adopted to that end, which are not prohibited, but consist with the letter of the Constitution, are constitutional. . . ."

Luther Martin had insisted in his argument that even if Congress had the authority to establish the bank, the state could still levy the tax in question. Marshall rejected this argument and laid down the general principle that the central government had constitutional power to "withdraw any subject from the action" of the states. "The power to tax," he declared, "involves the power to destroy." To permit Maryland to tax the bank's operations would place all federal programs at the mercy of the states. This facet of the McCulloch opinion gave rise to the doctrine of intergovernmental tax immunity.

Pertinent Literature

Beveridge, Albert J. *The Life of John Marshall.* Vol. IV: *Conflict and Construction, 1800-1815.* Boston: Houghton Mifflin Co., 1916.

In this authoritative four-volume work Albert Beveridge sympathetically reviews John Marshall's life as a frontiersman, soldier, legislator, lawyer, politician, diplomat, and jurist. Beveridge presents a comprehensive survey of the argument and opinion in *McCul-loch* v. *Maryland* and the uproar of criticism which it provoked. He devotes little or no attention to the political or historical setting of the controversy, but his account of the argument and recitation of the opinion are perhaps the fullest to be found in the literature on the subject. He makes a persuasive argument that Marshall had written the opinion before the case was argued in the Supreme Court. It is Beveridge's treatment of the reaction to the decision, however, which gives his work its special merit.

One of the harshest critics of the *McCulloch* v. *Maryland* decision was Hezekiah Niles, publisher of the widely read and influential *Weekly Register.* Niles, claims Beveridge, publicized the text of the opinion so extensively that *McCulloch* v. *Maryland* was the most widely read Supreme Court pronouncement up to that time, and in this connection rivaled *Gibbons* v. *Ogden* (the great commerce case) and *Dred Scott* v. *Sanford.* The chief elements of Niles' criticisms were that the rule of the case established Congress' power to grant monopolies and create corporations, that the opinion was "mysterious" for all except the judicial "priests," and that its thrust was decidedly in favor of propertied interests and hostile to the interests of the common people. Beveridge claims that, because of the wide circulation of Niles' *Register,* fundamental disagreements about the nature of the Constitution were made sharper than they had been since 1789.

Two other leading contemporary critics of the disposition of the McCulloch case, according to Beveridge, were Spencer Roane, Chief Judge of the Virginia Court of Appeals, and John Taylor of Caroline, a leading Virginia constitutional theorist. Niles had spoken to the common man, but Roane addressed his criticisms to the American legal profession. Using the friendly Richmond *Enquirer* as his forum, Roane attacked Marshall's constitutional arguments in such harsh terms that Marshall was provoked to reply in kind.

One point introduced by Beveridge in connection with his discussion of Roane's criticism of the *McCulloch* v. *Maryland* opinion needs to be stressed; the relationship of the constitutional status of slavery and the theory of secession to the *McCulloch* v. *Maryland* principles. Marshall's interpretation of the broad scope of the national government's power under the implied powers doctrine was understood as a fair warning that the national government could use its delegated powers to undermine the slavocracy. It appears that Roane's criticism prompted the introduction of resolutions in the Virginia legislature condemning the decision on the ground that it authorized Congress to lay down conditions upon which states would be admitted to the Union. Beveridge contends that the Virginians' interpretation of the opinion was correct, but he deplores their response. Taylor advanced his criticism in his *Construction Construed and Constitutions Vindicated,* of which five chapters out of a total of sixteen were devoted to a constitutional critique of the *McCulloch* v. *Maryland* opinion. All critics of the opinion attacked the opinion's justification of implied powers, arguing that Marshall had rendered the national government theoretically omnipotent by asserting that Congress could use whatever means it considered expedient to accomplish its goals. The action of the Ohio legislature in repudiating *McCulloch* v. *Maryland* as an encroachment on the sovereignty of states was consistent with Taylor's thesis. Ohio's lead was followed by the legislatures of Virginia, Pennsylvania, Indiana, and Illinois.

It is Beveridge's conclusion that Marshall's opinion in *McCulloch* v.

Maryland did more for the American people "than any single utterance, excepting only Washington's Farewell Address."

Hammond, Bray. *Banks and Politics in America, from the Revolution to the Civil War.* Princeton: Princeton University Press, 1957.

This work by the United States' outstanding historian of banks and banking is a major contribution to what might be called the political history of the monetary and fiscal development of the United States. While much of this ponderous book focuses on the experience with the First and Second Banks of the United States, there are chapters on the 1694-1781 period, the First American Bank of Philadelphia in 1781-1787, and banking prior to 1791 in New York, Boston, and Baltimore. The chapters devoted to the 1836-1865 era chronicle the banking policies of that turbulent time. A chapter on Canadian banking in 1792-1867 provides Hammond with the opportunity to make poignant comparisons and contrasts with banking practices of the two countries.

Hammond has provided what appears to be the most exhaustive discussion of the *McCulloch* v. *Maryland* case in terms of background and impact. His close scrutiny of the monetary straits of the bank and of the economy generally in the 1819 period leads him to suggest that the bank's precarious position in 1818 and 1819 led the Supreme Court to ignore the bank specifically as an institution entrusted with regulating monetary policy. This fact is shown, Hammond believes, by the irony of the bank's position. The bank came before the Court to protect its legality when, in reality, its solvency was in doubt.

There is here a basis for the argument that the Supreme Court's adoption of the broad construction position was a result of its being unable to be convincing about the bank in narrower, more specific terms. Hammond contends that the decision has been of greater importance to the evolution of federal power generally than in the field of monetary policy. Nevertheless, the ruling confirmed the general identification of the bank with strengthened federal authority. He provides extensive documentation for the generally held view that the Supreme Court's position in *McCulloch* v. *Maryland* was responsible for saving the Bank of the United States from destruction at the hands of the states. Hammond believes that the decision alarmed states' rights partisans who felt that the authority of the federal government was "invading" the states. For the federal government to create a bank in a state, which would be above the laws of that state, confirmed their fears that the concept of states' rights was slowly dying.

McCulloch v. *Maryland,* claims Hammond, was merely the most important act in a larger drama. Numerous important court cases stemming from the activities of the Second Bank of the United States, he contends, represented problems of morals, economics, and constitutional interpretation which profoundly affected the foundations of American society. Eighteenth century entrepreneurs, claims Hammond, had functioned under restraints imposed by tradition, restraints which had lost their hold by the late 1810's. Hammond suggests that the monetary machinations constituting the background of the *McCul-* *loch* v. *Maryland* case were the natural by-products of the greatly expanded use of credit and the opportunities for manipulation and embezzlement created by the growth of complex corporate structures. — *J.J.B.*

Additional Recommended Reading

Boudin, Louis B. *Government by Judiciary.* Vol. I. New York: William Goodwin, 1932. Boudin, who is generally highly critical of the judiciary's self-aggrandizement, considers the *McCulloch* v. *Maryland* decision to be the product of Marshall's "statesmanship" rather than his earlier penchant for being "legalistic." He is one of the few commentators who does not refer to the *McCulloch* opinion as Marshall's greatest, a distinction which he awards to *Gibbons* v. *Ogden* (1824).

Catterall, Ralph C. *The Second Bank of the United States.* Chicago: University of Chicago Press, 1903. This authoritative history of the Second Bank gives a full account of the financial technicalities and mismanagements underlying the bank's predicament at the time of the *McCulloch* v. *Maryland* case.

Channing, Edward. *A History of the United States.* Vol. V, ch. 10. New York: The Macmillan Company, 1921. Channing's discussion relates the *McCulloch* v. *Maryland* decision to the political setting of the Second Bank of the United States and to the general political and constitutional history of the period.

Corwin, Edward S. *John Marshall and the Constitution.* New Haven: Yale University Press, 1920. In this decidedly pro-Marshall judicial biography Corwin provides a relatively full account of the case and its background and significance; he claims that *McCulloch* v.*Maryland* was Marshall's first opportunity to "elaborate the tenets of his nationalistic creed."

Govan, Thomas P. *Nicholas Biddle: Nationalist and Public Banker, 1786-1844.* Chicago: University of Chicago Press, 1959. Although it does not focus on the *McCulloch* v. *Maryland* case, this excellent biography of Biddle contains much information on the operations of the bank and the politics of the era.

FOUNDING OF THE UNITARIAN CHURCH IN THE UNITED STATES

Type of event: Religious: secession of Congregationalists having liberal views
Time: 1819
Locale: Boston, Massachusetts

Principal personages:

WILLIAM ELLERY CHANNING (1780-1842), known as the "Apostle of Unitarianism," pastor of Federal Street Church, Boston

HENRY WARE (1764-1845), liberal minister at First Church in Hingham, Massachusetts, and Hollis Professor Divinity at Harvard University 1805-1840

JEDIDIAH MORSE (1761-1826), minister at Charlestown, Massachusetts, and founder of the *Panoplist*

LYMAN BEECHER (1775-1863), pastor of Park Street Church, Boston

HOSEA BALLOU (1771-1852), Universalist minister of Portsmouth, New Hampshire

JARED SPARKS (1789-1866), Unitarian minister and editor of *The Unitarian Miscellany*

CHARLES CHAUNCY (1705-1787), pastor of First Church, Boston

JONATHAN MAYHEW (1720-1766), pastor of West Church, Boston

Summary of Event

In May, 1819, William Ellery Channing, pastor of the Federal Street Church in Boston, traveled to Baltimore to preach at the ordination of a Unitarian minister, Jared Sparks. His sermon, "Unitarian Christianity," was a landmark in the founding of the Unitarian Church in the United States.

Channing delivered his sermon in the midst of the "Unitarian Controversy," a religious debate between liberal and orthodox Congregationalists which had begun officially in 1805 when Henry Ware was appointed Hollis Professor of Divinity at Harvard University but which reached back into the early eighteenth century. Religious liberalism, or "Arminianism" as it was called, emerged in the 1730's as a reaction against the rigorous Calvinism of men such as Jonathan Edwards and, later, Samuel Hopkins. In the pre-Revolutionary period, Charles Chauncy, pastor of First Church, Boston, and Jonathan Mayhew, pastor of West Church, Boston, were the foremost Arminian spokesmen, preaching anti-Trinitarianism, the benevolence of God, and human ability in salvation. Other denominations besides Congregationalism were affected by the liberal impulse. In the early 1780's, anti-Trinitarian views were heard in King's Chapel, which subsequently broke away from the Church of England. Universalists, such as Hosea Ballou of Portsmouth, New Hampshire, also embraced the liberal theology.

But liberalism was particularly strong in Boston and among Congregationalists, and it was within that denomination that the "Unitarian Controversy" occurred. At the beginning of the nineteenth century, orthodox Congregationalists, led by such men as Jedidiah Morse, minister at Charlestown, Massachusetts, and Lyman Beecher, pastor of Park Street Church, Boston, tried to fight the tide of liberalism. Morse founded the *Panoplist* to proselytize "the faith once delivered to the saints," and succeeded in uniting Hopkinsians and Old Calvinists in a common front against the liberals. When the Hollis Chair of Divinity at Harvard University became vacant in 1803, orthodox Congregationalists attempted to get a moderate Calvinist appointed. Having failed, they gave up Harvard as lost to heterodoxy and founded their own seminary at Andover in 1808.

In the decade following Ware's appointment at Harvard, the lines between orthodox and liberal Congregationalists hardened. Liberals—who preferred that title to the "Unitarian" label which their opponents succeeded in fastening on them—steadily gained strength, spreading their views by way of pulpit and press. The orthodox intensified their attack. In 1815 Morse distributed a pamphlet entitled *American Unitarianism,* a chapter from a British work which argued that New England liberals were Unitarians in the English sense, meaning that they avowed merely the humanity of Jesus. Morse also published a review of the

pamphlet in the *Panoplist,* which denounced liberal Congregationalists as heretics secretly conspiring to overthrow the true faith and called for their expulsion from the Congregational Church. As the leader of the Boston liberals, Channing answered the *Panoplist* attack by a public letter to Samuel C. Thacher, minister of the New South Church. This letter brought a reply from Samuel Worchester of Salem, who defended the review. A long pamphlet debate between Channing and Worchester followed, with the issue shifting from the *Panoplist* review to the more general question of the nature of Unitarianism. As the theological differences became clearer, liberals began to accept the once unpopular term "Unitarian," though they expanded and elaborated on its meaning.

It was in this context of bitter theological debate that Channing decided in 1819 to deliver the now famous Baltimore sermon which laid the foundations for the Unitarian Church in the United States. "Unitarian Christianity" provided a comprehensive statement of the beliefs of American Unitarians as well as an eloquent defense of their faith. Unitarians, Channing declared, interpreted the Scriptures by "the constant exercise of reason" and rejected any theological doctrines repugnant to reason and moral sense. Thus they believed in the unity of God, rejecting the "irrational and unscriptural doctrine of the Trinity." They also rejected the Calvinist God, worshiping instead a God who is "infinitely good, kind, and benevolent." Such a God offered salvation not to a few elect, but to all men. Unitarians rejected doctrines of natural depravity and predestination not only because of their "unspeakable cruelty" but also because such doctrines were "adverse" to the "Parental character" of God. Channing concluded his sermon on a conciliatory note. "We have embraced this system," he explained, "not hastily or lightly, but after much deliberation, and we hold it fast, not merely because we believe it to be true, but because we regard it as purifying truth, as a doctrine according to godliness, as able to 'work mightily' and to 'bring forth fruit' in them that believe. . . . We see nothing in our views to give offence, save their purity, and it is their purity which makes us seek and hope their extension through the world."

Despite its conciliatory tone, Chan-

ning's sermon made reconciliation between liberal and orthodox Congregationalists even less likely than before. Separation of Unitarians from Congregationalists and vice versa became commonplace, as one or the other group (usually the latter) within a church withdrew to form a new society. In 1825 the American Unitarian Association was founded "to diffuse the knowledge and promote the interests of pure Christianity." This was the final act of separation which divided Unitarians and Congregationalists into two denominations and ended the long theological conflict which had begun more than a quarter of a century earlier.

Pertinent Literature

Wright, Conrad. *The Beginnings of Unitarianism in America.* Boston: Starr King Press, 1955.

Although historians have given a great deal of attention to seventeenth century Puritanism and nineteenth century religious revivalism, they have tended to slight the intervening period. Conrad Wright, a student of Perry Miller, is an exception to this rule. His book, which won the Carnegie Award of the American Historical Association, is a study of "the liberal movement which developed within the Congregational churches of New England in the eighteenth century" and emerged in the nineteenth century as Unitarianism.

Religious liberalism, or "Arminianism" as it was called, was a phase in the decline of Puritanism. By 1750, following the bitter theological conflict waged over the Great Awakening, the lines between Calvinists and Arminians

were clearly drawn. Wright argues that the most important issue which divided Arminians from orthodox Congregationalists was not the freedom of the will, as Jonathan Edwards believed, but the Calvinist doctrines of the imputed guilt of Adam's sin and total depravity. Arminians rejected both. They also stressed the benevolence of God and man's ability in salvation. Indeed, Wright argues that the Arminian doctrine of justification and regeneration developed by the late 1760's "was in all essentials the same as that of the first generation of New England Unitarians," except that it was articulated in the traditional Christian vocabulary.

Although the differences between Arminians and Calvinists are the chief subject of this book, Wright is also careful to distinguish the liberals from other religious groups. He points out, for example, that Arminians emphasized the role of reason in religious matters but they were "supernatural rationalists" who supplemented natural religion with Christian revelation, unlike the Deists who rejected supernatural revelation altogether. It is significant that when American liberals began to adopt anti-Trinitarian views late in the eighteenth century, it was the Arian, not the Socinian, variety of anti-Trinitarianism which they espoused, a fact which distinguished them from the more radical English Unitarians. Indeed, Wright points out that "Arianism continued to be the commonest form of Unitarianism in New England until well into the nineteenth century." The comparisons with Deism and English Unitarianism reveal a degree of conservatism in New England Arminians. For all their liberalism in theology, they were unwilling to go so far as some other groups. Perhaps this religious conservatism was a function of the social conservatism of most Arminians, who tended to come from wealthy mercantile families. Perhaps too, this religious conservatism explains why, as Wright points out, Arminians were able in the 1790's to unite with Calvinists against "infidelity," by which they meant the views of Paine and the Deists, in much the same way that Hopkinsians and Old Calvinists would later unite against Unitarian "infidels." Wright suggests that "the French Revolution may have postponed for a decade the split between liberal and orthodox." The book ends with a discussion of the events surrounding the Ware appointment of 1805.

Wright's study is not of Unitarianism *per se,* but of the theological developments which paved the way for the "Unitarian controversy" and Channing's Baltimore sermon. It was the Arminians of the eighteenth century— men such as Jonathan Mayhew, Charles Chauncy and Ebenezer Gay— who "amassed the intellectual capital on which the liberals drew in the Unitarian controversy."

Edgell, David P. *William Ellery Channing.* Boston: Beacon Press, 1955.

William Ellery Channing, one of the central figures of early American Unitarianism, has been the subject of several biographies. Writing in 1955, William Edgell set himself the task of reintroducing the real Channing "as a man of his times," and determining "the nature of his thought and its relevance to the problems of his age and ours." In the process of fulfilling these twin goals, Edgell focuses more on Channing's thought than on the events of his life and times. Edgell's book thus provides a more analytical approach than, for example, the biographies of Madeleine Hooke Rice *(Federal Street Pastor,* 1961) and Arthur W. Brown *(Always Young for Liberty,* 1956). At the same time, Edgell challenges the interpretation of Robert L. Patterson *(The Philosophy of William Ellery Channing,* 1952) which viewed Channing as an original thinker who advanced a new religious philosophy. For Edgell, Channing's ultimate significance derives from "his position as a synthesizer of intellectual and ethical theories. . . ." As the embodiment, if not the creator, of religious and social liberalism, Channing played an important role in making it available and acceptable to "a dominantly middle class culture."

In describing the evolution of Channing's religious thought, Edgell emphasizes the gradual nature of Channing's drift away from orthodoxy. As late as 1809 Channing was preaching in orthodox terms, and "the public thought of him as an orthodox Hopkinsian, if not an orthodox Calvinist." During the first decade as pastor of the Federal Street Church, he was aligned with the religious moderates, as opposed to the "old-line Calvinists" on the one side and the "extreme liberals" on the other. Nevertheless, Channing's moderation did not shield him from attacks by the orthodox. It was these attacks which impelled him to rise to "the defense of the 'liberal Christians.' " In the process, he clarified his own ideas and moved beyond the middle-of-the-road position he had originally taken.

Edgell makes an interesting and persuasive case for the considerable influence of Samuel Hopkins on Channing's religious thought. Like Hopkins, Channing was primarily interested in morality. Though Channing rejected the earlier theologian's Calvinist view of God and man, he was greatly influenced by his idea of disinterested benevolence, a notion which he also found in the writings of Richard Price, Francis Hutcheson, and the Earl of Shaftesbury. Edgell views both Hopkins and Channing

as part of a "revolution in American theology." "Channing's own revolution," Edgell writes, "was a continuance of the Hopkinsian revolt. The new movement not only consolidated the gains of its predecessor, but also moved on to new positions—the denial of the Trinity, the virtual denial of hell, a belief in the perfectibility of man and the spiritual efficacy of good works, a faith in progress, and finally a new conception of the value of man as the source of whatever is truly divine."

In arguing that Channing's Unitarianism grew out of "the Hopkinsian revolt," Edgell seems to challenge Conrad Wright's thesis that the beginnings of Unitarianism lay in Arminianism. But this conflict of interpretation should not be emphasized, for the Federal Street Pastor was hardly a typical Unitarian. Throughout his later life Channing exhibited "a Transcendental bias" which set him apart from "orthodox" Unitarians such as Andrews Norton. Indeed, Channing's religious philosophy defies categorization. If it was not wholly original, it was nevertheless "something unique—something not quite Christian (in the orthodox sense), not quite rational (in the eighteenth century sense), not quite Transcendental (in the philosophic sense)." It was a "precarious equilibrium" which reflected and contributed to the metamorphosis of American religion in the early nineteenth century. — *A.C.L.*

Additional Recommended Reading

Haroutunian, Joseph. *Piety Versus Moralism: The Passing of the New England Theology.* New York: Henry Holt and Company, 1932. Haroutunian treats American Unitarianism as the final stage in the decline of Calvinism in New England, viewing it as a blend of religious liberalism and secular humanitarianism.

Parke, David B. *The Epic of Unitarianism: Original Writings from the History of Liberal Religion.* Boston: Starr King Press, 1957. A collection of primary sources in the history of religious liberalism, ranging from a sixteenth century treatise "On the Errors of the Trinity" by Michael Servetus, to James Luther Adams' "A Faith for Free Men" written in 1946. The documents, as well as the editor's notes, help to place American Unitarianism in the perspective of the larger movement.

Persons, Stow. *Free Religion: An American Faith.* New Haven: Yale University Press, 1947. In 1876 a group of young radicals broke away from the Unitarian church to form the "Free Religious Association." Persons analyzes the origins and development of the free religion movement which he credits with transforming Unitarianism "from a Christocentric religion to a pragmatic, humanistic theism. . . ." This is an important work for the history of nineteenth century Unitarianism.

Geffen, Elizabeth M. *Philadelphia Unitarianism, 1796-1861.* Philadelphia: University of Pennsylvania Press, 1961. Philadelphia Unitarianism differed from the New England variety in that it was not a native growth but an import from England. This book studies the institutional life of the Philadelphia society, with considerable attention to the role of its pastor, William Henry Furness.

Wilbur, Earl M. *A History of Unitarianism in Transylvania, England, and America.* Cambridge: Harvard University Press, 1952. The second of a two-volume work on the history of Unitarianism on the European continent, in England and America. Wilbur views American Unitarianism as largely an autonomous, indigenous development, similar in that respect to the movements in other parts of the world.

Rice, Madeleine H. *Federal Street Pastor: The Life of William Ellery Channing.* New York: Bookman Associates, 1961. This recent account of Channing's life and thought draws on the Channing Papers, a collection not utilized by previous biographers. It is carefully documented and well-written, though there is little in the way of critical analysis of Channing's religious philosophy.

THE FREE PUBLIC SCHOOL MOVEMENT

Type of event: Cultural: educational development
Time: 1820's and 1830's
Locale: Northeastern and Western States, and the Upper South

Principal personages:

HORACE MANN (1796-1859), secretary of the Massachusetts Board of Education 1837-1848

JAMES G. CARTER (1795-1849), Massachusetts educational reformer

CALVIN WILEY (fl. nineteenth century), first superintendent of common schools in North Carolina

HENRY BARNARD (1811-1900), editor of *American Journal of Education,* and commissioner of public schools in Connecticut and Rhode Island

CALEB MILLS (fl. nineteenth century), state superintendent of public instruction in Indiana

DEWITT CLINTON (1769-1828), Governor of New York

EDWARD EVERETT (1794-1865), Governor of Massachusetts

THADDEUS STEVENS (1792-1868), leader of free-school supporters in Pennsylvania House

CHARLES FENTON MERCER (1778-1858), Whig politician from Virginia

Summary of Event

The free public school movement of the late 1820's and the 1830's had its roots in the latter part of the eighteenth century when a number of states had drafted constitutions containing clauses or articles urging public aid to education. Nevertheless, the idea that education was a function of the government of the state rather than of family, church, or philanthropy took hold only gradually. It was not until the early nineteenth century, for example, that some states began to enact laws leading to the establishment of public or common schools. Even then, such schools were generally created for, and attended by, pauper children. Moreover, although most states established permanent school funds to supplement lo-cal support of schools, few states resorted to direct taxation as a means of financing education.

During the first two or three decades of the nineteenth century, religious and philanthropic institutions were more active than state governments in promoting free public schooling. The Sunday School movement contributed significantly to the growth of interest in public education. Even more important were the efforts of philanthropists working through benevolent societies. The Free School Society of the City of New York, later reorganized as the Public School Society of New York, was typical of such efforts, as was the Philadelphia Society for the Establishment and Support of Charity Schools.

Nevertheless, like existing state-supported institutions, these schools were mainly for the benefit of children of the poor.

Not until the late 1820's and the 1830's were demands heard for the establishment of a system of free public schooling equally open to all. In some of the larger cities, workingmen's parties called upon the state legislatures to establish public schools. Thus the workingmen of Boston declared in 1830 that "the establishment of a liberal system of education, attainable by all, should be among the first efforts of every lawgiver who desires the continuance of our national independence." At the same time, a number of educational reformers, influenced by the humanitarian reform movement which swept over the United States in the 1830's and 1840's, began to promote the cause of free public schooling. James G. Carter of Massachusetts wrote newspaper articles and pamphlets suggesting improvements in the educational system of his state; as a member of the Massachusetts House and chairman of the Committee on Education, Carter drafted the bill creating the Massachusetts Board of Education in 1837. Horace Mann, who was named secretary of the Board, left a promising legal and political career to dedicate himself to what he called "the supremest welfare of mankind upon the earth." During his twelve years on the board, Mann sustained a concerted campaign in behalf of public education. Largely as a result of efforts by Carter and Mann, Massachusetts led the way in establishing a system of public schooling. In Connecticut and Rhode Island, Henry Barnard promoted the public school cause. In the South and West,

where obstacles to free public schools were greater than in New England, other educational reformers worked to establish systems of public education and to improve facilities and teacher training. Calvin Wiley made North Carolina the center of educational reform in the South. Caleb Mills called for the establishment of a public school system in a series of six annual "Addresses" to the Indiana legislature. In neighboring Ohio, Calvin Stowe, a founder of the Western Literary Institute and College of Professional Teachers, contributed to the development of free public schools through his accounts of the Prussian educational system.

The efforts of educational reformers in promoting free schooling were aided by a number of politicians, including Governors, such as DeWitt Clinton of New York, Edward Everett and Marcus Morton of Massachusetts, and George Wolf of Pennsylvania. The New York Whig, William H. Seward, justified state support of common schools on much the same grounds as other internal improvements. In Pennsylvania, Thaddeus Stevens invoked humanitarian and democratic notions in support of a state law supporting public education. Robert Rantoul, Jr., the first Democratic member of the Massachusetts Board of Education, was another spokesman for free schooling. Publicists and editors, such as George Bancroft, William Cullen Bryant, and William Leggett, also lent their voices to the campaign for "universal education."

By 1850, the movement for free public schooling had largely achieved its basic objectives. The principle of public support for common schools was generally accepted throughout the Union. Every state, for example, had by midcentury established some type of permanent school fund. Moreover, every state except Arkansas had experimented with taxation as a means of school support. Taxation was not universally accepted and school tax laws were repealed in some states, but a precedent had been established which would serve as a basis for a unified system of compulsory taxation. Accompanying the principle of public support was the principle of public control of education. By 1850, according to Lawrence Cremin, "the people . . . largely controlled the schools which they had instituted with public funds." Thus the middle of the nineteenth century marked the end of the initial phase of the campaign for free public schooling, during which the essential groundwork was laid, and the beginning of a second phase of expansion and development was made. As Cremin observes: "The principles and precedents having been established, it remained only for the people to decide how good and how universal a common school education they desired for their young. This eventually would decide the extent to which they drew on their newly established tradition."

Pertinent Literature

Cremin, Lawrence A. *The American Common School: An Historic Conception.* New York: Bureau of Publication, Teachers College, Columbia University, 1951.

Professor Cremin in his study of the conceptual and practical beginnings of the public school system in the United States argues that the idea of a common school emerged in the early nineteenth century as a response to certain social and intellectual developments. One such development was the democratization of politics which conferred on the common man "a vital new political role." Accompanying the trend toward greater political equality was an increasing concern over the maintenance of social equality, particularly by workingmen and other members of the lower middle class who saw in growing industrialism a threat to their economic independence. New conceptions of man and society—perfectionism, humanitarianism, democratization— also shaped the culture of the middle period. Equally important was the swelling current of nationalism, which combined the optimism of "Manifest Destiny" with a growing pessimism regarding the assimilation of immigrant groups.

These intellectual and social developments prompted certain demands which in turn helped to shape the nineteenth century concept of the common school. For example, democratization prompted both liberals and conservatives to call for universal education of the newly enfranchised masses. Labor groups looked to equal education as a means of preventing class stratification, while other Americans saw the school as an institution peculiarly fitted to the task of Americanizing, and even Christianizing, newly arrived immigrants. Implicit in these demands was what Cremin calls "a new, functional, and positive conception of the school's role in society," a concept which emerged in the ideal of the common school formulated by nineteenth century educational reformers. According to Cremin, they conceived of the common school as an institution embracing the entire community—"common to the young of all classes and creeds"—and charged with the function of preparing students for the responsibility of citizenship by nurturing "a common core of sentiment, of value, and of practice." The type of school envisioned by these men was also "common" in the sense of being supported and controlled by the community as a whole.

As Cremin suggests, the ideal of the common school not only developed out of a new concept of education; it was also conceived as an answer to larger cultural and social problems besetting the young nation. In a period of growing concern over questions of national identity, loyalty, and patriotism, and what contemporaries referred to as "national character," educational reformers offered the common school as the one institution "uniquely capable of maintaining and perpetuating a republican society." Thus the common school was one of several efforts in the early nineteenth century to foster a sense of identity and cohesiveness among a strongly individualistic people. Its role in shaping the values and attitudes of young Americans was to become even more important in the late nineteenth and early twentieth centuries. As Cremin observes: "It remained for the facilities, insights, techniques, and methods emerging out of another century of educational endeavor for the school's power in this . . . sphere to be anywhere near adequately harnessed and realized."

Welter, Rush. *Popular Education and Democratic Thought in America.* New York: Columbia University Press, 1962.

Early educational reformers were not alone in looking to the common school as a bulwark of republican society. Indeed, Rush Welter argues that Americans tended to link ideas of public education and popular rule throughout the nineteenth and early twentieth centuries.

In analyzing "the idea of education in its essentially political applications and functions, Welter distinguishes between the republican theory of the post-Revolutionary and early national period—which viewed education as instrumental, hierarchical, authority-oriented, and limited in scope—and the democratic theory which emerged in the 1830's. "When Americans fully embraced democracy, education achieved a new status in their thought," according to Welter. Education became something more than "a democratic instrument of democratic politics." In effect, education absorbed politics and political structure, and was identified with them.

The nature of this revolution in educational thought, which mirrored the changes occurring throughout the whole of American society, is clearly revealed in the theory of democratic education advanced by the workingmen's parties of the late 1820's and early 1830's. The workingmen's demand for a system of public schools was in part an outgrowth of anti-monopoly and anti-aristocratic sentiment. In their fight against special privilege, they attacked not only legislative incorporation of banks, turnpikes, and other economic enterprises, but also state support of "colleges and universities . . . exclusively for the benefit of the wealthy." Just as they insisted upon equal rights in the economic sphere, so they demanded that "the means of equal knowledge" be made "the common property of all classes." Thus the workingmen repudiated the republican conception of education as hierarchical and class-oriented. At the same time, they modified the earlier idea of education as authority-oriented. In their view, popular education would curtail, not increase, the authority of established leaders; public schools were to serve a new authority, the people. Nor did the workingmen seek to limit the scope of education, as republican theorists had. Indeed, "education was the one function of democratic government that might continue to expand even when political evils had been dealt with by limiting the scope of government." In effect, workingmen sought legislation to create a system of universal education; once created, the system would "make unnecessary other forms of legislative activity." Education thus served ultimately as a kind of substitute for the activity of government. The workingmen's policy was what Welter calls "anarchy with a schoolmaster."

Welter maintains that the workingmen's theory of democratic education became "the most characteristic social theory of the age." Democrats and Whigs, liberals and conservatives eventually came to share the workingmen's faith in universal public education. This general commitment to democratic education was translated into legislation in the 1840's and 1850's, as various state constitutional conventions adopted "the principles of popular rule, limited government, and public education that had caused such a stir during the 1830's." The result, according to Welter, was to fix "the doctrines of educated anarchy irrevocably on American political thought." The idea of anarchy with a schoolmaster, first developed in the 1820's and 1830's, would dominate educational thought for almost a century, until World War I and the Great Depression of the 1830's subjected both educational and political beliefs to a sweeping reëxamination and redefinition. — *A.C.L.*

Additional Recommended Reading

Bailyn, Bernard. *Education in the Forming of American Society: Needs and Opportunities for Study.* Chapel Hill: University of North Carolina Press, 1960. Bailyn's seminal essay on the transformation of American education during the colonial period is crucial to an understanding of the origins of nineteenth century theories of public education. Viewing education "in its elaborate, intricate involvements with the rest of society," Bailyn shows how changes in family life, the nature of servitude, organized religion, and community life caused a total recasting of educational thought.

Cremin, Lawrence A., ed. *The Republic and the School: Horace Mann on The Education of Free Men.* New York: Bureau of Publications, Teachers College, Columbia University, 1957. As secretary of the Massachusetts Board of Education, Horace Mann wrote twelve annual reports defending popular education and discussing the variety of problems confronting the growing public school system. Cremin provides excerpts from the reports, in addition to a short introductory essay entitled "Horace Mann's Legacy."

Maddox, William A. *The Free School Idea in Virginia Before the Civil War: A Phase of Political and Social Evolution.* New York: Teachers College, Columbia University, 1918. The South lagged behind the rest of the nation in the development of free public schooling. This study of the development of the common school in Virginia sheds considerable light on the educational pattern followed by other Southern states.

Jackson, Sidney L. *America's Struggle for Free Schools: Social Tension and Education in New England and New York, 1827-1842.* Washington, D.C.: American Council on Public Affairs, 1941. Jackson examines the literature of the Common School Revival and relates it to the economic, political, and cultural conflicts occurring in New York and New England between 1827 and 1842. This thorough treatment includes an extensive bibliography.

Edwards, Newton and Herman G. Richey. *The School in the American Social Order: The Dynamics of American Education.* Boston: Houghton Mifflin Co., 1947. This text studies the development of educational policies and practices against the background of the general social and political history of the United States. A list of selected references encompassing a broad range of subject matter follows each chapter.

LAND LAW OF 1820

Type of event: Legal: legislation regulating the sale of the public domain
Time: April 24, 1820
Locale: Washington, D.C.

Principal personages:

WILLIAM HENRY HARRISON (1773-1841), Congressman from Ohio, who became ninth President of the United States in 1841

ALBERT GALLATIN (1761-1849) Secretary of the Treasury 1801-1814, who advocated the sale in small tracts with credit

ALEXANDER HAMILTON (1757-1804), first Secretary of the Treasury 1789-1795, who proposed use of the public domain as source of revenue for the central government

THOMAS HART BENTON (1782-1858), Senator from Missouri, advocate of cheap land policy

SAMUEL AUGUSTUS FOOT (1780-1846), Senator from Connecticut, who reflected the New England opposition to cheap lands

HENRY CLAY (1777-1852), Senator from Kentucky, Whig leader, and presidential candidate

THOMAS SKIDMORE (fl. 1820's), Eastern labor reformer interested in cheap land policy

NINIAN EDWARDS (1775-1833), Governor of Illinois, supporter of preëmption and liberal land policy

Summary of Event

The first settlers of the British colonies in North America early recognized that their chief source of wealth lay in the land and its cultivation. The extent of the land appeared to be limitless, its fertility of infinite duration. The colonial governments, in an effort to tap this treasure, quickly concerned themselves with the business of land grants. The Continental Congress believed no differently and assumed that the creation of a public domain would provide the government with funds through land sales. Thus, the states ceded their Western claims to the newly organized government and that government developed a system for the sale, survey, and political organization of the newly formed public domain. The Land Ordinance of 1785 provided for rectangular survey and the six-mile-square township unit of measurement. This system was utilized for all the public land states. Political organization was provided for in the famous Northwest Ordinance of 1787. But the question of how cheaply and quickly this land should be settled was not decided and became a principal political issue in the early Republic.

There were basically two schools of thought on the question of land prices. There were those like Alexander Hamilton, and later, Senator Samuel

582

Foot of Connecticut, who believed that the chief purpose of the public domain was to provide the government with a source of revenue. Prices should be kept at a fairly high level. In general, Easterners, at least through the 1820's, were opposed to cheap lands because they feared that the rapid development of the West would weaken the political power of the East in the councils of the nation.

In favor of cheap lands were Albert Gallatin, Secretary of the Treasury from 1801 to 1814, and Senator Thomas Hart Benton of Missouri, who pointed out that the ultimate value of the land depended upon quick settlement and agricultural exploitation. They also advocated settlement in small tracts with credit facilities. In the opening rounds of this struggle the opponents of cheap land prevailed and the Land Act of 1796 provided for sale in tracts of 640 acres (a section) at two dollars per acre.

The land policies of the United States became a perennial topic for political debate. The advocates of cheap land chipped away at both the price and minimum acreage provisions. The Harrison Land Act of 1800 decreased the size of the tracts to 320 acres while the price remained the same. But in 1804, the price was reduced to $1.64 per acre and the size to 160 acres. This act retained the four-year-credit provision of the Harrison Land Act. The system remained unchanged until 1820. Administration of the system was improved with the establishment of a General Land Office in 1812 as a bureau of the Treasury Department.

Beginning in 1803, with the admission of Ohio into the Union, and through 1821, seven public land states were admitted. Although settlement of the West had continued steadily during the Federalist and Jeffersonian years, the War of 1812 caused a decline in the rate of settlement. But by 1814-1815 the movement became a torrent. Over a million acres of public land were sold in 1814. Land offices had multiplied from eleven in 1810 to thirty-four in 1820, operating in nine states and territories. The population, at 9,600,000 in 1820, had increased by thirty percent since 1810. Speculation in land became a mania, and land indebtedness, due to the liberal credit provisions of the Harrison Land Act, grew apace. In 1819, the Secretary of the Treasury reported that the federal government had sold forty-four million dollars worth of land since 1789 but had received only half that amount. Arrears in payments increased by fourteen million dollars between 1815 and 1819.

This overextension of credit and capital in the purchase of public lands was part of a general overextension in the area of commerce and banking. The end of the War of 1812 reopened the market of the United States to British manufacturers. The states produced banks which in turn produced credit. The Second Bank of the United States, chartered in 1816, was unable to stem the tide of inflation. Specie was drained from the West to the East and from there to Great Britain. With a weakened currency, irresponsible banking practices, inflated prices, overexpansion in business, and the great sales of public lands, an economic reaction was inevitable. It came with the Panic of 1819 and a depression which lasted into the 1820's.

Since it was recognized that credits

originating from the provisions of the Harrison Land Act were a major cause of the panic, reform of the system was essential and provided for in the Land Law of 1820. In this act, credit was abolished, the price per acre was reduced to $1.25, and the minimum acreage was cut to eighty. A relief act followed in 1821 which allowed previous purchasers to give up the land for which they were in arrears and apply payments already made to a portion of the purchase to be retained. The Land Law of 1820 has been criticized because the requirement of cash purchase supposedly worked against the settler in favor of the speculator. Recent research has pointed out, however, that the speculators served a positive role in Western settlement by providing credit

as well as other services to immigrants.

This land reform act did not end discussion of the land system. If anything the tempo of discussion picked up as the West came into its own politically. Western leaders, such as Thomas Hart Benton, exploiting the sectional nature of American politics, held out hopes of Western support to political leaders of other sections in return for a liberalization of the land laws. Westerners now voiced their demands for graduation (the scaling down of the price of land according to the length of time it remained unsold), and preëmption (the official recognition of squatters' claims to land not yet on the market). Through skillful horse-trading, Western leaders achieved preëmption in 1841 and graduation in 1854.

Pertinent Literature

Hibbard, Benjamin H. *A History of the Public Land Policies.* New York: The Macmillan Company, 1924.

This volume is one of the multivolume *Land Economic* Series edited by Richard T. Ely of the University of Wisconsin. Professor Hibbard states that the aim of this volume "has been to put into one moderate-sized volume, a sketch of the historical development and operations of our federal land policies."

In his introductory chapter Professor Hibbard states that, from the earliest days of the nation, land was viewed as a primary national resource. Alexander Hamilton in his famous 1790 report on the public domain stated that the large expanse of unsettled land controlled by the national government should be used to reduce the national debt and to foster the rapid settlement of the nation's Western regions.

Thomas Jefferson also believed that the public domain should be used as a revenue generating source. The Virginian, however, differed with Hamilton in that the former believed that the land should be sold as cheaply as possible. Hibbard points out that in the long run neither Hamilton's nor Jefferson's ideas concerning land sale prevailed. It was the pioneer settler who eventually determined the land disposal program of the national government.

After the principle of the desirability of Western settlement was agreed upon, the disagreement over the actual method of settlement threatened to hinder the movement of settlers into the Trans-Appalachian region. Hibbard points out that there were two contesting settlement patterns: the

New England township system, which required all land to be surveyed and recorded before being opened for systematic settlement, and the Southern settlement system which allowed scattered settlement on unsurveyed land. The New England and Southern systems were compromised in the Ordinance of 1785. This land law required that unsettled land be surveyed, but it did not require the methodical township pattern of settlement, allowing the erratic settlement pattern prevalent along the southern frontier.

Attempting to increase governmental revenues and to strike at the speculators who were gaining control of the Western land, Congress liberalized the credit features of the land laws in 1796, 1800, and 1804. It was hoped that by reducing the price of land from $2.00 to $1.64 per acre and by increasing the time settlers could pay for their purchase, more land would be purchased by individual settlers.

The credit sales system worked well during the economically affluent years following the War of 1812. The Panic of 1819, however, brought a decline in land sales and many settlers defaulted in their payments.

In an attempt to remedy this situation, Congress passed the Land Act of 1820 which abolished the credit sales system. The 1820 act, furthermore, established a minimum price of $1.25 per acre and reduced the minimum amount of land to be purchased from 160 acres to eighty acres. Hibbard states that the reduction of the size of the purchase tract to eighty acres and the total purchase price to $100.00 brought access to the public lands within the reasonable grasp of most Western settlers. He further states that this reduction in acreage and price, although immediately reducing the amount of land sales, stabilized the whole system and gave the government time to recover some of its losses caused by the Panic of 1819.

The next major change in the government's land policy came during the 1830's when Congress recognized the principle of preëmption, the right to settle on, improve, and later purchase unappropriated public lands. Preëmption, however, was just a precurser to the Homestead Act of 1862. This latter legislation was intended to open the public domain to free settlement by allowing settlers to acquire 160 acres free of all charges, except for a small filing fee. Full title to the land was granted only after the homesteader had lived on the land for five years.

Hibbard concludes his study by explaining the operation of the Timber Culture and Desert Land Acts, both of which modified the Homestead Act, but neither of which fulfilled their purpose of getting more settlers onto Western lands.

Rohrbough, Malcolm J. *The Land Office Business: The Settlement and Administration of American Public Lands, 1789-1837.* New York: Oxford University Press, 1968.

In his introduction Rohrbough states that during the first half of the nineteenth century, "Land was the nation's most sought-after commodity," and that the effort in time and money spent by the settlers and speculators to obtain a piece of the public domain was one of the "dominant forces of the period."

Because land was such a dynamic

influence upon the new nation, the Confederation government was forced to take immediate steps to develop a workable land policy. The vast amount of Western land was viewed as a source of revenue and a protective barrier against the hostile Indians. Effective settlement, however, was necessary for either of these desired goals to be achieved. Accordingly, the Confederation Congress debated and eventually passed the Ordinance of 1785 which established the first systematic land survey and sales system.

The federal Congress continued the Confederation land policy by enacting the Land Law of 1796 which provided for the sale of 640 acre tracts at $2.00 per acre. The law also continued the rectangular survey system established by the Ordinance of 1785.

Because the 1796 law did not stimulate land sales and thereby generate vital revenue, in 1800, Congress acted to change the land sales system by establishing four land districts within Ohio Territory. Land was sold at public auction at each of these offices following proper public notification. The price of land remained at $2.00 per acre, but Congress authorized the government to grant credit to prospective purchasers. The 1800 act also reduced the minimum purchasable tract to 320 acres, thus giving settlers the opportunity to purchase land.

With the 1803 acquisition of the Louisiana Purchase region, the public domain of the United States almost doubled in size and Congress extended the Land Office districts as far west as St. Louis. The additional offices not only expanded the possibility for further settlement, but the surveys also increased the scientific and political knowledge of the new region as it developed. For as Rohrbough states, "No one was better stationed to observe the formation and transformation of the western country than the district land officers and the surveyors-general."

The Panic of 1819 abruptly ended the "boom days" of the early nineteenth century land sales. Before the advent of this economic depression, however, one of the nation's greatest migrations occurred, and five new states, all of them carved out of the Western domain, entered the Union: Indiana in 1816, Mississippi in 1817, Illinois in 1818, Alabama in 1819, and eventually Missouri in 1821.

The 1819 economic dislocation prompted a sharp congressional debate over the terms under which public lands were sold. The credit system had prompted the Western settler to assume financial obligations that extended beyond his ability to fulfill. In an attempt to remedy this situation Congress passed the Land Act of 1820. The new law slowed but did not entirely stop the westward flow of settlers seeking new lands. Although the post-1820 settlers were required to pay cash for their land, the problem of defaulting settlers still plagued the government.

During the 1820's, Congress passed several relief acts, but it was not until Andrew Jackson's Administration that effective relief was given the Western debtors, and, eventually, preëmption was recognized by the federal government as an acceptable means of securing individual claims to the public domain.

Preëmption stimulated land sales in western Missouri and Arkansas and the 1830's were another period of "boom days" in land sales. The Panic of 1837 ended the rush of Jacksonian land sales, and returned the system to a more orderly pace. — *J.G.C.*

Additional Recommended Reading

Treat, Payson J. *The National Land System, 1785-1820.* New York: E. B. Trent, 1910. A pioneer effort at scholarly treatment of the formative years of the public land system, which is still useful.

Robbins, Roy M. *Our Landed Heritage: The Public Domain, 1776-1936.* Princeton: Princeton University Press, 1942. Robbins attempts to relate land policy to forces in society other than, but including, politics and economics.

Gates, Paul W. *Frontier Landlords and Pioneer Tenants.* Ithaca: Cornell University Press, 1945. In studying the effects of cheap land, Gates discovers that there was considerable tenancy on the frontier.

Carlson, Theodore L. *The Illinois Military Tract: A Study of Land Occupation, Utilization, and Tenure.* Vol. XXXII: *University of Illinois Studies in the Social Sciences.* Urbana: University of Illinois Press, 1951. Carlson studies patterns of settlement in a part of the Illinois River Valley.

Chambers, William N. *Old Bullion Benton, Senator from the New West: Thomas Hart Benton, 1782-1858.* Boston: Little, Brown, and Company, 1956. A biography of the U.S. Senator from Missouri, who was a political associate of President Jackson and the leader of cheap land forces in Congress.

Carstensen, Vernon. *The Public Lands: Studies in the History of the Public Domain.* Madison: University of Wisconsin Press, 1953. A collection of some of the more important scholarly articles dealing with the public lands and their settlement.

OPENING OF THE SANTA FE TRADE

Type of event: Economic: desire to establish trade between a Spanish outpost and the Missouri frontier
Time: September, 1821-June, 1822
Locale: The greater Southwest

Principal personages:
WILLIAM BECKNELL (1790?-1832), trail-blazer credited with opening the Santa Fe route for trade purposes in 1821
THOMAS JAMES (1782-1847), St. Louis merchant also engaged in trade on the Santa Fe Trail in 1821
JACOB FOWLER (1765-1850), and
HUGH GLENN (1788-1833), traders who sold goods in Santa Fe in 1821
JOSIAH GREGG (1806-1850), caravan leader in 1831 and author of *Commerce on the Prairies,* the classic account of the Santa Fe trade

Summary of Event

In the early years of the nineteenth century, Santa Fe was an isolated outpost some fifteen hundred miles from the center of Spanish authority in Mexico City. Its inhabitants possessed an abundance of silver, furs, and mules; but they suffered from a lack of fabricated goods. Traders on the Missouri frontier were eager to obtain these products in exchange for inexpensive textiles, cutlery, utensils, and a wide variety of other items. The mutual advantage of trade was obvious, but venturesome traders arriving in Santa Fe between 1804 and 1820 were forcefully reminded that the Spanish empire was not open to foreigners. Those who failed to heed the warning had their property confiscated, and a few were imprisoned. The Mexican Revolution in 1820, however, brought an end to Spanish restrictions on commerce in New Mexico.

Frontier traders quickly seized the opportunity to sell or exchange their goods in Santa Fe, and even before news of Mexico's freedom had reached Missouri, several men already organized pack trains to penetrate the Rockies in 1821, carrying manufactured wares to exchange for furs trapped by the Indians. In the forefront was William Becknell, who had headed west in May with a party of twenty men and ascended the Arkansas river. In the vicinity of Raton Pass his party encountered an encampment of Mexican soldiers who told them Mexico had won its independence and would welcome American traders. The party immediately turned south to Santa Fe, where they sold their goods for quantities of Mexican silver and returned to Missouri in midwinter, arriving in the frontier town of Franklin in January, 1822. About two weeks after Becknell's departure fom Santa Fe, a St. Louis merchant, Thomas James, arrived with a trainload of goods. He remained in New Mexico from December until

588

June, experiencing difficulty in disposing of his stock of drab cotton fabrics. A third trading party, led by Jacob Fowler and Hugh Glenn, reached Santa Fe and enjoyed a profitable business. The next spring, William Becknell and a score of men returned to Santa Fe with three wagons of merchandise. Becknell thus gained celebrity as "Father of the Santa Fe Trade." Knowing that it would be difficult to cross Raton Pass with heavily-loaded wagons, Becknell pioneered a new route direct to Santa Fe from the Arkansas River Crossing through the Cimarron Desert.

Wagons were being used extensively on the trail by 1824, and the number of men and the amount of goods involved steadily increased each year until 1828 in spite of many difficulties. In addition to the problems of conducting a train across the treeless plains and waterless desert, another hazard was the probability of attack by the hostile Kiowa and Comanche Indians. Upon arriving in Santa Fe, traders had to pay an import tax that sometimes ran as high as sixty percent of the value of their goods, and to avoid this tax, they often resorted to bribery. The Mexican government, in 1839, countered by charging a tax of five hundred dollars on each wagon, which merely encouraged traders to use larger wagons and overload them. In spite of handicaps and uncertainties, the average wagon train earned a profit of between ten and forty percent.

In the total economy of the West, the value of the Santa Fe trade was minimal, averaging only $130,000 a year between 1822 and 1843. The best year was 1841, when the value of goods exchanged reached $450,000. The trade was temporarily stopped by the Mexican government between 1843 and 1844, but was revived during the Mexican War and attained a wartime peak of $1,752,250 in 1846. The business continued after the war, not as an international trade but as a means of supplying United States military forces on the frontier. Trade was brisk during the Civil War, and the Santa Fe Trail continued in use for commercial purposes until the railroad era.

The United States government was in the difficult position of trying to maintain a permanent Indian frontier along the western boundary of Missouri and of guaranteeing the Plains region to the tribes while at the same time encouraging and protecting traders who were intruding upon the Indians' domain. Major Stephen Cooper had led a company of thirty traders to Santa Fe in 1823. Two years later, the federal government appropriated thirty thousand dollars to mark the route within the limits of the United States and to seek concessions from the Indian tribes guaranteeing safe passage for the traders. Unfortunately, the markings made of earthen and stone mounds were placed upon the little used and longer "Mountain Route" that ascended the Arkansas river to Bent's Fort near present Pueblo, Colorado, thence south to Santa Fe, rather than along the Cimarron "cutoff." Fort Leavenworth was established in 1827, principally to guard the trail, but the following year Indians attacked the caravans headed for Santa Fe. Several traders were murdered, others were robbed, wagons were abandoned when the animals drawing them were killed, and at least one party had to walk home. Military escorts were pro-

589

vided at government expense in 1829, 1834, and 1843 to protect the traders as far as the United States boundary.

The Santa Fe trade not only initiated the disintegration of the permanent Indian frontier but also turned the attention of the United States toward the Mexican territory in the Southwest.

Reports of traders dispelled the illusion of Mexican military power and demonstrated the ease with which the United States might take over the area. In addition, Santa Fe traders assisted in destroying the concept of the Great Plains as "the Great American Desert."

Pertinent Literature

Duffus, Robert L. *The Santa Fe Trail.* New York: Longmans, Green, and Co., 1931.

This is still the first and only book available which attempts to discuss the major aspects of the history of the Santa Fe Trail. Duffus tells the story chronologically from the exploration of Coronado in 1541 to the entry of the first railroad train into Santa Fe in 1880. His account covers the activities of Spanish, French, and American explorers who traversed portions of the trail. He describes the adventures of traders who violated the Spanish border and were imprisoned or deported for their rashness; of entrepreneurs who later developed the route for commercial caravans; and of politicians and government servants who attempted to locate, mark and protect the road. Emphasis is placed on the use of the trail for military purposes, including the movement of troops in the Southwest during the Mexican War and in sustaining the military outposts there when the conflict ended. Three-fourths of the book is devoted to the period before 1848.

Duffus has succeeded in bringing together in a single volume much information that hitherto was scattered in many works. Writing in the style of a journalist, he has produced a delightful and entertaining narrative that will be of value to students and readers interested in the history of the West. He has delved deeply into the general literature and has allowed his imagination full play in handling this fascinating subject. Those interested in a broad coverage of the history of the Santa Fe Trail will find this volume rewarding.

Historical scholars have warned, however, that this book must be used with caution. In his attempt to turn a felicitous phrase, Duffus often makes statements that are historically incorrect, or at least questionable. His handling of the sources has been casual. Errors in factual details and misspelled names of persons and places are to be found throughout. Nevertheless, this book remains the best source available on the subject for the general reader.

Gregg, Josiah. *The Commerce of the Prairies.* Edited by Max L. Moorhead. Norman: University of Oklahoma Press, 1954. Various later revisions, the latest being: New York: Haskell House Publications, 1969.

First published in two volumes during 1844, Josiah Gregg's description of the Santa Fe trade has for many years

been recognized as the classic account of the subject. Written by a man with a cultivated mind who participated in the trade for nine years, all the time taking careful notes, this book is more accurate than the typical memoir. No one since Gregg has written on the subject without relying heavily on his work.

Born in 1806, Gregg grew up as a sickly child, too frail to work on the family farm in Missouri but with an interest in school and learning. He studied surveying, taught school for a time, and became a physician. When twenty-four years old, he was so ill that he resolved to travel to Santa Fe to improve his health. Leaving Independence in 1831 with a merchant caravan, he earned his way by keeping books for the traders. He regained his health quickly, and learned sufficient Spanish on the trail to be able to communicate effectively by the end of the journey. Thus inadvertently drawn into the Santa Fe trade, he made four round trips with wagon caravans, taking dry goods and hardware in exchange for Mexican silver and mules. One trip took him beyond Santa Fe to Chihuahua City and into the interior of Mexico.

Among other things, Gregg tells of the routine procedures and organization of a typical caravan. Early in May, traders arrived at Independence or other outfitting towns on the Missouri frontier to bring together their merchandise, men, and supplies. Each employee was paid from $25 to $50 a month according to his duties, and was guaranteed his rations calculated on the basis of fifty pounds of flour, fifty pounds of bacon, ten pounds of coffee, and twenty pounds of sugar for the entire trip. Buffalo and other game killed along the route were to provide meat.

As soon as the ground was passable, each trader moved his wagons westward to the rendezvous at Council Grove, Kansas, where the caravan was assembled and officers were chosen. After the organization was completed, the group moved west, traveling from eight to fifteen miles a day. Gregg not only provides detailed information on the business of trading, but also makes valuable comments on the terrain and on the flora and fauna. He describes life among the New Mexicans, including their religious superstitions, their *fandangos,* and even their methods of loading pack mules and rolling cigarettes by hand. His book is a veritable storehouse of information about the Southwest of the 1830's and 1840's.

The first edition of two thousand copies of Gregg's work sold so quickly that a second printing was immediately issued with the addition of an explanatory preface, an index, and a glossary of Spanish words. Numerous printings followed, including English and German editions. Between 1941 and 1944, the diaries and correspondence of Josiah Gregg were published for the first time. Taking advantage of this new information and recognizing that earlier editions of *Commerce of the Prairies* were out of print and difficult to obtain, Max L. Moorhead has prepared a new edition of exceptional merit. He identifies names, places, and incidents, thereby clarifying both Gregg's text and notes. He calls attention to a few errors of fact and interpretation by referring to other contemporary accounts and to recent historical research. In the introduction he sketches the life and personality of Gregg and gives the essential facts about the assistance which Gregg received in preparing his notes for publication. This volume is the most reliable historical publication on the Santa Fe Trail. — *W. T. J.*

Additional Recommended Reading

Coues, Elliott. *The Journal of Jacob Fowler, 1821-1822.* New York: Francis P. Harper, 1898. The classic work describing how Fowler and his partner Hugh Glenn followed the course of the Arkansas river and secured permission to trap and trade in Mexican territory in 1821.

Gregg, Kate L. *The Road to Santa Fe.* Albuquerque: University of New Mexico Press, 1952. A definitive account of the survey and marking of the Santa Fe Trail by the United States government, 1825-1827, including the journals and diaries of George Champlin Sibley and others.

Magoffin, Susan S. *Down the Santa Fe Trail and into Mexico: The Diary of Susan Shelby Magoffin, 1846-1847.* Edited by Stella M. Drumm. Revised ed. New Haven: Yale University Press, 1962. The account of an observant young woman who accompanied her husband, a veteran Santa Fe trader, to New Mexico and on south to Chihuahua City during the Mexican War.

Moorhead, Max L. *New Mexico's Royal Road: Trade and Travel on the Chihuahua Trail.* Norman: University of Oklahoma Press, 1958. A scholarly and interpretive study emphasizing the nature and importance of trade between Santa Fe and Chihuahua City and explaining its relationship to the Santa Fe trade.

Field, Matthew C. *Matt Field on the Santa Fe Trail.* Edited by John E. Sunder. Norman: University of Oklahoma Press, 1960. The vivid firsthand impressions of an able journalist who spent the summer of 1839 on the Santa Fe Trail and in the settlements of New Mexico.

Vestal, Stanley. *The Old Santa Fe Trail.* Boston: Houghton Mifflin Co., 1939. A readable popular account that attempts to recapture the experience of those who traveled to Santa Fe.

Young, Otis E. *The First Military Escort on the Santa Fe Trail, 1829.* Glendale, California: The Arthur H. Clark Company, 1952. A synthesis of available source materials to describe fully the attacks made on caravans traversing the Santa Fe Trail in 1828.

THE MONROE DOCTRINE

Type of event: Diplomatic: declaration of American foreign policy concerning independent countries in the Western Hemisphere
Time: December 2, 1823
Locale: Washington, D.C.

Principal personages:

JAMES MONROE (1758-1831), fifth President of the United States 1817-1825

JOHN QUINCY ADAMS (1767-1848), American Secretary of State 1817-1825

HENRY CLAY (1777-1852), leader, U.S. House of Representatives

RICHARD RUSH (1780-1859), American Minister to Great Britain

ROBERT STEWART (First VISCOUNT CASTLEREAGH) (1769-1822), British Foreign Secretary who committed suicide in 1822; also known as Marquis of Londonderry

GEORGE CANNING (1770-1827), succeeded Castlereagh as British Foreign Secretary

GEORGE IV (1762-1830), King of Great Britain 1820-1830

ALEXANDER I (1777-1825), Tsar of Russia 1801-1825

AUGUSTE JULES ARMAND MARIE DE POLIGNAC (PRINCE DE POLIGNAC) (1780-1847), French Ambassador to Great Britain

PRINCE KLEMENS VON METTERNICH (1773-1859), Austrian Chancellor; sponsor of monarchial balance of power system in Europe after 1815

Summary of Event

On December 2, 1823, President James Monroe stood before the Congress of the United States to read his annual message. Though most of his remarks concerned domestic matters, two widely-separated sections were destined to take on historic importance as the basis of a major declaration of American foreign policy. "The American Continents," Monroe announced, "by the free and independent condition which they have assumed and maintain, are henceforth not to be considered as subjects for future colonization by a European power." The President then turned to European colonial policy in the New World: "With the existing Colonies or dependencies of any European power, we have not interfered, and shall not interfere. But with the Governments who have declared their Independence, and maintained it, and whose Independence we have, on great consideration, and on just principles, acknowledged, we could not view any interposition for the purpose of oppressing them, or controlling in any other manner, their destiny, by any European power, in any other light than as the manifestation of an unfriendly disposition towards the United States."

Monroe's message contained three main points about foreign policy. First, the President announced to Europe that the United States would oppose any attempt to take over any independent country in the Western Hemisphere (the no transfer principle). Second, he promised that America would abstain from European quarrels (nonintervention) unless this nation's rights were endangered. Third, Monroe insisted that Europe must keep hands off any independent nation in the New World. In other words, Monroe meant that the United States would not take sides in European disputes but that, in return, there must be no tampering with the *status quo* in the Western Hemisphere.

Monroe's words offered no threat to such nations as Great Britain or France. In 1823 America lacked the power to force Europe to follow any specific course of action. Fortunately, however, Great Britain wanted just such a policy as Monroe suggested. The British fleet, not Monroe's words, helped maintain the independence of Latin America. Indeed, it was not until 1852 that anyone referred to Monroe's principles as the Monroe Doctrine. And it was not until the twentieth century that the United States had enough power to insist on international acceptance of the Monroe Doctrine.

Even so, Monroe's words reflected an altering of the unfriendly relations between Great Britain and the United States which had led to the War of 1812. The explanation lies in decisions made at the Congress of Vienna in 1815. Napoleon had been defeated; Prussia, Russia, Austria, France, and Great Britain set out to turn the clock back, through establishing a Quintuple Alliance to undo the changes wrought by Napoleon. This action led to a Concert of Europe which sponsored four congresses between 1818 and 1822. The congresses established the modern system of conference diplomacy though the various members failed to agree among themselves about the future of Europe. For one thing, in 1815 Tsar Alexander I of Russia invited the monarchs of Austria and Prussia to join him in a Holy Alliance, a group dedicated to upholding autocracy. Great Britain chose not to become affiliated with so openly reactionary an alliance but it continued as a member of the Quintuple Alliance.

Great Britain learned that it could not have things both ways. As a member of the Quintuple Alliance, Great Britain seemed to support a policy of reestablishing monarchy and opposing revolution. By refusing to join the Holy Alliance, however, it seemed to oppose appearing as a bastion of reaction. Great Britain's actions soon proved that it favored a system of monarchy, a balance of power for Europe, but not systematic suppression of revolution in other parts of the world.

Spain demanded the return of its colonies in the New World. In 1820, when Prince Metternich, the architect of reaction, suggested that the Concert of Europe had a sacred duty to crush revolution, Great Britain refused to go along with his proposal. It would have meant sending an army to Latin America to overthrow new republics. Great Britain distinguished between a balance of power system in Europe (where revolution would not be permitted) and a colonial empire in the New

World (where revolution would be allowed to occur). Besides, Spain had monopolized trade with its colonies; only as independent republics in Latin America could they maintain a profitable trade with the British.

The Russian Tsar also tried to extend his interests in North America. Through an imperial *ukase,* or decree, of September 14, 1821, Russia seemed to claim territory on the Pacific Coast south to the fifty-first parallel (or well into the Oregon country) by insisting that all foreign ships must remain a substantial distance from the coast that far south. Secretary of State John Quincy Adams vigorously opposed the *ukase,* citing the American principle of noncolonization. The Tsar's *ukase* was never enforced.

Lord Castlereagh, British Foreign Secretary, decided that Spanish and Russian claims to territory in the New World were less important to Great Britain than was the profitable trade with former Spanish colonies. Accordingly, the British began thinking of some sort of arrangement with the United States which would prevent European powers from taking new, or regaining old, colonies in the Western Hemisphere.

In August, 1823, George Canning, Castlereagh's successor as Foreign Secretary, suggested to Richard Rush, the American Minister to Great Britain, that the two countries jointly declare their intent to oppose further colonization of the New World. Rush was reluctant to agree to so bold a move without consulting his own superior, John Quincy Adams.

In the meantime, Canning began a series of conversations with Prince Jules de Polignac, the French ambassador in London, concerning some guarantee that France would not help Spain regain her lost colonies in America. On October 12, the Ambassador gave Canning the specific assurances he wanted in a document known to posterity as the Polignac Memorandum. France's promise to Great Britain, and not the Monroe Doctrine, ended any chance of Spain's regaining its colonies in the New World.

In Washington, Adams opposed a joint noncolonization declaration with Great Britain. He was unaware of the Polignac Memorandum. Instead, he suggested to President Monroe that the United States make a declaration opposing further European colonization attempts in the Western Hemisphere—but not in conjunction with Great Britain. The result was the Presidential statement of December, 1823. Only the British fleet gave the President's words any meaning as far as France and Spain were concerned.

Since 1823 Monroe's message has become of much greater significance. During the Civil War, France established a puppet in the person of the Austrian Archduke, Maximilian, as the head of the government of Mexico. In 1867, by invoking the Monroe Doctrine and threatening an invasion, the United States ensured the collapse of Emperor Maximilian's government. In December, 1904, President Theodore Roosevelt added a corollary to the Monroe Doctrine in which he stated that the United States would not interfere with Latin American nations that conducted their affairs with decency, but that should they fail to do so, the United States would intervene and exercise an international police power. In 1930, President Hoover formally repudiated the Roosevelt Corollary by revealing the publication of the Clark Memorandum abjuring any right of the United States to intervene in Latin America. The Monroe Doctrine would be applied only as originally intended —to protect Latin America from European intervention.

The United States, however, has found reasons for intervening in the affairs of countries in this hemisphere since 1930. As recently as 1965, President Lyndon Johnson ordered American troops into the Dominican Republic to prevent the takeover of that country by a Communist government, although the official justification for intervention was the protection of the lives of Americans and other nationals.

Pertinent Literature

Perkins, Dexter. *A History of the Monroe Doctrine*. Boston: Little, Brown, and Company, 1955.

This is the best one-volume history of the Monroe Doctrine during its first 120 years. Dexter Perkins, a leading American diplomatic historian, devoted much of his scholarly life to the study of the evolution of Monroe's 1823 message. This book represents a summary of his many earlier writings. Perkins believes that the origins of the Monroe Doctrine are to be found in European attempts to regain or take new colonies in the New World. Russia threatened to extend southward her Alaskan possessions; Spain threatened to have France help her regain her New World empire. The result, he suggests, was "a prohibition on the part of the United States against the extension of European influence and power to the New World."

Perkins notes how little the message was noticed in the years after 1823. He carefully explains that though America promised to remain neutral in European conflicts, this nation did not commit itself to a rigid policy of isolationism. Perkins shows that Monroe's message was very much in the self-interest of the United States, but he does not believe that economic considerations explain the origins of the Monroe Doctrine. On the other hand, he suggests that the same cannot be said for Theodore Roosevelt's Corollary to the Monroe Doctrine. Perkins, like most historians, has little to say for Roosevelt's threat to intervene forcefully in Latin America. As he suggests, "in the development of the Doctrine, indeed, one of the most extraordinary and interesting objects of study must be the evolution of a theorem intended for the protection of the Latin-American states by the United States into one that justified and even sanctified American interference in and control of the affairs of the independent republics of this continent."

Bemis, Samuel Flagg. *John Quincy Adams and the Foundations of American Foreign Policy*. New York: Alfred A. Knopf, Inc., 1949.

The Monroe Doctrine bears the name of the fifth President, and that is entirely appropriate, as he announced the doctrine to the world and had directed the consultations of which it was a product. Samuel Flagg Bemis grants that fact, but also rather convincingly demonstrates the crucial role that Monroe's Secretary of State, John Quincy Adams, played in the formation of the "most significant of all American state papers," and, indeed, in the formation and exercise of those principles that are fundamental in the United States' foreign policy. This biographical approach to the survey of foreign policy in the first three-quarters of the century of American independence focuses on the life of Adams and examines his role as creator and exemplar of those fundamental principles that were so clearly articulated in the Presidential message of 1823. In the last chapter of the work, Bemis identifies fourteen "classic principles" of American policy, some of them merely restatements or refinements of the three great principles of the Monroe Doctrine itself. Adams had a part in all of them; he grew up with the nation, really and figuratively, and his career in diplomacy, and later in the White House, provides a useful framework for the development of a history of those principles.

The Monroe Doctrine itself announces the principles of "Non-Colonization;" "Abstention by the United States from European affairs;" and "Hands-Off by the European nations of the Western Hemisphere." Bemis describes generally the origins of these principles as well as their instant emergence in Monroe's message, with particular attention to the involvement of John Quincy Adams. Without denigrating the role of President Monroe and his ultimate responsibility as President for it, Bemis assigns to Adams the chief authorship of the non-colonization principle. Adams, in earlier nego-

tiations with the Russians as Secretary of State and in his general demeanor during discussions with representatives of foreign states, had made clear his conviction that the interests of the United States as a continental power—a power which he had personally helped develop through his Transcontinental Treaty with Spain—precluded further colonization of the Western Hemisphere. The hands-off principle, announced in the Doctrine with non-colonization, Bemis maintains, is simply a corollary to the non-colonization principle. In the cabinet discussions occasioned by the correspondence with Great Britain over the possibilities of European intervention in Latin America to restore to Spain her dominions in this hemisphere, Adams was also the chief proponent of a vigorous adherence to the abstention principle—a principle as old as Washington's "Farewell Address." Monroe, defending the republican and liberal systems as they were emerging in Latin America, and assuming for the United States the role of defender of such principles outside its own borders, wished to go further than the Western Hemisphere. He wanted to associate the United States with both the struggle of Greece for independence from Turkey; and the struggle of liberal elements in Spain against the forces of despotism—the armed forces of France which were assigned by the Holy Alliance to crush constitutionalism in Spain. Adams, no less than Monroe, was a defender of human liberty; his later career after his Presidency would be marked by a vigorous assault on chattel slavery. He, however, resisted tendencies of the President and members of the Cabinet to involve the

United States in European affairs. He argued, as had others from the birth of the nation, that Europe had a political system that was inherently different from that system that was being built on this side of the ocean, and that the interests of the United States and ultimately the interests of human freedom were best served by a recognition of those differences and the abstention of the United States from European affairs when direct interests were not involved. Even Jefferson and Madison, who were consulted by Monroe before he had formulated the Doctrine, had been willing to depart from that policy to the extent of associating the nation with Britain in defense of Latin America. Adams won over the President and Cabinet, and the Monroe Doctrine announced the policy which the United States was to follow towards Europe into the twentieth century. Adams focused his attention on the development of the nation as the continental power it was to become and worked toward that end. The Monroe Doctrine asserted for the United States a role in this hemisphere that would have been difficult to have maintained, but it asserted that power independently. The doctrine is Monroe's, but Bemis' work illustrates that the work of his Secretary of State cannot be ignored because he was in fact the chief architect of this "foundation" of American foreign policy. — *D.H.C.*

Additional Recommended Reading

Dangerfield, George. *The Era of Good Feelings.* New York: Harbinger Books, 1963. One of the best accounts of the Monroe Presidency; Dangerfield's thesis about the origins of the Monroe Doctrine, "The Diplomacy of Coal and Iron," should not, however, be accepted uncritically.

Whitaker, Arthur P. *The United States and the Independence of Latin America, 1800-1830.* Baltimore: The Johns Hopkins University Press, 1941. Places the Monroe Doctrine in the context of Latin American independence.

Williams, William A. "The Age of Mercantilism: An Interpretation of the American Political Economy to 1828," reprinted in Williams' *The Shaping of American Diplomacy.* Vol. I. Chicago: Rand McNally, Inc., 1970. A brilliant article which suggests the importance of trading privileges with Latin America in the thinking of Adams and Monroe. Williams terms the Monroe Doctrine a "Manifesto of Empire." See also Charles Lyon Chandler. "United States Commerce with Latin America at the Promulgation of the Monroe Doctrine," reprinted in Williams' *The Shaping of American Diplomacy.* Vol. I, 104-108. Chicago: Rand McNally, Inc., 1970.

Bemis, Samuel Flagg. *The Latin American Policy of the United States: An Historical Interpretation.* New York: Norton Library, 1967. A controversial, pro-American account which explains the Monroe Doctrine as an act of idealism.

Rappaport, Armin, ed. *The Monroe Doctrine. American Problem Studies.* New York: Holt, Rinehart and Winston, 1964. A selection of excerpts from studies of the Monroe Doctrine and a helpful critical bibliography.

LaFeber, Walter, ed. *John Quincy Adams and American Continental Empire: Letters, Papers, and Speeches.* New York: Quadrangle Books, Inc., 1965. Primary material concerning Adams and the Monroe Doctrine.

Perkins, Bradford. *Castlereagh and Adams: England and the United States, 1812-1823.* Berkeley: University of California Press, 1964. A thoroughly researched volume which concentrates on Anglo-American relations after 1815.

FEDERAL GOVERNMENT ASSUMES CONTROL OF
INTERSTATE COMMERCE
(*Gibbons* v. *Ogden*)

Type of event: Legal: Supreme Court decision regulating interstate commerce
Time: March 2, 1824
Locale: Washington, D.C.

Principal personages:

JOHN MARSHALL (1755-1835), Chief Justice of the United States 1801-1835, author of the majority opinion in the case

WILLIAM JOHNSON (1771-1834), Associate Justice of the United States, author of the concurring opinion in the case

JAMES KENT (1763-1847), Chief Justice of New York and Chancellor of New York, author of the opinion in the case whose judgment Gibbons was appealing in the U.S. Supreme Court

DANIEL WEBSTER (1782-1852), chief attorney for Gibbons

ROBERT R. LIVINGSTON (1746-1813), amateur scientist and speculator in steamboats

ROBERT FULTON (1765-1815), inventor and builder of steamboats in partnership with Robert R. Livingston

AARON OGDEN (1756-1839), entrepreneur, former Governor of New Jersey, steamboat company owner and litigant in the case

THOMAS GIBBONS (1757-1826), wealthy Georgia lawyer, steamboat company owner and litigant in the case

Summary of Event

In order to provide the commercial relations of the United States with a sense of orderliness and uniformity that had been considerably lacking before 1787, the Constitution of the United States gave Congress the power to "regulate Commerce with foreign Nations, and among the several States, and with the Indian Tribes." Congress took advantage of this new-found power almost immediately in the field of foreign commerce by providing for the regulation of ships and commerce from foreign countries and by enacting the National Coasting Licensing Act in 1793 for the licensing of vessels engaged in coastal trade. It was left to the Supreme Court of the United States, thirty years later, to make the first national pronouncement regarding domestic commerce in the case of *Gibbons* v. *Ogden*.

The catalyst of this decision was the development of the steamboat as an economical means of transportation. This was accomplished in August of 1807 when Robert Fulton and Robert Livingston made a successful voyage up the Hudson river from New York to Albany. In April of 1808, the legislature of the State of New York responded to this success by giving Fulton and Livingston a monopoly to operate steamboats on New York waters

600

for a period of time not to exceed thirty years. All other steam craft were forbidden from navigating New York streams unless licensed by Fulton and Livingston; unlicensed vessels would, if captured, be forfeited to them. A similar grant was obtained from the legislature of Orleans Territory in 1811 thus conferring upon Fulton and Livingston control over the two great ports of the American Nation, New York City and New Orleans.

The commercial potential of steam transportation was too great to be left to the devices of two men. Rival companies came into being, and a commercial war reminiscent of the old Confederation erupted. New Jersey authorized owners of any boats seized under New York law to capture that state's boats in return. Connecticut would not allow Livingston and Fulton boats to enter her waters. Georgia, Massachusetts, New Hampshire, Vermont, and Ohio enacted "exclusive privilege" statutes for operators of steamboats on their waters. Finally, a number of New York citizens defied the state law and operated unlicensed steam vessels up the Hudson. Among these was one Thomas Gibbons, possessor of a license granted under the federal Coasting Act of 1793, operating in competition with a former partner, Aaron Ogden, who had secured exclusive rights from Livingston and Fulton to navigate across the Hudson river between New York and New Jersey. As early as 1812 the New York Court of Errors, and Chief Justice James Kent, one of America's most prominent jurists, had issued a permanent injunction against intruders on the monopoly. Gibbons persisted in the face of this injunction because of his federal license, and Ogden sought

a restraining order in the New York Court of Chancery. Kent, who was now Chancellor, upheld the monopoly once again, arguing that a federal coasting license merely conferred national character on a vessel and did not license it to trade, especially in waters restricted by state law. In short, there was no conflict between the act of Congress and the actions of New York state, for the power to regulate commerce was a concurrent one. Gibbons persisted in appealing to the New York Court of Errors, where Kent's decision was upheld. This set the stage for the final appeal to the United States Supreme Court.

It was expected that the case would be heard during the 1821 term of the court, but for technical reasons it was delayed until February, 1824. The oral arguments lasted four and one-half days in a setting that was by all accounts a great social and political occasion as well as one of the great moments in American constitutional history. Among the distinguished attorneys presenting the case was Daniel Webster, champion of a strong national government and the best known orator of his time. Webster opened his argument in broad sweeping terms by contending that the statutes of New York, and by implication all exclusive grants of others states, violated the United States Constitution. "The power of Congress to regulate commerce was complete and entire." Individual states have no concurrent powers in this area; the federal government's domain is exclusive. Moreover, he left no doubt that commerce included navigation. Opposing counsel necessarily wished to limit the notion of commerce to "traffic" or to the "buying and selling" of commodities, which would not include navigation. The regulation of New York, it contended, was a matter of internal trade and navigation, the province of the states.

The case before the Court, however, dealt with far more than the conflict between New York state law and a federal coasting licensing act. In the weeks immediately preceding and during the argument for *Gibbons* v. *Ogden,* Congress was debating whether or not it had the power to build roads and canals, a debate in which the association of slavery with national control over commerce became quickly apparent. If Congress could legislate over matters of internal commerce, it could easily prohibit the slave trade. Further, Marshall's former decisions, particularly *McCulloch* v. *Maryland,* and *Cohens* v. *Virginia,* were under fire in Congress, from the President, and in the press. In a sense, the forces arguing the two sides of the case represented national power and the potential for emancipation (some would add those who supported the protective tariff) on the one hand, and on the other, state sovereignty and the fear of emancipation (with some free trade proponents), a not altogether logical set of alliances. It was in this context, however, that one month later, on March 2, 1824, John Marshall delivered the decision of the Court.

Typically the opinion was a broad one, loaded with *dicta,* and not typically as nationalistic as expected, or as Webster would have desired. Marshall began by agreeing with Webster's definition of commerce:

> Commerce, undoubtedly, is traffic, but it is something more; it is intercourse. It describes the commercial intercourse between nations, and parts of nations, in all its branches, and is regulated by prescribing rules for carrying on that intercourse. The mind can scarcely conceive a system for regulating commerce between nations, which shall exclude all laws concerning navigation, which shall be silent on the admission of the vessels of the one nation into the ports of the other and be confined to prescribing rules for the conduct of individuals, in the actual employment of buying and selling, or of barter.

What did the Constitution mean when it said that Congress had the power to regulate such commerce "among the several States"?

> The word 'among' means intermingled with. A thing which is among others is intermingled with them. Commerce among the States cannot stop at the external boundary line of each State, but may be introduced into the interior.

Surprisingly, after having laid the logical groundwork for claiming complete and exclusive federal power to regulate such commerce, which was Webster's argument, Marshall retreats and states:

> It is not intended to say that these words comprehend that commerce which is completely internal, which is carried on between man and man in a State, or between different parts of the same State, and which does not extend to or affect other States. . . . Comprehensive as the word 'among' is, it may very properly be restricted to that commerce which concerns more States than one. . . .

The federal power over commerce was not exclusive as Webster maintained, although in this instance the state law was in violation of the federal coasting act. Actually the one concurring opinion in the case given by Justice William Johnson, ironically a Republican appointed by Jefferson, was stronger and more nationalistic than Marshall's. Johnson contended that the power of Congress "must be exclusive; it can reside but in one potentate; and hence, the grant of this power carries with it the whole subject, leaving nothing for the state to act upon." But, for Marshall if it was clear that the "acts of New York must yield to the Law of Congress," it was also evident that the "completely internal commerce of a state, then, may be considered as reserved for the state itself." The nationalist Chief Justice had unwittingly laid the basis for a multitude of legal perplexities by making a distinction between intrastate and interstate commerce (terms he did not use); and it would fall to less subtle judicial minds to interpret this as meaning commerce which does not cross state lines. Lest anyone misunderstand his position on the general enumerated powers of the Congress and on the theory of strict construction of the Constitution adopted by Ogden's counsel and by Chancellor Kent, Marshall concludes his opinion with these words:

> Powerful and ingenious minds, taking, as postulates, that the powers expressly granted to the government of the Union are to be contracted, by construction, into the narrowest possible compass, and that the original powers of the States are retained, if any possible construction will retain them, may, by a course of well digested, but refined metaphysical reasoning, founded on these premises, explain away the construction of our country, and leave it a magnificent structure indeed, to look

at, but totally unfit for use. They may so entangle and perplex the understanding, as to obscure principles which were before thought quite plain, and induce doubts where, if the mind were to pursue its own course, none would be perceived. In such a case, it is peculiarly necessary to recur to safe and fundamental principles. . . .

In other words, the courts should construe the Constitution and the powers of Congress broadly.

In immediate practical terms, Marshall had finally rendered a popular decision. The steamboat monopoly had come to an end. *Gibbons* v. *Ogden* was the first great antitrust decision given at a time when monopolies were decidedly unpopular. Lost in the public euphoria over the end of "exclusive grants," save to a few Jeffersonian Republicans, was the fact that Marshall had made the Supreme Court the future arbiter of matters involving congressional power over commerce and intervention into state police and taxing powers. In so doing he had struck one more blow for a broad view of the Constitution and of national power. Only when steam came to be used for land transportation would the full commercial implications of the Gibbons decision be clear. For, if as many maintain, half of the Constitution is the commerce clause, (the other half being the due process clause of the Fourteenth Amendment), the *Gibbons* v. *Ogden* case has been correctly termed the "emancipation proclamation of American commerce."

Pertinent Literature

Beveridge, Albert J. *The Life of John Marshall.* Vol. IV: *Conflict and Construction, 1800-1815.* 4 vols. Boston: Houghton Mifflin Co., 1919.

Beveridge's biography of John Marshall has become virtually synonymous with the saccharine, almost idolatrous treatment of the biographical subject.

Yet it is in Beveridge's discussion of the Gibbons case that one finds a full, accurate, even if glamorized, account of the case. Beveridge's is by far the most detailed assessment.

Early in the work, Beveridge gives an account of the Robert R. Livingston-Robert Fulton relationship, replete with a discursive footnote (borrowed from J. H. B. Latrobe) detailing the steamboat exploits of Nicholas J. Roosevelt, Livingston's agent in the United States. Along with the gothic embellishments, however, is a generous account of the development of steamboating in the United States with emphasis on the trend toward the granting of monoplies to promising entrepreneurs. Thus, a broad context of political history is established for the discussion of the *Gibbons* v. *Ogden* case.

Three considerations make Beveridge's treatment especially valuable— his discussion of the political machinations surrounding the interstate competition over steamboating and steamboat monopolies; his quite specific account of the New York litigation in the case under discussion; and his clarification of the relationship between the *Gibbons* v. *Ogden* case and the controversies over internal improvements and slavery.

Of these contributions, the narrative of the New York legal developments is perhaps the greatest, since he unravels a tangled mass of suits and countersuits in the labyrinthine New York state judicial hierarchy. The connection between sectionalism and internal improvements and the Gibbons case is also of considerable value. Beveridge makes it clear that the questions with which the Supreme Court dealt had

been thoroughly debated in the Congress. He gives enlightening highlights of the congressional debate, stressing quotes from a speech by John Randolph against the Internal Improvements Bill of 1824 at approximately the time the Supreme Court was hearing arguments on *Gibbons* v. *Ogden*. The slavery question was always ready to surface; an essential thread of Randolph's argument, suggests Beveridge, was that "If Congress possesses the power to do what is proposed . . . they emancipate every slave in the United States. . . ."

In closing his account of *Gibbons* v. *Ogden,* Beveridge makes a suggestive comment that warrants mention. The concurring opinion by Justice William Johnson espousing a more comprehensive view of the national power over commerce, suggests Beveridge, actually represented Marshall's true views.

> In view of the strong influence Marshall had, by now, acquired over Johnson, it appears to be not improbable, or that the Chief Justice availed himself of the political status of the South Carolinian, as well as of his remarkable talents, to have Johnson state the real views of the master of the Supreme Court.

Surprisingly, Beveridge is critical of Marshall at several points, but these criticisms are directed at Marshall's style more than the substance of his arguments. Thus, Beveridge claims that in dealing with the question of concurrent state and federal power over commerce, Marshall is "diffuse, prolix, and indirect," and in explaining the relevance of the coasting license argument, "falling into his characteristic over-explanation, Marshall proves the obvious by many illustrations."

Federal Government Assumes Control of Interstate Commerce

Crosskey, William W. *Politics and the Constitution in the History of the United States.* 2 vols. Vol. I, ch. 9. Chicago: University of Chicago Press, 1953.

Crosskey's thesis in this massive two-volume work is that the Constitution's framers intended to create a national government with plenary power over any aspect of life which the national government should find warranted regulation. His work is thoroughly scholarly in its style, approach, and documentation, but it apparently has been rejected as untenable by the historical and political science professions. The argument marshaled by Crosskey concerning the *Gibbons* v. *Ogden* case is both illustrative of his approach and crucial to his argument. He engages in an extended and elaborate presentation of the various nuances in which various words and phrases in the constitutional text were used at the time of the framing and at the time of the judicial construction. He, for example, considers at length the argument of the champions of the steamboat monopoly that "navigation" was not a part of "commerce" with a lengthy discussion of the meaning which lawyers ascribed to these terms in the late eighteenth and early nineteenth centuries.

Crosskey argues that Marshall could not possibly have meant to give support to what Crosskey calls the "interstate" theory of the commerce power, but that the Chief Justice really believed that Congress had the power to regulate, more or less, commerce fully and completely without regard to state boundaries. Crosskey contends that Marshall, however, was led to emphasize the coasting license argument and reject Webster's more appealing theory of plenary national power because probably "half the Court . . . all, very likely, but Story and Johnson—gave trouble to Marshall, in the Gibbons case." All but two of the Justices, he argues, had been appointed by the Jeffersonian ("anti-nationalist") party; four of the five Associate Justices sitting in *Gibbons* v. *Ogden* were Southerners. Marshall, nevertheless, managed to convey his true meaning to Professor Crosskey through highly sophisticated double-talk. Crosskey, for instance, finds that when Marshall wrote that the commerce clause gives Congress power to regulate that commerce which "concerns more States than one," the Chief Justice was using "concern" to mean "of interest or importance to" and that the delimiting statement which Marshall immediately introduces makes the opinion's nationalistic meaning clear.

The Crosskey thesis is intriguing, provocative, and undoubtedly stimulating. Unfortunately, the arguments made in its support rely so heavily on the "he must have known" or "must have meant" approach that they are not always convincing. That is not to say that Crosskey's work can be dismissed as frivolous; its impact has been considerable, since it has required its detractors to review the primary materials. — *C.L.E.*

Additional Recommended Reading

Dangerfield, George. "The Steamboat Case," in John A. Garraty's *Quarrels That Have Shaped the Constitution.* New York: Harper & Row Publishers, 1964. This brief and readable article contains much information about John R. Livingston (brother of Robert R. Livingston and his successor in steamboat development), Aaron Ogden, and Thomas Gibbons, the principals in the litigation. His account of the Court's opinion, however, is superficial and confused.

Faulkner, Robert K. *The Jurisprudence of John Marshall*. Princeton: Princeton University Press, 1968. Faulkner provides a comprehensive critique of Marshall's juridical thought. This affords the reader an opportunity to place the *Gibbons* v. *Ogden* case in perspective with regard to the Chief Justice's legal philosophy.

Frankfurter, Felix. *The Commerce Clause Under Marshall, Taney, and Waite*. Chapel Hill: University of North Carolina Press, 1937. In this collection of three lectures the great jurist assesses the impact of the *Gibbons* v. *Ogden* case on our constitutional development. Calling the opinion "either unconsciously or calculatedly confused," he goes on to find that the principles of Gibbons "became central to our whole constitutional scheme: The doctrine that the commerce clause, by its own force and without national legislation, puts it into the power of the Court to place limits upon state authority . . . Marshall's use of the commerce clause greatly furthered the idea that though we are a federation of states we are also a nation. . . ."

Haskins, George L. "Marshall and the Commerce Clause of the Constitution," in W. Melville Jones' *Chief Justice John Marshall: A Reappraisal*. Ithaca: Cornell University Press, 1956. Stresses the impact of *Gibbons* v. *Ogden* on our constitutional growth; its chief merit is that it traces the decision's importance to the New Deal and post-New Deal developments.

Loth, David G. *Chief Justice: John Marshall and the Growth of the Republic*. New York: W. W. Norton & Co., 1949. Although Loth gives a good brief account of the Gibbons case's political context, his main contribution is on the human side. He concentrates on the personalities in the controversy and on a colorful description of the argument before the Court and the reading of the opinion.

Warren, Charles. *The Supreme Court in United States History*. 2 vols. Vol. I, ch. 15. Boston: Little, Brown, and Company, 1926. This standard history of the Supreme Court does for the Court as an institution what Beveridge's *Marshall* does for the Chief Justice.

606

ELECTION OF 1824

Type of event: Political: Presidential election which ended the "Era of Good Feelings"
Time: November, 1824-February, 1825
Locale: Washington, D.C.

Principal personages:

JOHN QUINCY ADAMS (1767-1848), Secretary of State in the Monroe Administration 1817-1825, who became sixth President of the United States

HENRY CLAY (1777-1852), leading Republican and Speaker of the House of Representatives, who became Secretary of State in the Adams Administration 1825-1829

ANDREW JACKSON (1767-1845), military hero of the United States and a presidential candidate in 1824

WILLIAM H. CRAWFORD (1772-1834), Secretary of the Treasury in the Monroe Administration 1816-1825, and a presidential candidate in 1824

JOHN CALDWELL CALHOUN (1782-1850), Secretary of War in the Monroe Administration 1817-1825, and a presidential candidate in 1824 who withdrew

DANIEL WEBSTER (1782-1852), Congressman from Massachusetts

MARTIN VAN BUREN (1782-1862), New York politician and leader of the "Albany Regency"

THURLOW WEED (1797-1882), newspaper editor from Rochester and a rising politician in New York

Summary of Event

By 1824 the Federalist Party had ceased to exist, and the misnamed "Era of Good Feelings" was coming to a close. Five men in the Republican Party wanted to succeed the fifth President of the United States, James Monroe. Henry Clay of Kentucky put forth the most positive program. With his "American System," which involved high protective tariffs and federally supported internal improvements, Clay sought to consolidate the different sections of the country behind him. Andrew Jackson of Tennessee was the most popular choice and was the nation's premier military hero. He was the only candidate supported outside his own section, appealing not only to the West but also to small farmers in the South and workingmen in the East. John Quincy Adams of Massachusetts, Secretary of State in the Monroe Administration, was the choice of the conservative New Englanders. Though his statesmanship and personal honesty were admitted by all, his lack of tact and charm, and his unwillingness to become involved in the rough-and-tumble of politics, prevented him from gaining a popular following. John C. Calhoun of South Carolina soon withdrew rather than face such formidable

607

opposition for the Presidency, and became the sole vice-presidential candidate. William H. Crawford was the selection of a rump congressional caucus; Crawford's candidacy ended, however, when he suffered a stroke in mid-campaign. He had been supported by Monroe and Thomas Jefferson, and claimed to be the only true heir of the Jeffersonian tradition in the race. Born in Virginia and a resident of Georgia, Crawford supported the large plantation interests. He advocated the strict construction of the Constitution and emphasized states' rights.

Crawford was the last candidate nominated by the congressional caucus, a meeting of a party's entire congressional delegation which, until 1824, had picked all presidential candidates. By 1824, this system was under attack for its undemocratic features and for giving Congress too much power. State legislatures nominated the other candidates, and this new device continued in use until the nominating convention was generally adopted within the next decade.

The greatest difficulty for the nominees was a lack of issues. All the candidates were for some tariff reform, although Adams termed his tariff policy "cautious," and Jackson called his "judicious." Both Adams and Clay supported the American System, though Adams outstripped Clay in his support of internal improvements. To these "issues" Jackson added an attack on the caucus system and supported the right of the people to choose their Presidential electors directly. As there were no real political differences, the contest quickly became one of personalities. There was little campaigning and most of the excitement was provided by the press. With Crawford's physical infirmity virtually eliminating him, Adams assumed the favorite's position. He was expected to gain from the split in the South and West between Clay and Jackson.

In the election, Jackson received the greatest number of votes, but not a majority. The electoral vote was: Jackson, ninety-nine; Adams, eighty-four; Crawford, forty-one; and Clay, thirty-seven. As no candidate had received a majority, the choice of the President was passed to the House of Representatives. Clay was out of the race, for the Constitution stipulated that the House, voting by states, should choose between the three candidates receiving the highest electoral totals.

Clearly the choice was between Adams and Jackson, and Clay was in a unique position. As Speaker of the House, he could control many of the votes there, and was forced to choose between two men both of whom he heartily disliked. There was only one choice for Clay, as he considered Jackson unfit for the Presidency. On the other hand, both he and Adams supported the American System, and their differences were only personal. They agreed to meet and discuss "public affairs," and though both later denied that any deal was made, Clay was able to deliver several states into the Adams camp, notably Clay's own state of Kentucky, whose electors had been instructed to vote for Jackson. In the House election of February, 1825, Adams received thirteen votes to seven for Jackson and four for Crawford.

Rumors of a compact, or deal, between Clay and Adams were rampant. Indeed, in January there appeared in the *Philadelphia Columbian Observer*

608

an anonymous letter charging that Clay had sold out to Adams for an appointment as Secretary of State. Clay immediately denied the charge and published a "card" challenging his accuser to a duel. The duel was never fought, nor was any proof of the bargain ever provided. One of Adams' first acts as President was to appoint Henry Clay as his Secretary of State; thus, according to the Jacksonians, was the "corrupt bargain" consummated. Jackson wrote to one of his supporters, "So you see the Judas of the West has closed the contract and will receive his thirty pieces of silver. . . . Was there ever witnessed such barefaced corruption in any country before?"

Jackson and his supporters believed that he had been cheated out of the Presidency because he had refused to bargain with Clay. Jackson, they contended, was the obvious popular choice, and should have been named President. Indeed, many believed that Congress was morally bound to elect him. Both Adams and Clay were discredited in many eyes. Jackson resigned his Senate seat and returned to Tennessee, where he was immediately nominated as that state's presidential candidate in 1828.

The election of Adams in 1824 terminated the succession of the "Virginia dynasty" in the party. During Adams' Administration, moreover, the Jeffersonians split into two wings: the Adams-Clay wing, whose adherents went by the name of National Republicans; and the Jackson wing, whose membership became known as the Democratic Republicans. Adams was caught in the middle of this partisan strife, and, unwilling or unable to engage in personal politics, he lost popular support and was defeated by Jackson in 1828.

Pertinent Literature

Livermore, Shaw, Jr. *The Twilight of Federalism: The Disintegration of the Federalist Party, 1815-1830.* Princeton: Princeton University Press, 1962.

Believing that a major political party could not have suddenly disappeared from the American scene, Shaw Livermore, Jr. has written a history of the death struggle of the Federalists. Their problem, simply stated, was how to remain active in public life and still keep the Federalist identity in a period of Republican one-party government. Many Federalists found their proscription from public office unbearable. Indeed, these men, who had always believed themselves suited by birth and training to rule over others, were inordinately eager to obtain public office. But what influence could a proscribed, ambitious, and active minority have?

The Federalists soon abandoned hope of returning to power as a national party, but were still eager for national and state offices. Their strategy, according to Livermore, was to conciliate the Republicans on the national level while fighting them in the states. As they steadily lost power on both levels, the Federalists were forced to support and encourage the growth of Republican factionalism.

The election of 1824, which shattered all semblance of Republican unity, provided an opportunity for the Federalists to move out of their jobless state by actively supporting one of the Republican presidential candidates. All of the Republican candidates sought Federalist aid. Clay was hopeful that the Federalist *New York Post* would swing his way and was bitterly disappointed when it went for Crawford. Jackson was believed to have the best chance for Federalist support. He could freely appoint Federalists to office, because his Republicanism, unlike that of Adams, had never been challenged. Indeed, some letters from Jackson to President Monroe urging the Chief Executive to appoint deserving Federalists were made public. Since they were written in 1816, they could not possibly be construed as political in nature. Jackson did not disavow the sentiments expressed in the letters, and was not hurt politically by them. He still had many Federalists in his camp when the election went to the House. Adams, on the contrary, had been a Federalist until 1808, and any move on his part to advance their cause would immediately be suspect.

How then did Adams win? Livermore contends that Adams' election to the Presidency hinged upon a political deal, but not the "corrupt bargain" he allegedly made with Clay. Two crucial votes were needed by Adams after he acquired Clay's support. Daniel Webster, the Congressman from Massachusetts, delivered these votes by swinging the New York and Maryland delegations to Adams. Webster, says Livermore, wished to be the Minister of the United States to Great Britain, and he wanted his friends appointed to office. He visited Adams who gave him a letter, thereafter called the "Webster Pledge," promising that the Federalists would not be kept out of office during his administration. Webster's coup was the delivery of the two delegations that had been previously divided in their loyalties. To do so took the full talents of the "Godlike Daniel." He first convinced two influential members of the Maryland delegation to vote for Adams, thereby assuring a pro-Adams vote. All eyes next turned to New York where the deciding vote was held by an old patroon, Steven Van Rensselaer. The pressure applied to the old man was overwhelming. Knowing that Van Rensselaer was unbelievably suggestible, Webster and Clay drew him aside for a talk on the morning of the ballot. The persuasiveness of these two masters was too much for one man to withstand, and the old Dutchman voted for Adams. The addition of Maryland and New York gave Adams the thirteen votes needed for a majority over Jackson. Webster, however, did not reap the benefits of his labor.

Adams offered the post of Minister of the United States to Great Britain to another Federalist, Rufus King. This was an astute political move, for King had been chosen Senator from New York by a Republican legislature. Thus, though a Federalist, King was acceptable to both sides.

Livermore's study concentrates exclusively upon the Federalists in New England and the Middle Atlantic states. Centering his research in newspaper editorials, contemporary correspondence, and biographies, he has provided fresh interpretative insights into the local politics and shifting alliances of the post-Federalist period. *The Twilight of Federalism* is a significant contribution to our understanding of the "Era of Good Feelings."

Dangerfield, George. *The Era of Good Feelings.* New York: Harcourt, Brace, & World, Inc., 1952.

On February 9, 1825, a committee from the House of Representatives informed John Quincy Adams that he was the President-elect. Adams was not elated; rather, his appearance was that of a condemned man. If it were possible, he said, to decline the office and have an election that would bring about a clear result, he would do it. But since these conditions could not be met, Adams accepted the Presidency. In his personal diary he confided that "two-thirds of the whole people were adverse to the actual result." Adams had good reason to feel reluctant about assuming the Presidency. To have obtained the office without a clear majority was bad enough, but even worse was having to promise, to flatter, to electioneer, and to bargain. This, according to George Dangerfield, was almost too much for the New Englander.

Despite his best efforts, the President-elect had been forced to this extremity, and he was not happy with his part in the affair. But when he learned to what lengths others had gone to put him in the White House, his conscience almost rebelled. A perfect example of his friends' behavior was the manner in which they obtained New York's key electoral vote in the House. The prime mover in this affair was Thurlow Weed, a young newspaperman from Rochester.

The scene was Albany, New York, described by Dangerfield as "the greatest and probably the grubbiest school of political intrigue in the United States." It was there that Weed outmaneuvered Martin Van Buren, the leading New York politician and titular head of the Republican machine, the "Regency." By unbelievably involved politicking among the Clay and Adams supporters in the New York Assembly, Weed was able to defeat the Regency and its candidate for the Presidency, William H. Crawford. Adams emerged from the balloting needing only one vote for a majority, with the remaining votes held by Clay and Crawford supporters. Because he knew that most of the New York votes were his by questionable means, Adams could not bring himself to acknowledge Weed's contribution.

Eventually, the election went to the House where Clay, as Speaker, played the role of king-maker. By Christmas, 1824, it was common knowledge in informed political circles that Clay wished to become Secretary of State as a stepping stone to the Presidency. Adams was by then beginning to recognize that he could not become President without becoming personally involved in the political maneuvering. On January 1, 1825, therefore, he decided to have a talk with Clay, and, according to Dangerfield, Adams was too weakened by "Potomac fever" to resist reaching an "understanding" with the Kentuckian. Had he resisted, Jackson would have been President. Adams knew he needed Western support and, despite their personal differences, he and Clay had almost identical policies. The alliance was made and both went to work. Adams cultivated Daniel Webster in the East and Clay worked his magic in the West.

For Adams to have become involved with Clay politically was unfortunate for this sensitive man but was necessary for political success. Clay's conscience was neither corrupt nor bad; rather, it was political and amoral. Adams' conscience, on the other hand, was moral; indeed, it was the enemy of his political ambitions. Up to a point his integrity had resisted the evils of public life, but Adams could remain aloof no longer.

By February it was all accomplished. The final act was played out by Van Rensselaer, who, though cornered by Webster and Clay before the vote, was still unsure until he bowed his head in prayer in the House of Representatives. He asked for divine guidance and when he opened his eyes saw an Adams ballot on the floor before him. He picked it up and put it in the ballot box. Thus Adams was elected. And so, when the committee came to tell the President-elect of his good fortune, he received them with anguish.

George Dangerfield has written an excellent book about the period between the War of 1812 and the accession of Andrew Jackson to the Presidency. His treatment of the election of 1824 centers around John Quincy Adams and his struggle in accepting the seamy side of political life. The author is at his best in painting clear and penetrating portraits of the leaders of the period, and the reader suffers the anguish of conscience along with Adams. Factually and stylistically, the book offers little to criticize and is regarded as the standard work on this period. — *C.L.E.*

Additional Recommended Reading

Eaton, Clement. *Henry Clay and the Art of American Politics.* Boston: Little, Brown, and Company, 1957. This short biography of Clay places particular emphasis on politics and Clay's "fateful decision" in 1824. Eaton maintains that there was no corrupt bargain.

Roseboom, Eugene H. *A Short History of Presidential Elections.* New York: The Macmillan Company, 1967. Long and detailed, yet done in an easy style, this is a study of all the Presidential elections in the United States. Particular emphasis is placed on the intricate politicking of 1824.

Bemis, Samuel F. *John Quincy Adams and the Union.* New York: Alfred A. Knopf, Inc., 1956. The dean of American diplomatic historians has written a delightful book about John Quincy Adams and his trials. Only in an Era of Good Feelings could a man like Adams have been elected, according to Bemis.

Tugwell, Rexford G. *How They Became President.* New York: Simon and Schuster, 1964. Tugwell, an original member of Franklin D. Roosevelt's "Brain Trust," has written an account of Presidential elections well worth reading.

Bailey, Thomas A. *Presidential Greatness: The Image and the Man from George Washington to the Present.* New York: Appleton-Century Crofts, 1966. The story of 1824 in this Presidential survey is one of Adams' being caught in the middle of partisan brick-throwing. Unwilling or unable to stoop to conquer, Adams soon lost his popular support and was defeated in 1828.

THE HUDSON RIVER SCHOOL OF PAINTERS

Type of event: Cultural: founding of the first American school of painting
Time: 1825-1875
Locale: New York

Principal personages:

THOMAS COLE (1801-1848), English-born landscape painter who founded the Hudson River School

ASHER BROWN DURAND (1796-1886), leader of the Hudson River School after Cole's death

RALPH WALDO EMERSON (1803-1882), American essayist who popularized transcendental philosophy and also the demand for American cultural nationalism

THOMAS BIRCH (1779-1851), precursor of the Hudson River School of landscape artists

THOMAS DOUGHTY (1793-1856), early American landscape painter

FREDERICK STUART CHURCH (1842-1924), member of the later Hudson River School of landscape artists

ALBERT BIERSTADT (1830-1902), one of the last of the Hudson River School of landscape artists

Summary of Event

The Hudson River School of American painting marks the first appearance of a recognizable American style of painting which did not as a matter of course imitate the predominant European styles. The Hudson river had become the great national commercial artery of the young nation with the completion of the Erie Canal in 1825. By 1825 there were already demands for America to assert its cultural freedom from Europe, as well as the beginning of a new movement of nationalism in art which culminated with Ralph Waldo Emerson's lectures and essays. To a large degree the Hudson River School of painting realized much of Emerson's call for an American art, while at the same time the new school of American landscape painters re-flected the heavily European influences present in Emersonian transcendentalism. While much of the Hudson River School was indigenous to the new nation, its philosophy also reflected traditions in European painting, as well as worldwide manifestations of nationalism expressed in art.

Thomas Cole, the father of the school, was largely a self-taught artist. He came to America from England in 1819 at the age of eighteen. Cole had grown up in an industrial town in Lancashire where he underwent an early apprenticeship as a designer of calico prints. He continually dreamed of America, which seemed like a Utopia to him, and later he was to apply this dream in his painting. After settling briefly in Stubenville, Ohio, Cole began his painting career with no more training than merely watching an itinerant artist paint. Armed with this modest training, Cole set out to make his fortune as an artist in the new world. Fortunately for him, painting was much in demand in America, for the new nation was starved for culture. Cole was able to earn his way to Philadelphia where belatedly he began his formal artistic education at the Pennsylvania Academy. There he became familiar with the leading contemporary schools of art both in America and abroad. Landscape painting at the time was not a highly regarded form even though it was beginning a new vogue in Europe that would parallel its American development. Europeans favored the neoclassic style with an emphasis upon heroic paintings of historical or Biblical events. One of America's problems was its lack of history and historical traditions; historical paintings therefore had little relevance for Americans and found no ready buyers. The neoclassical mode so popular in Europe rejected anything specific or contemporary which might mar the perfect form it sought. For neoclassic theory, what was of the present was temporary and could be used only to illustrate timeless allegories which related to a moral law. In America, however, the present and the future were at the heart of the nation's experience and many Americans simply could not understand the educated allusions at the core of neoclassical painting.

Transcendentalism had become popular in America because of the influence of Emerson's lectures and writings, and it was in part as a result of this romantic view of the world that Cole and his style of painting became successful. Transcendentalism raised unspoiled nature to new heights as a reflection of God's grand design on earth. The new nation undeniably possessed in abundance new and unspoiled forests. Until Cole no one had thought of painting them; yet here was a cultural area in which Americans could excel, for the idea of the wilderness and the innocence of unsullied nature is a theme that has dominated the popular American dream of the West. One finds it expressed continually in American thought from Jefferson's agrarian hopes to Frederick Jackson Turner's Frontier Thesis of American development.

Cole found two landscape painters to his liking: Thomas Birch (1779-1851), and Thomas Doughty (1793-1856), who earned their living primarily as painters drawing scenes for engravers who then sold them as wall decorations. Thus, when Cole began his paintings of nature as it was found in wilderness America, he was working within an established tradition in American painting. However, in the hands of an idealist like Cole the tradition was quickly transformed. Indeed, Cole bridged the gap between the American taste which demanded a specific object set clearly in the present and usable as a house decoration, and his own romantic idealism which reflected the new romanticism of European art and imagination. Cole's triumph, while impelled by his idealism, was essentially affected by his technique, which took a normally prosaic scene and added exuberance, power, and range until the scene majestically reflected the entire untamed and primeval American continent.

Cole had become inspired with his

first journey up the Hudson river to Catskill, where he made his artistic home until his death in 1841. He also established the basic code of the Hudson River School—the primacy of nature itself—which opposed the teachings of Sir Joshua Reynolds (then influential in Europe) that the proper study of art belonged in the traditions of the past.

Asher Durand, subsequently the major painter of the established Hudson River School, was born in New Jersey in 1796 and became the most successful American engraver, specializing in bank notes and in gift books. He later became a landscape painter; with three other major Hudson River School painters, John W. Casilear, John F. Kensett, and Thomas P. Rossiter, Durand made the required educational pilgrimage to Europe in 1840-1841. Durand's home at Catskill Clove became the center of the movement after Cole's death in 1848. Durand and his followers were deeply committed to a philosophy of art which is set forth in Durand's *Letters on Landscape Painting* published in the art journal, *Crayon,* in 1855-1856 which argued that man was influenced by what he experienced, and that divinity was implicit within nature. The popularity of the Hudson River School is more easily understood in a society which valued the practical and useful; a landscape became the tangible word of God and as James Flexner points out, "A painting over the fireplace was as much of necessity as a Bible on the table."

The Hudson River School exalted America and rejected European values in a formative period of American life. As a popular art form it enabled artists not only to earn a living painting but also to begin an indigenous American art. It allowed later painters one more choice of a tradition within the American experience, and it influenced all of the romantic landscapists of the later nineteenth century. Most of all, it fulfilled the need of a new people for an immediate and useful art which reflected new world scenes and values.

Pertinent Literature

Flexner, James Thomas. *That Wilder Image: The Painting of America's Native School from Thomas Cole to Winslow Homer.* Boston: Little, Brown, and Company, 1962.

James Flexner has written the first comprehensive history of the vogue of artistic nationalism that swept America in the nineteenth century and which was best represented by the Hudson River School of painters. Flexner deals with the historical and philosophical antecedents of Thomas Cole and his followers as well as with the various offshoots of the Hudson River School itself. More than one hundred illustrations, an extensive bibliography, and comprehensive documentation make this an imposing scholarly and popular introduction to American art.

As Flexner points out in his foreword, the nineteenth century was a more propitious time for art in America than perhaps any other period of American history. Painters could readily sell paintings, and the best of American artists became wealthy and respected leaders in society.

After the Napoleonic Wars in Europe, the disillusionment with war caused a reaction from those who anticipated a golden age following the French Revolution. The disappointment caused European artists to turn away from reality and to turn either to neoclassicism or to experiment with romantic idealism. America after the War of 1812 was established as a young and vigorous republic; yet its cultural leaders were aware that there was no historical or cultural tradition to draw upon in the new nation, and instead of encouraging the strong tradition already present in American folk painting, they decided to impose the European neoclassical tradition upon the American public. The use of heavily historical paintings in the young American nation struck no responsive chords in the public, and depressed the market for art; artists as gifted as Samuel F. B. Morse finally turned to other fields in despair. Morse gave up painting for invention and his Morse Code is indicative of his varied talents if not his dedication to an unprofitable artistic career.

One of the great opportunities for native American artists existed precisely because of the lack of a cultured and educated populace. Most Americans read with difficulty and welcomed pictures. Thus, America had a mass audience for painting that was willing to support any art that eschewed the neoclassical theme with its irrelevant (to Americans) historical or philosophical allusions to universal values. Flexner argues that the native tradition which emphasizes the representation of familiar objects is the base by which more sophisticated forms of art become acceptable to a society. He cites England as an example in which landscape illustration was expanded by brilliant topographical watercolorists to form the base upon which Constable and Turner were building their revolutionary aesthetics.

In America, Cole was preparing to build in the same way. From the beginnings of American colonization, Americans had purchased engravings of the emerging cities. As the nation expanded westward this practice was enlarged to include engravings of any picturesque scene. As long as the purchase of a painting could not be construed as a useless act, Americans were prepared to buy cheap pictures that were more useful than artistic.

It was to this opportunity that Cole's particular imagination was drawn. Cole's landscape style did not so much change the native landscape style; rather, it transformed that style in a way that remained consonant with American values and reflected as well the new European romanticism.

Novak, Barbara. *American Painting of the Nineteenth Century: Realism, Idealism, and the American Experience.* New York: Frederick A. Praeger Publishers, Inc., 1969.

Barbara Novak's history of American art attempts to define the particularly American qualities of nineteenth century art by discussing a dozen major artists of the century and placing them in historical perspective. Included is a selective bibliography as well as a valuable appendix containing brief biographies of major American artists of the eighteenth and nineteenth centuries. Over 270 illustrations accompany the text. An introductory chapter and an epilogue provide the historical continuity between the eighteenth and twentieth centuries.

In the nineteenth century there developed an emphasis upon the moral value of the aesthetic experience. Awareness of landscape, as one writer observed, was not only connected with the "love of the good," but with the principle of "God's sensuous image of revelation." Thomas Cole was presented with the basic dilemma of ambitious American painters—how to satisfy their own imagination while at the same time producing recognizable landscape paintings that reflected reality. Throughout Cole's life, his own highly romanticized landscape conceptions caused patrons to question the specificity of the picture's subject, for often a particular view was so greatly transformed by Cole's imagination that it ceased to resemble the commissioned view. Novak points out that Cole's conception of the real was ill-suited to a period in which American taste was so naturalistic and nationalistic. Indeed Cole, in his attempts to substitute a "characteristic spirit" for the concrete, anticipated the synthesis of the later nineteenth century in which form clothes idea, and of the impressionist idea that nature was rarely right and had to be transformed by the artist's vision and imagination.

Despite the frustrations of his ambitions and the clashes with public taste, Cole was profoundly respected by a large American public, perhaps, as Novak speculates, for his moralism rather than his art. One unfortunate development following his death in 1848 was that his successors perpetuated Cole's compromises rather than following the implications of his polarities, which were well in advance of his time. The Hudson River School thus became a compromise style in which, while working from sketches, artists, such as Frederick Church and Albert Bierstadt, idealized the composition and then "materialized" the execution of the painting so that the details of the scenery remained substantially correct while the view as a whole was false. The Hudson River School's formula became in the hands of Cole's successors—Durand, Kensett, Church, and Bierstadt—an amalgam of bucolic sentiment, the idea of design based upon the conception of Claude Lorain, and "near-looking" detail.

Asher Durand's painting turned toward the opposite pole of the Hudson River School's real-ideal duality. Whereas Cole tended toward the real, Durand, after Cole's death the dean of the school, worked more toward the ideal. However, in one important technical attribute Durand left an enduring legacy. Instead of working from sketches he worked outdoors with paint, thus beginning the plein-air tradition in American painting in which the intrinsic components of the landscape determined the design, and the actual weather affected the color, atmosphere, and light. Durand's new approach paralleled the new landscape art of Gustave Courbet in France, and Cole's search for the "characteristic real" marks his work as an early precursor of Impressionism in America. Novak, however, makes several important distinctions between the American Impressionism of Winslow Homer and the imported French Impressionism practiced by the Americans, Childe Hassam and Jack Twachtman. Durand, unlike Courbet, never negated or changed local color, and one looks in vain for a purple or a pink tree in Durand's work. In a provocative conclusion to the Hudson River style, Novak shows that the very idea of the principle of landscape art in America as revelations from God precluded any future American experiments which involved breaking up the spectrum and subjecting it to coloristic analysis. The insistence upon the real that made American landscape painting acceptable in the nineteenth century made an indigenous Impressionism impossible. — *D.H.C.*

Additional Recommended Reading

Barker, Virgil. *American Painting.* New York: The Macmillan Company, 1950. A basic history of American painting.

Larkin, Oliver W. *Art and Life in America.* Revised and enlarged ed. New York: Holt, Rinehart & Winston, Inc., 1960. A basic social history of art including sculpture and architecture.

McCoubrey, John W. *American Tradition in Painting.* New York: George Braziller, Inc., 1963. A brief history that examines what is distinctively American in American painting.

Noble, Louis Legrando. *The Life and Works of Thomas Cole.* Edited by Elliot S. Vessell. Cambridge: Belknap Press, 1964. A reissue of the first biography originally published in 1853 which remains useful and contains much valuable source material and a new introduction.

Sweet, Frederick A. *The Hudson River School and the Early American Landscape Tradition.* Chicago: Chicago Art Institute, 1945. The illustrated catalog of the Whitney Museum and Art Institute.

Gardner, Albert Ten Eyck and Stuart P. Feld. *American Paintings: A Catalogue of the Collection of the Metropolitan Museum of Art.* Vol. I. New York: Metropolitan Museum, 1965. An invaluable reference work with brief biographies and comments on American painters in the Metropolitan collection who were born before 1815.

JEDEDIAH SMITH'S EXPLORATION OF THE FAR WEST

Type of event: Scientific: exploration of the Southwest and California
Time: August 22, 1826-Spring, 1828
Locale: The greater Southwest and the Pacific slope

Principal personages:

JEDEDIAH STRONG SMITH (1798-1831), partner in the Rocky Mountain Fur Company, and the Pathfinder to California

HARRISON G. ROGERS (fl. 1826), quartermaster of the expedition who wrote a chronicle of the first journey to California

JOSÉ MARÍA ECHEANDÍA (fl. 1826), Governor of California who questioned the right of Smith's party to enter the province and demanded that it leave

DR. JOHN MCLOUGHLIN (1784-1857), buyer for the Hudson Bay Company at Fort Vancouver who retrieved and purchased the furs which Smith lost to the Indians in southern Oregon

Summary of Event

In 1826, Jedediah Smith, loaded with a supply of goods from the East, arrived at the rendezvous of the Rocky Mountain Fur Company located at the Great Salt Lake. His express purpose was to explore the territory both south and west of the lake while his partners, David E. Jackson and William L. Sublette, conducted the fall hunt. Smith and a party of sixteen men left the Great Salt Lake between August 15 and 22, traveled southwest to the Utah Lake, and then by way of the Sevier river, crossed a mountain range to the Virgin river. Using this river to guide them, they came upon the Colorado river, crossed to its east bank, and then rode through the Black Mountain country of Arizona for four days before reaching the Mojave. After having rested with the Mojave Indians for longer than two weeks, all the while obtaining information about the sur-rounding territory, the Smith party set out across the Mojave Desert on November 10, 1826; they were guided by two Indians who had escaped from a southern California Spanish mission. Although their exact course for this stage of the journey is unclear, they undoubtedly traveled westward along the earlier Indian trade routes, which were much the same as that followed by the Santa Fe Railroad today. They crossed the Sierra Madre Range, prob-ably using Cajon Pass, and camped a short distance from the San Gabriel Mission. Thus, this was the first Ameri-can party to make the overland trip through the Southwest to California.

Although Mexican law forbade their presence in California, Smith and his men were hospitably received by the padres. Governor José Mariá Ech-eandía, however, viewed them as in-truders, and purposely delayed answering a letter from Smith requesting permission to journey through the province. After waiting for ten days, Smith went to San Diego to plead with the Governor in person. Mollified by this action and the gift of some beaver skins, Echeandía finally agreed not to imprison Smith and his men for violating the border on condition that they leave California over the route by which they had come. Smith disregarded this condition and led his party (less two men who had succumbed to the charms of mission life in California) back through the Cajon Pass and then either west across the Tejon or north across the Tehachapi Pass into the San Joaquin Valley. Leaving his men to trap beaver, with Silas Gobel and Robert Evans, Smith ascended the middle fork of the Stanislaus river to cross the towering Sierra. Starting on May 20, 1827, the three men took eight days to cross the mountains near Ebbetts Pass to the headwaters of the Walker river, which flowed into Walker Lake. Almost nothing is known of Smith's route across the Great Basin, but he probably went east to the vicinity of what is now Ely, Nevada, then northeast to the Great Salt Lake, where he and his associates arrived in June, 1827, after a punishing journey.

After a brief rest, Smith set out with nineteen men on July 13, 1827, to rejoin his hunters in California as he had promised. Traveling the route of the previous year the party arrived at the Mojave villages, where Indians surprised and killed ten of the company; the remainder abandoned most of their belongings and made forced marches across the desert to Mission San Gabriel. Smith quickly rejoined the hunt-

ers he had left in the San Joaquin Valley. The necessity for obtaining food and supplies caused him to travel to the Mission San Jose where he was arrested and placed in jail and denied access to the Governor for a time. Although he was finally permitted to talk with Echeandía in Monterey, only the intervention of several American ship captains prevented Smith's being sent to a Mexican prison. He was forced to post a thirty-thousand-dollar bond to guarantee his departure from California within two months. From Monterey, Smith's route took him northward to the head of the Sacramento, then west, probably along the Trinity river to the coast and on northward to the Umpqua river in Oregon. While encamped on this stream the party was attacked by Indians, and all but Smith and two of his men were massacred. All the furs were stolen. Among the dead was Harrison G. Rogers, clerk and quartermaster of the expedition. When Smith had returned to the Great Salt Lake the year before, he had left Rogers in charge of the party in the San Joaquin Valley, and Rogers had kept a journal of his experiences. The three survivors made their way to Fort Vancouver, the Hudson's Bay post on the Columbia river, where Dr. John McLoughlin, the chief factor, gave them aid and sent a party to regain the captured furs, which he subsequently purchased for twenty thousand dollars. The act was a generous one, for Smith had no means of transporting the furs back to the Great Salt Lake. However, McLoughlin exacted a promise that the Rocky Mountain Fur Brigade would not again penetrate the Northwest. In the spring of 1828, Smith and one companion made their way to Pierre's Hole on the western side of the Teton Mountains, where they rejoined Smith's partners, Jackson and Sublette.

Smith had explored a new route from the Great Salt Lake southwest into California, had made the first crossing of the Sierra, and had opened another route across the Great Basin desert to the Great Salt Lake. In marching to the Columbia river, his men were the first Americans to explore the great interior valleys of California. They opened a north-south route and made known California's potential for American traders and settlers.

Pertinent Literature

Morgan, Dale L. *Jedediah Smith and the Opening of the West.* Indianapolis: Bobbs-Merrill Co., Inc., 1953.

This standard work on Jedediah Smith is both more and less than a biography. It is less because the authentic historical material on Smith is so limited that no definitive biography which will dispel the legend surrounding his name can be produced; it is more because Morgan sketches the lives and characters of the mountain men with whom Smith was associated, and the list includes nearly all the leading participants in the fur trade. Smith, the central figure in the account, emerges as the grand exception to most generalizations about fur men. He was able to read and write, had received some formal education, proclaimed and practiced Christianity, did not smoke or swear, rarely took a drink, and never shared his bed with a squaw. His actions indicated that he was intelligent, responsible, and generous. He was reckless only in his determination to explore the wilderness and to overcome natural obstacles.

Morgan takes into account the international aspects of the British and American fur trade and the resulting impact upon the pattern of Western development. He also explains the ways in which the business of the fur trade was conducted, noting the evolutionary changes in fur trading and trapping. However, his primary concern is with geography, with "the opening of the West," as the title of his book states; Morgan gives extensive and detailed descriptions of Smith's travels and the terrain covered, naming rivers, mountains, and valleys unfamiliar to the general reader. To follow the narrative of exploration, a knowledge of the geography of the West or possession of a good map is essential. Such attention to detail is logical, for Smith is important because of his geographical discoveries during the nine years he spent in the Western fur trade. In this short period he made an "effective" discovery of the South Pass through the Rocky Mountains, although he was not the first to pass through it; he was the first man to cross overland from the American frontier, via the Great Salt Lake, to California; the first to traverse the length of Utah and the breadth of Nevada; the first to cross the Sierra Nevada; and the first to travel by land northward through California and Oregon. He startled the Mexican governor of California by his appearance in San Diego, and the chief factor of the Hudson's Bay Company by his arrival at Fort Vancouver. After eight years of exploration and hunting for new areas for trapping, Smith became interested in the Santa Fe trade. He was killed on the trail to Santa Fe in 1831 when he was thirty-two years of age.

Morgan's work is scholarly. He is familiar with the historical evidence, both printed and manuscript, on the exploits of Smith. He relies heavily upon the sources located by earlier writers, such as Harrison C. Dale and Maurice S. Sullivan, and he has added new material from diaries that have become available since those studies of Smith were prepared. In addition, Morgan has succeeded in organizing with clarity the complicated and fragmentary information. He skillfully analyzes and interprets the factual evidence, and he writes well.

Sullivan, Maurice S. *Jedediah Smith, Trader, and Trail Breaker.* New York: Press of the Pioneers, Inc., 1926.

After dedicated research and careful detective work Maurice S. Sullivan in 1934 published a volume entitled *The Travels of Jedediah Smith: A Documentary Outline, Including the Journal of the Great American Pathfinder.* It contains, among other documents, a portion of Smith's daily record of his movements, hitherto thought to be lost, which briefly describes Smith's entry into the fur trade, then skips a period of five years and continues the record from June 24, 1827, to July 3, 1828. In this last section are the details of Smith's trip across the Utah Desert, his second journey to California, his escape from the Mojave Indians, and his adventures in California and Oregon, including the massacre of most of his men and the loss of his furs. Sullivan published not only this important journal, but also Alexander R. McLeod's diary, located in the Hudson's Bay Company Archives. This diary describes the recovery of the furs seized by the Umpqua Indians and also reveals the reasons for the attack. From the Mexican Archives, another valuable letter announcing the death and terms of the will of Jedediah Smith is reproduced. Although Sullivan had made the greatest contribution of new evidence on Jedediah Smith since the publication of Harrison Clifford Dale's *Ashley-Smith Explorations* in 1918, he did not attempt a biography at this time.

Two years after the 1934 publication of *The Travels of Jedediah Smith,* Sullivan brought out *Jedediah Smith, Trader and Trail Breaker,* in which he incorporated new information. Although a significant and readable biography, the style is flamboyant. The volume appears to have been a labor of love. Readers will find it an exciting and dramatic narrative. Sullivan died after the work was completed but prior to its publication, and a brief foreword and bibliographical notes have been added by Rufus Rockwell Wilson. — *W.T.J.*

Additional Recommended Reading

Dale, Harrison C., ed. *The Ashley-Smith Explorations and the Discovery of a Central Route to the Pacific, 1822-1829.* Revised ed. Glendale, California: The Arthur H. Clark Co., 1941. First published in 1918 this monograph was for years the standard account of

Jedediah Smith's activities. New vistas of fur trade history were opened by Dale, who emphasized the interrelationship between trading and exploration.

Smith, Alson J. *Men Against the Mountains: Jedediah Smith and the South West Expedition of 1826-1829.* New York: John Day Co., 1965. A popular, well-written book, carefully based on the scholarly accounts of Dale, Morgan, and Sullivan.

Neihardt, John G. *Splendid Wayfaring: The Exploits and Adventures of Jedediah Smith and the Ashley-Henry Men.* Lincoln, Neb.: University of Nebraska Press, 1970. A recent analysis of the Ashley-Smith explorations.

BALTIMORE AND OHIO RAILROAD BEGINS OPERATIONS

Type of event: Economic: building of the first major railroad system in the United States
Time: 1828-1830
Locale: Baltimore and westward to the Ohio river

Principal personages:

PHILIP EVAN THOMAS (1776-1861), prosperous merchant of Baltimore, who was largely responsible for the promotion of the scheme for the Baltimore and Ohio Railroad

EVAN THOMAS (fl. 1828), brother to Philip E. Thomas and one of the first promoters of the Baltimore and Ohio Railroad

COLONEL JOHN EAGER HOWARD (1752-1827), prominent Baltimore resident in whose home the scheme for the Baltimore and Ohio Railroad was first discussed

CHARLES CARROLL (1737-1832), signer of the Declaration of Independence, who laid the first cornerstone for the construction of the B & O Railroad

COLONEL STEPHEN H. LONG (1784-1864), army officer hired by the management of the Baltimore and Ohio Railroad to oversee the survey and location setting for the line

JONATHAN KNIGHT (1789-1864), famed mathematician and chief engineer of the Baltimore and Ohio Railroad

Summary of Event

The quickening pace of American life achieved a new momentum in the early national period. The Westward movement acquired a national character as New Englanders pushed into the Ohio Valley and Virginians filled up Kentucky and Tennessee. The Eastern Seaboard, with its cities and port facilities, turned to the West for its food, and the grain-producing hinterland responded with increased production. New methods of transportation were required to bring the produce of the interior to the coast. Enterprising businessmen, pooling their capital resources, engaged in canal building and railroad construction. Private initiative, in the absence of a consistent gov-

ernment policy of promoting public works, laid the foundation of a national transportation system. This transportation system began with canals, but regions without navigable waterways had to find another method. The railroad provided the answer.

The development of transportation in the early national period took three forms; canals, roads, and railways. Canals, in areas of accessible rivers and lakes, were by far the cheapest. Horse-drawn barges could move heavy bulk commodities inexpensively, and the cost of maintenance was negligible. When the Erie Canal opened in 1825, Buffalo and New York City became *entrepôts* for Western trade. The Morris

Company Canal, under construction from 1824 to 1832, eventually connected New York Harbor to the mouth of the Lehigh river, and served to bring Lehigh coal to the seaboard. Other canals were enthusiastically promoted with the expectation of reaping huge profits from the Western trade. Pennsylvania, smarting from the Erie Canal, constructed the Pennsylvania Portage and Canal System between 1826 and 1840. This elaborate system of cable portages and short canals was a dismal failure. High construction costs and competition from railroads rendered this bold scheme obsolete before it opened.

The construction of roads had a much longer history. The Philadelphia-Lancaster Turnpike, completed in 1794, encouraged road building in other areas. In New England and the Middle states, where distances were relatively short, toll roads were constructed feverishly in the 1790's and early 1800's. Yet, road transportation was still more expensive than canal transportation. High freight costs precluded the movement of bulk commodities, and overland transportation declined rapidly with the rise of canals. By 1821, six hundred miles of new turnpike construction had been authorized, and nearly four thousand miles stood completed. The Old National Road, connecting Cumberland, Maryland, and Wheeling, on the Ohio river, fell into neglect after the opening of the Erie Canal. By 1825 the turnpike boom had passed.

The third form of transportation required the assistance of technology. In 1825, the Stockton and Darlington Railroad opened in England. Americans quickly recognized the railroad's potential for the United States. Within a few years, railroad construction in the United States surpassed that in Great Britain. Shortline railways were first, but with the incorporation of the Baltimore and Ohio Railroad, long distance rail transportation for goods and passengers became a reality.

Baltimore's decision to sponsor a railway into the interior was, in essence, a manifesto in its struggle for commercial supremacy with New York City. By 1827, Baltimore boasted a population of 80,000, of which nearly two-thirds earned their living in commerce or related industries. The completion of the Erie Canal threatened Baltimore's prosperity. The National Road, which had played a significant role in Baltimore's commercial success, could not compete with New York's all-water route. Hence, the idea of a railroad, an ambitious and fiscally dangerous scheme at best, soon found influential supporters in Baltimore's business community.

Discussion preceded organization. At a dinner party held at the home of Colonel John Eager Howard at Baltimore in 1826, the scheme for a railroad linking Baltimore with the Ohio Valley was first discussed. Evan Thomas, an influential member of Baltimore's business elite, who was to become the first president of the new railroad, had just returned from England, where he had viewed the operations of the Stockton and Darlington Railroad. Thomas was enthusiastic about the new enterprise, and he succeeded in arousing the interest of a few business leaders with his vivid descriptions of the English system. Most business leaders, however, remained reticent, and their cautious attitude prevented immediate action. Evan's brother, Philip E. Thomas, now took up the cause. As a prosperous merchant who felt threatened by New York City's ascendancy, Philip Thomas began pushing the idea at every available gathering. When New York City appeared to be running away with the Western trade, Baltimore's businessmen began to panic. The ideas of the Thomas brothers, so quietly received in 1826, now aroused unbridled enthusiasm in the early months of 1827.

On February 2, 1827, at a dinner party held at the home of George Brown, the Thomas brothers presented a discourse on the relative advantages of a railway trade route to the West. Twenty-five businessmen attended this affair, representing a good portion of Baltimore's business elite. After the discourse, a committee was appointed to investigate the feasibility of the scheme. One week later, the committee reported that immediate steps should be taken to "construct a railway between the city of Baltimore and some suitable point upon the Ohio River." The report further suggested that a company be formed and a charter of incorporation be obtained from the legislature. Business leaders received the report and took action immediately. A large edition of the report was published in pamphlet form and distributed publicly. News of the plan quickly spread beyond city limits, and throughout the state of Maryland tongues were wagging. Thus, when a formal petition for a charter of incorporation was submitted to the Maryland State Legislature on February 27, 1827, little opposition was present. The bill for incorporation passed easily the

next day, and America's first significant experiment in railroad building was under way.

The charter of the Baltimore and Ohio Railroad Company provided for a capital stock of $3,000,000 to be raised by the public sale of 15,000 shares at one hundred dollars a share. Ten thousand shares were reserved for subscription by the state of Maryland, and five thousand for subscription by the city of Baltimore. When ten thousand shares had been purchased, the corporation would be declared established and all its rights and privileges would take effect immediately. The fiscal organization of the Baltimore and Ohio Railroad transformed the city of Baltimore and the state of Maryland into a private corporation, and the citizens of the state into a public enterprise.

When the stock offer was made, an enthusiastic public responded. Money flowed into the company coffers. Parents took out stock in their children's names, and a wave of speculation swept the state. The stock books were opened on March 20, 1827, at the Farmers Branch Bank in Frederick and the Mechanics Bank in Baltimore. Twelve days later the books were closed. The Baltimore and Ohio Railroad stock was distributed among twenty-two thousand individuals; nearly every family in the state had a stake in the company. Private enterprise had created a public utility.

The actual construction of the line awaited the solution of many engineering problems. Americans were novices in railroad building, but what they lacked in practical experience, they more than made up for with energy. The federal government possessed the only repository of engineering knowledge, and the management of the Baltimore and Ohio Railroad raided the government for talent. Colonel Stephen H. Long was acquired from the army, and Jonathan Knight, a well-recognized mathematician, was obtained from the National Road project. Engineers were sent to England to study the British system, and preliminary surveys were made to determine the best route to take. Problems arose, but public impatience goaded the bureaucracy to action.

By the summer of 1828, enough progress had been made to allow a symbolic gesture. The historic significance of America's first long distance railroad was clearly seen. The citizens of Maryland felt themselves upon the threshold of a new era. To insure a conspicuous place in later history books, the management of the Baltimore and Ohio Railroad sought to commemorate the occasion with the laying of a cornerstone. To perform this symbolic act they chose Charles Carroll, the last surviving signer of the Declaration of Independence. And on July 4, 1828, in a ceremony preceded by parades and speeches, Charles Carroll laid the cornerstone for America's first interstate railway.

Two years later on January 7, 1830, the Baltimore and Ohio Railroad opened its line from Pratt Street through to Carrolton Viaduct for public riding. Four rail cars, with a total seating capacity of 120 persons pulled by teams of horses, made the first run.

The beginning was inauspicious, but the potential for public rail transportation created a railroad mania throughout the nation. Schemes for railroad construction took the public imagination by storm. By 1833, the South Carolina Canal and Railroad Company had completed its line from Charleston to Hamburg, South Carolina. In 1836, the Erie and Kalamazoo Railroad connected Toledo, Ohio, with Adrian Township, in the Michigan Territory. And in the twenty years from 1840 to 1860, an additional 28,000 miles were added to the nation's railroad system. Steam engines of greater efficiency soon replaced the smoking teakettle contraptions of the earlier years, and as horsepower per tonnage increased, freight costs dropped dramatically. What had begun as a private enterprise by Baltimore merchants to save their city became a national institution.

The railroad soon came to dominate internal transportation, but more importantly, the railroad created a need for corporate organization on a large scale. The phenomenal growth of American industry in the second half of the nineteenth century cannot be understood without reference to the impact of the railroads upon American economic life.

Pertinent Literature

Hungerford, Edward. *The Story of the Baltimore and Ohio Railroad.* 2 vols. New York and London: G. P. Putnam's Sons. The Knickerbocker Press, 1928.

Hungerford attempts to trace the history of the Baltimore and Ohio Railroad as a single example of corporate institutional growth. In a style perhaps too elliptical for modern reading tastes, Hungerford weaves his theme of all-conquering private enterprise into, under, around, and through the drab fabric of institutional history. The larger issues of national growth, Westward expansion, and sectionalism are often submerged beneath the murky waters of statistical analysis and erudite historical scholarship. The optimistic view of American industrial omnipotence reflects all too clearly the late 1920's, but Hungerford remains true to his sources and presents an accurate, if dull, narrative of the history of the Baltimore and Ohio Railroad.

The building of the Erie Canal forced the merchants of Baltimore to disregard traditional modes of transportation. Innovation, the child of progress, was a necessity; daring and ambition were the seeds of success. The railroad scheme required large sums of capital, and large sums of capital required large scale corporate organization. Baltimore rose to the occasion, while other cities pursued abortive and costly experiments in canal construction. The success of the Baltimore and Ohio Railroad speaks adequately for the enterprising spirit of American industrial leadership, but more significantly, the founding of the Baltimore and Ohio Railroad illustrates the strength of American democracy. The Baltimore and Ohio Railroad was more than a private enterprise; it was essentially a democratic undertaking on the part of the citizens of Maryland, and as such, the founding of the Baltimore and Ohio Railroad parallels the growth of American participatory government.

Hungerford's theme is perhaps too simplistic, but an element of truth is present. The fact is, the successful establishment of a corporate structure with a fluid capital base of $3,000,000 does speak well for the faith of Americans in their system. Stock holdings for the Baltimore and Ohio Company were relatively well-distributed across socioeconomic class lines, and most Marylanders held high hopes for the Company's success. The railroad saved Baltimore from economic extermination, and the "American nature" of the enterprise cannot be totally discounted.

Hungerford continues his narrative on through 1927, noting the contribution made by the Baltimore and Ohio Railroad to national growth and fiscal expansion. His theme suffers somewhat during the years of the Civil War, but the last half of the nineteenth century enables Hungerford to revive the patriotic call of American big business. Yet Hungerford's history continues to merit respect. The detailed analysis of business practices, the exceedingly interesting accounts of engineering feats, and the vast core of statistical data drawn from the business files of one of America's first great public utilities, allows the reader to draw his own conclusions about the Baltimore and Ohio Railroad Company. The outdated historical perspective notwithstanding, Hungerford's history of the Baltimore and Ohio Railroad today remains the most useful and informative history available.

Stover, John F. *American Railroads.* Chicago and Toronto: University of Chicago Press, 1961.

Stover's general history of the American railroad places the event of the founding of the Baltimore and Ohio Railroad in historical perspective. The rapid growth of American rail transportation is told in clear, concise language, devoid of heavy interpretive themes, and refreshing in its panoramic view. Stover's central theme is the "railroad problem" in American history, the complex and often perplexing puzzle of management, finance, and control.

Few nations have experienced such a rapid expansion of railroads as the United States. This expansion created enormous problems for government. The large corporate structures required by railroads became unmanageable. The private investors who contributed the major portion of the capital for the early railroads gave way after 1850 to Eastern banks, European monied interests, and large fiscal combines. The American people lost control of their own system. Government was too slow in meeting the challenge. As railroads became the major weapon in the "competitive municipal mercantilism" of the day, the weak controls established by governmental agencies broke down. In the quest for a national system of rails, private enterprise was allowed free reign. This laissez-faire attitude produced wasteful duplication, noncompetitive price fixing, and costly overexpansion.

Stover notes, with a touch of nostalgia, that America's failure to solve the "railroad problem" doomed the rail system to eventual extinction. Twentieth century America turned away from rail transportation when presented with the automobile as an alternative. Throughout the history of American transportation the tendency of each new phase to challenge and supplant the preceding phase is evident. The canals replaced the turnpikes only to be replaced by the railroads. Fortunately for the railroad, this trend stopped in the middle of the nineteenth century, but the coming of the automobile literally sounded the death knell of rail transportation in the United States. In the fifty years or so before the automobile supplanted the railroads, the American rail system had an adequate opportunity to grow, which it did.

Uncontrolled growth encouraged by government's inability to act prevented American railroads from achieving an efficient, integrated system which could meet the challenge of the twentieth century and the automobile. The result was evident by the 1950's. In 1959 rail mileage had actually declined to a level below that of 1906.

Stover concludes his book with an essay suggesting governmental actions to alleviate the "railroad problem." There is little evidence, however, to sustain the hope that governmental action, if it comes at all, will be adequate or in time. — *J.G.C.*

Additional Recommended Reading

Fishlow, Albert. *American Railroads and the Transformation of the Ante-Bellum Economy.* Cambridge: Harvard University Press, 1965. A controversial interpretation of the effect of railroad expansion upon the economy of pre-Civil War America. Fishlow concludes that during the period from 1828 to 1840 the expansion of railroads yielded negative returns since investment costs always exceeded dividends.

Kirkland, Edward C. *Men, Cities and Transportation: A Study in New England History, 1820-1900.* 2 vols. Cambridge: Harvard University Press, 1948. A sectional study analyzing the response of a highly urban and industrial area to its own transportation needs as well as competition from other areas.

Gates, Paul W. *The Illinois Central Railroad and Its Colonization Work.* Cambridge: Harvard University Press, 1934. Emphasizes the impact of this great North-South line in opening up the western areas of Illinois to settlement, and its promotional efforts to attract settlers.

Overton, Richard C. *Burlington West: A Colonization History of the Burlington Railroad.* Cambridge: Harvard University Press, 1941. Traces the efforts of a major railroad to settle its vacant Trans-Mississippi lands.

Fogel, Robert W. *Railroads and American Economic Growth: Essays in Econometric History.* Baltimore: The Johns Hopkins University Press, 1964. A specialized study that concludes that railroads were not nearly so important to economic growth as has been assumed.

Clark, John G. *The Grain Trade in the Old Northwest.* Urbana: University of Illinois Press, 1966. Demonstrates that the growth of the grain trade and of urban centers to handle that trade went hand in hand with transportation improvements.

Reed, Merle E. *New Orleans and the Railroads: The Struggle for Commercial Empire, 1830-1860.* Baton Rouge: Louisiana Historical Association, 1966. Describes the efforts of New Orleans to utilize railroads to protect and expand her commercial hinterland.

Philips, Ulrich B. *A History of Transportation in the Eastern Cotton Belt to 1860.* New York: Columbia University Press, 1908. Notes that railroads in the Eastern cotton belt and much of the South were influenced by conditions peculiar to the region.

ELECTION OF JACKSON
TO THE PRESIDENCY IN 1828

Type of event: Political: beginning of a new two-party system in Presidential elections
Time: 1828
Locale: The United States

Principal personages:
ANDREW JACKSON (1767-1845), Indian fighter and hero of New
Orleans, seventh President of the United States 1829-1837
JOHN QUINCY ADAMS (1767-1848), diplomat and sixth President of the United States 1825-1829

Summary of Event

The Presidential campaign of 1828 was among the bitterest in American history. It is also one of the most discussed and analyzed, partially because it symbolized a number of practices and trends which were developing in American society. The 1828 contest followed on the heels of the famous "corrupt bargain" election of 1824 and was a rematch between the same two major protagonists—John Quincy Adams, the President, and Andrew Jackson. These men, and two others, Secretary of the Treasury William H. Crawford and United States Representative Henry Clay of Kentucky, had run in 1824, each hoping to succeed President James Monroe. No candidate received a majority in the electoral college, so the election went into the House of Representatives, which voted by states. There, Henry Clay's influence helped to throw the victory to Adams, who then appointed Clay to be Secretary of State. This, the Jacksonians believed, constituted a "corrupt bargain," and, so convinced, Jackson decided to run again in 1828 and seek vindication.

The election occurred at a time when a number of major issues and developments could have provided the substance for meaningful campaign debate and dialogue. John Quincy Adams' Administration was characterized by advocacy of a strong national government deeply involved in the direction and planning of many domestic economic, social, and intellectual activities. The President's program was essentially the same as Henry Clay's "American System" and was so nationalistic as to alienate many segments of the population who favored a strict constructionist, states' rights philosophy. The two sides differed over many specific issues: the tariff, land policy, internal improvements, banking, and, locally, debtor-relief and bankruptcy laws. There were in the background manifestations of class differences. In an over-simplified sense this was to be a conflict of "democrats" versus "aristocrats," "haves" versus "have-nots," "aspiring capitalists" versus the entrenched forces of "privilege."

The campaign revolved around all of these elements, and yet none of them. The public personalities and reputations of Andrew Jackson and John

631

Quincy Adams, the personal rivalry and personality and stylistic contrasts between the men, became the focal points of the campaign. Although the reactions of voters to the two men seemed to be due to their personality, undoubtedly, they mirrored or reflected deeper, perhaps vaguely but strongly felt and unarticulated emotional reactions to the issues. The parties themselves, Adams' National Republicans and Jackson's Democratic Republicans, seemed anxious to avoid substantial issues—their supporters were mixed lots, and they wanted to avoid alienating any segment of the faithful. They also were appealing to the uncommitted, and preferred vague generalities to spread the widest possible net.

The contest developed into one of the greatest examples of mudslinging in American political history. No charge, however inaccurate or unfounded, seemed too extreme for the zealous campaigners. Each candidate was the target of vicious slander, as charges of murder, adultery, and pandering were slung back and forth. Adams was portrayed as a monarchist, the darling of the old Federalists, a profligate spender who presided over a corrupt squadron of insiders and office-holders who lived in undemocratic luxury at the voters' expense. The hoary details of the "corrupt bargain," that marriage between "the Puritan and the black-leg" were dredged up again and again by the Jacksonians. Jackson fared no better. He was, according to his enemies, a hot-tempered, overly-ambitious, would-be tyrant, who had lived in sin with his beloved Rachel, and who appealed to the basest emotions of "King Mob."

The outcome of the contest was never much in doubt, the glamorous soldier-statesman Jackson, "Old Hickory," the "Hero of New Orleans," was an easy victor over the cold and proper incumbent. Jackson won 647,286 popular and 178 electoral votes to the 508,064 popular and 83 electoral votes of Adams, who carried only the New England section and the states of New Jersey, Maryland, and Delaware. It was a resounding victory for the General, but what did it mean?

Some have seen Jackson's election as the symbol of an economic revolution. As one writer has expressed it: "With Old Hickory's election a fluid economic and social system broke the bonds of a fixed and stratified political order. Originally a fight against political privilege, the Jackson movement had broadened into a fight against economic privilege, rallying to its support a host of 'rural capitalists and village entrepreneurs.' " However, others do not believe that the lines were that clearly drawn or that the Jackson victory changed matters very drastically. They point out that economic gulfs continued to widen during the Jacksonian era.

The General's victory has also been interpreted as a triumph for "democracy" over "aristocracy." But was it? The often-heralded broadening of the suffrage and democratization of the political system neither started nor ended with Jackson. His introduction of the "spoils system" with its turnout of the old entrenched bureaucrats was not as drastic as it seemed to many. The caucus system for nominating presidential candidates was last used in 1824, and by 1832 national nominating conventions had replaced "King Caucus," while, on another front, all of the states except South Carolina gave the voters the power to elect Presidential electors, divesting the legislatures of that prerogative. These were all "democratic" changes, but they can not be truly considered results of Jackson's victory per se.

To many, Jackson's triumph seemed a victory for states' rights in the South; to others it symbolized the rise of the nationalistic West. Orators talked of the elevation of the "common man" to his rightful position of power in the republic. Perhaps the greatest significance of Jackson's victory was in fact the elevation to national leadership of a man who symbolized so many of the hopes, aspirations, and interests of many different segments of the American community. This does not mean, however, that his triumph totally lacked substance. Jackson's victory did signify the return of two-party competition to the United States and it did provide the average citizen with elaborate party machinery through which his interests could more directly affect the operations of government and the formulation of public policy. Politicians were now obliged at least to strive for mass support, and this in itself was enough to give real substance to the "Revolution of 1828."

Pertinent Literature

Remini, Robert V. *The Election of Andrew Jackson.* Philadelphia: J. B. Lippincott Company, 1963.

Robert V. Remini is a well-known scholar of the Jacksonian period and in this book he avoids mythology and hero-worship to provide a thoroughly-researched and documented analysis of the significance of the election of 1828. Remini's brief study is an important contribution to the history of the period, written in a lively style that will appeal to the average reader.

The book focuses upon the development of the political parties of the middle and late 1820's. Remini argues that Andrew Jackson's 1828 victory was due largely to the excellent political organization that backed his candidacy, and the author believes that Jackson himself, not Martin Van Buren as Remini had himself suggested in an earlier work, was the architect and leader of the Jacksonian organization. He was not, as some other writers have assumed, merely the titular head of the movement. Jackson is seen by Remini as a "superb" politician who operated comfortably in the political milieu and conducted "a careful campaign to wrest the Presidency from John Quincy Adams."

While he does not deny Jackson's heroic appeal and charisma, Remini does argue that personal popularity as the explanation for Jackson's victory has been over-emphasized by other writers, and that, in fact, Jackson could well have been defeated in 1828 if his opponents had been better organized. Jackson's triumph did not, then, symbolize the appearance of a great democratic upsurge, but rather the formation of an effective political organization through which the common man could transform his assumptions into public policy. Some may disagree with Remini's interpretations, but most will find his work informative and provocative.

633

Meyers, Marvin. *The Jacksonian Persuasion: Politics and Belief.* Palo Alto: Stanford University Press, 1957.

Marvin Meyers, like many other historians, is intrigued by the paradoxes of Andrew Jackson and the Jacksonian movement. The author rejects many of the emphases which other writers have placed on class and sectional conflict as keys to the Jacksonian democracy and singles out the "expressive role" of politics as providing a more adequate explanation of the Jackson appeal.

Beginning with the assumption that what a politician says and writes is as important a clue to his beliefs (and those of his followers) as what he does, Meyers attempts to discover what the Jacksonians actually believed by reading, and taking seriously, their political statements.

As one might expect, Meyers finds that the Jacksonians had many opinions on numerous public questions, and that not all of Old Hickory's supporters were in agreement on particular issues. This accounts in part, he believes, for the varying interpretations by recent historians on the meaning of Jacksonian democracy. Meyers says that in the course of his investigations he has found substantiation for all recent interpretations. Nevertheless, he declares, the elements "converge to form an urgent political message with a central theme." That theme, which Meyers calls a "persuasion" rather than an ideology or *"ethos,"* is fundamentally

that, while Americans were "boldly liberal in economic affairs,"—while they cleared the continent, industrialized the countryside, and built cities, railroads, and canals—they were not really ready for the uncertainties, rapid changes, complexities, and indirection of the new economic ways. Psychologically they longed for the imagined virtue and innocent purity of the old Jeffersonian republic. The Jacksonian democracy represented in part a "struggle to reconcile again the simple yeoman values with the free pursuit of economic interest, just as the two were splitting hopelessly apart." Thus, the typical American was what Meyers calls a "venturous conservative."

As Meyers has argued in another of his writings, the Jacksonians therefore appealed "not to some workingmen's yearning for a brave new world; not to the possibilities of a fresh creation at the western limits of civilization; not to the ambitions of a rising laissez-faire capitalism—not to any of these so much as to a *restoration* of old virtues and a (perhaps imaginary) old republican way of life."

The Jacksonian Persuasion is a well-researched and readable book that should stimulate interest in both the Jacksonian movement and the American political process.

Additional Recommended Reading

Schlesinger, Arthur M., Jr. *The Age of Jackson.* Boston: Little, Brown, and Company, 1945. Pulitzer Prize-winning study that emphasizes the role of Eastern labor in the triumph of Jackson.

Abernethy, Thomas P. *From Frontier to Plantation in Tennessee: A Study in Frontier Democracy.* Chapel Hill: The University of North Carolina Press, 1932. Rejects the idea of Jackson as a representative of frontier democracy.

Hofstadter, Richard. "Andrew Jackson and the Rise of Liberal Capitalism," in *The American Political Tradition and the Men Who Made It.* New York: Alfred A. Knopf, 1948. Agrees with Abernethy's view of Jackson as a mid-Tennessee nabob whose election represented a mandate for economic reform and opportunity.

Ward, John William. *Andrew Jackson: Symbol For An Age.* New York: Oxford University Press, 1955. A sophisticated analysis of Jackson as symbol and myth in America.

NOAH WEBSTER PUBLISHES *AN AMERICAN DICTIONARY OF THE ENGLISH LANGUAGE*

Type of event: Cultural: desire to assert American cultural independence
Time: November, 1828
Locale: New Haven, Connecticut

Principal personages:
NOAH WEBSTER (1758-1843), author of *An American Dictionary of the English Language*
SAMUEL JOHNSON (1709-1784), English lexicographer whose dictionary helped to set American standards before Webster published his own work
GEORGE MERRIAM (1803-1880), and
CHARLES MERRIAM (1806-1887), publishers who purchased the rights of publication of Webster's dictionary in 1843
JOEL BARLOW (1754-1812), "Connecticut Wit" whose poetry represented the desire to create a national literature
TIMOTHY DWIGHT (1752-1817), president of Yale College and another "Connecticut Wit," who viewed America as representing a new era in history

Summary of Event

Although the political independence of the United States had been achieved by 1783, the new nation remained in certain respects a cultural colony of Europe. This was particularly true of "high" culture; literature and the fine arts in America remained largely derivative and subservient to European standards. While it was natural that a frontier country should follow the cultural leadership of the metropolitan centers of Western civilization, American nationalism of the post-Revolutionary period demanded a national culture. The literary group known as the "Connecticut Wits," or the "Hartford Wits," although imitative, strained to give the United States a distinguished literature. Later, Ralph Waldo Emerson called for cultural independence, and the nature of American cultural relations with Europe re-

mained an issue into the twentieth century. One cogent symbol of the recurrent plea for a national culture was the publication by Noah Webster of *An American Dictionary of the English Language.*

Born in Connecticut in 1758, Noah Webster was graduated from Yale College at the age of 20. As a Yale graduate and member of "The Friendly Club" in Hartford, he associated with John Trumbull, Theodore and Timothy Dwight, and others of the "Connecticut Wits." Webster's early contributions to American culture were as an educator, a function which his lexicographical career continued on a broader scale. His biographers have found it natural to accord him the title of "Schoolmaster to America," or "Schoolmaster of the Republic." In this role he was the author of *A Gram-*

matical *Institute of the English Language,* eventually a three-volume textbook for schoolchildren. The first part of the *Grammatical Institute of the English Language* became famous as the "Blue-Backed Speller"; "no other book, the Bible excepted," according to Harry R. Warfel, "played so unifying a part in American culture. . . ." Parts II and III, a grammar and a reader respectively, also did much to mold the American consciousness.

Webster's concern with language usage stemmed partly from his conviction that language was an important national bond. He believed that linguistic independence would follow political, with the gradual evolution of a distinct American dialect of English. Indeed, he was eager to accelerate the process, not only through the sanctioning and encouragement of American usages, but also through his advocacy of a reformed American spelling. At one time, the adoption of a reformed phonetic alphabet seemed to Webster the best way in which to render the United States culturally independent of England, and he enlisted the support of Benjamin Franklin in a plan to have the new alphabet adopted by the Confederation Congress. Although Webster came to realize that radical changes could not win support, he remained the advocate of spelling reform, as in the removal of silent or unnecessary letters. His authority did eventually support such minor deviations of American English as the omission of the "u" in words such as "honour" and "colour," and he defended American pronunciations.

An American Dictionary of the English Language was the logical culmination of Noah Webster's career. Prior to Webster's lexicography, three small American dictionaries had been published, but Americans still depended primarily on British dictionaries, such as that of Samuel Johnson. Not only did Johnson's dictionary fail to fit American needs, but its author was frequently mistaken, Webster believed, in his etymology. Webster himself was well-qualified by training and temperament to compile a dictionary. His learning was broad; he had practiced law, written about epidemic diseases, conducted laboratory experiments, and studied business conditions. He "delighted in etymological investigations," and learned other languages (eventually more than twenty) in order to understand the roots and relationships of English. He is characterized as America's first notable comparative philologist. Finally, Webster possessed extraordinary diligence and patience in the compilation and investigation of words.

Webster's masterwork was preceded by the publication in 1806 of his *Compendious Dictionary of the English Language,* which claimed the addition of five thousand words to the number found in the best English dictionaries. An abridgement intended for use in schools was published in 1807. Another two decades of labor remained before the two large volumes of *An American Dictionary of the English Language* came from the press in 1828. It listed seventy thousand words (twelve thousand more than the contemporary edition of Johnson's dictionary) and included an introduction in which Webster expounded his ideas on language and etymology. Webster made use of a preface to assert the parity of American with British English, and to defend James Madison, James Kent, Washington Irving, and others as authorities equal to the best British masters of the language.

Webster's dictionary soon became the lexicographical standard in the United States. After Webster's death in 1843, George and Charles Merriam purchased the rights of publication, and the Merriam Company has published many successive editions of the dictionary. Complete revisions have been made in 1864 (the famous *Unabridged*), 1890, 1909, 1934, and 1961, maintaining the identification of Noah Webster's name with American English.

Pertinent Literature

Warfel, Harry R. *Noah Webster: Schoolmaster to America.* New York: The Macmillan Company, 1936.

Harry R. Warfel's biography of Noah Webster is a highly sympathetic treatment of its subject as a consistent nationalist who played an important and multifarious role in the early history of the United States. Webster is presented as a man with something of the versatility and "many-sided intellectual quality of Benjamin Franklin," although retaining "the iron mantle of New England Calvinism." Tempered by a more modern humanitarianism, his religious orthodoxy supported a melioristic, but also sternly moralistic, brand of patriotism, disseminated through his schoolbooks and dictionaries.

Warfel emphasizes Webster's role in fostering "a consciousness of nationality." Replacing British textbooks, which naturally provided British geography and history, Webster's texts offered American orations on the Boston Massacre, Washington's Farewell Orders to the Army, and accounts of the Revolutionary War. *Rudiments of English Grammar* (1790) contained "A Federal Catechism," a basic explanation of the Constitution and the American system of government. At the same time, Webster discountenanced regional differences, attempting in particular to bring about the demise of regional variations of pronunciation and to standardize the national language. Although acknowledging his subject's increasing political conservatism, Warfel associates his nationalism with a "democratic idealism." He notes that Webster was by no means an abstract purist as a grammarian, being willing to defer to general usage in order to admit the correctness of "vulgar" or idiomatic expressions. "Just as the popular will should rule in speech, so should it rule in Church and State. . . . Our first teacher," Warfel rather hyperbolically adds, "was our first democrat."

As presented by Warfel, Webster's cultural nationalism was certainly of the same ilk as his political views. In the period following the Revolution, Webster was an early advocate of a strengthened American union. In a 1785 pamphlet, *Sketches of American Policy* (influenced strongly in its underlying philosophy by Rousseau's *Social Contract*), he urged the creation of a "supreme power at the head of the union," capable of compelling obedience to national laws. At this time, according to Warfel, Webster's Federalism was based on a "humanitarian, perfectionist philosophy." He supported ratification of the Constitution, wrote a widely disseminated pamphlet in its defense, and is credited by his biographer with a significant role in its adoption. He became a staunch Federalist and a supporter of the Hamiltonian program of developing American manufacturing and promoting national self-sufficiency.

Warfel's interpretation of Webster as a democratic idealist is somewhat embarrassed by his subject's drift to the political right and increasing qualms about popular government. Like so many early defenders of the French Revolution, he was disillusioned with its excesses, and, by Warfel's admission, became an "apologist of the old order." As a Federalist pamphleteer he tangled bitterly with Thomas Jefferson, accusing the third President of inverting the established order of society. With other New England Federalists he opposed the War of 1812, but, main-taining his fundamental nationalism, he did not entertain disunionist ideas.

Nationalism, indeed, is the constant quality in Warfel's portrayal of Webster, and the latter's crowning achievement, the publication of *An American Dictionary of the English Language,* emerges as its best expression. Warfel interprets this assertion of cultural independence against the background of a continuing struggle between national and colonial impulses in American life. The publication of Webster's dictionary was thus a manifestation of the same sentiment which called for a distinctively American legal system, demanded a national literature, and fostered the patriotic hagiography represented at its most frivolous by Mason Weems's story about the cherry tree in his *Life of Washington.* If Noah Webster's proposals for an American orthography sometimes seem as strained as Weems's myth-making, his solid lexicographical work was a necessary part of national self-definition.

Howard, Leon. *The Connecticut Wits.* Chicago: University of Chicago Press, 1943.

The phenomenon of cultural nationalism, of which Noah Webster is so outstanding an exemplar in early American history, is discussed in a related context by Leon Howard. Howard's study of Webster's fellow Connecticut literati, although it deals with Webster himself only peripherally, helps to place the lexicographer in perspective as a Yankee nationalist.

Making no attempt to discuss the entire group of writers known as the "Connecticut Wits," Howard concentrates on four older and major figures: John Trumbull, Timothy Dwight, David Humphreys, and Joel Barlow. All of these, like Webster, attended Yale College before or during the American Revolution, and all were known personally to Webster. Coming of age virtually at the same time as American independence, the "Connecticut Wits" sought to found a national literature. Their efforts, as Howard makes clear, were largely unsuccessful. For all their self-conscious patriotism, they remained loyal to European literary standards, and their attempts to create an American epic poetry seem today both provincial and pretentious. At most, Howard suggests, the "Connecticut Wits" helped to "fix the sense of direction" which their countrymen needed.

The "Connecticut Wits" shared the conviction that the founding of the United States represented a new era in human history. For some, indeed, it presaged the fulfillment of the ancient prophecy of the millenium. This conception of the national destiny joined men of such otherwise disparate views as Joel Barlow and Timothy Dwight. Barlow was egalitarian and anticlerical; he became a Jeffersonian Republican and died in 1812 while American minister to Napoleonic France. Dwight was a strong Federalist and a champion of Congregationalist orthodoxy. Both were nationalists.

Barlow decided as early as 1779 to compose an American epic. The result was his long poem, *The Vision of Columbus,* later revised as the *Columbiad.* The vision was one of progress according to "Heaven's extended plan," which included construction of the Erie, Suez, and Panama Canals, advances in medical science, and a league of nations. It reflected, Howard suggests, the "curious union between a complacent belief in the westward course of empire and an orthodox belief in the biblical millenium" prevalent among Americans. Barlow's nationalism was later manifested in a proposal that Congress establish a national university, and he proposed Webster as professor of philology. The two men were already associated in their interest in spelling reform, and Barlow later gave Webster some help with the dictionary.

To Dwight also the settlement of America represented a new epoch, and even prior to the Revolution he had prophesied in verse "the future glory of America in science, art, morality and religion until the coming of the millennium." Despite its biblical theme, Dwight's most ambitious poem, *The Conquest of Canaan,* seemed to embody an American nationalism; it was, Howard remarks, "full of eighteenth-century Americans with Hebrew names who talked like Milton's angels and fought like prehistoric Greeks." Still optimistic in 1787 when he began *Greenfield Hill,* Dwight contrasted European and American social institutions to the latter's advantage. America offered equal rights, liberty under law, popular education, and "pure religion." The poem concluded with "The Vision, or Prospect of the Future Happiness of America." Despite his later disillusionment with a republicanism tainted with "infidel philosophy," Dwight defended the United States from foreign criticism. He was particularly sensitive, like Noah Webster, to "the English disease of finding fault with the language of Americans."

For Webster as well as Barlow, Dwight, and the other "Connecticut Wits," language was the key to national identity. As self-conscious as was much of their epic poetry and the movement for a reformed orthography, they perceived the foundations of national culture in the way that Americans spoke and wrote. — *M.D.C.*

Additional Recommended Reading

Shoemaker, Ervin C. *Noah Webster: Pioneer of Learning.* New York: Columbia University Press, 1936. Shoemaker's study emphasizes Webster's educational role, but contains a careful discussion of his concern with language reform and his authorship of the dictionary.

Scudder, Horace E. *Noah Webster.* Boston: Houghton, Mifflin Co., 1881. While characterizing Webster as "the first aggressive American in our literature," Scudder also finds that the lexicographer "had no conception of the enormous weight of the English language and literature when he undertook to shovel it out of the path of American civilization."

Dangerfield, George. *The Awakening of American Nationalism, 1815-1828.* New York: Harper & Row Publishers, 1965. This volume in the *New American Nation* series provides useful background in discussing the political nationalism of the period in which Webster was compiling his dictionary.

Krout, John A. and Dixon R. Fox. *The Completion of Independence, 1790-1830.* New York: The Macmillan Company, 1944. Headed by a quotation from Webster urging Americans to unshackle their minds, this social history helps to relate his cultural nationalism, especially in the realm of education, to contemporary American society.

Perry, Bliss. *The American Spirit in Literature: A Chronicle of Great Interpreters.* New Haven: Yale University Press, 1918. Perry's theme is cultural nationalism as manifested in literature; his basic assumption is that "American literature is something different from English literature written in America."

Spencer, Benjamin T. *The Quest for Nationality: An American Literary Campaign.* Syracuse: Syracuse University Press, 1957. Webster appears frequently in this study of literary nationalism, concerned primarily with the nineteenth century.

THE HUMANITARIAN REFORM MOVEMENT

Type of event: Sociological: impact of evangelical religion on reform movement
Time: 1830's and 1840's
Locale: Northeastern and Western United States

Principal personages:

CHARLES GRANDISON FINNEY (1792-1875), revivalist and president of Oberlin College

WILLIAM LLOYD GARRISON (1805-1879), American abolitionist and editor of the *Liberator*

THEODORE DWIGHT WELD (1803-1895), American Anti-Slavery Society agent and organizer of a group of itinerant reformers known as the "Seventy"

ARTHUR TAPPAN (1786-1865), and

LEWIS TAPPAN (1788-1873), wealthy New York philanthropists and participants in founding the American Anti-Slavery Society

NEAL DOW (1804-1897), Maine prohibitionist, and president of World Temperance Convention of 1853

LUCRETIA MOTT (1793-1880), Quaker reformer, and organizer of Seneca Falls Convention

JAMES GILLESPIE BIRNEY (1792-1857), abolitionist and Liberty Party presidential candidate in 1840

ELIHU BURRITT (1810-1879), editor of the *Advocate of Peace and Universal Brotherhood*

ADIN BALLOU (1803-1890), founder of the Hopedale Community

Summary of Event

"In the history of the world the doctrine of Reform had never such scope as at the present hour," declared Ralph Waldo Emerson in 1841. Indeed, the wave of reform which swept over much of the United States in the 1830's and 1840's seemed to prove Emerson's theory that man was "born . . . to be a Reformer, a Remaker of what man has made; a renouncer of lies; a restorer of truth and good, imitating that great Nature which embosoms us all, and which sleeps no moment on an old past, but every hour repairs herself. . . ." In those decades Americans enlisted in a variety of causes and crusades, some of which were of a conservative nature while others challenged basic institutions and beliefs.

The antebellum reform movement was partly a response to economic, social, and political changes following the War of 1812. Such change provoked feelings of anxiety among some Americans, generating anti-Mason, anti-Catholic and anti-Mormon crusades. But it also generated a feeling of optimism and confirmed the almost universal faith in progress which characterized early nineteenth century

Americans. Evangelical religion played an important role in the origins of the reform movement. The shift from the Calvinistic doctrine of predestination to what William McLoughlin has called an "Arminianized Calvinism," which emphasized man's efforts in achieving salvation, nourished ideas of perfectionism and millenarianism. Not only could individuals achieve "perfect holiness" but the world itself, as evidenced by the movements for reform, was improving and moving toward the long-awaited thousand-year reign of the Kingdom of God on earth. Besides evangelicalism, the legacy of the Enlightenment and the American Revolution (the natural rights philosophy and the faith in man's ability to shape society in accordance with the laws of God and nature) were a stimuli to reform. So was the nineteenth century's romantic conception of the individual. "The power which is at once spring and regulator in all efforts of reform," Emerson wrote, "is the conviction that there is an infinite worthiness in man, which will appear at the call of worth, and that all particular reforms are the removing of some impediment."

Antebellum reformers attacked a variety of evils. Dorothea Dix urged humane treatment for the mentally ill; Thomas Gallaudet and Samuel Gridley Howe founded schools for the deaf and blind. Prison reform engaged the efforts of some Americans, and a campaign to abolish imprisonment for debt made slow but sure progress in the pre-Civil War period. Horace Mann championed common schools, and free public schooling gradually spread from New England to other parts of the United States. Elihu Burritt, the "learned blacksmith," urged the aboli-

tion of war and related evils. Communitarians, inspired by religious or secular principles, withdrew from society to found utopian experiments, such as Brook Farm, Oneida, or New Harmony. Lucretia Mott, Elizabeth Cady Stanton, Lucy Stone, and others championed higher education, the suffrage, and legal and property rights for women.

Temperance and abolition were the two most prominent crusades of the period. Both of them passed through several phases, moving from gradualism to immediatism and from persuasion to legal coercion. Thus the temperance movement began with an appeal for moderation in the consumption of alcoholic beverages, and shifted by the late 1820's to a demand for total abstinence. The Reverend Lyman Beecher's *Six Sermons,* published in 1826, were instrumental in effecting this shift to total abstinence; the "teetotal" position was further popularized in the 1840's by the Washington Temperance Society of reformed drunkards and the children's Cold Water Army. Similarly, the antislavery movement moved from a position favoring gradual emancipation and colonization in the 1820's, to a demand for immediate abolition of the sin of slavery. William Lloyd Garrison's *Liberator* and Theodore Dwight Weld's "Seventy" preached the immediatist doctrine, and it was adopted by the American Anti-Slavery Society which had been founded in 1833. In the 1840's some elements of both temperance and antislavery reformers, disillusioned by the lack of results being produced by education and "moral suasion," turned to politics as a means of achieving their goals. Some abolitionists supported the Liberty and

Free-Soil Parties, and later the Republicans, and sought legislation preventing the extension of slavery into the territories. Temperance advocates succeeded in getting state-wide prohibition and local option laws passed in a number of states in the early 1850's.

In most cases, the vehicle of reform was the voluntary association. Virtually every movement had a national organization, with state and local auxiliaries, which sponsored speakers, published pamphlets, and generally coördinated efforts in behalf of its cause. Though such societies were often rent by factionalism, they proved remarkably effective in arousing the popular conscience on the moral issues of the day. By 1850, for example, there were almost two thousand antislavery societies with a membership close to 200,000, compared to about five hundred such societies in 1826.

Although most of the reform movements had their largest following in the northeastern and western part of the United States, their impact was not confined to those sections. Southerners, though hostile to abolitionism and other radical causes, were receptive to pleas for educational and prison reform, and for better treatment of the insane and the blind. The temperance crusade made considerable headway in the South. Thus, to a greater or lesser degree, depending on the particular cause, the antebellum humanitarian reform movement was a truly national phenomenon.

Pertinent Literature

Cross, Whitney R. *The Burned-Over District: The Social and Intellectual History of Enthusiastic Religion in Western New York, 1800-1850.* Ithaca: Cornell University Press, 1950.

This book is a study of an area in western New York which was particularly susceptible to religious enthusiasm and reform movements in the 1820's and 1830's. The "Burned-Over District" was populated primarily by Yankees from New England; it was an area of bitter interdenominational strife; and, under the impact of the Erie Canal it had recently emerged from the frontier stage into "a period of relatively stable agrarian maturity." In addition, the inhabitants of the area enjoyed a certain amount of leisure time, were fairly well educated, and had access to a wide range of newspapers, periodicals, and tracts. All of these social, cultural, and economic factors made the area a fertile ground for revivalism and reform.

Cross singles out five "catalytic agents" which aided the release of the Burned-Over District's potential enthusiasm. The completion of the Erie Canal set the economic stage. Both the rise of anti-Masonic excitement and the spectacular growth of benevolent movements in the district stimulated a kind of religious enthusiasm, which made the inhabitants "easy targets" for the next revival. Thus Charles Grandison Finney, another catalytic agent, found the ground already prepared for him. His revivals of 1826 and 1831 succeeded in uniting revivalism and humanitarian movements, according to Cross. One other excitement served as a portent of things to come—the emergence of Mormonism under the leadership of Joseph Smith.

By the mid-1830's the Burned-Over District had reached a stage of heightened religious emotionalism which contemporaries called "Ultraism." Itinerant revivalists, employing Finney's "new measures," kept emotion at a fever pitch. They preached a radical religion characterized by belief in direct inspiration by the Holy Ghost and the imminence of the millennium, and by an intense preoccupation with sin. Ultraism was, Cross observes, almost "an impossible state of mind." Its existence was "only momentary, for its nature prohibited concerted and prolonged agreement by any considerable group of persons." Nevertheless, Cross believes that ultraism was "the precedent condition to all the ensuing crusades."

If Ultraism generated movements of "moral reformation" in the 1830's, it also determined their demise at the end of the decade. Cross attributes the demand for total abstinence in the temperance crusade and for immediate emancipation in the antislavery move-ment to Ultraistic thinking. At the same time, Ultraism's inherent tendency toward factionalism also infected the reform movements it fostered. In the late 1830's, temperance and abolition disintegrated in the wake of conflict over goals and methods. The depression of 1837 also played a role, though not the most important one, in dispersing Ultraist reform movements. In the 1840's, reformers moved into "more practical channels"; nevertheless, Cross argues that Ultraist thinking persisted as a powerful force in the Burned-Over District until mid-century.

Although this book is primarily concerned with religious ultraism and the social and economic factors which generated it, it is indispensable for understanding the origins and character of reform in the 1830's. Few writers on the antebellum period have been able to demonstrate the relation between revivalism and reform on the one hand and social and economic conditions on the other as precisely as does Cross.

Griffin, Clifford S. *Their Brothers' Keepers: Moral Stewardship in the United States, 1800-1865.* New Brunswick: Rutgers University Press, 1960.

Clifford Griffin views the antebellum reform movement as essentially a conservative effort aimed at preserving stability, sobriety, and order in society. Reformers were men of wealth and social prestige who sought to control society for personal reasons, in order to retain their economic and moral influence. Their goal was to persuade, or if necessary, to force others to conform to their way of thinking. Thus they "condemned as vicious and evil every practice in which they did not indulge, and they damned as ungodly men with different ideas."

The impulse behind the reform movement, according to Griffin, was the "combined idea of benevolence and trusteeship." Benevolence was more than simply a feeling of good will or philanthropic activity. "Benevolence was an infinite concern for other men's souls and other men's deeds." It was "the obligation that Christians had to make others good," to make sinful men obey the will of God. The notion of trusteeship was embodied in the reformers' concept of themselves as specially chosen by God to oversee the conduct of their fellow men. Although Griffin admits that this notion has a long tradition in American history, he argues that it had a special appeal in the 1820's and 1830's. Confronted with what appeared to be a decline of religion, morality, and order, a small group of self-appointed "trustees" formed national societies to combat what were seen as national ills. The purpose of the Bible and tract societies, the American Home Missionary Society, and the American Sunday School Union—as well as the National Temperance, Anti-Slavery, and Peace Societies—was to promote both personal piety and secular order, the basic components of a Christian society.

In the 1830's, the trustees tried to bring about conformity to their moral standards and social ideas by means of persuasion. In support of their views they offered not only religious arguments but also secular inducements, pointing to alleged social and economic benefits to be derived from their programs. When persuasion failed, the stewards turned in the late 1830's to another means of reform—political action. Working against popular disapproval of the legislation of religion and morality, they made slow progress. Yet the trustees remained committed to

"reform by compulsion" until the time of the Civil War, though Griffin argues that moral suasion continued to play an important role. Not only did temperance and antislavery reformers work for legislation favorable to their cause; such organizations as the Bible Society and Sunday School Union also employed political tactics in their efforts to get their publications into the public schools. Significantly, the shift to political action caused "a broadening of the benevolent impulse" to include politicians and political appointees who might assist the reformers. Thus Neal Dow not only urged temperance supporters to transcend their political affiliations and vote for prohibition men, but he also enlisted the aid of state and local politicians in order to get the famous Maine Law of 1851 passed. Griffin also suggests that the Republican Party was formed partly as a vehicle of reform by compulsion.

Griffin sees the antebellum reform movement as one phase of a long tradition of trusteeship. His interpretation of the movement as a conservative effort based on the notion of stewardship suggests a strong element of continuity between the Puritans, pre-Civil War reformers, and late nineteenth century advocates of the Gospel of Wealth. — *A.C.L.*

Additional Recommended Reading

Davis, David Brion, ed. *Ante-Bellum Reform.* New York: Harper & Row Publishers, 1967. Davis brings together recent significant articles on the psychological, social, and religious aspects of reform. His introduction and notes suggest an overall interpretation of the movement.

Tyler, Alice Felt. *Freedom's Ferment: Phases of American Social History from the Colonial Period to the Outbreak of the Civil War.* Minneapolis: University of Minnesota Press, 1944. A survey of the various reforms agitated in the century preceding the Civil War. Though some of its interpretations have been challenged by more recent works, it remains a valuable source of information.

Smith, Timothy L. *Revivalism and Social Reform in Mid-Nineteenth Century America.* New York: Abingdon Press, 1957. Smith stresses the perfectionist impulse behind reform movements of the 1840's and 1850's, and their concern with urban problems, such as poverty, industrialism, and immorality.

Thomas, John. "Romantic Reform in America, 1815-1865," in *American Quarterly* (Winter, 1965), 656-81. Written by the biographer of Garrison, this brilliant interpretive article deals with the antebellum reform movement as a whole. Thomas argues that the primary impulse behind the movement was "romantic perfectionism," which was in turn a product of the radical "transformation of American theology" in the early nineteenth century.

Filler, Louis. *The Crusade Against Slavery, 1830-1860.* New York: Harper & Row Publishers, 1960. A volume in the *New American Nation* series, Filler's book surveys the abolitionist movement and relates it to other reforms of the antebellum period, such as temperance, women's rights, education, and free speech.

Byrne, Frank L. *Prophet of Prohibition: Neal Dow and His Crusade.* Madison: State Historical Society of Wisconsin for the Department of History, University of Wisconsin, 1961. The Maine Law of 1851 was a victory for reformers seeking prohibition through state legislation. Byrne's book is a brief study of the man who championed that law, and of his efforts on behalf of prohibition in other states, Canada, and Britain.

Lewis, W. David. *From Newgate to Dannemora: The Rise of the Penitentiary in New York, 1796-1848.* Ithaca: Cornell University, 1965. Lewis analyzes two different approaches to prison reform in New York: one embodied in the work of Thomas Eddy at Newgate, and the other represented by the "Auburn system." The author relates the ideas of the reformers to the underlying assumptions of the society in which they lived.

Krout, John A. *The Origins of Prohibition.* New York: Alfred A. Knopf Inc., 1925. This is a comprehensive and well-documented study of the origin and development of the temperance movement to 1851, with a valuable bibliography of primary sources.

THE "PRO-SLAVERY ARGUMENT"

Type of event: Sociological: creation of a Southern consensus in support of the "peculiar institution"
Time: 1830-1865
Locale: The slave states

Principal personages:

GEORGE FITZHUGH (1806-1881), Virginia writer and social philosopher

JAMES HENRY HAMMOND (1807-1864), South Carolina lawyer, editor, and politician

THOMAS R. DEW (1802-1846), professor of political economy at William and Mary College

JOHN CALDWELL CALHOUN (1782-1850), South Carolina politician and political philosopher

JOSIAH NOTT (1804-1873), physician and author of *Types of Mankind*

THORNTON STRINGFELLOW (fl. 1850), Baptist minister of Culpeper County, Virginia

Summary of Event

In the quarter-century preceding the Civil War, Southerners advanced a wide range of arguments and theories —some old, some new—to justify the institution of chattel slavery. The distinctiveness of proslavery thinking during the years before the Civil War lay less in its content than in its tone or spirit., Spokesmen for the South's "peculiar institution" were no longer on the defensive; their mood was no longer apologetic. Unlike most of their predecessors, they did not merely tolerate slavery; they glorified it. They took the offensive in behalf of slavery partly in response to the attacks of Northern abolitionists. One objective, perhaps the primary objective of their aggressive proslavery campaign, was to dispel the doubts of Southerners as to the justice of slavery and to convince nonslaveholders and slaveholders alike (and especially the latter) that it was

sanctioned by religion, science, and morality, as well as by economic and political considerations.

Some of the proslavery arguments and theories advanced in the pre-Civil War period were used during the seventeenth and eighteenth centuries: the Biblical and historical arguments; the appeal to the alleged inferiority of the Negro; and the notion of entailment, which blamed the introduction of slavery on the British and predicted that social catastrophe would result from its abolition. But proslavery thought during the pre-Civil War period was highlighted by the "positive good" theory which emerged in the 1820's. In that decade Southerners began to argue that slavery was not a necessary evil, but a positive good. Dr. Richard Furman, Whitemarsh Seabrook, Edward Brown, and Dr. Thomas Cooper published pamphlets

648

expounding this point of view. In 1829 Governor Stephen D. Miller declared to the South Carolina legislature, "Slavery is not a national evil; on the contrary it is a national benefit." During the 1830's the "positive good" theory was championed by Southern Congressmen, including John C. Calhoun, who declared that slavery was "a good—a positive good," "a great blessing to both of the races," and "the great stay of the Union and our free institutions, and one of the main sources of the unbounded prosperity of the whole." Probably the most influential spokesman of the positive good theory in the thirties was Thomas R. Dew, professor of political economy at William and Mary College, whose *Review of the Debate in the Virginia Legislature of 1831 and 1832* served as a model for later proslavery writers. By the late 1830's, Southern sentiment had become consolidated in favor of slavery. The South Carolina politician and political philosopher John C. Calhoun observed in 1837 that "Many in the South once believed that [slavery] was a moral and political evil. That folly and delusion are gone. We see it now in its true light and regard it as the most safe and stable basis for free institutions in the world."

During the 1840's and 1850's Southern proslavery writers continued to employ some of the older arguments justifying slavery. For example, Thornton Stringfellow, the Baptist minister of Culpeper County, Virginia, invoked the Scriptures in a widely circulated defense of slavery. Others romanticized the system as a beneficent and paternalistic institution. James Henry Hammond, the South Carolina lawyer, editor, and politician, drew on earlier notions of Negro inferiority and of the hierarchical structure of society in his notorious "mud-sill" speech delivered in the Senate in 1858. "In all social systems there must be a class to do the menial duties," he declared. Such a class was necessary for the existence of "that other class which leads progress, civilization and refinement." Fortunately, the Senator observed, the South had found the Negro perfectly adapted to serve as "the very mud-sill of society and of political government," "a race inferior to her own, but eminently qualified in temper, in vigor, in docility, in capacity to stand the climate, to answer all her purposes."

Increasingly in the 1850's Southern proslavery writers turned to new sources and stratagems. Such men as George Fitzhugh, Henry Hughes, and George Frederick Holmes drew on the infant academic discipline of sociology to buttress their proslavery views. Josiah Nott, a physician, and Samuel Cartwright cited ethnological findings which offered "scientific" proof that the Negro was not only inferior but a member of a distinct species. Many proslavery writers did not confine themselves to the support of slavery; they also proclaimed the superiority and distinctiveness of Southern society. Some even went on to criticize free society in the North and in Europe. The best known of these writers, though not the most typical, was George Fitzhugh, the social philosopher from Virginia. In *Sociology for the South* and *Cannibals All!* he argued that the principles of freedom and equality which operated in the Northern states resulted in moral and social chaos, in contrast to the harmony and security prevailing in the South. Free competition made the

North a place of class warfare and cutthroat competition; preaching "moral cannibalism," it arrayed capital against labor, and rich against poor. Indeed, Fitzhugh declared, "free society" was a misnomer. In the North only the strong were "free"—to exploit the weak in a White Slave Trade "far more cruel than the Black Slave Trade, because it exacts more of its slaves, and neither protects nor governs them," making their "freedom" an "empty and delusive mockery." Thus capitalists were really slave owners by virtue of their command over labor, but they were "masters without the obligations of masters"; and laborers in turn were "slaves without masters," cruelly exploited, insecure, and unprotected. As a substitute (and cure) Fitzhugh advocated a patriarchal society which recognized "slavery as right in principle, and necessary in practice, with more or less of modification, to the very existence of government, of property, of religion, and of social existence."

As Fitzhugh's work suggests, "the pro-slavery argument" had become much more than a justification of slavery by the 1850's. It was a defense of the entire Southern way of life, whose culture, social structure, and economy were believed to depend on the institution of slavery. Undoubtedly, the intensity and unanimity with which Southerners defended their "peculiar institution" had much to do with the fact that they came increasingly to identify the system of slavery with Southern society as a whole.

Pertinent Literature

Jenkins, William S. *Pro-Slavery Thought in the Old South.* Chapel Hill: University of North Carolina Press, 1935.

William Jenkins has made an exhaustive survey of Southern proslavery writings, as his forty-six-page bibliography of primary sources indicates. Although historians, such as Louis Hartz, Ralph E. Morrow, and C. Vann Woodward, have recently offered new interpretations of certain aspects of "the pro-slavery argument," this book remains the definitive and most complete work on the subject.

Jenkins considers the Southern defense of slavery from two angles. He first offers a history of proslavery thought, dividing its development into three stages. In the initial period, 1790-1820, proslavery thinking was "quiescent," "passive," "apologetic," even "apathetic." During this period, Southern thought shifted away from the Enlightenment, rejecting social contract and natural rights theories and replacing them with an organic theory of society. There was a corresponding reaction against abstract speculation and idealism and a movement toward a philosophy of pragmatism and realism. History and experience, rather than philosophy, became the guides for political and social theory; "practical utility," rather than morality, came to be considered "the best test of the merit of an institution."

The second stage of proslavery thinking saw the development of the "positive good" theory. Among the factors impelling an open justification of slavery, Jenkins cites the Missouri controversy, the Charleston Insurrection of 1820, and the activity of the

Colonization Society, all of which appeared to threaten the "peculiar institution." Jenkins emphasizes that the "positive good" theory emerged in the 1820's. It was, therefore, not a response to Garrisonian abolitionism, as it antedated that movement by almost a decade.

From a positive justification of slavery, Southerners moved to a glorification of the system. During the third stage, 1835-1860, "the entire product of the collective mind of the South was colored by this one absorbing interest," according to Jenkins. Indeed, the "proslavery argument" was not confined to the ideological plane; it also manifested itself in practical activity. Two movements appeared in the 1850's which Jenkins regards "as the logical consummation of the idea that slavery must be defended as a 'positive good.' " One was a reform movement aimed at ridding the system of abuses and making it conform to the glowing descriptions offered in its defense. The other was the movement to reopen the slave trade, revealing clearly the militant posture which proslavery thought had assumed by the 1850's.

Besides narrating the historical development of proslavery thought, Jenkins also dissects the argument itself, analyzing its various elements. In defending the "peculiar institution," Southerners developed an elaborate ideology which embraced a variety of theories: some dealt with the origins and nature of slavery, while others explained its relation to government and the church, or its implications for social and economic structure; and still others argued for the plural origins and diversity of the races. Very few of the theories were original; Jenkins notes that proslavery writers often relied on European sources, modifying them to suit the American situation.

During the first half of the nineteenth century, the justification of slavery was the central preoccupation of the South. Like other historians, Jenkins explains this overriding preoccupation as a consequence of Southerners' identification of slavery with the whole of their civilization. In his view, the identification was not only unwarranted but costly: "mental energy was so much used up in the perfection of an irrefutable justification of slavery that the finer features of Southern life were neglected, and consequently imperiled." By 1863, the South had lost much more than the battle for slavery.

Fitzhugh, George. *Cannibals All: Or, Slaves Without Masters.* Edited by C. Vann Woodward. Cambridge: Harvard University Press, 1960.

Hartz, Louis. *The Liberal Tradition in America: An Interpretation of American Political Thought Since the Revolution.* New York: Harcourt, Brace & World, Inc., 1955. Also in paperback by the same publisher.

In the pre-Civil War years, George Fitzhugh became for many Northerners a symbol of Southern militancy. Many later historians have also viewed him as a representative Southerner. In shifting the defense of slavery to "higher ground," Fitzhugh was typical of proslavery theorists of the 1850's. But as C. Vann Woodward points out in the introduction to the John Harvard Library edition of *Cannibals All!*, he was atypical in most other respects.

Unlike other defenders of slavery, Fitzhugh was neither a fanatic nor a racist. He opposed nullification and secession, and feared disunion. In contrast to many nineteenth century Americans, especially Southerners, he was not an agrarian and he opposed free trade. John Taylor of Caroline, John Randolph of Roanoke, and even John C. Calhoun remained to some extent followers of John Locke and the Enlightenment. Fitzhugh completely and utterly rejected the state of nature and social contract theories, and with them the idea of progress, classical economics, notions of equality and inalienable rights, government by consent, and "*a priori* speculations" in the form of constitutions, declarations, and bills of rights. He viewed society as an organism, inequalitarian and hierarchical, and man as a social animal who was "fundamentally irrational, guided not by reason but by instinct, custom, habit, and requiring tradition and religion and stable institutions to keep him in line." Distrusting abstract theories, he looked instead to experience, history, and tradition for guidance.

Woodward disagrees with those historians who have characterized Fitzhugh's thought as either feudal or reactionary. In particular, he challenges the thesis of Louis Hartz, author of *The Liberal Tradition in America,* who contends that Fitzhugh and his contemporaries "exchanged a fraudulent liberalism for an even more fraudulent feudalism." Fitzhugh "did not go back to feudalism nor forward to Maistre" for his social and political theory, Woodward argues. Rather, he based much of his thinking on Sir Robert Filmer, whose emphasis on the patriarchal family fitted the "anthropological, sociological,

and political realities of Virginia society." Thus, Woodward declares, "it was not 'simple fraud' that led George Fitzhugh to seize upon Filmer in his search for some ideological basis on which to construct his defense and his understanding of Virginia society, even in mid-nineteenth century. As a sociologist he had got hold of some firm anthropological data. It is rather more a wonder that the patriarchs of Revolutionary Virginia should have temporarily embraced Locke than that their sons should have returned to Filmer."

If Fitzhugh drew on Filmer for his defense of Southern society, his critique of free society suggests a parallel with Karl Marx. Not only did the Virginian cite many of the sources Marx later used in writing *Das Kapital;* he also employed "something rather similar to the Marxian dialectic of class struggle" in refuting the Whiggish interpretation of history, and with it the idea of progress. Instead of an increase in liberty, Fitzhugh saw a decline of it. Of course, he was not the only American to criticize free society. What sets him apart is the severity of his critique. According to Woodward, "the ferocity of Fitzhugh's indictment of the capitalist economy surpasses that of John Taylor at the beginning of the century and the Southern Populists toward its close, and is equaled only by the severity of the socialist attack."

In Woodward's view, George Fitzhugh was "*sui generis*"; he was "an American original" who "deviated all down the line." "He saw retrogression in what others hailed as progress, embraced moral pessimism in place of optimism, trusted intuition in preference to reason, always preferred inequality to equality, aristocracy to democracy, and almost anything—including slavery and socialism—to laissez faire capitalism." As Woodward makes clear, it is precisely for this reason that it is appropriate to study Fitzhugh's thought, "for the sharp relief in which it throws the habitual lineaments of the American mind." — *A.C.L.*

Additional Recommended Reading

Sellers, Charles G., Jr. "The Travail of Slavery," in Sellers' *The Southerner as American.* Chapel Hill: University of North Carolina Press, 1960. Discusses the effect of the deeply rooted traditions of liberalism and Christianity in the South's attempt to justify slavery, and argues that the dogmatism and militancy of proslavery thought were responses to Southern feelings of guilt regarding the "peculiar institution."

McKitrick, Eric L., ed. *Slavery Defended: The Views of the Old South.* Englewood Cliffs: Prentice-Hall Inc., 1963. McKitrick's collection of writings justifying slavery demonstrates the "considerable range of talents, temperaments, and ingenuity" which engaged in the defense of the "peculiar institution."

Wish, Harvey. *George Fitzhugh: Propagandist of the Old South.* Baton Rouge: Louisiana State University Press, 1943. Wish provides an able treatment of Fitzhugh's life and thought, viewing him as "no ordinary slavery propagandist, but a challenging observer of his milieu who conceived of a national issue in terms of a world historical setting, reviving the timeless human problem of freedom versus organization, of liberty versus order, and of experimentalism versus authority."

Stanton, William. *The Leopard's Spots: Scientific Attitudes Toward Race in America, 1815-1859.* Chicago: The University of Chicago Press, 1960. This analysis of racial theories and attitudes of the antebellum period throws considerable light on the Southern argument in defense of Negro slavery.

Morrow, Ralph E. "The Proslavery Argument Revisited," in *Mississippi Valley Historical Review,* XLVII (June 1961). Morrow provides a useful corrective to earlier studies of the proslavery argument by emphasizing that defenders of slavery aimed their appeal primarily at Southerners (both slaveholders and nonslaveholders) and only secondarily at Northern and world public opinion.

RISE OF TRANSCENDENTALISM

Type of event: Intellectual: development of an American philosophy as a reaction against Unitarianism
Time: 1830's and 1840's
Locale: New England

Principal personages:

RALPH WALDO EMERSON (1803-1882), former Unitarian minister whose poems, essays, and lectures made him the central, if not the most typical, figure of the Transcendental movement

HENRY DAVID THOREAU (1817-1862), protégé of Emerson, author of *Walden* and "Civil Disobedience"

MARGARET FULLER (1810-1850), editor of *The Dial,* and author of *Woman in the Nineteenth Century,* a pioneer statement in the crusade for women's rights

GEORGE RIPLEY (1802-1880), former Unitarian minister, one of the founders of the Transcendental Club, president of the Brook Farm Association, and editor of *The Harbinger*

ORESTES AUGUSTUS BROWNSON (1803-1876), editor of *The Boston Quarterly Review*

THEODORE PARKER (1810-1860), editor of *The Massachusetts Quarterly Review*

AMOS BRONSON ALCOTT (1799-1888), educational reformer and writer who founded Fruitlands

Summary of Event

In the 1830's the Transcendental movement emerged among a small group of intellectuals living in Boston and Concord. In their lectures and writings, at meetings of the Transcendental Club, and in such periodicals as *The Dial* and *The Western Messenger,* they advanced what one of them, Ralph Waldo Emerson, called the "new views" a synthesis of imported and home-grown notions which produced the distinctive configuration of ideas known as American Transcendentalism.

The Transcendentalists drew on a wide variety of foreign sources including Platonism and Neoplatonism, German philosophical idealism, Swedenborgianism, the ideas of the French Eclectic School and the English romantics, and, somewhat later, the Oriental scriptures. There was no unanimity among them, but most Transcendentalists subscribed to an intuitive idealism, the concept of an organic universe, and a belief in the divinity of man. They were antiformalists in religion and literature, and they protested the commercial materialism of nineteenth century America. Though small in number and confined primarily to New England, they represent a significant influence in the history of American thought. Not only

654

did they question prevailing notions about the universe, man, and God, but they also challenged neoclassical artistic standards, introducing a new aesthetic theory based on the use of symbolism.

Philosophically, American Transcendentalism represented a repudiation of the Lockean philosophy of sensationalism and materialism which had dominated American thought during the eighteenth century and which survived, though in a somewhat modified form, in the Scottish common sense philosophy of the early nineteenth century. The Transcendentalists elevated intuition over sense experience as a source of knowledge, and they emphasized the superiority of the faculty of "reason" over that of the "understanding." Transcendentalists, George Ripley explained ". . . believe in an order of truth which transcends the sphere of the external sense." In Emerson's words, they "respect the intuitions and . . . give them . . . all authority over our experience."

But American Transcendentalism was not primarily a philosophical movement. As Perry Miller has shown, though the Transcendentalists argued their case against the dominant culture in the language of philosophy and literature rather than that of theology, they were nevertheless engaged in "a religious demonstration." Just as they repudiated Lockean philosophy, they also rejected its religious equivalent—what Emerson called "the corpse-cold Unitarianism of Brattle Street and Harvard College." The Transcendental movement emerged out of the "Unitarian Controversy" of the 1830's—a theological debate among Boston Unitarians which focused on the question

of miracles, but which ultimately extended to such issues as the divinity of Christ, the supernatural interpretation of Christianity, and the organization of the church.

The essence of what opponents called "the latest form of infidelity" may be seen in Emerson's Divinity School Address of 1838. First, Emerson attacked the Unitarian concept of miracles as an interruption of the natural order. "The word Miracle, as pronounced by the Christian churches, gives a false impression; it is Monster. It is not one with the blowing clover and the falling rain." For Emerson, as for other Transcendentalists, belief in an immanent God eliminated the traditionalism between the natural and the supernatural. The former Unitarian minister also condemned "historical Christianity," including Unitarianism, because it did not preach the "infinitude of man," and because "the soul is not preached." Christ's message, "that God incarnates himself in man," was distorted by later ages, Emerson declared. So was Christ's emphasis on "the eternal revelation in the heart." These two beliefs—the divinity of man and his capacity to apprehend spiritual truth at first-hand, by intuition, not mediated by any external authority—formed the heart of Transcendental religion. The immanence of God and the humanity of Jesus also formed a part of the Transcendentalists' creed.

The social philosophy of the Transcendental movement embodied two contrasting outlooks. Some Transcendentalists were led by their belief in the divinity of man to espouse an uncompromising individualism. Repudiating the "tyranny of the majority," they preached self-culture and self-reliance.

Rejecting the demand for conformity to social norms, they argued that each individual must be true to the moral law within. Emerson's "Self-Reliance" (1841) and Thoreau's "Civil Disobedience" (1849) are the classic expositions of Transcendental individualism and its political and social implications. Other Transcendentalists emphasized the unity of mankind and stressed cooperation rather than individualism as the key to social improvement. Orestes Brownson, editor of the *Boston Quarterly Review,* represents this side of Transcendentalism. The communitarian experiment at Brook Farm, founded in 1841, also reflects the unifying side of Transcendentalism. The issue between the two wings of the Transcendental movement was clearly drawn in Emerson's response to an invitation to join the Brook Farm community. "It seems to me a circuitous and operose way of relieving myself of any irksome circumstances, to put on your community the task of my emancipation which I ought to take on myself," he declared. Nevertheless, despite their disagreement as to the proper means of reform, Transcendentalists were united in protesting against such things as slavery, war, and the evils of capitalism. Thus, in its social philosophy, as in its religious and philosophical outlook, the Transcendental movement represented a trenchant critique of the dominant ideology and culture of antebellum America.

Pertinent Literature

Whicher, Stephen E. *Freedom and Fate: An Inner Life of Ralph Waldo Emerson.* Philadelphia: University of Pennsylvania Press, 1953.

Freedom and Fate is, as the author tells us, a reconstruction of "the inner life" of Ralph Waldo Emerson based on his writings, especially the journals. Beneath Emerson's quiet, composed exterior, Whicher perceives "a drama of ideas" which reveals the sources and consequences of the Transcendental philosophy as he lived it.

Emerson's early life—a time of ill health, religious doubt, and philosophical skepticism—determined the two basic themes of his inner life. On the one hand, the early journals convey a sense of helplessness, an awareness of the important role played by necessity or fate. Yet, at the same time, Whicher finds an intense longing for freedom, a refusal to accept a condition of dependence and submission. Emerson's release from doubt and dependence came with his discovery in 1831, "that God is within." According to Whicher, this "amazing revelation of my immediate relation to God" brought a "genuine rebirth," of which Emerson's resignation from the Unitarian ministry in 1832 may be taken as an outward sign. In Whicher's view, Emerson's new faith bears a striking resemblance to "the Calvinistic pietism that Unitarian moralism had left behind—new in that it is based on a vision of man's power rather than on a conviction of his sinfulness, but reviving the same sense of the living presence of a power not our own before which man is nothing." Thus, Emerson recovered "something of the flame of holy love that the Puritans had brought to New England two hundred years before."

The legacy of Puritanism, and even

Unitarianism, is also seen in Emerson's worship of moral perfection. This aspect of his Transcendental faith combined a sense of duty or conscience (derived from Unitarianism) with the notion (from Calvinism) that God endows man with the capacity to obey. But if one aspect of Emerson's newfound faith was linked to the past, another struck a "startling new note" in the history of American thought. Whicher discerns in Emerson a "radical egoistic anarchism" that was unique even among the Transcendentalists. It was an assertion of man's complete freedom and self-sufficiency which offered a way of meeting, and escaping, the pressures of the outside world. It explains Emerson's ambivalence toward the reform movement of the 1830's, his "deep sympathy" with the general idea of reform and his "progressive disillusionment with all actual reforms." Faced with a choice between reform activity on the one hand and his freedom on the other, Emerson chose the latter.

The year 1840 marked the beginning of a period of intellectual unsettlement during which Emerson became increasingly aware of the limitations that time and circumstance imposed on the freedom of the soul. The result was "a basic adjustment of belief," according to Whicher. By the mid-1840's Emerson had moved away from Transcendentalism to an empiricism which, while it continued to assert the "divine potentiality" of man, also recognized his "mortal limits." Acquiescence succeeded egoistic rebellion, optimism replaced the earlier millennialism, the demand for perfect freedom was superseded by a recognition of the possibility of partial freedom. The result was a philosophy in which freedom and fate balanced each other. One consequence of this intellectual reorientation was a lessening of Emerson's hostility toward society.

Even in his Transcendental period, Emerson was not typical of the Transcendentalists. Nevertheless, Whicher's study of the inner life of one of the most prominent members of that group is an indispensable introduction to the Transcendental movement as a whole.

Hutchinson, William R. *The Transcendentalist Ministers: Church Reform in the New England Renaissance.* New Haven: Yale University Press, 1959.

Of the twenty-six persons associated with the Transcendental Club, seventeen were Unitarian ministers, and eleven of them remained within the ministry. For the majority who remained within the Unitarian fold, and for the minority who resigned the pulpit, Transcendentalism supplied an impulse to religious as well as to philosophical and literary reform. *The Transcendentalist Ministers* focuses on the program of church reform proposed by these men, especially Emerson, Ripley, Parker, Brownson, Frederic Henry Hedge, James Freeman Clarke, and William Henry Channing.

Hutchinson divides the Unitarian Controversy into two phases. The first, which centered on the question of miracles, began in 1836 when Ripley published an article on the subject in the *Christian Examiner.* Emerson's Divinity School Address in 1838 further elaborated the Transcendentalist position. Although Andrews Norton, the Unitarian "pope," quickly branded the Transcendental point of view "atheism," other Unitarians hesitated to go so far. Hutchinson argues that the majority of Unitarians pursued a policy of moderation toward their critics. Consequently, the first phase ended in a stalemate, with conservative Unitarians caught between "the conflicting demands of free inquiry and Christian confessionalism."

The second phase of the Controversy began in 1841 and focused on Theodore Parker. His rejection of supernaturalism forced Unitarians "to rediscover and define [their] theological position." In the process of meeting Parker's challenge, the denomination was forced to compromise its policy of free inquiry and free expression, pursuing an exclusionist policy toward dissenters in order to preserve its doctrinal tradition. Moreover, in 1853 the Executive Committee of the American Unitarian Association adopted a declaration of opinion which, Hutchinson points out, "strongly resembled a creed." By then, he concludes, "Unitarians . . . had come reluctantly to the decision that some ideals must be sacrificed in order to preserve the organic integrity of the church. They had, therefore, made their affirmative beliefs explicit and had declared that whatever the consequences for traditions of 'free inquiry,' a Christian church must take its stand with the Christian confession."

Much of the reform program of the Transcendentalist ministers related to ecclesiastical matters. Hedge and Clarke, for example, described a "Church of the Future" whose membership accepted Christ as Savior and coöperated in humanitarian activity. The Church of Disciples, which Clarke served, was one religious society founded on Transcendental religious notions, and received financial support on a voluntary basis; pews were neither rented nor sold. The church sponsored discussion groups, prayer meetings, and reform activities; it also increased congregational participation in the worship service. Ripley, Brownson, Channing, and Parker made similar innovations in religious societies which they formed.

Hutchinson's general thesis, that Transcendental religious ideas played a constructive rather than a purely negative role in the early nineteenth century, is a persuasive one. Indeed, his work suggests the necessity of a reconsideration not only of Transcendentalism but of Unitarianism as well. — *A.C.L.*

Additional Recommended Reading

Frothingham, Octavius B. *Transcendentalism in New England: A History.* New York: G. P. Putnam's Sons, 1876. This is an account of the Transcendental movement written by an insider converted to Transcendentalism under the impact of Theodore Parker's preaching. Besides offering a valuable survey of the movement as a whole, Frothingham succeeds in catching its mood in a way that few later historians have been able to do.

Matthiessen, Francis O. *American Renaissance: Art and Expression in the Age of Emerson and Whitman.* New York: Oxford University Press, 1941. This monumental work analyzes the writings of Emerson, Thoreau, Hawthorne, Melville and Whitman, focusing on their concepts of literature and their common "devotion to the possibilities of democracy."

Kern, Alexander. "The Rise of Transcendentalism, 1815-1860," in Harry Hayden Clark, ed. *Transitions in American Literary History.* Durham, North Carolina: Duke University Press, 1954. This brief but comprehensive survey of American Transcendentalism is indispensable for an understanding of the movement. Kern describes the shift from earlier to Transcendental views in the realm of philosophy, religion, literature, and social thought.

Miller, Perry. *The Transcendentalists: An Anthology.* Cambridge: Harvard University Press, 1950. Perry Miller has collected the writings of the more typical, if lesser known, Transcendentalists, as well as some of their adversaries. The notes and general introduction, which deal with the origins and implications of New England Transcendentalism, elaborate his thesis as to the "inherently religious character" of the movement.

Paul, Sherman. *Emerson's Angle of Vision: Man and Nature in American Experience.* Cambridge: Harvard University Press, 1952. Paul analyzes Emerson's view of the relation between man and nature in terms of the Transcendental notion of "correspondence."

WEBSTER-HAYNE DEBATE OVER STATES' RIGHTS

Type of event: Political: debate over Western land policy which intensified the struggle between states' rights and nationalism
Time: January, 1830
Locale: Washington, D.C.

Principal personages:

ANDREW JACKSON (1767-1845), seventh President of the United States 1829-1837

JOHN CALDWELL CALHOUN (1782-1850), Vice-President of the United States under Jackson

DANIEL WEBSTER (1782-1852), Senator from Massachusetts, the nation's greatest orator at the time

ROBERT YOUNG HAYNE (1791-1839), Senator from South Carolina, Webster's antagonist

THOMAS HART BENTON (1782-1858), Senator from Missouri

SAMUEL AUGUSTUS FOOT (1780-1846), Senator from Connecticut

Summary of Event

In December, 1829, Connecticut Senator Samuel A. Foot presented a resolution to the United States Senate suggesting the temporary restriction of the sale of public land. Only those lands already surveyed and placed for auction were to be sold. This seemingly inoffensive resolution precipitated America's most famous debate.

A liberal land policy was vital for the continued growth of the West. Thomas Hart Benton, representing the West as a Senator from Missouri, jumped to his feet to attack the resolution as a bare-faced attempt to keep the emigrant laborer out of the West and to force him to remain in the East as an industrial wage-slave. The endeavor to check the development and prosperity of the West was nothing new, suggested Benton; rather, it was another sign of the hatred of the East toward the West which had so often plagued the forum of national politics. The Missourian

ended by saying that the hope of the West lay "in that solid phalanx of the South" which in earlier times had saved that section when in danger.

The Southern political leadership was anxious to make an alliance with the West to secure its support for the slavery issue. The Southern planter and the Western farmer in alliance could more than offset the Eastern manufacturing interests in controlling the federal government. The hope for such a combination led South Carolina's Senator Robert Y. Hayne to step forward and take up the fight.

Hayne offered Southern support to the West and deftly shifted the argument from land to state sovereignty. If the Eastern proposals were put into effect, said Hayne, the price of land would increase. The income derived from the sale of the higher priced land would provide a "fund for corruption" which would add to the power of the

660

federal government and correspondingly reduce the independence of the states. Preaching strict constructionist and states' rights views against federal intervention, the South Carolinian declared that "the very life of our system is the independence of the states and there is no evil more to be deprecated than the consolidation of government." In the course of his remarks Hayne made a bitter attack upon New England and that section's disloyalty during the War of 1812. This was too much for Daniel Webster, Senator from Massachusetts, who rose to defend his state and section: "Sir . . . I deny that the East has at anytime shown an illiberal policy toward the West." Fearful that he might further alienate the West, Webster ignored Benton and addressed his remarks to Hayne. Attacking the Southerner's views on the consolidation of government, Webster deplored the tendency of some to "habitually speak of the Union in terms of indifference and even disparagement," and then challenged Hayne to meet him on the grounds of states' rights versus national power.

Thus a discussion which had started on the subject of public land policy shifted to a debate over the nature and meaning of the federal Union. Both nationalism and state sovereignty were debated by two of their most capable champions. Hayne was an able lawyer, a skilled debater, and a splendid orator. Tall and graceful, with cordial and unaffected manners, he was the epitome of the Southern aristocrat. As the defender of the South and the advocate of that section's doctrines, Hayne stood second only to his mentor and fellow statesman, John C. Calhoun, then the Vice-President. Webster was the country's greatest orator. Further, he was a man of commanding appearance, with a large head, dark and penetrating eyes, and a deep and resonant voice. It has been said that no man could be as great as Daniel Webster looked. Indeed, his countenance was so overpowering and his oratorical style so effective that even trivial and commonplace statements sounded profound when presented by the "god-like Daniel."

In an age when political debates were loved by the American people, this battle between two brilliant speakers attracted wide attention. The Senate chamber, a small semi-circular room where only forty-eight members sat, was crowded to capacity and the galleries were packed. At one time so many Congressmen came to listen that the House of Representatives could not carry on its normal business.

Hayne answered Webster with a slashing defense of states' rights as it had been outlined by Calhoun. He spoke with logic and eloquence as Calhoun looked down from the Speaker's chair smiling and occasionally nodding his approval. Hayne's defense was based upon the Virginia and Kentucky Resolutions of 1798, and he asserted that each state, while assenting to the federal Constitution, reserved the right to interpret that document within its own borders; that is, the people of any state, if they believed themselves offended, could declare an act of the federal government null and void. Otherwise, Hayne continued, the federal government would have the capacity to "proscribe the limits of its own authority," and this made it a government without any restriction of its powers. The states and the people would be entirely at the mercy of the federal government.

Webster, in what has been called the greatest speech ever made in the Senate, upheld the doctrines of nationalism. A state could not, he said, annul an act of Congress except "upon the ground of revolution." He believed that the Constitution, as the supreme law of the land, was created by the people, not the states. The primary question, Webster maintained, was not the right of revolution against oppression, but that of determining whose prerogative it was to decide on the constitutionality of the laws. For him there was only one answer: the Constitution was the nation's highest law, and the ultimate appeal lay with the Supreme Court. He ended his endeavor with this peroration: "When my eyes shall be turned to behold for the last time the sun in heaven, may I not see him shining on the broken and dishonored fragments of a once glorious Union; on states dissevered, discordant, belligerent; on a land rent with civil feuds, or drenched, it may be, in fraternal blood! Let their last feeble and lingering glance rather behold the glorious ensign of the republic, known and honored throughout the earth, still full high advanced, its arms and trophies streaming in their original lustre, not a stripe erased or polluted, nor a single star obscured, bearing for its motto, no such miserable interrogatory as 'What is it all worth?' nor those words of delusion and folly, 'Liberty first and Union afterwards:' but everywhere . . . that other sentiment, dear to every true American heart,—Liberty *and* Union, now and forever, one and inseparable!"

The *Philadelphia Gazette* summed up the result of the debate: "The opposition party generally contend that Mr. Webster overthrew Mr. Hayne; while, on the other hand, the result is triumphantly hailed by the friends of the administration as a decisive victory over the eastern giant." Whoever won, the debate clarified the issues and intensified the struggle between states' rights and nationalism. It furnished both North and South with powerful arguments and thus accentuated the ardor with which each defended its cause.

Pertinent Literature

Fuess, Claude M. *Daniel Webster.* 2 vols. Boston: Little, Brown, and Company, 1930.

Though written forty years ago, Claude Fuess' biography of Daniel Webster remains the standard work on the great orator.

Webster's entire life and public career are covered in detail: the New Hampshire boyhood; life in Portsmouth as a young lawyer; his period as a leading citizen of Boston; and finally the various stages of his career in Washington. Fuess does not engage in hero worship; he is not blinded by the "god-like Daniel." Webster is painted in all his human frailty as well as his greatness—a man of genius, but with defects of character. Vanity, inebriation, constant indebtedness and a willingness to accept gifts all too carelessly were weaknesses which made politics a luxury Webster could scarcely afford. His love of material possessions made him dependent upon merchants and bankers, and made their cause his.

All, of course, was not weakness and

despair, and Fuess shows the positive side of Webster's nature equally well—the shrewd lawyer, the friendly fellow and boon companion, Secretary of State, giant of the Senate, and America's greatest orator. Both aspects of this restless, unsatisfied, ambitious and immortality-craving man are shown with force and compassion. Webster's desire for fame, particularly his eagerness to be President, led him downward from a position of statesman to mere politician.

Perhaps the outstanding service he performed for the nation was to present a clear view of an indissoluble Union, and to rally the conservative forces of the nation around it. Webster, as much as any man, deserves the title of "defender of the Union." This work began, says Fuess, with the Webster-Hayne debate and did not end until the Compromise of 1850 had been passed. For his part in the Compromise, and especially for his "Seventh of March" speech, Webster was never forgiven by his constituents.

With regard to the Hayne affair, Fuess does not paint Webster as the victor, nor does he assert that the New Englander's logic was more powerful than Hayne's. Webster was open to attack for his narrow sectionalism, and his sensitiveness to Hayne's attack betrayed this. Indeed, Fuess admits that Hayne delivered some telling blows because Webster had been inconsistent.

Webster began his career as a champion of New England shipping interests in favor of free trade, but after the War of 1812, with the growth of domestic manufacturers in his section, Webster caught the spirit of industrialism and by the late 1820's had become an aggressive advocate of the protective tariffs which fostered America's young industry. Webster's answers defending this change were not entirely creditable. Also, his attitude toward the West was strangely lacking in vision. He had little interest in Oregon and once remarked that California and New Mexico were "not worth a dollar." His anti-war stands in 1812 and 1846 are described as factious, wrongheaded and out of touch with the times.

The turning point in Webster's life may well have been the double tragedy of 1829, when both his wife and his brother died. Fuess implies that after remarrying, Webster simply let himself go and gave in to his desire for food and drink. "The effect was shown in certain physical and temperamental changes. He grew portly and slow in his movements. . . . The old Webster was there, but after 1829, he was both greater and smaller than he had been in 1825." Fuess' facile pen has produced a biography of admirable historical quality. It is dynamic and dramatic, written, as all history should be, with thoroughness, impartiality, and balance.

Jervey, Theodore D. *Robert Y. Hayne and His Times.* New York: The Macmillan Company, 1909.

Theodore D. Jervey has not written a narrative of the life and times of Robert Y. Hayne; rather, availing himself of the Charleston Library's rich holdings in contemporary newspapers and pamphlets, he has written about the city of Charleston and South Carolina from 1791 to 1839. Hayne's life is simply the unifying theme. Jervey asserts that Hayne was more than Daniel

Webster's antagonist in one of our nation's greatest debates. Eloquent, upright, devoted, and loyal, he was one of South Carolina's greatest sons, and his eminent public services, both before and after his debate with Webster, are cited as proof.

Regarding the Webster debate, Jervey's assertion that the New Englander did not demolish Hayne is still generally accepted. He also maintains that Hayne, except for his ideas on nullification, was more nearly correct than Webster on the nature of the Union, for the Founding Fathers were not aware that they were creating a perpetual Union. The debate demonstrates another basic difference between Hayne and Webster. Hayne was looking to the past, to a written instrument, and to a Union bound by definite limitations; Webster, perhaps unconsciously, was anticipating a future in which an aggressive and aspiring people would expand the boundaries of a more powerful Union.

Apart from this monumental debate, Hayne's services to his state and nation were impressive. His rise in public life was meteoric; apparently his abilities were recognized early and never challenged. He assumed a commanding position and never gave it up. Only thirty-two when elected to the Senate, Hayne achieved prominence after only five months in the chamber because of his opposition to Henry Clay's tariff of 1824. Ironically, it was Daniel Webster who led the opposition to this bill in debate in the House of Representatives. By 1828, when he had arrived in the Senate, however, Webster was wavering in his tariff opposition. Indeed, Webster's constituents were so unsure of him that a group of Boston merchants opposing the tariff of 1828 presented their protest to Hayne rather than to Webster, and the South Carolinian pleaded the Massachusetts case before the Senate. South Carolina opposed the tariff on economic grounds, and when it was passed, Hayne joined in his beloved state's resort to the ultimate appeal—nullification. Resigning his seat in the Senate, Hayne returned to South Carolina to become Governor and carry on the fight at the local level. Jervey insists that Hayne did not resign to make room for John C. Calhoun in the Senate. Most South Carolinians believed that the fight would be at home and not in Congress. Once the nullification crisis ended, Hayne devoted himself to the industrial development of South Carolina. He believed that transportation was the key to the South's survival, and that Charleston had to be tied to the rapidly growing West. To obtain this end Hayne became president of the Louisville-Cincinnati Railroad, but it had not been completed when he died in 1839.

Jervey idolizes Hayne. Where most historians see Hayne speaking Calhoun's lines, Jervey makes Hayne, far more than Calhoun, the chief proponent of the lost cause. Indeed, throughout the book there is an undercurrent of hostility toward Calhoun. Nevertheless, Jervey makes his point. Hayne was more than the man to whom Webster replied, and the debate was only an incident in a brilliant career. — *J.H.D.*

Additional Recommended Reading

Sydnor, Charles S. *The Development of Southern Sectionalism, 1819-1848.* Vol. V: *A History of the South.* Baton Rouge: Louisiana State University Press, 1948. This broad treatment of the South between 1819 and 1848 traces the progressive and humanitarian ideals which existed in spite of the section's defensive attitude and growing sectionalism.

Bowers, Claude G. *Party Battles of the Jackson Period.* Boston: Houghton Mifflin Co., 1922. This interesting work covers the eight-year period spanned by the administration of Andrew Jackson, with emphasis on the outstanding individuals of the period: Clay, Webster, Calhoun, Van Buren, and Jackson.

Van Deusen, Glyndon G. *The Life of Henry Clay.* Boston: Little, Brown, and Company, 1937. A first-class biography with little attempt to make a hero of Clay, this distinguished piece of scholarship and historical writing also discusses the men and times around the "Great Compromiser."

McMaster, John B. *Daniel Webster.* New York: The Century Company, 1902. This popular biography, though somewhat outdated, is pleasantly written and easy to read.

Current, Richard N. *Daniel Webster and the Rise of National Conservatism.* Boston: Little, Brown, and Company, 1955. With emphasis on social and economic history, Webster's life is traced from demigod to symbol and legend; yet throughout this splendid historical interpretation, Webster stands firm in about the same position his contemporaries placed him.

Garnett, James M. *Hayne's Speech.* New York: Charles E. Merrill Co., 1894. This small volume is devoted mainly to Hayne's speeches against Webster; however, it does contain a short biography of the South Carolinian.

PASSAGE OF THE INDIAN REMOVAL ACT

Type of event: Sociopolitical: exchange of Indian lands in the East for government lands in the West
Time: 1830
Locale: Washington, D.C.

Principal personages:

ANDREW JACKSON (1767-1845), seventh President of the United States 1829-1837, who aggressively pushed forward the removal policy of his predecessors

THOMAS L. MCKENNEY (1785-1859), humanitarian-minded head of the Indian Office, who favored removal

JEREMIAH EVARTS (1781-1831), secretary of the American Board of Commissioners for Foreign Missions, who led the attack on the removal policy during Jackson's Administration

THEODORE FRELINGHUYSEN (1787-1862), Senator from New Jersey, who strongly attacked the removal bill in the Senate

WILSON LUMPKIN (1783-1870), Congressman from Georgia and later, Governor and Senator, who urged the removal of the Indians from the Southern states

JOHN ROSS (1790-1866), Cherokee leader, who fought unsuccessfully to prevent removal

JOHN MARSHALL (1755-1835), Chief Justice of the United States, who upheld the Cherokees in their opposition to Georgia's efforts to force them from the state

Summary of Event

By the end of the 1820's, Indian affairs in the United States had reached a crisis. The Indian tribes in the East were surrounded by white settlers, who pressed upon the Indian lands and wanted the tribes out of the way. The solution to the problem adopted by the United States government was the exchange of Indian lands in the East for lands in the West, a policy that sought to satisfy the whites and at the same time save the Indians from destruction. The Indian Removal Act of May 28, 1830, marked the final adoption of the policy.

Thomas Jefferson was in favor of removing the Indians to unencumbered lands west of the Mississippi river, and in 1803 the Louisiana Purchase made such removal feasible. Before the end of Jefferson's Administration gentle pressure was put upon the Cherokee Indians of northern Georgia and eastern Tennessee to exchange their lands for land in the West. A few Cherokees went west, at first to hunt and then to settle, but there was no exchange of lands until 1817, when provision was made for the Indians who had gone to the region along the Arkansas river.

Much of the trouble in the 1820's came from the special circumstances surrounding the Cherokees in Georgia, and to a lesser extent, the Creeks,

Chickasaws, and Choctaws in Alabama and Mississippi. The Cherokees were settled on lands they had always held, and they had developed an agricultural economy, astute political leaders, and laws modeled on those of the whites. They had a deep affection for their lands and were determined to hold them at all costs. The United States government, however, had signed a compact with Georgia in 1802, by which the state had ceded to the federal government her Western land claims. The United States in return had agreed to extinguish the Indian titles to lands in Georgia as soon as it could be done peaceably and on reasonable terms. As the land hunger of the whites increased, Georgia accused the federal government of failing to live up to its part of the bargain, for the Cherokees were still in the state. The Governor of Georgia censured the federal government for its tardiness and weakness and asserted that the Indians were mere tenants who had only a temporary right to use the lands for hunting.

President James Monroe saw that some change in the situation was necessary. He denied any obligation on the part of the government to force the Indians to move involuntarily, but he believed that the Indians would either have to emigrate to the West or be absorbed by white society. In a special message on removal, drawn up by Secretary of War John C. Calhoun, Monroe urged Congress on January 27, 1825, to provide "a well-digested plan" for governing and civilizing the Indians, which would not only "shield them from impending ruin, but promote their welfare and happiness." The President was convinced that such a plan was practicable and that it could

be made so attractive to the Indians that all of them would agree to it. Congress, however, did not act, and as the years passed the situation grew more critical. In 1827 the Cherokee Nation adopted a written constitution, which asserted that it had complete jurisdiction over its own territory. The government of Georgia was angered by this "presumptuous document" and countered the Cherokee move by plans to extend state authority and law over the Cherokee lands.

When Andrew Jackson became President in 1829, he refused to support the Indians' contentions against Georgia and in his State of the Union Address on December 8, 1829, bluntly advised the Cherokees either to emigrate across the Mississippi or submit to the laws of Georgia. Following Jackson's lead, a new bill was introduced in Congress, authorizing the President to negotiate for the Indians' removal.

The bill occasioned long and bitter debate in Congress and in the public press. In the Senate the attack was led by Senator Theodore Frelinghuysen of New Jersey, who spoke for six hours against the bill, bringing in all possible arguments to support the Indians in their claims to independent authority over their lands and to protection of these rights by the federal government against the pretensions of Georgia. Missionary groups, led by the American Board of Commissioners for Foreign Missions in Boston, deluged Congress with memorials against removal, and writers, such as Jeremiah Evarts, the secretary of the American Board, wrote strong articles in support of the Indians' rights. The church groups implied, if they did not state outright, that all morality and right were on their side

667

of the question.

But Jackson had supporters, too, and not all of them acted only for political reasons. Many knowledgeable men, of whom Thomas L. McKenney, head of the Indian Office, was preëminent, saw in removal the only hope for saving the Indians as a race. Since the process of civilization and assimilation upon which the humanitarians had pinned their hopes proceeded much more slowly than they had envisaged, these men turned to removal as a means of giving the Indian race more time to change, in a place beyond the pressure of avaricious whites or federal-state jurisdictional disputes. They denied that all true friends of the Indians were opposed to the removal bill. When the votes were counted in May, 1830, the measure had passed by a small majority.

The Cherokee Indians had found it impossible to preserve the integrity of their Nation. In July, 1829, gold had been discovered on their lands. A Georgia law of December, 1828, meanwhile, had proclaimed that all laws of the Cherokee Nation would become void after June 1, 1830. Another resolution provided that after January 1, 1830, Cherokee Indians would be denied the right to serve as witnesses or be parties in a legal case which involved a white man. Free from fear of legal redress, whites could thus appropriate Cherokee lands.

Fighting to maintain their position within Georgia, the Cherokees carried two cases to the United States Supreme Court. In *Cherokee Nation* v. *Georgia* (1831), Chief Justice John Marshall denied that the Court had the authority to prohibit Georgia from laying claim to Cherokee land since the Cherokees did not comprise an independent foreign nation within the meaning of the Constitution. In *Worcester* v. *Georgia* (1832), however, Marshall declared that the federal government had jurisdiction in lands occupied by the Cherokee Nation. President Jackson is reported to have responded to the new Supreme Court decision: "John Marshall has made his decision, now let him enforce it." In any event, Georgia defied the Court with Jackson's blessings.

President Jackson pushed forward with removal negotiations. One by one the Southern Indians (Choctaws, 1830; Creeks, 1832; Chickasaws, 1832) signed removal treaties and began their painful movements to the West. The Cherokees held out until 1835, when a small group within the nation signed a treaty of removal. The Seminoles in Florida resisted by force, and only after several years of war were they rounded up and deported. In the North the process of removal was carried on during the same period, though less dramatically and with less public notice. By 1840 most of the Eastern Indians had been removed beyond the so-called "permanent Indian frontier," which ran along the western borders of Arkansas and Missouri and extended northeasterly through Iowa and Minnesota to the Mississippi river.

Pertinent Literature

Abel, Annie H. *The History of Events Resulting in Indian Consolidation West of the Mississippi.* Annual Report of the American Historical Association for the Year 1906. Washington, 1908, I, 233-450, reprinted, New York: AMS Press, Inc.

This monograph is the standard work on the origin and development of the Indian removal policy; despite its age, it has not been superseded. The completeness of its documentation and the general balance of its presentation make this study indispensable for anyone interested in the Indian Removal Act of 1830.

The author begins her historical narrative with Thomas Jefferson, who united schemes for colonization of the Indians in the Louisiana Purchase with the simpler policy of merely clearing Eastern lands of Indian occupancy. This combination of elements, Abel says, served "to distinguish the real philanthropists, such as Issac McCoy and, perhaps, Thomas McKenney, from the self-seeking and aggressive politicians who cared not what became of the aborigines so long as their presence was not allowed to obstruct the onward path of the white men." After Jefferson the policy moved gradually ahead, with greater emphasis on the South, where the pressures on the Indian land were greater and where the Indian nations were more able to resist. President Monroe strongly advocated voluntary removal, and President John Quincy Adams, Abel notes, "took up the work where Monroe laid it down and carried it on unflinchingly along the lines of no coercion."

The author sees a sharp contrast to the policy of Monroe and Adams in that of Andrew Jackson and speaks of "two policies diametrically opposed— the voluntary removals of Monroe and of Adams and the coercive of Jackson." Under Jackson's "force" policy Indian removal became a party question, she notes, something it had not been before, and many religious denominations ranged themselves against Jackson's Indian policy. The party feeling exhibited itself in the debate over the removal bill. "Removal under the direction of the Georgians and the Jackson party generally," Abel writes, "could be nothing more or less than compulsory. Therefore philanthropists and the friends of Adams took issue against it. It was pretty nearly a case of North against South, but not quite." She gives a careful history of the progress of the bill through Congress and concludes her monograph with a brief account of removal treaties and the difficulties involved in both the negotiations and the actual removals.

Abel's harsh view of Jacksonian policy reflects the position of Jackson's contemporary critics, especially those among the Indian missionary groups, and she pays little attention to philanthropic support of removal. But the fullness of her story and the exhaustive footnotes provide an excellent base upon which a student may build a full understanding of the removal bill and the policy it represented.

In her final paragraph, Abel essays a balanced appraisal of removal. She regrets that proposals for Indian self-government in the West, which were part of the full removal plan, never materialized. "The best criticism that can be passed upon Indian removal," she concludes, "is that it was a plan too hastily and too partially carried into execution for its real and underlying merits ever to be realized. That it had merits none can gainsay. But since it stopped short of self-government, for which some of the tribes were even then well fitted, it was bound to be only a temporary expedient." She notes that the titles given in the West proved less substantial than those in the East, and as a consequence, "before the primary removals had all taken place, the secondary had begun, and the land that was to belong to the Indians in perpetuity was in the white man's market."

Foreman, Grant. *Indian Removal: The Emigration of the Five Civilized Tribes of Indians.* Norman: University of Oklahoma Press, 1932.

The decade following the passage of the Indian Removal Act of 1830 was filled with negotiations with the tribes to sign removal treaties and with the actual work of migration. The story of these events as they pertained to the Southern Indians—the Choctaws, Creeks, Chickasaws, Cherokees, and Seminoles—is the subject of Foreman's book. For each of the tribes, the author writes first of the treaties and the machinations that too often were part of the negotiations, as the government, determined now upon removal, sought to convince the Indians that they must comply. Then he presents a detailed narrative of the actual emigration, frequently a pitiful tale of hardship as the Indians were forced to leave their ancestral homes and begin life anew in a strange land to the west. The American officials who advocated the removal policy, indeed, had little understanding of the toil and misery that such an uprooting of a people would entail.

The Choctaws moved first. By the Treaty of Dancing Rabbit Creek on September 27, 1830, the tribe ceded to the United States all land owned east of the Mississippi and was given three years to move to the lands designated for it in the West. "There was much resentment against the treaty," Foreman reports, "as a majority of the tribe was opposed to it." But tribal politicians, eager for government largess, committed the tribe to emigration, and during 1831 and 1832 the mass of the Indians moved, amid great distress, which Foreman fully describes. Next came the Creeks, who on March 24, 1832, agreed to part with their lands. The treaty provided for allotments of lands to individual families for a five-year period, but whites pushed in upon the tribe and defrauded the Indians of their allotments. By 1836 the smoldering troubles broke out into war, which was put down by the United States Army. The subdued Creeks were sent to the West, followed soon by the friendly factions of the nation. The Chickasaws signed a removal treaty on October 20, 1832, and the bulk of that tribe emigrated in 1837 with relatively little disturbance.

The Cherokees were firmly determined to resist removal, and not until December 25, 1835, in the treaty of New Echota, did a small faction of the nation agree to removal. Those who were opposed, led by John Ross, refused to emigrate voluntarily and did not leave until the army was sent to enforce the treaty. The Cherokees'

"Trail of Tears," as they moved to the West in 1838, is described by Foreman at great length. The Seminoles are treated in the final section of the book. "In the dishonorable record of our dealings with the Indians," Foreman writes, "there is perhaps no blacker chapter than that relating to the Seminole people."

Foreman insists that the book was not written "to excite sympathy for the Indians," nor to indict the people of the South for mistreatment of the Indians. "The author has undertaken here merely a candid account of the removal of these southern Indians," he says in his preface, "so that the reader may have a picture of that interesting and tragic enterprise as revealed by an uncolored day-by-day recital of events. Nor has he attempted an interpretation of these events or of the actions and motives of the people connected with them." Despite these disclaimers, the numerous extensive extracts from contemporary journals and reports which Foreman includes emphasize the tragedy and injustice of the undertaking, and the tone of the author, if not his explicit words, reveals a strongly critical judgment on Indian removal that has passed into the general historiography on the topic. — *F.P.P.*

Additional Recommended Reading

Foreman, Grant. *The Last Trek of the Indians.* Chicago: University of Chicago Press, 1946. This volume tells of the removal of the Northern tribes. It is a companion to the author's treatment of the Southern tribes in Indian Removal.

Van Every, Dale. *Disinherited: The Lost Birthright of the American Indian.* New York: William Morrow and Company, 1966. Van Every presents a moving narrative of the removal of the Southern Indians, with extensive quotations from contemporary sources.

Wilkins, Thurman. *Cherokee Tragedy: The Story of the Ridge Family and the Decimation of a People.* New York: The Macmillan Company, 1970. Wilkins tells the story of the faction of the Cherokees that ultimately favored removal and signed the Treaty of New Echota of 1835. It is a sympathetic account of this minority group and of the internal conflicts within the nation that resulted from the removal policy.

Prucha, Francis P. *American Indian Policy in the Formative Years: The Indian Trade and Intercourse Acts.* Cambridge, Mass.: Harvard University Press, 1962. This history of Indian policy from 1790 to 1834 places the removal policy in the general context of federal Indian relations. It sees a positive relationship between removal and the philanthropists' hopes to civilize the Indians.

Young, Mary E. *Redskins, Ruffleshirts, and Rednecks: Indian Land Allotments in Alabama and Mississippi, 1830-1860.* Norman: University of Oklahoma Press, 1961. This book describes the complications and fraud resulting from allotment provisions in removal treaties. It treats of an essential part of the full Indian removal story.